Java the UML Way

Java the UML Way

Integrating Object-Oriented Design and Programming

Else Lervik and Vegard B. Havdal
Sør Trondelag University College, Trondheim, Norway

Translated and sponsored by tisip

JOHN WILEY & SONS, LTD

First published in the Norwegian language as *Programmering i Java*, © 2000 Else Lervik and Vegard B. Havdal, *The TISIP Foundation*, and *Gyldendal Akadernisk*

English language edition
Copyright © 2002 by John Wiley & Sons Ltd,
                    Baffins Lane, Chichester,
                    West Sussex PO19 1UD, England

                    National   01243 779777
                    International (+44) 1243 779777
                    e-mail (for orders and customer service enquiries): cs-books@wiley.co.uk
                    Visit our Home Pag on http://www.wileyeurope.com

Library of Congress Cataloguing in Publishing Data (applied for)

British Library Cataloguing in Publication Data

A catalogue record for this book is available from the British Library

ISBN 0 470 84386 1

Typeset by Cybertechnics Ltd, Sheffield
Printed and bound in Great Britain by Biddles Ltd, Guildford and King's Lynn
This book is printed on acid-free paper responsibly manufactured from sustainable forestry,
in which at least two trees are planted for each one used for paper production.

Contents

Preface

This textbook was designed for higher education in technological fields where Java and object-orientation form the basis of programming education. This book covers both basic and more advanced programming.

The book assumes a general familiarity with computers, operating systems, and the most common tools (such as, for example, word processors and browsers). Readers should be familiar with concepts like "file" and "directory" and know the difference between internal memory (RAM) and storage (for example, the hard disk).

A foundation in object-orientation

When using Java as an educational language, it makes sense for readers to deal with object-oriented ways of thinking as soon as possible. To a large extent, modern programming consists of using ready-made components and classes. It's possible to make a Java program that draws geometric figures, displays images, and plays sound files without using anything more complicated than sequential control structure. We believe that graphics and graphical user interfaces will motivate further study into both object-orientation and programming in general, more so than difficult control structures and textual user interfaces.

Readers will be introduced to the Java API for the first time in chapter 3. We'll introduce the standard `JOptionPane` class which makes it possible to create programs with primitive graphical user interfaces. We'll also use the `Random` and `String` classes. This will teach readers to use ready-made classes and at the same time provide a general introduction to object-oriented ways of thinking.

Once readers have used ready-made classes, we believe they will want to find out what these classes look like inside. We devote quite a bit of space to creating our own classes, a broad and comprehensive topic. In chapter 4, the readers will get to create their own applets with simple geometrical figures where they can control the shape, colors, and fonts themselves.

With this as a foundation, more classes follow to demonstrate the need for selection and loop control structures.

Object-oriented thinking and modeling go hand in hand with programming throughout this whole book. Nevertheless, for beginners to be able to run Java programs, their first read-through of the book will probably focus on programming details. Later perusals will contribute more to readers lifting their gazes up beyond the details of the code.

Using ready-made classes is part of developing the ability to think abstractly and understand encapsulation. We've chosen to make do with this in the first half of the book. We consider event handling, which is required to write programs with "real" graphical user interfaces, to be so complicated that the time for it comes only after most of the pieces of the Java language and object-orientation in general are in place. If it is included too early on, we believe that the degree of "mystery" behind it remains too high.

This book is not just for beginners

Because of an early, and therefore very thorough focus on object-orientation, we believe that this book is suited to professional programmers with backgrounds in non-object-oriented solution methods and programming languages. These readers will be able to sail through many of the programming details in the earlier chapters and concentrate instead on the object-orientation aspect, as illustrated with simple code examples.

Readers with backgrounds from another object-oriented programming language, C++ for example, will recognize quite a bit in the first part of the book. They should, however, peruse this material quickly, primarily because there are a number of essential differences between Java and C++, but also because the conceptual apparatus differs somewhat between the two languages. Examples of where Java differs from C++: in Java, arrays are objects with built-in knowledge of their own length, exceptions are thrown if you try to refer to an array element with an invalid index, space has to be allocated for all objects using the new operator (you cannot put objects on the stack), objects that no longer have references are removed automatically, it's not possible to program true multiple inheritance, there's no operator-overloading, it's not possible to manipulate pointers, etc.

Java's rich Application Programming Interface (API) will be of particular interest to readers with backgrounds in other languages. The Swing library makes it possible to create platform-independent graphical user interfaces. The classes for managing strings and arrays of dynamic length are easy to use. Familiar data structures such as linked lists, trees, and hashtables are built in as part of the Java API. Remote Method Invocation (RMI) makes it easy to create distributed systems in the form of objects that cooperate over the network. Java Database Connectivity (JDBC) is a collection of classes that can communicate via database drivers with just about any database system. JavaServer Pages (JSP) is a technique for programming dynamic Web pages. The programs run on the web server and generate customized Web pages.

Unified Modeling Language (UML) as a modeling language

One of the most welcome events in recent years in the field of object-oriented analysis and design was when three gentlemen, Booch, Jacobson, and Rumbaugh, joined forces and created a *single* common modeling language, Unified Modeling Language (UML). This language is a standard accepted by the Object Management Group (OMG), and we will gradually introduce elements of the language as we proceed. We start with a class diagram that illustrates a single class in chapter 3, and gradually add more classes using associations and generalizations. We use an activity diagram to illustrate control structures, threads, and other parallel processes. Sequence diagrams are very convenient for showing how objects send messages to each other. In the last few chapters of the book, we use deployment diagrams to show how the different parts of a distributed system depend on each other and run on physically different machines.

Software

The software necessary for writing Java programs can be downloaded free from the Internet. This book builds on the Java 2 SDK. The SDK is available on Sun's Web pages (http://java.sun.com/). This book explains how the package is used. In addition, you'll need a good editor. Alternatively, you can use an integrated development environment, for example JBuilder Foundation, which you can get from Borland's pages on the Internet (http://www.borland.com/jbuilder/).

To develop dynamic Web pages with JavaServer Pages (chapter 21), the reader needs a web server. The book gives instructions on installation and use of a free web server, LiteWebServer from http://www.gefionsoftware.com/.

Resource page on the Internet

This book has its own Internet page, http://www.tisip.no/JavaTheUmlWay/, where you'll find all the examples, as well as answers to all the shorter problems and many of the programming problems. The page also includes a number of relevant links.

Teaching aids

The book includes several teaching aids: every chapter starts with the chapter's learning goals and ends with a list of the new concepts introduced, review problems, and more involved programming problems. In addition, most subchapters end with shorter problems, where the reader is encouraged to actively work with the material that was just covered.

The book's Internet page (see above) includes a set of overheads that go with each chapter. The overheads are based primarily on the book, but also contain some examples and figures not found in the book.

The book's structure

The basics

The first nine chapters provide the requisite foundation in programming.

The first chapter introduces the topics of programming and Java and lays out the prerequisites we're assuming the readers have. This chapter also covers the various typographical elements used in the book.

Chapter 2 provides a necessary introduction into the topics of variables, data types, and expressions. Chapters 3 and 4 focus on object-orientation and the goal of the chapters is for the readers to learn to use ready-made classes and to make their own classes. Readers will become familiar with important object-oriented concepts like servers, clients, attributes, messages, and operations. They will understand that there's a difference between objects in reality and objects in programs. Readers will create their own first applets with simple geometrical figures in chapter 4.

Chapters 5 and 6 cover the control structures of selection and loops.

Object-orientation is again the focus in chapter 7, where we'll look at message exchanges between objects. This requires a thorough understanding of how arguments are passed between objects, and we'll go through a number of programming details, some of them difficult.

We now believe the reader is ready to use the online documentation that comes with the SDK. Chapter 8 offers a brief introduction to this. Using the ready-made classes that come with the SDK requires familiarity with exception handling in Java. Therefore, this is also covered in chapter 8.

Chapter 9 covers arrays of primitive data types. Simple sorting and searching are discussed. The chapter also covers the use of ready-made methods for this purpose.

Intermediate topics

This part of the book will prepare readers to make comprehensive programs with graphical user interfaces. This requires extensive use of the Java API and a thorough understanding of the concepts in an object-oriented system (such as associations and generalizations, for example).

Arrays of reference types are essentially different in their structure and behavior from arrays of primitive data types. Therefore, we've chosen to treat these in a separate chapter along with the ArrayList class, which is a class that hides reference arrays with dynamic lengths. For many practical purposes, this class is better suited than an ordinary array of reference type. Chapter 10 also covers classes with prepared sort-and-search methods including classes that make it possible to take a country's character sets into consideration.

Chapter 10 introduces further relationships between objects in the form of associations. We emphasize a demonstration of the transition from class diagram to program code.

Chapter 11 deals with communication between programs and data files. The chapter covers both text and binary transfers as well as direct access to a file. Serialization is a simple, but very useful technique that we'll cover here.

Chapter 12 deals with some of the more important topics in object-orientation, namely inheritance and polymorphism. Modeling is important here. Readers will learn the difference between association and generalization. It's important to thoroughly understand the conceptual apparatus to program inheritance correctly.

With a solid foundation in object-oriented programming, readers should now be in a position to understand the event model used to program graphical user interfaces in Java. Chapters 13–15 cover this topic. The most common graphical components are covered and emphasis is placed on distinguishing the classes that describe the problem to be solved from the classes that describe the user interface. Readers will create both applets and applications.

Introduction to advanced topics

Chapter 16 covers thread programming. Threads make it possible to multitask internally within a single program. The Java interpreter makes extensive internal use of threads—for example, in conjunction with graphical user interfaces.

Chapter 17 shows how the Java API can be used to create and handle the traditional data structures—linked lists, queues, stacks, trees, and hashtables. Recursion is also covered in this context.

Chapter 18 covers applets in a larger context. We look at the purpose for applets and security in connection with them. The chapter also goes through communication between applets and the browser.

Chapter 19 deals with programming distributed systems. There's a brief introduction to socket programming, but the primary topic of the chapter is RMI. We will create relatively complex distributed systems with callbacks.

The topic of chapter 20 is programming with databases. The chapter shows how to use JDBC to get a Java program to communicate with a relational database using SQL statements.

Chapter 21 is an introduction to server programming for the Internet. We'll see how to use JSP to create systems for the Internet where users see customized Web pages and where communication with databases is central.

We would like to thank...

Many people have made the work on this book possible: first and foremost, TISIP, whose economic support has made it possible to carry out this project. We'd also like to thank the Norwegian Technical Literary Fund [Det Faglitterære Fond] for its financial support.

A number of people have contributed opinions, ideas, and materials for the book. We would especially like to express our gratitude to the following: Assistent Professor Mildrid Ljosland and Associate Professor Tore Berg Hansen read carefully through the entire manuscript and contributed extremely useful technical comments. Engineer Simon Thoresen wrote answers for well over 30 programming problems. The solutions for many of the most complicated problems present material that supplements the contents of the book.

We would especially like to thank the three lecturers who dared to believe that this would become instructional material that they could use during the 1999/2000 school year: Assistent Professor Bjørn Klefstad, Associate Professor Jan H. Nilsen, and Lecturer Grethe Sandstrak. Along with approximately 100 students, they worked with preliminary and unfinished course materials—their experiences were very helpful to us.

The chapter on JavaServer Pages is not a part of the Norwegian edition, and Assistant Professor Tomas Holt has contributed to this chapter with tips and comments in an indispensable way.

Translator Tara F. Chace did an excellent job in translating all the text from Norwegian into English during a very short period. Thanks to her!

Else Lervik

and

Vegard B. Havdal

Introduction

1

Learning goals for this chapter

After reading this chapter, you should understand:

- The relationship between Java and the Internet

- The concept of a computer program

- The basics of compilation

After reading this chapter you should be able to:

- Compile and run a small program you have entered into the computer

The sun was probably shining in San Francisco on the 23rd of May 1995, when the head of research at Sun Microsystems, John Gage, and perhaps the Internet[1] world's biggest celebrity, Netscape founder Marc Andreessen, officially presented the programming language Java and associated technology.

It was no wonder that Gage was one of the two men on the stage, as the language in question first saw the light of day during a research project at Sun named Green. Andreessen had been part of the small group of students who made the first graphical browser for the WWW (Web), Mosaic. This program, and its successor Netscape, had revolutionized the computing world during the early 1990s. The new cooperation between Netscape and Sun would let small programs written in Java make Web pages interactive and more alive. These plans received a lot of attention, and there were plenty of ideas about programming toasters over the Web, and more.

Even today, Java is strongly associated with the Internet, and many people think the language is exclusively for use on the Web. This is absolutely wrong. Java is a complete programming language, with its own distinctive features, and more and less typical fields of use.

---

1. If these words are new to you, there is a glossary of terms in section 1.8 of this chapter.

Java is a young programming language. Six or seven years is not long. As a result, computing professionals or students need to keep up with the continuing evolution of Java and its associated programs. Writing computer programs in a language that's undergoing constant refinement may seem like an impossible task, but in the case of Java, it is not. This is thanks to the language's design and philosophy. In this book, we hope to give you a basis for understanding this.

1.1 Preliminaries for Reading This Book

Everyone starts their computing career as the user of one or more available program(s). The term *end user* is also common. For instance, you might be using a word processing program to write letters or school reports, or an invoicing program at the store where you work. In addition, you are also a user of the computer's operating system. The operating system keeps track of the programs we are running, and lets us use hard disks, floppy drives and the rest of the hardware.

In this book, you will learn how such programs are created. What is taken for granted is that you have been using a PC for a while. You should be familiar with the terms file, directory and sub-directory. This means that when you are clicking your way through the Windows Explorer, you know that you're dealing with a structure of files in directories on a hard disk.

Programs in Windows are files with the suffix *exe*. If you double-click on one of these files, you start that program. We call them *program files*. If you double-click a *doc* file, the program Word will usually start. Try these things in Explorer yourself, if you wish.[2] It is important to note that this does not mean that the *doc* file is a program. It is just how Windows keeps track of the fact that these files are meant for the program Word, which must be started first. A *doc* file is data for the program Word.

There is also an important distinction between text-based and graphical programs. The vast majority of Windows programs have a *graphical user interface*. The user interface is how we communicate with the computer. This might be done using written commands entered on the keyboard, or we may point and click on menus and buttons using a mouse. Occasionally in Windows we use the former, a textual user interface. Then the textual dialogue takes place at the MS-DOS prompt, or the *console* as we call it in this book. In Windows NT there is no MS DOS. There it is called a command prompt. It is nevertheless depicted with an MS DOS symbol, because MS DOS programs can be run. In the MS DOS console we navigate through the directories with the command *cd*, change directory. When we feel like it, we can run a program that is located in our current directory by typing its name. Some people are familiar with using a computer this way, whereas many are not. Because

---

2. Keep in mind that Windows Explorer is often configured to hide the suffix of registered file types, displaying a graphical icon instead. You can check this by looking at View, Options: Hide extensions for known file types. We recommend not hiding the file extensions, to give you better control and avoid confusion when several files have the same prefix.

we will start working with Java through a console window, you will have to learn basic textual navigation. We will try to make this easy as we go along. If you need to read more about this, do a Web search for "MS-DOS commands" or an equivalent phrase. Or look at the book's Web pages on *http://www.tisip.no/Java-TheUmlWay/*, where we have links to some primers.

When it comes to the physical construction of the computer, we have already mentioned that there is usually a hard disk inside where files are arranged in directories. Furthermore, it is good to know that there is a central "brain" called the *microprocessor* and that the computer has *internal memory* that is often called RAM, Random Access Memory. Another name for the microprocessor is CPU, Central Processing Unit. It would be hard to avoid these terms in a book on programming.

The hard disk is an example of *secondary memory*. Even if we turn the computer off, our data and programs will still be intact on the hard disk. All the contents of the aforementioned internal memory disappear when the power is turned off. The internal memory is used by the microprocessor to store the running programs, and their data.

We have published additional information and numbered examples on the Web. Hence we are assuming that the reader is familiar with using the Internet, at least browsing a page on the Web and changing the basic configuration of the Web browser. Try to go to *http://www.tisip.no/JavaTheUmlWay/* and see if you can find your way around.

1.2 Contemplating a Computer

It's no easy task to describe the workings of a computer to a beginner. When you click on Windows Explorer there are several things taking place between you and the chip on the motherboard inside the computer, the microprocessor. Dividing the computer system into layers, see Figure 1.1, can help us see the bigger picture here. Each layer is one or more running program (*processes* is more widely used in this context), which makes up part of the operating system.

You start in the center, where there's a small program known as the kernel. This program uses a small number of commands to perform operations in the hardware of the computer. This is where it all starts.

Outside the kernel is the next layer, for instance the MS DOS text-based console. Here the user can work with the computer using a number of textual commands and run different programs. For each thing the user does in the console, several operations will be executed in the kernel.

Outside the textual console interface, we usually find a graphical user interface. This is familiar to most; using a mouse or another mechanical device we operate the computer by pointing and clicking to start programs, move files, etc.

In Figure 1.1, we put a computer in the center to symbolize computer hardware like disk drives, memory, screen and keyboard. The operating system kernel hides this hardware so that the outside layers don't have to know details about the hardware covered by the kernel. Outside the kernel, we can see a textual console layer and a window system. The program that implements the console layer in MS-DOS is called *command.com*. When we type the command *dir* in MS-DOS, we imagine a number of operations being executed in the kernel.

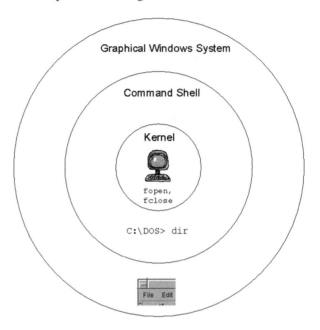

Figure 1.1 Layers in a computer system

How well defined the boundaries between layers are, varies from system to system, system being for instance Macintosh, Windows, Linux. In some systems you can use different combinations of the various layers depending on your needs. For instance, you might choose the graphical window system you like best. In other systems you are tied to one window system because the layers are not clearly separated.

For the person who is about to program these computers, this division into layers is a great advantage: we only need to deal with the level we are working on. It's possible that we are working on the graphical window system directly. In that case, programming consists of specifying when and where to open a window with the buttons OK and Cancel, and some text or specifying a pull-down menu with some selections. Microsoft Visual Basic is an example of a tool for this type of programming. On the other hand, we might program with the textual console interface as the base. Communication with the program will be through textual messages, but it is also common to create graphical user interfaces in this type of programming. It is just that in that case, it doesn't all begin with the graphics. This is how we set out to write Java programs in this book. We start by using text for the user interface, then move on to writing graphical user interfaces when we consider it necessary.

The goal of a programming language is for a programmer to describe the solution to a problem to the computer, solutions which are helpful for a number of users who will use the program or refine it further. It's the computer's job to execute this solution. The problems we're discussing are usually the kind that are too difficult or time consuming for human beings to solve. That's about all there is to say about programming languages in general, because the ways these problems are solved are incredibly diverse. There are numerous traditions and styles of programming in terms of how the programmer works, how the programs are written and how the user utilizes them. In Java, a technique called object orientation or OO is the key issue. Among other things, this is a means of organizing the computer program that is going to solve a given problem. We solve a problem by creating a model of objects that exist in the real world. This method is commonly linked to Java's relative in the world of computer languages, C++, but other languages, like Smalltalk, are also based on OO. The invention of this technique is commonly attributed to two Norwegians, Kristen Nygaard and Ole-Johan Dahl. They designed the first object oriented language, SIMULA, at the Norwegian Computing Centre in the mid-1960s.

1.3 Java Applications and Java Applets

As mentioned earlier, the language Java has received a good deal of publicity because of its connection to the Web and the Internet. There are two main important types of Java programs in use today: standalone Java programs, or *applications*, and Java *applets*. (We might also consider *servlets* as a third type.) Applets are what we see on the Web and they're what made Java unique at the time of its birth.

Most computer users are familiar with browsing the Web using Netscape, Internet Explorer or some other browser. We know that we come across pages with text and pictures, all of them placed on a Web *server* for us to fetch and view. The browser, or maybe the machine we run the browser on, is an example of a *client*. There are lots of clients all over the place fetching information from a single server. One would expect the server to be big and the clients small. That is often the case. The computer running the server is a powerful machine, while the client machine is a common desktop computer. The *programs* running on the server and client machines are related the other way around; a Web browser is a much more complicated program than a Web server.

The pages we find on the Web have been formatted in the language *HTML* (Hypertext Markup Language), which will give us header texts with different appearances and links to other documents. In addition, we see pictures and tables. Every now and then we run across a sound clip or maybe a small movie and then we might need an extra program module in our browser. Common to all these things we fetch from the Web to look at is that they are passive. We only deal with static information files, stored on some server somewhere in the world for us to retrieve and look at. Not so with Java applets. When we fetch one of those from the Web, it is a Java program that we load from the Web into our browser. When that is done, it is run, and it is allowed to communicate actively with the user of the browser. Instead of retrieving a "dead" HTML file, we now have a small computer program, and it is the responsibility of the browser in our own living room to arrange for this program to start and run. Web and applets are good examples of *distributed systems*. In a computer network context, with several computers interconnected, we always try to distribute the amount of work in a reasonable way between the different computers. When a Web page has 1000 hits in a short period of time and this page contains some applets, all 1000 clients will all fetch the applets, and start to run them. This is work that the Web servers would have to do otherwise, and it could easily have become much too big a task to keep track of all the information for all the browsers. But this server serves Java applets to the browsers, saying, "You can do this work yourselves, here is the program."

The other main type of programs are what we call applications. This is something more traditional; an application consists of program files that altogether make up a computer program. It is not linked to the Web. In this case, the entire program is run on the computer we are working on. There are no necessary network implications. We may also bring the program files home from the office with us and run the program there. But there are important differences between Java applications and traditional programs in the form of *exe*-files. For example, Java program files are not named *archive.exe* and cannot be run by typing their name or double-clicking on them. They have suffix *class* and require a separate program to be run. But we will look into this later.

Another very important attribute of programs written in Java is that they are not tied to a particular brand of computer. We say that the language is *architecture neutral* or platform independent. This means that you can write a program on your Windows NT Workstation at work and run it. Then you can bring it home to your Macintosh or Linux PC and run the same program. If we think back to applets, we see that this is clearly a prerequisite for applets to work as they were intended. There are several types of computers used to navigate the Web and if they are all going to be able to use the applets, which is more or less the situation today, the applet cannot be written in a way that is usable for only one type of computer. For example: if a language allows the programmer to write something that is particular to one specific computer's internal memory layout, that language is not architecture neutral.

1.4 JavaScript and JSP

There is also a programming language called JavaScript. But unlike Java, which can be used to write large, standalone applications, JavaScript is a language used solely in Web pages and browsers. JavaScript was created by Netscape. It is used in small bits of program code inside HTML documents to allow more advanced navigation using the mouse, more flexible use of graphics, etc. Hence, pages containing JavaScripts are not totally passive.

So what does this have to do with Java? The answer is almost nothing, except for the name. At times, the program code in JavaScript is reminiscent of Java, but it *is* something completely different. You will be introduced to JavaScript in Chapter 21.

JSP, or Java Server Pages, is another Java-related technology for advanced Web applications. You will learn more about that in Chapter 21 also.

1.5 How This Book is Structured

At the beginning of this text we concentrate on Java applications and then later on we cover applets. Furthermore, we will start by using textual communication with the user. This means that we start out with the most minimal type of Java programming. By doing this, we provide a basis for understanding the whole workings of both applets and graphical user interfaces. We do this by gradually explaining the mechanisms of the language, before taking on graphics and applets. Small graphical user interfaces are still used quite early, for the sake of simplicity.

New students of programming languages often start by writing the world's smallest program. It is commonly referred to as "Hello world!", because its only task is printing that greeting to the user. The program only has to print one line of text on the screen. We will also do this, but there is a certain antagonism between writing tiny programs and studying Java's fundamental construction, object orientation. Tiny Java programs don't make much sense in an OO context. Only when the programs become larger will the power of OO begin to show. The conclusion is this: things that seem odd to begin with become important in a larger context. Don't pay too much attention to things looking strange in a small program.

Vocabulary

The use of terms in computer science is not trivial. Different aspects of computer science put different meanings into the same term. In this book, we stick to the terms used by Java's main developers, Gosling, Joy and Steele, in their language specification [Gosling, Joy, Steele 1996]. We also use the vocabulary of the main designers of UML, our modeling language [Rumbaugh, Jacobson, Booch 1999]. In the event that these two sources differ in their terminologies, we will choose those of the Java designers.

Language references

The language Java can be said to be minimal. That means that there is a small number of constructs and keywords in the language, but a large amount of ready-to-use code for all sorts of functions. You need to learn to use this code and find your way around it as well. In this book we will provide references to the core of the language and ready-to-use functionality in two types of boxes in the text. This is our way of trying to systematize this. An example of a reference box relating to the language core follows here. What's inside it is only included as an example.

Java Core

Example of language core reference: class

The reserved word `class` is used at the beginning of the definition of all classes in Java. `class` is followed by a start-bracket, {, next is the member variables and methods of the class, and finally the class definiton is closed by a closing bracket, }. Example:

```
class Patient {
    /* Contents */
}
```

When we wish to describe parts of the ready-to-use program libraries included with Java, the *API*, we do that in a box marked API Reference. Here is an example:

API Reference

Example of API reference: the class java.lang.String

Methods:

```
public int length()
```

The method returns the length of this `String` object.

Pay particular attention to the Note boxes.

Type faces

We have used different type faces for various parts of the text. The aim of this is to make it easy to read. The text in the book is printed in Giovanni. If we include words of program code inside a paragraph, like `int age = 0;`, we use a typewriter face, Courier. We do the same when including examples of program-user interaction in the console, for instance how to compile and run a program:

```
c:\javaprograms\> javac MyProgram.class
c:\javaprograms\> java MyProgram
Hello, you lot!
```

As you see, the user input is in *italics*.

Often, we need to include larger amounts of Java code in a paragraph. We have chosen to use a more space-conserving type face for that.

```
public class BouncingBall {
  public static void main(String[] args) {
    Dimension windowDim = new Dimension(500,500);
    BouncingBallWindow myWindow
      = new BouncingBallWindow(windowDim.width, windowDim.height);
    myWindow.setVisible(true);
  }
}
```

When we refer to file names in the text, like *autoexec.bat* or *javac.exe*, we use italics.

References

Instead of including them verbatim in the text several times, we have collected our references to literature and Web pages in a list in Appendix G. A reference to a Web page in this list from the text itself looks like this: [URL Java book] and a reference to a book looks like this: [Larman 2000]. The exact addresses and details are included in the list of references.

Coding standards

When we write computer programs, the appearance of the *program code* adheres to a particular style. This has to do with indentations, upper and lower case letters, etc. The point of this is keeping the code tidy and easy to read. Sun has published a standard for this, which we use to a large extent. You can find it on [URL Coding standard]. We recommend sticking to this standard for the appearance of your code and most of the code in this book does. There are a few things we do differently to enhance readability. These exceptions of ours are summarized in Appendix F.

Figures

In the book you will learn about a standard for modeling program systems called UML, Unified Modeling Language. This refers to various types of diagrams used mainly in the design phase of a program system. Figures that are UML are marked as such in the captions.

1.6   A Small Example Program

Now it's high time to introduce our first Java program. We do not intend to explain all of its aspects, but wish to give the reader an idea of what a Java program is. We have already used the term program code for what you can see in program listing 1.1, and it is also called *source code*.

Program Listing 1.1

```
/*
 * PrintText.java VBH 2001-08-28
 * Prints text several times
 *
 */
class PrintText {
  public static void main(String[] args) {
    System.out.println("Our first program...");
    for (int i = 0 ; i<10 ; i++) System.out.println("About to learn Java!");
  }
}
```

Program listing 1.1 details a small Java program, or if you like, a (very) small application. Let's look at the first lines. There is text in English there, and you might guess that this is for humans, not computers. The lines between / * and * / are *comments*. Comments are essential in all programming. The point is to explain and elaborate on aspects of the program. This is for another person who has to read the program at a later stage, make corrections, or put it to use. But it can also be useful to you if you need to change something in a program you wrote several years ago. It is universally regarded as very important to write comments for difficult and complicated pieces of the code, but it is not uncommon to fail to do so, especially in an educational context. We think this is because the usefulness of comments is not apparent in the short term.

Comments make computer programs useful in the long run as well, for instance when other developers have to work with them. It is important to acquire the habit of commenting your code well.

The first comment line in the example shows the name of the file where we have stored this program, *PrintText.java*. In other words, we imagine that we have typed this into a *text file* with Notepad, for instance, and saved it as *PrintText.java*. The files do not contain images or headers, and are by no means similar, for example, to a *doc* file that Word uses. Text files are widely used, but tend to be less familiar to Windows users. The *ini* configuration files in Windows are text files. E-mail and the majority of all services on the Internet are also based on the same type of text coding. In all programming languages, the program code itself is also stored in plain text. A text file is a text file, computer type (almost) notwithstanding, and this has been the case for a few years. But in Windows 95/98 and MS-DOS there are complications, since ASCII (a common character set, see the new concepts in section 1.8) with certain modifications is often being used here.

We mentioned that one may write, save and edit these files using Notepad in Windows, but this is very far from being a satisfactory tool. We want more functionality, like having several files open for editing at the same time. One might use Word and always save as plain text, but this is needlessly cumbersome. So we suggest using a program named WinEdit. It is a handy text editing tool, or *editor*, a short introduction to which is given in Appendix A.

Back to the example program. We had stated that the file in which the program is stored is called *PrintText.java*. It is not a coincidence that the first actual code line in the program is `class PrintText`. In this case, `class` denotes the start of our program. It is true that a program is always a class in Java, but the reverse is not true. A class can be other things besides a program. Notice the brackets, `{ and }`. They are used in Java to mark *blocks*. Blocks are groups of code lines that belong together and that we need to delimit. If you look closely at the example, there are two such blocks here, one inside the other. The outer block is the class `PrintText`, where we see `class PrintText` and its block. The next block is the *method* `main`. It is named by `public static void main(String[] args)` and the brackets. To summarize, you are looking at one class with one method. In other programming languages, methods are called *subroutines* or *functions*.

So what does this program actually do? A computer program is a way for a computer to solve a problem. In this example, this solution is what is inside the `main()` method. This is always where a Java application starts. The program prints the following text in the console window:

```
Our first program...
About to learn Java!
About to learn Java!
About to learn Java!
About to learn Java!
About to learn Java!
About to learn Java!
About to learn Java!
About to learn Java!
About to learn Java!
About to learn Java!
```

This is done with something called a loop, which we will come back to later. We print "Our first program..." once and "About to learn Java!" ten times. We won't describe in detail what causes this to happen right now, but we will mention that the words `System.out.println` handle the printing of one sentence.

How we run a program

Our little program has been saved in the file *PrintText.java*. The computer can't run this directly from the Java source code. We need to translate it into a type of code that the computer understands. This is the process referred to as *compilation*, even though the actual details differ a bit from language to language. The compiler is the program that handles this translation.

It has been most common for PCs that the compiler translates from source code into *machine code*. The machine code is the language the microprocessor uses. It is practically unreadable to humans and that is certainly one of the reasons we have programming languages like Java. Compiling into machine code can be illustrated as in Figure 1.2. In this example, a file written in the language Pascal, with file name *HelloWorld.pas*, is to be compiled.

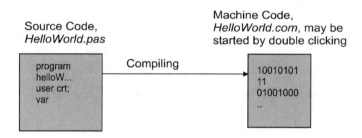

Figure 1.2 Compiling to machine code

We have indicated the machine code with the digits 0 and 1. Data made up of only these digits is called *binary data* and this is how the microprocessor "thinks". But we don't. The finished machine code is stored in the file *HelloWorld.com* and it can be started by double clicking on it. Today, an *exe* file is more common than *com*, but an *exe* file is not necessarily machine code.

In Java it is a slightly different story. Instead of creating a completely self-contained file of machine code, the compiler produces *byte code*, stored in a *class* file. This class file can't run by itself. Another program, known as the *interpreter*, is required to run it. We have illustrated this in Figure 1.3.

In Figure 1.3 we have illustrated the contents of the class file with random characters. It is not legible to us either.

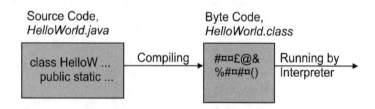

Figure 1.3 Compiling to byte code

The outcome of all this is that we need two programs to run a Java program we have written: a compiler to create the *class* file, and an interpreter to run it. Sometimes, the interpreter is also called a compiler, because in the process of running the program it translates it into machine code internally. A Just-In-Time Compiler is an interpreter. But in this book, "Java compiler" means the program that translates from source code into byte code, unless we say otherwise.

Note that the file with the source code has the suffix *.java* and the file with the byte code (which we call the *class* file) always has the suffix *.class*. This is mandatory.

But why this middle stage in the form of the class files? The most important answer lies in what we said earlier about architecture neutral languages. A *class* file can be used on all types of computers that support Java, i.e. all types of computers for which a Java interpreter is available. Only when the interpreter starts to run the *class* file will machine-specific issues start to play a role at all. Anything pertaining to a type of computer (say a Macintosh) is the concern of the interpreter alone. Ideally, the *class* files will work everywhere. If you have a *class* file program and an interpreter, you are ready to run that program. This is where the slogan "Write once, run everywhere" comes from.

The interpreter is also refered to as JVM, Java Virtual Machine. This is an abstract, theoretical model for a computer that will run Java and the interpreter program implements this model.

Another attribute of the *class* files is their small size: they are usually significantly smaller that the file with the source code. This makes them quicker to transmit through a network, like applets on the Web.

In this book, we are working with the compiler and interpreter that are included in Sun's freely distributed package Java Development Kit, or *JDK*. Newer JDK releases are called *SDK* (Software Development Kit). Short and sweet, the Java compiler is called javac, Java Compile, and the interpreter is called java. The installation and use of these programs are outlined in Appendix A. Henceforth we assume you have installed SDK, and we will now show a brief example of typing, compiling and running a program on a PC.

1. First, type the code in Program Listing 1.1 in your favourite text editor, for instance WinEdit.

2. Then save the file in the directory on your hard drive you wish to store Java files on: let's use *c:\javaprograms*. The file may, but is not required to, be saved as *PrintText.java*, because `PrintText` is the name of the class containing the method `main()`.[3]

---

3. If you are using Notepad, you need to make sure the file wasn't named PrintText.java.txt. Notepad insists on naming all text files *.txt*, which is completely wrong. You might quote the file name when saving.

3. Then you start an MS-DOS window and go to the program directory with the following command:

```
c:\windows> cd c:\javaprograms
c:\javaprograms>
```

4. Then compile by typing the following text. If it works out fine, you will get the prompt back and it will look as if nothing happened.

```
c:\javaprograms> javac PrintText.java
c:\javaprograms>
```

If, on the other hand, you get an error message, you have to recheck the source code for typos. Another common mistake is to spell the name of the file wrong.

5. If you didn't get any errors, you can start the program this way and look at its output:

```
c:\javaprograms> java PrintText
Our first program...
About to learn Java!
About to learn Java!
About to learn Java!
About to learn Java!
About to learn Java!
About to learn Java!
About to learn Java!
About to learn Java!
About to learn Java!
About to learn Java!
c:\javaprograms>
```

Notice that it is incorrect to type

```
c:\javaprograms> java PrintText.class (Mistake!)
```

even though it is the class file that is to be started.

The example showed a rather optimistic course of events. It is far more common to get some sort of *error message* from the compiler, indicating a mistake in the source code. After some corrections and new mistakes in the source code, you will eventually get it right, but errors may also arise during the execution of the program. This is all in a day's work for a computer programmer, and you have to get used to a certain amount of hassle getting things to work. Fortunately, there are techniques and tools to simplify things as much as possible.

Other tools for working with Java

We use SDK from Sun. This is the most official development tool for Java. We have seen that it consists of simple programs which we basically need to start by hand by giving textual commands. Many people prefer to work in this way, but many others will prefer menus and buttons for compiling and running. Luckily there are products that provide this.

With text editing tools like WinEdit, we can compile and run programs from menus, in addition to editing text. These menu choices automatically run javac and java for us, making WinEdit into a sort of shell around the SDK. Every now and then, problems arise in the communication between the editing tool and SDK, for instance with particular types of Java programs. It will then be very useful to go to a console window (like the MS-DOS prompt) and do the compiling by hand. So we recommend learning to use the SDK from the console as an auxiliary solution.

Another category are tools specializing in keeping track of the programmer's files graphically, creating graphical user interfaces with powerful tools, and of course compiling and running. Examples of such products are Borland JBuilder and IBM VisualAge. In our opinion it is still always useful to know how to use the console tools. That gives the programmer full control over the development process and all the associated file types.

In the tool Microsoft Visual J++, changes to the language itself have been added, but not in conformance with Sun's official Java standards. This has been very controversial and we will not cover these extensions in this book.

1.7 Examples of Applets

With an Internet connection, you can look at a simple example applet we have written. Many readers may have seen applets on the Web before. Our example is found at *http://www.tisip.no/JavaTheUmlWay/examples/SimpleApplet.html* [URL Simple Applet].

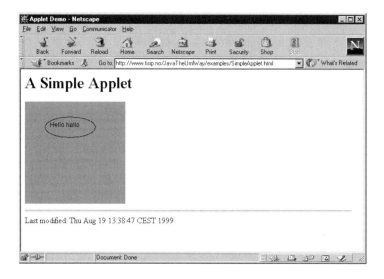

Figure 1.4   Very simple applet

The address reveals that it is an HTML document. Applets must lie within HTML files, or to be precise, the reference to the applet's *class* file must lie within a HTML file. So where there is an applet, there is always an accompanying HTML document. When you load this address, you will get a small document, and the applet runs inside a rectangular area on the page. This applet is very simple: it only prints a text with a circle around it. Figure 1.4 shows a piece of the browser, where the applet is running.

So what is so interesting here? The text and the circle you see are created by the little applet running in your browser. It is not a part of the static document you fetched from *www.tisip.no*. This is the reason why you probably need to wait a while for something to happen with the applet, compared to the rest of the document. A small program has to run. In this example, there is certainly no need for an applet. We could have included the text and the circle in the HTML document, because it is static. But the applet could have moved and received input from you, the user

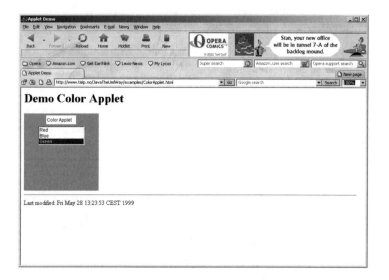

Figure 1.5 A slightly more advanced applet

Our second example does just that: [URL Color Applet]. Here you are presented with the option of choosing the applet's background color from a menu. It is in fact a tiny graphical user interface. This applet is active: it communicates with you by itself, after being completely downloaded from the Web server. Figure 1.5 shows how this might look in your browser, although we cannot show the colors.

The applet in Figure 1.5 could not have been made in HTML, as it is not static. Small and graphical, it could have been written in JavaScript, but that would have given us serious limitations if we wanted to expand its functionality, and speed decreases significantly as the size of the little "system" increases.

Possible problems with the applets

There is a chance that you will have trouble seeing any applets in these Web pages. That has to do with the low degree of homogeneity on the Web. There are a plethora of computers, operating systems and browsers. Java applets are meant to work in most cases, but it is inevitable that they occasionally fail to work correctly. This problem is much more pronounced with applets than with applications, because there are not as many different Java interpreters as there are browsers. Here are some possible causes for you not seeing any applets at all:

- Your browser does not support Java applets. This means that the browser program hasn't been provided with this functionality. Netscape 4.0 and Internet Explorer 3.0 and newer should support certain versions of Java. Your solution is to download a newer browser.

- Your browser has the Java applet functionality disabled. In your configuration menu (Options, Preferences or the like) you may switch off running applets encountered on the Web. The solution to this problem is obvious: enable applet support in the browser.

- Your browser does not support applets written in the version of Java this applet is written in. This usually implies that you are using an older browser. Published applets tend to be written in the newest version of Java commonly supported at that time. The solution is to get a newer browser and perhaps an additional module for Java support.

You *may* run across other problems, but these three are very common.

1.8 New Concepts in This Chapter

Concept	Brief Explanation
API	Application Programming Interface. A standard program library that comes with the Java software. See also chapter 8.
applet	A Java program that's executed inside a Web browser. It is part of a Web document.
application	A standalone program meant to run by itself, not needing a browser, for example.
architecture neutral	A key element in Java. Nothing in the language ties a program to a particular type of computer.
ASCII	American Standard Code for Information Interchange. A commonly used character set. See also text file.
browser	A program for viewing pages ("surfing") on the Web. Examples: Internet Explorer and Netscape Navigator.

Concept	Brief Explanation
byte code	Something between machine code and source code.
client	A program or a computer that asks for services from a server, usually over a network.
compiler	A program that accepts source code as input and produces, for example, machine code or byte code.
compiling	The process of translating source code into machine code or byte code.
console	A text window where we communicate with a text-based program.
CPU	See microprocessor.
data file	Files with information used by the programs.
directory	The files on a computer are arranged in directories. The directories are organized like a tree, with directories under others.
distributed system	Consists of several programs running on several computers and communicating with each other.
file	An amount of information that serves a purpose to the computer. Often stored on a hard disk.
HTML	Hypertext Markup Language. The formatting language for Web documents.
interactive	A situation where a continuous dialogue takes place between human and computer.
Internet	A world-wide network of computers. It is special because it consists of several types of computers and sub-networks. Used for Web, e-mail, discussion groups and countless other things.
Java interpreter	A program in charge of executing a Java program.
JDK	See SDK.
JVM	Java Virtual Machine. The theoretical model for a computer, which the Java interpreter realizes.
machine code	The language of the microprocessor.
method	A named part of the source code which we use whenever needed. See also chapters 3 and 4.
microprocessor	The "brain" of a computer.
object orientation (OO)	A way to design computer programs. An example of a principle is: Everything that has to do with a certain thing in the program is gathered in a certain module. An object oriented language is a language in which this principle is a key point.
operating system (OS)	The program that administers the hardware so that the user can use it easily. Also keeps track of the different programs running on the computer. The most widely used operating systems today are Windows 98 and NT.
platform independent	See architecture neutral.

Concept	Brief Explanation
process	A more general term for a program running on a computer. We often start several processes when we start a program by double-clicking on it. See also chapter 16.
program code	See source code.
program file	A file that is a program we can run.
programming language	A set of rules for instructions to a computer. A programming language is a whole lot more exactly defined than German, for example.
SDK	Software Development Kit. A standard development tool for Java.
server	A program or computer that performs tasks at the request of clients.
source code	The text which constitutes a program. The source code is to be found on one or more text files.
text file	File containing only plain text. The standard for plain text in Europe is ISO 8859-1, or latin-1. 8 bits per character are used. The Unicode character system, which Java uses, is larger, with 16 bits per character. The characters in ISO 8859-1 match Unicode. ASCII is an older character set with regional variants. The standard part of ASCII is part of ISO 8859-1.
Unicode	A newer and larger character system than ASCII. See also text file.
UNIX	Common name for a large class of operating systems. It is widely used for large, heavy applications.
URL	Uniform Resource Locator. An address on the Web, like *http://www.tisip.no/* eller *ftp://ftp.gnu.org/*.
user interface	The part of a program visible to the user. The user interface may be graphical. In that case, the user will use buttons and windows. If it's textual, the user communicates with the computer using written commands.
Web (WWW, World Wide Web)	A service on the Internet where different documents are presented. They usually contain links to other documents, that can be navigated between using a mouse.
Windows Explorer	The program in Windows that we use to explore disks, diskettes and more. It allows us to move and copy files, etc.

1.9   Review Problems

1. What is a programming language? Name three.

2. What is Java SDK? Where do you get it?

3. What is byte code?

4. Explain how we compile and run a Java program.

1.10 Programming Problems

1. Enter the program `PrintText` in a text editor, save, compile and run it. Verify that the printout is correct, which is to say that the program works. Implied in this is that SDK has been installed on your machine.

2. Change the program `PrintText` so that it prints the greeting 50 times instead of 10. Compile it and check to see that it works.

3. Find out what happens if you try to run the program by typing

   ```
   C:\javaprograms> java PrintText.class
   ```

   Try to explain what you see.

4. Find out what happens if you try to run an applet, for instance *SimpleApplet.class*, in the usual way with the program java, and not in a Web page.

Variables, Data Types, and Expressions

2

Learning goals for this chapter

After completing this chapter, you will understand the following concepts:

- Variables—how the contents are interpreted depending on the type of data

- Algorithms, input data, output data, test data sets

- Sequential execution, blocks, statements, keywords, and names

- Assignment, casting

You will be able to

- Write programs that perform mathematical calculations and print the results to the console

- Set up a test data set for these types of programs

This chapter will cover a number of fundamental language elements in Java. There are equivalent language elements in just about every programming language.

We'll start by introducing an example that we will work with as we proceed through the book, a program that calculates what it will cost to fix up a condominium.

In order for the computer to be able to perform these calculations, it needs quite a bit of information about the condominium. We will look at how to input this information into a program. We will also look at how to write the program so that it does the calculations for us and displays the results on the screen.

2.1 Example

You just bought an old condominium that you're going to renovate. You've decided that the bathroom, kitchen, and the electrical installations are fine. However, you want to replace the flooring in a couple of the rooms and paint and wallpaper some of them.

You need to perform a number of calculations:

- How much paint, or wallpaper, will you need for a wall?

- How many square meters of parquet flooring, or other flooring, will you need for a floor?

- What will the renovation cost for each individual wall, each individual room, and the entire renovation project?

We will work quite a bit with this example over the course of this book. We'll start with a very simple program that calculates the area of a wall, and we'll end up with a program with a graphical user interface that will be a useful tool in planning a renovation (see Figure 15.8). Between these two extremes, we will write smaller programs that can be used to calculate, for example, how many rolls of wallpaper we need to cover a wall.

This book is about object-oriented programming. That means that we always start by finding the objects that are going to be modeled. These can be walls, floors, wallpaper, etc. The purpose of the program will be to perform certain tasks using these objects—for example, estimating the number of liters of paint we will need for a wall.

In this chapter, we'll look at how to solve minor, individual problems without thinking so much about the objects.

2.2 Data and Variables

Now we will write a program that calculates the area of a rectangular surface that could be a wall or a floor. We'll ignore windows and doorways.

We need to know the answers to three key questions to be able to solve this problem:

1. What is the purpose of the program? What results do we expect to get? This is the data the program prints on the screen. We call it *output data*. Notice that we are looking at this from the computer's point of view. The program *writes* and the program's user reads this data on the screen.

Answer: Output data is the area, measured in square meters.

2. What data needs to be input in order for the program to be able to calculate these results? This is data that the program's user will use the keyboard to input. The program *reads* this data. We call it *input data*.

Answer: The formula for the area of a rectangle is the length times the height. Thus the input data is the length and height, measured in meters.

3. What happens between the data being input and the results printing out?

Answer: The program calculates the area based on the formula provided.

The program that solves this little problem will communicate with the user via the screen and keyboard. When we put this into a larger context, we will be able to say instead that the surface object performs services for a so-called client object, which in turn communicates with a user interface object. In an object-oriented program we will have to ask ourselves these three questions for every single object: What do we expect the object to tell us, and what does it need to know about itself to be able to tell us this? What formulas and problem-solving methods does the object need to know? These questions show that an object in a program has very different characteristics from an object in reality. More about this in chapter 3.

The following sketch of a textual user interface in the console window is sufficient for our simple problem:

```
The length of the wall (meters): 5
The height of the wall (meters): 2.3
The area of the wall is 11.5 square meters
```

What the user types is indicated in *italic*. The user can calculate the area of several walls by running the program several times.

Actually, it's very difficult to do something as basic as inputting two numbers into Java. Therefore we start by inputting the length and height directly into the program (see Program Listing 2.1). Now the user interface is even simpler than shown above. Only the result prints out. Look at the end of the program listing. You'll find "Example Run". By enclosing this in /* and */, the compiler regards this as a comment. Most of the program listings in this book that contain complete programs with a textual user interface show example program runs at the end.

If the user wants to calculate the area of several walls, she has to open the program in an editor and edit the length and height each time. Then she has to compile and run it again.

Program Listing 2.1

```
/*
 * WallCalculations.java   E.L. 2001-08-09
 */
```

```
class WallCalculations {
  public static void main(String[] args) {
    double length = 5.0;
    double height = 2.3;
    double area = length * height;
    System.out.println("The area of the wall is " + area + " square meters.");
  }
}

/* Example Run:
The area of the wall is 11.5 square meters.
*/
```

Get the program from [URL Java book], compile it, and run it.

The lines of code are performed in the order they are listed. This is called *sequential execution*.

We remember from section 1.6 that the program does what is in the `main()` method. The program sets aside room for data in the computer's internal memory. For example:

```
double length = 5.0;
```

Storage spaces like this are called *variables*. Each variable can contain only one data value. The program fills the variables with reasonable contents immediately after they're formed. Here, the variable `length` receives the value 5.0.

All the variables in the program are outlined in Figure 2.1.

Once `length` and `height` are created and have each received their values, the area is calculated. The result of the multiplication is placed in the variable named `area`:

```
double area = length * height;
```

Finally, the results of the calculations are printed:

```
System.out.println("The area of the wall is " + area + " square meters.");
```

We're familiar with `System.out.println()` from chapter 1. Inside the parentheses we indicate what will be printed on the screen. If we are going to print out several things, we use + to link them together. Text that is going to be printed exactly as it is is placed in double quotes. Text without double quotes can be the name of a variable, such as `area`. That means that the program will get the contents of the variable and print that on the screen. In this example, the printout looks like this:

Figure 2.1 The variables in the program that calculate the area of a wall

```
The area of the wall is 11.5 square meters.
```

Let's look a little more closely at the variables:

The computer's internal memory is made up of many small electronic components. We can think of these as switches that can be either on or off. A switch that can be on or off can be associated with the digit 1 or 0. This type of digit is called a *bit* ("binary digit"). Eight bits make a *byte*. The variables we are storing information in consist of one or more bytes. By allowing the different switches in a variable to be on or off, we can create many different combinations of zeroes and ones. Each combination means a specific number, letter, or character. In the program code, we indicate how the contents of the variables will be interpreted by setting the data type before the name of the variable.

The data type for `length`, `height`, and `area` is `double`. That means that the contents of the variables will be interpreted as decimal numerals.

Data input from the user

Program Listing 2.2 shows the same program with data input from the user. Compile and run the program. Compared to the previous version of the program the advantages are obvious. There we had to insert new values into the source code for every new wall that was going to be calculated, and then compile before we could run the program again. This new version can calculate the area of a number of different walls without requiring changes in the program code.

Nonetheless, the program code in Program Listing 2.2 is quite complicated. We will explain the details in the next chapter.

Program Listing 2.2

```java
/*
 * WallCalculations2.java   E.L. 2001-06-16
 */
import javax.swing.JOptionPane;
class WallCalculations2 {
  public static void main(String[] args) {
    String lengthInput = JOptionPane.showInputDialog("The length of the wall (meters): ");
    String heightInput = JOptionPane.showInputDialog("The height of the wall (meters): ");
    double length = Double.parseDouble(lengthInput);
    double height = Double.parseDouble(heightInput);
    double area = length * height;
    JOptionPane.showMessageDialog(null,
            "The area of the wall is " + area + " square meters.");
    System.exit(0);
  }
}
/* Example Run:
Length: 5.8 m
Height: 2.4 m
The area of the wall is 13.92 square meters.
*/
```

Using comments in program code

We can tell the Java compiler that text is commentary in two ways:

- By using /* and */. All text between /* and */ is ignored by the compiler. There can easily be several lines of text between /* and */.

- By using //. The rest of the line is ignored.

In this book, the comments are used in the following manner:
/* and */ are always used if the comment consists of at least one line of text. We use // if the rest of the line should be interpreted as a comment. For example:

```
double price = 140.50;   // price in Swedish Crowns
```

There's usually a *header comment* at the top of a file. In this book, that will include the file name, the author's initials, the date of the most recent version of the file, and often a short description of the file. In larger programming systems, the header comment can contain far more comprehensive information.

Otherwise, comments are used to explain bits of code that might not be obvious. On the other hand, it's usually assumed that the reader is familiar with the programming language. The comment shouldn't repeat what the code statement says. An example of a superfluous comment:

```
double number = 4; // declares a variable named number, and sets it equal to 4
```

However, in some places in this book we will use comments like this to explain new things. In another situation these comments would be considered superfluous.

Problems

1. Change the length and height in the program in Program Listing 2.1 so that it calculates the area of another wall.

2. Expand the program so that it also calculates the perimeter of the wall. Print out the result.

2.3 Algorithms, Programming Errors, and Test Data

An *algorithm* is "a limited and ordered set of well-defined rules for solving a problem".[1] Note that the rules (instructions) are clearly defined—they shouldn't be ambiguous. This doesn't necessarily mean that they are very detailed—we can have algorithms with many different degrees of detail. Having different levels of detail in algorithms is key in non-object-oriented programming, which we won't go into here. In object-oriented programming the problem at hand is almost always

---

1. [Hofstad, Løland, Scott 1997, p. 19.]

smaller, and there's rarely a need for algorithms on multiple levels. An algorithm's rules are "ordered" by definition. That means that they have to be carried out in a specific order. Usage instructions and cake recipes are familiar examples of algorithms. The program in the previous example builds on the following algorithm:

1. Read the length and height.

2. Calculate the area using the stated formula.

3. Output the area.

We say that a program that goes through the compiler without error messages has no *syntax errors*. The program's syntax is correct. That means that we have combined words and punctuation in the program in such a way that the compiler can translate it to a series of byte code instructions.

Errors can arise when you run the program. There may be errors that stop the program from running, or it may be that the program doesn't solve the problem that it was intended to solve. The reason for this might be that the algorithm is programmed wrong, or that the algorithm is wrong. Errors of this type are called *logical errors* (the expression *semantic errors* is also used, "semantic" meaning "of or relating to meaning"). The compiler doesn't help us find logical errors. We can find logical errors by running a carefully thought-out set of test data through the program.

A *test data set* is a set of input and output data values whose purpose is to detect logical errors in the program. Test data of course has to be realistic data, but it's also important to choose data that will test the program's outer limits. A program for organizing books in a library has to work for zero books and for 200,000 books (or whatever the upper limit is). In this case, realistic data will be somewhere between these two outer limits.

We set up the test data for our program as shown in Table 2.1.

Table 2.1 Test data set for a program that calculates the area of a wall

Data Set No.	Length	Height	Expected Results	
1	0.0	0.0	0.0	no wall
2	100	10	1000	a large wall
3	2.3	4.5	10.35	a "normal" wall
4	-2.5	3	error message	

If we run the program with data set number 4, it will calculate that the area is -7.5. We don't get any message that negative length is meaningless. That's because the program doesn't check that the input data is correct before the calculations are performed. Program Listing 2.3 demonstrates how we can do this. We use the language elements `if` and `else`: *if* a condition is satisfied (here: both height and length are greater than zero), then we will calculate the area; *if not*, then we will send a message to the user. This is covered thoroughly in chapter 5. Until then, we'll get by without checking the input data.

We've seen the need for test data. There are also other ways to find logical errors in a program. *Inspections* are used a great deal. Briefly, this is when other people formally go through the code. The benefit to this, over testing, is that this type of debugging can take place early on in the development process. The earlier an error is detected, the cheaper it will be to fix.

Program Listing 2.3

```
/*
 * WallCalculations1.java   E.L. 2001-08-09
 */

class WallCalculations1 {
 public static void main(String[] args) {
  double length = -2.5;
  double height = 3;
  if (length > 0 && height > 0) { // if length > 0 and height > 0
    double area = length * height;
    System.out.println("The area of the wall is " + area + " square meters.");
  } else {                    // ...otherwise....
    System.out.println("The length and/or the height has a non-positive value.");
  }
 }
}

/* Example Run:
The length and/or the height has a non-positive value.
*/
```

Problem

Test the program above with the test data set in table 2.1.

2.4   Statements, Blocks, and Names

A program consists of many statements. A *statement* is an instruction to the computer. It ends with a semicolon(;). A group of statements surrounded by curly braces {} is called a *block*. In some contexts, a block can also be considered a statement.

A statement consists of keywords, names (identifiers), and special characters. A programming language has a well-defined set of *keywords*. These words are reserved for particular purposes in the language and cannot be used for anything else. The Java keywords are listed in Appendix B.

In Program Listing 2.1 the following keywords appear: `class`, `public`, `static`, `void`, `double`.

In addition to the keywords, there are words that are explained in standard classes that come with Java: `String`, `System`, `out`, `println`. We say that the words are declared there. *Declaring* means introducing a new name and explaining to Java what it's a name for.

In addition to all the declarations that come with Java, we also make our own declarations. There are six such declarations in the example: we declare the variables `length`, `height`, and `area`. We also explain that `WallCalculations` is a class and that `main()` is a method in this class. `args` is a parameter for the `main()` method. We'll come back to its exact meaning further on in the book.

Java Core

Name

A name (or identifier) can consist of letters,[2] digits, the underscore character _, and $. The first character cannot be a digit. Names cannot include spaces. Upper- and lower-case letters are distinct characters. There are no limits on the number of characters in the name.

Examples of different valid names: `number`, `Number`, `numberOfChildren`, `student21`.

Naming conventions

In addition to the rules, there are also some recommended guidelines for names. These guidelines primarily come from [URL Coding standard] with our adaptations, which are described in Appendix F. We'll discuss these recommendations as they become relevant. For the time being, the following suggestion is important:

Names should evoke immediate associations to the reality the program is modeling. That means, for example, that `p1`, `yy`, and `hj` are rarely good names.

---

2. Because the Unicode character set is used in Java, it is possible to have other letters than a to z in names. This is often practical to non-English programmers. But be aware of using such letters in class names if you are working in a mixed Windows/MS-DOS environment, because a class name will correspond to a filename. And the special letters do not necessarily have the same codes in Windows as in MS-DOS.

Many development environments require the file where we save a Java program to have the same name as the class that contains main(). Upper- and lower-case letters also have to be consistent. The file always has to have a *java* extension at the end. Thus, the program in Program Listing 2.1 is in a file named *WallCalculations.java*, while the program in Program Listing 2.2 is in the file *WallCalculations2.java*.

Problems

1. Which of the following words are permissible in Java?

```
To day            #hit
TheBookOfMary The_bike_of_Eve
NUMBER           _Number34
100Number        History###
```

2. Study the following program:

```
class Conversion {
  public static void main(String[] args) {
    final double factor = 4.2;
    double numberOfCalories = 500;
    double numberOfKJoules = numberOfCalories * factor;
    System.out.println("The number of kJ is " + numberOfKJoules);

  }
}
```

Type the program in and run it. Answer the following questions:

(a) What keywords are used? (Use the list in Appendix B.)

(b) What variables are defined? Draw a figure similar to the one in Figure 2.1.

2.5 Variables and Constants

The contents of a variable can vary as the program runs, or it can remain constant.

It's normally possible to change the content of a variable. For example, we want to be able to input values for the variable, or to calculate the value it will have.

A variable has to have a value before it can be used. We often give the variable a value at the same time as we declare its name—we say that we *initialize the variable*. For example:

```
double sum = 3.7;
```

We can achieve the same effect with the following two statements, but there's rarely any advantage to splitting them up this way:

```
double sum;
sum = 3.7;
```

We can also change the content of a variable several times:

```
perimeter = 15.6;
perimeter = 1670.5;
perimeter = 2 * (length + height); // the perimeter of a rectangle
```

Variables that are declared inside a method are called *local variables*. All the variables we look at in this chapter are declared inside the main() method, hence they are local.

The *scope* of a name (a declaration) refers to the part of the program where we can use the name without indicating more precisely where it is. A local variable's scope is the rest of the block where the variable is declared. A local variable cannot be used outside its scope.

Local variables have to be given a starting value in the program. Study how the different variables in Program Listing 2.1 get their values.

Java Core

Declaring a local variable

Syntax:

> *dataType variableName;*

or

> *dataType variableName = initialValue;*

A variable is a storage location in the computer's memory. The size corresponds to the data type in question. The program can change the variable's contents.

A local variable is always declared inside a method. The variable has to be given a value before it can be used. A variable's scope is the rest of the block where that variable is declared.

Examples:

```
double area = length * height;
int sum;
int number = 4;      // the number of triangles
```

There's a new data type in the example in the Java Core box. The int data type means that the variable's content will be interpreted as an integer.

Also notice that the syntax is written in italics. Text written this way is a description of what the syntax rules require. For example:

> *dataType variableName = initialValue;*

The word "dataType" has to be replaced with a valid data type, while "variableName" has to be a valid name, and "initialValue" a value permissible for the data type. The punctuation marks shown in the syntax description always have to be included.

In some circumstances, we want the contents of a variable to be constant. We can, for example, have a variable with the name upperLimit. Here we set the content to 30, and that cannot be changed by the program. We declare a *named constant* this way:

```
final int upperLimit = 30;
```

Now if the program tries to change the content of the variable upperLimit, the compiler will send an error message.

final is a *modifier*—in other words, a keyword that modifies the original meaning of what follows it.[3] In this case, upperLimit becomes a variable with a constant content.

Why should we declare a name for the number 30? Can't we just use the number 30 when we need it? There are several reasons to give the number a name:

- In a formula, the name upperLimit will tell the reader a good deal more than the number 30.

- If the limit changes, we only have to change the number 30 in one place—namely, where the variable upperLimit is declared.

- For decimals, we're assured of using the same number of decimal places everywhere, not 3.14 in one place and 3.14159 in another.

- If we have large numbers or numbers with a lot of decimal places, it's easier and safer to write the name than the number.

We call the number 30 and other constants that come up in the program *anonymous constants* or *literals*. In Program Listing 2.1 we have the following literals:

```
5.0
2.3
"The area of the wall is "
" square meters"
```

---

3. The following modifiers exist: public, protected, private, final, static, transient, volatile, abstract, synchronized, native. We cover most of them in this book (see the index at the end of the book).

Java Core

Declaring a named constant

Syntax:

> final *dataType variableName = initialValue*;

The keyword `final` makes the contents of a variable constant. The program will not be able to change the contents of this type of variable. The variable has to be initialized. The value can be an anonymous or previously named constant, or a constant expression.

Examples:

```
final int number = 100;
final int numberOfParts = 5;
final int numberPerPart = number / numberOfParts;
final int size = 125;
final double cmPerInch = 2.54;
```

Conventions for naming variables

We don't distinguish between the names of variables and constants. Here are some recommendations (remember that these are recommendations, not syntax rules):

- Variable names should be lower case.

- If a name is composed of more than one word, every new word should start with a capital letter. For example: `numberOfCitiesInBelgium`.

- Avoid using underscore and $.

Problems

The following statements are given:

```
final int numberOfYears = 35
double Amount = 40,95;
final aConstant = 789.6;
DOUBLE number = 15.7;
Amount = Amont * 100;
```

1. Insert these statements into a program and run it. You will get several compile-time errors. Try to explain them. Correct the errors so that the program compiles.

2. Which of the names are inconsistent with the naming conventions used in this book?

2.6   Data Types

A *data type* (or just "type") describes a set of values. The data type also determines which operations can be performed on these values—for example, comparison or addition.

Here we will go through the *primitive data types*, which are data types for integers, decimal numerals, characters, and boolean values. To be thorough, we'll consider all of them. You probably won't need all of them or see the point to all of them until later on in the book.

The size of the set of values that belongs to the different data types varies, and that means that variables of different types use different size of storage in the internal memory. For the primitive data types the size varies from 1 to 8 bytes.

We'll also look at the `String` data type, which is used for texts. This is not a primitive data type and for now we'll only include what we need in order to write simple programs that handle texts.

The integer types

The most commonly used integer type is `int`. Examples of literals of this data type are:

    105
    -67
    0

Earlier we learned that variables are actually composed of zeros and ones. The contents of a variable are therefore easily interpreted with respect to a base 2 binary system, and this gives us an integer value. For details on number systems, see Appendix C.

Table 2.2 shows the integer types that exist in Java. The `char` data type is included with the integer types, but we use variables of this type to store letters and other characters. It will be treated in a paragraph of its own.

Table 2.2 Data types for representation integers

Name	Number of Bytes	Range
byte	1	[-128, 127]
short	2	[-32,768, 32,767]
int	4	[-2,147,483,648, 2,147,483,647]
long	8	[-9,223,372,036,854,775,808, 9,223,372,036,854,775,807]
char	2	[0, 65,535], see separate section

The range indicates the maximum and minimum numbers that can be stored in a variable of this type. The int data type describes the set of all integers from -2,147,483,648 to +2,147,483,647. We say that the *range* for int is [-2,147,483,648, +2,147,483,647]. We need four bytes to store a value of this data type. The bigger the range, the more room it requires. There's room for more combinations of zeros and ones in an 8-byte variable than in a 4-byte variable.

An integer literal has the type int if it's not followed by the letter L. If it is, then it's type is long. We could also use a lower-case l, but since those are easy to confuse with the digit 1, we avoid doing so. Examples of long type literals:

```
-123456789L
223372036854775808L
90000l // we used a lower-case l here—difficult to read
```

An integer literal that starts with the digit 0 is interpreted according to the base 8 system. This very thing has been the cause of many "inexplicable" errors. If the literal starts with the characters 0x or 0X, it's interpreted according to the base 16 system. You can confirm this by inserting the following bit of code into a program and running it:

```
System.out.println("Printing 056 gives " + 056);  // value 46
System.out.println("Printing 0x00e6 gives " + 0x00e6); // value 230
```

We don't get an error message if the result of an integer calculation doesn't have room in the integer variable we're trying to store the result in. The only thing that happens is that the answer is wrong. Therefore, we have to be careful not to perform calculations where this can occur.

If we try to divide an integer by 0, on the other hand, we get an error message and the program stops.

Data types for decimal numerals

Variables of the double data type are used to store decimal numerals[4] in the computer. Literals of this type look like this:

```
1.25
-0.0067
6.7e10      (= 6.7·10^10)
3.256e-5    (= 3.256·10^-5)
```

Very large and very small numbers should be written with powers of 10 using e (or E).

---

4. Also called floating point numbers, which tells us something about how decimal numerals are represented internally in the computer, without going into any more detail about that here.

The range for double is approximately $\pm[10^{-308}, 10^{+308}]$. Notice that the range is divided in two, from a large negative numerical value to a small negative numerical value, and then from a small positive numerical value to a large positive numerical value. In addition, there is the number 0.0. This type of variable takes up 8 bytes (64 bits).

Decimal calculations never give 100% accurate results. We work with an approximate number of significant digits. Certain types of calculations are significantly less accurate. We'll look at this more closely in Chapter 5.

Variables of the data type float can also be used to store decimal numerals. The range, number of significant digits, and storage requirements for float and double are shown in Table 2.3.

A decimal numeral literal will be of the type double, if it's not followed by the letter F (or f). For example: 3.5F

Remember from the last section that when you divide an integer by 0 you get an error message and the program stops. This is not the case if at least one of the operands is a decimal numeral.

From math, we know that 0/0 is an indeterminate expression. If we ask a Java program to calculate this, and the operands are decimal numerals, we get the value NaN. This means "not a number."

Dividing by the decimal numeral 0.0 gives the value Infinity. This also agrees with what we know from math.

The following lines:

```
System.out.println("Zero divided by zero: " + 0.0 / 0.0);
System.out.println("Division by zero: " + 10.0 / 0.0);
```

gives the output:

```
Zero divided by zero: NaN
Division by zero: Infinity
```

Despite getting results from dividing by 0, we should be careful with this. These results won't be of any use in further calculations.

Table 2.3 Data types for representing decimal numerals

Name	Number of Bytes	Range
float	4	approx. $\pm[10^{-38}, 10^{+38}]$. Number of significant digits is about 7.
double	8	approx. $\pm[10^{-308}, 10^{+308}]$. Number of significant digits is about 15.

When you run the programs in this book, you will probably be irritated that decimal numerals are frequently output with an unnecessarily large number of decimal places. Getting outputs with a specific number of decimal places requires the use of classes and several lines of programming code. We'll cover this in Section 8.3.

A data type for boolean values

Little by little, we'll see that we often need variables that can store a boolean value (true or false). This type of variable contains the value `true` or the value `false`. The data type is called `boolean`. Examples:

```
boolean allWallsArePainted = false;
allWallsArePainted = true;  // now all the walls are finished
```

A data type for characters

The `char` data type is used to handle letters and other characters. Examples of literals of the `char` data type:

```
'O'
'Z'
'_'
'7'
'#'
```

A literal of this type is enclosed in single quotes.

A variable of the `char` type takes up two bytes.

Because it is not possible to store anything but numbers in the computer, every character has its own number. There are many numbering systems. Most programming languages use the ASCII character set. This character set is defined so that each character uses one byte of memory. That means that it can only contain 256 different values. Of these, only the values 0 to 127 are standardized. The other values vary from platform to platform and from country to country. This is, of course, unfortunate in a world that's becoming ever more international. Therefore, Java uses the Unicode character set.[5] With two bytes per character at its disposal, it's possible to store 65,536 different characters. The characters with numbers from 0–127 correspond to the characters with the same numbers in ASCII. Appendix D shows the standardized portion of the ASCII character set.

Also note that the *digit characters* have their own values. The digit character '5', for example, has the number 53.

We can speculate in which way we should write the character '. We *don't* write three single quotes. Instead, we use a backslash followed by two single quotes, like

---

5. Currently, Windows NT and several UNIX variants use the Unicode character set. More information about Unicode at [URL Unicode].

this `'\''`. There are a number of other characters that we have to write the same way. For example, `'\n'` denotes a newline. See table 2.4.

Table 2.4 Special characters written with a backslash before the character

Name	Character
newline	`'\n'`
backslash	`'\\'`
double quote, after the backslash: double quote and single quote	`'\"'`
single quote, after the backslash: two single quotes	`'\''`
tabulator	`'\t'`

A data type for texts

Frequently we need to work with texts. We might need to output a result to the screen, or we need to read, for example, a name or an address. It's possible to handle these texts using the `char` data type, but it's relatively difficult. Therefore, a `String` class has been created that makes it possible for us to work on a more abstract level. Every individual character in the text is represented by a `char`, but we deal with the text as a whole. We say that we're working with instances of the `String` class. We call these instances *text strings*, or just *strings*.
Examples of string literals:

```
"This is a string."
"This is a longer string."
"1"
"Next is an empty string."
""
"Here are \"double quotes\" and 'single quotes'"
```

The last example demonstrates that we can insert special characters directly into the string, as long as we use the backslash before the character. There is one exception: we can insert single quotes without using the backslash.

We're used to using string literals in output statements. We can also declare `String` variables. Examples of strings in use:

```
String city = "Trondheim";
String text = "This is four words.";
int number = 17;
System.out.println("We have " + number + " groups");
String cities = city + " Bergen";
System.out.println(cities);
```

Even if we can use the + operator to concatenate, or link together, strings and numbers, we can't use the - operator to cut strings. The program excerpt above gives the following output:

```
We have 17 groups
Trondheim Bergen
```

The following statement prints three words with newlines between them:

```
System.out.println("Line1" + "\n" + "Line2" + "\n" + "Line3");
```

We use *single quotes* when we make literals of the char type. Examples: `'a'` `'9'` `'7'`

We use *double quotes* when we make string literals. Examples: `"hi"` `"a"` `"this was a little complicated"`

Problems

1. What data type do the following literals belong to?

```
12.45
"Hello!"
"\""
'\"'
12345L
0456
true
3.245e-5
```

2. We need to store some merchandise information. What data type should we use to represent the following?

   (a) Price

   (b) Quantity of merchandise measured in kilograms

   (c) Quantity of merchandise measured in number

   (d) Color code (a letter)

   (e) Bar code

   (f) Name

3. What is output if the following statements are inserted into a program and it's run?

```
String firstName = "Ann";
String middleName = "Isabelle";
String lastName = "Adams";
```

```
String fullName = firstName + " " + middleName + " " + lastName;
System.out.println(fullName);
double number = 2.3e-2;
System.out.println("The number is " + number);
char symbol = 'a';
System.out.println("The symbol is " + symbol);
```

2.7 Assignments and Arithmetical Expressions

An expression has exactly *one* value. From math, we are familiar with arithmetical expressions formed using arithmetical operations (addition, subtraction, multiplication, division).

An expression consists of operands and operators. The *operands* correspond to the variables and constants in the expression. In the expression

```
number * price * 0.5
```

number, price, and 0.5 are operands. We use *operators* to deal with the variables and constants (operands) in an expression. In the expression above, we perform two multiplications using the operator *.

The four basic arithmetic operators

The four operations are addition (the + operator), subtraction (the - operator), multiplication (the * operator) and division (the / operator).

Expressions are usually, but not always, interpreted from left to right. In a composite expression, operations with * and / are performed first, then those with + and -. We say that * and / have *operator precedence* (priority) over + and -. For example, 5 + 7 * 5 = 40. If we have several operations with the same priority, these are interpreted from left to right.

We can use parentheses to override the predefined order. For example:

```
8 + 7 * 2 = 22
(5 + 7) * 5 = 60
6.0 / 3.0 *4.0 = 8.0
6.0 / (3.0 * 4.0) = 0.5
```

In addition to the operators for the four types of calculations, we usually also have the *modulo operator* in programming. In Java, this operator is written as a percentage sign. This gives the remainder of a division. Examples:

```
3 % 4 = 3        -3.7 % 2 = -1.7
10 % 3 = 1       -5.5 % -2.2 = -1.1
-6 % 4 = -2      0 % 5 = 0
```

The modulo operator has the same priority as multiplication and division.

Dividing integers results in *integer division* (in other words, the result will be the quotient except for the remainder of the division):
5 / 2 = 2-5 / 2 = -2
1 / 3 = 0-1 / -3 = 0
2 / 3 * 5 = 0-5 / -2 = 2
2 * 5 / 3 = 30 / 5 = 0

The unary operators + and -

Usually, + and - take two operands, and we say that they're binary. A unary operator takes one operand. There are unary versions of the operators + and -. We can write +a and -b. In and of itself, this might not be very interesting, but eventually we'll discover that sometimes we need to multiply a number by -1. Instead of setting up the multiplication, we use the unary operator -

```
number2 = (-1) * number1;  // not like this
number2 = -number1;  // but like this
```

Here we see examples of assignment—the right side is calculated first, then the result is stored in the variable on the left side. More on this below.

Assignment

In the example calculations in the section above, we used the = sign the same way we do in math, namely with the meaning "is equal to" (for example, 5 / 2 = 2).

If we use = in the program code, it's an operator, and the operation performed is called *assignment*. Whatever's on the right side of = is calculated first. The resulting value is placed in the variable on the left side. We say that the right side is "assigned" to the left side.
Examples:

```
sum = 4;
sum = sum + 5;  // NB! Not exactly the same as in math!
```

After these two statements are executed, sum has the value 9.

We can also perform an equivalent operation with strings:

```
String result = "This is the beginning,";
result = result + " and this is the continuation.";
System.out.println(result);
```

If we insert this bit of code into a program and run it, we get the following output:

```
This is the beginning, and this is the continuation.
```

Note that the left side of the assignment operator always has to be the name of a variable.

The assignment operation has the lowest priority of all the operators, and it is interpreted from right to left.

Because the assignment character is an operator, the assignment will be an expression with a specific value. The value of the expression is equal to the contents of the variable on the left side of the assignment character after the assignment is completed.

The value of the expression `number2 = 4` is 4. For example, this makes it possible for us to write:

    number1 = number2 = 4

First, `number2` is set to equal 4, and the value of the expression `number2 = 4` calculates to 4. Then `number1 = 4` is carried out.

Problems

We have the following variables with integer contents: a is equal to 10; b is equal to 5; c is equal to 3; d is equal to 2. And we have the following variables where the contents are to be interpreted as decimal numerals: p is equal to 2.8; q is equal to 3.3. These variables are used in problems 1–3 below.

1. Draw out the variables the way it was done in Figure 2.1.

2. Which of the following statements is legal?

    5 = 5;
    b = b + c;
    d = d;
    10 = b * 2;
    b = a : 2;
    p := q;

3. What is the value of each of the following expressions?

    c + d * a
    a * b / c + a
    c % d
    d % c
    p % q
    q % p
    c % d % a + b / c
    a = b = 16

4. Compose expressions for the following formulas:

$$b^2 - 4ac$$
$$x^2 + y^2 + z^2$$
$$x^3$$
$$(a - b) \ (a + b)$$

$$\frac{a + b}{c + d}$$

2.8 Type Conversion

There's no requirement that both of the operands in an operation have to be of the same type. If the operands are of different types, they will automatically be converted to the same type before the calculation is carried out. The operands are converted to the data type with the largest range. If automatic conversion is not possible, an error message is generated.

For example, if one of the operands is a decimal numeral, the other operand will be converted to a decimal numeral before the calculation is performed.

```
double sum = 5674.33;
int number = 14;
double average = sum / number;
```

The average is calculated as 5,674.33 / 14.0, and the result will be 405.31.

Sometimes we need to control the type conversion. Earlier, we saw that integer division results in an integer (5/2 = 2). This is not always desirable. If that's the case, we can ensure that the operands are converted to decimal numerals before the calculation is carried out. We do this by placing (double) in front of the operand that will be converted. This type of conversion is called *casting*. For example:

```
int theNumberOfKids =  5;
int theNumberOfApples = 23;
double applesPerKid  = (double) theNumberOfApples / (double)
theNumberOfKids;
```

After this section of the program is carried out, applesPerKid will have the value 4.6. Strictly speaking, it's enough to cast only one of the operands in an expression, then the others will be converted automatically.

In casting, the contents of the variables do not change. The value of the variable theNumberOfApples is obtained, and then this value is converted.

Note that it's *not* enough to have a double variable on the left of the assignment character. Then an integer division is performed. After that, the result of this will be converted to double, and we get 4.0 as the end result.

Conversion from decimal numeral to integer always has to be done with casting, and the result is truncated, not rounded. Both 2.8 and 2.3 will have the value 2. Examples:

```
int a = (int) 1.7;
int b = (int) (1.6 + 1.7);
int c = (int) 1.6 + (int) 1.7;
System.out.println(a + " " + b + " " + c);
```

The output will be 1 3 2.

We can add 0.5 to the original value to get rounding to occur:

```
double d1 = 3.2;
double d2 = 3.9;
double d3 = 4.0;
double d4 = 4.5;
int p = (int) (d1 + 0.5);
int q = (int) (d2 + 0.5);
int r = (int) (d3 + 0.5);
int s = (int) (d4 + 0.5);
System.out.println(p + " " + q + " " + r + " " + s);
```

The output here will be 3 4 4 5.

Java Core

Type conversion in calculating expressions

The following rule applies for automatic conversions:

Before the calculation, both of the operands are converted to the largest type that is included in the expression. The following order applies (from largest to smallest): `double`, `float`, `long`, `int`, `short`, `byte`. This means, for example, that if at least one operator is `double`, the other will also be converted to `double` before the calculation is performed. This type of conversion will always be valid.

If we want to convert to a smaller type, this must be done with casting. Java doesn't give you any error message if there's not enough room for the number in the new type. So, the result will be wrong. For example, it doesn't work to cast the `double` value 3e12 (= $3 \cdot 10^{12}$) to `int` because the range for `int` does not cover numbers that big.

It's not possible to convert to or from the `boolean` type.

What happens if we try to convert from `char` to `int`? For example:

```
char symbol = '5';
int digit = symbol;
```

This works fine because `char` is a smaller type than `int`. The `digit` variable gets the number assigned to the character '5' in the Unicode system (i.e., 53).

The `digit` variable can get the value 5 this way:

```
int digit = symbol - '0';
```

The character '0' has the number 48, and since the numeric characters have progressive numbers in the Unicode system, `digit` will have the value 5.

Problems

We have the same variables as in the problems after section 2.7:

a is equal to 10; b is equal to 5; c is equal to 3; d is equal to 2; p is equal to 2.8; and q is equal to 3.3.

Note that Java only considers a single (partial) expression at a time. For example:

double result = 3.7 + 3 / 4;

The division is performed first as an integer division, then the addition is carried out. The result will be 3.7. If we don't want the integer division, we have to cast:

double result = 3.7 + (double) 3 / 4;

1. What is the value of each of the following expressions?

p + (double) a / q
p + a / q
(int) p + (int) q
(int) (p + q)

2. Assume we have the variables stated before problem 1. One of the expressions below has to be cast before assignment can occur. Which one? What will the content of the variables be after the statements below are carried out?

d = d / b;
b = d * c;
a = p + q;
a = a + 4;

3. What is output when the following section of code is run?

long a = 2000000000 * 30;
long b = 2000000000L * 30L;
System.out.println("a = " + a + ", b = " + b);

2.9 Calculations for Our Renovation Project

We will need several formulas for our renovation project. We can check the formulas with the following data:

- The wall is 7.2 meters long and 2.35 meters high.

- The roll of wallpaper is 54 cm wide and 12.5 meters long. A roll of wallpaper costs $10.

- The paint covers 10 m^2 per liter. Three coats are recommended. The paint costs $8 per liter.

In the program, these numbers will be input data. Output data will be the number of rolls of wallpaper and number of liters of paint that are necessary for the wall, and the price for them.

How many liters of paint do we need to buy?

The area of the wall is given by the following formula:

    double area = length * height;

The number of liters of paint needed can be calculated as follows:

    double noOfLiters = area * noOfCoats / noOfSqMPerLiter;

We'll round up to the nearest half liter. First we find the number of whole liters:

    int noOfLitersInteger = (int) noOfLiters;

Then we find out how much we have beyond the number of whole liters:

    double more = noOfLiters - noOfLitersInteger;

If this is over 0.5, we should add another whole liter. If not, we'll add a half liter.

Numerical example: Area = 7.2 * 2.35 m^2 = 16.92 m^2. Number of liters of paint: 16.92 * 3 / 10 = 5.08. We round up to the nearest half liter; in other words, we have to buy 5.5 liters of paint. That will cost $8 * 5.5 = $44.

What does it cost to wallpaper a wall?

First we have to calculate how many rolls of wallpaper we need. We start by calculating the number of wallpaper widths necessary:

    int noOfHeights = (int) (lengthSurface / widthPerRoll); // length is the wall's length

We remember that casting int leads to truncation. If we had rounded the number, it wouldn't have helped very much. Even if it's only a few centimeters over, we have to calculate an entire height in addition. Therefore, we have to add one height if the division doesn't come out even.

Numerical example: Number of heights is equal to 7.2/0.54 = 13.33. In other words, we need 14 heights of wallpaper.

We have to avoid horizontal seams in the middle of the wall. By throwing out remnants that occur this way, we can calculate how many heights we'll get from one roll:

    int noOfHeightsPerRoll = (int) (lengthPerRoll / heightSurface);

The number of whole rolls we need will be:

    int noOfRolls = noOfHeights / noOfHeightsPerRoll;

If there are remnants, we have to add one roll. The remnants from this roll may be usable on the next wall, but our program won't take that into consideration.

Numerical example: The length of a roll is 12.5 meters. The number of heights per roll is 12.5/2.35 = 5.32, or 5 whole heights. The remnant is set aside. The number of rolls is thus 14/5 = 2.8, which is to say that we need three rolls to wallpaper the wall. These three rolls will cost 3 * $10 = $30.

2.10 New Concepts in This Chapter

Concept	Brief Explanation
algorithm	A limited and ordered set of well-defined rules for solving a problem.
anonymous constant	A constant in the program, examples: `23`, `"Mary"`.
assign	To calculate an expression and then store the result in a variable. Uses the operator =.
binary operator	An operator that requires two operands.
bit	"Binary digit." One of the digits 0 or 1 when they are used in the base 2 system.
block	A group of statements surrounded by {}.
byte	8 bits.
casting	Asking the program to convert from one data type to another data type. May give the wrong result because the range of the second data type may be too small to contain the value.
data type	A data type describes a set of values. It also determines which operations we can perform on these values.
declare	Introduce a name to the compiler, and tell what it's a name for.
`final`	Modifier that's used, among other things, to declare a named constant.
floating point numbers	Decimal numerals stored on the computer with respect to a representation form called the floating-point system.
header comment	Comment lines located at the top of a file. In this book they contain the file name, the author's initials, the date of the most recent version of the file, and often also a description of the file's contents. In larger programming systems, header comments often contain more comprehensive information.
`Infinity`	The result of dividing by 0.0 and other calculations with decimal numerals that give result values that are too large.
initialize	Give a value to a variable when it is declared.
input data	Data that the program reads, for example, from the keyboard.
inspection	Letting someone other than the author read the source code in a formal manner to find logical errors.
integer division	The result that when two integers are divided by each other, the remainder from the division is deleted, e.g. 5/3 = 1.
keyword	Word with predefined significance, cannot be used in any way other than that specified in the syntax of the language.
literal	See anonymous constant.

Concept	Brief Explanation
local variable	A variable that is declared inside a method.
logical error	The program gives the wrong answer, or the execution is stopped part-way through (we thought things out wrong when we wrote the program).
modifier	A keyword that modifies the original meaning of that which follows.
modulo operator	Gives the remainder of a division, written %, e.g. 5%3 = 2.
named constant	A variable with constant content, which is given its value using an anonymous constant.
NaN	"Not a Number"—result of a mathematically indeterminate expression, the division 0.0/0.0.
operator precedence	Controls the interpretation order in a composite mathematical expression. For the operators we covered: the operators * / and % have the highest priority, then come + and - and lowest =
output data	Data that the program prints to the screen. The user reads this data.
primitive data type	A predefined data type where the type name is a keyword: byte, short, int, long, char, float, double, boolean.
scope	The portion of the program where we can use a name (declaration) without stating more precisely where it is declared (without "qualification," see chapter 4).
semantic error	See logical error.
sequential execution	Program statements are executed, one by one, in the order they're in.
statement	Instruction to the computer; ends with a semicolon. In some contexts, a block is considered a statement.
string	An object that contains a text; the object is an instance of the String class.
String	Predefined type (class) for handling texts.
syntax	Rules that we have to follow when setting up a program so that the compiler will understand what we mean.
syntax error	Error that the compiler discovers; our program doesn't follow the syntax rules.
test data set	A set of input and output data values whose purpose is to detect errors in the program. These values are often more "extreme" than realistic data.
text string	The same as "string."
type	See data type.
unary operator	An operator that only requires one operand.
variable	A storage location that can contain a value of a given data type.

2.11 Review Problems

1. Explain what input and output data mean.

2. What's a variable?

3. What's an algorithm?

4. What are the characteristics of a keyword? Where can you find a synopsis of all the keywords in Java?

5. What data types belong to the group "primitive data types"?

6. What are the relative priorities of the operators covered in this chapter (+ - * / %)?

7. What is the value of the expression (5 * 6 / 7 + 5 % 3)? Change the value of the expression by adding parentheses in different places.

8. Why can it be detrimental to have the digit 0 first in an integer literal?

9. How do you write the number $3.67 \cdot 10^7$ in Java?

10. What happens when you divide by zero?

11. When do you use single quotes? When do you use double quotes?

12. What is Unicode?

13. What's the difference between the use of the character = in programming and its use in math?

14. What is casting? When is it necessary? When is it impossible?

2.12 Programming Problems

Since reading data is so complicated in Java, you can assign values to variables directly in the program for these problems.

If you want to input data, you can copy the method used in Program Listing 2.2 for decimal numerals. Integers are parsed from strings as follows:

```
int number = Integer.parseInt(numberInput);
```

Problem 1

Write a program that converts from inches to centimeters. An inch is 2.54 centimeters. Set up a test data set, and test the program.

Problem 2

Write a program that converts hours, minutes, and seconds into a total number of seconds. Set up a test data set and test the program.

Problem 3

Write a program that inputs a number of seconds and calculates how many hours, minutes, and seconds this is (hint: use integer division). Set up a test data set and test the program.

Using Ready-Made Classes

Learning goals for this chapter

After completing this chapter, you will understand the following concepts:

- Object, the difference between objects in reality and in a program
- Attribute, message, operation, class, client, server, encapsulation
- Method, constructor, parameter, argument, client program. Class constants and class methods. Package and `import`

You will be able to:

- Draw a class diagram based on an informal description of the class
- Use methods in the `JOptionPane` class to communicate with the user
- Use the most important methods in the `String` class

There are several systematic ways to solve programming problems. Previously, one would approach a problem like this by focusing on an algorithmic abstraction. One started by setting up an algorithm at a very high level of abstraction. For example: input data – perform computations – print results. Then one took each step of this algorithm separately and added further detail, often on many levels depending on the complexity of the problem. It wasn't uncommon that one would discover at a low level that the problem was one that had been solved before. Isolating program bits that solved specific problems became, and still is, of great use in program development. Libraries of routines, for example, for mathematical computations, graphics, and handling large quantities of data in archives (databases) are common. Of course, even if the data is important, there is no clear connection in these libraries between the data and the algorithms that do things to the data.

Many people believe that one of the reasons it's so difficult to create large and complex systems lies in this method of approach. Data and algorithms should be viewed in context. Software libraries should not consist merely of handling routines for data, but of a type of modules where these routines are indissolubly linked to the data they can handle. These types of modules are called classes. We can have classes that describe students, that describe cars or books.

Approaching a programming problem this way is called object orientation. It's not required, but is an absolute advantage, to create the program using an object-oriented programming language. Java is just such a language. In this chapter, we will see how we use ready-made classes. In the next chapter, we will create classes ourselves. Mastering classes is completely fundamental to everything we will do later on in this book.

3.1 Objects as Models of Reality

A *model* is a simplification of reality. Models help us to understand complicated realities. From everyday life, we are familiar with differing models of the same thing—a house can be modelled both as a blueprint and as a three-dimensional minihouse made of plastic. Different models of the same thing help us understand different aspects of reality. The blueprint makes it easy for us to form an image of the overall floor plan. Detailed measurements are included. The three-dimensional model gives us an impression of how the house will look from the outside. It's also important to be clear about the fact that a model isn't just the real thing in miniature—it also has characteristics that do not conform to reality. The blueprint is two-dimensional; the three-dimensional model is made out of a different material than the house and doesn't have glass in its windows.

The objects are the core of an object-oriented model. An *object* is a model of a thing that our problem is about. An object can model something concrete like a chair, a table, a person, or a bus, or something abstract like a meeting or an agreement. Objects are always nouns. We are focusing on *responsibility*. An object can be responsible for knowing a number of things about itself.

Examples:

- A car has knowledge of its own license plate number, make, and model. It knows how it starts, how it drives, and how it stops.

- A student knows her own student ID number, her own grades, name, birth date, and address. She knows how to get to her campus and how she will answer the questions on the test.

- A meeting knows where it's being held, who's participating, when it starts, and when it's scheduled to end. Later, it also knows who participated, and when it actually ended.

Objects in reality and in programming

An object in an object-oriented model is essentially different from the real object that it models. The model object has a great deal of knowledge about itself, regardless of whether the real object is alive, dead, or abstract. All the same, we almost always take the real objects as the basis when making the model objects.

In continuation, when we talk about objects, we mean the model objects. If we want to refer to the real objects, we say that in plain text.

Very soon we will study the three examples named earlier in more detail. First, however, we need to look at the concepts of *client*, *server*, *message*, and *operation*.

Client and server are roles that objects play.[1] Objects collaborate when a client object requests a service by sending a message to a server object. The server carries out an operation as a reaction to the message. The server can send responses back to the client.

In Figure 3.1 we see Greta and her car. Greta sends messages to the car: start, speed up, brake, stop, etc. Greta is a client object; the car is a server object. As a reaction to the message, the car performs the right operation: start, speed up, brake, stop, etc.

client   server

Greta sends a message to
her car: "speedUp"

Figure 3.1   The object Greta plays the role of client, while the car object plays the role of server

Especially in this example, it's relatively easy to imagine some of the knowledge that must lie in the server object. A driver is used to the car having the responsibility for how the operations of starting, driving, etc. will be performed. He needs to know very little about the complicated processes that take place in reality. In addition to knowledge of the operations, the model also requires that the car object have knowledge of the license plate number, make, and model. In the real world, this information is part of the car's surroundings, but since it is part of characterizing the car object, we say that the object itself will have this knowledge.

Let's look at example number two: Of course a student has knowledge of her student ID number, address, and how she will respond to the questions in the

---

1. In chapter 1, the concepts of client and server were used in a very specific context. There we were discussing computers as Web servers and Web clients. The program we are running on a computer determines the role the computer plays.

exam. In the real world she is responsible for updating the information and taking the initiative to sign up for the class. In a way, she is both client and server. She sends messages to herself. It's possible to allow a single object to be both client and server, but usually two different objects play these roles. In an object-oriented model, the client will send the message "take the exam" to the student object. A client will also be able to send the message "this is your grade" to the student object.

In the third example, we will model something as abstract as a meeting. What will a meeting object be responsible for? A meeting is characterized by a location, a start and end time, participants, etc. A client should be able to send, for example, the following messages to a meeting object: start the meeting, move the meeting, change the timetable for the meeting.

An object has a *state*. The state for an object is "a condition or situation during the life of an object during which it satisfies some condition, performs some activity or waits for some event."[2] The student can sit in the exam room and wait for the tests to be given out. When the exams are passed out, she changes over to a new state.

An *attribute* is a named quality with a defined range of values. In the student example, the student ID number and address are attributes. The values for these attributes could, for example, be "1234567" and "56 University Ave." The "student ID number" attribute always consists of seven digits. The range of values is therefore all seven-digit integers. The "address" attribute can be defined as a text, or it can be one of a more precisely specified number of addresses.

An object has an *identity*. All real objects can be distinguished from each other. The same is true of our model objects. We distinguish the object with student ID number 1234567 from all other objects.

An object has a *behavior*. The object is capable of performing a number of tasks. Anne can change her address, and she can go to a lecture. An object's behavior is given as a quantity of operations that the object can perform.

Encapsulation is an important characteristic of objects. Information about how an object solves tasks is hidden inside the object. The client object doesn't need to know how the server object solves the task, just that it can be solved. A client object only relates to the behavior that is defined for the server object. Thus, the client can only send a limited selection of messages to the server object. Whoever constructs the object gets to decide which services the object will offer.

A *class* is a description of a quantity of objects that have the same attributes and same behavior in common.

It's common to illustrate a class using a *class diagram*. This is a standard notation that is a part of *Unified Modeling Language* (UML).[3] UML is independent of the programming language. We will, of course, be programming in Java, but other pro-

---

2. [Rumbaugh, Jacobson, Booch 1999, p. 433]

3. The main UML reference is [Rumbaugh, Jacobson, Booch 1999]. This is a reference work. The same three people have also written a more practically oriented user guide: [Booch, Rumbaugh, Jacobson 1999].

gramming languages can also be used where a UML model is the basis. Figure 3.2 shows an excerpt of the diagram for the class Car. The names in the class diagram are chosen such that we can use them in a program later. The first letter in a class name is usually a capital.

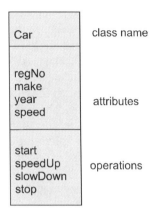

Figure 3.2   Class diagram (UML)

Problems

1. In the text above, you find an informal description of the classes Student and Meeting. Draw class diagrams.

2. Make a description of an object that models a microwave oven. Draw a class diagram with attributes and operations. Set up some states that the oven can be in.

3.2   Using Ready-Made Classes

Object-oriented programming means that we are composing objects in the program code with characteristics as described before. A class describes a collection of objects with the same attributes and behavior. An object is an *instance* of a class.

In chapter 2 we went through the primitive data types. We use these data types to represent, for example, integers and decimal numerals. Classes are also data types. Every class describes a specific data type. This kind of data type is called a *reference type*. By studying the class, we find out how we can use this type.

The Car type

The messages we can send to instances of the Car class are given by the operations in the class diagram in Figure 3.2 and can be set up as follows:

```
void start( )
void speedUp(int increase)
```

```
void slowDown(int decrease)
void stop( )
```

When operations appear this way in program code, we usually use the programming language's conceptual apparatus. In Java we call these *methods*. All methods can have *parameters*. Parameters describe data that the client has to send along with the message to the server object. The parameters are set up in parentheses after the name of the method. Every parameter has a data type and a name. In the example, the `speedUp()` and `slowDown()` methods each have a parameter, while `start()` and `stop()` don't have any parameters.

This type of description of messages that can be sent to an object will be the *interface* for the object. The outside world communicates with the object through this interface. There aren't any other ways to communicate with the object.

We call the program code behind the interface the *implementation* of the class. In chapter 4, we'll see how we implement classes.

We use ready-made classes by composing objects that we send messages to. In that way, our program functions as a client, while the object is the server. We say that we have composed a *client program*.

Let's say that in `main()` we have a car object that's called `theCarOfGreta`. (We'll get to how we create objects very soon.) We send a message to this object by putting a method name after the object name. The object name and the method name will be separated by a period. We give the instruction for the car to start:

```
theCarOfGreta.start();
```

We send a message to speed up:

```
theCarOfGreta.speedUp(30);
```

We send the value 30 along with the message. This is in accord with the description of the method. In this case, along with the message, we will send a data value of the `int` type. We call values like this *(actual) arguments*.[4] An argument is an actual value for a parameter. We also refer to sending messages to an object in this way as *calling a method*. In this case, it is implicit which object it applies to.

If the method is going to send a message back to the client, this must be done using a *return value*. The data type for this value is called the method's *return type* and comes in front of the method name in the description of the method. If it says `void` there, that means that the method doesn't send any value back. In our example, all the methods are of the `void` type.

A class is also responsible for making it possible to instantiate objects of its own type. *Constructors* are used to create instances of a class. Constructors are similar to methods, but they don't have a type name in front of their name, and their name is always the same as the class name. Example:

---

4. We are using the words parameter and argument the way they are used in the Java Language Specification [Gosling, Joy, Steele 1996] and in UML [Rumbaugh, Jacobson, Booch 1999]. In other literature you may find the expressions actual and formal parameters, or actual and formal arguments. The "actual" is what we call an argument. The "formal" is what we call a parameter.

Car(String regNo, String make, int year, int initSpeed);

A constructor is always used with the keyword new to create an instance of a class. The statement

Car theCarOfGreta = new Car("VD-12345", "Volvo", 1998, 0);

leads to an instance of Car class being composed. Figure 3.3 shows how room is set aside in the computer's internal memory when we create an instance of the Car class. Notice that it's the little square with an arrow on it that's called theCarOfGreta. This variable contains what we call a *reference* (actually the address) to the place where the data are stored (hence the reference type designation). The object is symbolized with a circle. The data values are stored for every instance of a class in the machine's internal memory, while information concerning permitted methods is indicated by the class the object belongs to.

An example of a complete client program:

```
class CarTrip {
  public static void main(String[] args) {
    Car theCarOfTom = new Car("AA-45456", "Saab", 1995, 0);
    theCarOfTom.start();
    theCarOfTom.speedUp(50);
    theCarOfTom.slowDown(20);
    theCarOfTom.stop();
  }
}
```

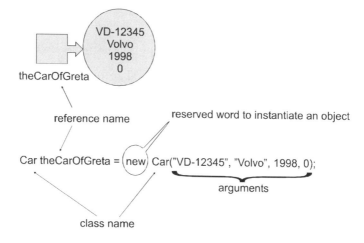

Figure 3.3 The reference theCarOfGreta refers to an instance of the Car class

The name of a variable of a reference type is the name of a *reference* to an instance of the class in question. For the sake of simplicity, we are using the name as if it was the name of the object, and not of a reference to it. We are also talking about the fact that a reference *points* to the object. (See the arrow in the figure.)

In the beginning:
The car objects have one reference each

theCarOfGreta   theCarOfAnne

Then we execute the statement
theCarOfGreta = theCarOfAnne;
and get the following:

There is no longer any reference to the other object; it'll be removed from the memory.

theCarOfGreta   theCarOfAnne

Figure 3.4 A reference is set to equal another reference

A reference can be given the value `null`, for example:

theCarOfGreta = null;

With this, the reference doesn't point to any object, and attempts to call methods in connection with the reference will result in a `NullPointerException`, and the program stopping.

If we set a reference equal to another, we get two references to the same object (see Figure 3.4). This has both advantages and disadvantages, which we will see as time goes by.

Java Core

Using classes in a client program
Syntax:

To instantiate an object:

> *className nameOfInstance* = new *className(listOfArguments)*;

The arguments in the argument list have to agree in type and number with the parameter list for a constructor. An argument can be a constant, an expression, or a variable. If the argument is a variable, the name of the variable doesn't need to be the same as the name of the parameter.

A name of a variable of a reference type is always a reference to an instance of the class. We can't get to the object any other way than through the reference. If we set a reference equal to another, we get two references to the same object.

Method call:

> *nameOfInstance.nameOfMethod(listOfArguments)*

What is said about arguments to the constructor (above) applies to arguments to methods, as well.

If the return type is something other than `void`, we can (but don't have to) use the method call in an expression.

Examples:

```
aMerchandise.increasePrice(20);
double price1 = aMerchandise.getPriceWithoutTax(quantity);
System.out.println("The price of " + quantity + " kg is $" +
                    aMerchandise.getPriceWithoutTax(quantity) + " without tax");
```

If `quantity` is 100, and the price without tax is calculated to be $6.75, the output from this last statement will be as follows:

```
The price of 100 kg is $6.75 without tax
```

What does it mean that the argument type has to agree with the parameter type? The type doesn't need to be the same. It's enough that the argument can automatically be converted to the parameter type. Example: the method

> `void increasePrice(double increase)`

will accept the following calls:

```
aMerch.increasePrice(20); // argument type is int, automatically converted into double
aMerch.increasePrice(12.50); // argument type is double, no conversion
```

Other number types that are less than `double` are also accepted as arguments (see section 2.8).

Problems

1. Sketch out figures that correspond to Figure 3.3 when the following statements are executed. Explain which things are references, which are objects, and which are variables of primitive data types.

```
int speed = 70;
final int speedLimit = 80;
Car thisCar = new Car("XX-55555", "Saab", 1987, 0);
Car thatCar = new Car("XY-66666", "Saab", 1989, 0);
```

2. Find possible errors in the following statements:

```
theCarOfJohn = new Car(1234, "Mazda", 1990, 0);
Car myCar = new yoursCar("ZD-44444", "Peugeot");
theCarOfJohn.start(12.5);
theCarOfJohn.speedUp(80);
theCarOfJohn.slowDown();
Car.stop();
```

3. Write statements that do the following: Create an instance of the Car class. Start the car, speed up a few times, slow down, and stop.

4. Among others, the Student class offers the following methods:

```
void takeExam(String classNo);
void setGrade(double grade, String classNo);
void applyForStudentLoan();
```

The constructor looks like this:

```
Student(String studID, String name);
```

Write statements that create an instance of the Student class. Have the student take exams in three classes, and record grades for these three classes. Have the student apply for a student loan.

3.3 The Random Class

Many ready-made classes come with the Java compiler. There are classes for programming graphical user interfaces, for communicating with databases, for communicating over networks, for programming with sound and images, and much more.

Up to this point, we have used the System class to display text on the screen. The use of this specific class is slightly specialized, and now we will look instead at classes that are more typical in the way they're used. We'll start with the Random class that describes objects that generate random numbers. In the next section, we'll go through the String class that describes strings.

Sometimes we need random numbers—for example, in lottery drawings. Many algorithms have been developed to automatically generate so-called pseudo-random numbers.[5] An algorithm like this is usually based on a start value (a "seed"). With the same seed value, we always get the same sequence of pseudo-random numbers (hence the term "pseudo").

---

5. See for example [Weiss 1998].

We can imagine having a machine that comes up with these kinds of numbers for us. Every time we want a new number, we send a message to this machine (see Figure 3.5).

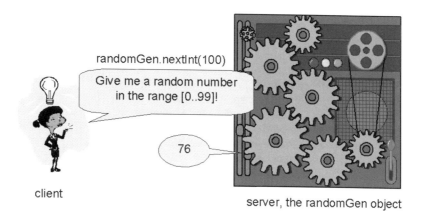

randomGen.nextInt(100)

Give me a random number
in the range [0..99]!

76

client

server, the randomGen object

Figure 3.5 A client asks a random number generator for a number

In our program, the random number generator will be modeled as an object. We give the object the name `randomGen`. The object belongs to the `Random` class that comes with the Java compiler. We instantiate the object this way:

    Random randomGen = new Random(seed);

`seed` is the seed for the random number algorithm. To create the best possible number sequences, seeds should be prime numbers. Here, `seed` is a constant with a value equal to 17.

The `Random` class provides a method for drawing an integer from a specific interval. We receive the integer and store it in a local variable, like this:

    int number1 = randomGen.nextInt(limit);

`limit` is 1 greater than the upper limit of the interval. The lower limit is 0. By setting `limit` equal to 100, we get a number in the interval [0..99].

Program Listing 3.1 shows a program that stores and prints pseudo-random numbers in the interval [0..99].

The `Random` class is in a "package" called `java.util`. We have to tell the compiler this by "importing" the class before we can use it:

    import java.util.Random; // this statement has to be the first in a file, if it is to appear

The concepts of "package" and "import" are explained later in this chapter.

Program Listing 3.1

```
/*
 * TestRandom.java   E.L. 2001-05-21
 */
import java.util.Random; // NB!
class TestRandom {
  public static void main(String[] args) {
    final int limit = 100; // wants numbers in the range [0..99].
    final int seed = 17; // the seed should be a prime number
    Random randomGen = new Random(seed);
    int number1 = randomGen.nextInt(limit);
    int number2 = randomGen.nextInt(limit);
    int number3 = randomGen.nextInt(limit);
    int number4 = randomGen.nextInt(limit);
    System.out.println(
      "Here you have four random numbers in the range [0.." + (limit - 1) + "]: " +
              number1 + " " + number2 + " " + number3 + " " + number4);
  }
}

/* Example Run:
Here you have four random numbers in the range [0..99]: 76 20 94 16
*/
```

Below you'll find the book's first API reference. These references describe classes that come with the Java compiler. The descriptions are not complete but contain the most important constructors and methods.

 API Reference

The java.util.Random class

The class is used to generate pseudo-random numbers.

Constructors:

```
public[6] Random()
public Random(long seed)
```

The first constructor uses the machine's clock to make a seed and uses that to generate different number sequences each time. The second constructor takes a seed as its argument. The same value gives the same number sequence.

Methods:

```
public double nextDouble()
```

---

6. We'll go through the `public` modifier in the next chapter.

This method returns the next decimal numeral uniformly distributed in the interval [0.0..1.0>.

```
public int nextInt()
public long nextLong()
```

These methods return the next integer, uniformly distributed over all possible integers, positive and negative. The `nextInt()` method draws the number from the interval for the data type `int`, while `nextLong()` draws from the interval for the data type `long`.

```
public int nextInt(int n)
```

This method returns the next integer, uniformly distributed in the interval [0..n-1].

Problems

1. Write a program that creates and outputs the following pseudo-random numbers:

   (a) Three integers selected from the entire numerical range for the data type `long`

   (b) Three integers in the interval [0..1000]

   (c) Two decimal numerals in the interval [0.0..1.0>

   (d) Two integers in the interval [-500..500]

   (e) Two decimal numerals in the interval [0.0..100.0>

   Hint for e): Multiply the results from `nextInt()` and `nextDouble()` respectively by a suitable factor.
   Run the program several times, with and without a specific seed value.

2. We can output the random number without storing it in a variable:

   ```
   System.out.println("A random number: " + randomGen.nextInt());
   ```

   Study Program Listing 1.1 where the statement "About to learn Java!" is printed 10 times. Try to make a program that writes, for example, 20 random numbers under each other.

3.4 The String Class

The `String` class is used to handle strings. From chapter 2, we have the following examples:

```
String city = "Trondheim";
String text = "Here are four words";
```

The String class is special because we can create instances of the class without using the word new. The statements above can also be written in the following manner:

```
String city = new String("Trondheim");
String text = new String("Here are four words");
```

We have two references as shown in Figure 3.6.

Thus, Figure 3.3 doesn't tell the whole truth. The object that theCarOfGreta refers to contains two references of its own (see Figure 3.7).

Figure 3.6   References to strings (instances of the String class)

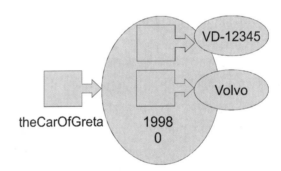

Figure 3.7   theCarOfGreta refers to an object that contains two references of its own

The String class provides close to 50 methods. We will look at the simplest of these. Program Listing 3.2 shows examples of some of these methods in use. Study the program code and the output. There are several things to take note of:

- There are methods for converting from lower to upper case and vice versa. These methods also work for special letters outside the English/American a-z alphabet, such as the German ö and ü, when run on Windows. If you write to the MS-DOS window, it will look as though the methods aren't working for these letters, but that's because of the character set that MS-DOS uses.

- None of the methods change the contents of the object. The toUpperCase() and toLowerCase() methods create new instances of the String class and return references to them.

- To retrieve a single character, use the charAt() method. The length() method gives the number of characters in the string, including blank spaces. The characters are numbered from 0 on. If the length is 5, the characters will be numbered 0, 1, 2, 3, 4.

The short form for creating instances of the String class is used a lot. Example:

    String name = "John";

However, it's important to remember that this is exactly the same as if we had written:

    String name = new String("John");

Figure 3.8 shows the room that is set aside by the machine's internal memory when running the program. We have:

- Four variables of reference types. These contain references to instances of the String class: text, noTrailingOrLeadingSpaces, upper, lower.

- Four instances of the String class.

- Three variables of primitive data types: initial and secondLetter are of the char data type, while noOfChars is of the int data type.

Program Listing 3.2

```
/*
 * TestString.java   E.L. 2001-05-21
 */
class TestString {
  public static void main(String[] args) {
    String text = "Anne Smith";
    String noTrailingOrLeadingSpaces = text.trim();
    String result = "Spaces removed: " + noTrailingOrLeadingSpaces;
    String upper = text.toUpperCase();
    result = result + "\nOnly upper case letters: " + upper;
    String lower = text.toLowerCase();
    result = result + "\nOnly lower case letters: " + lower;
    char initial = text.charAt(0);
    result = result + "\nInitial letter: " + initial;
    char secondLetter = text.charAt(1);
    result = result + "\nSecond letter: " + secondLetter;
    int noOfChars = text.length();
    result = result + "\nThe length of the string: " + noOfChars;
    System.out.println(result);
```

```
    }
}
/* Example Run:
Spaces removed: Anne Smith
Only upper case letters: ANNE SMITH
Only lower case letters: anne smith
Initial letter: A
Second letter: n
The length of the string: 10
*/
```

text → (Anne Smith)

initial → [A]   secondLetter → [n]

no TrailingOrLeadingSpaces → (Anne Smith)

noOfChars → [10]

upper → (ANNE SMITH)

lower → (anne smith)

Figure 3.8 Room reserved in the memory in connection with the string handling in Listing 3.2

API Reference

The java.lang.String class

The class is used to handle strings.

All methods with the `String` return type return a reference to a new instance of this class.

Constructor:

    public String(String text)

Methods:

    public char charAt(int index)

This method returns the character in the position stated (the index). The positions are numbered from 0 on.

```
public int indexOf(int character)
public int indexOf(int character, int fromIndex)
public int indexOf(String subString)
public int indexOf(String subString, int fromIndex)
```

These methods are used to search for an individual character or a substring in the string. The data type for the `character` parameter is `int`. Nevertheless, you can send in a regular character (the data type `char`) as argument. The methods return the position for the character or position at the beginning of the substring. If the character or substring doesn't exist, the methods return -1. The first position in the string has the number 0. Two of the methods take `fromIndex` as their argument. This makes it possible to start the search in a position (index) other than 0. If `fromIndex` is less than 0, the search starts at the beginning of the string. If `fromIndex` is greater than or equal to the string's length, -1 is returned.

```
public int lastIndexOf(int character)
public int lastIndexOf(int character, int fromIndex)
public int lastIndexOf(String subString)
public int lastIndexOf(String subString, int fromIndex)
```

These methods correspond to the methods named `indexOf()`, but here the search is done backwards.

```
public int length()
```

This method returns the number of characters the string consists of, including all blank spaces.

```
public String substring(int beginIndex)
public String substring(int beginIndex, int endIndex)
```

These methods return a part of the string. The first method returns the whole string starting from `beginIndex`, while the second one returns the string starting from the position `beginIndex` up to and including the position (`endIndex - 1`). Invalid argument values (example: `endIndex` greater than the length of the string) give an `IndexOutOfBoundsException` message.

```
public String replace(char oldChar, char newChar)
```

This method returns a string where all occurrences of a specific character (first parameter) are replaced with another character (second parameter).

```
public String toLowerCase()
public String toUpperCase()
```

These methods return strings that are equal to the original string, but where all letters are lower- or upper-case respectively. These methods work for letters outside the English/American alphabet, too.

```
public String trim()
```

This method returns a string that is equal to the original string, but where blank spaces in the beginning and end of the string have been removed. Blank spaces in the middle of the string are retained. Blank spaces don't just mean the character ' ', but also a number of other invisible characters, such as, for example, carriage returns and tabs.

Program Listing 3.3 shows the search methods described above in use. The program creates the string `"This is a testing text with many e's"` and then undertakes a number of searches in it. All the different forms of the methods `indexOf()`, `lastIndexOf()` and `substring()` are tested. Study the source code and the output.

Program Listing 3.3

```java
/*
 * TestStringSearch.java   E.L. 2001-05-25
 */
class TestStringSearch {
  public static void main(String[] args) {
    String text = "This is a testing text with many e's";
    System.out.println("Testing the text: " + text);
    System.out.println("This text's length is: " + text.length());
    System.out.println("The positions are numbered from 0, and up to and including "
        + (text.length() - 1));

    /* Searching from the beginning with the method indexOf() */
    int pos = text.indexOf('e');
    System.out.println("The first e is at the position: " + pos);
    pos = text.indexOf('e', pos + 1);  // The search continues after the first e
    System.out.println("The next e is at the position: " + pos);
    pos = text.indexOf("text");
    System.out.println("The first occurrence of \"text\" is at the position: " + pos);
    pos = text.indexOf("text", pos + 1);
    System.out.println("The next occurrence of \"text\" is at the position: " + pos);

    /* Searching from the end with the method lastIndexOf() */
    pos = text.lastIndexOf('e');
    System.out.println("The last e is at the position: " + pos);
    pos = text.lastIndexOf('e', pos - 1);  // The search continues before the last e
    System.out.println("The last but one e is at the position: " + pos);
    pos = text.lastIndexOf("text");
    System.out.println("The last occurrence of \"text\" is at the position: " + pos);
    pos = text.lastIndexOf("text", pos - 1);
    System.out.println("The last occurrence but one of \"text\" is at the position: " + pos);
```

```
/* Finding substrings */
String partOfText = text.substring(10);
System.out.println("From position 10: " + partOfText);
partOfText = text.substring(7, 14);
System.out.println("From position 7 including position 13: " + partOfText);

/* Replacing all e's with a's */
String newText = text.replace('e', 'a');
System.out.println("The new text with a's instead of e's: " + newText);

System.out.println("None of all these operations has changed the original text: "
   + text);
 }
}
/* Example Run:
Testing the text: This is a testing text with many e's
This text's length is: 36
The positions are numbered from 0, and up to and including 35
The first e is at the position: 11
The next e is at the position: 19
The first occurrence of "text" is at the position: 18
The next occurrence of "text" is at the position: -1
The last e is at the position: 33
The last but one e is at the position: 19
The last occurrence of "text"  is at the position: 18
The last occurrence but one of "text"  is at the position: -1
From position 10: testing text with many e's
From position 7 including position 13:  a test
The new text with a's instead of e's: This is a tasting taxt with many a's
None of all these operations has changed the original text: This is a testing text with
many e's
*/
```

Problems

1. The following declarations are stated:

```
final String continent  = new String("Europe");
String country = "Spain";
String city = new String("Madrid");
char regLetter = 'E';
```

Create a sketch corresponding to Figure 3.8. Write a description of the figure. Use the words variable, reference, primitive data type, reference type, and object in your text.

2. What is output when the following code bit is run?

```
String song = new String("Yesterday");
song = song.toLowerCase();
```

```
char letter = sang.charAt(0);
System.out.println(song + letter + song.length());
```

3. Find the errors in the following code bit:

```
String text = 'Yellow Submarine';
String vocalist = new ("Ringo Starr");
int noOfChars = vocalist.length;
String lastLetter = vocalist.charAt(noOfChars);
System.out.println("The length of the vocalist's name is: " + noOfChars
    + " The last letter is " + lastLetter);
vocalist.toUpperCase();
System.out.println("The vocalist's name in upper case: " + vocalist);
```

4. What is output when the following code bit is run?

```
String text = "This is one of many problems.";
System.out.println(text.indexOf('.'));
System.out.println(text.indexOf("is"));
System.out.println(text.lastIndexOf("is"));
text.replace('e', 'u');
System.out.println(text);
text = text.replace('u', 'a');
System.out.println(text);
text = text.replace('e', 'a');
System.out.println(text);
```

5. The following is stated:

```
String text = "Today it's June 16th. In two weeks the summer holiday is here.";
```

Compose a code bit that uses the different versions of the indexOf() method to find the position of:

```
The first and second periods.
The number '16'.
The word "In".
Find out what happens if you try to find the next "In" (there isn't one).
```

3.5 Organizing Classes in Packages

Random and String are only two of a great many classes that come with the Java compiler. To keep people from losing the general view, these classes are organized into *packages*. Most of the classes we are creating in this book belong to a nameless package. That means that we don't need to think very much about packages when it comes to the classes we are composing ourselves.

Classes that may come to be used in broader contexts should, however, be stored in a package with a name. The name of the package will usually be identical to the name of the subdirectory where the classes that belong to the package are located.[7] The package name is a part of the class name.

For the classes that come with the compiler, we need to use the complete class name for all classes that don't belong to the package java.lang. Package names that consist of several words denote that we have several subdirectories before we find the class.

The Random class belongs to the java.util package. The complete name of the class is java.util.Random. The first part of Program Listing 3.1 looks like this:

```
import java.util.Random;
class TestRandom {
  public static void main(String[] args) {
    .....
    Random randomGen = new Random(seed);
```

The import declaration says that the java.util.Random class will be accessible in the program. If we want all the classes in the java.util package to be accessible, we can use *:

```
import java.util.*;
```

It's very common to use the asterisk even if only one class is going to be accessible.

The import declaration makes it so that the compiler will understand the incomplete class name Random, assuming that it's unique in the *java* file.

We can have several import declarations in a program. They must be placed before all other program code (except comments) in the *java* file.

Instead of using import, we can write out the entire class name:

```
java.util.Random randomGen = new java.util.Random(seed);
```

Note that an asterisk in an import declaration can only replace class names. It cannot replace package names. In other words, we can't write, for example

```
import java.*.*;  // not allowed!
```

3.6 Class Methods and Class Constants in the Java Library

Now we have seen several examples where we instantiate objects and send messages to them. This is the usual, and most correct, way to do object-oriented

---

7. This is the most common. Certain development environments organize the packages in a database. That won't be covered in this book.

programming. The methods are called *instance methods*, because we always call them in connection with an instance of a class.

At the same time, a library should also provide a few methods of a more general nature, which can be used without being linked to a specific object. These types of methods are called *class methods*, and examples are methods for mathematical computations (square root, sine, cosine, etc.) as well as methods for sorting and searching.

In a class description, a class method is marked with the modifier `static`, and in the `java.lang.Math` class, we find the following methods, among others:

```
public static double sqrt(double number)
public static double sin(double number)
```

We call a class method by putting the class name before the method call.

For example:

```
double sqRoot = Math.sqrt(15678);   // finding the square root of 15678
```

In Program Listing 3.1, we composed a `Random` object that we then sent messages to. In the Java library, we also find a class method that creates a random number. The `random()` method in the `java.lang.Math` class generates a pseudo-random number in the interval [0.0..1.0>.

Very shortly we will need to use class methods when inputting data from the user. All data, even numbers, are input as strings. If we want to use the numbers in computations in the program, we have to convert them from strings to numbers. In order to understand the necessity of this conversion, we have to take a detailed look at how characters and numbers are stored in the internal memory. For the time being we'll have to make do with stating the fact that they are stored in different ways, and for that reason, the conversion is necessary.

Class methods have been created for this conversion. The methods are called `parseInt()` and `parseDouble()`. They belong to the `Integer` and `Double` classes respectively, which are both part of the `java.lang` package. Therefore, we can use the methods without setting up the classes in an `import` declaration.

The following little code bit creates two strings and then converts them to numbers:

```
String text1 = "2345";
String text2 = "45.3";
int number1 = Integer.parseInt(text1);  // interpreting text1 as integer
double number2 = Double.parseDouble(text2); // interpreting text2 as decimal numeral
System.out.println(number1 + " " + number2);
```

As expected, the output is:

```
2345 45.3
```

Of course, it can happen that it's not possible to convert the string to a number. For example, `text2` above cannot be converted to an integer. Then the program stops with an error message.

The Java library also contains many constants. Each constant is common for all the objects the class describes. Therefore, it is declared as a *class constant*. In the API reference a class constant may look like this:

```
public static final double PI  // this is 3.141592....
```

and is used like this:

```
double circumference = Math.PI * 2 * radius;
```

The most familiar example of a class method, however, isn't part of the Java library. It's our own `main()` method. When we start a program with the Java interpreter, it will look for `main()` in the class we declare. The method is started without any instances of the class being made.

3.7 Reading Data from the User

We use class methods in the `javax.swing.JOptionPane` class to read data from the user.

Figure 3.9 shows a run for the program in Program Listing 3.4. We see dialog boxes, as we recognize them from graphical user interfaces. We will use boxes like this to communicate with the user without making *real* graphical user interfaces for that purpose. In a real graphical user interface, those kinds of dialogs will be smaller parts of a larger system of windows, menus, etc. Programming graphical user interfaces requires that we build up the part of the program that has to do with user communication in a completely different way than we are doing now. We will come back to this in chapter 13.

Let's take a closer look at the program that created Figure 3.9.

The class method `showInputDialog()` returns a reference to a string that contains whatever the user has entered. We use `parseDouble()` (see section 3.6) to convert from string to decimal numeral. The method `showMessageDialog()` writes a message on the screen and can be compared to `System.out.println()`. There is, however, one important difference: We can't write a new message unless the user has closed the window with the last message in it. Test this by inserting another printout in the program.

Note that the `showMessageDialog()` method takes two arguments, while the `showInputDialog()` takes one. For the time being, the first argument in `showMessageDialog()` will be `null` for our purposes.

Note that we still can't handle the case where the user pushes down the "Cancel" button, or where he closes the window by clicking in the upper right corner.

In order for a program that uses dialogs this way to stop in the usual fashion, we have to insert the statement

    System.exit(0);

at the end of it.

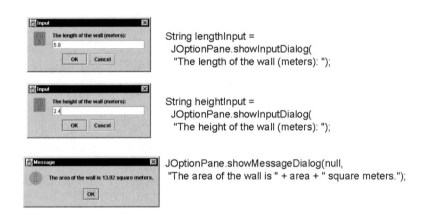

Figure 3.9   Running the program in Program Listing 3.4

Program Listing 3.4

```
/*
 * WallCalculations2.java   E.L. 2001-06-16
 */
import javax.swing.JOptionPane;
class WallCalculations2 {
  public static void main(String[] args) {
    String lengthInput = JOptionPane.showInputDialog("The length of the wall (meters): ");
    String heightInput = JOptionPane.showInputDialog("The height of the wall (meters): ");
    double length = Double.parseDouble(lengthInput);
    double height = Double.parseDouble(heightInput);
    double area = length * height;
    JOptionPane.showMessageDialog(null,
            "The area of the wall is " + area + " square meters.");
    System.exit(0);
  }
}
/* Example Run:
Length: 5.8 m
Height: 2.4 m
The area of the wall is 13.92 square meters.
*/
```

Figure 3.10 shows several examples of message boxes. The `showMessageDialog()` method is described in its entirety in the API reference below. The third example uses a homemade image as an icon. The image is in a file in the same directory as the program. The `ImageIcon` class is in the `javax.swing` package and has to be imported.

```
JOptionPane.showMessageDialog(null,
   "The simplest message dialog");
```

```
JOptionPane.showMessageDialog(null,
   "To the left you see the error message icon",
   "The method with four parameters",
   JOptionPane.ERROR_MESSAGE);
```

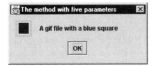
```
ImageIcon image = new ImageIcon("blue.gif");
JOptionPane.showMessageDialog(null,
   "A gif file with a blue square",
   "The method with five parameters", 0, image);
```

Figure 3.10 Examples of message dialogs

API Reference

The javax.swing.JOptionPane class

Methods:

Message dialogs:

```
public static void showMessageDialog(Component parent, Object message)
public static void showMessageDialog(Component parent, Object message,
                         String title, int messageType)
public static void showMessageDialog(Component parent, Object message,
                         String title, int messageType, Icon icon)
```

The dialogs display a message with an OK button.

Input dialogs:

```
public static String showInputDialog(Component parent, Object message)
public static String showInputDialog(Component parent, Object message,
                         String title, int messageType)
public static String showInputDialog(Object message)
```

These methods let the user enter a text that is returned to the client.
The methods have several parameters in common:

- `parent` will be `null` as long as the dialog box doesn't belong to an ordinary window in a graphical user interface.

- `message` is the text that is written in the dialog. Even if the parameter type is `Object`, it works well with `String` as an argument.[8]

- `title` is the text that appears at the top of the title line in the dialog.

- `messageType` determines the icon on the left in the box and can be one of the following class constants: ERROR_MESSAGE, INFORMATION_MESSAGE, WARNING_MESSAGE, QUESTION_MESSAGE or PLAIN_MESSAGE (no icon).

  If we use one of the methods where the message type is not going to be stated, we get a default icon.

- `icon` represents an image. The parameter type is `Icon`. The argument can be of the type `ImageIcon`,[9] which is well suited when we have the image in a file. This argument overrides the argument for `messageType`.

The methods return `null` if the user hits the Cancel button or closes the dialog by clicking in the upper right corner.

Problems

1. Write statements that input an integer, a decimal numeral, and a text. Use the simplest of the `showInputDialog()` methods. Sketch how you think the dialog boxes will look.

   Make a program out of this and run it.

   Try out the most complicated of the `showInputDialog()` methods.

2. Do a change to the program in problem 2, section 2.4. The number of calories will be input by the user. The result will be displayed in a message box.

---

8. Because the parameter type is `Object`, the argument can be an instance of any class whatsoever. It can be a GUI component (chapter 13), or it can be an instance of the `ImageIcon` class. In other cases, the object's `toString()` method is used (see chapter 10).

9. `Icon` is an interface (see chapter 10). The argument can be of any class whatsoever that implements this interface.

3.8   New Concepts in This Chapter

Concept	Brief Explanation
argument	The value the client sends with a method or a constructor. The term "actual argument" is also used.
attribute	Information that an object is responsible for knowing about itself, a named property with a defined range of values.
behavior	The set of operations an object can execute.
class	A description of a set of objects with the same attributes and behavior.
class constant	A variable in a class, with the modifiers `static final` and a given value. The constant is common for all instances of the class, and it may be accessed even if no instances of the class exist.
class diagram	Graphical presentation of one or more classes, and the connection between them, with respect to UML. For the time being, our class diagrams will only consist of individual classes.
class method	A method declared with the modifier `static`. Outside the class the method is invoked by qualifying it with the class name.
client	A role that an object can play. The role entails the object requesting another object (the server) for a service, or asking another object a question. Also used as short form for "client program", see this.
client program	A program that sends messages to one or more objects. The term is often used about the method `main()`.
constructor	Used to make an instance of a class.
encapsulation	Information about data representation and how operations are performed are hidden inside the object. The client deals with the object's interface.
identity	Objects have identity because they model things in the real world that are identifiable.
implement	To program the classes (see chapter 4). Also used about creating programs in general.
`import`	Keyword to say that the program uses classes that belong to a named package. The alternative is to write the complete class name (including the package name) every time it is referred to the class.
instance	Synonym for object. [Booch, Rumbaugh, Jacobson 1999, p. 185] says : "Instance and object are largely synonymous. [...] From common usage, the concrete manifestation of a class is called an object. Objects are instances of classes, so it's excruciatingly proper to say that all objects are instances, although some instances are not objects (for example, an instance of an association is really not an object, it's just an instance, also known as a link). Only power modelers will really care about this subtle distinction."

Concept	Brief Explanation
instance method	Represents an operation. Often just called "method" if there's no danger of misunderstandings. Outside the class the method is invoked by qualifying it with the name of an instance of the class.
instantiate	Synonym for the process of creating an object. The dictionary says: "to represent (an abstraction) by a concrete instance <heroes instantiate ideals -- W. J. Bennett>" [URL Merriam-Webster]
interface	A description of the messages that can be sent to an object. The description of a method contains return type, method name, and parameter list.
message	An instruction or a question that the client object sends to the server object. Data is sent along as (actual) arguments.
method	Declarations of operations at the program code level.
method call	The act of a client sending a message to a server object.
model	A simplification of reality. Created to place the focus on a specific portion of the reality.
new	Keyword for creating an instance of a class.
null	A variable of a reference type may be set to null. It means that it doesn't refer to any object.
object	A model of a thing, concrete or abstract, which our problem is about.
operation	The instructions that the server object executes in response to a message.
package	A collection of classes. We distinguish between unnamed and named packages.
parameter	Describes a value that a client can send together with a message or a constructor. The description includes the data type and a descriptive name. The term "formal parameter" is also used.
reference type	A data type that is described using a class declaration.
return type	The data type for the return value from a method.
return value	The data value that a method sends back to the client. It will be the server's response to a query from the client.
server	A role that an object can play. The role entails the object answering a question or performing a task following instructions from another object (the client).
state	"A condition or situation during the life of an object during which it satisfies some condition, performs some activity or waits for some event." [Rumbaugh, Jacobson, Booch 1999, p. 433]
UML	Unified Modeling Language—a modeling language.
unnamed package	Classes that are in files that don't contain the package statement belong to the unnamed package.

3.9   Review Problems

1. Explain why we say that an object is a model. Why do we need to distinguish between objects we use in programming and objects in the real world?

2. What do client and server mean? Find examples of an object playing both roles.

3. What differentiates the use of class methods from the use of other methods? What do we call the other type of methods?

4. How can we get a program to generate random numbers?

5. What is encapsulation?

6. What's the purpose of the `parseInt()` method and how do we use it?

7. How are the concepts of object and class related?

8. What's the difference between a parameter and an argument? Illustrate with examples.

9. Explain how we use the keyword `import`.

10. The data types can be divided into two groups: the primitive data types and the reference types (the classes). One of the differences between these two groups is the space reserved in the internal memory. Explain this difference using examples and figures. Can you think of other differences between these two groups of data types?

11. What happens if we set one reference equal to another? Demonstrate with an example and a figure.

3.10 Programming Problems

Problem 1

Write a program that does the following (in this order):

* Input two integers.
* Calculate the quotient and print the result.
* Input two decimal numerals.
* Calculate the quotient and print the result.

    Set up a test data set and test the program. Test portions of the program at a time.

Problem 2

Write a program that inputs a text. The following will be output:

* The text in lower-case letters.

- The text in all capitals.

- The number of characters in the text.

- The first and last characters in the text.

   Create a test data set and test the program.

Problem 3

Write a program that inputs a text, and outputs the following:

- The position of the first, second, and third occurrence of a specific character. This character will be input. (If the character isn't in the text, -1 will output. That's OK.)

- The position of the last occurrence of a word in the text. This word will be input. (If the word isn't in the text, -1 will be output. That's OK.)

- The text where all occurrences of a specific letter are replaced with another letter. Both of the letters will be input.

Constructing Your Own Classes

Learning goals for this chapter

Once you've completed this chapter, you will understand the following concepts:

- Instance variables, instance methods

- A method's signature, head and body

- Private and public members

- Constructor, default constructor

- Overloading names

- Mutable and immutable class

- Accessors and mutators (get and set methods)

- Pixel, graphics context and the `paintComponent()` method

You will be able to:

- Start with an informal description of a class, and program it with class constants, instance variables, constructors and instance methods

- Program applets for simple graphics (circles, rectangles and lines, colors and different fonts)

Now that you have some experience using ready-made classes, this chapter will focus on how you can program your own classes.

We will start by looking at how we find out what objects will be formed and then how we construct the classes.

This chapter contains many coding details and offers several examples of programmed classes. Some of the classes are applets that draw simple graphics on the screen.

4.1 Creating Classes

Constructing classes is central to object-oriented programming. This makes it possible to develop programs using the building block principle. There are several advantages to this:

- By dividing the problem up into a number of pieces (classes), we can concentrate on one thing at a time. Each class takes care of itself, as independently as possible from the other classes. This way, we can forget the rest of the problems and concentrate on this part.

- Several people can cooperate on a program. When they are each working on their own parts, they can work independently from each other.

- The building blocks can be tested and modified independently. We can program one class at a time and test it before we go on to the next. During the course of the development process, we will probably discover smarter ways to solve earlier problems. If we don't alter the interface for the class, we can change the implementation as often as we want, without affecting the other classes.

- If we create the building blocks carefully, we can make some of them general enough that they can be used later on. We have already seen several examples of uses for ready-made classes. Gradually, we will build up our own library of classes.

 Classes make it possible to maintain perspective over the entire program and make it feasible to create larger programs. Experienced developers put much effort and consideration into selecting classes and distributing responsibilities between classes. Classes maintain information about attributes and operations. The more you manage to keep a class distinct from all the other classes, the better.

Before we can create our own classes, we have to develop an understanding of what part of reality we want to model as classes. A class will be a description of a collection of objects with the same attributes and operations. Therefore, we have to start by asking what should be modeled as objects.

Let's look at the renovation case study from chapter 2. The things our problem deals with should be the basis for the objects in our model. We remember that objects are always nouns and, from the description in the beginning of chapter 2, we can make the following list of objects:

- The whole apartment

- Floor

- Wall

- Flooring

- Wallpaper

- Paint

What information do we have to keep track of in a system like this?

- Length and width/height of the walls and floors

- Length and width of a roll of wallpaper

- Width of the flooring

- The paint's coverage ability and number of coats

- Prices for everything

What calculations will we have to be able to do?

- Area of walls and floors

- How many rolls of wallpaper are necessary for one wall

- How many meters of flooring are necessary

- How many liters of paint are necessary for a wall or a floor

- How much everything costs

The next stage is to divide the responsibility for maintaining information and carrying out calculations between the objects in question. The division should be done in such a way that each object is as independent as possible from the other objects.

These objects have to be described. Therefore, we need a class for each type of object. A proposal for the division of responsibilities is shown in the class diagram in Figure 4.1. Let's see if we can reason our way through this figure.

First let's look at the information that will be stored in the system. Generally, this information will become attributes.

A wall knows about its own height and length. A floor has information about its length and width. *As clients, therefore, we can ask the wall about this.* If we're going to paint, we need to know the area of the wall or the floor. Again, as clients, we ask the wall, "How big are you?".

Now we can draw an important conclusion that will simplify the rest of our work. We see that, in this context, there is no difference between the floor and the walls. We can generalize and combine the descriptions of these objects into a class, the Surface class. We have also included the operation "Get circumference" in the Surface class. For pedagogical reasons, we want a few more operations and this will also make the class more useful in other contexts.

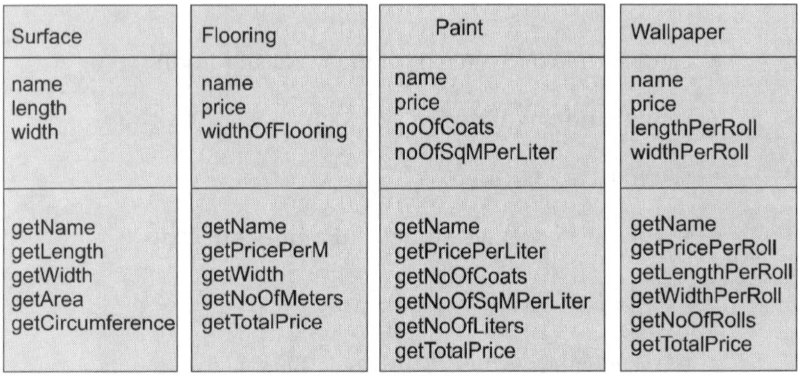

Surface	Flooring	Paint	Wallpaper
name length width	name price widthOfFlooring	name price noOfCoats noOfSqMPerLiter	name price lengthPerRoll widthPerRoll
getName getLength getWidth getArea getCircumference	getName getPricePerM getWidth getNoOfMeters getTotalPrice	getName getPricePerLiter getNoOfCoats getNoOfSqMPerLiter getNoOfLiters getTotalPrice	getName getPricePerRoll getLengthPerRoll getWidthPerRoll getNoOfRolls getTotalPrice

Figure 4.1   Class diagram – the renovation case study (UML)

The flooring has information about its width and price per meter. The paint knows what it costs, how many square meters it covers per liter, and how many coats are recommended. The roll of wallpaper knows about its own width, length and price.

The most difficult thing is dividing responsibility for the calculations when several objects are involved.[1] Should the wallpaper or the wall bear the responsibility for calculating the number of rolls needed? If we let the roll of wallpaper figure it out, we have to give it information about the size of the wall. If the wall is going to calculate it, it has to know the length and width of a roll of

---

1. It should be mentioned that a fair amount of work has been done in trying to systematize the division of responsibility. "Patterns" are central. For example, see [Larman 2000].

wallpaper. In addition, if we are going to calculate the cost, we have to give the wall information about the price of the wallpaper. Both of these alternatives are fairly good, but in this case we let the wallpaper be responsible for this calculation. We ask the roll of wallpaper, "How much of you do we need if you are going to be used to wallpaper a wall that is 5 m long and 2.3 m high? And how much will it cost?". "Get number of rolls" and "Get total price" thereby become operations for objects in the `Wallpaper` class. We give the operations the method names `getNoOfRolls()` and `getTotalPrice()`.

We go through a similar reasoning process for paint and flooring. The paint is responsible for calculating the number of liters needed for a given surface, and the flooring will have to calculate the number of meters needed for a floor.

4.2 Programming a Class

Here we will create the `Surface` class along with a simple client program.

Our file now contains two classes, the `Surface` class and the class that contains `main()`. We call this last class `FloorCalculations`. See Program Listing 4.1. Here we have placed the class that contains `main()` at the end of the file. This is a convention we use in this book. We could easily have placed the class first in the file – it doesn't make any difference. We could also have placed each of the two classes in its own file.

The program's execution always starts with the method `main()` in the class you name when you start the Java interpreter. Most development environments therefore require that the *java* file has the same name as the class where `main()` is. The statements in `main()` control the program execution. Depending on what it says there, the program control "jumps" to program code (methods or constructors) in other classes. The program control "jumps" back to where it came from when it's finished with the method or constructor in question. We tried to illustrate this with the line numbers in Figure 4.2. Only those statements where processing occurs are numbered. The lines that are not numbered are remarks or pure declarations.

First we'll look at the client program. The purpose of this program is to test the `Surface` class.

Testing a class

We create an object as an instance of the class, input data into the object and then retrieve the data to see if we got it into the right place. We also make the possible calculations to see if the object is performing its calculations correctly. This is a standard way to test a class.

Program Listing 4.1

```
/*
 * FloorCalculations.java   E.L. 2001-08-10
 *
```

```
 * In this file you'll find two classes:
 * The Surface class and the FloorCalculations class.
 * The main() method is found in the FloorCalculations class,
 * and this method acts as a test program for the Surface class.
 */

class Surface {
  private String name;  // for identification purposes
  private double length;
  private double width;

  public Surface(String initName, double initLength, double initWidth) {
    name = initName;
    length = initLength;
    width = initWidth;
  }

  public String getName() {
    return name;
  }

  public double getLength() {
    return length;
  }

  public double getWidth() {
    return width;
  }

  public double getArea() {
    return width * length;
  }

  public double getCircumference() {
    return 2 * (length + width);
  }
}

/*
 * We are going to test the Surface class.
 * First we instantiate an object of the class,
 * then we retrieve the data from the object and
 * present them to the user. By doing this we will
 * prove that the object really contains the correct data
 * and performs its calculations correctly.
 */
class FloorCalculations {
  public static void main(String[] args) {

    /* Step 1: We instantiate an object of the class. */
    Surface aFloor = new Surface("Mary's floor", 4.8, 2.3);

    /* Step 2: We retrieve data from the object,
       and we let the object perform calculations. */
```

```
    String name = aFloor.getName();
    double width = aFloor.getWidth();
    double length = aFloor.getLength();
    double area = aFloor.getArea();
    double circumference = aFloor.getCircumference();

    /* Step 3: We present the results on the screen for control. */
    System.out.println("Information about the floor with the name: " + name + ":");
    System.out.println("Width: " + width);
    System.out.println("Length: " + length);
    System.out.println("Area: " + area);
    System.out.println("Circumference: " + circumference);
  }
}
/* Example Run:
Information about the floor with the name: Mary's floor:
Width: 2.3
Length: 4.8
Area: 11.04
Circumference: 14.2
*/
```

```
class Surface {
    private String name;  // for identification purposes
    private double length;
    private double width;

    public Surface(String initName, double initLength, double initWidth) {
2.  name = initName;
3.  length = initLength;
4.  width = initWidth;
    }
    public String getName() {
6.  return name;
    }
    public double getLength() {
10.  return length;
    }
    public double getWidth() {
8.  return width;
    }
    public double getArea() {
12.  return width * length;
    }
```

Figure 4.2 The order the statements are performed in (continued overleaf)

```
        public double getCircumference() {
14.     return 2 * (length + width);
        }
    }

    class FloorCalculations {
    public static void main(String[] args) {

        /* Step 1: We instantiate an object of the class. */
1.      Surface aFloor = new Surface("Mary's floor", 4.8, 2.3);

        /* Step 2: We retrieve data from the object,
        and we let the object perform calculations. */
5.      String name = aFloor.getName();
7.      double width = aFloor.getWidth();
9.      double length = aFloor.getLength();
11.     double area = aFloor.getArea();
13.     double circumference = aFloor.getCircumference();

        /* Step 3: We present the results on the screen for control. */
15.     System.out.println("Information about the floor with the name: " + name + ":");
16.     System.out.println("Width: " + width);
17.     System.out.println("Length: " + length);
18.     System.out.println("Area: " + area);
19.     System.out.println("Circumference: " + circumference);
        }
    }
```

Figure 4.2   (continued)

Now we'll look more closely at the Surface class. See Figure 4.3.

For the time being, let's ignore the so-called "access modifiers" private and public. We'll look at these in section 4.3.

Attributes become variables in the class. If we don't specify anything else, these will receive 0 as their initial value. Attributes represent the data information for an object. These variables are generally called *instance variables* because every instance of a class has its own set of values.

The operations we have linked to the objects become *instance methods* (or just "methods") in the class. One of the methods looks like this:

```
public double getArea() {
    return width * length;
}
```

An instance method can use all the instance variables directly. Here we see that the getArea() method uses the instance variables length and width.

A method declaration consists of a *method head* and a *method body*. The method head is what comes before the first brace {. The rest of the method is *the contents of the method*, or simply the method body. Anyone who is going to use the class only needs to recognize the method head. It's the method heads that form the interface for an object of the class. The method head contains a list of parameters. This list can be empty as is the case in all the methods in this example.

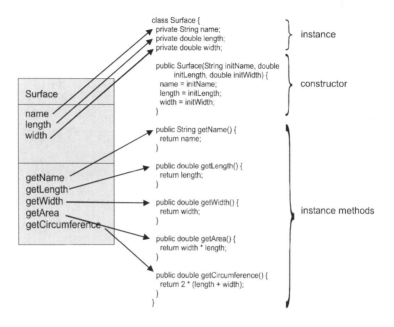

```
                                            class Surface {
                                              private String name;                    ⎫
                                              private double length;                  ⎬  instance
                                              private double width;                   ⎭

                                              public Surface(String initName, double
                                                 initLength, double initWidth) {       ⎫
  ┌──────────────────┐                           name = initName;                      ⎬  constructor
  │     Surface       │                           length = initLength;
  │                  │                           width = initWidth;                    ⎭
  │  name            │                         }
  │  length          │
  │  width           │                         public String getName() {              ⎫
  │                  │                           return name;                          │
  ├──────────────────┤                         }                                      │
  │                  │                                                                 │
  │  getName          │                         public double getLength() {            │
  │  getLength        │                           return length;                       │
  │  getWidth         │                         }                                      │
  │  getArea          │                                                                ⎬  instance methods
  │  getCircumference │                         public double getWidth() {             │
  └──────────────────┘                           return width;                         │
                                              }                                        │
                                                                                       │
                                              public double getArea() {                │
                                                return width * length;                 │
                                              }                                        │
                                                                                       │
                                              public double getCircumference() {       │
                                                return 2 * (length + width);           │
                                              }                                        ⎭
                                            }
```

Figure 4.3 The connection between a class diagram and a class declaration

In addition to instance variables and instance methods, we will probably find one or more constructors in a class. A constructor always has the same name as the class. Constructors differentiate themselves from each other by having parameter lists that differ in their number and/or type of parameters. A client uses a constructor to instantiate an object of a class. From the example, we have the following (see point 1 in Figure 4.2):

```
Surface aFloor = new Surface("Mary's floor", 4.8, 2.3);
```

We are entering the values "Mary's floor", 4.8 and 2.3 as arguments. The arguments can also be expressions or names of variables.

Let's follow the order in the statements from Figure 4.2 to see what happens next. Now we come to the constructor, and the parameters receive values equal to the arguments in question.The parameters should be viewed as local variables in the method. We can imagine that the following occurs behind the scenes:

```
String initName = "Mary's floor";
double initLength = 4.8;
double initWidth = 2.3;
```

Now we're in the constructor. Three statements are executed:

```
2. name = initName;
3. length = initLength;
4. width = initWidth;
```

The instance variables now receive values that control the initial values mentioned before.

Then we're back in the client program. We have now finished creating the object aFloor. In the next statement, we are sending a message to this object:

    5. String name = aFloor.getName();

In other words, we are asking the floor, "What's your name?"

Now we'll go back to the class. This method has no parameters and the next statement is:

    6. return name;

The value of the instance variable name is returned to the client and there it is stored in the client's variable, which also is called name. The reserved word return takes care of the return transmission.

We skip to point 11 in the client program:

    11. double area = aFloor.getArea();

We return to the class and the following statement is performed:

    12. return width * length;

width and length are instance variables that now have the values 4.8 and 2.3. These are multiplied together and the result is returned to where the method was called from. Thus, the area variable in the client program receives the value 11.04.

Overview: local variables, parameters and instance variables

Local variables are declared in a method and can only be used in the block where they are declared. Local variables are not given any definite initial value. That's up to the programmer. Parameters function as local variables with initial values provided by the argument list in the method call.

Instance variables are declared in a class, but outside all the methods. They can be used by all the methods in the class.

Instance variables are automatically given initial values according to their data type. Variables of a number type get the value 0, while boolean variables get false, and variables of a reference type get the value null.

Problems

1. Change the program in Program Listing 4.1 so that the user enters the width and length.

2. The following assertions or Java statements are all incorrect. Explain what the error in each one is:

    (a) Edward Johnson is a class.

    (b) void getSalary("January")

(c) 1756 is a parameter.

(d) The attribute name has an object person.

(e) `getSalary(String month)`

(f) The argument value is called a parameter.

(g) Attributes have a head and a body.

(h) A local variable can be accessed in all methods in the class.

3. Correct the mistakes in the following class:

```
class Circle {
  private radius;
  public circle(double initRadius) {
    radius = initRadius;
  }
  public int getArea() {
    return Math.PI * radius * radius; // Math.PI is a pre-defined constant that is used
                                      //  this way
  }
  public double getCircumference() {
    circumference = 2.0 * Math.PI * radius;
    return circumference;
  }
}
```

4. The following client program uses the class from the previous problem. Fill in what is missing (marked with --------).

```
class CircleCalculations {
  public static void main(String[] args) {
    ------- aCircle = new -------;
    double area = aCircle.-------;
    System.out.println("The area is calculated to be " + area);
    ------- ------- = aCircle.getCircumference();
    System.out.println("The circumference is calculated to be " + circumference);
  }
}
```

5. Name the local variables, the instance variables and the parameters in Program Listing 4.1.

4.3 Access Modifiers – Private and Public

In the example in Program Listing 4.1, the instance variables have the modifier `private` in front of them. This means that these variables are not available outside the class. The constructor and the methods have the modifier `public` in front of them. This means that they can be used anywhere, including outside the class. The use of these two modifiers lends support to a basic principle of object orientation – an object's interface is defined by the messages a client can send to the object. This is achieved by stating that the methods that represent these messages will be `public`, while the variables, which give the internal data representation of an object, are stated to be `private`. A class may have private methods in addition to the public ones; we'll see that such methods may be useful later on in the book.

Before we can state some rules about accessibility, sufficient for beginners, we'll find it practical to define the concept of a member: the *members* of a class are defined as the methods and the variables in the class. Constructors are not members.

If we don't use the modifier `private` or `public`, the constructor or the member will be accessible in the package the class belongs to. We call this *package access*. This is most significant if we create large systems with a number of named packages.

The accessibility for public members and constructors can be limited by the class's accessibility.

The class has to be public for the public members and constructors to be accessible outside the package the class belongs to.

To make a class public, we have to set the modifier `public` in front of the class, for example:

```
public class Surface {
```

Most of the classes in this book are not public; they have package access.

A *java* file cannot contain more than one public class.

4.4 Contents of a Class

In this section, we will look at a number of rules and several examples involving the contents of a class.

The members of a class

The members of a class consist of the methods and variables that are declared in the class. The constructors are not considered members.

The scope of the members is the whole class body.

Outside the scope, we have to *qualify* the name, i.e. we have to set up the name of an object or the name of the class before the name of the member. The two names are separated by the dot operator; examples: `aFloor.getArea()` and `Math.PI`.

Overloading names

It's possible to have several methods with the same name in a class if the methods' signatures are different. Then we say that the name is *overloaded*. The *signature* for a method consists of the method name, number and type of parameters. Neither the return type nor the parameter names are a part of the method's signature.[2]

We have the following example from the `String` class (section 3.4):

```
int indexOf(int character)
int indexOf(int character, int fromIndex)
int indexOf(String subString)
int indexOf(String subString, int fromIndex)
```

These methods search the string and find the position of an individual character or a substring.

Constructors and initializing instance variables

Instance variables can be given values in the declaration. Examples:

```
private String name = "";
private double length = 5;
```

If the variables are not given values this way, they get the value 0. Boolean variables are given the value `false`, while reference variables get the value `null`.

A constructor is used to create an object as an instance of a class. This means that memory is allocated for all the instance variables, and that the instance variables are initialized with their initial values.

A constructor often provides values for the instance variables. These values will control the initial values given in the declaration. The following code extract shows three different constructors for the `Surface` class:

```
public Surface(String initName, double initLength, double initWidth) {
    name = initName;
    length = initLength;
    width = initWidth;
}

public Surface(double initLength) {
    length = initLength;
}

public Surface() {
}
```

The first constructor gives values for all the instance variables. The second only gives a value for length, while the last doesn't give a value for any of the instance variables.

If we don't create any constructors in a class, a *default constructor* will be created. The constructor's parameter list and body will be empty. If we created constructors in a class, this default constructor would not be created. If we then want a constructor with empty parameter list to exist, we have to create it ourselves.

---

2. The definition of the term "signature" that we are using in this book refers to the programming language Java. The UML definition of signature also includes the return type, name and direction (in, out, in/out) of the parameters.

Note that the signature has to be different for all the constructors in a class.

Instance methods

The return type from a method is either a primitive data type or a reference type. Examples from Program Listing 4.1:

```
public double getCircumference() { // the return type is a primitive data type
  return 2 * (length + width); // returns a value that goes with the return type
}

public String getName() { // the return type is a reference type
  return name; // returns the reference to an object
}
```

If the method doesn't return any value, the reserved word void should be used as the return type. As an example, suppose we expand the Surface class with the following method:

```
public void setWidth(double newWidth) {
  width = newWidth;
}
```

This method changes the contents in an instance variable. Example of call:

```
aFloor.setWidth(5.3);
```

Here we are sending the message "Hi, you will have a new width of 5.3 meters!" to the object aFloor. Often, methods of this type don't need to send data back to the client, and therefore they are of the void type.

Since it's not very realistic that a floor would change its width, this method is not included in the Surface class. In other contexts, this type of method can be very appropriate, for example to change the price of a piece of merchandise.

A *mutable class* is a class that contains methods that change the values for the instance variables. An *immutable class* is a class that does not contain these types of methods.

Methods that implement operations that get attribute values or calculate results from these values are called *accessors*. Accessors don't change the variables in a class. An immutable class only has accessors.

Methods that implement operations that change the attribute values are called *mutators*.

An instance method can contain its own local variables. We usually use these to store results from intermediate calculations. For example, the method getCircumference() in the Surface class could have the variable sum as the storage location for the sum of the length and width, before this is multiplied by 2 and returned:

```
public double getCircumference() {
  double sum = length + width;
  return sum * 2;
}
```

In this case there isn't much point to a local variable like this serving as intermediate storage, but in more complicated methods we will see that these are indispensable.

If the return type is different from `void`, the method must contain at least one `return` statement. For the time being there is no need for more than one `return` statement, but later on we will see examples where this is appropriate.

A `return` statement consists of the reserved word `return` followed by an expression of the same type as the return type, or of a type that can be automatically converted to the return type (for automatic conversion, see section 2.8). If the program control runs into a `return` statement, it immediately jumps out of the method regardless of whether there are more statements in the method or not.

A method with the return type `void` can also contain the statement `return;`. The effect is the same as if a value was returned.

All the methods in a class must have different signatures.

Constants, variables and methods with the static modifier

In section 3.6 you learned about class constants and class methods in the Java Library. We declare a class constant in this way:

```
private static final double VAT = 23.0;
```

If the constant is of interest outside the class, it can be given the access modifier `public`.

There can also be *class variables*. These can be useful in very specific situations. See problem 4 at the end of this section. There you'll learn to make class methods as well.

But in object-oriented programming, class methods are rare and, with the exception of `main()`, we will create very few methods of this type in this book.

Hiding names and the reserved word this

If a local variable (or a parameter) has the same name as an instance variable, it is the local variable that applies. We say that the local variable *is hiding* the instance variable. Example:

```
private double length;
private double width;
public Surface(double length, double width) {
    ....
}
```

Writing the statement `length = length;` in this constructor body has no effect since both the right and left sides of the assignment operator refer to the parameter. If we insist on having the same name for the parameters as for the instance variables, we can use the reserved word `this` to distinguish them from each other:

```
public Surface(double length, double width) {
  this.length = length;
  this.width = width;
}
```

`this` is a reference that always points to the object the Java interpreter is busy with at any given time. We will not use `this` much in this book. Instead, we prefer to let the parameters have different names from the instance variables.

Programming conventions for classes

Note that these are the code conventions we are using in this book. There are no rules that the compiler requires us to stick to. In chapter 12 we will go through several subjects that will somewhat expand the guidelines below.

- Class names start with a capital letter. Variable names and method names start with lower-case letters. If the name consists of several words, a capital letter is used for the first letters of the second word and words that follow it. The underline character and $ are not used.[3]

- Instance variables have the access modifier `private`.

- Constructors have the access modifier `public`.

- Methods have the access modifier `public` or `private`.

- Class variables and class methods are rarely used.

- Constructors and members are grouped in the order shown in the syntax description below.

- Accessors and mutators whose jobs are to get or change an attribute have standardized names:

    public void set*NN(type value)* // gives a value to the attribute NN
    public *type* get*NN*() // gets the value for the attribute NN

    If the attribute is of the data type `boolean`, the following method heads will be used:
    public void set*NN*(boolean *value*)
    public boolean is*NN*()

- In this book we have chosen to mark the parameter name in the mutator with the prefix `new`. Example:

    public void setLength(double newLength)

---

3. Exception: We are using the underline character in class names for answers to problems to indicate which problem we're referring to, for example `Problem5_4_2`. This class shows the solution to problem 2 after section 5.4.

Java Core

Declaring a class

These rules are not complete, but cover what we've covered in this chapter. Syntax rules for abstract classes, subclasses and inheritance are found in Chapter 12. Inner classes are discussed in Chapter 13.

A class declaration specifies a new reference type.

Syntax:

```
accessModifier class className {
  classConstants
  classVariables
  instanceVariables
  constructors
  classMethods
  instanceMethods
}
```

The order of constructors and members in the class is not a part of the syntax. They can be arranged in random order, but we recommend the grouping and order shown here.

Syntax for constructors and members is shown in Table 4.1.

Problems

There are more problems here than usual and we recommend that you do as many of them as possible. This material is both difficult and fundamental.

1. Suppose we create the `Surface` class without constructors. Is it then possible to create instances of the class?

2. What is wrong with the following method that is supposed to set a value for the variable `width` in the `Surface` class?

```
public void setWidth(double width) {
  width = this.width;
}
```

3. These problems are based on the example in Program Listing 4.2. Download the file, compile, and run the program. Make the changes stated below. Test the program after each change. The program contains the class constants:

```
private static final double VAT = 20.0;
private static final double VATfactor = 1.0 + VAT / 100.0;
```

These are constants that are communal for all the instances of the class. Any method in the class can refer to these constants. For example, see the method `getPriceWithVAT()`.

Table 4.1 Syntax for constructors and members in a class

class constant	*accessModifier* static final *dataType name = value*; A class constant is communal for all instances of the class.
class variable	*accessModifier* static *dataType name*; or *accessModifier* static *dataType name = initialValue*; A class variable is communal for all instances of the class. If no initial value is given, it is automatically set to the value 0 (or `false`, or `null`, depending on the type). Class variables are rarely used.
instance variable	*accessModifier dataType name*; or *accessModifier dataType name = initialValue*; Every instance of a class has its own set of instance variables. If an instance variable isn't given an initial value, it is automatically set to the initial value 0 (or `false`, or `null`, depending on the type).

constructor	*accessModifier className(parameterList)* {
	   statements
	}
	If we don't program any constructors, a constructor with an empty parameter list and without contents (the default constructor) is created. If the constructor has a parameter list, we have to pass arguments that agree in number and type with the parameter list.

class method	*accessModifier* static *returnType methodName(parameterList)* {
	   statements
	}
	A class method is called on behalf of the class. The most familiar class method is `main()`. About parameter list, see constructor, above. If the return type is not equal to `void`, the method has to return a value that agrees with the type. The client can, but does not have to, make use of this value.

instance method	*accessModifier returnType methodName(parameterList)* {
	   statements
	}
	An instance method is used when we want to send a message to an object. About parameter list, see constructor, above. About returntype, see class method, above.

Problem (a)
A merchandise object has information about its own name, number and price. A client must therefore be able to ask the merchandise for this information. Create a method that gets the merchandise's product number. The method will not print the product number, but send it back to the client. Enter a method call in the client program so that you can test the method.

Problem (b)
Do the same for a method that gets the merchandise name.

Problem (c)
As mentioned above, it is possible to give instance variables initial values. Example:

```
private String merchandiseName = "NN";
private int merchandiseNo = 0;
private double price = 0.0;
```

Insert this into the class. Give initial values in the client program using a constructor. Find out which values are significant after an object is created.

Problem (d)
Expand the class with information about how much of the merchandise is in stock. Let this be an integer. Change the constructor such that the initial value for the amount of merchandise in stock can be set in addition to the other initial values. Create methods to get, increase and decrease the amount of merchandise in stock. You don't need to consider the possibility that the amount in stock could be negative.

4. This problem shows how class variables work. This is not recommended for beginners since it's easy to confuse this with instance variables.

Enter the following class:

```
class Room {
  private static int lastUsedRoomNo = 0;  // a class variable
  private String name;
  private int roomNo;
  private int noOfSeats;

  public Room(String initName, int initNoOfSeats) {
    name = initName;
    noOfSeats = initNoOfSeats;
    lastUsedRoomNo = lastUsedRoomNo + 1; // increases the class variable
    roomNo = lastUsedRoomNo;
  }

  public String getName() {
    return name;
  }
```

```java
      public int getRoomNo() {
        return roomNo;
      }
    }
```

`lastUsedRoomNo` is a class variable, i.e. a variable that is communal for all the instances of the class. For every new instance that is created, this variable is increased by 1, which is to say that the room objects are numbered 1, 2, 3, etc.

Problem (a)
Create a client program that creates three room objects. Print the room number for each of the room objects.

Problem (b)
Create a class method that gets the room number that was used most recently. Test the method.

Problem (c)
The method from b) works if it is made into an instance method. Will an instance method that is made into a class method work without any other changes?

Program Listing 4.2

```java
    /*
     * PriceCalculations.java   E.L. 2001-08-10
     *
     * This program is calculating the price of a given amount (kilo) of merchandise.
     */
    class Merchandise {
      private static final double VAT = 20.0;
      private static final double VATfactor = 1.0 + VAT / 100.0;

      private String merchandiseName;
      private int merchandiseNo;
      private double price; // price per kilo, without VAT

      public Merchandise(String initMerchandiseName,
                                    int initMerchandiseNo, double initPrice) {
        merchandiseName = initMerchandiseName;
        merchandiseNo = initMerchandiseNo;
        price = initPrice;
      }

      public Merchandise(String initMerchandiseName, int initMerchandiseNo) {
        merchandiseName = initMerchandiseName;
        merchandiseNo = initMerchandiseNo;
        price = 0.0;
      }
```

```
    public double getPriceWithoutVAT(double noKilo) {
      return price * noKilo;
    }

    public double getPriceWithVAT(double noKilo) {
      return price * noKilo * VATfactor;
    }

    public void setPrice(double newPrice) {
      price = newPrice;
    }
}

class PriceCalculations {
  public static void main(String[] args) {
    final double amount = 2.5;
    final double kiloPrice1 = 7.30;
    final double kiloPrice2 = 7.90;
    Merchandise aMerchandise = new Merchandise("Brie", 123, kiloPrice1);
    double price1 = aMerchandise.getPriceWithoutVAT(amount);
    double price2 = aMerchandise.getPriceWithVAT(amount);
    System.out.println("The price per kilo without VAT: " + kiloPrice1);
    System.out.println("The price for " + amount + " kilos is " + price1 + " without VAT");
    System.out.println("The price for " + amount + " kilos is " + price2 + " with VAT");

    aMerchandise.setPrice(kiloPrice2);
    System.out.println("New price per kilo without VAT: " + kiloPrice2);
    System.out.println("The price for " + amount + " kilos is "
      + aMerchandise.getPriceWithoutVAT(amount) + " without VAT");
    System.out.println("The price for " + amount + " kilos is "
      + aMerchandise.getPriceWithVAT(amount) + " with VAT");
  }
}

/* Example Run:
The price per kilo without VAT: 7.3
The price for 2.5 kilos is 18.25 without VAT
The price for 2.5 kilos is 21.9 with VAT
New price per kilo without VAT: 7.9
The price for 2.5 kilos is 19.75 without VAT
The price for 2.5 kilos is 23.7 with VAT
*/
```

4.5 One More Class and Some New Operators

Let's say that we're going to create a program that can handle yes/no votes. People can call a number if they want to vote "yes" and a different number if they want to vote "no," or they can vote a different way by, for example, writing their names on lists.

The main object here will be a counter that can be updated with new individual votes and with new bundles of votes. Which is to say that it has to be possible and easy to add a single new vote and to add a number of new votes. See Figure 4.4.

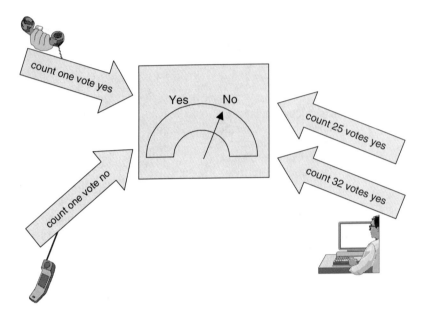

Figure 4.4 Different clients send messages to a counter

A client could be an answering machine that consecutively sends messages about each individual vote that comes in, or it could be a program that a person runs to record, for example, 20 yes votes and 35 no votes. In chapter 6, we will program the first version of this client program. In Chapter 19, we will make a distributed system out of this, where people can sit around on different PCs and update a communal counter object. In this chapter, we will stick to creating the class. You will write a test program yourself in problem 1 at the end of this section.

The class diagram might look like Figure 4.5. Notice that we have included parameter lists in the operations. We have done this to show two pairs of operations for increasing the number of yes and no votes respectively. Two by two operations have the same name, but different parameter lists. There are no strict requirements for how complete the contents of a class diagram have to be. It depends on what level of the development proess we're at when we make the diagram. At a very early stage, this class diagram would probably contain only one operation to increase the number of yes votes and one to increase the number of no votes.

A parameter declaration (or an attribute declaration) in UML is written with the name first, then a colon and a space, then the data type, for example: `increase: int`

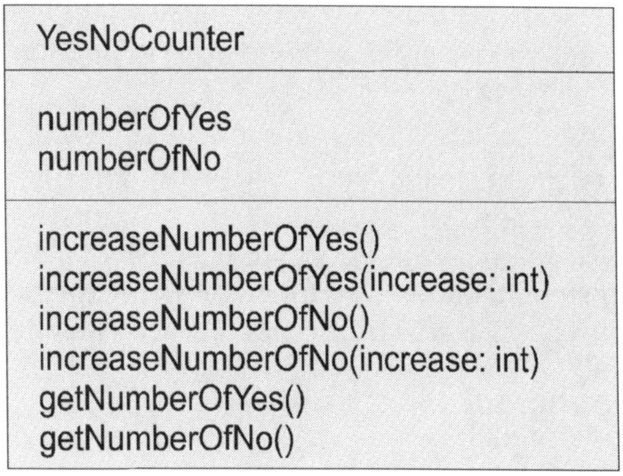

Figure 4.5   The class yesnocounter (UML)

The program code is shown in Program Listing 4.3.

The class offers operations for increasing the number of yes votes (or no votes) by 1 or by a given number. We create two methods with the same name, but different parameter lists. Let's look more closely at the methods `increaseNumberOfYes()`, first the method that increases the number of yes votes by 1:

```
public void increaseNumberOfYes() {
    numberOfYes++;
}
```

The operator ++ is called the *increment operator*, and it's used when the contents of a variable are to be increased by 1. The statement

```
numberOfYes++;
```

is the same as

```
numberOfYes = numberOfYes + 1;
```

We have a corresponding *decrement operator*, --, which reduces the value of a variable by 1.[4]

---

4. The complete names for these operators are the postincrement operator and the postdecrement operator, "post" because the operator is placed after the variable name. We can also place ++ and -- before the variable name, and then the operators are called the preincrement and predecrement operators. The difference is that for the postfix versions the value of the variable will be changed *after* it has been retrieved from memory. The prefix version changes the value of the variable *before* it's retrieved. It is possible to use expressions with these operations as part of larger expressions. Then the pre and post distinction can become meaningful. We discourage this use of the operators since expressions of this type are difficult to read. In this book we use only the postfix versions of the operators, and we don't let the expressions be part of larger expressions.

The following method has an integer as an argument and increases the contents of the instance variable `numberOfYes` by this amount:

```
public void increaseNumberOfYes(int increase) {
    numberOfYes += increase;
}
```

The statement `numberOfYes += increase;` is thus the same as `numberOfYes = numberOfYes + increase;`. We call the operator `+=` a *compound assignment operator*. We have similar compound assignment operators for subtraction, multiplication, division and the modulus operation.

Table 4.2 shows the connection between new and familiar operators.

Program Listing 4.3

```
/*
 * YesNoCounter.java   E.L. 2001-08-15
 *
 */

class YesNoCounter {
  private int numberOfYes = 0;
  private int numberOfNo = 0;

  public void increaseNumberOfYes() {
    numberOfYes++;
  }

  public void increaseNumberOfNo() {
    numberOfNo++;
  }

  public void increaseNumberOfYes(int increase) {
    numberOfYes += increase;
  }

  public void increaseNumberOfNo(int increase) {
    numberOfNo += increase;
  }

  public int getNumberOfYes() {
    return numberOfYes;
  }

  public int getNumberOfNo() {
    return numberOfNo;
  }
}
```

Table 4.2 Increment and decrement operators and compound assignment operators

expressions with new operators	expressions with familiar operators
value++	value = value + 1
value--	value = value - 1
value += 3	value = value + 3
value -= 3	value = value - 3
value *= 3	value = value * 3
value /= 3	value = value / 3
value %= 3	value = value % 3

Problems

1. Write a test program for the class `YesNoCounter`.

2. What is printed when the following bit of code is run?

```
int value = 2;
value++;
value--;
System.out.println(value);
value += 5;
value *= 2;
value %= 3;
System.out.println(value);
```

3. Find out what the variables a, b and c contain after the following bit of code is run:

```
int a = 10;
int b = 20;
int c = b % a;
a++;
b++;
c += a;
a *= c;
b--;
c /= 2;
c %= 2;
```

4.6   Introduction to Applets

Many example applets follow with the online SDK documentation. You can also find many examples on the Internet. The "fanciest" applets are relatively complicated to program and fall outside the scope of this book.

For now, we will look at very simple applets that draw one or more geometric figures. In chapter 13 we will fill the applets with push buttons, text fields and other components you're familiar with from the usual graphic user interfaces.

Program Listing 4.4 displays the code for the applet in Figure 1.4.

Program Listing 4.4

```
/*
 * SimpleApplet.java  V.H & E.L. 2001-08-10
 */

import java.awt.*;
import javax.swing.*;

public class SimpleApplet extends JApplet {
  public void init() {
    Container content = getContentPane();
    Drawing aDrawing = new Drawing();
    content.add(aDrawing);
  }
}

class Drawing extends JPanel {
  public void paintComponent(Graphics window) {
    super.paintComponent(window);  // Remember this!
    setBackground(Color.green);
    window.drawString("Hello hello", 50, 50);
    window.drawOval(40, 30, 100, 40);
  }
}
```

The program consists of three parts:

1. `import` statements

2. The class `SimpleApplet`

3. The class `Drawing`

We will go through these three parts in detail.

import statements

The `import` statements tell us that we are using classes from two packages: the package `java.awt` contains, among other things, classes that make it possible to draw on the screen (the `Graphics` class), while the package `javax.swing` contains the JApplet class, which is required in all applets in this book.[5] Both of the packages contain classes for the familiar graphic components such as, for example, push buttons, list boxes, windows, etc. The components in the javax.swing package are the newest and most useful. Therefore, those are the ones we'll use in this book. We will come back to these components in chapter 13. Here we are only using the class Container that we can think of as a container where we put our drawings. Container belongs to the java.awt package.

The class SimpleApplet

(This section contains very difficult material. However, it's completely possible to create applets without understanding all the details. We will come back to these details in other contexts throughout the book, so that it will sink in gradually.)

The applet class will be constructed the same way in all the examples in this chapter.

The SimpleApplet class is the class we refer to in the HTML file (see Appendix E). The access modifier public is at the very beginning of the class head. This means that the class is public and can therefore be accessed from all locations. All applets have to be public.

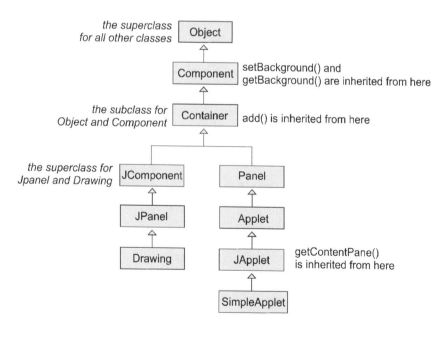

Figure 4.6   A segment of the class tree in java (UML)

---

5. Applets of this type require Java version SDK2. Currently very few browsers support this version. There is a way round: search for the product HTMLConverter at [URL Javasoft].

After the class name comes `extends JApplet`. This means that the class is a *subclass* of the `JApplet` class. We can imagine that the class `JApplet` describes the set of (almost) all possible applets. The `SimpleApplet` class only describes applets that look exactly like our small, simple one. This will be a subset of the first, large set of applets. Everything that is true for the set of all applets is also true for our special applet. We say that the `SimpleApplet` class *inherits* everything that applies to all applets.

Figure 4.6 shows a segment of the *class tree* in Java. There isn't room in this UML diagram to write more than the class names in the boxes. The relationship between the classes is the main point of the class tree. At the bottom right we find the classes mentioned before. We see that `JApplet` is a subclass of `Applet`, which in turn is a subclass of `Panel`, etc. A subclass inherits methods from all classes above it in the tree. Therefore we say that not only the `Applet` class is a subclass of the `Panel` class, but also that all classes under `Applet` are subclasses of `Panel`.

On the other hand, `Panel` is a *superclass* for `Applet`, and for all classes under `Applet`.

If we want to emphasize that a class comes directly above or below another, we talk about *direct superclass* or *direct subclass*.

The `Container` class has two direct subclasses under it, namely `JComponent` and `Panel`.

In the UML diagram, the arrow goes from the subclass to the direct superclass.

Figure 4.7 shows how the objects in a subclass are a subset of the objects in the superclass. For example, the objects that are described by the `Applet` class are a subset of the objects that are described by the `Panel` class.

We will say a lot more about subclasses and inheritance in chapter 12.

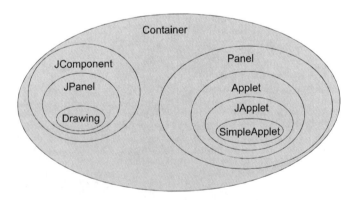

Figure 4.7 The objects the different classes describe form sets

The `SimpleApplet` class contains one method, `init()`. This is a method we have in all applets, much the same way that we have `main()` in all applications.

As opposed to `main()`, this isn't a class method, but an instance method. That means that an applet object has to exist for the method to be carried out.

 The Web browser instantiates the applet object and sends the message `init()` to it. This starts the applet.

Of course the contents of `init()` will vary, but we will usually have to get a reference for a container where we place what is going to be displayed on the screen:

    Container content = getContentPane();

We see that there is no object name before `getContentPane()`. That means that the applet object (which we are now inside) is sending this message to itself. The method `getContentPane()` is a method that is inherited from the `JApplet` class. We will gradually see more examples of objects sending messages to themselves, and they don't have to be only inherited methods. Any instance method can be of interest.

The return type from `getContentPane()` is `Container`. Among other things, we can send the message `add()` to these types of objects. And what are we "adding" to a container? Well, the components that will be displayed in the applet window. There's a drawing here.

This example doesn't show it, but it is of course possible to use the dialogs in `JOptionPane` to communicate with the user. On the other hand, output from `System.out.println()` statements are displayed in the console window, which in a Web browser is called "Java Console", or something like that.

The class Drawing

All the applets in this chapter consist of a simple drawing. A drawing should be a subclass of the `JPanel` class.

Drawing on the screen occurs when the Java interpreter goes through all the components that make up the window and sends the message `paintComponent()` to every single one of them. It is these components that we have "added" to the "content pane", cf. previous section.[6]

Therefore, the class `Drawing` has to contain a method named `paintComponent()`. The method head and first line always have to be as follows:

    public void paintComponent(Graphics window) { // can use a name other than "window"
    super.paintComponent(window); // Remember this!

---

6. If we want to have more than one component in the window, we have to think about the so-called layout-manager. See chapter 13.

The statement `super.paintComponent()` sees to it that the superclass's drawing method is called. `window` is a parameter name. As in other methods, we are free to choose this name when we create the method. The data type, however, has to be `Graphics`.

The Java interpreter creates an object that represents the surface we are drawing on, the *graphics context*. This becomes the argument for the method `paintComponent()`. This method is called by the interpreter. When the program control gets into this method, the `window` parameter will refer to the graphics context.

The method starts by setting the background color to green:

```
setBackground(Color.green);
```

As shown in Figure 4.6, `setBackground()` is a method that is inherited from the `Component` class. Again we see an example of the object (here it's the drawing) sending a message to itself. `green` is a class constant in the `Color` class.
  Then we draw the text and an oval:

```
window.drawString("Hello hello", 50, 50);
window.drawOval(40, 30, 100, 40)
```

We send messages to `window`. The numbers determine the size of the oval, and the location of the text and the oval on the screen. There's more about the `Graphics` class in the next section.

API Reference

The javax.swing.JApplet class

Method:

```
public Container getContentPane()
```

The method returns a reference to a container that can be filled with GUI components.

The java.awt.Component class

This class is the superclass for most graphics components.

Methods:

```
public Color getBackground()
public void setBackground(Color newColor)
```

These methods are used to get and set new background colors. The `Color` class is covered in the next section.

The java.awt.Container class

The class describes a container for graphics components. These components include buttons, lists, text fields, etc. In this chapter we are only putting a drawing we produced ourselves into the container.

Method:

        public Component add(Component comp)

The method places a component in the container. The method returns a reference to the component. We rarely have to worry about that return value.

4.7 Introduction to Graphics

The screen being drawn on has a certain resolution. By *resolution* we mean the number of addressable points on the screen. Typical resolutions are 1280×1024 points and 1024×768 points. One of these points is usually called a pixel. "A *pixel* is the smallest element in a display surface that can be assigned color or intensity independently."[7] Drawing means assigning certain pixels specific colors.

The window being drawn in is a section of the screen. We decide where the drawing will be by indicating x and y coordinates relative to the origin in the upper left-hand corner of the window. See Figure 4.8. The system of coordinates is inverted with respect to what we are used to from mathematics.

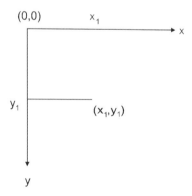

Figure 4.8 The system of coordinates' origin is in the upper left-hand corner

In the `paintComponent()` method we draw by sending messages to the `window` object. In Program Listing 4.4 two messages are sent:

7. [Hofstad, Løland, Scott 1997, p. 207]

```
window.drawString("Hello hello", 50, 50);
window.drawOval(40, 30, 100, 40)
```

The first message makes sure that the text "Hello hello" is drawn with a start position of x = 50 and y = 50. The second message draws an oval. The two first arguments designate the position in the upper left-most corner of the surrounding rectangle. The last two arguments state the diameter of the oval along the x and y axes respectively. If these are equal, a circle is drawn.

The summary below shows a few drawing operations that can be used for objects that belong to the `Graphics` class.

API Reference

The java.awt.Graphics class

Methods:

> public void drawLine(int x1, int y1, int x2, int y2)

The method draws a straight line from point (x1, y1) to point (x2, y2).

> public void drawOval(int x, int y, int width, int height)
> public void fillOval(int x, int y, int width, int height)

The methods draw an open, possibly filled, oval with the stated width and height. The point (x, y) is in the upper left-most corner of the surrounding rectangle.

> public void drawRect(int x, int y, int width, int height)
> public void fillRect(int x, int y, int width, int height)

The methods draw a rectangle with the given width and height. The point (x, y) is in the upper left-most corner of the rectangle.

> public void drawArc(int x, int y, int width, int height, int startAngle, int arcAngle)

The method draws an arc. The point (x, y) is in the upper left-most corner of the rectangle that surrounds the oval that the arc is a part of. The size of this rectangle is given by the width and height. The arc starts at `startAngle` and stretches over an arc indicated by `arcAngle`. The angles are measured in degrees. Positive angles are counterclockwise and negative angles are clockwise. For an example of use, see Figure 4.9.

> public void drawString(String text, int x, int y)

The method draws the text. The point (x, y) is in the lower-most left-hand corner of the text.

> public void setFont(Font newFont)

The method sets a specific font to apply in the window. The `Font` class is described below.

> public void setColor(Color newColor)

The method sets a specific color to apply for drawing in the window. The `Color` class is described below.

    public Font getFont()

The method gets the font that will be used.

    public Color getColor()

The method gets the color that will be used.

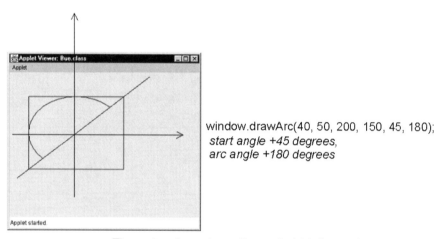

window.drawArc(40, 50, 200, 150, 45, 180);
start angle +45 degrees,
arc angle +180 degrees

The rectangle encloses the oval which the arc is a part of:
window.drawRect(40, 50, 200, 150);

Figure 4.9 Example of drawing an arc

A class for colors: Color

A color consists of a red, a green and a blue component. Each component has a numerical value between 0 and 255 depending on the contribution from the component in question. The `Color` class offers a constructor that takes three numbers as an argument. This makes it possible to construct any color. However, there are 13 standard colors. We can make these lighter or darker and this covers most needs. See the example in Figure 4.10.

The program code is shown in Program Listing 4.5. We will go through some of the statements:

    Color color = Color.gray;

The `color` object receives the standard color `gray` as a value. This is a class constant in the `Color` class. We set this as the drawing color in the window and draw the first of five rectangles:

```
window.setColor(color);
window.fillRect(40, 50, 20, 120);
```

The next rectangle will be a shade lighter. We create a new color and set it to apply:

```
color = color.brighter();
window.setColor(color);
```

We continue this way until all five rectangles have been drawn. The method `darker()` makes the color darker.

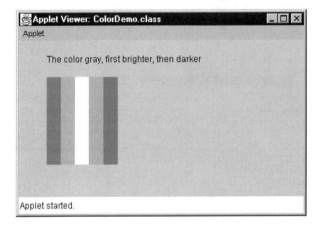

Figure 4.10 Using the method `brighter()` followed by `darker()`

Program Listing 4.5

```
/*
 * ColorDemo.java   E.L. 2001-08-21
 */

import javax.swing.*;
import java.awt.*;

public class ColorDemo extends JApplet {
  public void init() {
    Container content = getContentPane();
    Drawing aDrawing = new Drawing();
    content.add(aDrawing);
  }
}

class Drawing extends JPanel {
  public void paintComponent(Graphics window) {
    super.paintComponent(window);
    window.drawString("The color gray, first brighter, then darker", 40, 30);
```

```
        Color color = Color.gray;
        window.setColor(color);
        window.fillRect(40, 50, 20, 120);
        color = color.brighter();
        window.setColor(color);
        window.fillRect(60, 50, 20, 120);
        color = color.brighter();
        window.setColor(color);
        window.fillRect(80, 50, 20, 120);
        color = color.darker();
        window.setColor(color);
        window.fillRect(100, 50, 20, 120);
        color = color.darker();
        window.setColor(color);
        window.fillRect(120, 50, 20, 120);
    }
}
```

API Reference

The java.awt.Color class

The standard colors are public constants in the Color class:

Color.black	Color.gray	Color.orange	Color.yellow
Color.blue	Color.green	Color.pink	
Color.cyan	Color.lightGray	Color.red	
Color.darkGray	Color.magenta	Color.white	

Methods:

```
public Color brighter()
public Color darker()
```

These methods generate a new color object in a somewhat lighter or darker shade.

A class for fonts: Font

An object that is an instance of the Font class contains information concerning the font. A font has a name, a style and a size. The names are the same as the ones we are familiar with from word processing. There are a great many fonts and the number of fonts depends on what is installed on the computer in question. In order to have a common basis, five logical names are defined that will always correspond to existing physical fonts. These five are SansSerif, Serif, Monospaced, Dialog and DialogInput. In Windows, for example, SansSerif will always correspond to Arial. Three of the fonts are shown in Figure 4.11. The four possible styles are also shown here: normal, **bold**, *italic*, and the combination of ***bold and italic***.

The size of the font is expressed by a number of points. This is a measurement unit derived from typography and it does not correspond to the number of pixels. It is possible to find the size of letters by using the FontMetrics class. This class is not covered in this book. With a little more experience, however, you will be able to find out how this class is used by studying the documentation that comes with Java.

The program code that gives Figure 4.11 is shown in Program Listing 4.6. Together with the description of the Font class below, it should be possible to read the program code without any additional guidance.

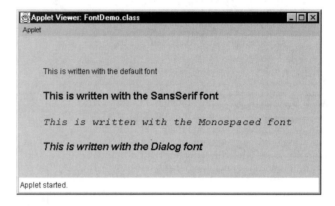

Figure 4.11 Demonstration of various fonts

Program Listing 4.6

```
/*
 * FontDemo.java   E.L. 2001-08-30
 */

import javax.swing.*;
import java.awt.*;

public class FontDemo extends JApplet {
  public void init() {
    Container content = getContentPane();
    Drawing aDrawing = new Drawing();
    content.add(aDrawing);
  }
}

class Drawing extends JPanel {
  public void paintComponent(Graphics window) {
    super.paintComponent(window);
    window.drawString("This is written with the default font", 40, 60);
    Font theFont = new Font("SansSerif", Font.BOLD, 16);
```

```
    window.setFont(theFont);
    window.drawString("This is written with the " + theFont.getName() + " font", 40, 100);
    theFont = new Font("Monospaced", Font.ITALIC, 16);
    window.setFont(theFont);
    window.drawString("This is written with the " + theFont.getName() + " font", 40, 140);
    theFont = new Font("Dialog", Font.BOLD + Font.ITALIC, 16);
    window.setFont(theFont);
    window.drawString("This is written with the " + theFont.getName() + " font", 40, 180);
  }
}
```

API Reference

The java.awt.Font class

Constructor:

```
public Font(String name, int style, int size)
```

This constructor is used to achieve a specific font, style and size. The name of the font is either a logical name (SansSerif, Serif, Monospaced, Dialog and DialogInput) or the name of a font we know is found on the computer running the program. No error message is sent if the name is invalid. The style is one of the class constants cited below. The size of the font is expressed in a number of points, which are not the same as the number of pixels.

Class constants:

```
public Font.BOLD
public Font.ITALIC
public Font.PLAIN
```

These class constants describe valid styles. The constants are integers. We can also set up the sum (Font.BOLD + Font.ITALIC), which gives fonts that are both bold and italic.

Methods:

```
public String getName()
public int getSize()
public int getStyle()
```

These methods are used to get information about the font.

```
public boolean isBold()
public boolean isItalic()
public boolean isPlain()
```

These methods are used to ask if the font is in a given style.

Problems

1. Try the `ColorDemo` class with colors other than gray. Also try different combinations of `brighter()` and `darker()`.

2. Change the `SimpleApplet` class in the following way:

   Draw a filled oval instead of an empty one. Write the text under the oval. The oval and the text should be in different colors.

3. Try different fonts by making changes to the `FontDemo` class.

4.8 New Concepts in This Chapter

Concept	Brief Explanation
access modifier	The modifiers `public` and `private` (and `protected`, see chapter 12) control access to classes, constructors and members. The class's access controls the constructors' and the members' access if it's stricter.
accessor	Method that gets an attribute value or a calculated result. The method doesn't change the attribute values.
class body	The contents of the class, i.e. the part of the class declaration that follows the class head, surrounded by {}.
class head	A class head consists of a possible modifier, the word `class` and then the class name.
class tree	A tree that shows the relationship between classes and subclasses. In Java, all classes are connected in a single tree, with the class `java.lang.Object` at the top.
class variable	A variable that is communal for all the instances of a class, declared with the modifier `static`. The variable may be accessed even if no instances of the class exist.
compound assignment operator	`+= -= *= /= %=` The operators change the contents of a variable, for example, `value *= 3;`
create an object	An object is an instance of a class, and we create an object with the reserved word `new` and a constructor. Memory is allocated for all the instance variables, which are given their initial values.
decrement operator	`--`, decreases the contents of a variable by 1, for example, `number--;`
default constructor	A constructor which is made automatically if you do not supply one. The default constructor does not take any arguments.
direct subclass	A class directly under the class in question in the class tree. The reserved word `extends` is used in the class head followed by the name of the class that this class will be a direct subclass of. If `extends` is not used, the class becomes a direct subclass for `java.lang.Object`.
direct superclass	The class directly above the class in question in the class tree. See also direct subclass.

Concept	Brief Explanation
`extends`	The keyword that denotes subclassing. `class A extends B` means that A becomes a direct subclass of B.
font, logical	The following five font types will correspond to a font on the computer running the program: SansSerif, Serif, Monospaced, Dialog, DialogInput.
get method	Method that gets the value for an attribute.
graphics context	The surface our program is drawing on, for example, a specific screen type.
immutable class	A class that does not contain mutators.
increment operator	++, increases the contents of a variable by 1, for example, `number++;`
inheritence	Members that are inherited from a superclass can be used the same way in the subclass as if they were declared in the subclass. Also see the definition in chapter 12.
instance variable	Represents an attribute. Has to be declared in a class, but outside all the methods in the class. Each instance of a class gets its own set of the instance variables.
member	All instance variables and methods, and all class variables and methods, are members of the class. Constructors are not members.
method body	The part of the method declaration that follows the method head, surrounded by {}.
method head	A method head consists of possible modifiers, then the method's return type (possibly `void`) and then the method name and parameter list.
mutable class	A class that contains mutators.
mutator	Method that changes one or more attribute values.
`null`	The value for a reference that doesn't point to any object.
overloading a name	Inside a class, methods and constructors with the same name can be kept apart by having different signatures. We say that the names are "overloaded".
package access	The class, constructor or member is accessible in the package the class belongs to. Package access applies if no access modifier is used.
pixel	The smallest element in a graphics interface that can be assigned color or intensity independently. [Hofstad, Løland, Scott 1997, p. 207]
postdecrementoperator	See decrement operator.
postincrementoperator	See increment operator.
predecrement operator	The operator -- located in front of the variable. Not used in this book. See footnote in section 4.5.
preincrement operator	The operator ++ located in front of the variable. Not used in this book. See footnote in section 4.5.
primitive name	Last part of a qualified name.

Concept	Brief Explanation
private	A member or a constructor with the access modifier `private` is not accessible outside the class where it's declared. Constructors are rarely private.
public	A member or a constructor with the access modifier `public` is accessible anywhere as long as the class the member is part of is also declared `public`.
qualified name	A name that consists of several parts separated by a period.
qualifier	All the parts of a qualified name, except the last part.
qualify a name	Necessary when we use the name outside its scope. The qualifier will be a package name, a class name or the name of an object.
reference type	A data type described in a class declaration.
return statement	A statement that begins with the reserved word `return`. Makes sure that the program control immediately exits the method and returns to the place it was called from. If the return type is anything other than `void`, `return` has to be followed by an expression of the same type as the method's return type, potentially a type that can be automatically converted to the return type. `return` is rarely used if the return type is `void`.
screen resolution	Number of addressable points a screen is divided into.
set method	Method that changes the value for an attribute.
signature	The name of the constructor or method and the number and type of parameters. Neither the return type nor the parameter names are a part of the signature.
static	Modifier that states class constants, class variables or class methods.
subclass	A class one or more levels below the class in question in the class tree. All messages that can be sent to an instance of a class can also be sent to instances of this class's subclasses. See also direct subclass.
superclass	A class one or more levels above the class in question in the class tree. See also direct superclass.
this	This keyword is used in a method and it's a reference to the object the method is being carried out for.
void	Keyword that says the method doesn't return any value.

4.9 Review Problems

1. Explain the building block principle in programming.

2. What is a constructor?

3. Are there other ways to give initial values to instance variables than by using constructors?

4. Why shouldn't constructors be private?

5. What distinguishes local variables from instance variables?

6. What is the relationship between local variables and parameters?

7. How do we make a named constant that will be used in several methods?

8. What does it mean that `main()` has the word `static` before it?

9. State differences and similarities between reference types and primitive data types.

10. What do we mean by members in a class?

11. How can a class have more than one constructor when a constructor has to have the same name as the class?

12. What's the difference between the scope of a name declared inside a class and the scope of a name declared inside a method?

13. What's the difference between a method's signature and the method head?

14. What is a "graphics context," and what is the relationship between it and the method `paintComponent()`?

4.10 Programming Problems

In problems 1–3 you will create classes. You should make at least one constructor in each class. Make a test data set and client program to try out the class. Use the class `JOptionPane` class to communicate with the user.

Problem 1

You are going to create a `Person` class. Suggest attributes. Create methods that make it possible to get every single one of the attributes. Evaluate which of the attributes you should be able to change the values of. Create methods that make that possible.

Problem 2

Create a `ForeignCurrency` class. It should have methods to calculate conversions from and into your own country's currency. The client program will create several objects to represent different currencies.

Problem 3

Create a `Project` class. The project title, name of the person responsible and budget (only one number) will be entered at the start of the project. The project will also be able to keep track of its own finances. The class will have methods to get all the information and a method that records that a sum of money is accrued to the project.

The client program will create several project objects. Also set up statements that change the objects you have created.

Problem 4

Create an applet that draws a smiley face ☺

Problem 5

Create an applet that inputs the attributes for a rectangle and then draws the rectangle. While drawing, the area and circumference of the rectangle will be printed. Let the background texts give hints for reasonable values, so that the rectangle doesn't go outside the applet window.

Selection as a Control Structure

Learning goals for this chapter

After completing this chapter, you will understand the following concepts:

- The selection control structure

- Boolean expression

- Nested `if` and multiple choice statements

You will be able to

- Create an activity diagram to illustrate selections

- Use boolean variables and boolean expressions in programs

- Structure the program code in a legible manner using indents and braces

- Program multiple choices using nested `if` statements and `switch`

- Program decision tables

All of the client programs we've written up to this point have been sequential in nature. Their statements are performed in the order they appear. With the multitude of ready-made classes available, it's possible to achieve relatively complicated programs this way.

The opportunity to choose between several alternative execution ways can make a client program more flexible. In this chapter, we'll look at how to program `if` statements, as the selection mechanism is called.

We will also benefit a great deal from using the `if` statement inside methods in classes we create.

The recurrent example in this chapter will be a very simple calculator.

5.1   A Simple Calculator

Before we start looking at new material, we will create a simple calculator that can perform the four arithmetical operations: addition, subtraction, multiplication, and division. See the class diagram in Figure 5.1.

The program code is displayed in Program Listing 5.1. Read through it. In the first problem at the end of this section, you will create a little test program for the class.

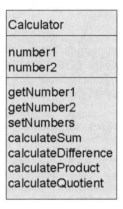

Figure 5.1   A calculator class (UML)

Program Listing 5.1

```
/*
 * Calculator.java   E.L. 2001-08-10
 *
 */

class Calculator {
  private double number1;
  private double number2;

  public Calculator(double initNumber1, double initNumber2) {
    number1 = initNumber1;
    number2 = initNumber2;
  }

  public double getNumber1() {
    return number1;
  }

  public double getNumber2() {
    return number2;
  }
```

```
public void setNumbers(double newNumber1, double newNumber2) {
  number1 = newNumber1;
  number2 = newNumber2;
}

public double calculateSum() {
  return number1 + number2;
}


public double calculateDifference() {
  return number1 - number2;
}


public double calculateProduct() {
  return number1 * number2;
}

public double calculateQuotient() {

  /* Division by zero gives special results:
   * Both numerator and denominator are 0: Result: Double.NaN ("not-a-number")
   * Only denominator is 0: Result: Double.NEGATIVE_INFINITY or
   *                  Double.POSITIVE_INFINITY.
   * Printing these values gives "NaN" and "Infinity".
   */
  return number1 / number2;
  }
}
```

Problems

1. Write a little program that tests all the methods in the `Calculator` class. Remember to specially test what happens in the `calculateQuotient()` method if one or both of the numbers is zero.

2. Expand the class with a method that solves a linear equation: $ax + b = 0$. Test the method.

3. Modify the `Calculator` class so that it can solve a second-degree equation. There is a ready-made method for calculating the square root of a number. The usage example follows:

```
double root = Math.sqrt(number);  // finds the positive root
```

Hint: You have to create a method for each of the two roots. As a test, you can use the equation $2x^2 - 4x - 16 = 0$. It's solutions are $x_1 = 4$ and $x_2 = -2$.

5.2   A Selection is a Control Structure

We're familiar with the concept of an algorithm from before. An algorithm is "a limited and ordered set of well-defined rules for solving a problem" (see section 2.3). That an algorithm is ordered means that the instructions have to be carried out in a specific order. This specific order doesn't necessarily have to be a straight line from beginning to end. We can decide that we will execute the same instructions several times over, or depending on a given situation, we will do one thing or the other. There are three categories of execution order: sequence, selection, and loop. We call these the three different *control structures*. The programs we've seen up to this point have all had sequential structures.

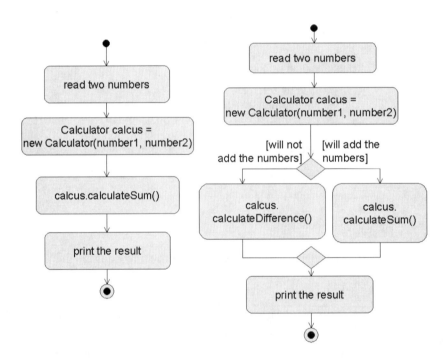

Figure 5.2   A client object sends messages to the `calcus` object (UML)

Selection is a control structure that enables the program to choose one set of instructions or another depending on what it will do in a given situation. If we instantiate an object of the `Calculator` class, we will send messages to this instance, depending on whether we want to add, subtract, multiply, or divide the two numbers in question. The selection control structure is the theme of this chapter.

A *loop* is a control structure that makes it pc
sequence of instructions several times. This makes
makes it possible, for example, to do several tr
account or to calculate the renovation costs for se
The loop control structure is the topic of the next c

We use *activity diagrams* to illustrate control structu.
of UML.

Figure 5.2 shows examples of the sequence and selection cc
We're inside the client program. The client program can be consideic
object that goes from state to state. Every "box" in the figure represents a stu.
activity. The client object is active in this state. The client object on the left can only
add two numbers together. The one on the right gives the user a choice between
addition and subtraction. We'll program this shortly. Later, we'll find out how to
let the user choose between all four arithmetical operations.

The notation used in an activity diagram is presented in Figure 5.3.

Each individual selection always has to be worded as a yes/no question. The
activity diagram doesn't show the questions, only the pertinent answers stated as
assertions, or conditions. A condition has two possible values: true or false. Hence,
the condition "will add the numbers" is the opposite of the condition "will not add
the numbers". The question is, "Should the numbers be added?" On the right, the
answer is "yes". On the left, the answer is "no". The conditions set up in the
diagram should be the opposite of each other, as the example shows. We can't write
[will subtract from each other] on the left. In that case, we would have had to ask
another yes/no question.

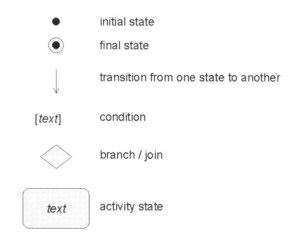

Figure 5.3 Notation used in activity diagrams (UML)

…ure 5.4 shows data input for the calculator. The `showConfirmDialog()` method in the `JOptionPane` class makes it possible to ask yes/no questions. Study Program Listing 5.2 along with Figure 5.4. The user presses one of the buttons[1], and the method returns an integer value depending on which button was pressed. By comparing this value with class constants, we can make sure that the program is doing what the user want.

JOptionPane.showInputDialog("First number: ");

JOptionPane.showInputDialog("Second number: ");

JOptionPane.showConfirmDialog(null,
"Add the numbers?", "Calculator",
JOptionPane.YES_NO_OPTION);

JOptionPane.showMessageDialog(null, result);

Figure 5.4   Running the program testcalculator1

The method for asking the user yes/no questions has the following head:

```
public static int showConfirmDialog(Component parent,
                    Object message, String title, int combinationOfButtons)
```

The button combination is a constant in the `JOptionPane` class. We used `YES_NO_OPTION` (there are other possibilities in the API reference below).
 The program uses the method this way:

```
int answer = JOptionPane.showConfirmDialog(null, "Add the numbers? ",
                    "Calculator", JOptionPane.YES_NO_OPTION);
```

Depending on the value of the answer, the program will add or subtract. We use what we call an `if` statement:

---

1. The user should click with the mouse or press Alt-N to get the No-button pressed. Just tab and pressing the Enter-key do not work (at least not in the Windows environment).

```
if (answer == JOptionPane.YES_OPTION) { // NB! Notice the double equal sign!
  calculatedAnswer = calcus.calculateSum();
  operator = '+'; // will be part of the result that prints
} else { // otherwise
  calculatedAnswer = calcus.calculateDifference();
  operator = '-';
}
```

We read this section of code as follows:

If the user pressed the Yes button,

add the numbers and set `operator` equal to '+',

otherwise,

subtract the numbers from each other and set operator equal to '-',.

Note that the statements that will be executed in the first case are collected in a block, as are the statements that will be executed in the second case. The `calculatedAnswer` and `operator` variables have to be declared before both of these blocks so that they will be available to print out at the end of the program.

Program Listing 5.2

```
/*
 * TestCalculator1.java   E.L. 2001-08-10
 *
 */
import javax.swing.JOptionPane;
class TestCalculator1 {
 public static void main(String[] args) {

  /* Reading data */
  String number1Read = JOptionPane.showInputDialog("First number: ");
  String number2Read = JOptionPane.showInputDialog("Second number: ");
  double number1 = Double.parseDouble(number1Read);
  double number2 = Double.parseDouble(number2Read);
  int answer = JOptionPane.showConfirmDialog(null, "Add the numbers? ",
          "Calculator", JOptionPane.YES_NO_OPTION);

  /* Calculating results */
  Calculator calcus = new Calculator(number1, number2);
  double calculatedAnswer;
  char operator;
  if (answer == JOptionPane.YES_OPTION) { // Yes is pressed
    calculatedAnswer = calcus.calculateSum();
    operator = '+';
  } else { // No or Esc is pressed, or the dialogue is closed
    calculatedAnswer = calcus.calculateDifference();
    operator = '-';
  }

  /* Printing results */
  String result = "Our calculation: " + calcus.getNumber1() + " " +
```

```
                        operator + " " + calcus.getNumber2();
            result += "\nThe answer is " + calculatedAnswer;
            JOptionPane.showMessageDialog(null, result);
            System.exit(0);
        }
    }
    /* Example Run:
    See figure 5.4
    */
```

API Reference

The javax.swing.JOptionPane class

See also Section 3.7.

Methods:

Confirm dialogs:

```
        public static int showConfirmDialog(Component parent, Object message)
        public static int showConfirmDialog(Component parent, Object message,
                    String title, int combinationOfButtons)
        public static int showConfirmDialog(Component parent, Object message,
                    String title, int combinationOfButtons, int typeOfMessage)
        public static int showConfirmDialog(Component parent, Object message,
                    String title, int combinationOfButtons, int typeOfMessage, Icon icon)
```

These are dialogs with different combinations of OK, Yes, No, and Cancel buttons.

The parameters `parent`, `message`, `title`, `typeOfMessage`, and `icon` are explained in Section 3.7.

`combinationOfButtons` can be one of the following class constants: `DEFAULT_OPTION`, `YES_NO_OPTION`, `YES_NO_CANCEL_OPTION`, or `OK_CANCEL_OPTION`. The simplest version of the method doesn't require any button combination to be indicated. In that case, `YES_NO_CANCEL_OPTION` applies.

The method returns information about which button the user pressed. The alternatives are given with the class constants `CANCEL_OPTION`, `OK_OPTION`, `YES_OPTION`, `NO_OPTION`, or `CLOSED_OPTION` if the user closed the dialog.

Option dialogs:

```
        public static int showOptionDialog(Component parent, Object message,
                        String title, int combinationOfButtons, int typeOfMessage, Icon icon,
                        Object[] options, Object initialOption)
        public static Object showInputDialog(Component parent, Object message,
                        String title, int typeOfMessage, Icon icon, Object[] options,
                        Object initialOption)
```

These methods make it possible for the user to choose between several alternatives. They are relatively difficult to use, and we recommend that you study the example in Section 5.5 before reading the facts below. See also Figure 5.7 and table 5.1 later in this chapter.

`showOptionDialog()` shows the options as pushbuttons, while `showInputDialog()` shows the options in the form of a list (dropdown list if fewer than 20 alternatives).

The parameters `parent`, `message`, `title`, `typeOfMessage`, and `icon` are explained in Section 3.7. `combinationOfButtons` is explained above. `options` is an array of the possible options. They can be e.g. texts or icons. `initialOption` shows what will be selected if the user doesn't make a choice of his own.

`showOptionDialog()` returns the number of the option selected. The first option has number 0. If the user presses Cancel, the dialog closes and the constant `CLOSED_OPTION` is returned.

`showInputDialog()` returns a reference to the object selected. If the user presses Cancel, `null` is returned.

Problem

Modify the program so that it gives the user the choice between multiplying and dividing.

5.3 Blocks inside Methods

A block is a group of statements surrounded by curly braces {}. A method contains at least one block.

We call variables that are declared inside methods local variables. From chapter 2 we remember that a local variable's scope is the rest of the block where the variable is declared.

Figure 5.5 shows a revised version of the calculator program where the scope of the various variable names is indicated.

Here the result string gets its final value inside the same block that the result is calculated in. Then we can declare `calculatedAnswer` inside the innermost block. Declaring a variable near where it is used is a good habit to get into.

In this program, we have two different variables with the name `calculatedAnswer`, each in its own block. We can't declare two variables with the same name in the same block. This means that if we've declared the name `calculatedAnswer` in an outer block, we can't redefine this name in an inner block.

{ } placement and using indents

Pay attention to where the curly braces { } go and how we use indents in the program. The way we do this helps make a program easier to read. No matter what, the compiler ignores the indents.

We recommend that { always be placed at the end of the line. Indent the following statements two spaces.[2] Keep this increased indent until you get to }. Decrease the indentation when you write }. Having several blocks inside each other will lead to many indentations before we begin decreasing the indentation again.

The curly brace } that ends a block will usually have a line to itself. This means that there's a little bit of space in the program in a logical place.

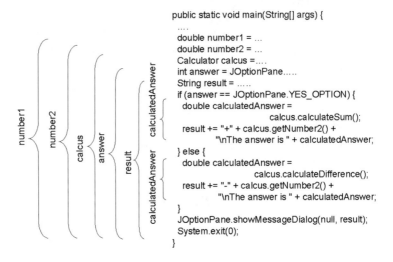

Figure 5.5 The scope for names in the revised calculator program

Problems

1. The following is given:

```
double sum = 0.0;
int value = 10;
if (value > 5) sum += value;
else sum -= value;
```

What is the value of sum after this section of a program is executed?

2. The following is given:

---

[2]. In the examples in this book, it will often look as though the indentation is less than two positions. This is because we are writing program code in a proportional font out of space considerations. If you look at the *java* files in an editor, you will see that a two-position indent is used.

```
if (a > 10) {  // start block 1
  int number1 = 60;
  int number2 = 50;
  System.out.println("number1 = " + number1 + ", number2 = " + number2);
  if (b < 20) { // start block 2
    int number3 = 20;
    number1 = 30;
    number2 = 100;
    int number4 = number1 + number2 + number3;
    System.out.println("number1 = " + number1 + ", number2 = " + number2);
    System.out.println("number3 = " + number3 + ", number4 = " + number4);
  } else { // end block 2, start block 3
    int number3 = 65;
    System.out.println("number3 = " + number3);
  } // end block 3
  System.out.println("number1 = " + number1 + ", number2 = " + number2);
} // end block 1
```

(a) How many variables are declared in this segment of a program?

(b) Number the lines 1–17. What are the scopes of the different variables?

(c) What is printed in the output statements if both *(a > 10)* and *(b < 20)* are true?

(d) What is printed in the output statements if *(a > 10)* is true and *(b < 20)* is false?

5.4 The if Statement

There are two versions of the `if` statement (see Figure 5.6). Notice that in both cases, the activity diagram runs together before we proceed to the next instruction following the `if` statement.

statement1 and *statement2* can be blocks – i.e., a set of statements enclosed in { }.

The selection can always be worded as a yes/no question. In the previous example, we see that the question is programmed as a comparison:

```
if (answer == JOptionPane.YES_OPTION).....
```

We call the contents of the parentheses a *boolean expression*. Other examples of boolean expressions are:

```
if (price1 > price2)...  // greater than
if (a + b < c)...      // less than
if (number1 == number2)...  // equal to
if (personFound)... // boolean type variable
```

The value of a boolean expression is either `true` or `false`.

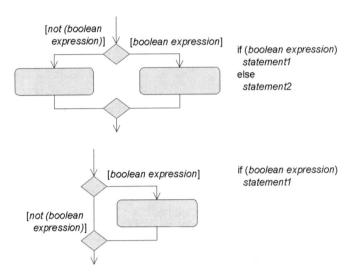

Figure 5.6　The two versions of the if statement (UML)

 Java Core

The if statement

Syntax:

> if (*booleanExpression*)
> 　statement1

or

> if (*booleanExpression*)
> 　statement1
> else
> 　statement2

statement1 and/or statement2 can be a block.

The boolean expression is evaluated. If the value is true, statement1 is executed. If the value of the boolean expression is false, one of two things takes place:

- If the if statement doesn't contain an else section, the program execution proceeds to the first statement following the if statement.

- If the program contains an else section, *statement2* is executed.

Examples:

```
if (number > 10) {
  number = 0;
  System.out.println("Number is set to 0");
} else {
  number++;
  System.out.println("Number is increased by 1");
}
if (number1 > number2) number1 = number2;
```

A return statement inside the if or else block abruptly completes the method you're in.

Look at the following bit of code:

```
if (a > b);
else a = b;
```

Notice that there's a semicolon at the end of the first line. This is an *empty statement*. It has no contents. Nothing happens if a > b.

There are rarely good reasons for using empty statements. The section of code above should, of course, be written this way:

```
if (a <= b) a = b;
```

More on the use of curly braces and indents

Let's look more closely at the coding style for if statements. The most complicated of the if statements takes the following form:

```
if (booleanExpression)
  statement1
else
  statement2
```

If *statement1* and/or *statement2* consist of more than one individual statement, the statements have to be enclosed in curly braces {}. Otherwise, it's not necessary to use curly braces. However, for the sake of readability, and to decrease the chance of errors, we also recommend using curly braces if only one individual statement is to be executed and there isn't room for it on the same line as if or else.

We will try to explain the reasons for this assertion. Suppose we have written the following bit of code:

```
if (a > b)
  sum += a;
```

After some time, we've found an error in the program. In addition to the statement sum += a; we will also change b if a > b. We modify the bit of code so that now it looks like this:

```
if (a > b)
    sum += a;
    b++;
```

This gives the visual impression that the two statements form a block that will be executed if a > b. This doesn't happen. The statements aren't enclosed in {}. Therefore, the statement b++; will be executed regardless of whether a > b or not.

If the statement that is to be executed is in a line by itself, it should be enclosed in {} to prevent errors from cropping up during later maintenance of the program. The pieces of code above should therefore look like this:

```
if (a > b) {
    sum += a;
}
```

and

```
if (a > b) {
    sum += a;
    b++;
}
```

Problems

1. Set up if statements for the following:

   (a) If number is greater than 20, code will be set to 'M' (for "many"), otherwise, code will have the value 'F' (for "few").

   (b) If "body mass index" (BMI) is greater than 25, print out "You weigh too much", otherwise, nothing will happen. BMI is calculated according to the formula (weight / (height * height)). Weight is measured in kilograms, height in meters.

2. Write the following segment of code according to the recommendations for indenting and {} given above. Then find the values for all the variables after the code segment has been executed.

   ```
   int a = 20;
   int b = 30;
   int p = 20;
   int q = 40;
   int r = 30;
   int s = 15;
   if (a < b) a = b; b = 10;
   if (p == 20) q = 13; else q = 17;
   ```

```
if (r > s) { q = 100;
} s = 200;
```

3. What do the following statements do?

```
if (size > 38);
else System.out.println("Small!");
```

How should this section of code be written?

5.5 Nested if and Multiple-Choice Statements

If one of the two alternatives in an `if` statement is a new `if` statement, we get `if` statements that are inside each other. This is a *nested if*. Example:

Depending on the value of the variable `temperature` we want to print out the text "Degrees below zero", "Zero degrees", and "Degrees above zero". A possible solution is:

```
if (temperature > 0) {
  System.out.println( "Degrees above zero.");
}
if (temperature == 0) {
  System.out.println("Zero degrees.");
}
if (temperature < 0) {
  System.out.println("Degrees below zero.");
}
```

This method works. However, if the `temperature` is positive, we notice that the second and third tests are unnecessary. The number of unnecessary tests increases with the number of alternatives. What we want is for the second and third tests not to be performed if `temperature` is positive. We also want the third test not to be performed if `temperature` is equal to zero. We can accomplish this with the following lines of code:

```
if (temperature > 0) {
  System.out.println("Degrees above zero.");
} else {
  if (temperature == 0) {
    System.out.println("Zero degrees.");
  } else {
    System.out.println("Degrees below zero.");
  } // end of the innermost if-else statement
} // end of the outermost if-else statement
```

We can nest `if` statements as much as we want, but have to be careful that we get the logic right. In the example, we use {} to demonstrate the complexity that generally ensues with only two nested `if` statements. Here the blocks consist of just an individual statement and there's room for this statement on the same line as `if` and `else`. We should make use of this to improve the readability. We write the example in the following manner:

```
if (temperature > 0) System.out.println("Degrees above zero.");
else {
  if (temperature == 0) System.out.println("Zero degrees");
  else System.out.println("Degrees below zero.");
} // end of the outermost if-else statement
```

Furthermore, we observe that there's actually only *one* statement, namely an `if` statement, after the first `else`. Even if this statement doesn't fit on one line, we usually omit {} in *multiple choice statements* like this. Now the lines can be written this way:

```
if (temperature > 0) System.out.println("Degrees above zero.");
else if (temperature == 0) System.out.println("Zero degrees");
else System.out.println("Degrees below zero.");
```

Letting the user choose between the four math operations

Program Listing 5.3 shows a client program where the user gets to choose between all four of the arithmetical operations in the `Calculator` class. You'll find an activity diagram that describes this situation in the solution to problem 1 at the end of this section. Before you peek at the solution, you can, of course, try to diagram it yourself.

Run the program. Four pushbuttons allow you to choose between the four arithmetical operations[3]. We'll see how we use the `showOptionDialog()` method to present these choices.

The last two parameters look like this (see the API reference in section 5.2): `Object[] options, Object initialOption`.

- What does the `Object` data type mean? From Figure 4.6 we see that the `Object` class is a superclass to all the other classes. That means that the description given for the `Object` class applies to all possible objects. In practice, this means that if the parameter type is `Object`, then the argument can be of any class.

- What does the symbol [ ] mean? We want to present the user with multiple choices—this symbol says that the parameter `options` can receive more than one value as its argument. We submit an "array" of all the possible choices.[4] We make the array this way:

---

3. Note that you have to click on the correct pushbutton with the mouse, just tabbing with the tab-key and pressing Enter do not work (at least not in the Windows environment).

4. Arrays are covered in chapters 9 and 10. For now, we're just mentioning what we need to use these methods.

```
String[] options = {"plus", "minus", "multiply", "divide"};
```

The elements in the array are numbered starting with 0. We submit the default value to be selected as the argument for the parameter `initialOption`. Here we set this value equal to the first value in the array. We write it like this: `options[0]`.

The method call for `showOptionDialog()` looks like this:

```
int option = JOptionPane.showOptionDialog(null, "Choose operator",
    "The four arithmetical operations", 0, JOptionPane.PLAIN_MESSAGE,
    null, options, options[0]);
```

The choice the user made is now stored in the variable `option`. Here we find the number for the element selected in the `options` array. In other words, `option` equal to 0 means "plus," `option` equal to 1 means "minus," `option` equal to 2 means "multiply," and `option` equal to 3 means "divide."

Table 5.1 and the left part of Figure 5.7 illustrate the relationship between parameters and arguments in the `showOptionDialog()` method. The right part of the figure shows what the dialog box looks like if we use `showInputDialog()` instead. In that case, the call in the program will look like this:

```
Object option = JOptionPane.showInputDialog(null, "Choose operator",
    "The four arithmetical operations", JOptionPane.DEFAULT_OPTION,
    null, options, options[0]);
```

The return type from the method is `Object`, and we have to compare the return value to the array elements:

```
if (option == options[0]) {  // "plus" was pressed
```

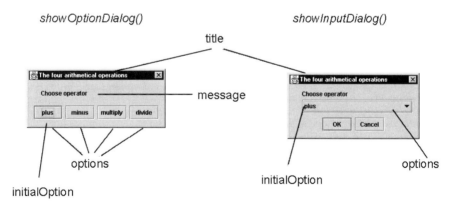

Figure 5.7 Example using `showOptionDialog()` and `showInputDialog()`

Let's go back to Program Listing 5.3.

We will construct a string that contains the math problem in question. The string is printed in a message box. (Example: 2.3 + 5.6 = 7.9.) The operator depends on the operation, and we store it in the variable `operator`.

A boolean variable `ok` keeps track of whether or not errors occur. The only error of interest here occurs if the user asks to divide by zero. Then `ok` is set equal to `false`, and the division is not performed.[5] We also set `ok` equal to `false` if the user hits the Esc key or closes the dialog. In these cases, the variable `option` is set to equal the value `CLOSED_OPTION`.

Table 5.1 The relationship between parameters and arguments in the `showOptionDialog()` method

Parameter	Argument (example)	Explanation
Component parent	null	Argument equal to `null` means that the dialog isn't part of a larger system of windows, etc.
Object message	"Choose operator"	See Figure 5.7.
String title	"The four arithmetical operations"	See Figure 5.7.
int combination-OfButtons	0	The buttons that will be displayed are determined by `options`. As long as `options` is different from `null`, the value of this parameter is insignificant.
int typeOfMessage	JOptionPane. PLAIN_MESSAGE	The icon that will be displayed on the left in the dialog is indicated here. No icon is displayed in the example. `QUESTION_MESSAGE` is an alternative to `PLAIN_MESSAGE`.
Icon icon	null	If you want your own icon instead of one of the standard icons, you can set it up here. For an example, see Figure 3.10.

---

5. We execute the test `if (number2 == 0.0)` ... We can do this because the numbers are input. If the numbers have been computed, we can't use a test this simple between variables that contain decimal numerals. We will spend more time on this at the end of this chapter.

Parameter	Argument (example)	Explanation
`Object[] options`	`options`	Here you submit an array that contains the choices, e.g. an array of `String` or an array of `ImageIcon`.
`Object initialOption`	`options[0]`	When the dialog box comes up on the screen, one of the buttons will be marked as selected. In the example it will be the first alternative in the `options` array.

Program Listing 5.3

```
/*
 * TestCalculator2.java   E.L. 2001-08-10
 *
 */
import javax.swing.JOptionPane;
class TestCalculator2 {
  public static void main(String[] args) {

    /* Reading data */
    String number1Read = JOptionPane.showInputDialog("First number: ");
    String number2Read = JOptionPane.showInputDialog("Second number: ");
    double number1 = Double.parseDouble(number1Read);
    double number2 = Double.parseDouble(number2Read);
    String[] options = {"plus", "minus", "multiply", "divide"};
    int option = JOptionPane.showOptionDialog(null, "Choose operator",
       "The four arithmetical operations", 0, JOptionPane.PLAIN_MESSAGE,
       null, options, options[0]);

    /* Calculating results */
    Calculator calcus = new Calculator(number1, number2);
    double calculatedAnswer = 0.0;
    char operator = ' ';  // uses this in the result string
    boolean ok = true;
    if (option == 0) {
      operator = '+';
      calculatedAnswer = calcus.calculateSum();
    } else if (option == 1) {
      calculatedAnswer = calcus.calculateDifference();
      operator = '-';
    } else if (option == 2) {
      calculatedAnswer = calcus.calculateProduct();
      operator = '*';
    } else if (option == 3) {
```

```
  operator = '/';
  if (number2 == 0.0) ok = false;  // we have to avoid division by zero
  else calculatedAnswer = calcus.calculateQuotient();
} else { // Esc is typed, or the dialog is closed
  ok = false;
}

/* Printing the result */
String result;
if (ok) result = number1 + " " + operator + " " + number2 + " = " + calculatedAnswer;
else result = "It is not possible to calculate a result.";
JOptionPane.showMessageDialog(null, result);
System.exit(0);
  }
}

/* Example Run:

First number: 12.5
Second number: 3.56
Choose the operation "multiply"
Result: 12.5 * 3.56 = 44.5

First number: 12.5
Second number: 0.0
Choose the operation "divide"
Result: It is not possible to calculate a result.
*/
```

A possible trap...

Try to find out what prints out when the following bit of code is run:

```
int a = -10;
int b = 20;
if (a > 0) {
  if (b > 10) b = 10;
}
else a = 0;
System.out.println(a + " " + b);

a = -10;
b = 20;
if (a > 0)
   if (b > 10) b = 10;
else a = 0;
System.out.println(a + " " + b);
```

Aside from the fact that the bottom section of the code doesn't contain curly braces in the prescribed locations, is there any difference between these two pieces of code? The indentation gives the impression that the author means the same thing—namely, that a is set equal to 0 if a is not greater than 0.

Running this piece of code results in the printout:

```
0 20
-10 20
```

This is explained by the fact that the bottom `else` belongs to the `if` statement immediately above it, so that a is set equal to 0 only if b is not greater than 10. We come to the following conclusion:

If you use multiple `if` statements inside each other (nested `if`), and an `else` block doesn't belong to the closest preceding `if`, it *has* to be marked with {}.

Decision tables

A special application of multiple choice statements is programming decision tables. Table 5.2 shows an example of a decision table.

A method that calculates the grade, when the point total is given as an instance variable, looks like this:

```
public char getGrade() {  // returns an 'X' if too many points, a 'Z' if too few points
  if (points > 100) return 'X';
  else if (points >= 90) return 'A';
  else if (points >= 80) return 'B';
  else if (points >= 70) return 'C';
  else if (points >= 60) return 'D';
  else if (points >= 0) return 'F';
  else return 'Z';
}
```

Note that the order of the `if` statements is not arbitrary. How would the program behave if we change around the tests for the two upper limits (90 and 80)?

Table 5.2 A decision table to determine the grade when the point total is known

Points	Grade
90-100	A
80-89	B
70-79	C
60-69	D
0-59	F

Problems

1. Make an activity diagram for the client object in Program Listing 5.3.

2. Rewrite the code below so that the indentation and {} placement follow the recommendations listed earlier. Then find out what is printed out.

```
int a = 20;
int b = 30;
int c = 40;
if (a > b) a = b; else { a = c;
b = 50;
if (a > 50) a = 100;}
System.out.println("a = " + a + ", b = " + b + ", c = " + c);
```

3. Rewrite the coding for the decision table above so that you're using "less than" tests instead of "greater than or equal to" tests.

4. Program the class that the method `getGrade()` belongs to. Write a little test program.

5.6   Boolean Expressions

A *boolean expression* has the value `true` or `false`.

The *logical-complement operator* ! reverses the expression's value. This means that (`!true`) is equal to `false` and vice versa. The operator ! is also often called the *not-operator*.

A boolean variable is a boolean expression. Notice that it's not necessary to compare the boolean variable with the values `true` and `false`; we use the variable's value directly:

```
if (personFound)..... // like this, but not like this: if (personFound == true)....
if (!cityFound).... // like this, but not like this: if (cityFound == false)...
```

We can also create boolean expressions using the *comparison operators*. The comparison operators are[6]:

<	less than
<=	less than or equal to
>	greater than
>=	greater than or equal to
!=	not equal to
==	equal to

Note that the operators that consist of two characters have to be written without spaces between the characters.

---

6. There is also the `instanceof` comparison operator. This is covered in chapter 11.

Examples:

```
numberOfStudents < lowerLimit
price * number != 5
numberOfMen + numberOfWomen == totalNumber - numberOfChildren
```

The arithmetical operators have higher priority than the comparison operators. The last two expressions are calculated as if they said:

```
(price * number) != 5
(numberOfMen + numberOfWomen) == (totalNumber - numberOfChildren)
```

Constants and variables of the data type char can also be compared. The extent to which a character is "greater" or "less" than another character is determined by where the character comes in the Unicode ranking. The letters a-z are in alphabetical order so that we can use the operators to sort.[7]

We can create more complex expressions by combining simple boolean expressions using the following two operators:

&&   conditional-and (or only: "and")
|| conditional-or (or only: "or")

The operators are listed in order of priority. Table 5.4 summarizes the operators we've covered up to this point. Operators in the same group have the same priority. If we have several operators in an expression with the same priority, they are interpreted according to *associativity*. Most are interpreted from left to right. Expressions with assignment operators are interpreted from right to left. In most practical cases, however, it's sufficient to think about left-associativity, which, for example, means that the expression (5 * 10 / 2) is evaluated from left to right, like this: (5 * 10) / 2.

Here are some examples of combining simple boolean expressions:

- We want to know if the number of students is in the closed interval [20, 30]. We *can't* write this the way we would in math: 20 <= number <= 30. Instead we have to create a compound boolean expression:

  ```
  number >= 20 && number <= 30
  ```

- We want to know the opposite: is the number of students outside the interval [20, 30]? We can write it like this:

  ```
  number < 20 || number > 30
  ```

  or

  ```
  !(number >= 20 && number <= 30)
  ```

---

7. Those who use an alphabet with letters outside a-z should take care and check the ordering of the letters. See [URL Unicode].

Compound boolean expressions are interpreted according to what we call "truth tables." A *truth table* contains the value of a boolean expression for all possible combinations of true and false: see table 5.3.

Pay special attention to the fact that OR actually means what we call and/or in everyday speech. If both of the operands are true, the value of the expression "operand1 OR operand2" is also true.

Let's see how a relatively complicated boolean expression is evaluated. The expression

    a >= 0 && a <= 4 || a >= 10 && a <= 15 || a == 20

is true if a is in the interval [0, 4], or in the interval [10, 15], or equal to 20. Suppose a equals 16. Figure 5.8 shows how the result of the expression is calculated.

Table 5.3 Truth tables for the conditional-and and conditional-or operators

operand1	operand2	operand1 AND operand2	operand1 OR operand2
true	true	true	true
true	false	false	true
false	true	false	true
false	false	false	false

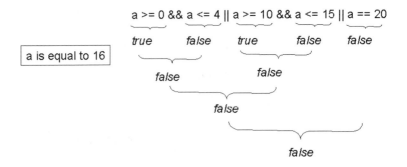

Figure 5.8   Calculating a complex boolean expression

Comparing strings

A method call with the return type `boolean` will be a boolean expression. As an example, we'll look at the possibilities in the `String` class for comparing strings. First we try the `equals()` method. The piece of code: (top of page 148)

Table 5.4 Operators in the same group have the same priority, highest at the top of the table

Operator	Name/Description	Associativity
.	to qualify names, the period operator	left
( )	parenthesis	
method call		
!	not, logical-complement	right
+	unary plus	
-	unary minus	
++	increment	
--	decrement	
(*type*)	casting	
new	instantiate an object	
*	multiplication	left
/	division	
%	modulo	
+	addition	left
-	subtraction	
<	less than	left
<=	less than or equal to	
>	greater than	
>=	greater than or equal to	
==	equal to	left
!=	not equal to	
&&	conditional-and	left
||	conditional-or	left
=	assignment	right
+=	compound assignment operator	
-=	compound assignment operator	
%=	compound assignment operator	
*=	compound assignment operator	
/=	compound assignment operator	

```
String name1 = "Margaret Eliza";
String name2 = "Maya";
if (name1.equals(name2)) System.out.println("The names are the same.");
else System.out.println("The names are not the same.");
```

yields the printout: "The names are not the same." Then we use the compareTo() method on the same names:

```
int result = name1.compareTo(name2);
if (result < 0) System.out.println(name1 + " comes first.");
else if (result > 0) System.out.println(name2 + " comes first.");
else System.out.println("The names are the same.");
```

Now the printout is: "Margaret Eliza comes first."

We can use the operator == between operands of the String type. The expression is true if both of the operands point to the *same* String object. To compare the contents of the String objects, we have to use methods in the String class.

API Reference

The java.lang.String class

See also Section 3.4.

Comparison methods:[8]

    public int compareTo(String theOtherString)

This method compares two strings according to their Unicode order. It returns a negative value if the string we're sending the message to comes before theOtherString in the order, a positive value if it comes after, and 0 if the strings are equal.

    public boolean equals(Object theOtherObject)

This method returns true if the strings are equal, otherwise false. Even if the parameter is of the Object type, it works fine to submit a string as an argument.

---

8. For those with an alphabet with letters outside a-z: With the exception of the equals() method, you should check if the methods work for letters outside a-z. In chapter 10, we will see that it's relatively easy to achieve a comparison that works for these letters as well, without using multiple choice statements that treat the characters specially, as we often have to.

```
public boolean equalsIgnoreCase(String theOtherString)
public int compareToIgnoreCase(String theOtherString)
```

These methods are identical to the previous two, except that they don't take the difference between upper- and lower-case letters into consideration.

Short-circuit evaluation

If a boolean expression contains && or ||, Java uses *short-circuit evaluation*. That means the computation ends as soon as the result is determined. If there's an "and" between the expressions, the evaluation continues as long as the expressions are true. The instant the Java interpreter encounters the first expression which evaluates to false, the compound expression as a whole will be false, and it can terminate the computation. If there's an "or" between the expressions, the opposite happens. The interpreter keeps going as long as the expressions are false. The instant one of them is true, it can stop, because then the whole expression is true.

For example: we want to find out if the square root of a number is less than limit. But we don't want to try to figure out the square root at all if the number is negative. So we can write

```
if (number >= 0 && Math.sqrt(number) < limit) ....
```

The value of the expression number >= 0 is evaluated first. Only if this expression is true will the computation continue such that the square root is calculated.

Problems

1. Set up the boolean value for each of the following expressions:

   (a) 5 * 3 / 4 + 3 < 10

   (b) !(4 > 3)

   (c) 2 < 20 && 4.5 > 20

   (d) 2 < 20 || 4.5 > 20

2. Set up boolean expressions to express the following conditions:

   (a) The number of students will be *between* 20 and 30 – i.e., 20 and 30 aren't legal numbers.

   (b) The winning lottery numbers are 3, 18, and 25.

   (c) The answer to the question should be an upper- or lower-case 'Y' (for "yes").

   (d) The temperature has to be outside the closed interval [15, 25].

   (e) The sum will be positive and outside the open interval <10, 100>.

   (f) The character has to be a letter (A-Z), capital or lower-case.

(g) The character will be a digit (0–9).

3. What is the boolean value of the expression

$$a == -20 \;||\; a >= 0 \;\&\&\; a <= 10 \;||\; a >= 15 \;\&\&\; a <= 20 \;||\; a > 100$$

where a has the values 17, 120, -30? Draw figures corresponding to Figure 5.8.

5.7 The Multiple-Choice Statement switch

If each case in a multiple-choice statement corresponds to a specific integer value or a character, it may be practical to use the switch statement. Before we look at an example, we have to define the concept of a label. A *label* is a point in the program that has a specific name. The label name is followed by a colon. The program control can "jump" to a label from another location in the program. An example of a label:

```
aPlace:
```

In this book, we limit the use of labels to case and default labels in switch statements. The multiple choice statement in Program Listing 5.3 can be programmed using switch:

```
switch (option) {
  case 0:
    operator = '+';
    calculatedAnswer = calcus.calculateSum();
    break;
  case 1:
    calculatedAnswer = calcus.calculateDifference();
    operator = '-';
    break;
  case 2:
    calculatedAnswer = calcus.calculateProduct();
    operator = '*';
    break;
  case 3:
    operator = '/';
    if (number2 == 0.0) ok = false;
    else calculatedAnswer = calcus.calculateQuotient();
  default:
    ok = false;
    break;
}
```

In short, the statement works such that the program control jumps to the right case label depending on the value of the option variable. The statements are executed up to the keyword break. If option has a value that doesn't conform to any of the case labels, the program control jumps to the default label. There are a great many rules and limitations associated with the switch statement. These are listed in the following syntax description:

Java Core

The switch statement

Syntax:

```
switch (expression) {
  case constantExpression:
    statements
    break;  // may be skipped
  case constantExpression:
    statements
    break;  // may be skipped
  case ...
    ....
  default: // may be skipped (skipping not recommended)
    statements
    break;
}
```

The data type for *expression* has to be char, byte, short, or int. In other words, decimal numerals cannot be used.

The number of case labels in a switch block is random, but all the labels have to represent different *constantExpression* – in other words, separate values. Thus, it's not possible to provide an interval or a list of values here.

A switch block cannot contain more than one default label.

The switch statement is evaluated as follows:

- The value of *expression* is calculated. The program control jumps to the label with a constant expression equal to the calculated value. If no such label is found, the program control jumps to the default label. If the default label can't be found, the program control jumps out of the switch block.

- If the program control encounters break, it jumps out of the switch block. Otherwise it continues through the other labels up to the first break, potentially to the end of the switch block.

- If the program control encounters a return statement, it jumps immediately out of both the switch block and the method this is inside.

Example:

```
String text = JOptionPane.showInputDialog("Which place? ");
int place = Integer.parseInt(text);
```

```
switch (place) {
  case 1:
    JOptionPane.showMessageDialog(null, "Gold!");
    break;
  case 2:
    JOptionPane.showMessageDialog(null, "Silver!");
    break;
  case 3:
    JOptionPane.showMessageDialog(null, "Bronze!");
    break;
  case 4:
   /* falls through */
  case 5:
   /* falls through */
  case 6:
    JOptionPane.showMessageDialog(null, "You have points!");
    break;
  default:
   int luckyNumber = (int) (100 * Math.random() + 1);
   JOptionPane.showMessageDialog(null, "Thank you for honourable achievement!\n" +
                                       "Your lucky number is: " + luckyNumber);
    break;
}
```

If break is skipped, we recommend the comment /* falls through */ as shown in the example above.

The class method Math.random() is used in the example. This method creates a random decimal numeral in the interval [0.0, 1.0>. By multiplying by 100, we get a random number between 0.0 and 100.0. By adding 1 and converting the result to int using casting, we end up with a "lucky number" in the interval [1, 100].

Problem

Point out errors and weaknesses in the following switch statement:

```
switch (dayOfWeek) {
  case 1, 2:
    System.out.println("In the beginning of the week");
  case 3, 4:
    System.out.println("In the middle of the week");
  case 5:
    System.out.println("Near the end of the week");
  case 6, 7:
    System.out.println("Weekend");
};
```

5.8 Comparing Computed Decimal Numerals

What will the value of number3 be after the following bit of code is executed?

```
double number1 = 1.0e20;
double number2 = number1 + 1.0;
double number3 = number2 - number1;
```

We'll lose accuracy here. When we add 1 to the number $1.0 \cdot 10^{20}$ (an extremely large number, 1 followed by 20 zeros), we get the number $1.00000000000000000001 \cdot 10^{20}$. Because double doesn't operate with more than about 15 significant digits, the digits at the end are truncated and thus the number 1 that we tried to add disappears. Therefore, number3 will be 0.

A special field called "numerical mathematics" estimates the size of errors and sets up algorithms so that the results of calculations involving decimal numerals are as correct as possible. The most important conclusion in our context is this:

Never use the operators == and != to compare results from calculations involving decimal numerals. Instead, check that the difference between the numbers is less than a given tolerance:

```
final double tolerance = 0.00001;
if (Math.abs(number1 - number2) < tolerance) {
  System.out.println("The numbers are almost the same");
} else System.out.println("The numbers are different.");
```

Remember to use the absolute value of the difference between the numbers.

The size of tolerance has to be in proportion with the size of the numbers that are being compared. For instance, in this example, numbers where both are smaller than 0.00001 will be considered as equal regardless of how different they are.

5.9 The Conditional Operator ?:

This is the only operator that takes three operands.

Java Core

The conditional operator ?:

Syntax:

booleanExpression ? expression1 : expression2

The value of the expression as a whole is determined by the value of the boolean expression. If the boolean expression is true, the value is equal to *expression1*; otherwise, the value is equal to *expression2*.

The operator is left-associative and it's prioritized just above the assignment operators.

For example:

```
max = (number2 > number1) ? number2 : number1;
```

is the same as:

```
if (number2 > number1) max = number2;
else max = number1;
```

Many people find expressions that use this operator difficult to read. Therefore, we don't use this operator in this book.

5.10 New Concepts in This Chapter

Concept	Brief Explanation
activity diagram	Shows how an object goes from activity(state) to activity(state).
AND-operator	The && operator; another name is conditional-and.
associativity	Direction of interpretation (from the left or from the right) in an expression.
boolean expression	An expression that has the value true or false.
break	Keyword that interrupts sequential program flow. break means that the program control jumps out of the switch block (and other blocks, but this isn't used in this book).
comparison operator	Operators that make it possible to compare values (less than <, greater than >, etc.).
compound boolean expression	Two or more comparisons combined using conditional-and and/or conditional-or operators.
conditional-and	The AND-operator &&
conditional operator	The operator ?: Can be used if a variable will have one value if a condition is true and another value if this condition is false.
conditional-or	The OR-operator ||

Concept	Brief Explanation
control structure	A way that statements in a program can be gone through. There are three control structures: sequence, selection, and loop.
empty statement	In practice, an unnecessary semicolon. Example: `if (a > b);` The semicolon after the last parenthesis is interpreted as a statement.
`if` statement	Statement that makes it possible to program alternative ways of execution (selections).
label	A point in the program with a specific name.
logical-complement operator	The NOT-operator `!` This operator reverses the value of a boolean expression.
multiple-choice statement	Makes it possible to choose between more than two alternatives; programmed with `if - else if - else if - else` or with `switch`.
nested `if`	Several `if` statements inside each other.
NOT-operator	The `!` operator; another name is logical-complement operator.
OR-operator	The `||` operator; another name is conditional-or.
short-circuit evaluation	A technique for calculating a compound boolean expression that entails the evaluation stopping once the result is reached.
`switch` statement	A multiple-choice statement that can be used in certain situations.
truth table	A table that shows the value of a boolean expression for all possible combinations of true and false.

5.11 Review Problems

1. Explain what an activity diagram is.

2. Provide examples of the two different forms of the `if` statement.

3. Describe the recommended use of curly braces and indentation in conjunction with `if` statements and blocks. Compare this with what the syntax requires.

4. What's the difference between an arithmetical and a boolean expression?

5. Name and show the comparison operators.

6. Name and show the symbols for the conditional operators.

7. Why shouldn't we write

   ```
   if (add == true)...
   if (divide == false)...
   ```

   What should we write instead?

8. What's wrong with the following boolean expression?

>   if (number != 10 || number != 20)...

What do you think the programmer is trying to say?

9. What is a multiple-choice statement and how do we program it?

5.12 Programming Problems

Problem 1

Create a class `NumberAnalysis`. It should offer the following methods with boolean return values:

- Is the number positive?

- Is the number divisible by a given number?

- Is the number in a given closed interval?

- Is the number in a given open interval?

  The number should be an integer.
  Set up test data and test the class.

Problem 2

The tax office provides help on tax returns. You should ask for help in a specific room depending on what day of the month you were born in. Create a class that keeps track of the relationship between birthday and room (see table 5.5).
   The reason that every office can't take the same number of days is that they are staffed differently.
   Set up test data and test the class.

Table 5.5 Relationship Between Birthday and Room

Birthday	Room
1-8	113
9-14	120
15-25	125
26-31	134

Problem 3

In this problem, you will use the `ForeignCurrency` class from programming problem 2, chapter 4.

Make an activity diagram that shows how a client object (client program) lets the user choose which direction the currency exchange will take place in.

Write the client program.

Problem 4

A year is a leap year if it's divisible by 4. Years ending in 00 are the exception—they have to be divisible by 400. Write a program that inputs a year from the user and finds out if it's a leap year.

Problem 5

We will write a program that helps us with the following problem: ground meat from brand A costs $3.60 for 450 grams, while ground meat from brand B costs $3.95 for 500 grams. Which brand is cheaper?

Create a `Brand` class. Suggest attributes and methods that are relevant for this problem.

Make an activity diagram that shows how a client object (client program) can use instances of this class to find out which of the two brands is cheaper.

Write the client program.

Loops as a Control Structure

Learning goals for this chapter

After completing this chapter, you will understand the following concepts:

- Initializing loops

- Loop conditions

- Counter-controlled loops

- Loops controlled by a general condition

- Endless loops

You will be able to:

- Formulate loops by identifying the different parts of the loop and selecting the right loop statement (`while`, `for`, or `do-while`)

- Create test data for a loop

In this chapter, we'll cover the third control structure, loops. Up to this point, we've written several programs to test classes. We've had to run the programs again for each new set of test data. Now we'll find out how to program this reiteration.

Loops can also be used in many other contexts. We'll look at a graphics example. Further on in the book, we'll use loops to search for data values, sort data, and much more.

There are three different loop statements in Java. The `while` and `for` statements can, in principle, be used for the same thing, but they have come to be used somewhat differently in practice. The `do-while` statement is useful when inputting data from the user, and especially if the program is going to test the validity of this data.

6.1 Counter-Controlled Loops

The following little program is given:

```java
class PrintManyLines {
  public static void main(String[] args) {
    int counter = 0;
    while (counter < 5) {
      System.out.println("This is a line.");
      counter++;
    }
  }
}
```

Running the program prints the following output to the console:

```
This is a line.
This is a line.
This is a line.
This is a line.
This is a line.
```

Figure 6.1 shows an activity diagram for this program. After counter is set to 0, the following yes/no question is asked: "Is `counter < 5`?". If yes, print a text and increase `counter` by 1. Then go *back* and ask the same yes/no question again. This is repeated until the answer to the question is no.

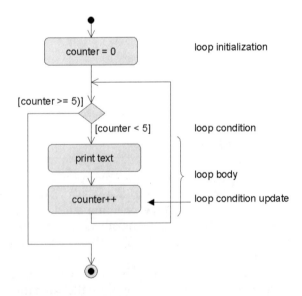

Figure 6.1 A client object prints five lines of text (UML)

It's the `while` statement in the program code that causes a set of instructions to be executed multiple times. In this context, `while` can best be interpreted as "as long as": as long as `counter` is less than 5, the following will be done: print a text and increase `counter` by 1.

In the previous chapter, we covered `if` statements. The main difference between `while` and `if` is that a block in a `while` statement can be executed many times, while a block in an `if` statement is never executed more than once. `else` cannot be used in conjunction with a `while` statement.

A *counter-controlled loop* is a loop where the number of iterations is known in advance. In the example, we decided to print out five lines and we use a "counter" to keep track of the number. In the next section, we will look at loops where the number of iterations is not known in advance.

Every loop consists of the following parts:

- Initialization

- Loop condition

- Loop body (this is synonymous with the "contents of the loop")

- Condition update (this will be a part of the loop body)

These parts have to be identified for all loops.

We will look more closely at what these concepts entail by tying them to the simple example above (see also the right side of Figure 6.1):

- Initialization: This is program code that makes it possible to answer the yes/no question in the `while` statement the *first* time the program control reaches it. Here the question is: "Is `counter` < 5?". In order to answer this, `counter` needs to have a value. Initialization consists of setting `counter` to equal 0 just before the `while` statement.

- Loop condition: This is the yes/no question. The condition is a boolean expression as in an `if` statement. In the example, the loop condition is `(counter < 5)`.

- Loop body: This is comprised of the statements that will be executed if the loop condition is true. If there's more than one statement to be executed, the statements have to be collected in a block using {}. The recommendations for using {} and indentation are the same as for `if` statements. In the example, the loop body consists of the following statements:

```
System.out.println("This is a line.");
counter++;
```

- Update condition: The loop body must include a statement that changes the value of the loop condition from true to false. If this is not the case, the loop will never stop and will be an *endless loop*. In the example, it's the statement `counter++;` that finally makes the loop condition false. Usually we find the loop update condition near the end of the loop body.

It's customary to start the counter for a counter-controlled loop at 0 and not 1. If the loop is to be run N times, the condition will be (`counter < N`).

Java Core

The while statement

Syntax:

```
while (loopCondition)
    statement
```

The `loopCondition` is a boolean expression.

The `statement` can be a block and forms the loop body.

The value of the loop condition is evaluated. If the value is true, the loop body is executed. The value of the loop condition is evaluated again and the loop body is executed again if the value is still true. This is repeated until the value of the loop condition is false. The instant that happens, the program proceeds to the first statement after the `while` statement.

If the value of the loop condition is false the first time it's evaluated, the loop body won't be executed at all.

The loop body must contain statements that, sooner or later, mean that the value of the loop condition has the value "false". If that's not the case, then the loop is endless.

If the program control encounters a `return` statement inside the loop body, it immediately exits both the loop and the method the loop is part of.

Example:

```
int counter = 0;
while (counter < 5) {
    System.out.println( );  // writes a blank line
    counter++;
}
```

Problem

The loop in the example is executed exactly five times. Modify the example so that the loop is executed 0 times, and then an infinite number of times.

6.2 A Loop with a General Condition

In general, it's possible for a loop to be executed zero times. This is especially true when searching through data, where the process starts by determining if there is any data to search through in the first place. If there isn't, the control jumps over the whole loop.

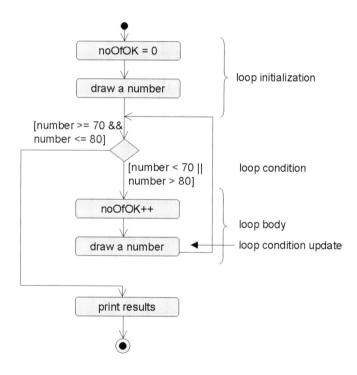

Figure 6.2 Drawing numbers until an invalid number is drawn (UML)

As storing large quantities of data is rather complicated, we'll create a somewhat artificial example to illustrate this situation.

We'll run in a loop and draw numbers from the interval [1, 100]. We'll continue until we get a number in the interval [70, 80]. The numbers drawn until such a number is drawn are considered to be alright and will be counted. Of course, it could happen that the first number drawn is invalid. The activity diagram is shown in Figure 6.2 and the program code in Program Listing 6.1. The Math.random() method is described at the end of Section 5.7.

Program Listing 6.1

```
/*
 * SearchForNumbers.java   E.L. 2001-08-12
 *
 */
class SearchForNumbers {
  public static void main(String[] args) {
    final int limit1 = 0;
    final int limit2 = 70;
    final int limit3 = 80;
    final int limit4 = 100;

    int noOfOK = 0;
    int number = (int) ((limit4 - limit1) * Math.random() + 1);

    while (number < limit2 || number > limit3) {
      noOfOK++;
      System.out.println(number);
      number = (int) ((limit4 - limit1) * Math.random() + 1);
    }
    System.out.println("We had to draw " + noOfOK +
            " numbers until we got an illegal one: " + number);

  }
}
/* Example Run:
97
12
45
We had to draw 3 numbers until we got an illegal one: 74
*/
```

Loop constructions always need to be tested. We always have to formulate test data that will catch the following situations:

- The loop runs 0 times. The test data must make the condition false the first time the program control comes to the `while` statement. Do all the variables have reasonable values after the loop statement, even if the program control isn't in the loop body at all?

- The loop runs exactly one time.

- The loop runs several times (the most common situation).

- Is it possible to construct data that never makes the loop condition false? If yes, that means you've created something that can become an endless loop. The loop wouldn't stop unless it's interrupted from the outside in some way. This is usually a mistake.

If you have problems getting the loop to work, insert print statements (`System.out.println()`) in appropriate locations to check that the data has relevant values and to check if the number of iterations is correct.

Problems

1. In the section of code below, random numbers in the interval $[1, 500]$ should be drawn. Insert this drawing for the numbers into the right place. Also fill in anything else that's missing in the following section of code:

```
int smallNumbers = 0;
int bigNumbers = 0;
while (.....) {  // finish when the number 250 is encountered
   ....if number is greater than 250 increase bigNumbers by 1,
   ....otherwise increase smallNumbers by 1.
}
```

2. Find logical errors in the following program that should calculate x^n, where n >= 0:

```
import javax.swing.JOptionPane;
class Problem6_2_2 {
  public static void main(String[] args) {
    String inputBase = JOptionPane.showInputDialog("What is the base? ");
    String inputExponent = JOptionPane.showInputDialog("What is the exponent? ");
    double x = Double.parseDouble(inputBase);
    int n = Integer.parseInt(inputExponent);
    double answer = 0;
    int counter = 1;
    while (counter < n) {
      answer *= n;
      n++;
    }
    JOptionPane.showMessageDialog(null, "The answer is " + answer);
    System.exit(0);
  }
}
```

3. Make a test data set for the program in the previous problem.

4. The situations below can be formulated as loops. In each case, identify the individual parts the loop consists of. Make activity diagrams.

   (a) Edward will water all the flowers in the living room.

(b) Jane forgot the key. She has to look for an open window she can climb in through.

(c) Matthew will count how many days he biked to and from school in May.

6.3 A Graphics Example

Loops are very applicable to graphics. We'll look at how we construct the applet shown in Figure 6.3. The black spots are filled circles drawn with the `fillOval()` method. The lines are drawn with the `drawLine()` method. The placement of the spots is randomly distributed inside the coordinates that comprise the window. The `Math.random()` method is used to find these random numbers.

We need a loop that is iterated a certain number of times. How many? There are 10 lines and 11 spots in the figure. We need to draw both a line and a spot in each iteration of the loop. That means we'll have 10 iterations. We draw the first spot before we enter the loop for the first time. Each line starts at the point where the previous line stopped. In other words, one line's stopping point has to be *remembered* for the next iteration of the loop.

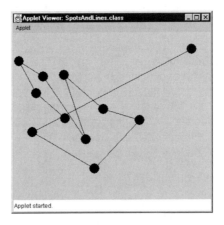

Figure 6.3 The spots are spread randomly throughout the window

We have a counter-controlled loop with a condition (`counter  <  10`). Updating the condition will consist of increasing `counter` by 1. How should we set up the initialization and in what order should we insert the instructions in the loop body? Initialization, in addition to setting `counter  =  0`, will consist of finding the first point and drawing the first filled circle. The loop body will thus consist of drawing a line, followed by drawing a circle with the line's end point as its center.

Study Program Listing 6.2. Pay special attention to how the variables `lastX` and `lastY` are used to keep track of the end point of the previous line. The first time, `lastX` and `lastY` are equal to the first point. The arguments `x` and `y` for the `fillOval()` method denote the upper left corner of the square that surrounds the circle that will be drawn. Thus diameter is subtracted from the height and width of the window when it's time to determine x and y.

Program Listing 6.2

```java
/*
 * SpotsAndLines.java   E.L. 2001-08-12
 *
 * An applet with filled circles and lines between the circles.
 * The applet window is 400 pixels in the horizontal direction,
 * and 300 pixels in the vertical direction.
 */
import java.awt.*;
import javax.swing.*;

public class SpotsAndLines extends JApplet {
  public void init() {
    Container content = getContentPane();
    Drawing theDrawing = new Drawing();
    content.add(theDrawing);
  }
}

class Drawing extends JPanel {
  private static final int windowWidth = 400;  // have to agree
  private static final int windowHeight = 300;   // with the html file
  private static final int diameter = 20;
  private static final int center = diameter / 2;
  private static final int noOfLines = 10;

  public void paintComponent(Graphics window) {
    super.paintComponent(window);
    int x = (int) ((windowWidth - diameter) * Math.random() + 1);
    int y = (int) ((windowHeight - diameter) * Math.random() + 1);
    window.fillOval(x, y, diameter, diameter);
    int counter = 0;
    while (counter < noOfLines) {
      int lastX = x;
      int lastY = y;
      x = (int) ((windowWidth - diameter) * Math.random() + 1);
      y = (int) ((windowHeight - diameter) * Math.random() + 1);
      window.drawLine(lastX + center, lastY + center, x + center, y + center);
      window.fillOval(x, y, diameter, diameter);
      counter++;
    }
  }
}
```

Problems

1. Modify the applet so that the last filled circle is connected to the first filled circle by a line.

2. Modify the applet so that every other circle is filled and every other circle is open.

6.4   The for Statement

All kinds of loops can be created using `while` statements. However, the custom is to use a `for` statement if the loop is counter-controlled. In that case, the example from Section 6.1 looks like this:

```
class PrintManyLines {
  public static void main(String[] args) {
    for (int counter = 0; counter < 5; counter++) {
      System.out.println("This is a line.");
      counter++;
    }
  }
}
```

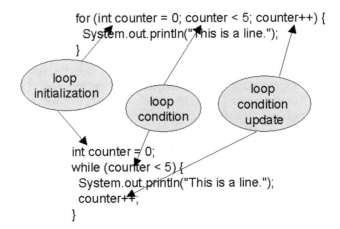

Figure 6.4 The relationship between `while` and `for` statements

The relationship between `while` and `for` statements is shown in Figure 6.4. Notice that we can (but don't have to) declare the counter inside the `for` statement. In this case, the counter's scope will be the for statement. If we're going to make another `for` loop, we have to declare `counter` again.

Java Core

The for statement

This description has been simplified.

Syntax:

> for (*loopInitialization*; *loopCondition*; *loopConditionUpdate*)
>   statement

corresponds to the following `while` statement:

> loopInitialization
> while (*loopCondition*)
>   statement incl. loop condition update

`statement` can be a block.

Variables declared in the initialization portion of the `for` statement have the loop body as their scope.

It's customary to use a `for` statement for counter-controlled loops, and for loops where an integer variable increases or decreases by a fixed value for every iteration.

Example:

```
/* draws 30 circles one after the other */
int x = 0;
int y = 50;
for (int counter = 0; counter < 30; counter++) {
  window.drawOval(x, y, 20, 20);
  x += 20;
}
```

Other `for` statements:

```
for (int number = 1000; number > 500; number--) {   // counts down from 1000 to 501
for (int xPos = 100; xPos < 800; xPos += 5) {  // increases by 5 for every iteration
for (int membNo = 101; membNo <= 900; membNo++) { // member no. from 101 to 900
```

Problem

In the syntax description above, there's a small section of code that draws 30 circles. Insert this into an applet and run it. Modify it so that the size of the circles increases by 2 pixels in diameter for every iteration. Every other circle should be filled, and every other one open.

6.5 Nested Control Structures

Just as `if` statements can be nested inside each other, loops can be contained within other loops. We can also have `if` statements inside loops or loops inside `if` statements. We say that these control structures are *nested*.

Program Listing 6.3 demonstrates an example of two `for` loops inside each other. Study the program code carefully. Notice that the counters must have different names if the `for` loops are inside each other. Inside the innermost loop, we use the statement `System.out.print()` to print. It works the same way that `System.out.println()` does, but without a new line at the end.

Program Listing 6.3

```
/*
 * SumNumbers.java   E.L. 2001-08-12
 *
 * The program calculates and prints all sums in the interval [0, 9]
 */

class SumNumbers {
  public static void main(String[] args) {
    for (int lineCounter = 0; lineCounter < 10; lineCounter++) {
      int sum = 0;
      for (int number = 1; number <= lineCounter; number++) {
        sum += number;
        System.out.print(number + " ");
      }
      System.out.println("The sum is: " + sum);
    }
  }
}

/* Example Run:
The sum is: 0
1 The sum is: 1
1 2 The sum is: 3
1 2 3 The sum is: 6
1 2 3 4 The sum is: 10
1 2 3 4 5 The sum is: 15
1 2 3 4 5 6 The sum is: 21
1 2 3 4 5 6 7 The sum is: 28
1 2 3 4 5 6 7 8 The sum is: 36
1 2 3 4 5 6 7 8 9 The sum is: 45
*/
```

Problems

1. What is printed when the following program runs?

```
public class Problem6_5_1 {
  public static void main(String[] args) {
    String text = "ABVVUIHJV";
    char luckySymbol = 'V';
    int noOfTimes = 1;
    for (int counter = 0; counter < text.length(); counter++){
      char character = text.charAt(counter);
      if (character == luckySymbol) {
        noOfTimes *= 2;
        for (counter = 0; counter < noOfTimes; counter++) {
```

```
        System.out.print(character);
      }
      System.out.println();
     }
    }
   }
  }
```

2. Modify the applet in Program Listing 6.2 so that, instead of each filled circle, it draws out concentric (i.e. with the same center) open circles—the first time 1, the second time 2, etc. The smallest of the circles will have a diameter of 6 pixels. Then the size increases by 4 pixels for every circle. The x and y values are found this way:

```
x = (int) (windowWidth * Math.random() + 1);
y = (int) (windowHeight * Math.random() + 1);
```

6.6 The do-while Statement

The third loop statement, the `do-while` statement, distinguishes itself from the others in that its loop body is always executed at least once. It is important to understand this limitation of the statement. In the `do-while` statement, control of the loop condition comes *after* the loop body, while this control comes *before* the loop body in `while` and `for` statements.

Java Core

The do-while statement

Syntax:

```
do
  statement
while loopCondition
```

The `loopCondition` is a boolean expression.

`statement`, which can be a block, is executed first. Then the value of the loop condition is evaluated. If the value is true, `statement` is executed again. This is repeated until the value of the loop condition is false.

Example:

```
int noOfStudents;
do {
  String inputText = JOptionPane.showInputDialog("How many students (max. 30)? ");
  noOfStudents = Integer.parseInt(inputText);
} while (noOfStudents < 0 || noOfStudents > 30);
```

We will write a client program that uses the `YesNoCounter` class from chapter 4. The program will be used to register results from yes and no lists that people have signed themselves up on. We have, for example, the following:

```
12 yes answers
14 no answers
32 yes answers
20 no answers
71 no answers
etc.......
```

We let an instance of the `YesNoCounter` class keep track of this. Let's call the instance `addingMachine`. The appropriate message, depending on the yes or no answers, is sent to the instance. This is repeated as long as there's data to input into the program.

We need a loop and have to identify the parts that the loop will consist of: we already know something about the loop body. It will consist of sending the right message to `addingMachine`. What will the condition be? The condition for continuing is that the user has more data to input. How should we word it? We can't use a counter-controlled loop since we can't insist that the user count the lists in advance. At a given point in time, the user will have to tell the program that there's no more data to input. How should we do that? Let's look at the input data for the program.

The number of yes and no votes is input data. These are integers different from 0 with additional information about the type of vote. We are not yet able to create a custom graphical user interface. What can we do? We can input an integer, and for every number ask the user if they were yes or no votes. And for every number we can also ask if there are more results to be input. In the long run, this is very inconvenient for the user. Instead, we assume that yes votes are input as positive integers, while no votes are input as negative. Then we're left with a number that isn't used, namely 0. We can let the user write 0 to indicate that now there's no more data to enter.

Now we can write the loop condition: `number != 0`.

Updating the loop condition will consist of reading a new number.

What about initializing the loop? This initialization will differ depending on whether we choose a loop construction where the test of the condition comes at the beginning of the loop (`while` or `for`) or a loop construction where the test of the condition comes at the end of the loop (`do-while`).

Since the program's purpose is to input data, we can assume that the loop will always be run through at least once. Therefore, we choose to use a `do-while` loop. (If we think the user might change his mind after he's started the program, but before any data has been input, then we should use a `while` loop.) What is then the initialization? See Program Listing 6.4. What's required for the loop to work? The object `addingMachine` needs to exist, and the variable `number` has to be declared outside the loop because this variable is part of the condition.

Program Listing 6.4

```
/*
 * TestYesNoCounter.java   E.L. 2001-05-31
 */
import javax.swing.JOptionPane;
class TestYesNoCounter {
  public static void main(String[] args) {
    int number = 0;
    String inputLog = ""; // logs all input
    YesNoCounter addingMachine = new YesNoCounter();
    do {
      String numberInput = JOptionPane.showInputDialog("Number of votes" +
          "\nPositive number = yes votes, negative = no, 0 = exit: ");
      inputLog += "\nInput number: " + numberInput;
      number = Integer.parseInt(numberInput);
      if (number > 0) addingMachine.increaseNumberOfYes(number);
      else if (number < 0) addingMachine.increaseNumberOfNo(-number);
    } while (number != 0);

    JOptionPane.showMessageDialog(null, inputLog +
      "\n\nThe result is " + addingMachine.getNumberOfYes() +
      " yes votes and " + addingMachine.getNumberOfNo() + " no votes.");
    System.exit(0);
  }
}

/* Example Run:

Input number: 23
Input number: -56
Input number: 101
Input number: 24
Input number: 0

The result is 148 yes votes and 56 no votes.
*/
```

6.7 Choosing the Right Loop Statement

Here are some guidelines for choosing a loop statement:

- Use a `for` statement if the number of iterations of the loop is known in advance, or if there is an integer variable that increases or decreases by a fixed value for every iteration.

- Use a `while` statement if the number of loop iterations is controlled by a general condition.

- Use a `do-while` statement if the number of loop iterations is controlled by a general condition and the loop will *always* be gone through at least once.

In addition, we have the following warnings:

Think things through one more time if you find out that the loop body in a `do-while` loop has to contain an `if` statement with the same condition as the loop. Then you probably actually need a `while` loop, which will permit a test before the loop body.

If the loop is going to count something, this number should be correct after the program is out of the loop. It shouldn't be necessary, for example, to reduce this number by 1. Then there would be something wrong with the initialization of the number or the placement of the update of the number.

Similar considerations apply to other variables that change their values inside the loop body.

6.8 Controlling Input Data

With loops at our disposal, we can write programs where we ask again if the user has entered invalid data. These are general problems independent of specific objects, and therefore we will now create some of the book's few class methods.

Program Listing 6.5 shows methods for inputting text, decimal numerals, and integers. Data control is added according to the following specifications:

- If the user presses Cancel, or closes the window or doesn't enter any data, the message "You have to enter data!" appears.

- If numbers should be entered, and the user enters a text that cannot be interpreted as a number, the message "Invalid integer!" or "Invalid decimal numeral!" comes up.

The methods ask again and again until the user enters valid data.

Program Listing 6.5

```
/*
 * TestInputReader.java  E.L. 2001-08-12
 */
import javax.swing.JOptionPane;
class InputReader {

  public static String inputText(String prompt) {
    String text = JOptionPane.showInputDialog(prompt);
    while (text == null || text.trim().equals("")) {
      JOptionPane.showMessageDialog(null, "You have to enter data!");
      text = JOptionPane.showInputDialog(prompt);
    }
```

```
      return text.trim();
    }
    public static int inputInteger(String prompt) {
      int number = 0;
      boolean ok = false;
      do {
        String theInputText = inputText(prompt);
        try {
          number = Integer.parseInt(theInputText);
          ok = true;
        } catch (NumberFormatException e) {
          JOptionPane.showMessageDialog(null, "Invalid integer!\n");
        }
      } while (!ok);
      return number;
    }
    public static double inputDecimalNumeral(String prompt) {
      double number = 0;
      boolean ok = false;
      do {
        String theInputText = inputText(prompt);
        try {
          number = Double.parseDouble(theInputText);
          ok = true;
        } catch (NumberFormatException e) {
          JOptionPane.showMessageDialog(null, "Invalid decimal numeral!\n");
        }
      } while (!ok);
      return number;
    }
  }
  class TestInputReader {
    public static void main(String[] args) {
      String text = InputReader.inputText("Enter a text: ");
      double decimal = InputReader.inputDecimalNumeral("Enter a decimal numeral: ");
      int integer = InputReader.inputInteger("Enter an integer: ");
      System.out.println("You entered this: ");
      System.out.println(text);
      System.out.println(decimal);
      System.out.println(integer);
      System.exit(0);
    }
  }
```

Let's look more closely at the individual methods. We'll start with the
inputText() method. We use showInputDialog() to input data. This
method returns null if the user presses Cancel or closes the window. The

following section of code checks this and prints out the message "You have to enter data!" before the user is asked again:

```
String text = JOptionPane.showInputDialog(prompt);
while (text == null || text.trim().equals("")) {
  JOptionPane.showMessageDialog(null, "You have to enter data!");
  text = JOptionPane.showInputDialog(prompt);
}
```

Notice how the loop is constructed. The program control only goes into the loop if the text is not valid.

We can use a `do-while` statement if we aren't going to print out a message about the error:

```
String text;
do {
  text = JOptionPane.showInputDialog(prompt);
} while (text == null || text.trim().equals(""));
```

Don't succumb to the temptation to use `do-while` if a message will be printed! Then you would need an `if` statement after the input inside the loop body, and that's not very elegant.

The methods for inputting numbers are more difficult. As you know, we use `parseInt()` or `parseDouble()` to convert text to numbers. Up to this point, if the text can't be converted to a valid number, an error message comes up in the console window and the program stops. This is, of course, an unfortunate situation, and now we'll find out how to catch this situation and also ask the user again.

We use the `inputText()` method discussed above to input the text. We can call this method directly, without qualifications, since we're in the same class.

```
String theInputText = inputText(prompt); // calls another method in the same class
```

We can interpret the text and handle any potential errors that arise:

```
try { // we'll try to convert the text to numbers
  number = Integer.parseInt(theInputText); // we try here
  .....we only end up here if it succeeds
} catch (NumberFormatException e) { // we end up here only if it didn't succeed
  JOptionPane.showMessageDialog(null, "Invalid integer!\n");
}
```

There's quite a bit of unfamiliar material here.

The call to `parseInt()` is inside a block that starts with the keyword `try`. It signals that we are going to try something with an outcome we're unsure of. What we are going to try is to convert the text into a valid number. If it's not successful, a so called "exception object" will be thrown (someplace inside the `parseInt()` method there's actually a `throw` statement). We have to do something with this object, otherwise the user will get the ugly error message mentioned above. What we'll do is to "catch" the object. That happens in a `catch` block a little further down in the program code.

Study the comments in the code above. Notice which statements are executed when the error occurs, and which are executed if everything is successful.

In the `inputInteger()` method, we use a boolean variable, `ok`, to keep track of whether the conversion was successful or not. We set the variable equal to `false` in the beginning of the method, and it is only set to equal `true` if we get through the call to `parseInt()` without any errors occurring.

Don't despair if you find this difficult. Exception handling is covered in chapter 8, and we'll spend more time on the details of it then. Until then, copy the class and use the methods where you need them. Remember to qualify it with the class name:

```
String text = InputReader.inputText("Enter a text: ");
```

Problems

Modify the program `WallCalculations2` from listing 3.4 in this way:

(a) If the user enters data that cannot be converted into valid numbers, let the program ask again.

(b) Limit valid lengths to between 1 and 15 meters, and valid heights to between 1.5 and 7 meters. Let these numbers be named constants.

6.9 New Concepts in This Chapter

Concept	Brief Explanation
counter-controlled loop	A loop where the number of iterations is known in advance.
do-while	Keyword to make a loop statement that has at least one iteration.
endless loop	A loop whose loop condition is always true.
for	Keyword to make a general loop statement, usually used for counter-controlled loops and other loops where the contents of an integer variable increase or decrease by a fixed value from one iteration to the next.
loop	Control structure where a statement or a block can be reiterated multiple times.
loop body	The statement or block that will be reiterated.
loop condition	The boolean expression that controls the number of times the loop will be reiterated.
loop condition update	The statement(s) that sooner or later should result in the loop condition being false.
loop counter	An integer variable that keeps track of the number of iterations for a counter-controlled loop.

Concept	Brief Explanation
loop initialization	Program code that sets the prerequisites for the loop to be executed correctly.
`while`	Keyword to make a general loop statement.

6.10 Review Problems

1. Study the following bit of code:

```
int sum = 0;
int unEvenNumber = 1;
while (unEvenNumber < 1000) {
  sum += unEvenNumber;
  unEvenNumber += 2;
}
```

What happens in the loop? Explain the different parts that make up the loop (initialization, condition, loop body, condition update).

2. Describe how to test a loop.

3. What's the relationship between `while` and `for` statements? When is it customary to use a `for` statement?

4. What distinguishes the `do-while` statement from the other two loop statements? Why should we be careful when using a `do-while` statement?

6.11 Programming Problems

Problem 1

Create an `Account` class. The pertinent instance variables are account number, name, and balance. Create methods that get the values of these instance variables. Also create methods to deposit and withdraw money. It shouldn't be possible to withdraw more money than there is in the account.

Write a client program that runs in a loop and inputs several transactions from the user. The balance should be output for each transaction performed. A message should be printed out if a transaction is illegal.

Problem 2

Write a program that finds out if a number is prime.

Problem 3

Write a program that converts between the base 10 system and some other numbering system with a base number 2–9. See Appendix C for a discussion about number systems.

Problem 4

Create an applet that draws a polygon line by line. Input the number of corners from the user. Generate the polygon's corner coordinates with a random number generator.

Problem 5

Create an applet that draws various geometric figures in random colors scattered around in a window. Use the random number generator to determine the type of figure, its color, and its location. Limit the number of different types of figures and the number of different colors to three. There should be 15 figures in total.

Collaboration Between
Objects

Learning goals for this chapter

After completing this chapter, you will understand:

- What collaboration between objects entails

- Similarities and differences between passing arguments of a primitive data type and a reference type

You will be able to:

- Program collaboration between objects

- Draw a sequence diagram that shows collaboration between objects

In order to complete tasks, objects often have to collaborate. Examples from reality:

- The teacher sends the message "Complete this task" to a student. The student searches for help from other students, and searches on the Internet or in books to complete the task.

- Elisabeth turns her CD player on. It has to collaborate with the CD to be able to make music.

In programs, we get an object to collaborate with another object by sending messages to it. We program this by calling methods on behalf of the object we are going to send the message to. With that, an object can collaborate with another object if it can send messages to it. Example: We send the message "Play this CD!" to the myCDplayer object in this way:

```
myCDplayer.play("Four Seasons");
```

The myCDplayer object can now collaborate with (send messages to) its own instance variables (the parts the CD player is made up of) and the "Four Seasons" object which it has received via the parameter list.

In this chapter, we will work with the renovation example. We will program several of the classes and create a simple, menu-driven client program that can be used to find the materials required and prices for wallpapering, painting, and laying flooring.

Collaboration between objects must necessarily lead to our having references to the same object from several locations in the program. We will look at the consequences this can have.

7.1 Examples of Collaboration Between Objects

We will work with the renovation project and create a simple client program that can be used to calculate the materials required and prices. We will see how material objects have to collaborate with surface objects to solve this problem. In this case, instances of the classes Flooring, Paint, and Wallpaper have to collaborate with an instance of the Surface class.

We figured out most of the formulas in Section 2.9. The class diagram is shown in Figure 4.1. Program listing 7.1 shows the Flooring and Wallpaper classes. We programmed the Surface class in chapter 4. The Paint class is the solution to one of the problems in this section.

Program Listing 7.1

```
/*
 * Flooring.java   E.L. 2001-05-17
 *
 */
class Flooring {
  private static final double limit = 0.02; // limit for one more width

  private String name;  // for identification purposes
  private double price;  // price per meter
  private double widthOfFlooring;   // meter

  public Flooring(String initName, double initPrice, double initWidth) {
    name = initName;
    price = initPrice;
    widthOfFlooring = initWidth;
  }

  public String getName() {
    return name;
  }

  public double getPricePerM() {
    return price;
  }
```

```java
public double getWidth() {
  return widthOfFlooring;
}
/*
 * We are going to calculate the amount which is needed to cover one surface.
 * The flooring is always placed crosswise relative to the length of the surface.
 * If you want to find the amount the other way, you have to change
 * width and length in the surface argument.
 */
public double getNoOfMeters(Surface aSurface) {
  double lengthSurface = aSurface.getLength();
  double widthSurface = aSurface.getWidth();

  int noOfWidths = (int)(lengthSurface / widthOfFlooring);
  double rest = lengthSurface % widthOfFlooring;
  if (rest >= limit) noOfWidths++;
  return noOfWidths * widthSurface;
}

public double getTotalPrice(Surface aSurface) {
  return getNoOfMeters(aSurface) * price;
}
}
/*
 * Wallpaper.java   E.L. 2001-05-17
 */
class Wallpaper {
  private static final double limit = 0.02; // limit for one more width

  private String name;  // for identification purposes
  private double price;  // price per roll
  private double lengthPerRoll; // meter
  private double widthPerRoll; // meter

  public Wallpaper(String initName, double initPrice, double initLengthPerRoll,
      double initWidthPerRoll) {
    name = initName;
    price = initPrice;
    lengthPerRoll = initLengthPerRoll;
    widthPerRoll = initWidthPerRoll;
  }

  public String getName() {
    return name;
  }

  public double getPricePerRoll() {
    return price;
  }
```

```java
public double getLengthPerRoll() {
  return lengthPerRoll;
}

public double getWidthPerRoll() {
  return widthPerRoll;
}

/*
 * This method calculates the number of rolls needed to paper a surface.
 */
public int getNoOfRolls(Surface aSurface) {
  double lengthSurface = aSurface.getLength();
  double heightSurface = aSurface.getWidth();

  /* calculate the number of heights */
  int noOfHeights = (int) (lengthSurface / widthPerRoll);
  double remnant = lengthSurface % widthPerRoll;
  if (remnant >= limit) noOfHeights++;

  /* calculate the number of rolls */
  int noOfRolls;
  int noOfHeightsPerRoll = (int) (lengthPerRoll / heightSurface);
  if (noOfHeightsPerRoll > 0) {
    noOfRolls = noOfHeights / noOfHeightsPerRoll;
    remnant = noOfHeights % noOfHeightsPerRoll;
    if (remnant >= limit) noOfRolls++;
  } else {  // the roll is shorter than one height (rarely!)
    double totalNoOfMeters = noOfHeights * heightSurface;
    noOfRolls = (int) (totalNoOfMeters / lengthPerRoll);
    if (totalNoOfMeters % lengthPerRoll >= limit) noOfRolls++;
  }
  return noOfRolls;
}

public double getTotalPrice(Surface aSurface) {
  return getNoOfRolls(aSurface) * price;
}
}
```

We create a little client program:

```java
class FlooringClient {
  public static void main(String[] args) {
    Surface theSurface = new Surface("Margaret's Floor", 5, 6);
    Flooring theFlooring = new Flooring("Fitted carpet", 24.50, 5);
    double noOfMeters = theFlooring.getNoOfMeters(theSurface);
    double price = theFlooring.getTotalPrice(theSurface);
    System.out.println("You need " + noOfMeters + " meters, price $" + price);
  }
}
```

Here we instantiate a `Surface` object and a `Flooring` object and send two messages to the `Flooring` object. First we ask it to find the number of meters required, then what that costs. The output from the program looks like this:

```
You need 6.0 meters, price $147.0
```

Example 1: the getNoOfMeters() method

Let's take a closer look at the message `getNoOfMeters()`. The object named `theFlooring` will figure out how many meters are required to cover a specific surface. To find that out, these two objects have to collaborate. Therefore, along with the message `getNoOfMeters()`, we send in a reference to the surface that is going to be covered.

References as arguments

We send a message to object A by calling a method. In order for object A to be able to collaborate with object B in completing a task, a reference to object B often has to be an argument for the method. In this way, object A can send messages to object B.

In the example, A is equal to `theFlooring`, while B is equal to `theSurface`. Method head:

```
public double getNoOfMeters(Surface aSurface)
```

Call:

```
double noOfMeters = theFlooring.getNoOfMeters(theSurface);
```

Read through the program code for the `getNoOfMeters()` method. It sends messages to the `Surface` object to get the length and width:

```
double lengthSurface = aSurface.getLength();
double widthSurface = aSurface.getWidth();
```

A *sequence diagram* shows how messages are sent from object to object (see Figure 7.1).[1] The italics in this diagram explain the use of symbols in the diagram and are not a part of UML. Here we follow the objects over time (vertical axis). We can read the following message exchange from the figure:

1. The client instantiates an object named `theFlooring`.

2. The client instantiates an object named `theSurface`.

---

1. UML offers something called collaboration diagrams, too. Sequence diagrams and collaboration diagrams express similar information, but show it in different ways. For this text we have found sequence diagrams to be the most appropriate.

3. The client sends the message getNoOfMeters() to theFlooring object. theSurface is sent along as argument.

4. theFlooring sends the message getLength() to theSurface.

5. theSurface sends a response back to theFlooring.

6. theFlooring sends the message getWidth() to theSurface.

7. theSurface sends a response back to theFlooring.

8. theFlooring sends a response back to the client.

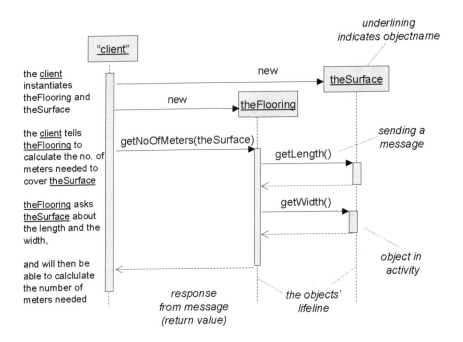

Figure 7.1 Sequence diagram (UML)

The dotted vertical lines represent the object's life span. The narrow vertical rectangles that partially overlap the life lines show the period of the life when the object is active.

A sequence diagram is usually used to show how the objects collaborate to perform a specific task. The object named theFlooring can be active in other periods of its life when there are other tasks to be done. But that isn't shown in this figure.

Note the difference between an activity diagram (chapter 5) and a sequence diagram. Both types of diagrams show things that happen in a time perspective.

Our activity diagrams show what's happening on a detail level[2] with an object in a part of its life that is represented by a narrow, vertical rectangle in a sequence diagram. Example: An activity diagram for the `getNoOfMeters()` method in the `Flooring` class shows what happens with the object named `theFlooring` while it's active (inside the vertical rectangle in the middle of the figure).

Example 2: the getTotalPrice() method

From the client program above, we have the following statement:

```
double price = theFlooring.getTotalPrice(theSurface);
```

The `getTotalPrice()` method looks like this:

```
public double getTotalPrice(Surface aSurface) {
    return getNoOfMeters(aSurface) * price;
}
```

We will find out what it costs to cover the surface with the flooring in question. In order to do so, we first have to determine the number of meters required, and then multiply this by the price. Of course the `Flooring` class already has a method that finds the number of meters, so we will use that. The object sends the message `getNoOfMeters()` to itself.

Example 3: two objects of the same class collaborate

An object can collaborate with another object of the same class to complete a task. Let's expand the `Surface` class with a method that compares the area of this surface with another surface. It's common for a comparison method to return 0 if the objects are the same, a negative value if the first one is smaller, and a positive value if the first one is bigger. We can use the `compareAreas()` method this way:

```
Surface surface1 = new Surface("A", 5, 4);
Surface surface2 = new Surface("B", 4, 4);
int result = surface1.compareAreas(surface2);
if (result < 0) System.out.println(surface1.getName() + " is the smaller one.");
else if (result > 0) System.out.println(surface2.getName() + " is the smaller one.");
else System.out.println("The surfaces have the same area.");
```

We see that we send a message to `surface1`. The argument for the comparision method is `surface2`. How should we program the method?

It's clear that `surface1` has to collaborate with `surface2` to come up with an answer. First it has to find its own area, then the area for `surface2`, and then compare them (see Figure 7.2). Notice how we draw an object sending a message to itself.

The program code looks like this:

```
public int compareAreas(Surface theOtherSurface) {
    final double precision = 0.00001;
```

---

2. However, activity diagrams are often used to show the control flow on a higher level.

```
    double area1 = getArea();
    double area2 = theOtherSurface.getArea();
    if (Math.abs(area2 - area1) < precision) return 0;
    else if (area1 < area2) return -1;
    else return 1;
}
```

We are comparing results from calculations with decimal numerals and have to remember that these calculations are not completely accurate. Therefore, we say that the areas are equal if the difference between them is less than the constant `precision`.

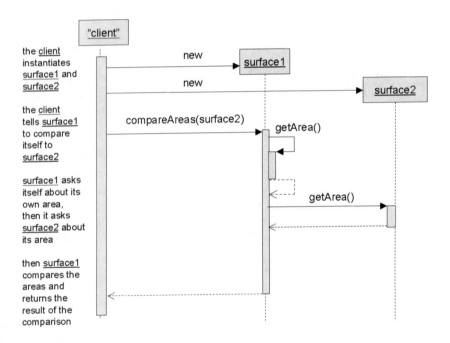

Figure 7.2 An Instance of the `Surface` class sends a message to itself and to another instance of the same class to complete a task (UML)

Notice that the parameter named `theOtherSurface` is set equal to the argument `surface2` when we call the method. When we say `theOtherSurface` inside the method, this then means the client object named `surface2`.

The `length` and `width` instance variables are private. Access to private members is limited to the *class*, not to the actual object we are in. In other words, as an alternative to calling the `getArea()` method, we can calculate the area for `theOtherSurface` inside the `compareAreas()` method this way:

```
double area2 = theOtherSurface.length * theOtherSurface.width;
```

Instances of the same class have access to each other's private members.

Problems

1. Program listing 7.1 shows the implementation of the `Wallpaper` class. Assume that the following lines of code are performed:

   ```
   Surface theSurface = new Surface("Margaret's wall", 5, 2.5);
   Wallpaper theWallpaper = new Wallpaper("Brocade wallpaper", 8.50, 12, 0.6);
   int noOfRolls = theWallpaper.getNoOfRolls(theSurface);
   ```

   (a) Draw a sequence diagram that shows what's going on here.

   (b) Draw an activity diagram that shows what happens when the object named `theWallpaper` carries out the activity `getNoOfRolls()`.

2. Program the `Paint` class according to the specifications given in the class diagram in Figure 4.1. The paint required should be rounded up to the nearest half liter.

3. The `Person` class is given:

   ```
   class Person {
     private String name;
     private int yearOfBirth;

     public Person(String initName, int initYearOfBirth) {
       name = initName;
       yearOfBirth = initYearOfBirth;
     }

     public String getName() {
       return name;
     }

     public int getYearOfBirth() {
       return yearOfBirth;
     }
   }
   ```

   In a client program, two instances of this class are instantiated:

   ```
   Person p1 = new Person("Peter", 1980);
   Person p2 = new Person("Jane", 1984);
   ```

   You will compose several instance methods in the `Person` class. For every method, you should set up a usage example for the method by sending messages to `p1` in the client program. Create methods that:

   (a) find out if the person is the same age as another person, return type `boolean`

(b) compare the person's age with the age of another person, return type `int` (younger than, same age, older than)

(c) find out if the person is more than x years older than another person, return type `boolean`

7.2 A Menu-Driven Program

We will write a program that we can use to estimate the materials required and the price for renovating a surface (wall or floor). The program runs in a loop and makes it possible to do several calculations in a row. See the activity diagram in Figure 7.3 that shows the client's activities. The client begins by printing some lines of instructions for the user, so that the user gets an idea of what the program can do and what he has to do as a user.

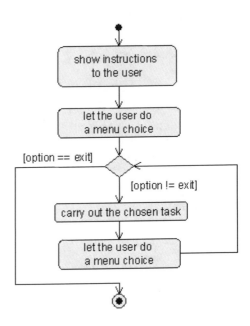

Figure 7.3 The activity for a client object that's estimating the materials required for renovation (UML)

We create the menu using the `showOptionDialog()` method in the `JOptionPane` class (see Figure 7.4).

Of course, we need the `Surface`, `Flooring`, `Paint`, and `Wallpaper` classes to create the program. We looked at these earlier in the chapter.

Figure 7.4 The user can select the renovation materials

The communication with the user is more complicated than we've seen in the programs we've covered up to this point. We need an object that can be responsible for carrying out the tasks in the activity diagram. Let's call the class this object belongs to `ProjectChap7`. See the class on the left in Figure 7.5. We'll introduce a little bit of new notation in this class diagram:

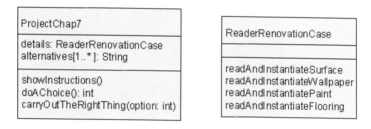

Figure 7.5 Classes with responsibility for communication with the user (UML)

- Up to this point, the number of values an attribute can have for a specific object has been 1. However, the number of alternatives in a menu is usually more than one. We use the notation [1..*], or more generally, [m..n], to indicate this. The first number indicates the lower limit for the number of values; the second number indicates the upper limit. An asterisk instead of a number (as in the figure here) says that there is no upper limit on the number of values.

- In this case we have found that it's correct to include parameter lists for the operations. The extent to which we do this depends on how far we've come in the development process. The data type and parameter name are indicated the same way for parameters as for attributes.

- Here we have indicated the return type for operations that return values. The operation `doAChoice()` returns an integer. We express that by putting a colon and the data type after the operation.

For a task associated with a menu selection to be carried out, data concerning surfaces and materials has to be input. New objects have to be instantiated and calculations have to be performed. As an example, we will look at what has to happen when the program runs to estimate how much paint will be used:

1. Input data about the surface that will be painted (name, length, width).

2. Create an instance of the `Surface` class.

3. Input data about the paint that will be used (name, price, number of coats, number of square meters per liter).

4. Create an instance of the `Paint` class.

5. Ask the paint object how much paint is needed to cover the given surface and what it will cost.

6. Output the answers.

We can place all this in the `ProjectChap7` class or we can compose a new class that is responsible for the portion of these tasks that may be useful in other contexts. We choose to separate out points 1 and 2 on their own, and points 3 and 4.

We compose a new class with methods for inputting information and instantiating objects. See the `ReaderRenovationCase` class on the right in Figure 7.5.

We distinguish between tasks that are linked directly to the specific client program we are writing now (the `ProjectChap7` class) and tasks of a somewhat more general nature (the `ReaderRenovationCase` class).

We let an instance of the `ReaderRenovationCase` class be an attribute for an instance of the `ProjectChap7` class. In this, we make it possible for there to be collaboration between these objects.

The client program is in the same file as the `ProjectChap7` class (see Program Listing 7.2). Notice that we have named the integers that represent the menu selections. This makes the program code easier to read and also has another important benefit: one of these constants (`exit`) is used in `main()` to terminate the loop. Now we can insert several menu selections into the `ProjectChap7` class and still have the selection `exit` at the end of the menu. Even if `exit` changes value to, for example, 4, this doesn't mean anything to `main()`. The value of the constant is only changed in one place.

The `ProjectChap7` class contains three methods:

- The `showInstructions()` method prints the user instructions in a message box. All programs of a certain size should contain a little guidance for the user.

- The `doAChoice()` method presents the menu to the user and returns the selection to the client.

- The `carryOutTheRightThing()` method makes sure the task associated with the menu selection is carried out.

The `ReaderRenovationCase` class is shown in Program Listing 7.3. Each method reads data and creates an object that is returned to the client.

Figure 7.6 shows how the client collaborates with other objects to find the wallpaper requirements.

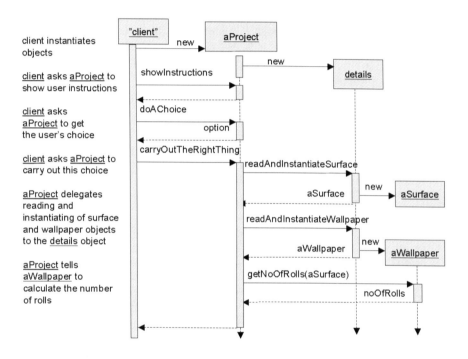

Figure 7.6 Objects collaborate to estimate the wallpaper needed (UML)

Problems

Respond to the following questions in conjunction with Program Listings 7.2 and 7.3:

1. Name all the classes that are used. Show where instances of the classes are created.

2. Suppose that we replace the `while` loop in `main()` (starting with "`int option = ...`") with the following `do-while` loop:

```
do {
  option = aProject.doAChoice();
```

```
aProject.carryOutTheRightThing(option);
} while (option != ProjectChap7.exit);
```

Why doesn't this work satisfactorily?

3. In the beginning of the `ProjectChap7` class, the constants `wallpaper`, `paint`, `flooring`, and `exit` get values. Explain why they can't get values other than the ones they receive here.

Program Listing 7.2

```java
/*
 * RenovationChap7.java   E.L. 2001-06-19
 *
 */
import javax.swing.JOptionPane;
class ProjectChap7 {
  public static String[] alternatives = {"Wallpaper", "Paint", "Flooring", "Exit"};
  public static final int wallpaper = 0
  public static final int paint = 1;
  public static final int flooring = 2;
  public static final int exit = 3;
  private ReaderRenovationCase details = new ReaderRenovationCase();

  public void showInstructions() {
    String instruction =
      "The program calculates the price and amount needed to renovate surfaces,\n" +
      "such as floors and walls. First, you are presented a menu where you\n" +
      "choose between materials: wallpaper, paint, or flooring. Then you have to enter\n" +
      "data about the surface and about the chosen material.\n" +
      "The area of the surface, the price and amount of material are then output.\n" +
      "After that you are back into the menu again.\n";

    JOptionPane.showMessageDialog(null, instruction);
  }
  public int doAChoice() {
    return JOptionPane.showOptionDialog(null, "What do you choose:", "Renovation",
      JOptionPane.DEFAULT_OPTION, JOptionPane.PLAIN_MESSAGE, null,
      alternatives, alternatives[0]);
  }
  public void carryOutTheRightThing(int option) {
    Surface aSurface = details.readAndInstantiateSurface();
    String result =
      "\nThe area of " + aSurface.getName() + " is: " + aSurface.getArea() + " sq m.\n";
    switch (option) {
      case wallpaper:
        Wallpaper aWallpaper = details.readAndInstantiateWallpaper();
        result += ("You will need " + aWallpaper.getNoOfRolls(aSurface) +
          " rolls of wallpaper " + aWallpaper.getName() + ", price $" +
```

```
                aWallpaper.getTotalPrice(aSurface));
         break;
       case paint:
         Paint aPaint = details.readAndInstantiatePaint();
         result += ("You will need " + aPaint.getNoOfLiters(aSurface) + " liters of paint " +
                aPaint.getName() + ", price $" + aPaint.getTotalPrice(aSurface));
         break;
       case flooring:
         Flooring aFlooring = details.readAndInstantiateFlooring();
         result += ("You will need " + aFlooring.getNoOfMeters(aSurface) +
                " meters of flooring " + aFlooring.getName() + ", price $" +
                aFlooring.getTotalPrice(aSurface));
         break;
       default:
          break;
     }
     JOptionPane.showMessageDialog(null, result);
   }
}
class RenovationChap7 {
  public static void main(String[] args) {
    ProjectChap7 aProject = new ProjectChap7();
    aProject.showInstructions();
    int option = aProject.doAChoice();
    while (option != ProjectChap7.exit) {  // we have to qualify the name exit
      aProject.carryOutTheRightThing(option);
      option = aProject.doAChoice();
    }
    System.exit(0);
  }
}
/* Sample data:

Input:
Margaret's wall: 7.2 m x 2.35 m,
      Wallpaper Sungold: price $9.50, length: 12.5 m, width: 0.54 m.
Anne's wall: 7.2 m x 2.35 m, paint 056789: price $9.90, 3 coats, 10 sq m/l.
John's floor: 5 m x 4 m, Flooring Berger XX: price $34.00 , width: 5 m.

Output:
The area of Margaret's wall is: 16.92 sq m.
You will need 3 rolls of wallpaper Sungold, price $28.50
The area of Anne's wall is: 16.92 sq m.
You will need 5.5 liters of paint 056789, price $54.45
The area of John's wall is: 20.0 sq m.
You will need 4.0 meters of flooring Berger XX, price $136.0
*/
```

Program Listing 7.3

```java
/*
 * ReaderRenovationCase.java   E.L. 2001-08-12
 *
 * This class has the responsibility to read input about surface,
 * wallpaper, paint and flooring, and to instantiate objects of these classes.
 * References to these objects are returned to the client program.
 */
import javax.swing.JOptionPane;
class ReaderRenovationCase {

 public Surface readAndInstantiateSurface() {
  String nameSurface = InputReader.inputText("The name of the surface: ");
  double lengthSurface =
       readPositiveDecimalNumeral("The length of the surface (meter): ");
  double widthSurface  =
       readPositiveDecimalNumeral("The width of the surface (meter): ");
  Surface aSurface = new Surface(nameSurface, lengthSurface, widthSurface);
  return aSurface;
 }

 public Paint readAndInstantiatePaint() {
  String namePaint = InputReader.inputText("Name or number to identify this paint: ");
  double price = readPositiveDecimalNumeral("Price per liter: ");
  int noOfCoats = readPositiveIntegralNumeral("How many coats? ");
  double coverage = readPositiveDecimalNumeral("How many square meters per liter?");
  Paint aPaint = new Paint(namePaint, price, noOfCoats, coverage);
  return aPaint;
 }

 public Wallpaper readAndInstantiateWallpaper() {
  String nameWallpaper = InputReader.inputText(
          "Name or number to identify this wallpaper: ");
  double pricePerRoll = readPositiveDecimalNumeral("The price per roll of wallpaper: ");
  double lengthRoll = readPositiveDecimalNumeral("The length of the roll (meter): ");
  double widthRoll = readPositiveDecimalNumeral("The width of the roll (meter): ");
  Wallpaper aWallpaper =
          new Wallpaper(nameWallpaper, pricePerRoll, lengthRoll, widthRoll);
  return aWallpaper;
 }

 public Flooring readAndInstantiateFlooring() {
  String nameFlooring = InputReader.inputText(
          "Name or number to identify this flooring: ");
  double pricePerMeter = readPositiveDecimalNumeral("Price per current meter: ");
  double widthFlooring = readPositiveDecimalNumeral("Width of the flooring (meter): ");
  Flooring aFlooring = new Flooring(nameFlooring, pricePerMeter, widthFlooring);
  return aFlooring;
 }
```

```
/* Private utility methods */
private static int readPositiveIntegralNumeral(String prompt) {
  int number = 0;
  boolean ok = false;
  do {
    number = InputReader.inputInteger(prompt);
  } while (number <= 0);
  return number;
}

private static double readPositiveDecimalNumeral(String prompt) {
  double number = 0;
  boolean ok = false;
  do {
    number = InputReader.inputDecimalNumeral(prompt);
  } while (number <= 0);
  return number;
}
}
```

7.3   Several References to the Same Object

Collaboration between objects usually means that we have several references to the same object. That can be difficult to keep track of if these references are in different methods or perhaps even in different classes. We'll look at two concrete cases:

1. An access method gains access, via the parameter list, to an object that "belongs" to the client.

2. An instance variable refers to an object that it has received via the parameter list for a constructor or a mutation method. The object is created on the client.

A reference type as a parameter for an access method

Suppose that in a client program we have the following:

```
Flooring theCarpet = new Flooring("AutumnBrown", 23.50, 5.0);
Surface myFloor = new Surface("Anne's floor", 4.2, 3.5); // length 4.2, width: 3.5
double noOfMeters = theCarpet.getNoOfMeters(myFloor);
```

theCarpet has to collaborate with myFloor to find the number of meters. The method call in the last line gives the getNoOfMeters() method a reference to the myFloor object.

What happens when we move into the method? When a method is called, each individual parameter is set to equal the accompanying argument. Here, that means that the following occurs:

Surface aSurface$_{\text{the method}}$ = myFloor$_{\text{client}}$;

`aSurface` thus becomes a reference for the object that contains the data about Anne's floor (see Figure 7.7).

What do we do with `aSurface` inside the method? See Program Listing 7.1. We send messages where we ask about the length and width:

```
double lengthSurface = aSurface.getLength();
double widthSurface = aSurface.getWidth();
```

Flooring theCarpet = new Flooring("AutumnBrown", 23.50, 5.0);
Surface myFloor = new Surface("Anne's floor", 4.2, 3.5);

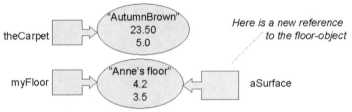

double noOfMeters = theCarpet.getNoOfMeters(myFloor);

What happens when the method getNoOfMeters() is invoked?
Behind the scenes: Surface aSurface$_{\text{the method}}$ = myFloor$_{\text{client}}$;

Figure 7.7 What happens during a call to the `getNoOfMeters()` method?

Assume that the `Surface` class is mutable (i.e., that it contains methods that change the data contents), and that it contains the following method:

```
public void setLength(double newLength) {
  length = newLength;
}
```

What can we do *then* with `aSurface` inside the method `getNoOfMeters()`? Follow along in Figure 7.8. We can change the contents of the object. The statement

```
aSurface.setLength(5.7);
```

leads to an object that "belongs" to the client changing contents. The object is declared as a variable in the client program, and in this way we can say that it belongs to the client. With the statement above inside the `getNoOfMeters()` method the object changes its value far away from its owner. Such changes can quickly lead to our losing the overall picture. One way of assuring ourselves that this will never happen is simply to not make the class mutable. On the other hand, this is often far from the reality that we are modeling. When the real objects change values, our model objects should, too.

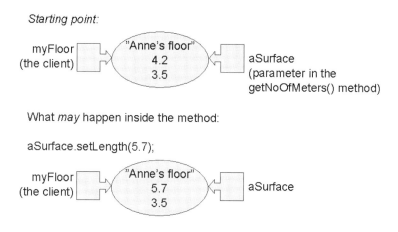

Figure 7.8   A method can change a parameter of reference type

An instance variable refers to an object that is created by the client

Suppose we expand the `Surface` class with the attribute `flooring`. This attribute indicates which type of flooring we will be using on the surface.

The constructor can now look like this:

```
public Surface(String initName, double initLength, double initWidth,
                Flooring initFlooring) {
    name = initName;
    length = initLength;
    width = initWidth;
    flooring = initFlooring;
}
```

The client program creates an instance of the class:

```
Flooring theCarpet = new Flooring("AutumnBrown", 23.50, 5.0);
Surface myFloor = new Surface("Anne's floor", 4.2, 3.5, theCarpet);
```

The last argument is a reference to an object that was created by the client. The constructor makes sure that the instance variable `flooring` in `myFloor` points to this object (see Figure 7.9). Also note that for the brief period of time that the program control is inside the constructor, we have a third reference to this object, namely the parameter `initFlooring`.

Here it's natural to say that the ownership of `theCarpet` object is transferred from the client program to the `myFloor` object. Nevertheless, the client will be able to change the contents of the objects by using the mutation methods that may exist.

If the Flooring class is mutable, we ought to evaluate whether the constructor should create a copy of the object instead:

```
public Surface(String initName, double initLength, double initWidth,
                      Flooring initFlooring) {
    name = initName;
    length = initLength;
    width = initWidth;
    flooring = new Flooring(initFlooring.getName(), initFlooring.getPrice(),
                             initFlooring.getWidth());

}
```

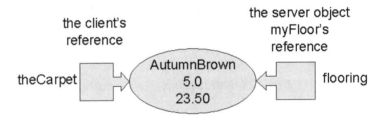

Figure 7.9 An instance variable in the server object points to the same object as a variable in the client object

Several references to the same object

A mutable object can be changed in all methods that have access to a reference to the object. Hence, one risks losing the overall picture of where the data contents in the object are changed.

This is why it's important to evaluate whether or not to use immutable classes. If you know that the objects are seldom changed once they've received their start values, you should compose immutable classes. If, once in a while, the object will be changed, you have to create a new object with the altered values instead. The String class is an example of an immutable class.

A constructor or a method that takes a reference to a mutable object as its argument can usually create a copy of this object. In this case, you should evaluate the extent to which it's desirable to have copies of the objects around in the system.

You should try to construct classes so that you get the fewest possible connections between them.

Finally, one small thing: What happens to all the objects as time goes by? Does the memory finally fill up if you constantly create new objects? Java uses a technology called *automatic garbage collection*. At regular intervals, Java cleans up the memory. When no more references to an object exist, the object is deleted. Not all programming languages clean up after themselves. A C++ programmer, for example, has to be careful to free up space that is no longer needed. Java also provides methods that let the programmer request a cleanup in special situations.

Problems

1. Suppose that the `Surface` class has the following method:

```
public void setLength(double newLength) {
  length = newLength;
}
```

The following program is produced:

```
class Playground {
  private String name;
  private Surface theSpot;

  public Playground (String initName, Surface initSpot) {
    name = initName;
    theSpot = initSpot;
  }

  public Surface getSpot() {
    return theSpot;
  }

  public void changeSpot(double newLength) {
    theSpot.setLength(newLength);
  }
}
class Problem7_3_1 {
  public static void main(String[] args) {
    Surface spot1 = new Surface("spot1", 4.5, 3);
    Playground aPlayground = new Playground("playground1", spot1);
    System.out.println("A: " + spot1.getName() + " length: "
            + spot1.getLength() + " width: " + spot1.getWidth());
    aPlayground.changeSpot(8.5);
    spot1.setLength(5.0);
    spot1 = aPlayground.getSpot();
    System.out.println("B: " + spot1.getName() + " length: "
            + spot1.getLength() + " width: " + spot1.getWidth());
  }
}
```

(a) Draw a figure that shows which objects are created, and which references there are to these objects. The figure will show the situation before the first print statement.

(b) What has changed when we come to the next print statement?

(c) What will be output when the program runs?

2. In this section, we expanded the `Surface` class with the attribute `flooring`. Create a set-method that changes the value for this instance variable. Create two versions of the set-method—one makes a copy of the client's flooring object, the other doesn't.

7.4   Summary: Argument Passing

We've seen that a method can change an object that "belongs" to the client, if a reference to the object is an argument to the method. Let's review a little and ask the following question: can a method, in a similar fashion, change a variable of a primitive data type?

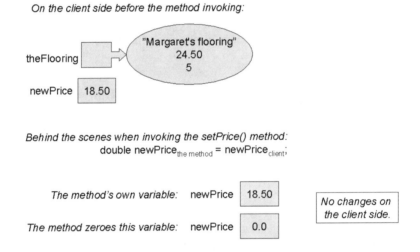

Figure 7.10   Variables on the client

Let's expand the `Flooring` class with the following methods that change the price of the flooring:

```
public void setPrice(double newPrice) {
    price = newPrice;
    newPrice = 0.0;
}
```

The method zeroes the variable `newPrice` after it's used. Does this have any effect on the client? Let's say that the client creates an instance of the class, and then inputs a new price from the user:

```
Flooring theFlooring = new Flooring("Margaret's flooring", 24.50, 5);
String newPriceRead = JOptionPane.showInputDialog("New price: ");
double newPrice = Double.parseDouble(newPriceRead);
theFlooring.setPrice(newPrice);
```

Figure 7.10 shows which variables exist in the client program. What happens when we send the message `setPrice()` to `theFlooring`? The parameter `new-Price` is set equal to the argument `newPrice` (here the parameter and the argument have the same name; they may just as easily have different names, which we've seen many examples of). Hence, the method gets its own copy of the primitive variable. Of course, the method can change the value for this variable without that affecting the variable `newPrice` in the client program.

Passing arguments during method calls

See Figure 7.11. In a method call, the *values* for the arguments are always passed. The method works with a *copy* of the argument. We differentiate between the following two cases:

- The parameter is of a primitive data type: if the method changes the value for this variable, that doesn't affect the argument at all.

- The parameter is a reference: a copy of the argument means that the method and the client each have their own reference to *the same object*. If the method makes changes to the object, they will, of course, apply to the object that the argument points to, since that's the same object we're talking about.

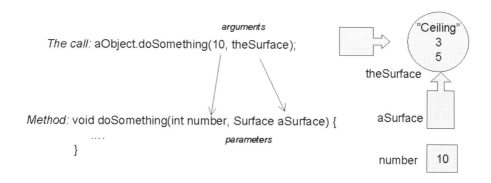

Figure 7.11 Passing different types of arguments

Problems

1. What is printed when the following code bit runs?

```
int number1 = 3;
int number2 = 4;
System.out.println("Before: " + number1 + " " + number2);
int help = number1;
number1 = number2;
number2 = help;
System.out.println("Afterwards: " + number1 + " " + number2);
```

2. Suppose that we have inserted number swapping in a method:

```
public void swapNumbers(int t1, int t2) {
  int help = t1;
  t1 = t2;
  t2 = help;
}
```

The method belongs to the Nonsense class and we do the following in a client program:

```
Nonsense aObject = new Nonsense();
int a = 10;
int b = 4;
System.out.println("Before: " + a + " " + b);
aObject.swapNumbers(a, b);
System.out.println("Afterwards: " + a + " " + b);
```

What is printed now?

3. We create the following two methods to change the contents of the two objects:

```
public void swapObjects1(Surface f1, Surface f2) {
  Surface help = f1;
  f1 = f2;
  f2 = help;
}

public void swapObjects2(Surface f1, Surface f2) {
  Surface help = new Surface(f1.getName(), f1.getLength(), f1.getWidth());
  f1 = new Surface(f2.getName(), f2.getLength(), f2.getWidth());
  f2 = help;
}
```

None of these work. Explain why.

4. Is it possible to create a method that changes the contents of two objects in the Surface class? If so, how?

7.5 New Concepts in This Chapter

Concept	Brief Explanation
garbage collection	Cleaning the internal memory so that space taken up by data that's no longer in use is freed up.
sequence diagram	A UML diagram that shows which messages are sent between objects that are collaborating. The diagram shows the order of the messages along a time axis.

7.6 Review Problems

1. Name examples of objects having to collaborate to complete tasks. How do we program collaboration?

2. Name similarities and differences between activity diagrams and sequence diagrams.

3. We have two UML rectangles in front of us. Inside one it says `Person` and in the other, `person`. How should we interpret these two rectangles? We used each of these two types of rectangles in its own diagram. Which type of rectangle belongs in which type of diagram?

4. Explain which graphical elements are included in a sequence diagram.

5. When is an object ready for garbage collection?

6. When should we copy objects?

7.7 Programming Problems

Problem 1

Compose a `Person` class with the attributes `firstName`, `lastName`, and `YearOfBirth`. The class should have a get method for each attribute and be immutable.

Compose an `Employee` class with the attributes `personalia` (data type `Person`), `employeeNo`, `yearOfAppointment`, `monthSalary`, and `tax-Percent`. In addition to get methods for all the attributes, the following operations should be available:

• Find the employee's monthly tax

• Find the gross annual salary

• Find tax withholding per year. To our employees June is tax free, and in December there's only half the usual tax.

- Find name (in the format: last name, first name. Example: Johnsen, Ann)

- Find age

- Find number of years employed at the company

- Find out if the person has been employed for more than a given number of years (parameter)

- Set methods to change attributes that it makes sense to change

Find out in which cases an instance of the `Employee` class has to collaborate with its `personalia` object in order to complete these tasks. Draw sequence diagrams for these operations.

The following code lines will tell you the current year:

```
java.util.GregorianCalendar calendar = new java.util.GregorianCalendar();
int year = calendar.get(java.util.Calendar.YEAR);
```

Write a simple program that puts data into an instance of the `Employee` class and calls all the methods you've created. Check that the results are correct.

Write a menu-driven program that makes it possible for the user to change the data contents in the object. Let the program run in a loop such that several changes can be made. For every run-through of the loop, the program will send suitable get messages to the object and print their results so that it's possible to check that the changes were made.

Problem 2

Compose a class, `Poster`. The poster will have three lines. Every line will have its own font, color, and upper- and lower-case letter designation. The text is also an attribute for the line. Think about which class should be responsible for the lines' placements.

The classes will be used in an applet. Therefore, you also need methods for painting. The parameter for `paintComponent()` has to be passed to the paint methods you create in the `Poster` class and possibly in the `Line` class.

Create the applet.

Problem 3

Compose a class to handle books. Name, author, publication year, number of pages, and publisher are pertinent attributes for a book. In addition to get methods, you will create operations that compare the ages of two books, that compare the number of pages, and that find out if two books were written by the same author or if they were published by the same publisher.

Write a simple program that tests the class.

(To find the current year, see problem 1.)

Java Libraries and Exception Handling

Learning goals for this chapter

After completing this chapter, you should be able to:

- Use the part of the Java documentation that describes the Java API

- Create and use your own packages of classes

- Write the program code so that `RuntimeExceptions` don't happen

- Handle exceptions of other types using `try` statements, possibly `throws`

- Throw your own exception objects (`throw`), possibly of specially created exception classes

You've probably already figured out that an enormous number of ready-made classes come with SDK. We usually call this the Java API (API = Application Programming Interface). No textbook can train you fully in everything it enables. (There wouldn't be any point in it, either.) Hypertext technology is ideal for information about these classes. By accessing Sun's Web pages, you're also guaranteed to get the most up-to-date information.

In practice, most programmers turn out to need access to the class descriptions so often that they choose to download this documentation when they download SDK. Then you're assured of having the description that best suits the version of SDK you're using. You still shouldn't forget to visit Sun's Web pages from time to time—you can also sign up for a newsletter.

In this chapter, you'll find a brief introduction to using the portion of the SDK documentation that describes the Java API. As examples of classes, we'll look at how to format printouts of decimal numerals, and how to get an applet to play a music file and display images.

To use ready-made classes, you have to be familiar with the package concept (Section 3.5) and know what the Java class tree is. We saw a section of the class tree in Figure 4.6. Here, we will look at how to construct package structures that make class names globally unambiguous. We'll also look at how to create our own libraries for classes of a more general nature.

We'll look at how to handle exceptions so that we can avoid having them show up on the screen as messages that result in a program abortion. We'll look at various types of exceptions—which ones you should try to program around and which ones you should catch and take care of.

8.1   The Online API Documentation

In the previous chapters, you learned about the `JOptionPane` class, the `String` class, and some other ready-made classes. In this chapter, we will look at more of the classes that come with the SDK. However, it's not practically possible to describe all the classes that are included in the SDK this way. Therefore, we'll cover how to use the online documentation. First check to see if you downloaded this. It should be in the *docs* subdirectory under the directory named *jdk1.4*.[1] If you don't have this directory, or if it's empty, you have to download the documentation from Sun's Web pages the same way you downloaded SDK.

We're assuming now that you've installed the documentation. Open the file *docs/index.html* in your browser by, for example, going into Windows Explorer and clicking on it. You will get something that looks more or less like Figure 8.1. As you can see, you have access to many interesting pages here. Click on "API and Language". The page that comes up is not shown here. But, once there, you should click on "Java™ 2 Platform API Specification." Then the page in Figure 8.2 will come up. API is short for "Application Programming Interface" and can be defined as "The specification of how a programmer writing an application accesses the behavior and state of classes and objects".[2] In practice, this means that you find a brief description of the class along with public methods and variables. The links the class has to other classes are also included. From now on, we'll call this the online API documentation. Make a bookmark for this page—you're guaranteed to use it later.

In order to make use of Java's class libraries, it's imperative to be able to use this window. The following section covers the different parts of the window.

On the right side, there's a summary of all the packages that exist. The brief description of each package gives you an idea of the scope of the Java API. Click on one of the packages. You'll get a list of the interfaces (covered in chapter 10) and classes that are included in this package. Take a look at some of the classes—we'll come back to the class descriptions shortly.

---

1. The name of this directory may change as new versions come out.

2. This definition is from [URL Java glossary] where you'll find definitions for many of the current concepts.

Click back to the page shown in Figure 8.2. On the left there's a summary of all the classes in the Java API. Click on the `String` class. At the top are all the superclasses for the `String` class:

```
java.lang.Object
 |
 +--java.lang.String
```

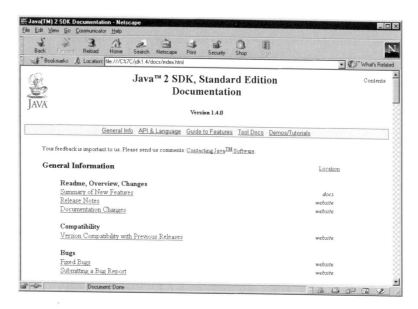

Figure 8.1 The main page for "Java^TM 2 SDK, Standard Edition Documentation Version 1.4.0"

Notice that `String` is right under the `Object` class. Other classes may be far from the class on the top, which is always the `Object` class.

The class tree and superclass concepts were covered in Section 4.6 in connection with applets. For a brief review, look at Figures 4.6 and 4.7. Absolutely all objects belong to the `Object` class. The `Component` class, which is a direct subclass of `Object`, describes a subset of all the objects. The further down the class tree we go, the more restricted the sets are. Public variables and methods declared in a class are inherited by all subclasses. That means they can be used as if they were declared in the subclass.

Back to the online documentation: a class description always begins with a text that describes the purpose of the class and often also includes usage examples. A lot of useful information can be found here. Read what it says for the `String` class. You understood most of it, right? Go down to the "Constructor Summary" section. This shows you all the constructors that can be used to instantiate objects of the `String` class. Note that some of the constructors are marked *"Deprecated"*. That means you shouldn't use them. Sooner or later they will disappear from the Java API. You'll find this label on many methods and constructors in the Java API. Most of these methods are from the earliest and most incomplete versions of the Java API.

In Chapter 3 you were introduced to one of the `String` constructors. Do you see it on the list? Clicking on it will give you a somewhat more detailed description.

Most of the other `String` constructors have a parameter of a type that includes the [ ] characters. This means that the argument has to be an array (we'll cover this in chapter 9).

Let's keep going and look at the methods. There are a great many methods—in most cases you'll find what you need.

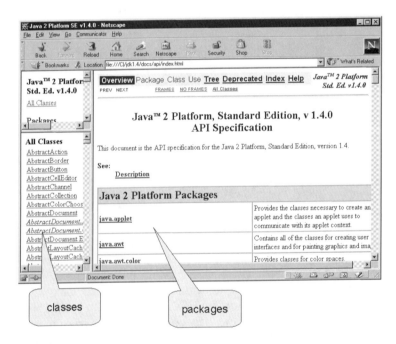

Figure 8.2 The main page for "Java™ 2 Platform API Specification"

Other sections you might find useful:

- Field Summary: This section is at the top. It contains public variables, as a rule, class constants. If you look here under the `Color` class, you'll find the colors `red`, `black`, `white`, etc. Notice that you have to put the class name in front of class constants if you are going to use them outside the class. For example:

```
Color myColor = Color.red;  // we have to qualify the name red
```

• Methods inherited from class xxx: This section is below the methods section. Methods listed here are methods that are inherited from a (direct or indirect) superclass. Look up the JApplet class. You'll find that JApplet inherits from all its superclasses. Do you recognize any of these methods?

Problems

1. How do you find a method that will find a number's absolute value?

2. By no means does the list on the left side of the documentation window show all the classes without scrolling. How can you limit this list to show only the classes in a specific package?

3. Look up the StringBuffer class. What's the main difference between the String class and the StringBuffer class?

8.2 Making Your Own Libraries

All the classes in the Java API belong to named packages. Examples of packages are javax.swing and java.applet. Our example programs usually belong to unnamed packages. The vast majority of Java installations create one unnamed package per subdirectory.

However, we should put classes we make, which we believe will be generally useful to us or to others, into named packages. The advantage to this is that we don't need to copy the classes when we use them in different directories. Thus, we also avoid maintaining multiple copies of these classes.

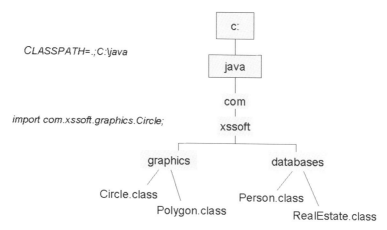

Figure 8.3 The package structure for classes from the XSSoft company

Suppose that we buy a number of Java classes from a company called XSSoft. Among other things, the company produces classes for graphics and managing archives of people and real estate. It's a plus for customers who use these classes that they have names that won't conflict with the other classes they're using. Is it possible to construct globally unambiguous class names? Yes, you can be reasonably sure that the class name is unambiguous if you let the class belong to a package named with the URL of the company's home pages on the Internet. Our fictional company's home page is *http://www.xssoft.com*. XSSoft.com is unique on the Internet, and that should also be adequate for the Java classes the company produces. It's common to create a package structure whose top part consists of the names contained in the URL, but in the reverse order. An example of a class from the company XSSoft is `com.xssoft.graphics.Circle`. Furthermore, the package structure is identical to the directory structure on the hard disk (see Figure 8.3). The `Circle` class is in a subdirectory named *graphics*, which in turn is a directory under *xssoft*. Above *xssoft* we find *com*. Notice how the `import` statement looks in a program where we will use the `Circle` class:

```
import com.xssoft.graphics.Circle;
```

Or we can write

```
import com.xssoft.graphics.*;
```

and gain access to all the classes in the `com.xssoft.graphics` package.

But what about the directory structure above *com*? This depends on where the person installing the software puts the packages. The figure shows that we placed the packages under *c:\java*. (In the following, we are assuming that we're working in MS Windows.)

When we run a Java program that uses the packages from XSSoft, we have to tell the Java interpreter where these packages are. This problem is solved by assigning values to an environmental variable called CLASSPATH. You may be familiar with the PATH variable; CLASSPATH is similar in that it contains a series of paths separated by semicolons. The paths indicate where the Java interpreter should look for packages. (See also appendix A.) In our case, then, CLASSPATH will contain *c:\java*. In addition, if the environmental variable CLASSPATH exists on the computer, then it also has to contain the path to the actual directory, where we usually have a number of classes. The path to the actual directory is a period. Then CLASSPATH will look like this:

```
CLASSPATH=.;c:\Java
```

Large class libraries are often delivered as packaged files. The zip and jar formats are common. *jar* files can be created with the Java tool jar, and are basically *zip* files with some additional information. The documentation for the compiler has more information about the jar tool and *jar* files. Both *zip* and *jar* files can be included directly in CLASSPATH. In that case both the path and file name should be included in CLASSPATH.[3]

---

3. There's an example in Section 20.1, where we include a database driver.

Java Core

The package declaration

Syntax:

> package *packageName*;

A class that belongs to a named package has to be declared in a file that starts with a package declaration.

The class has to be public so that it can be accessed outside the package.

Example:

> package com.xssoft.graphics;
> public class Circle {
>   ...

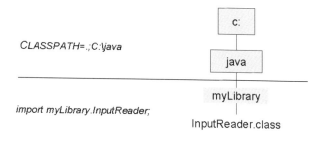

Figure 8.4 The myLibrary package contains the InputReader class

The myLibrary package

If you've copied the book's examples from [URL Java book], you've got a subdirectory named myLibrary. This directory contains the package myLibrary, which among other utility classes contains the class Input-Reader from Section 6.8. Many of the examples in the rest of the book will require that the package myLibrary exist, so you have to set up the environment variable CLASSPATH to include the path up to (but not including) this directory, as explained above. (See Figure 8.4 too.)

Let's take a look at the file *InputReader.java* in the *myLibrary* directory. The first lines in the file are as follows:

```
package myLibrary;
import javax.swing.JOptionPane;
public class InputReader {
```

Note the differences from Section 6.8.

Near the end of the class you'll find the test program. We have put `main()` into the class. For a utility class it's a good idea to put the test program into the class. When you start the Java interpreter you input the name of a class, and the interpreter looks for the `main()` in that class. Now we'll try the test program.

If you've set up CLASSPATH correctly, it'll be possible to run `main()` from any directory (but there may be problems from an editor):

```
>java myLibrary/InputReader
```

Notice the direction of the slash—this direction also applies if the console window is an MS-DOS window! Here you're indicating that you are going to run the `myLibrary.InputReader` class. When you start the program from the command line, write the slash instead of a period.

Now work out what happens if you move to the directory *myLibrary* and write

```
>java InputReader
```

Try to explain why this happens.

8.3 Localization

By *formatting*, we mean how, for example, a number is displayed on the screen or on another output unit. Formatting doesn't affect the value itself. Assume the variable `number` contains the value 35645.4. The numerical value can be output (formatted) in several ways:

```
35,645.4      English/American locale
35 645,4      Some European locale
35 645,40     Some European locale
35645         Likely to be anyone
```

As you see, a main difference between locales is the decimal separator. Some use period, others use comma.

The contents of the variable `number` remain the same, regardless of the output format.

Formatting decimal numerals is a mere fragment of what is called *localization*. This refers, for example, to currency units, date formats, alphabet sort orders, and also—of course—language. Java provides classes for creating programs that support settings like this.

A specific *location* is identified by its language and country, and possibly also its language variant. We'll ignore the variants here.

Look up the `Locale` class in the online API documentation. Browse through the page quickly. The `Locale` class is used to specify which language and which country the format should be set for. The country and language designation follow international standards. The `Locale` documentation contains URLs for these standards. For example, the German language is designated as "de" and the country of Germany as "DE". We specify that the formatting should follow the German standard this way:

```
Locale german = new Locale("de", "DE");
Locale.setDefault(german);
```

The `java.text.NumberFormat` class provides class methods for formatting numbers according to the rules that apply for the location that is designated. For example:

```
Locale german = new Locale("de", "DE");
Locale.setDefault(german);
double number = 0.757;
NumberFormat numberFormat = NumberFormat.getNumberInstance();
NumberFormat percentFormat = NumberFormat.getPercentInstance();
NumberFormat currencyFormat = NumberFormat.getCurrencyInstance();
System.out.println("As decimal numeral: " + numberFormat.format(number));
System.out.println("As percent: " + percentFormat.format(number));
System.out.println("As currency: " + currencyFormat.format(number));
```

gives the following output:

```
As decimal numeral: 0,757
As percent: 76%
As currency: 0,76 DM⁴
```

Notice that the contents of the variable `number` are not changed. The `format()` method returns a string with the characters that will be output—in one case the string contains "0,76 DM", in another case, "76%".

It's possible to control the details concerning the number of decimal places and symbols that will be included in the formatting. Refer to the online API documentation if you're interested in learning about this. Here, we'll stick to looking at the `DecimalFormat` class. It's used to control the output format for decimal numerals. We indicate the format as a string that says how the number will look. The most important codes are shown with examples in table 8.1.

Thus

```
Locale locc = new Locale("en", "US");
Locale.setDefault(locc);
DecimalFormat theFormat = new DecimalFormat("###0.00");
String text = theFormat.format(13.4);
System.out.println(text);
text = theFormat.format(-3456789.4);
System.out.println(text);
```

gives the output

---

4. With version 1.4 of SDK, you'll get the symbol (euro) from 01.01.2002 for countries of the European Monetary Union.

```
13.40
-3456789.40
```

Try this bit of code without setting location. Then you should get a result reflecting the environment your program is running in ("Regional Settings" in Windows).
We see that even if the format is too restrictive, the number prints out.

Table 8.1 Codes to create patterns for the DecimalFormat constructor. The codes can be combined

Code	Interpreted as	Example	France ("fr", "FR")	Great Britain ("en", "GB")
0	A numeric character.	"0000.00"	6.7 becomes 0006,70	6.7 becomes 0006.70
#	A numeric character, but don't show it if there's a zero at the beginning or end of the number.	"####.##"	6.7 becomes 6,7	6.7 becomes 6.7
.	Placement of decimal point.	see above		
,	Placement of group separator.	"###,###.##"	56786.7 becomes 56 786,7	56786.7 becomes 56,786.7

API Reference

The java.text.DecimalFormat class

Constructor:

> public DecimalFormat(String pattern)

The pattern is composed the way we want the formatting (see table 8.1).

Method (inherited from java.text.NumberFormat*):*

> public String format(double number)

This method formats the number and stores the result in a string. The string is returned to the client.

Printing numbers out in columns

What we're lacking is a code that will insert blank spaces if there is an introductory zero at the beginning of the number. This code is useful when printing numbers out in columns. If we have such a code, the decimal points will line up, assuming we're using a nonproportional font.[5]

In the package `myLibrary`, which you should have installed (see the last part of Section 8.2), you'll find a class that can be used in cases like this. The constructor for the `MyDecimalFormat` class takes two arguments, the number of places before and after the decimal point. The class contains one method, the `format()` method, which takes a number as an argument and returns a string with the formatted number.

Example of the class in use:

```
myLibrary.MyDecimalFormat format1 = new myLibrary.MyDecimalFormat(5, 2);
double aNumber = 8.5;
for (int i = 0; i < 8; i++) {
  System.out.println(format1.format(aNumber));
  aNumber *= 10;
}
```

gives the output (with the English/American locale):

```
     8.50
    85.00
   850.00
  8500.00
 85000.00
850000.00
```

We see that it works well as long as the format is large enough. When the number is larger than the format, printing the right numerical value is prioritized over printing the right format (with the wrong numerical value).

Problem

This will familiarize you with the `DateFormat` class.

Create an instance of the class by using, for example, the class method `getDateTimeInstance()`. The style will be a class constant: FULL, LONG, MEDIUM, or SHORT. This instance now contains information about the format for the date and time.

Today's date can be obtained with:

```
Date toDay = new Date();
```

Write a program that prints today's date in several different styles.

---

5. This is a font where all the characters take the same amount of room (see the "Monospaced" font in Figure 4.11).

8.4 Sound and Images

A number of examples come with the SDK. See the comment in Program Listing 8.1.

The applet assumes that both of the files are in the same directory as the applet (see Program Listing 8.1).

First the applet gets information about where it was downloaded from. This is saved in an instance of the URL class. This URL is used to download the music and image files.

The painting takes place in the `paintComponent()` method, as usual. For details on the methods that are used, see the API reference below.

Program Listing 8.1

```
/*
 * SoundAndImage.java   E.L. 2001-08-13
 *
 * The image file duke.running.gif and the audio file spacemusic.au
 * should be in the same directory as this applet.
 * The image file is from version 1.3 of SDK (demo/jfc/Java2D/images/),
 * while the music file is found in version 1.4 (demo/applets/Animator/audio/)
 */
import java.net.*;
import java.awt.*;
import javax.swing.*;
import java.applet.*;

public class SoundAndImage extends JApplet {
  public void init() {
    Container content = getContentPane();
    URL codebase = getCodeBase(); // where the applet resides

    AudioClip music = getAudioClip(codebase, "spacemusic.au");
    music.play();

    Image theImage = getImage(codebase, "duke.running.gif");
    Drawing theDrawing = new Drawing(theImage);
    content.add(theDrawing);
  }
}

class Drawing extends JPanel {
  private Image image;

  public Drawing(Image newImage) {
    image = newImage;
  }

  public void paintComponent(Graphics window) {
    super.paintComponent(window);
    /*
     * The arguments to drawImage() are:
```

```
                * First the image, then
                * the x- and y-coordinates for the top-left corner,
                * the width and the height of the image (it may be resized),
                * background color,
                * ImageObserver, see the online API-documentation.
                */
              window.drawImage(image, 0, 0, 200, 200, Color.red, this);
            }
          }
```

 ## API Reference

The java.applet.Applet class

Methods:

```
    public URL getCodeBase()
```

The return type is URL. The URL class is part of the `java.net` package. This method gives the applet's URL. This makes it possible to access files that are in the same subdirectory as the applet.

```
    public AudioClip getAudioClip(URL url)
    public AudioClip getAudioClip(URL url, String relativeURL)
```

These methods return sound objects of the `AudioClip` type (see below) from the stated URL. The latter method makes it possible to indicate this URL relative to the URL that is given as the first argument. This method is usually used together with the `getCodeBase()` method. The methods return immediately. The file isn't downloaded until the music plays. No message is sent if the URL doesn't exist.

```
    public Image getImage(URL url)
    public Image getImage(URL url, String relativeURL)
```

These methods create instances of the `Image` class the same way the methods above make `AudioClip` objects. The `Image` class belongs to the package `java.awt`.

`JApplet` is a subclass of the `Applet` class, and therefore inherits these methods.

The java.applet.AudioClip interface[6]

Methods:

```
    public void play()
    public void loop()
    public void stop()
```

---

6. AudioClip is an interface, not a class. The distinction doesn't mean anything in practical use here. We will cover interfaces in chapter 10.

These three methods respectively play the music file once, play it infinitely many times, and stop it from playing. It's possible to play several music files at one time.

The java.awt.Graphics class

See also Section 4.7.

Methods:

```
public boolean drawImage(Image image, int x, int y, ImageObserver observer)
public boolean drawImage(Image image, int x, int y, int width, int height,
                            Color background, ImageObserver observer)
```

x and y are the coordinates for the upper left corner of the image. width and height are the size of the image, measured as a number of pixels.

Calling the method registers that an image should be painted. A new thread (see chapter 16) is started by downloading the image. Then the original program thread returns to the client. Thus two program threads, or processes, run in parallel until the image is downloaded. The last argument in the method call can be an object that is alerted about how the download of the image is progressing. In our examples, we use this as an argument here.

Problem

Try the applet with other file formats for sound and images.

8.5 Introduction to Exception Handling

Before we examine Java's exception objects, we take a more general approach to exceptions.

An *exception* is a state that can arise during runtime, but which is a deviation from normal. Examples of exceptions that a program should be able to handle without aborting:

- The program tries to divide by zero, find the square root or logarithm of a negative number, or some other mathematical "impossibility".

- The program tries to get a character in an invalid position in a string. For example: in the "Example" string, 0, 1, 2, 3, ..., 6 are valid positions, but position 7 is not.

- A number falls outside some valid interval.

The program has to handle the exception states that arise during runtime in a sensible manner. Depending on the circumstances, the programmer has to tackle the possibilities that may arise, and program a way out of them.

We haven't programmed much error handling up to this point. From chapter 6 we have the following:

```
String text = JOptionPane.showInputDialog(prompt);
while (text == null || text.trim().equals("")) {
  JOptionPane.showMessageDialog(null, "You have to enter data!");
  text = JOptionPane.showInputDialog(prompt);
}
```

If the user enters the wrong data, she'll expect to see a message on the screen and have the opportunity to try again. If unusual situations arise in other contexts, it's hardly to be assumed that a message should print out on the screen. In object-oriented programming, a problem often arises when a server object performs a task for a client object. The natural thing is for the server object to then send a message to the client about the situation, and in this way leave it to the client to decide which steps to take.

How can a server object alert the client that it didn't manage to perform the task as intended? One way is for the method in question to return an error code. From Section 5.5, solution to problem 4, we have the following:

```
class Grade {
  private int points;

  public Grade(int initPoints) {
    points = initPoints;
  }

  public char getGrade() {  // returns an 'X' if too many point, a 'Z' if too few points
    if (points > 100) return 'X';
    else if (points >= 90) return 'A';
    else if (points >= 80) return 'B';
    else if (points >= 70) return 'C';
    else if (points >= 60) return 'D';
    else if (points >= 0) return 'F';
    else return 'Z';
  }
}
```

The `getGrade()` method returns an 'X' or a 'Z' if the point total is invalid. The client has to check the return value:

```
Grade theGrade = new Grade(points);
char grade = theGrade.getGrade();
if (grade == 'Z') {
  JOptionPane.showMessageDialog(null, "Negative number of points not allowed.");
} else if (grade == 'X') {
  JOptionPane.showMessageDialog(null, "Max. number of points is 100");
} else {
  JOptionPane.showMessageDialog(null, points + " points gives the grade " + grade);
}
```

For simple error situations, the `boolean` return type can be used. Then the return value `false` will mean that something has gone wrong, while the return value `true` is used if everything is normal.

Exception objects

From now on, an exception will mean a Java exception object.

In Program Listing 6.8 we saw that `parseDouble()` and `parseInt()` threw exception objects if the text in question couldn't be converted to a number. Now we will see what an "exception object" is, and what it means to "throw" one.

This method of handling errors is essentially different from the procedure described above. The mechanism is based on creating and dealing with instances of the so-called `Throwable` classes where `Exception` is an important subclass.

First let's look at the problems that can occur if we are using the simple exception handling described in the previous section.

What if all possible characters were valid return values from the `getGrade()` method? How would we warn the client then if something was wrong? And how can we warn the client about errors that occur in a constructor? Exceptions make it possible to send feedback to the client without using a return value.

File handling (covered in chapter 11) is an occasion where you can imagine things going wrong. Briefly, that means that the program reads and writes data to a file instead of (or in addition to) communicating with the user. This makes it possible to store data from run to run. Communication with a file can always go wrong—for example, it could happen that parts of the file are damaged. After every single file operation, therefore, it's important to check that everything went well so that you can continue:

> *establish a connection to the file*
> *if this was successful*
>   *read a little data from the file*
>   *while this was successful and there is more data*
>   *read data from the file*
>   *end the connection to the file*

There can be many messages to the file object inside the `while` loop. *Every single one of these* can go wrong. This can lead to very complicated control structures with many `if` statements embedded inside each other.

What is a Java exception?

A Java exception is an object that contains information about the error. If something goes wrong inside a method, the method throws an exception object. This object doesn't come through the return value from the method.
The client can catch this object or throw it without handling it.

Exceptions make it possible to handle these errors in one place in the program. Now the program outline from before will look like this:

> *try*
>   *establish a connection to the file (exception object may be <u>thrown</u>)*
>   *read a little data from the file (exception object may be <u>thrown</u>)*
>   *while there is more data*
>   *read a little data from the file (exception object may be <u>thrown</u>)*
>   *end the connection to the file (exception object may be <u>thrown</u>)*
>   *<u>catch</u> any exception object*
>   *common error handling*

We're trying to do a number of things with this file. If an error occurs inside a file method, this method will throw an exception object. We can catch it (as we did here), or we can throw it again.

As you may remember from chapter 6, the keywords in this context are `throw`, `throws`, `try`, and `catch`.

Figure 8.5 shows how `main()` handles an error that may occur in the `getData()` method. Notice that the method head says that this method throws ("throws") an exception if an error occurs.

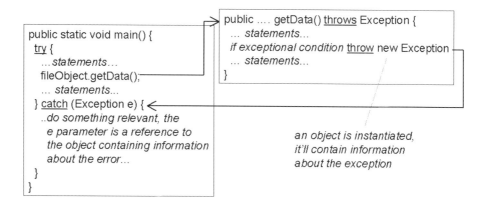

Figure 8.5 `main()` catches an exception object that is generated in the `getData()` method

In Figure 8.6 it's `methodX()` that calls the `getData()` method. An exception object is generated in this method and sent back to `methodX()`. It says in the method head that exceptions will be thrown (`throws Exception`). In this case, the exception object is handled by `main()`. We can also imagine that `main()` sent the object on—then a message would print out on the screen and the program would stop.

An exception object is an instance of (a subclass of) the `Throwable` class. See Figure 8.7. At some places in the class tree, we find three dots. That means that there are more classes on this level than those that are shown.

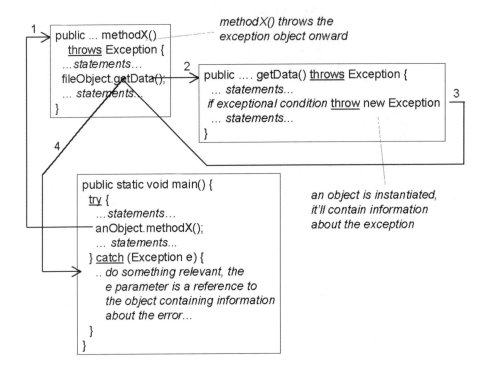

Figure 8.6   `methodX()` receives an exception object from `getData()`, which it sends on to `main()`

Exception handling for beginners

Exception handling is a difficult subject. Beginners need to understand the concept to avoid the error messages that come up during compiling and running. Here's a simple approach for beginners:

- If the compiler says that the exception has to be caught or thrown onwards, it's easiest to throw it onward. Write `throws Exception` in the method head. If that doesn't work (for example, in the `init()` method in an applet),[7] enclose the block that contains the problematic method with `try` and `catch`.

---

7. Why doesn't this work? See the "Java Core" description later on in this chapter.

- If the exception causes the program to stop when it's running, you should try to change the program to avoid that happening (see the examples below).

- The online API documentation covers all the exceptions a method can throw.

We can find information about a specific class of exceptions by looking up the class name in the online API documentation. The exceptions a method throws are also described there.

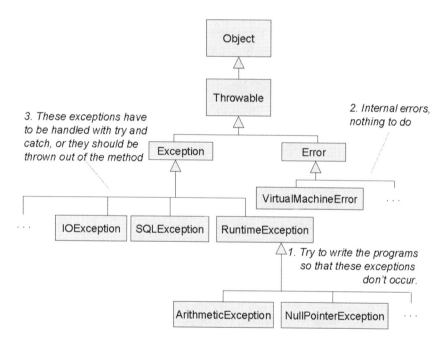

Figure 8.7 Three different types of exceptions (UML)

Exceptions that should not occur in a program

These exceptions are subclasses of RuntimeException and belong to type 1 in Figure 8.7. In most cases it's easy to write programs so that exceptions of this type don't occur.

In chapter 2 we encountered an ArithmeticException, which is thrown, among other reasons, when we try to divide an integer by zero. We avoid this exception with a simple if test:

```
if (number2 != 0) result = number1 / number2;
```

You may also see the message `NullPointerException` on your screen. That means that you're trying to use a reference before you've set it to point to a concrete object. For example:

Suppose we've declared the following instance variable in the `Person` class:

```
private Car myCar;
```

The variable automatically gets the value `null`. If we don't give it some other value (in a constructor, for example), it will still have the value `null` when we do the following inside an instance method:

```
myCar.start();
```

We are trying to send a message to a non-existent object, and that is of course not possible. Thus a `NullPointerException` is thrown.

It's not always easy to program your way around an exception of type 1. For example, in Program Listing 6.5 we instead used the data control in `parseDouble()` and `parseInt()` and let these methods throw an exception object if the text in question cannot be converted into a number.

Problem

What is printed out when the program below runs?

```java
class Problem8_5_1 {
  public static void main(String[] args) {
    try {
      for (int i = 0; i < 5; i++) {
        System.out.println("The value of i: " + i);
        System.out.println(1/i);
      }
    } catch(ArithmeticException e) {
      System.out.println("Division by zero!");
    }

    System.out.println("For-loop no. 2 starts here:");
    for (int i = 0; i < 5; i++) {
      try {
        System.out.println("The value of i: " + i);
        System.out.println(1/i);
      } catch(ArithmeticException e) {
        System.out.println("Division by zero!");
      }
    }
  }
}
```

8.6 Exception Handling in Detail

It may be beneficial to read the rest of this chapter as the need for more advanced exception handling arises.

Three types of exceptions

We can divide exceptions into three groups as shown in the class tree in Figure 8.7. We've already covered group 1, subclasses of `RuntimeException`.

Only rarely will we run into exceptions in group 2, subclasses of `Error`. Normally we don't deal with them since there's little we can do in this type of situation. If they occur, it's usually because of a programming error, for example infinite recursion (Chapter 17).

Group 3, subclasses of `Exception` except for `RuntimeException`, requires a little more thorough treatment. We have not seen any examples up to this point of this type of exception, but in Program Listing 11.1 we have:

```
class MaintainNameArchive {
  public static void main(String[] args) throws Exception {
    ...file handling...
  }
}
```

Here we let the `main()` method throw the exception onwards. In this case, that means that it appears on the screen and the program stops.

We can also write:

```
class MaintainNameArchive {
  public static void main(String[] args) {
    try {
      ...file handling...
    } catch (Exception e) {
      System.out.println("Program aborted: " + e);
    }
  }
}
```

Here we catch the exception. There's not much of a practical difference between this example and the previous. In the latter case, the text "Program aborted: xxxxx" prints out. Then the program stops because there's nothing else to do.

If we compile the example in Program Listing 11.1 without doing anything about the exceptions, we get a lot of compile errors, an example:

```
C:\Temp\ExChap11\MaintainNameArchive.java:13:
unreported exception java.io.FileNotFoundException; must
be caught or declared to be thrown:

FileReader readingConnToFile = new FileReader(filename);
                                                ^
```

The conclusion is that we *have to* do something with exception objects of type 3 in the figure. We have to either catch the exception or throw it out of the method. We should make our decision based on the following guidelines:

- The main() method should catch all exceptions to avoid "ugly" messages on the screen and program abortions. In simple examples and test programs, of course, this is less important.

- Other methods should only catch exceptions that can be handled reasonably. Other exceptions are thrown on so that the client can handle them.

How precise do you have to be when you declare the type of exception?

Figure 8.7 shows the class tree for the Throwable class with subclasses. Remember that in a way the class tree shows sets and subsets of objects. The exceptions we need to worry about belong to the set of exceptions described by the Exception class. Using Exception after throws or as a parameter type for catch will cover all the pertinent types of exceptions.

By indicating the name of a subclass, you're being more specific and therefore excluding other types of exceptions.

If you use multiple catch blocks under each other, you have to be careful to put the most specific one first.

Java Core

try statements

Syntax:

```
try {
    statements
} catch (parameter) {
    statements
} catch (parameter) {
    statements
} finally {
    statements
}
```

Here there's a try block, two catch blocks, and a finally block.

We can have zero, one, or more than one catch blocks as long as the parameter is of a different type. Every catch block has exactly one parameter. The parameter has to be of the Throwable type or one of its subclasses.

The finally block is only needed in specific situations and otherwise can be omitted. The contents of this block are *always* executed, regardless of what happens in the try block. Common uses for the finally block, for example, are closing files or releasing database resources.

What's actually happening?

The statements in the try block are executed. If no exceptions are thrown, the program continues to the contents of any finally block that might be there and then executes the statements after the try statement.

If an exception is thrown in the `try` block, the program control jumps over the rest of the `try` block to the first `catch` block that has a parameter that fits the exception that was thrown. That means that the parameter has to belong to the same class as the exception, or a superclass of this. The contents of this `catch` block are executed. Then the program continues to the contents of any `finally` block that's there and then executes the statements after the `try` statement.

If an exception is thrown in the `try` block, and no `catch` block matches, the contents of any `finally` block are executed before the program control jumps out of the method (with an exception thrown out of the method).

If no `catch` blocks fit the exception, and the exception is also not thrown out of the method, then depending on the type of exception either the compiler protests or the program execution is aborted.[8]

Example 1 (Program Listing 11.2):

```
public static void main(String[] args) {
  String filename = "numberFile.txt";
  try {
    ...establish connection to the file...
    int sum = 0;
    try {
      ...read text from the file...
      ...convert the text into number, and update sum...
    } catch (IOException e) {
      System.out.println("IO-Error when reading from file: " + filename);
    } catch (NumberFormatException e) {
      System.out.println("Error when converting from text to number.");
    }
    ...close the file...
    ...print the sum...
  } catch (FileNotFoundException e) {
    System.out.println("File not found: " + filename);
  } catch (IOException e) { // all other IO errors are caught here
    System.out.println("IO-Error when opening/closing the file: " + filename);
  }
}
```

Example 2 (Program Listing 20.2):

```
public ArrayList getAll() throws SQLException {
  ...some initializations...
  try {
    ...search through the database, exceptions may be thrown out of this method...
  } finally {   // the statements below are executed regardless of exceptions thrown
    ...release database resources, in every case, also if exceptions are thrown...
  }
}
```

---

8. Actually, the running thread is aborted. Other threads continue. More about threads in Chapter 16.

throws specification in a constructor or method head

Syntax:

> throws *class1, class2, ...*

The classes after `throws` have to be `Throwable` or subclasses of it.

Example (Program Listing 11.2, slightly revised):

```
public static void main(String[] args) throws Exception {
  String filename = "numberFile.txt";
  try {
    ...establish connection to the file...
    ...read text from the file...
  } catch (FileNotFoundException e) {
    System.out.println("File not found: " + filename);
  }
}
```

Here, all exceptions other than `FileNotFoundExceptions` are thrown out of `main()`.

If the method is a redefinition of an inherited method, it can't throw any more type 3 exceptions (see Figure 8.7) than the method it redefines. For example, the `Applet` class declares the following method:

> public void init()

For all intents and purposes, the `init()` method in any applet will be a redefinition of this inherited method. We are trying to let the method throw an exception of type 3, then an exception of type 2:

```
public void init() throws IOException { // not ok, results in a compiling error
public void init() throws VirtualMachineError { // ok, but not much point?
```

throw statements

Syntax:

> throw *expression*;

The value of *expression* has to be a reference of the `Throwable` type or a subclass of this class. The statement means that, after any possible `finally` block is executed, the program control will immediately jump out of the method it's in and over the other methods to the first `try` statement that handles the exception in question. If no such `try` block is found, the program control jumps to the end of `main()`, and the program is aborted.

Example (from the source code[9] for the `String` *class):*

```
public char charAt(int index) {
  if ((index < 0) || (index >= count)) {
    throw new StringIndexOutOfBoundsException(index);
  }
  return value[index + offset];
}
```

The `return` statement gets the character in question and returns it.

The parameter in the catch clause of the try statement

This is a parameter, equivalent to a parameter in a method or a constructor. The argument will be a reference to the actual exception object that's thrown, i.e. an instance of a subclass of `Throwable`. This class is described in the API reference below. For example, we often let the program print out the parameter in this way:

```
System.out.println("An error has occurred: " + e);
```

This is the same as:

```
System.out.println("An error has occurred: " + e.toString());
```

`toString()` is a standard name for a method that returns a string that describes the contents of an object. An object name in the `println()` statement will be interpreted such that the `toString()` message is sent to the object and the returned string will be printed out.

API Reference

The java.lang.Throwable class

This class is the superclass of all the exception classes.

All subclasses, according to convention, have two constructors of the same type as the constructors for `Throwable`.

Only a few of the subclasses introduce new methods in addition to the methods that are inherited from the `Throwable` class.

Constructors:

```
public Throwable()
public Throwable(String message)
```

---

9. The *src.jar* file contains the source code for all the classes that come with the SDK. It can be downloaded along with the SDK from Sun's Web pages. The contents of the file can be extracted using, for example, WinZip.

The constructor with the parameter is used if you want to insert a specific message in the exception object.

Methods:

    public String getMessage()

If the object was instantiated with the constructor with a parameter, the message that was inserted is returned, otherwise `null` is returned.

    public String toString()

This method returns a brief description of the exception object. If the object was created with the constructor with a parameter, a string is returned that consists of the name of the class the object is an instance of, followed by a colon and the message that was entered when the object was instantiated. If the object was instantiated with the constructor without parameter list, the name of the class the object is an instance of is returned.

Creating your own exception objects

If the data don't conform to our requirements, we may choose to throw an exception object:

```
try {
  number = InputReader.inputInteger("Enter an integer: ");
  if (number < limitNo1 || number > limitNo2) throw new NumberFormatException();
} catch (NumberFormatException e) {
  System.out.println("Invalid number.");  // or something else
}
```

However, instantiating exception objects with their subsequent handling is a relatively resource-intensive operation, and we should use it with caution. The case above is definitely best solved without throwing an exception:

```
int number = InputReader.inputInteger("Enter an integer: ");
if (number < limitNo1 || number > limitNo2) {
  System.out.println("Invalid number.");  // or something else
}
```

As an example of a situation where it's expedient to instantiate our own exception objects, we will look at an error discovered in a constructor. A constructor cannot return any value and it absolutely should not contain any output. Throwing exceptions is a good way of reporting errors from a constructor.

The Employee class describes an employee with number, name and salary per hour (see Program Listing 8.2). The number should be a four digit number, and there is a minimum rate of $6 per hour. The initial values are sent in as arguments for the constructor. If the number or the salary is invalid, an instance of the IllegalArgumentException class is thrown out of the constructor. In principle, we can use any of the ready-made exception classes, but this one is chosen because it describes the problem fairly well. It's the argument for the constructor that there's something wrong with.

Notice how we insert an appropriate message into the call for the exception object's constructor:

```
if (initSalary < limitSal) {
  throw new IllegalArgumentException("Salary: " + initSalary +
                                "\nThe salary should be at least $" + limitSal);
}
else if (initNumber < limitNo1 || initNumber > limitNo2) {
  throw new IllegalArgumentException("Number: " + initNumber +
          "\nThe number should be in the interval [" + limitNo1 + ", " + limitNo2 + "].");
} else {
  ....
```

The `try-catch` statement in the client program is placed inside the `while` loop, and if the exception is thrown, we get the message on the screen:

```
JOptionPane.showMessageDialog(null, e.getMessage() +
                          "\nStart over again with this employee");
```

Program Listing 8.2

```
/*
 * TestEmployee.java E.L. 2001-08-14
 *
 */
import myLibrary.InputReader;
import javax.swing.JOptionPane;
import java.util.ArrayList;
class Employee {
  private static final int limitNo1 = 1001;  // lower limit, employeeno.
  private static final int limitNo2 = 9999;  // upper limit, employeeno.
  private static final int limitSal = 6;    // minimum salary per hour ($)

  private int number;
  private String name;
  private int salary; // per hour

  public Employee(int initNumber, String initName, int initSalary)
                            throws IllegalArgumentException {
    if (initSalary < limitSal) {
      throw new IllegalArgumentException("Salary: " + initSalary +
                "\nThe salary should be at least $" + limitSal);
    }
    else if (initNumber < limitNo1 || initNumber > limitNo2) {
      throw new IllegalArgumentException("Number: " + initNumber +
          "\nThe number should be in the interval [" + limitNo1 + ", " + limitNo2 + "].");
    } else {
      number = initNumber;
      name = initName;
```

```
        salary = initSalary;
      }
    }
    public int getNumber() {
      return number;
    }
    public String getName() {
      return name;
    }
    public int getSalary() {
      return salary;
    }
    public String toString() {
      return "No. : " + number + ", name: " + name + ", salary: " + salary + "\n";
    }
  }
  class TestEmployee {
    public static void main(String[] args) {
      ArrayList employees = new ArrayList(); // see chapter 10.
      int number = InputReader.inputInteger("Employee no. (0 for exit): ");
      while (number != 0) {
        try {
          String name = InputReader.inputText("Name: ");
          int salary = InputReader.inputInteger("Salary, per hour: ");
          Employee emp = new Employee(number, name, salary);
          employees.add(emp);
        } catch (IllegalArgumentException e) {
          JOptionPane.showMessageDialog(null, e.getMessage() +
                        "\nStart over again with this employee");
        }
        number = InputReader.inputInteger("Employee no. (0 for exit): ");
      }
      System.out.println("Control output:\n");
      for (int i = 0; i < employees.size(); i++) System.out.println(employees.get(i));
      System.exit(0);
    }
  }
```

We can go another step further and create our own exception class. This class can describe the error in question, and it must be a subclass of the Throwable class or of one of the subclasses under Throwable. By letting the class be a subclass of Exception (but not of RuntimeException) we get the compiler to force the client to handle the exception in one way or another. If the exception is an instance of a subclass of RuntimeException (group 1, Figure 8.7), like IllegalArgumentException, handling is not required.

The class can look like this:

```
class InvalidEmployeeException extends Exception {
  public InvalidEmployeeException() {
    super("Invalid employee data");
  }

  public InvalidEmployeeException(String message) {
    super(message);
  }
}
```

Like the other exception classes, it contains two constructors, a constructor with empty parameter list, and a constructor with a string as parameter.

In a class tree, the constructors are called successively up the tree. The constructor that will be used on one level is stated on the level below. If nothing is stated, the constructor with empty parameter list is used. To specify a constructor with parameters, the keyword `super` has to be used followed by a parenthetical statement with the actual arguments. The constructors for `InvalidEmploye-eException` contain `super` with a string as its argument. This means that the equivalent constructor in the `Exception` class is used.

The constructor for the `Employee` class has to be changed to use the new exception class:

```
public Employee(int initNumber, String initName, int initSalary)
                                        throws InvalidEmployeeException {
  if (initSalary < limitSal) {
    throw new InvalidEmployeeException("Salary: " + initSalary +
              "\nThe salary should be at least $" + limitSal);
  }
  else if (initNumber < limitNo1 || initNumber > limitNo2) {
    throw new InvalidEmployeeException("Number: " + initNumber +
        "\nThe number should be in the interval [" + limitNo1 + ", " + limitNo2 + "].");
  } else {
    number = initNumber;
    name = initName;
    salary = initSalary;
  }
}
```

And the equivalent in the client program:

```
try {
  .....
} catch (InvalidEmployeeException e) {
  .....
```

Problems

1. Change the constructor in Program Listing 8.2 in such a way that it handles the case where *both* the number *and* the salary are invalid.

2. (You may solve this problem after you've read chapter 11.) The program in Program Listing 11.2 will abort if it encounters an invalid number. Change the program in such a way that invalid numbers will be skipped. Valid numbers will be summed.

8.7   New Concepts in This Chapter

Concept	Brief Explanation
API	"The specification of how a programmer writing an application accesses the behavior and state of classes and objects" (see [URL Java glossary]).
catch	Keyword that introduces a code block where an exception of a specific type is handled. Part of the try statement.
deprecated	In the API documentation, some methods (and classes) are marked as "deprecated". This means that they are scheduled to be removed in a future version of the SDK. Therefore we shouldn't use these types of methods.
exception	Generally: a condition that can arise during runtime, but that is an aberration from normal. At the same time, most often used in a slightly more specialized meaning, namely about objects which are instances of subclasses of Throwable. These objects contain information about the exception encountered.
finally	Keyword that introduces a code block that is always executed regardless of whether exceptions are thrown or not. Part of the try statement.
format data	To display data in a specific way. Formatting doesn't affect the contents of the variable where the data value is.
location	Language, country, and possibly variant—determines how, for example, numbers and dates will be formatted (see the Locale class).
package	Keyword to indicate that a class belongs to a specific package. The package name has to be the same as the name of the subdirectory where the package is.
throw	Keyword to throw an exception. The program control jumps out of the method (but see finally).
throws	Keyword to throw an exception on, used in the method or constructor head.
try	Keyword that introduces the try statement. The statement starts with a block of instructions where errors can occur.

8.8   Review Problems

1. Why is it important to know the methods and variables that a class inherits?

2. Why shouldn't we use methods that are marked "deprecated"?

3. What do we mean when we say "formatting" data?

4. How do we set the formatting of numbers, dates, etc. so that it will follow, for example, the French standard?

5. Explain how we use the keywords `package` and `import`.

6. What's the purpose of CLASSPATH?

7. What does the concept of an "exception" involve?

8. We should write programs such that some types of exceptions don't occur. Which ones? Name examples.

9. What are the characteristics of the two other types of exceptions?

10. What does the keyword `finally` mean?

8.9 Programming Problems

Problem 1

(Difficult.)
Create a `MyDate` class. Use the `GregorianCalendar` class, possibly the `Date` class (but avoid using the methods that are marked "deprecated").

The `MyDate` class will be immutable and offer the following services:

• A constructor for today's date

• A constructor for a given date

• Create a new date that is equal to this date plus a specific number of days (this number can be negative)

• Compare two dates (before, after, or the same)

• Number of days between two dates

Problem 2

The `String` class contains a great many methods. Now we'll create more.
Create a class called `MyString`. It should have an instance variable of the `String` class. The `MyString` class will be immutable and offer the following services:

• A constructor that takes an instance of the `String` class as an argument

• An abbreviation. The abbreviation will be made by combining the first character in every word. Use a space as the separator between words. For example: "this sentence can be abbreviated" will be abbreviated "tscba." Hint: use a `while` loop and, for example, the `String` methods: `substring()`, `indexOf()`, and `charAt()`.

- Deleting a character. For example: if the character 'e' is removed from the text "this sentence can be abbreviated," then we're left with "this sntnc can b abbrviatd." Hint: use a `while` loop and, for example, the `String` methods `indexOf()` and `substring()`.

Problem 3

Let the `MyString` class from problem 2 contain an instance of the `String-Buffer` class instead. Otherwise, let it offer the same services. Decide for yourself whether the class should be mutable or immutable.

Arrays of Primitive Data Types

Learning goals for this chapter

After completing this chapter, you will understand the following concepts:

- One-dimensional and two-dimensional arrays

- Index, array length, when an index is valid

- Sorting and searching

You will be able to:

- Evaluate when it makes sense to use an array

- Evaluate whether the array should be one- or two-dimensional

- Program different processing routines for the elements in an array, including a simple sorting method

- Program a sequential search in an array

- Use what the `java.util.Arrays` class has to offer

In this chapter, we will look at an easy way to handle large quantities of data of the same type. As an example, we will look at a month's worth of precipitation data and a year's worth of sales data.

A *data structure* is a collection of data that is stored in the internal memory under one name. The data structure for storing lots of data of the same type is called an array. An object is also a data structure. In an array, the individual data elements are numbered, whereas in an object they have name (the name of the instance variables).

The data in an array can be of any data type. In this chapter, we will limit ourselves to the primitive data types.

9.1   What is an Array?

Suppose we're going to write a program that handles precipitation data. We will store the number of millimeters of rain for each day, and calculate the maximum, minimum, and average. Let's look at the precipitation that falls over the course of a month. The `Month` class might look like the one shown in Figure 9.1. The `precipitation` attribute has 28–31 values depending on the number of days in the month.

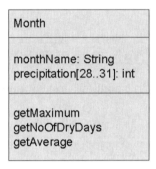

Month
monthName: String precipitation[28..31]: int
getMaximum getNoOfDryDays getAverage

Figure 9.1   The month class (UML)

How should we set up the instance variables?

```
private String monthName;
private int precipitation1;
private int precipitation2;
private int precipitation3;
private int precipitation4;
    .....
private int precipitation31;
```

is a possibility. Of course, this is extremely tiresome and especially so when you go to find, for example, the largest value (how many `if` statements will this require?).

Storing and handling many data values of the same type is such a common task in programming that almost all programming languages provide the *array* mechanism. An array is specially created to make it easy to store and work with data of one type.

Figure 9.2 shows an array of integers. The array is called `march`, and it has a *length* of 31. That means that it's divided into 31 *elements*. Every element is a storage location for a numerical value of the `int` type. The data type for the array is `int[]`. The elements are numbered according to the position they have in the array. The first element is numbered 0, the last, 30. This number is called the *index* for the element.

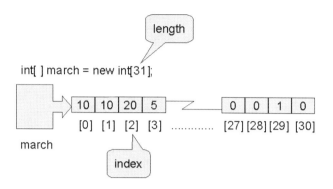

Figure 9.2 An array of precipitation data for march

As shown in the figure, the name of an array is a reference. And the array itself is an object with special characteristics. The statement

```
int[] march = new int[31]; // note the square brackets!
```

declares the array `march` and reserves room for 31 integers. Just as with ordinary objects, it's possible to declare the array without reserving space. Space can be reserved when you know how large an array is needed:

```
int[] month;   // months have different lengths
month = new int[31];
```

We can use every single element in the array as if it were an individual variable of the `int` type. The name of the element is the array name followed by its index in square brackets. To begin with, all the elements have a value of 0. This is true both if the array is a local variable and if it's an instance variable. (For simple variables, the zero setting will not apply if they're local.) We can assign an individual element a specific value, for example:

```
march[0] = 20; // 20 mm of precipitation on the first day of the month
march[15] = 0; // no precipitation on the 16th of the month
march[30] = 10; // 10 mm of precipitation on the last day (31st) of the month

int oneDay = march[15]; // the precipitation for March 16th is stored in the variable oneDay
int sum = march[0] + march[1] + march[2]; // compute the total rainfall for March 1st-3rd
```

It's important for the index to be valid. Invalid indices are meaningless. In this example, a valid index has one of the values 0, 1, 2, 3, ..., 30. If there's any doubt about the validity of the index, we have to test it with an `if` statement. If the program discovers that we're trying to use an invalid index, it throws an `ArrayIndexOutOfBoundsException` and then stops.

The following lines print out the precipitation on the different days of the month:

```
for (int i = 0; i < 31; i++) {
    System.out.println("Precipitation on March " + (i + 1) + "th was " + march[i] + " mm.");
}
```

This is a counter-controlled loop, where i is the counter. It is very common to use names like i, j, k, etc. for counters that are indices in arrays. It is important to remember that the array index is one smaller than the number of the day so we use (i + 1) in the print statement. Notice that we need to put parentheses around the expression so that it's interpreted before being combined with the string. Suppose that i is equal to 3, and that march[i] is equal to 10. Then the statement

```
System.out.println("Precipitation on March " + i + 1 + "th was " + march[i] + " mm.");
```

will print

```
Precipitation on March 31th was 10 mm.
```

With the parentheses around the expression i + 1, it will be calculated first and the printout will be:

```
Precipitation on March 4th was 10 mm.
```

As mentioned above, an array is an object with special characteristics. A public constant, length, is always declared. This denotes the length of the array. We usually use this instead of an anonymous or named constant to indicate the length. The length of an array cannot be changed once the array is created.

The index for the first element in an array is always equal to 0. This makes standardized formulations of, for example, if tests and for loops possible:

```
if (index >= 0 && index < array.length) {   // valid index
for (int i = 0; i < array.length; i++) {  // sequential handling of all the elements in the array
```

If, through communication with the user, we instead want to number them starting with, for example, 1, we insert this in the background texts for the user. For example:

```
System.out.println("The number of pupils in the  " + (i + 1) + "th grade is " + noOfPupils[i]);
```

We can input precipitation data as follows (with InputReader from chap. 6.8):

```
for (int i = 0; i < march.length; i++) {
    march[i] =
        InputReader.inputInteger("No. of mm on March " + (i + 1) + "th: ");
}
```

Notice that this loop also works if the array is empty (i.e., when march.length equals 0). Then the loop body won't be executed at all.

It's possible to initialize an array directly:

    int[] oneWeek = {12, 0, 13, 12, 10, 0, 0};

The length of the array will be indicated by the number of values in the curly braces. An array element that has received a value this way can, like other array elements, be changed later in the program:

    oneWeek[2] = 5;

Java Core

The data structure array

Syntax:

> *dataType*[] *name*;
> *name* = new *dataType*[*length*];

or:

> *dataType*[] *name* = new *dataType*[*length*];

or:

> *dataType*[] *name* = {*initialValue0*, *initialValue1*, *initialValue2*, ...};

In the last case, `initialValueN` is the start value for an element with the index N. The length of the array will be equal to the number of values in the curly braces.

If the array is not explicitly initialized this way, all the elements receive a start value of 0.

The `dataType` can be any data type. Reference types are covered in the next chapter.

`length` has to have the data type `int`, or a type that can be automatically converted to `int` (in other words `short`, `byte`, or `char`). The data type `long` is not allowed here.

The elements in the array are numbered from 0 to `length` - 1. This number is called the element's index.

The same requirements apply to the index's data type as for the data type for `length`. If the index is invalid (less than 0 or >= length) an `ArrayIndex-OutOfBoundsException` is thrown.

An array element can be used wherever a simple variable of the same type can be used.

An array is an object and has a public constant (`public final`) named `length`, which indicates the array's length.

Examples:

    final int noOfClasses = 10;
    int[] noOfPupils = new int[noOfClasses];

```
noOfPupils[2]++; // a new pupil in the 3rd grade
noOfPupils[5] -= 2;  // two fewer pupils in the 6th grade

int sum = 0;
for (int i =0; i < noOfPupils.length; i++) { // sum of all the pupils
  sum += noOfPupils[i];
}
```

If possible, we should wait to set aside room for the array until we know how large it's going to be. If that's not possible, we have to create an array that is large enough and then keep track of how much of the array is full. However, it's often hard to know how large "large enough" is. The result may be that we have to set aside quite a bit of room and risk this space not being used.

A better solution is to use something called array lists. This is a type of array that expands as needed. We will look at array lists in the next chapter.

Problems

1. (a) Create an array that will have room to store the number of days in every month. Assign values to all the array elements by initialization. The number of days in February is set to equal 28.

   (b) Write code that asks the user if it's a leap year. If it is, the number of days in February should be set to equal 29.

2. Create an array of the data type char. It should be initialized with the values 'A,' 'N,' 'N,' 'E'. Write program code that prints these values out in the opposite order.

3. The integer array myArray is initialized with the values: 3, 8, -5, 5, 6, 0, 3, -2, 8, 9.

   Then the following statements are executed:

   ```
   myArray[2] = myArray[6] + 5;
   int a = myArray[8];
   myArray[7] = a + myArray[0] * myArray[0];
   myArray[4] = myArray[4] + 1;
   myArray[5] = myArray[3] + myArray[9];
   myArray[3] = myArray[2*myArray[0]];
   ```

   Now what are the contents of the array?

9.2 Copying Arrays

We declare and initialize two arrays:

```
int[] array1 = {1, 4, 6, -2};
int[] array2 = {7, 14, -6, 0};
```

Then we try to set `array2` equal to `array1`:

    array2 = array1;

What happens? Since arrays are objects, `array1` and `array2` will be references. Now we've got two references to the same array. The array that `array2` originally pointed to is no longer accessible (see Figure 9.3).

We can copy element by element using a `for` statement (see Figure 9.4):

    for (int i = 0; i < array1.length; i++) {
      array1[i] = array2[i];
    }

This presupposes that `array1` is not longer than `array2`. Whole arrays or parts of arrays can also be copied using the class method `arraycopy()` that is described below (see Figure 9.5).

API Reference

The java.lang.System class

Method:

    public static void arraycopy(Object fromArray, int fromIndex, Object toArray,
                                 int toIndex, int number)

The first two parameters indicate the array to be copied from and the start index for the copying. The next two parameters indicate the array that will be copied to and the start index for where the data will be placed. The last parameter indicates the number of values that will be copied.

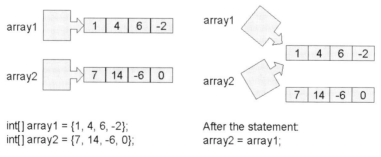

```
int[] array1 = {1, 4, 6, -2};
int[] array2 = {7, 14, -6, 0};
```

After the statement:
array2 = array1;

Figure 9.3 Setting `array2 = array1` means that we get two references to the same array

```
int[] array1 = {1, 4, 6, -2};
int[] array2 = {7, 14, -6, 0};
```

Copying each element:

```
for (int i = 0; i < array1.length; i++) {
    array1[i] = array2[i];
}
```

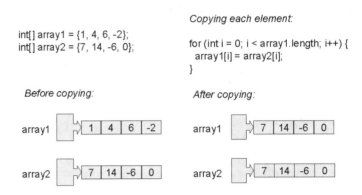

Before copying: *After copying:*

Figure 9.4 Copying an array element by element

```
int[] array1 = {1, 4, 6, -2};
int[] array2 = {7, 14, -6, 0};
```

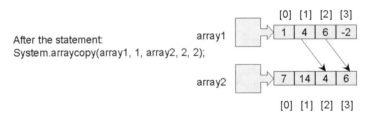

After the statement:
System.arraycopy(array1, 1, array2, 2, 2);

Figure 9.5 The contents of an array can be copied to another array using `System.array-copy()`

Problems

1. `array1` and `array2` are given as at the top of Figure 9.5. Set up a `for` loop that copies the contents from `array1` to `array2`, but so that the values in `array2` end up in the reverse order from `array1`. In other words, after copying, `array2` will contain the values in the following order: -2, 6, 4, 1.

2. Use the online API documentation and find out what exceptions `arraycopy()` can throw. Which of these should you prevent from happening? And how do you do that?

3. We can use `arraycopy()` to shift elements internally in an array. What is printed out when you run the following?

```
char[] month1 = {'S', 'e', 'p', 't', 'e', 'm', 'b', 'e', 'r'};
char[] month2 = {'N', 'o', 'v', 'e', 'm', 'b', 'e', 'r'};
System.arraycopy(month2, 0, month1, 0, 3);
System.arraycopy(month1, 4, month1, 3, 5);
for (int i = 0; i < month1.length; i++) System.out.print(month1[i]);
System.out.println();
char[] month3 = {'M', 'M', 'M', 'a', 'y'};
System.arraycopy(month3, 2, month3, 0, 3);
for (int i = 0; i < month3.length; i++) System.out.print(month3[i]);
System.out.println();
```

9.3 The Month Class for Precipitation Data

We will create the Month class with operations for precipitation statistics. The class diagram is shown in Figure 9.1. The program code with several more methods than are shown in the diagram is reproduced in Program Listing 9.1.

We have the month and an array of rainfall data as instance variables. This array gets the right size and contents in the constructor. As an argument for the constructor, we have an array created in the client program. We let every single instance of the Month class get its own array of rainfall data. To give other objects access to the rainfall data, we've created methods that find the number of days (the length of the array) and the precipitation on a given day (index). If the client inputs an invalid index for the last method, -1 is returned.

Let's look at the method getMaximum(). The local variable max will contain the maximum value. After checking that the array has a length larger than zero, we start by setting max equal to the first element in the array:

```
max = precipitation[0];
```

Then we run through the rest of the array:

```
for (int i = 1; i < precipitation.length; i++)
```

Every time we find an element that's larger than max, this becomes max's new value:

```
if (precipitation[i] > max) max = precipitation[i];
```

The getAverage() method adds up all the rainfall and finally divides by the length of the array (= number of days). Note that you have to check that the length of the array is not equal to zero to avoid dividing by zero. Since both sum and the length of the array are integers, we have to make sure to convert at least one of them so that integer division doesn't take place. An average should be a decimal numeral.

There's not much to say about the getNoOfDryDays() method. Remember to zero number!

The getDaysMax() method is somewhat more complex. This method will find out which days had rainfall equal to the maximum value. We start by calling getMaximum() to find the maximum value. Then we run through all the precipitation days to find out which days had this amount of precipitation. But that's not enough—we also have to store these days. For example: if we have a maximum precipitation on the days with indices 0, 5, and 17, these indices have to be stored. We create an integer array with the same size as the precipitation array. Theoretically, in the worst conceivable case, all the days will have precipitation that equals the maximum value. Then we'll run in a loop and check every individual precipitation value against the maximum value. If they are equal, we take note of the *index* and increase noOfMax by 1.

It is important that the client receives an array of the right size. We do this by creating a new array, the maxDays array, and copying over the data.

It's possible to engineer this in other and more efficient ways, but the method shown here is probably the most "straightforward." Here we see what problems come up when we don't know the exact size of the array we need in advance. These problems are elegantly solved in the java.util.ArrayList class (chapter 10).

At the very end of the program listing we find a short test program. Notice that the class is tested for arrays with lengths of 0 and 1, as well as for an array with a more "normal" length. Instead of a length of 30, we've used a length of 5, which is a much more manageable array size for testing.

Program Listing 9.1

```
/*
 * PrecipitationStatistics.java   E.L. 2001-08-14
 *
 */
class Month {
  private String monthName;
  private int[] precipitation;

  /*
   * The constructor makes a copy of the precipitation data.
   * The client may therefore use the same data structure to hold data
   * for other months. Every one instance of the Month class holds
   * its own precipitation data, independent of the client's data.
   * (See Section 7.3).
   */
  public Month(String initMonthName, int[] initPrecipitation) {
    monthName = initMonthName;
    int noOfDays = initPrecipitation.length;
    precipitation = new int[noOfDays];
    for (int i = 0; i < noOfDays; i++) precipitation[i] = initPrecipitation[i];
  }

  public String getMonthName() {
    return monthName;
  }
```

```java
public int getNoOfDays() {
  return precipitation.length;
}
/*
 * The method returns the precipitation for one special day.
 * Returns -1 if invalid index.
 */
public int getPrecipitation(int index) {
  if (index >= 0 && index < precipitation.length) return precipitation[index];
  else return -1;  // invalid index
}
/*
 * The method returns the maximal rainfall in one day in the month.
 */
public int getMaximum() {
  int max = 0;  // Remember: Local variables always have to be given a value.
  if (precipitation.length > 0) {
    max = precipitation[0];
    for (int i = 1; i < precipitation.length; i++) {
      if (precipitation[i] > max) max = precipitation[i];
    }
  }
  return max;
}
/*
 * The method returns the average daily precipitation in the month.
 */
public double getAverage() {
  int sum = 0;
  for (int i = 0; i < precipitation.length; i++) {
    sum += precipitation[i];
  }
  if (precipitation.length > 0) return (double) sum / (double) precipitation.length;
  else return 0.0;
}
/*
 * The method returns the number of days without raining.
 */
public int getNoOfDryDays() {
  int number = 0;
  for (int i = 0; i < precipitation.length; i++) {
    if (precipitation[i] == 0) number++;
  }
  return number;
}
```

```java
/*
 * The method returns an array holding the indices of days
 * with precipitation equal to the maximum precipitation.
 */
public int[] getDaysMax() {
  int max = getMaximum();

  /* Prepare for the worst;
     we create an array with room for all the days in the month. */
  int [] array = new int[precipitation.length];
  int noOfMax = 0;
  for (int i = 0; i < precipitation.length; i++) {
    if (precipitation[i] == max) {
      array[noOfMax] = i;
      noOfMax++;
    }
  }
  /* Now we create an array with correct size, and copy the data */
  int[] maxDays = new int[noOfMax];
  for (int i = 0; i < noOfMax; i++) maxDays[i] = array[i];
  return maxDays;
  }
}


class PrecipitationStatistics {
  public static void main(String[] args) {
    int[] precipitation = {1, 4, 0, 4, 3};  // a very short month for testing
    /*int[] precipitation = {};  // We have tested with arrays of
     *int[] precipitation = {1}; // length 0 and 1, too. */
    Month oneMonth = new Month("January", precipitation);
    System.out.println("Statistics " + oneMonth.getMonthName());
    System.out.println("Maximum: " + oneMonth.getMaximum());
    System.out.println("Average: " + oneMonth.getAverage());
    System.out.println("No. of dry days: " + oneMonth.getNoOfDryDays());

    for (int i = 0; i < oneMonth.getNoOfDays(); i++) {
      System.out.println("Precipitation day no. " + (i + 1) + ": "
        + oneMonth.getPrecipitation(i));
    }

    int[] maxDays = oneMonth.getDaysMax();
    for (int i = 0; i < maxDays.length; i++) {
      System.out.println("Max. precipitation day no.: " + (maxDays[i] + 1));
    }
  }
}
/* Example Run:
Statistics January
Maximum: 4
```

```
Average: 2.4
No. of dry days: 1
Precipitation day no. 1: 1
Precipitation day no. 2: 4
Precipitation day no. 3: 0
Precipitation day no. 4: 4
Precipitation day no. 5: 3
Max. precipitation day no.: 2
Max. precipitation day no.: 4
*/
```

Problems

You will write several more methods for the `Month` class. They will be tested by expanding the client program.

1. Create a method that finds the total number of days with precipitation equal to the maximum.

2. Create a method that finds the number of days when it rained less than a given number of millimeters. This number will be a parameter.

3. Create a method that finds the average deviation from the mean value (standard deviation). You may have to look the formula up in a statistics book.

9.4   Sorting

Sorting an array means putting the elements in order depending on their size. We distinguish between *ascending sorts*, where the smallest value comes first and the largest last, and *descending sorts*, where the largest comes first.

As examples of the need for sorting data, we can mention ranking the participants in a competition, sorting names in a telephone directory, and ranking cities according to the price of local services.

We assume that there is room in the internal memory for the whole array which will be sorted. As elsewhere in the chapter, we will limit ourselves to data belonging to a primitive data type—in other words, numbers or characters (the numeric characters '0'–'9' and the letters 'a'–'z'). Sorting names, for example, will mean that we have to sort instances of the `String` class.

Sorting an array often means that you have to compare the values of the individual elements and let them change places until all the elements are in the right order. Now let's look at an algorithm for the sorting method "Sorting by selection."

In this method, we choose an element and place it in the right spot in the array. We can summarize this algorithm as follows:

```
for (start = 0; start < array.length; start++) {
    find the index for the smallest element in the interval [start, array.length - 1]
```

replace smallest element with the element in the start position
}

Follow along in Figure 9.6. Remember that the positions in the array are numbered starting with 0. The first time, `start` will equal 0. Then we'll search through the whole array for the smallest element. We find the number -5 in position 2. This changes place with the first one. Now we're done with the first element. The small end of the array is sorted. In the next run through the loop, `start` will equal 1. We search through the rest of the array and find that -2 in position 7 is the smallest. That trades place with the element in the position with the index `start`. Now the first two elements are in the right place. Continue in this manner until you think you've got the knack of it. The vertical line marks how much of the array is already sorted.

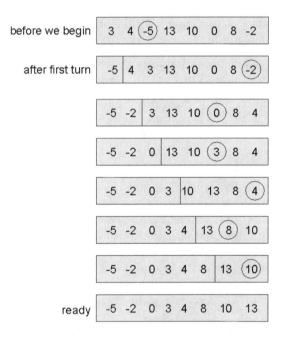

Figure 9.6　Sorting by Selection

The algorithm in more detail:

1. Details on "find the index for the smallest element in the interval [start, array.length - 1]".

Earlier we looked at how to find the largest element in an array (the `getMaximum()` method in Program Listing 9.1). Now we'll find the index for the smallest element, not in the whole array, but starting from the `start` index. The principle is the same as in Program Listing 9.1. We store the index for the smallest element in the variable `smallestToNow`. We start by setting this to equal `start` and then going through the rest of the array to find any elements that might be smaller:

```
int smallestToNow = start;
for (int i = start + 1; i < array.length; i++) {
  if (array[i] < array[smallestToNow]) smallestToNow = i;
}
```

2. Details on "replace smallest element with the element in the `start` position."

We exchange the contents of the two variables. To accomplish this, we have to use an auxiliary variable for store-and-forward:

```
int help = array[smallestToNow];
array[smallestToNow] = array[start];
array[start] = help;
```

Program listing 9.2 shows the sorting algorithm programmed as a class method. It's in the `Sort` class in the `myLibrary` package (see Section 8.2). It's being created as a class method so that we can use it if we need to sort an array of numbers, regardless of the class the array belongs to.

The following little program shows how the `Sort()` method is used:

```
import myLibrary.*;
class TestSort {
  public static void main(String[] args) {
    int[] test = {3, 4, -5, 13, 10, 0, 8, -2, 22, 15, 11, 9, 17};
    Sort.sortIntegerArray(test);
    System.out.println("Sorted array: ");
    for (int i = 0; i < test.length; i++) System.out.print(test[i] + " ");
    System.out.println();
  }
}
```

What happens when the `sortIntegerArray()` method is called? When we enter the method, the `array` parameter will point to the same array object as `test` in the client program. Giving a new value inside the method by permutating the individual elements in `array` has direct consequences for the `test` array in the client program because we actually are dealing with one array (see Figure 9.7).

Program Listing 9.2

```
/*
 * Sort.java  E.L. 2001-08-14
 *
 */
package myLibrary;
public class Sort {
  public static void sortIntegerArray(int[] array) {
```

```
for (int start = 0; start < array.length; start++) {
  int smallestToNow = start;
  for (int i = start + 1; i < array.length; i++) {
    if (array[i] < array[smallestToNow]) smallestToNow = i;
  }
  int help = array[smallestToNow];
  array[smallestToNow] = array[start];
  array[start] = help;
}
}
/* This class consists of two more methods, see chapter 10. */
}
```

Method invocation:
Sort.sortIntegerArray(test);

What's happening behind
the scenes:
int[] array$_{sortIntegerArray}$ = test$_{client}$

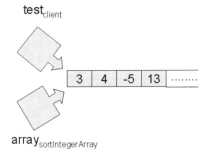

Figure 9.7   An array as an argument gives the method a reference to the array object that belongs to the client

What if we wanted to sort decimal numerals? We would have to write a sorting method where the parameter is of the `double[]` type and the `help` variable is of the `double` type. The same applies to other primitive data types. Luckily this has been done for us and with a much more efficient sorting algorithm than the one covered here. Later in the chapter, we'll look at what the `java.util.Arrays` class has to offer.

Problems

1. Change the `sortIntegerArray()` method so that it sorts the numbers in descending order.

2. Write a class method that takes an array as an argument and that returns a sorted version of this array, but such that all duplicates are removed.

3. Create a class method that takes two equally long arrays as arguments. The method will create a new array where every element is equal to the sum of the corresponding elements in the two arrays. The method will return the new array. If the arrays are not the same length, the value `null` will be returned.

9.5 Searching

Searching in an array means finding the element or elements that satisfy specific criteria. For example, we indicate a value and go to find the index for the element or elements that have this value. We also have to consider the possibility that this value may not be found at all. Sometimes it's enough to find one occurrence of the value; at other times we have to find all occurrences.

In Program Listing 9.1 there are two search examples:

- The `getNoOfDryDays()` method searches for the value 0. It counts the number of times this value occurs.

- The `getDaysMax()` method finds the indices for all the occurrences of a specific value.

The traditional search problem is searching for a specific value. We expand the `Month` class with a method that finds the index for a day on which there was a specific amount of precipitation (although this method may not be of much practical use):

```
public int getDay(int value) {
  for (int i = 0; i < precipitation.length; i++) {
    if (precipitation[i] == value) return i;      // value found
  }
  return -1; // value not found
}
```

If the value is not found, we have to tell the client this. We do that by returning a negative value. This is meaningful here because an index never has a negative value. If the array is sorted, we can stop the search as soon as the values are larger than or equal to the one we're searching for.

In the search we immediately exit the `for` loop when the value is found. We should avoid immediately exiting loops in long methods (for example, more than 10 lines). That can make the method difficult to read. It's best if we can divide large methods up into several smaller ones. If that's not possible, we should formulate the condition to avoid exiting abruptly. Let's look at two alternative formulations of the search above.

To avoid exiting abruptly, we include the exit condition as part of the loop condition. We can still use the `for` statement, but the condition is no longer linked to only a counter, and it makes just as much sense to use a `while` statement:

```
int dayNo = 0;
while (dayNo < precipitation.length && precipitation[dayNo] != value) dayNo++;
if (dayNo < precipitation.length) {
   ...do what should be done if the value is found...
} else {
   ...do what should be done if the value is not found..
}
```

The condition contains a boolean expression that consists of two comparisons. The order of these comparisons is important. We check first that the index is valid (dayNo < precipitation.length), then we use the index. This works because Java uses short-circuit evaluation (see Section 5.6) when calculating the condition. If the first part is false, the second part won't be computed at all. (precipitation[dayNo] with an invalid index will throw an ArrayIndexOutOfBoundsException.)

Sometimes the search condition is so complicated that it's a good idea to introduce a boolean variable that keeps track of when the value is found:

```
boolean found = false;
int dayNo = 0;
while (dayNo < precipitation.length && !found) {
  if (precipitation[dayNo] == value) found = true;
  else dayNo++;  // increase only if not found
}
if (found) {
  ...do what should be done if the value is found...
} else {
  ...do what should be done if the value is not found...
}
```

In the next section, we'll look at the search methods available in the java.util.Arrays class.

Problems

1. Create a class method that searches for a specific value in an integer array. Assume that the numbers in the array are sorted in ascending order. The method will return the index for the value. If the value doesn't exist, -1 is returned. Use return from the loop body.

2. Program the method in problem 1 without using return from the loop body. The return statement should be at the very end of the method.

9.6   The java.util.Arrays Class

This class contains a number of class methods for handling arrays of various types. They assume that the array is full of data. If it isn't, we have to create a new array of the correct length and copy the data over. We've already seen an example of this in the getDaysMax() method in Program Listing 9.1, where array is the array that isn't full:

```
int[] maxDays = new int[noOfMax];  // maxDays is the new array with the correct length
for (int i = 0; i < noOfMax; i++) maxDays[i] = array[i];  // copies from array to maxDays
```

java.util.Arrays uses a well-known algorithm called quick-sort as a sorting method (see for example [Weiss 1998]).

The search method is called binary search, and it requires the array to be sorted beforehand. Binary search works like this: in a sorted array we know that small values are at the beginning of the array and large values at the end. If we compare the value of the middle element with the one we're searching for, we can find out if what we're searching for is in the first or last half of the array. Then we can just forget about the half of the array that the element is not in. Then we evaluate the value of the middle element in the half that is still of interest and again rule out the half that does not contain the element. We continue like this until we either get to the element we're looking for or there are no elements left, in which case we can establish that the value isn't there.

API Reference

The java.util.Arrays class

Methods that take an index interval as their argument only operate on this part of the array. The other methods operate on the whole array.

Here we'll only look at methods for the primitive data types, in other words `byte`, `char`, `short`, `int`, `long`, `float`, or `double`.

Class methods:

> public static int binarySearch(*dataType*[] array, *dataType* searchValue)

The method presuppose that the array is sorted. It returns the index for an element with the value equal to the `searchValue`. If multiple elements have values equal to the search value, there is no clear definition of which one the method will return the index for.

If the value is not present in the array, the return value will tell us which position the value should have in the array in order for it to remain sorted. If we put the value that is returned in the `index` variable, the position will be equal to (-`index` - 1).

An example: Given the array {-5, -2, 0, 3, 4, 4, 4, 8, 9, 11, 11}. We search for the value 7. This value is not in the array, and the method returns -8. Thus the value 7 should be inserted at position (-(-8)-1) which is equal to 7. And this is correct. The resulting array is:{-5, -2, 0, 3, 4, 4, 4, 7, 8, 9, 11, 11}.

> public static boolean equals(*dataType*[] array1, *dataType*[] array2)

This method compares two arrays with elements of the same type. The method returns `true` if the arrays are equal in length, and `array1[i]` is equal to `array2[i]` for all pertinent i. Otherwise, the method returns `false`.

> public static void fill(*dataType*[] array, *dataType* value)
> public static void fill(*dataType*[] array, int fromIndex, int toIndex, *dataType* value)

These methods set a specific value for all the elements in the entire array or for portions of an array (from `fromIndex` inclusive to `toIndex` exclusive). For example: `Arrays.fill(array, 3, 7, 14)` gives the value 14 to the elements with indices 3, 4, 5, 6. If `toIndex == fromIndex`, no elements will receive values. The methods throw exceptions:

- `ArrayIndexOutOfBoundsException` if `fromIndex` or `toIndex` is less than 0 or greater than `array.length`

- `IllegalArgumentException` if `fromIndex > toIndex`

  These exceptions should be avoided with necessary tests before the method call.

  ```
  public static void sort(dataType[] array)
  public static void sort(dataType[] array, int fromIndex, int toIndex)
  ```

These methods sort the entire array or parts of an array (from `fromIndex` inclusive to `toIndex` exclusive).

The method throws exceptions under the same conditions as the `fill()` method.

Problems

1. Write a program that tests both of the `fill()` methods. Remember to check the indices before calling the second of the two methods.

2. The `binarySearch()` method returns a negative value if the value you're searching for doesn't exist. It indicates where this value would have been in the array (see the API reference above). What do you have to do to get this value into that place in the array? Write code that does this.

9.7 Two-Dimensional Arrays

Let's look at sales data for a department in a business. Sales data for every day for one year (52 weeks, 5 days per week) can be presented as shown in Table 9.1.

Table 9.1   Sales data for every day for one year

	Day 0	Day 1	Day 2	Day 3	Day 4
Week 0	100	200	150	210	300
Week 1	230	200	160	300	450
Week 2	120	210	180	400	
Week 3					
Week 4					
Week 5					
......					
Week 51					

The possible operations for a sales object might be:

- Register a new sales number

- Find the sales for a given day

- Find the sales for a given week

- Find the total sales for a given day of the week

- Find the most profitable day of the week on average over the course of the whole year

- Find the total sales for the whole year

In computer contexts, we call the arrays we've seen up to this point *one-dimensional*. We can store the array layout above in a data structure that we call a *two-dimensional array*. A two-dimensional array is an array that consists of a series of one-dimensional arrays. The sales data can be stored in 52 one-dimensional arrays (i.e., an array for each week).

Figure 9.8 shows a two-dimensional array of sales data where we've restricted ourselves to four weeks. We create a two-dimensional array in the following manner (example):

```
int[][] sales = new int[4][5];
```

Every line is viewed as a one-dimensional array with the following name:

```
sales[0]
sales[1]
sales[2]
sales[3]
```

As we now know, we can access an element in a one-dimensional array by putting the index after the array name. An element with the index 3 in the `sales[1]` array is therefore accessed as `sales[1][3]`. We can use these elements the same way we use a simple variable of the same data type:

```
sales[1][3] = 400;
int theSale = sales[0][4];
int sum = sales[3][0] + sales[3][1];
```

The two-dimensional array at the figure can be initialized as follows:

```
int[ ][ ] sales = {{100, 200, 150, 210, 300}, {230, 200, 160, 300, 450},
                   {120, 210, 180, 400, 120}, {300, 310, 250, 240, 200}};
```

The data in each line is placed in curly braces, separated by commas. The lines are separated by commas and the whole thing is enclosed in an outer pair of curly braces.

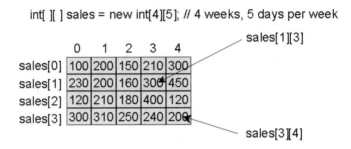

Figure 9.8   A Two-Dimensional Array with Four Lines and Five Columns

Program Listing 9.3 shows the `Sales` class with the operations mentioned above implemented. In the problems at the end of this section, you will create a client program that works with an instance of this class. You will also create some more methods.

Program Listing 9.3

```java
/*
 * Sales.java   E.L. 2001-08-14
 *
 */
class Sales {
  private String department;
  private int[][] theSales;

public Sales(String initDepartment, int noOfWeeks, int noOfDays) {
  department = initDepartment;
  theSales = new int[noOfWeeks][noOfDays];
}

public String getDepartment() {
  return department;
}

public int getNoOfWeeks() {
  return theSales.length;
}

public int getNoOfDaysPerWeek() {
  if (theSales.length > 0) { // no of weeks
    return theSales[0].length;
  }
```

```
    return -1;  // no data
}
/*
 * Three utility methods to control the index validity.
 * These methods are of no interest for the clients,
 * therefore they are made private.
 */
private boolean validWeekNo(int weekNo) {
  if (weekNo >= 0 && weekNo < theSales.length) return true;
  else return false;
}

private boolean validDayNo(int weekNo, int dayNo) {
  if (theSales.length > 0 // at least one week has to be registered
     && dayNo >= 0 && dayNo < theSales[weekNo].length) return true;
  else return false;
}

private boolean validIndices(int weekNo, int dayNo) {
  if (validWeekNo(weekNo) && validDayNo(weekNo, dayNo)) return true;
  else return false;
}
/*
 * The method registers the sales for a given day.
 */
public boolean setSales(int weekNo, int dayNo, int newSales) {
   if (validIndices(weekNo, dayNo)) {
   theSales[weekNo][dayNo] = newSales;
   return true;
 } else return false;  // return false if invalid day or week
}
/*
 * The method gets the sales for a given day.
 */
public int getSales(int weekNo, int dayNo) {
   if (validIndices(weekNo, dayNo)) {
     return theSales[weekNo][dayNo];
 } else return -1;  // return -1 if invalid day or week
}
public int getSalesForAWeek(int weekNo) {
 if (validWeekNo(weekNo)) {
   int sum = 0;
   for (int i = 0; i < theSales[weekNo].length; i++) {
     sum += theSales[weekNo][i];
   }
   return sum;
 } else return -1;  // return -1 if invalid weekNo
}
```

```
public int getSalesForAWeekDay(int dayNo) {
  if (validDayNo(0, dayNo)) {
    int sum = 0;
    for (int i = 0; i < theSales.length; i++) {
      sum += theSales[i][dayNo];
    }
    return sum;
  }
  return -1;   // either no data, or invalid day
}
public int getTotalSales() {
  int sum = 0;
  for (int i = 0; i < theSales.length; i++) {
    for (int j = 0; j < theSales[i].length; j++) {
      sum += theSales[i][j];
    }
  }
  return sum;
}

  public int getMostProfitDay() {
    if (theSales.length > 0) {
      int mostProfitToDay = 0;
      int sumMaxSales = getSalesForAWeekDay(0);
      for (int i = 1; < theSales[i].length; i++) {
        int theSales = getSalesForAWeekDay(i);
        if (theSales > sumMaxSales) {
          mostProfitToDay = i;
          sumMaxSales = theSales;
        }
      }
      return mostProfitToDay;
    }
    return -1; // no data
  }
}
```

Now we'll go through some of the methods in Program Listing 9.3.

As opposed to the Month class, the Sales class is mutable. The constructor in the Month class took the entire rainfall array as its argument. It made a copy of it, and after that no client could change these values.

The constructor in the Sales class sets up the array, but doesn't put any values in. That means that the default value 0 is entered for all the values in the array. Then the client uses the setSales() method to register sales for a specific day in a specific week.

The class contains private methods to check valid indices. The methods are called validWeekNo(), validDayNo(), and validIndices(). In a class that manages arrays, we need to constantly check that the indices used are valid.

Instead of repeating this test multiple times, we created methods that are called when such a test is needed. A client has no interest in these methods, so we've made them private. In these methods we also see how `length` is used in conjunction with a two-dimensional array. The number of lines (in other words, the number of one-dimensional arrays in the `sales` array) is given by `sales.length`. The length of the line with the index `weekNo` is `sales[weekNo].length`. All the lines have the same length. In the next example, we'll see that the lines can have different lengths.

Various kinds of errors may occur in many of the methods. The methods return `false` or a negative value if this happens.

Notice the similarities and differences between the `getSalesForAWeek()` and `getSalesForAWeekDay()` methods. The former method adds up all the sales numbers in a line, while the latter adds up all the sales numbers in a column.

The `getTotalSales()` method adds up all the numbers in the entire array. The outer `for` loop runs through all the weeks and the inner `for` loop all the days in a week.

The `getMostProfitDay()` method finds out which day of the week is the most profitable for all the weeks combined. We use the `getSalesForA-WeekDay()` method to find the sales for a given day of the week. If multiple days of the week have sales that equal the maximum sales amount, this method only finds the first of these days.

Lines with different lengths

As mentioned above, the lines in a two-dimensional array can differ in length. Study the little example in Program Listing 9.4. There we create an array with three lines. The first line (index 0) has a length of 5, the second has a length of 4, and the last has a length of 2.

Program Listing 9.4

```
/*
 * LinesWith DiffLength.java E.L. 2001-08-14
 */
class LinesWithDiffLength {
  public static void main(String[] args) }
    /* An array where all the lines may be of different length. */
    int[][] myArray = new int[3][];    // second index is not given

    /* We create three small arrays, which represent the lines */
    myArray[0] = new int[5];
    myArray[1] = new int[4];
    myArray[2] = new int[3];

    /*
     * We put test values into the array, one line at a time.
```

```
* The length of line no. i is given by myArray[i].length
*/
for (int i = 0; i < myArray[0].length; i++) myArray[0][i] = i;
for (int i = 0; i < myArray[1].length; i++) myArray[1][i] = i;
for (int i = 0; i < myArray[2].length; i++) myArray[2][i] = i;

/* We print the lines. */
for (int i = 0; i < myArray.length; i++) { // myArray.length is equal to the no. of lines
    System.out.print("The length of line: " + myArray[i].length + " Data: ");
    for (int j = 0; j < myArray[i].length; j++) System.out.print(myArray[i][j] + " ");
    System.out.printin();
  }
 }
}

/* Example Run:

The length of line: 5 Data: 0 1 2 3 4
The length of line: 4 Data: 0 1 2 3
The length of line: 2 Data: 0 1
*/
```

One use for this technique might be if we want to collect rainfall statistics for the whole year in a two-dimensional array. Then the lengths of the lines would correspond to the lengths of the different months.

Problems

1. Set up the following statements in a client program that works with the `Sales` class (Program Listing 9.3):

(a) Make an object named `theYear2001`. It should have room for sales data for 52 weeks, 5 days per week.

You will send messages to the object `theYear2001`. Messages d) through g) will be worded so that the responses from the object print out on the screen (use `System.out.println()`):

(b) Register sales of $10,000 for Monday of week 10.

(c) Register sales of $12,100 for Thursday of week 8.

(d) Find total sales for week 5.

(e) Find sales for Monday of week 6.

(f) Find total sales for the whole year.

(g) Find out which day of the week (day number) is the most profitable and how much was sold on this day of the week.

2. Create several methods for the `Sales` class:

   (a) Find average sales per week.

   (b) Create a method that finds the most profitable weeks.

3. (a) Define an array to keep track of the results of a soccer series. For every team, register the number of games won, drawn, and lost.
   (b) Assume that the array in problem a) is an instance variable in a class. Create a method that calculates how many points each team got. (They get 3 points for every game they won, 1 point for a draw, and 0 points for a loss.) Put the results in an array that is returned to the client.

9.8 More Than Two Dimensions

It's very possible to create arrays with more than two dimensions. Suppose the sales data in the example above is divided per salesperson. If we have five salespeople, we'll have a two-dimensional array with sales numbers for each salesperson. We can think of these as being stacked on top of each other and then we have three dimensions. We create the array this way:

```
int[][][] sales = new int[noOfSalespersons][noOfWeeks][noOfDays];
```

The number of numerical values in the array will be `noOfSalespersons` multiplied by `noOfWeeks` multiplied by `noOfDays`. Access to the individual sales numbers and handling the array works the same as for two dimensions. Some examples:

Finding out how much the salesperson with the index `salespersonNo` has sold in the week with index `weekNo`:

```
int sum = 0;
for (int i = 0; i < sales[salespersonNo][weekNo].length; i++) {
  sum += sales[salespersonNo][weekNo][i];
}
```

Finding out how much the salesperson with the index `salespersonNo` has sold in total:

```
int sum = 0;
for (int weekNo = 0; weekNo < sales[salespersonNo].length; weekNo++) {
  for (int dayNo = 0; dayNo < sales[salespersonNo][weekNo].length; dayNo++) {
    sum += sales[salespersonNo][weekNo][dayNo];
  }
}
```

Finding the total sales:

```
int sum = 0;
for (int salespersonNo = 0; salespersonNo < sales.length; salespersonNo++) {
```

```
for (int weekNo = 0; weekNo < sales[salespersonNo].length; weekNo++) {
  for (int dayNo = 0; dayNo < sales[salespersonNo][weekNo].length; dayNo++) {
    sum += sales[salespersonNo][weekNo][dayNo];
  }
 }
}
```

Problem

We have three fields of apple trees, with ten trees each. We want to find out if there's any difference between the fields and register the number of kilos of apples on each tree. We take measurements five years in a row.

(a) Define a three-dimensional array to record the apple crop.

(b) Assume that the array is an instance variable in a class. Create a method that finds the total number of kilos for each field. The results will be returned to the client in an appropriate data structure.

9.9 Multidimensional Arrays and Object-Oriented Programming

Multidimensional arrays aren't used very much in object-oriented programming. The reason is that we make arrays of objects instead, where each object contains an array with additional information directly linked to the array.

We can store rainfall data for a year in a two-dimensional array. Rainfall data for several years can be stored in a three-dimensional array. The only additional information we've put in the Month class in Figure 9.1 is the name of the month. That single bit of information can be read from the two-dimensional array by looking at the line number. But by using a multidimensional array instead of an array of Month objects, we tie ourselves to this structure. We won't be able to easily add more information in the future linked to each month or each year (such as the person taking the measurements, where they were taken, and information about special meteorological conditions). If we keep the monthly rainfall as an object, we will be able to add the information mentioned above by expanding the Month class with more instance variables.

We can collect all the Month objects that belong to the same year in an instance of the AnnualPrecipitation class. There will be room for several years in an instance of the Statistics class.

The structure is outlined in Figure 9.9.

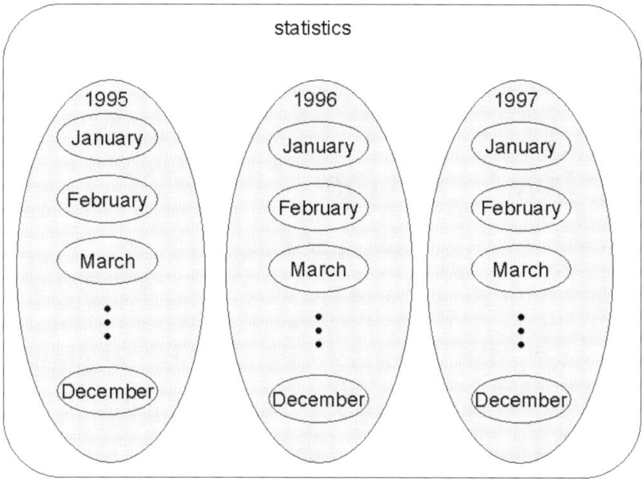

Figure 9.9   Objects with monthly statistics are hidden inside objects with annual statistics, which are collected into one large statistics object

We should be able to deal with arrays where the elements are objects. This is the topic of the next chapter.

Multidimensional arrays are useful if we need to *handle* data in multiple dimensions. In the array of sales numbers, we needed to do computations for both lines and columns.

9.10 New Concepts in This Chapter

Concept	Brief Explanation
array	A data structure where all the data is of the same type and where each data value has an index and can be accessed by indexing.
component	See element. "Component" is used here in the list of concepts as defined in the Java Language Specification [Gosling, Joy, Steele 1996, p. 193]. In other parts of the book we use "component" in other ways.
data structure	A collection of data stored in the internal memory under a name.
element	The smallest building block that makes up an array; has room for a single value. Multidimensional arrays are divided into components until a component itself is no longer an array. Then the component is an element. See component.

Concept	Brief Explanation
index	The position of a component or an element in an array. The positions are numbers from 0 to (length - 1) inclusive.
indexing	A component or an element in an array can be accessed by indexing—the array name is stated followed by square brackets that contain the index for the component or element (example: `array[5]`).

9.11 Review Problems

1. Name some examples of data structures.

2. Assume that a and b are declared as two integer arrays, each with a length of 10. Draw the arrays. Explain why we can't copy the contents of a over to b by writing b = a. What do we have to do to copy the contents?

3. Why are `for` loops important when handling arrays?

4. Name some examples of methods found in the `java.util.Arrays` class.

5. What do one- and two-dimensional arrays have in common?

6. Explain why the lines, but not the columns, in a two-dimensional array can have different lengths.

9.12 Programming Problems

Problem 1

Make a class that contains an array of prices for products. The product number corresponds to the index in the array. The class has to have a variable, `noRegistered`, that keeps track of how many products are registered at any given time. This variable will have a value of 0 before the first product is registered.
Create methods to

- Register a new product

- Register a new price for a product with a given number

- Find the price for a given number

- Change the price of a product that is already registered. The change will be given as a percentage.

- Find out how many products cost more than a given amount. The amount will be a parameter.

Remember that the methods have to return an error code if, for example, invalid product numbers are given.

Create a menu-driven client program (hint: see Program Listing 7.2).

Problem 2

Create a `Temperature` class. It will contain a two-dimensional array of temperatures for every hour of the day for a month.

The class will offer methods that make it possible to find

(a) The mean temperature for each day of the month

(b) The mean temperature for every hour of the day for the month

(c) The mean temperature for the whole month

(d) The number of days with a mean temperature in the following groups: less than -5 °C, between -5 °C and 0, between 0 and 5 °C, between 5 °C and 10 °C, and over 10°C

Hint: The methods in problems a), b), and d) will return references to arrays that contain the results that are requested.

Write a simple client program that can be used to test the class. Keep the number of hours in a day and the number of days in a month minimal when testing.

Problem 3

Create a `Matrix` class. It will contain a two-dimensional array and correspond to a matrix in mathematics. Create methods to

- Add a matrix to this matrix

- Multiply this matrix by another matrix

- Transpose the matrix

The class will be immutable. In other words, all the methods have to make new matrices that are returned. If the operations are impossible, the methods will return `null`.

Write a simple client program that can be used to test the class.

Arrays of Reference Types and Array Lists

Learning goals for this chapter

Once you've completed this chapter you will understand the following concepts:

- Array list, an array list's capacity and size

- Wrapper class

- Interface with the keywords `interface` and `implements`

- Association with name and multiplicity

You will understand the difference between

- Arrays of a primitive data type and arrays of a reference type

- Arrays and array lists

You will be able to:

- Create and use arrays of reference type and create and use array lists

- Use ready-made sort and search methods for arrays and array lists

- Understand parameters of the `Object` type

- Set up one-to-many associations between a small number of classes and know how to program these

The elements in an array can be objects, or more correctly, *references* to objects. In this chapter, we will look at differences and similarities between arrays of reference types and arrays of primitive data types.

As we have seen earlier, the length of an array cannot be changed after the array has been created. The `java.util.ArrayList` class solves this problem for us. This class contains an array of references and offers methods for, among other things, inserting and removing elements from this array. If the array is too small, the class creates a new, larger array and copies the references over. As a user of the class we don't need to think about the array filling up.

To demonstrate the use of array lists we will create a program to calculate what it costs to paint surfaces in an apartment with different types of paint. In this context, we will also look at what an association is and how this fits into the class diagram.

Finally, we'll see how to sort arrays of reference types. We will look especially at how we deal with sorting strings according to location. We will also look at library methods for sorting arrays of reference types and array lists.

10.1 An Array of Reference Type

Up to this point, we have only been able to create arrays whose elements were numbers or characters (primitive data types). This has placed significant limitations on what we have been able to do. We need to be able to make arrays of objects, or more precisely, *references* to objects − for example, arrays of names or arrays of merchandise information, personnel information, etc.

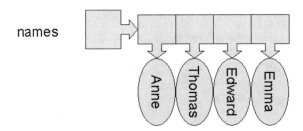

Figure 10.1 An array of reference type is an array of references. The objects have to be created individually

We make an array of reference type the same way we make an array of a primitive data type, but we also have to create each individual object. As an example, let us declare an array of the `String` type:

```
String[] names = new String[4];
```

This is an array of references. Every individual instance of the `String` class has to be created:

```
names[0] = new String("Anne");
names[1] = new String("Thomas");
```

Instances of the `String` class can also be created by using the shortened form:

```
names[2] = "Edward";
```

Or we can input the name:

```
names[3] = JOptionPane.showInputDialog("Write a name: ");
```

See Figure 10.1.

An array of references can also receive values by initialization:

```
String[] names1 = {new String("Anne"), new String("Thomas"), new String("Edward"),
                   new String("Emma")};
String[] names2 = {"Anne", "Thomas", "Edward", "Emma"};
```

Both of these arrays have the length 4.

Figure 10.2 shows what happens if we copy an array of references. The objects are not copied. We just get two sets of references to each object.

Otherwise, the same rules for arrays of reference types apply as for arrays of primitive data types. For example, we can use an element in all the places we can use a simple variable of the reference type. The following loop converts all the names in the `names` array to upper case:

```
for (int i = 0; i < names.length; i++) {
  names[i] = names[i].toUpperCase();
}
```

Just to review before we proceed: What happens in the assignment statement here? We send the message `toUppercase()` to the object that `names[i]` is referring to. The `String` class is immutable, i.e. the method `toUpperCase()` doesn't change the object in question, but instead creates a new object. This new object is returned. The reference `names[i]` is now set to refer to the new object, while the old one disappears the next time the Java interpreter does garbage collection (if there aren't other references to this object).

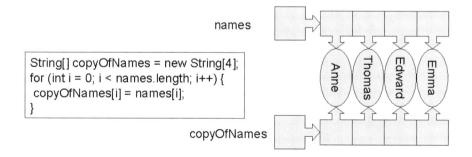

Figure 10.2 Copying an array of references does not copy the objects

Array elements of primitive data type vs. reference type

The elements in an array of a primitive data type contain the data values. Comparisons and assignments between elements directly affect the data values. They are compared and copied.

The elements in an array of reference type are references.

We can't use comparison operators other than == and != on elements like these. The operator == returns true if the elements refer to the same objects.

Assignment means the reference changes value, in other words it is set to refer to another object. The objects remain untouched. They are neither moved nor copied.

The references in an array get the initial value null. This occurs independently of whether the array is a member in a class or a local variable. Every individual reference in the array has to be set to refer to an object before it can be used. If we try to use an array element that does not refer to any object, a NullPointerException is thrown.

Problems

1. Find the error(s) in the following bit of code:

```
Merchandise[] items = new Merchandise[3];  // see Program Listing 4.2
items[1].setPrice(320.50);
items[2].setPrice(123.70);
items[3].setPrice(120.65);
```

2. Suppose that the names array is as shown in Figure 10.1. In addition, we have the variable aName:

```
String aName = "Martha";
```

Set up statements that do the following:

(a) names [1] will refer to a new String object with the text "Paul".

(b) names [3] will refer to the same object that aName refers to.

(c) Store the sum of the lengths for all four of the strings in the variable sumLength. Use a for statement.

(d) Find the number of 'r's in all the strings (hint: use indexOf () and a for statement).

3. In [URL Java book] under chapter 10, you'll find a revised version of the class Merchandise from Program Listing 4.2. Download this and do the following:

(a) Create an array of the `Merchandise` class with four elements. Fill the array with data. Decide on suitable values for the attributes yourself.

Set up bits of code that do the following with a `Merchandise` array of general length:

(b) Print the names of all the merchandise items.

(c) Find the most expensive item.

(d) Increase the price of all the items by 7%.

4. The `names` array is as given in Figure 10.1. Figure 10.2 shows the result of copying the array elements. Rewrite the body in the `for` loop in the figure so that `copyOfNames` will refer to copies of the objects in `names`. Hint: the `String` class has a constructor that takes a reference to a `String` as an argument.

5. The parameter for `main()` is `String[] args`, i.e. an array of strings. If we run the program from the command line, the words we write after the program name will end up in this array. Example:

```
>java aProgram London Paris Rome
```

Create a `main()` method that prints all the elements in the array `args`, and run the program as shown here. Then the city names will print out.

10.2 Array Lists

One problem with arrays is that their size cannot be changed after the array has been created. If we find out that the original array is too small, we have to create a new array that is larger and copy all the elements from the first array over into the new array. The `java.util.ArrayList` class solves this problem for us.

The `ArrayList` class has a built-in array of references and maintains its size as required. The size of the array is called the array list's *capacity*.[1] The array list keeps track of how much of the capacity is being used at any point in time. While necessary, the capacity is increased. As users of the class we do not need to think of this.

The following bit of code declares an array list and inputs an unknown number of texts that are stored in the array list. The code runs in a loop that stops if an empty text is input:

```
ArrayList texts = new ArrayList();
String aText = JOptionPane.showInputDialog("Write a text: ");
while (aText.length() > 0) {
  texts.add(aText);  // inserts a reference to the text into the array list
```

---

1. We can fine tune both the start capacity and the way this increases and decreases. See the online API documentation.

```
aText = JOptionPane.showInputDialog("Write a text: ");
}
```

Notice how the loop is constructed. The order of the statements prevents the empty text from being inserted into the array list. `add()` is a method in the `ArrayList` class with the following method head:

```
boolean add(Object obj)
```

The method inserts a new reference into the array list. The parameter is of the `Object` type. You read earlier (Figure 4.6) that absolutely all classes are subclasses of the `Object` class. This means that the argument in the method `add()` can be of any class. The method always returns `true` (!). Therefore, it's not necessary to check the return value.

 If a parameter is of the `Object` type (i.e. `java.lang.Object`), the argument can be from any reference type whatsoever.

The number of elements in the array list is called the *size* of the array list and is given by the method `size()`. This must not be confused with the capacity. `size()` gives us the number of elements that contain meaningful data. In all practical work, it is the size that is of interest for us, not capacity. The elements are numbered the same way as in an array. Therefore, we can print out all the elements in the array list this way:

```
for (int i = 0; i < texts.size(); i++) {
    String thisText = (String) texts.get(i);
    System.out.println("Text no. " + i + ": " + thisText);
}
```

We are using the `get()` method. The return type is `Object`. Therefore we have to cast to the right type. An exception is thrown (`ClassCastException`) if we try to cast to the wrong type.

 If the return type from a method is `Object`, we have to cast the return object to the right class before we can send messages to it.

This is a slight simplification. Strictly speaking, casting is not necessary if we use methods inherited from `Object`. And in the example above, we do. In printing, the method `toString()` is used implicitly if we don't write it out in clear text. We will say more about `toString()` later on in this chapter.

When getting data from an array list, we have to be just as careful as when getting data from an array. We have to check the validity of the index:

```
if (index >= 0 && index < texts.size()) { // valid index
    we can safely get data with the method get()
}
```

If we use an invalid index, the `get()` method throws an `IndexOut-OfBoundsException`.

API Reference

The java.util.ArrayList class

Note that the array list does not contain the objects itself, but *references* to the objects.

Constructor:

> public ArrayList()

The constructor creates an empty array list with a given start capacity. If this eventually turns out not to be enough, the capacity is increased, if necessary several times.

Methods:

It is generally true that methods that take an index as an argument throw an `IndexOutOfBoundsException` if the index is invalid. If nothing else has been specified, a valid index is from 0 up to, but not including, `size()`.

> public int size()

This method returns the number of elements in the array list.

> public boolean add(Object obj)

This method inserts a reference at the end of the array list. The method always returns `true`. If the capacity is too small, it is expanded without our having to think about it. `obj` can be `null`.

> public void add(int index, Object obj)

This method makes room for a new reference by moving all references down one position starting with `index`. The new reference is placed in the position `index`, which can be equal to `size()`. This means that the reference is inserted at the end of the list. `obj` can be `null`.

> public Object get(int index)

This method returns the reference with the stated `index`. Casting may be necessary if we are going to send messages to the returned object.

> public Object remove(int index)

This method removes a reference from the array list. The elements are transferred one position closer to the beginning of the array list, starting with the position where there was an empty space and proceeding from there. The method returns the reference. Casting may be necessary if we are going to send messages to the returned object.

```
public Object set(int index, Object obj)
```

This method replaces the reference in the stated index with the reference to another object. obj can be null.

Problems

Use the class Merchandise that you'll find under chapter 10 in the [URL Java book] in these problems as well.

1. Create an array list named items. Write program code that inserts instances of the Merchandise class into the array list. The product number will be equal to the index + 100, i.e. 100, 101, 102, 103, etc. The objects will be created by the program running in a loop and for each item of merchandise, the merchandise name and price are input. Find suitable termination criteria for the inputting actions yourself.

2. Write program code that runs through the whole items array list and prints out the input information.

3. Write program code that searches for a product with a given name. We are assuming that the product name is unambiguous.

4. Write program code that removes the product found in Exercise 3.

10.3 Wrapper Classes – Integer, Double, etc.

An array list cannot contain values of the primitive data types. The elements in an array list have to be references. But it's not hard to imagine a need for number arrays with dynamic lengths. We can use so-called *wrapper classes* for this. This type of class "wraps" something else, in this case a value of a primitive data type. (The point of all classes is that, to the extent possible, they will package something. Nevertheless, the designation wrapper class is used in a slightly specialized way.) In addition to a constructor to instantiate an object that contains a value of the primitive data type, the classes offer methods for getting the value, for converting between numbers and text, constants that give the maximum and minimum value in the data type, etc.

All the wrapper classes are in the java.lang package, and they have the following names: Integer, Long, Float, Double, Byte, Character and Boolean.

The statement

```
Integer integerObject = new Integer(50);
```

creates an instance of the `Integer` class and place the number 50 in this object. The following bit of code inputs positive integers from the user, converts them to an integer object and inserts them into the array list. The input is completed when the user enters a non-positive number:

```
ArrayList numbers = new ArrayList();
int aNumber = InputReader.inputInteger("Write a positive number: "); // see chap. 6.8
while (aNumber > 0) {
  Integer integerObject = new Integer(aNumber);
  numbers.add(integerObject);
  aNumber = InputReader.inputInteger("Write a positive number: ");
}
```

API Reference

Wrapper classes for primitive data types

All the classes are immutable.

All the classes implement the `Comparable` (see Section 10.7) and `Serializable` (see Section 11.10) interfaces.

All the classes implement their own version of the following two methods (see Section 10.4):

```
public String toString()
public boolean equals(Object obj)
```

All the classes have a constructor that takes a value from the corresponding primitive data type as argument:

```
public wrapperClass(dataType value)
```

All the classes, except `Character`, also have a constructor that takes a string as its argument:

```
public wrapperClass(String text)
```

For numbers, this constructor throws a `NumberFormatException` if it's not possible to convert the string to a value of the type in question. In order to give the object a sensible value and also if the text cannot be converted to a number, this exception should be handled with `try` and `catch`. Example:

```
/*
 *  We may handle a NumberFormatException in this way:
 */
String text = "23..5";
Double numberObject;
try {
 numberObject = new Double(text);
```

```
} catch (NumberFormatException e) {
    numberObject = new Double("0.0"); // possible error message
}
System.out.println(numberObject.doubleValue());  // gets the numerical value
```

The printout will be 0.0 because the text "23..5" cannot be converted to a decimal numeral.

If the constructor is going to create an instance of the `Boolean` class, the string `"true"`, despite a combination of upper and lower case letters, is converted to `true`. All other strings, including `null`, are converted to `false`.

The java.lang.Number class

This class declares a number of methods that are all implemented in the subclasses `Byte`, `Integer`, `Short`, `Long`, `Float` and `Double`. That means that all these methods can be used for objects which are instances of these six classes.

Methods:

```
public double doubleValue();
public float floatValue();
public int intValue();
public long longValue();
public short shortValue();
```

These methods get the value of the object after the necessary conversion is done. An exception is not thrown if the type it is converted to is too small, but the result will not be correct.

The java.lang.Integer class

Class constants:

```
public static final int MAX_VALUE;
public static final int MIN_VALUE;
```

The constants contain the maximum and minimum value for the data type `int`.

Class methods:

```
public static int parseInt(String text)
```

The method converts `text` to an integer and returns the integer value. The exception `NumberFormatException` is thrown if the conversion is not successful. For exception handling, see Program Listing 6.5, method `inputInteger()`.

The java.lang.Double class

Among other things, the class includes treatment of the special values "Not-A-Number" and "Infinity". See Section 2.6.

Class constants:

> public static final double MAX_VALUE
> public static final double MIN_VALUE
> public static final double NaN
> public static final double NEGATIVE_INFINITY
> public static final double POSITIVE_INFINITY

Class method:

> public static double parseDouble(String text)

The method converts `text` to decimal numerals and returns the value. The exception `NumberFormatException` is thrown if the conversion is not successful. For exception handling, see Program Listing 6.5, method `inputDecimalNumeral()`.

Methods:

> public boolean isInfinite()

The method returns `true` if the `Double` object contains a value that is infinitely large (positive or negative).

> public boolean isNaN()

The method returns `true` if the `Double` object contains the special value NaN.

Problems

1. Write statements that

(a) Wrap the number 15 into an object named `anInteger`.

(b) Wrap the letter 'S' into an object named `initial`.

(c) Retrieve the integer from the object `anInteger` and store it in the variable `number` (data type `int`).

(d) Create a string that contains the character in the object `initial`.

(e) Create a string that contains the integer in the object `anInteger` as text.

2. Write a bit of code that tries to convert a text into an integer. If the conversion does not succeed, the message "This text cannot be converted to a number" is printed.

10.4 The Methods – equals() and toString()

All wrapper classes implement their own versions of the methods

```
public String toString()
public boolean equals(Object obj)
```

These are methods that are declared in the Object class. All classes inherit these methods because they are all subclasses of Object. The methods are implemented in the following way in the class Object:

- equals() compares the reference this (see Section 4.4) to the reference obj. If they are equal (i.e, they refer to the same object), the method returns true, otherwise false.

- toString() returns the name of the class the object is an instance of, followed by '@' and a numeric code.

If this implementation doesn't suit a class, the class can have its own version of the method.

Many library classes have their own versions of these methods. For any given class, these methods should be programmed this way:

- equals() should compare the contents of the objects.

- toString() should return a string that can be used to print out the data contents of an instance of the class.

The method toString() is often used in printouts. For example, we can program it for the class Flooring:

```
public String toString() {
  return "Flooring: Name: " + name + "price: " + price + ", width: " + widthOfFlooring;
}
```

The method returns a string that says what class the object is an instance of ("Flooring") and then rattles off the values for the individual instance variables. The method toString() is special in that it is implied if an object is linked to a string with the operator +. In the example, we write:

```
return "Flooring: Name: " + name + ", ....
```

That's the same as:

```
return "Flooring: Name: " + name.toString() + ", ....
```

toString() is usually used either to create a new toString() for another class (the way we have used toString() in the example here), or to display data. Example:

```
JOptionPane.showMessageDialog(null, "" + myFlooring);
JOptionPane.showMessageDialog(null, "" + myFlooring.toString());
JOptionPane.showMessageDialog(null, myFlooring.toString());
JOptionPane.showMessageDialog(null, myFlooring);
```

These four statements all have the same effect.

Problem

In the text above, `toString()` is programmed for the class `Flooring`. Program this method for the class `Paint` as well. Write a little test program.

10.5 Associations

Previously, we have looked at how objects can collaborate to solve a problem. In those cases, we are describing a connection that exists during the short instant it takes to solve the task. Meanwhile, we also discussed that in order for this to be possible, there has to be an underlying structural relationship. An object can collaborate with an object that is, for example, a parameter or an instance variable.

Let's look at a relationship type called *association*. An association between classes means that there is a connection between instances of the classes. In the class diagram, an association is drawn as a straight line between the classes. In the examples in this section, we are focusing on the associations. Therefore, the boxes contain only the class name. We can link names and multiplicity to an association.

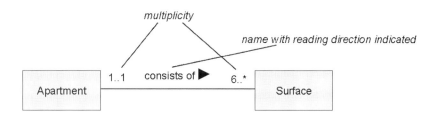

Figure 10.3 An association between the classes `Apartment` and `Surface` (UML)

Figure 10.3 shows an association between the class `Apartment` and the class `Surface`. The figure demonstrates that there is a relationship between an apartment and the surfaces (ceiling, walls, floor) it is composed of.

The *name* of the association is "consists of", and the arrow shows that the association should be read from left to right. In this book, we have chosen to set the reading direction *from* the class that needs to know about the other class. Now, you can imagine that both of the classes need to know about each other and then you can choose the name and the reading direction you think will tell the most, maybe even set up both directions. In the figure shown here, we are demonstrating that an apartment has to know which surfaces it is made of. A given surface, however, does not need to know what apartment it belongs to.

The *multiplicity* says something about the number of instances of each class that are included in a given relationship. It can be stated as an interval in the form of "minimumvalue..maximumvalue". There's a "1..1" on the left side. This means that both the minimum and the maximum value are 1. There is exactly 1 apartment in this situation. On the right it says "6..*". That means that an apartment has to consist of at least 6 surfaces (4 walls, a ceiling and a floor). The star means that the maximum number of surfaces is arbitrary. There could be dividing walls, and the individual walls can be divided into smaller surfaces.

If we only state a single number, that means an interval with the length 1. "1" means exactly 1, "2" means exactly 2. But if we write an asterisk and don't state a lower limit, that means any value whatsoever, including 0. We can also state individual values with a comma between them or combinations of single values and intervals, for example, "3, 7, 10..20".

A very common association is 1 on the one end and * on the other end. We call this a *one-to-many association*.

Figure 10.4 shows other types of associations: a one-to-one and a many-to-many association. Designing associations is almost a subject unto itself. In this book, we will only be looking at relatively simple associations.

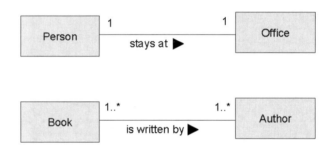

Figure 10.4 A one-to-one and many-to-many association (UML)

Let's look at our renovation case study. We will now create a solution with the following limitations and possibilities:

The apartment consists of an arbitrary number of surfaces. While the number of surfaces can be anything whatsover, in this version we want to limit ourselves to only one type of renovation material, namely paint. For every surface, we record the type of paint. We want to maintain a register of all the surfaces and a register of all the paint types and connect paints to surfaces as we wish. See Figure 10.5. We have a one-to-many association between `Paint` and `Surface`. A specific type of paint can be used on many surfaces, but each surface can only be painted with one type of paint.

We choose to combine the two registers (surfaces and paint types) in an object described by the class `RenovationProject`. Operations for this object will be, for example, registering a new type of paint, registering a new surface, finding a specific type of paint, etc. Thus, our renovation project has to know which surfaces and which types of paint are recorded, which why we read in the direction *from* the class `RenovationProject`.

What about the relationship between `Surface` and `Paint`? Does a type of paint need to know what surfaces it is going to paint and/or does the surface need to know what type of paint it is going to be painted with? We are choosing to be satisfied with the latter – the surface has to know what type of paint is going to be used on it. Therefore, we name the association so that we read from `Surface` to `Paint`: A surface "uses" a specific type of paint.

Problems

1. Use the class `Merchandise` that you'll find in chapter 10 in the [URL Java book]. Set up an association between the class `MerchandiseRegister` and the class `Merchandise`. The register should contain lots of merchandise. Suggest operations linked to the class `MerchandiseRegister`.

2. Describe what is in the associations in Figure 10.4 in words.

3. Look at the bottom of Figure 10.4. Suppose that books and authors are going to be stored in a register. We also want to have the relationship between them as shown in the figure. What changes do we have to make to the class diagram?

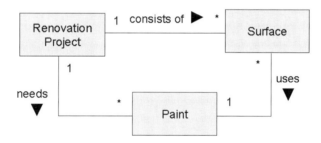

Figure 10.5   Surfaces and paint types included in a renovation project (UML)

10.6 A Bigger Example

We are going to program the system described in Figure 10.5.

In addition to the number of liters of paint, we will calculate the price for each individual surface and the total price. When we calculate the amount of paint needed, we round it up to the nearest half litre. The program will run in a loop and be menu-driven. We are using the `JOptionPane` input dialog with the menu as a dropdown list showing all registered surfaces as well as the choices "New Surface" and "Exit". See Figure 10.6.

Registering a new surface occurs in the following way: we have to enter a name to identify the surface with length, width and type of paint. The type of paint can be one that is already registered or it can be new. See the list box on the right in Figure 10.6. A type of paint is identified by name. In addition, the number of coats, number of square metres per litre and price per litre are entered.

If we choose a surface that's already registered in the list box on the left, that means that we want to change the type of paint for this surface and the list box on the right comes up.

In constructing the classes, we distinguish between the classes that belong to the problem area that we are going to treat and the classes that belong to the user communication. We begin with the first group.

A wall and a ceiling with different type of paint

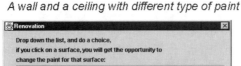

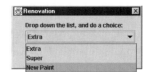

Now we use the same paint on both surfaces:

Figure 10.6   User interface for renovation project with many surfaces and many types of paint

Figure 10.7 shows the class diagram with attributes and operations.

Compared with Figure 4.1, the class `Paint` has not been changed and it contains information about name, number of coats, covering ability and price. It offers get methods for each attribute and also methods that calculate the need for paint and the price.

The class `Surface` has information about length, width, area and circumference calculations. In addition, it can get and change the type of paint. The type of paint is not set up as an attribute, but is obtained through the association to `Paint`.

Now let's see how we program the associations in the figure.

A register emerges as a one-to-many association between a class that is responsible for maintaining the register (here, `RenovationProject`) and the class that is describing the objects that are included in the register.

We create a register by creating an array list. This array list will contain references to the objects that are stored in the register.

The class `RenovationProject` has one-to-many associations to both the class `Surface` and the class `Paint`. Thus, the class will contain two array lists, one for surfaces and one for types of paint:

```
class RenovationProject {
  private String name;
  private ArrayList allSurfaces = new ArrayList();
  private ArrayList allPaints = new ArrayList();
```

We have a one-to-many association from `Paint` to `Surface`. Should we program it the same way? In other words, should we create an array list in the class `Paint`?

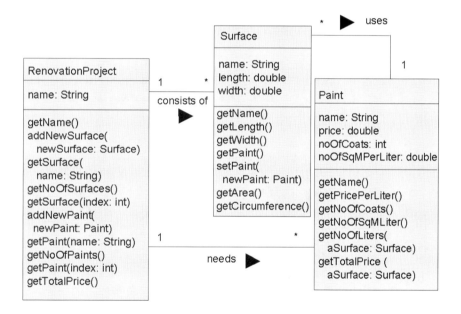

Figure 10.7 Class diagram – renovation project (UML)

In order to answer that, we have to look at the application. Earlier we decided that the surface needs to know about the type of paint, but not the other way around. Therefore, we will not have an array list with surface objects in the class `Paint`. Instead, we will have a reference to the right type of paint in the class `Surface`:

```
class Surface {
  private String name;  // for identification purposes
```

```
private double length;
private double width;
private Paint paint;
```

We refer to [URL Java book] for the complete program list of the classes `Surface` and `Paint`.

Programming a one-to-many association

Suppose that we have the class A on the 1-side of the association and the class B on the many-side.

If an instance of class A has to recognize all the instances of class B that it is linked to, we create an array list in class A. This array list contains references to all the pertinent instances of class B.

If an instance of class B has to know which instance of class A it is linked to, we create a reference to this instance in class B.

We are going to look at how we program the different methods in the class `RenovationProject`. See Program Listing 10.1. We satisfy ourselves by looking at the treatment of the register for paint types. The `Surface` register is treated the same way.

- A client has to be able to insert a new element in the register. In the example, it's the method `addNewPaint ()` that takes care of this task. We have to be careful here to check possible requriements to the object, before we accept it and register it. In the example, we assume that all the paint types have different names. Therefore, we check that before we put the element in place. If there already is a paint type registered with this name from before, the new element is not put in place and the method returns a reference to the type of paint that is already registered. If, on the other hand, the registration succeeds, the method returns a reference to the new paint type. The client can use this:

```
aPaint = details.readAndInstantiatePaint(); // creates a new paint object
if (project.addNewPaint(aPaint) != aPaint) {
  JOptionPane.showMessageDialog(null, "Paint with this name is already registered.");
}
```

- We have to offer the client the ability to look at the elements in the array list. In general it should be possible to look at one element at a time. Then we need a method that finds the number of elements and one that gets an element (a reference) with a given index. In the example, this general need is covered by the methods `getNoOfPaints ()` and `getPaint (int index)`. A client can use these methods in the following way:

```
for (int i = 0; i < project.getNoOfPaints(); i++) {
  Paint thisPaint = project.getPaint(i);
  .....do something with thisPaint..
}
```

Notice that by getting the reference to an object the client can change the object the reference refers to. That will not be the case here since `Paint` is an immutable class. But this is generally the case. Because we don't really want different parts of the program working with their own copies of the object, do we? It's clear that situations like this can easily lead to our losing the overall perspective. We should aspire to have the least amount of dependence between classes as possible, potentially limiting the dependence to clearly delimited groups of classes. See Section 7.3. Notice that this is documented at the top in the program code in Program Listing 10.1.

Program Listing 10.1

```
/*
 * RenovationProject.java   E.L. 2001-08-15
 *
 * This class maintains a register with surfaces and different types of paint.
 * The class works with references to the objects all the time. No copies of
 * objects are created.
 * A client may add new references to the register, or it may retrieve a
 * reference to an object. In this way it may change the content of the object
 * in the register, if the object belongs to a mutable class.
 */
import java.util.ArrayList;
class RenovationProject {
  private String name;
  private ArrayList allSurfaces = new ArrayList();
  private ArrayList allPaints = new ArrayList();

  public RenovationProject(String initName) {
    name = initName;
  }

  public String getName() {
    return name;
  }
  /*
   * This method adds a new surface to the register. If a surface
   * with this name already exists, a reference to this object is returned,
   * if not a reference to the newly added object is returned.
   */
  public Surface addNewSurface(Surface newSurface) {
    Surface thisSurface = getSurface(newSurface.getName());
    if (thisSurface == null) {
      allSurfaces.add(newSurface);
```

```
      Paint thisPaint = newSurface.getPaint();
      if (thisPaint != null) addNewPaint(thisPaint);
      return newSurface;
    }
    else return thisSurface;  // surface with this name already registered
  }

  /*
   * This method searches for a surface with a given name.
   * If not found, the method returns null.
   */
  public Surface getSurface(String nameOfSurface) {
    for (int i = 0; i < allSurfaces.size(); i++) {
      Surface thisSurface = (Surface) allSurfaces.get(i);
      if ((thisSurface.getName()).equals(nameOfSurface)) return thisSurface;
    }
    return null;
  }

  /* This method is constructed in the same way as addNewSurface() */
  public Paint addNewPaint(Paint newPaint) {
    Paint thisPaint = getPaint(newPaint.getName());
    if (thisPaint == null) {
      allPaints.add(newPaint);
      return newPaint;
    }
    else return thisPaint;
  }

  /* This method is constructed in the same way as getSurface() */
  public Paint getPaint(String nameOfPaint) {
    for (int i = 0; i < allPaints.size(); i++) {
      Paint thisPaint = (Paint) allPaints.get(i);
      if ((thisPaint.getName()).equals(nameOfPaint)) return thisPaint;
    }
    return null;
  }

  /* This method calculates the total price of the project */
  public double getTotalPrice() {
    double totalPrice = 0.0;
    for (int i = 0; i < allSurfaces.size(); i++) {
      Surface theSurface = (Surface) allSurfaces.get(i);
      Paint paint = theSurface.getPaint();
      if (paint != null) totalPrice += paint.getTotalPrice(theSurface);
    }
    return totalPrice;
  }

  /* The following methods may be used to run through all the paints
   * or all the surfaces in a sequential way.
```

```
    */
    public int getNoOfPaints() {
      return allPaints.size();
    }

    public Paint getPaint(int index){
      if (index >= 0 && index < allPaints.size()) {
        return (Paint) allPaints.get(index);
      }
      else return null;
    }

    public int getNoOfSurfaces() {
      return allSurfaces.size();
    }

    public Surface getSurface(int index){
      if (index >= 0 && index < allSurfaces.size()) {
        return (Surface) allSurfaces.get(index);
      }
      else return null;
    }
}
```

Now let's look at the classes that take care of communication with the user. We construct them the same way as in Section 7.2. The client program looks like the one in chapter 7:

```
public static void main(String[] args) {
  ProjectChap10 aProject = new ProjectChap10();
  aProject.showInstructions();

  int option = aProject.doAChoice();
  while (option != ProjectChap10.exit) {
    aProject.carryOutTheRightThing(option);
    option = aProject.doAChoice();
  }
  System.exit(0);
}
```

We're going to go through what distinguishes the class ProjectChap10, Program Listing 10.2 , from the class ProjectChap7, Program Listing 7.2. Read the text along with the program code and the comments written there.

First we have to go through how we create the contents of the list on the left in Figure 10.6. This is an array with strings, one string for each line. The array of strings is created in the method setOptions(). The number of strings will be equal to the number of registered surfaces + 3. The last three strings contain the total price, the text "New surface" and the text "Exit".

We find the number of registered surfaces by sending the message getNoOfSurfaces() to project, which is an instance of the RenovationProject class.

We use a `for`-loop to run through all the registered surfaces. First we get the surface and then the paint this surface is going to be painted with. We calculate the paint needs and price by sending messages to the paint object. This way we can construct the string the usual way. For decimal numerals we use a format object that shows decimal numerals with two decimal places. Decimal separator and currency formatting are according to the running environment (Windows: Regional Settings).

Then we can turn our attention to the beginning of the class `ProjectChap10`.

As is clear from the description of `setOptions()` above, the value for the menu selection "Exit" will vary from time to time. We let the constant `exit` receive a value that cannot be a menu selection, namely -1. If the user selects "Exit", the method `doAChoice()` returns this value. The client can compare the return value from `doAChoice()` with `exit` and in this way find out when the program will be terminated.

The method `carryOutTheRightThing()` is very different from the corresponding method in chapter 7.

If the selection has a value less than the number of surfaces, that means that the user has clicked on one of the lines that describes surfaces and by doing that she is signalling that she wants to try another paint type on this surface. After a paint type is selected (the method `getPaint()`, right box in Figure 10.6), we get a reference to the surface object and change the paint type for this surface.

As in chapter 7, the user also has to register new surfaces and new paints. We are using a sligthly revised `ReaderRenovationCase` class from Program Listing 7.3. See [URL Java book].

Program Listing 10.2

```
/*
 * RenovationChap10.java   E.L. 2001-08-15
 *
 */
import java.text.*;
import javax.swing.JOptionPane;
import myLibrary.InputReader;  // see chap. 6.8
class ProjectChap10 {
  public static final int exit = -1;

  private ReaderRenovationCase details = new ReaderRenovationCase();
  private RenovationProject project = new RenovationProject("My Flat");
  private DecimalFormat numberFormat = new DecimalFormat("###0.00"); // see ch.8.2
  private DecimalFormat currencyFormat =
          (DecimalFormat) NumberFormat.getCurrencyInstance();

  public void showInstructions() {
    String instruction =
      "This program calculates the price and amount needed to paint several surfaces\n" +
      "with different kinds of paint. You may choose to change the type of paint on\n" +
      "a registered surface, or to register a new surface. You have to register a new \n" +
```

```
      "surface as the first thing you do. Every time you do a change, the amount of\n " +
      "paint and the price are shown in the list box.";
    JOptionPane.showMessageDialog(null, instruction);
  }

  public int doAChoice() {
    String[] options = setOptions();
    String selectionDone = (String) JOptionPane.showInputDialog(null,
      "Drop down the list, and do a choice, " +
      "\nif you click on a surface, you will get the opportunity to " +
      "\nchange the paint for that surface:",
      "Renovation", JOptionPane.DEFAULT_OPTION, null, options, options[0]);
    int selection = getSelectionAsInt(options, selectionDone);
    if (selection == options.length - 1) return exit;
    else return selection;
  }

  public void carryOutTheRightThing(int option) {
    if (option < project.getNoOfSurfaces()) { // changes paint
      Paint thePaint = getPaint();
      Surface theSurface = project.getSurface(option); // get a reference to the surface object
      theSurface.setPaint(thePaint);
    } else {   // new surface is to be registered
      Surface aSurface = details.readAndInstantiateSurface();
      if (project.addNewSurface(aSurface) == aSurface) { // ok, finds the paint
        Paint thePaint = getPaint();
        aSurface.setPaint(thePaint);
      } else {
        JOptionPane.showMessageDialog(null,
                "Surface with this name is already registered.");
      }
    }
  }

  /*
   * This method creates a String array to be presented to the user as a menu.
   * The array will contain all registered surfaces with their paint and price,
   * and in addition the total price and the items "New Surface" and "Exit".
   */
  private String[] setOptions() {
    int noOfSurfaces = project.getNoOfSurfaces();
    int noOfOptions = noOfSurfaces + 3;
    String[] options = new String[noOfOptions];
    for (int i = 0; i < noOfSurfaces; i++) {
      Surface thisSurface = project.getSurface(i);
      Paint thePaint = thisSurface.getPaint();
      if (thePaint != null) {
        double noOfLiters = thePaint.getNoOfLiters(thisSurface);
        String noOfLitersFormatted = numberFormat.format(noOfLiters);
        double price = thePaint.getTotalPrice(thisSurface);
```

```
    String priceFormatted = currencyFormat.format(price);
    options[i] = thisSurface.getName() + ", paint: " + thePaint.getName() + ", "
            + noOfLitersFormatted + " liters, price: " + priceFormatted;
  }
  else options[i] = thisSurface.getName() + ", paint not registered.";

}
options[noOfSurfaces] = "The total price is: "
                + currencyFormat.format(project.getTotalPrice());
options[noOfSurfaces + 1] = "New Surface";
options[noOfSurfaces + 2] = "Exit";
return options;
}

/*
 * This method finds the correct paint, or registers a new one.
 * In this case, the method returns null if a paint with the
 * same name already is registered.
 */
private Paint getPaint() {
  int paintIndex = getPaintIndex();  // the user choose the right paint
  Paint aPaint;
  if (paintIndex < 0) {  // we are going to register a new paint
    aPaint = details.readAndInstantiatePaint();
    if (project.addNewPaint(aPaint) != aPaint) {
    JOptionPane.showMessageDialog(null, "Paint with this name is already registered.");
    }
  }
  else aPaint = project.getPaint(paintIndex);
  return aPaint;
}

/*
 * This method lets the user choose between all existing paints, or he may
 * choose to register a new paint. In the first case the method returns
 * the index of the chosen paint, in the second case the method returns -1.
 */
private int getPaintIndex() {
  int noOfPaints = project.getNoOfPaints();
  if (noOfPaints > 0) { // there are paints registered
    int noOfOptions = noOfPaints + 1;
    String[] options = new String[noOfOptions];
    for (int i = 0; i < noOfPaints; i++) {
      Paint thisPaint = project.getPaint(i);
      options[i] = thisPaint.getName();
    }
    options[noOfPaints] = new String("New Paint");

    /* We show the menu list to the user, and we note his choice. */
    String selectionDone = (String) JOptionPane.showInputDialog(null,
      "Drop down the list, and do a choice:",
```

```
        "Renovation", JOptionPane.DEFAULT_OPTION, null, options, options[0]);
        int thePaint = getSelectionAsInt(options, selectionDone);
        if (thePaint < options.length - 1) {
          return thePaint; // Return, we are going to use the paint with this index
        }
      }
      return -1;  // Return, we are going to register a new paint
    }
    private int getSelectionAsInt(String[] options, String selectionDone) {
      for (int i = 0; i < options.length; i++) {
        if (options[i].equals(selectionDone)) return i;
      }
      return -1;
    }
  }
class RenovationChap10 {
  public static void main(String[] args) {
    ProjectChap10 aProject = new ProjectChap10();
    aProject.showInstructions();

    int option = aProject.doAChoice();
    while (option != ProjectChap10.exit) {
      aProject.carryOutTheRightThing(option);
      option = aProject.doAChoice();
    }
    System.exit(0);
  }
}
/* Example Run:

Data:
Surfaces: A wall in Mary's room: 3 x 4 m, Ceiling in the corridor: 6 x 1 m,
Paints: Heimdal Extra: 3 coats, 10 kvm/l, 100 NOK/l,
        Heimdal Super: 2 coats, 12 kvm/l, 80 NOK/l

In this example we use Norwegian crowns as currency. The program
will use the currency given by the regional settings.

The output window, see figure 10.6.
*/
```

Problems

Expand the class `RenovationProject` with the following methods:

1. A method to remove a surface.

2. A method to remove a paint type. A paint type can only be removed if no surfaces have references to it.

   Create your own test program to try out these methods.

10.7 The Comparable and Comparator Interfaces

An *interface*, simply put, is a collection of method heads. A class can choose to implement an interface. Then all the methods in the interface have to be programmed. A class can easily implement more methods than the interface promises, but in any case it has to implement the methods specified in the interface.

An interface is similar to a class. It contains only method heads, not method bodies. A method head is followed by a semicolon. An interface is introduced by the reserved word `interface` followed by the name of the interface. An example from the `java.lang` package is:

```
public interface Comparable {
  public int compareTo(Object obj);
}
```

The method `compareTo()` will be used when comparing objects. It should be implemented such that it will return a negative value if `this` is smaller than `obj`, a positive value if `this` is larger than `obj`, and 0 if `this` and `obj` are equal.

A class signals that it is implementing *all* the methods in the interface by setting the reserved word `implements` followed by the name of the interface after the class name in the class head. Example:

```
class Surface implements Comparable {
  public int compareTo(Object obj) { // comparing areas
  Surface theOtherSurface = (Surface) obj;
  double area1 = getArea(); // the area of this
  double area2 = theOtherSurface.getArea();
  if (area1 < area2 - 0.0001) return -1;    // comparing decimal numerals, see chap. 5.8
  else if (area1 > area2 + 0.0001) return 1;
  else return 0;
  }
```

The method heads in the class and in the interface have to be exactly equal.

The class `String` is another example of a class that implements the interface `Comparable`. The class head looks like this:

```
public final class String implements java.io.Serializable, Comparable {
```

This class also implements the interface `java.io.Serializable`. You can tell from the online API documentation whether a class implements an interface.

Example of the use of `String`'s `compareTo()`:

```
String text1 = JOptionPane.showInputDialog("Enter text no. 1: ");
String text2 = JOptionPane.showInputDialog("Enter text no. 2: ");
if (text1.compareTo(text2) > 0) {
  JOptionPane.showMessageDialog(null, "Text 2 is the first one acc. to Unicode");
}
else if (text1.compareTo(text2) < 0) {
  JOptionPane.showMessageDialog(null, "Text 1 is the first one acc. to Unicode");
```

```
        }
        else JOptionPane.showMessageDialog(null, "The texts are equal.");
```

The interface `java.util.Comparator` looks like this:

```
public interface Comparator {
    /* comparing two objects, notice the difference from Comparable */
    int compare(Object o1, Object o2);
    /* comparing two instances of classes that implement Comparator */
    boolean equals(Object obj);
}
```

An instance of a class that implements `Comparator` will contain information about the sorting order of objects. It is of little interest to us to create classes like this, but we will use the ready-made class `Collator` to sort texts according to localization. We'll need to know about the interfaces if we want to use the sorting methods in the Java API, too. More about this in the next section.

API Reference

The java.lang.Comparable interface

Method:

> public int compareTo(Object obj)

This method will return a negative value if `this` will come before `obj` in sorting order, a positive value if `this` will come after `obj`. If the objects are equal, 0 is returned.

The java.util.Comparator interface

Methods:

> public int compare(Object o1, Object o2); // comparing two objects
> public boolean equals(Object obj); // comparing two instances of classes
> // that implement Comparator

It's not of current interest to us to create classes that implement this interface.

We will go through more about interfaces in chapter 12.

Problem

Change the class `Merchandise` (use the version found in [URL Java book] in chapter 10) so that it implements the interface `Comparable`. The merchandise should be sorted by product number. Create a little program that tests out the method `compareTo()`.

10.8 Sorting Arrays and Array Lists

We are going to create a string variant of the sorting method from Section 9.4. What changes do we have to make in the method aside from changing the name and the data type in the parameter list? The variable `help` has to be of the type `String`. What about the comparison:

```
if (array[i] < array[smallestSoFar])...
```

Here we receive a compiling error. Variables of reference type cannot be compared by using the "less than" operator. The class `String` implements `Comparable` (see previous section), but this isn't good enough either. The method `compareTo()`, as implemented in the class `String`, makes comparisons according to Unicode. Character by character, the two strings are compared and one character is considered smaller than the other if it has a lower numeric value in the Unicode character set. See Appendix D. Even if we only look at the letters A–Z, this is wrong. All words with capitalized first letters end up before all words with lower case first letters. If we want the comparison to deal with upper and lower case letters the same way, we use the method `compareToIgnoreCase()`. The sorting method is shown in Program Listing 10.3, and is part of the `Sort` class in `myLibrary`. Here is a simple test program:

```java
public static void main(String[] args) {
  String[] names =
     {"Anna", "Edward", "Paul", "Barbara", "James", "Thomas", "Margaret"};
  myLibrary.Sort.sortText(names);
  String result = "Sorted names: \n";
  for (int i = 0; i < names.length; i++) {
    result += names[i] + "\n";
  }
  javax.swing.JOptionPane.showMessageDialog(null, result);
  System.exit(0);
}
```

Program Listing 10.3

```java
/*
 * Sort.java  E.L. 2001-08-14
 *
 */
package myLibrary;
public class Sort {
  /*
   * Sorting strings according to the Unicode character set.
   * Upper and lower case letters are treated the same.
   */
  public static void sortText(String[] array) {
    for (int start = 0; start < array.length; start++) {
```

```
                int smallestToNow = start;
                for (int i = start + 1; i < array.length; i++) {
                if (array[i].compareToIgnoreCase(array[smallestToNow]) < 0) smallestToNow = i;
                }
                String help = array[smallestToNow];
                array[smallestToNow] = array[start];
                array[start] = help;
            }
        }
    }
```

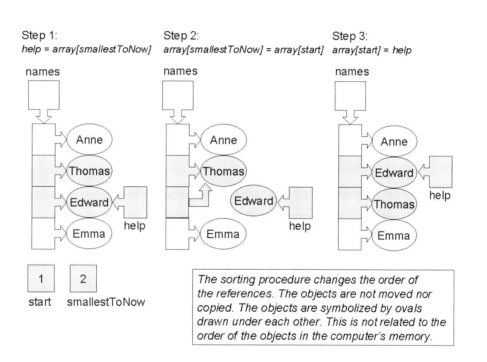

Figure 10.8 Interchanging the contents of two references

Figure 10.8 shows what happens when you swap two values in the string array. We have come to the second round of sorting. In other words, the first element ("Anne") is in the right place. The value to start is 1 ("Thomas"). We go through the rest of the array and first find "Edward" who will trade places with "Thomas". The value of smallestToNow is 2. What happens during the exchange?

- Step 1: The reference that refers to "Edward" should refer to "Thomas" instead. Therefore, we have to take care of the reference to the object "Edward". We do this by setting `help` to refer to this object: `help = array[smallest-ToNow];`

- Step 2: Now we can set `array[2]` to refer to "Thomas": `array[smallestToNow] = array[start];` Now we have two references to "Thomas".

- Step 3: The reference that originally referred to "Thomas" will be set to refer to "Edward". We have taken care of the reference to "Edward" in the variable `help`. Therefore we can write: `array[start] = help;`

Sorting according to location

But what if our alphabet contains letters others than A–Z? This is the case with many European alphabets, e.g. the Norwegian, the Swedish, the Danish, the German, etc.

In Section 8.3 we learned about the class `java.util.Locale`. Decimal numerals, currencies and dates, be printed in a format suited to the country and language where the program is running. The class `java.text.Collator` implements `Comparator` (see previous section), and performs string comparsion according to a given location. You'll find the most important methods in the `Collator` class in the API reference below.

We may use a collator when sorting texts. See Program Listing 10.4. This method works well for all kinds of alphabets.

Program Listing 10.4

```
/*
 * Sort.java  E.L. 2001-08-14
 *
 */
package myLibrary;
public class Sort {
  /*
   * Sorting strings according to the "default location".
   * In Windows it means language and country as set in "Regional Settings".
   * "Sorting by selection" is used as sorting method.
   */
  public static void sortTextLocale(String[] array) {
   Collator collator = Collator.getInstance();
   for (int start = 0; start < array.length; start++) {
    int smallestToNow = start;
    for (int i = start + 1; i < array.length; i++) {
     if (collator.compare(array[i], array[smallestToNow]) < 0) smallestToNow = i;
    }
```

```
            String help = array[smallestToNow];
            array[smallestToNow] = array[start];
            array[start] = help;
         }
      }
   }
```

API Reference

The java.text.Collator class

The class is used to compare strings with respect to a given location (language, country).

The class implements the interface `Comparator`.

Class methods:

```
public static Collator getInstance()
public static Collator getInstance(Locale givenLocation)
```

The first method creates an object that is suited to the environment the program is running in (Windows: Regional Settings). The second creates an object suited to the specified location.

Instance methods:

```
public int compare(String text1, String text2)
```

The method returns a negative value if `text1` comes before `text2` in the alphabet, 0 if they are equal, and a positive value if `text1` comes after `text2`.

```
public boolean equals(String text1, String text2)
```

The method returns `true` if the strings are the same, otherwise `false`.

```
public void setStrength(int newStrength)
public int getStrength()
```

There are three degrees of comparison detail, expressed by the following class constants (remember the qualifiers if you are going to use them, for example, `Collator.PRIMARY`):

```
public static final int PRIMARY // ignores accent marks and case differences
public static final int SECONDARY // ignores case difference, but not accent marks
public static final int TERTIARY // ignores nothing, this is the default value.
```

Sorting methods in the Java API

In Section 9.6 we saw sorting methods from the Java API for arrays of primitive data types. We also have methods like that for arrays of reference types. These methods use a sorting algorithm called mergesort[2] and are of course far more effective than the simple sorting method we went through above.

A method that will sort objects needs methods to compare the objects. There are two types of ready-made sorting methods in Java:

1. In addition to the array or array list that is going to be sorted, the methods take an instance of a class that implements `Comparator` as its argument. An example of a class like this is the class `Collator` (see above), which describes the sorting order of strings relative to a given location (country and language).

   With this we can sort strings in the following way:

   ```
   java.text.Collator collator = java.text.Collator.getInstance();
   java.util.Arrays.sort(names, collator);   // sorts array
   ```

   Methods for sorting array lists are completely equivalent and we find them in the class `java.util.Collections`. We sort an array list that contains strings in the following way (`collator` is the same as in the bit of code above):

   ```
   java.util.Collections.sort(strings, collator); // sorts array list
   ```

2. Methods of the other type do not take a class that implements `Comparator` as their argument. They then require that the objects in the array (array list) are instances of a class that implements the interface `Comparable`. We may then sort an array of surfaces in this way:

   ```
   java.util.Arrays.sort(surfaces);
   ```

   The Java interpreter will protest with `ClassCastException` if the `Surface` class does not implement the `Comparable` interface. If we sort strings with this method, the result will be as without localization.

API Reference

The java.util.Arrays class

See also Section 9.6.

The class offers class methods for sorting and searching in arrays.

Methods that don't have a parameter of the type `Comparator` assume that the objects in the array (array list) are instances of a class that implements the interface `Comparable`. If not, a `ClassCastException` is thrown.

Class methods:

```
public static int binarySearch(Object[] array, Object[] value)
public static int binarySearch(Object[] array, Object[] value, Comparator comp)
```

---

2. See, for example, [Weiss 1998].

These methods assume that the array is sorted. They return the index for an element that is equal to `value`. If the value is not found in the array, the return value will tell us where the value should be placed in the array so that it will still be sorted. If we store the returned value into the variable `index`, the position will be equal to (- index - 1). For an example of using this return value, see the method with the same name in Section 9.6.

```
public static void sort(Object[] array)
public static void sort(Object[] array, int fromIndex, int toIndex)
public static void sort(Object[] array, Comparator comp)
public static void sort(Object[] array, int fromIndex, int toIndex, Comparator comp)
```

The methods sort all or parts (from `fromIndex` inclusive to `toIndex` exclusive) of an array. The method throws out exceptions:

- `ArrayIndexOutOfBoundsException` if `fromIndex` or `toIndex` is smaller than 0 or greater than `array.length`.

- `IllegalArgumentException` if `fromIndex` > `toIndex`.

In addition, we have object versions of the other methods presented in Section 9.6. See the online API documentation for further details.

The java.util.Collections class

The class offers class methods for sorting and searching in array lists.

The `ArrayList` class implements an interface called `List`. This is the reason the first parameter in the methods below is of the `List` type.

Methods that don't have a parameter of the `Comparator` type assume that the objects in the array (array list) are instances of a class that implements the interface `Comparable`.

Class methods:

```
public static int binarySearch(List arrayList, Object value)
public static int binarySearch(List arrayList, Object value, Comparator comp)
public static void sort(List arrayList)
public static void sort(List arrayList, Comparator comp)
```

The methods have the same functionality as the corresponding methods in the `java.util.Arrays` class (see above).

Problems

1. (a) Make an array with five strings. The strings will contain the following names: Maud, Amy, Nella, Louis, John.

   (b) Create program code that stores these names into the array list `list1`.

(c) Create a `list2` that is a copy of `list1`. Elements with the same index in the two array lists will refer to the same object.

(d) Create a figure that shows all objects and references.

(e) Sort `list2` using the `sort()` method in the `java.util.Collections` class.

(f) Create a new figure showing the result.

2. In the exercise in Section 10.7 you changed the class `Merchandise` so that it implements the interface `Comparable`. Create an array of merchandise. Sort the merchandise using the `sort()` method in the `java.util.Arrays` class.

3. Typical Norwegian names shown in alphabetical order are: "Einar", "Petter", "Synnøve", "Øyvind", "Åsmund". Create a little program which sorts these names. Remember to insert them into the array (or array list) in another order than the alphabetical, to check the sorting. You have to sort according to the Norwegian locale (`new Locale("no", "No")`).

10.9 New Concepts in This Chapter

Concept	Brief Description
array list	An instance of the `java.util.ArrayList` class. An "array" with dynamic length. Can only store data of reference types.
association between classes	There is a connection between instances of the involved classes. An instance of the one class is linked to one or more instances in the other class.
capacity of an array list	Number of elements there is room for in the array list. It takes care of expanding the capacity gradually by itself if necessary.
collator	Something that organizes elements in a definite order independent of the original order.
`implements`	Keyword that says that a class implements an interface.
interface	A set of method heads. (Somewhat simplified, see chapter 12.)
`interface`	Keyword that declares an interface.
length of an array list	See "size of an array list".
multiplicity	Two numbers, which in connection with associations, state the number of instances of each class that are participating in the association.
size of an array list	Number of elements in the array list. The size is obtained by sending the message `size()` to the array list.
wrapper class	A class whose purpose is to "wrap" something else, here used about wrapping values of primitive data types.

10.10 Review Problems

1. Describe the similarities and differences between an array of a reference type and an array of a primitive data type.

2. Explain why an array list is often preferable to an array.

3. Set up a summary of arrays versus array lists: how to find the size, how to add a new element and how to view an element that has already been added.

4. What is the purpose of wrapper classes, as they are described in this chapter?

5. What are the wrapper classes called and what common qualities do all the wrapper classes described in this chapter have?

6. Explain how we program one-to-many associations.

7. What is a Java interface?

8. What does it mean to say that a class is implementing a Java interface?

9. The interfaces `Comparable` and `Comparator` are used in different contexts. What contexts?

10. An interface contributes to a standardization of method names. Why is this sometimes necessary?

11. What is a collator? What do we use the class `Collator` for? Give examples.

12. There are two types of library methods for sorting array lists and arrays. What are the two types and what is the difference between them?

10.11 Programming Problems

Problem 1

Create a register of employees. The class `Employee` is itemized in programming problem 1, chapter 7. The register should offer the following services to a client:

- Register new employees

- Find the number of employees

- Look at employees one by one, given the index

- Find an employee, given the employee number

- Find the average salary

- Find the employee number for the oldest employee(s)

- Find employee number for employees who have worked for the company for more than five years

Create a menu-driven client program.

Problem 2

Use the class `Merchandise` from Program Listing 4.2. Expand the class with a suitable `toString()` method.

Create a register to keep track of the merchandise. The register will offer the following services:

- Register a new item

- Remove an item

- Get the number of registered items

- Get items one by one

- A `toString()` method that returns a string of all the merchandise information, sorted by product name. Use a blank line as a divider between items.

Create a client program to test out the register.

Extensions:

Expand the class `Merchandise` with information about how much merchandise is in stock and also information about the lower limit for ordering merchandise. In other words, if the amount in stock falls below this limit, the merchandise will be ordered. The order will be for four times this limit.

Expand the register class with suitable operations for handling this. Among other things, it should be possible to get an order list.

Using Data Files and Streams

Learning goals for this chapter

After completing this chapter, you will understand the following concepts:

- Streams, opening and closing files, reading data from a file, writing data to a file

- Text and binary data transfer, file pointer, sequential versus random access

- Serialization

You will be able to:

- Program the different forms of reading and writing to data files

---

Up to this point, we have been writing programs that communicate with the world through the keyboard and the screen. Programs can also communicate with data files. A program can read input data from a file, and output data can be written to a file instead of to the screen.

Data files make it possible for the program to *remember* data from run to run. This is practical for us users—we don't need to reenter data if we run a program several times with only minor changes in the input data.

You're already familiar with data files. All the files you work with in word processors, spreadsheet programs, and editors are data files. You open the application, open the data file (the text document, spreadsheet, or whatever it is), make any necessary changes, and save it for later use.

Now we will look at how we program the handling of data files: how a program assigns the connection to a data file, how the data is input into the program, and how it is rewritten to the file. We can transfer data from a program to a file in two ways:

- All data is converted into text before saving. People can read files created in this way using an editor. Programs written in languages other than Java may be able to read these files, too.

- The data is not converted before saving. We're talking about binary transfer of data, and files created in this way can only be read by programs where the data is represented internally the same way as in the program that saved the file.

It is also easy to store entire objects in a file. The transfer is binary and the process is called *serialization*.

The `java.io` package contains over 60 classes and interfaces for file handling. We include only a small selection of them here.

11.1 Data Files and Streams

We can think of the data that is sent between a program and a file as a *stream*. The data streams from a source to a destination. We start by opening the stream. We fill it up with more data ("write" to the stream) if the stream is going from the program to the file. If the stream is going in the opposite direction, the program empties the stream of data as the data is "read." Finally, we close the stream. We also use the stream model if the program is communicating with the console. Sometimes we need to think of the console as a data file. In MS-DOS/Windows, the filename is "con". UNIX distinguishes between a file the program is reading from ("stdin"), a file the program is writing to ("stdout"), and a file the program is writing error messages to ("stderr").

We start by attaching a stream object to the file we want to read from or write to. We say that we are *opening the file*. This stream is the object we are working with in the program. We send read and write messages to the stream object. The communication with the physical file is hidden in the implementation of the stream classes. When we finally close the stream object, this leads to the termination of the connection to the physical data file. We say that we are *closing the file*. Closing a file means releasing internal resources allocated to the stream object. If we forget to close a file that the program is writing to, we can also risk losing data.

There are many classes that make stream objects. We have to study the individual class descriptions and see what possibilities they offer. We make the stream objects in a somewhat special way: an instance of one stream class will preferably become an argument for the constructor for another stream class. We can continue with this in several steps before we get a stream we are satisfied with. In this chapter, we will look at different types of streams. We start by concentrating on streams of texts.

A text consists of a number of characters. In Java, every character takes up two bytes, and is interpreted based on the Unicode character set. Most other programs, for example the editor you are using, are using a byte-oriented character set, for instance an ASCII extension. The translation from Unicode to the byte-oriented character set is hidden in the `OutputStreamWriter` class, which is used for writing to a file. The reverse process is hidden in the `InputStreamReader` class, which is used for reading. Therefore, we do not need to think about the fact that different operating systems, platforms and programs use different byte-oriented character sets.

11.2 An Example of a Data File

We will create a program that maintains a simple list of names. The program will be able to print all the names on the screen and it will be possible to add new names.

The list of names is in a file. The file is called *nameFile.txt*, and we have entered the first few names in an editor. Actually, the editor is the easiest tool for keeping this data file in order, but we will also create a Java program that does some of the work. The main purpose of the program is to illustrate reading from and writing to a file with a simple example.

Suppose that the file has the following contents before we run the program:

```
Tony Kingsley
Ken Brown
Margaret Gibson
```

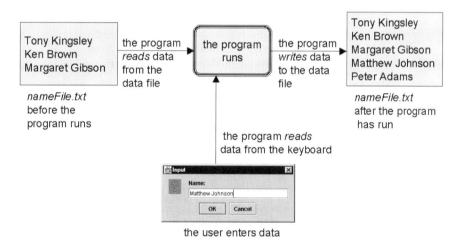

Figure 11.1 A program communicates with a data file

Then we run the program: see Figure 11.1. The program reads the contents of the data file and displays them in a message box on the screen (not shown in the figure). Then it asks the user if there are more names to add in. The user says "yes" and enters two new names. The program writes these names to the data file, after the ones that were already there from before. If we take the file into an editor now, we see that it has the following contents:

```
        Tony Kingsley
        Ken Brown
        Margaret Gibson
        Matthew Johnson
        Peter Adams
```

The program is shown in Program Listing 11.1. We'll go through this program line by line in the next two sections.

Program Listing 11.1

```java
/*
 * MaintainNameArchive.java   E.L. 2001-08-15
 *
 */
import java.io.*;
import javax.swing.JOptionPane;
class MaintainNameArchive {
  public static void main(String[] args) throws Exception {
    String filename = "nameFile.txt";
    /*
     * Reads all the names, and prints them on the screen.
     */
    FileReader readConnToFile = new FileReader(filename);
    BufferedReader reader = new BufferedReader(readConnToFile);

    String result = "The register:\n";
    String oneName = reader.readLine();
    while(oneName != null) {  // null means end-of-file
      result += oneName + "\n";
      oneName = reader.readLine();
    }
    JOptionPane.showMessageDialog(null, result);
    reader.close();

    /*
     * Does the user want more names to be registered?
     */
    int answer = JOptionPane.showConfirmDialog(null, "Do you want to add more names?",
            "Archive", JOptionPane.YES_NO_OPTION);
    if (answer == JOptionPane.YES_OPTION) {
      FileWriter writeConnToFile = new FileWriter(filename, true);
      PrintWriter printer = new PrintWriter(new BufferedWriter(writeConnToFile));
      while (answer == JOptionPane.YES_OPTION) {
        String newName = JOptionPane.showInputDialog("Name: ");
        printer.println(newName);
        answer = JOptionPane.showConfirmDialog(null, "Do you want to add more names?",
                "Archive", JOptionPane.YES_NO_OPTION);
      }
```

```
          printer.close();
      }
      System.exit(0);
  }
}
/* Example Run:
=> The data file before program run:
Tony Kingsley
Ken Brown
Margaret Gibson

=> The user enters two new names:
Matthew Johnson
Peter Adams

=> The data file after program run:
Tony Kingsley
Ken Brown
Margaret Gibson
Matthew Johnson
Peter Adams
*/
```

11.3 Reading Text from a File

We'll go through the first part of Program Listing 11.1. First, let's look briefly at how we can assign a file name in a program. A file name is a text, and, for example, we can write:

    String filename = "nameFile.txt";

The file has to be in the same directory as the program. If the file is not in the same directory, we can either assign the path to the file relative to the directory the program is running from:

    String filename = "dataFiles/nameFile.txt";

or we can assign an absolute path:

    String filename = "c:/data/myData/dataFiles/nameFile.txt";

In this connection, we may use the forward slash / instead of the backslash \ in the Windows environment. If we choose to use \, we have to use two slashes, because \ is a special Java character (see table 2.4), for example: `"dataFiles\\nameFile.txt"`.

Or we may use the `File.separator` constant. This contains the right file directory separator for whichever environment the program is running in:

    String filename = "dataFiles" + File.separator + "nameFile.txt";

The `File` class is in the `java.io` package. This class contains many methods for handling files and directories. For more information, refer to the online API documentation.

When we look at the program, we see that `main()` throws `Exception`:

```
public static void main(String[] args) throws Exception {
```

Most methods that have to do with handling files and streams can throw exceptions that we have to deal with, or throw away (see Section 8.5). Here we do the easiest thing, we throw them away. This means that an error will abort the program. This is acceptable in a simple program like this.

We link a stream object to the physical file with the following statement:

```
FileReader readConnToFile = new FileReader(filename);
```

For the program to read from a file, the file has to exist in advance. If the file does not exist, the constructor `FileReader()` throws a `FileNotFoundException`.

A program that reads data from a file can read individual characters, or a line, depending on the input instruction that is used. Every input will mean that the program has to contact the disk to retrieve the data that is being requested. This takes time. Therefore, the speed of the program will depend on whether we are inputting characters one at a time or as whole lines. To avoid this, it is common for the data to be input into a *buffer* (an area in the internal memory that functions as temporary storage) first. This way, the program's read statements retrieve data from the buffer and not directly from the disk. In practical terms, this means that character-by-character input goes just as fast as line-by-line input. A buffer of this type is often much larger than the amount of data the program demands in an instruction. The standard size for a buffer used to buffer input data from a file into a Java program is 8192 characters. A read instruction in the program retrieves the data from the buffer. The buffer is filled with new data from the disk gradually as read instructions in the program empty it. The disk is accessed less often with buffering than without it, which helps to increase a program's speed. In the example above, all three of the names will be input during one disk access.

We accomplish buffered reading by wrapping an instance of the `BufferedReader` class around an instance of the `FileReader` class:

```
BufferedReader reader = new BufferedReader(readConnToFile);
```

Another reason to use the `BufferedReader` class is that this class offers a more practical input method than the `FileReader` class. In the `BufferedReader` class, we find the `readLine()` method that we use to read a line of text at a time. The input looks like this:

```
String oneName = reader.readLine();
```

The input always starts at the beginning of the stream and continues sequentially through the stream. The `readLine()` method returns `null` when there is no more data to read. If there's an error during reading, the method throws an `IOException`.

The program in Program Listing 11.1 runs in a loop, adding the input text to the result string and inputting new texts from the stream until there is no more text to read.

Finally, the stream is closed:

    reader.close();

More details on reading files

This section may be studied later.

The connection-statement

    FileReader readConnToFile = new FileReader(filename);

can be thought of as a short form for the following:

    FileInputStream inFile = new FileInputStream(filename);
    InputStreamReader readConnToFile = new InputStreamReader(inFile);

The first statement creates a stream with a connection to the file with the given name. The second statement makes sure that this byte stream is interpreted as Unicode characters. This form gives us more possibilities than the short form. For example, we can specify which ASCII extension we want used to interpret the input data.

The next statement in both cases is:

    BufferedReader reader = new BufferedReader(readConnToFile);

Now we'll think about the relationship between the physical file and the messages we are sending to the `reader` object. We'll look at the `readLine()` message as an example.

We construct the different stream objects by sending in other objects to the constructor as arguments. `inFile` is sent in to the `InputStreamReader()` constructor as an argument and thus becomes an instance variable in the `readConnToFile` object. Therefore, the `readConnToFile` object can send messages to the `inFile` object. Correspondingly, `readConnToFile` becomes an instance variable in the `reader` object, and the `reader` object can send messages to the `readConnToFile` object. Follow along in Figure 11.2[1] (note that both object and class names are in the rectangles at the top of the figure):

1. The client program sends the message `readLine()` to the object `reader`.

2. If there is data in the buffer, the data is fetched from the buffer and sent back to the client.

3. If the buffer is empty, the `reader` object sends itself a message (`fill()`) to fill the buffer. The buffer is an array of `char`.

---

1. You can find even more details here by looking in the source code for the classes. It may have to be downloaded and unpacked. Then it will be in the *src* directory under *jdk1.4*. You will find the rest of the directory structure by following the package name.

4. The `fill()` method sends the message `read()` to the `readConnToFile` object.

5. The `readConnToFile` object sends the message `read()` to the object `inFile`.

6. The `read()` method in the `FileInputStream` class is "native," i.e., it is programmed in platform-dependent code, probably C or C++. The method will fetch data from an external physical unit, and this process is not platform-independent.

7. The bytes are sent back to `readConnToFile`.

8. The `readConnToFile` object converts these bytes into Unicode characters and sends these as an array of `char` back to the `reader` object, which has had its buffer filled in this way.

9. The `reader` object retrieves a line from the buffer and returns to the client.

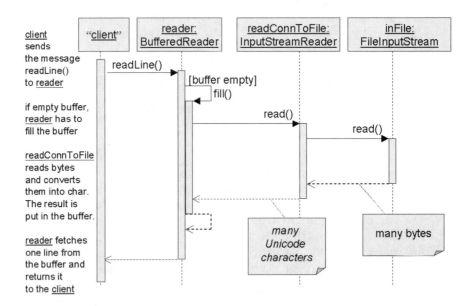

Figure 11.2   Reading from a file using streams (UML)

Problem

Write a program that reads lines of text from the data file *mineData.txt*. The program will count the number of lines read and display this number on the screen.

(a) Try the program without the file existing. What happens?

(b) Create the file, but do not store any data in it (use an editor). Now the number of lines read should be 0. Is that right?

(c) Enter data in the file. Try the program. Are the results right? Put the file in a subdirectory called *MineData*. What changes do you have to make to the program now?

11.4 Writing Text to a File

The second part of the program in Program Listing 11.1 inputs more names from the user. New names are written to the file after the ones that were already there. We open the file for writing:

    FileWriter writeConnToFile = new FileWriter(filename, true);

If we want to write over what was in the file from before, we set the last argument to `false`.[2]

The next statement takes care of buffering and also creates an instance of the `PrintWriter` class:

    PrintWriter printer = new PrintWriter(new BufferedWriter(writeConnToFile));

The reason we use `PrintWriter` and don't stick to `BufferedWriter` becomes apparent when we look at the methods the different classes offer. The class `BufferedWriter` offers output of strings or simple characters, while the class `PrintWriter` offers exactly the same methods we are familiar with from previous use of `System.out`.

The class `PrintWriter` flushes (empties) the buffer every time a new line is output.

We write a line to the stream in the following manner:

    printer.println(newName);

We close the stream with the `close()` method:

    printer.close();

Any buffers that are not empty are flushed. In other words, the contents are written to the disk. Therefore, it is especially important to remember to close streams that are being written to.

Problem

Continue working with the problem from the previous section. The lines that are input from the file *mineData.txt* will be translated into all capitals and output to the file *yoursData.txt* gradually as they are input.

---

2. As described in the details section for input, we have to mention that this can be considered a short form of the following two statements:
   FileOutputStream outfile = new FileOutputStream(filename, true);
   OutputStreamWriter writeConnToFile = new OutputStreamWriter(outfile);

11.5 Data Files: Summary and Class Descriptions

We'll begin by pointing out the following:

- Data files are opened for reading *or* writing. Reading always starts at the beginning of the file. Writing can happen at the beginning of the file or after what is already there from before.[3]

- For a file to be read, it has to exist in advance.

If a file to be written to does not already exist, it will be created automatically.

Table 11.1 provides a "recipe" for reading and writing to files, as we have covered it so far (*append* has the value `true` if we want to write after what is already in the file, otherwise the value is `false`).

Table 11.1 Reading and writing to a file

	To read from a file	To write to a file
To open a file	`FileReader connection = new FileReader(fileName)`	`FileWriter connection = new FileWriter(fileName, append)`
To create a read stream object or a write stream object	`BufferedReader reader = new BufferedReader( connection)`	`PrintWriter printer = new PrintWriter(new BufferedWriter( connection))`
To read/write to the stream object	`reader.readLine(...)`	`printer.print(....)` `printer.println(....)`
To close the stream object	`reader.close()`	`printer.close()`

We became acquainted with the statement `System.out.println()` in chapter 1. We have now progressed to the point where we can analyze it a little more closely. `System` is a class. By looking it up in the API documentation, we find that it belongs to the package `java.lang`. We also find that `out` is a class constant in this class. It is an instance of the class `PrintStream`, which is a class that does not take the conversion from Unicode to ASCII into consideration. Java

---

3. In Section 11.9, we will see how we can move forward and backward in a file. This method of handling a file also makes reciprocal rereading and rewriting possible.

provides two groups of classes for handling input and output data. The older group (JDK 1.0, Figure 11.3) ignores the conversion between Unicode and ASCII. The classes in this group are subclasses of the classes `InputStream` and `Output-Stream`. They have names that end in `Stream`. The classes that belong to the new group (JDK 1.1, Figure 11.4) handle the conversion between the two character sets as well as the different ASCII extensions that exist around the world. The new classes are also more efficient. These classes are subclasses of the classes `Reader` and `Writer`, and they have names that end in `Reader` and `Writer`.

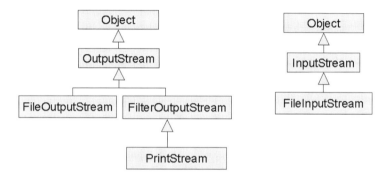

Figure 11.3   A small selection of the input and output classes in JDK 1.0 (UML)

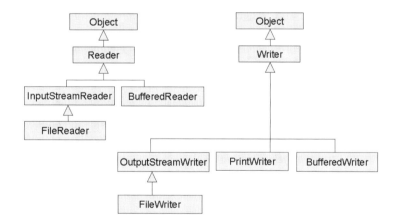

Figure 11.4   A small selection of the input and output classes in JDK 1.1 and newer versions of java (UML)

API Reference

Nearly all constructors and methods may throw IOException.

The java.io.InputStreamReader class

This class bridges between byte streams and character streams. It reads bytes and converts them into Unicode characters.

Constructor:

    public InputStreamReader(InputStream in)

An instance of this class reads bytes with reference to the code set in the environment the program is running in. For specifying other code sets, see the online API documentation.

Method:

    public void close()

This method closes the stream.

The java.io.FileReader class

An instance of this class corresponds to a FileInputStream combined with an InputStreamReader.

Constructor:

    public FileReader(String fileName)

The constructor throws a FileNotFoundException if the file does not exist.

The java.io.BufferedReader class

Constructor:

    public BufferedReader(Reader in)

The argument can be an instance of the class FileReader. The standard buffer size is 8192 bytes.

Methods:

    public String readLine()

This method reads a line of text. The return value does not contain the end-of-line character(s). The method returns a null if there is no more data to read.

    public long skip(long n)

The method skips a maximum of n characters. The return value states the number of characters skipped.

```
public void close()
```

This method closes the stream.

The java.io.OutputStreamWriter class

Constructor:

```
public OutputStreamWriter(OutputStream out)
```

An instance of this class converts characters in the Unicode character set to bytes in the code set stated in the environment the program is running in.

Methods:

```
public void flush()
```

This method flushes the buffer. Flushing means emptying the buffer of unwritten data and sending this data to the stream.

```
public void close()
```

This method closes the stream.

The java.io.FileWriter class

Constructors:

```
public FileWriter(String fileName)
public FileWriter(String fileName, boolean append)
```

If the file does not exist already, it is created. If you want the writing to occur *after* what is already in the file, you have to use the latter constructor with the second argument set to `true`.

The java.io.BufferedWriter class

Constructor:

```
public BufferedWriter(Writer out)
```

The argument can be an instance of the class `FileWriter`. The standard buffer size is 8192 bytes. The buffer is flushed for every end-of-line that is output.

The java.io.PrintWriter class

Constructor:

```
public PrintWriter(Writer out)
```

The argument is usually an instance of the `BufferedWriter` class.

Methods:

These methods can also be used for `System.out`.

public void println()

This method outputs a blank line. The new line can be a single character or several characters, depending on the platform. This method uses the string returned from the method `System.getProperty("line.separator");`

public void print(*dataType* value)
public void println(*dataType* value)

The former outputs the value without the newline after it. The latter ends the printout with a newline.

The *dataType* can be `boolean`, `char`, `char[]`, `double`, `float`, `int`, `long`, `Object`, or `String`. That the data type can be an `Object` means that the argument can be of any class. In these cases, the class's implementation of the method `toString()` is used (see Section 10.4). The method `String.valueOf(dataType)` is used for the primitive data types.

public void flush()

This method flushes the buffer.

public void close()

This method closes the stream.

11.6 Reading Numbers from a Data File

We link a stream to the file in the regular way. Then what do we do if we want to read a line of numbers from this text stream? The answer is as follows:

- All the data in a text stream has to be input with the method `readLine()`. There are no methods for reading a number or just a single word.

- To find spaces in a string, we use the class `java.util.StringTokenizer`.

- A string is converted into a number using the familiar methods `parseInt()` and `parseDouble()`.

Program listing 11.2 shows a program that inputs many numbers from a text stream and calculates the sum of these numbers.

We have a `try-catch` block to handle the exceptions that might occur. Then we have a loop where each run deals with one line. Each line consists of many numbers. The loop body in the innermost loop deals with one number.

We are using the class `StringTokenizer` to find the numbers. This class parses a string that consists of several parts ("tokens") separated by delimiters. Standard delimiters are spaces, tabs, newlines, and carriage returns. This works well for us. We can also define our own delimiters. The method `nextToken()` returns the next portion of the string, while the method `hasMoreTokens()` returns `false` when there are no more portions to be retrieved.

Program Listing 11.2

```java
/*
 * ReadManyNumbers.java   E.L. 2001-08-15
 *
 * Reads many lines of numbers, and adds them together.
 */
import java.util.*;
import java.io.*;
class ReadManyNumbers {
  public static void main(String[] args) {
    String fileName = "numberFile.txt";
    try {
      FileReader connToFile = new FileReader(fileName);
      BufferedReader reader = new BufferedReader(connToFile);

      int sum = 0;
      try {
        String aLine = reader.readLine();
        while(aLine != null) {
          StringTokenizer text = new StringTokenizer(aLine);
          while (text.hasMoreTokens()) {
            String s = text.nextToken();
            int number = Integer.parseInt(s); // may throw NumberFormatException
            sum += number;
          }
          aLine = reader.readLine();
        }
      } catch (IOException e) {
        System.out.println("IO-Error when reading from file: " + fileName);
      } catch (NumberFormatException e) {
        System.out.println("Error when converting from text to number.");
      }
      reader.close();
      System.out.println("The sum of all the numbers is " + sum);

    } catch (FileNotFoundException e) {

      System.out.println("File not found: " + fileName);

    } catch (IOException e) {
      System.out.println("IO-Error when opening/closing the file: " + fileName);
    }
```

```
    }
}
/* Example Run:
Data file:
23 45 678 1 -56
-42 898 7
3 56 -90 0 67
4

Output:
The sum of all the numbers is 1594
*/
```

API Reference

The java.util.StringTokenizer class

This class makes it possible to parse a string into tokens. Two tokens have to be separated by one or more delimiters. The delimiters are not part of the tokens that the string is divided up into.

Constructors:

```
public StringTokenizer(String text)
public StringTokenizer(String text, String delimiters)
```

The first constructor uses the following delimiters: spaces, tabs, newlines and carriage returns. The second gives us the opportunity to specify a number of pertinent delimiters.

Methods:

```
public boolean hasMoreTokens()
```

The method returns `true` if the string contains more tokens from the position where we are. Otherwise, the method returns `false`.

```
public String nextToken()
```

The class maintains an internal "pointer" that is used to search in the string. In the first call of this method, the pointer is at the beginning of the string. The method returns the string's first token. At the same time, the pointer gradually moves through the string as more and more tokens are returned using this method. The method throws a `NoSuchElementException` if the string does not contain any more tokens.

```
public int countTokens()
```

This method returns the number of tokens left in the string. The method does not move the internal pointer forward.

Problem

Create a class that contains two methods, one to read a line of integers and another to read a line of decimal numerals from a file. The numbers will be returned to the client in an array.

The class will have an instance variable of the `BufferedReader` type.

Create a program that makes it possible to test the class. Input several lines of numbers.

11.7 Communication with the Console

We have been writing to the console since chapter 1:

```
System.out.println("Our first program...");
```

But we have avoided reading data from the console in this book. Instead, we have used the class `JOptionPane`.

The following code bit links the console to a buffered text stream for inputting, then printing a background text, and then inputs a line of text:

```
InputStreamReader readConnConsole = new InputStreamReader(System.in);
BufferedReader reader = new BufferedReader(readConnConsole);
System.out.print("Your first name: ");
System.out.flush();   // flushes the buffer after print() is used
String firstName = reader.readLine();
```

We have to flush the buffer to be sure that the text "Your first name: " is printed on the screen before the program control comes to the input statement.

Otherwise, this is very similar to reading from a file. The difference is that we are using the `InputStreamReader` class instead of `FileReader`. The argument for the constructor is not the file name, but the class constant `System.in`. This is an instance of the `InputStream` class, which belongs to the "old" byte-oriented classes. The `InputStreamReader` class belongs to the new classes and takes care of the conversion to the Unicode character set.

Problem

Write a program that reads a number of numerals from the console and calculates their sum. The program will run until it encounters "file end." The end of the file is indicated by (Ctrl+Z) in MS-DOS and (Ctrl+D) in UNIX. "File end" has to be on its own line.

11.8 Binary Transfer of Data

People can read all the data files we have seen up to this point using an editor. In order for this to be possible for both numbers and text, the numbers must be converted from binary representation to text representation. We say that the data is *transferred as text*. The conversion between binary and text representation occurs without our needing to think about it. Nevertheless, we will look briefly at what this conversion entails. This is necessary in order to understand the difference between this method of transferring data and something that is called "binary transfer" of data.

As an example, we will illustrate what is happening in the text transfer of numbers: The number 25 is located in the internal memory in a variable of the type `int`. The variable contains the number 25 in binary form (the base-two system, see Appendix D): 11001.[4] This is converted to the string "25" when it is output. (The method `String.valueOf(25)` is called behind the scenes.) This string consists of two variables of the type `char`. The first represents the character '2' (numeric value 50, binary 110010), while the second represents the character '5' (numeric value 53, binary 1100101).

The reverse process is carried out when inputting to numeric variables. See Figure 11.5.

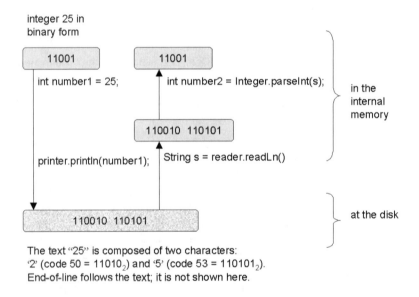

The text "25" is composed of two characters:
'2' (code 50 = 11010_2) and '5' (code 53 = 110101_2).
End-of-line follows the text; it is not shown here.

Figure 11.5 Numbers are converted to and from text through text transfer of data

There can be a number of reasons for this conversion to be done. The data file can be read by people and can be read by programs written in languages other than Java. If we do not have requirements of this type for our files, transferring data without converting it to text is a good alternative. That means that the data is stored in the same form on the disk as in the internal memory. Transferring data without converting to text is called *binary transfer of data*. The number 25 is stored as 11001 both in the internal memory and on the disk.

---

4. It is not important for you to understand the exact order of the zeros and ones. What is important is that you understand that this order differs depending on whether the number is represented in binary form or in text form.

The conversion from binary form to text takes time and is particularly unsuitable if there are decimal numerals to transfer. To maintain accuracy in the text form of the number, a `double` has to be written to a file with 15 digits.

A variable that is transferred without conversion from the internal memory to the disk takes just as much room on the disk as in the internal memory. The amount of space taken up by variables of the different data types is given in Section 2.6.

Methods for transferring data without converting it are specified in the interfaces `DataInput` and `DataOutput`. As an example of a class that implements these interfaces, we will look in the next section at the class `RandomAccessFile`, which gives us random access to the contents of a file. In connection with this class, we will go through several of the methods in the two interfaces. Other classes that implement these interfaces are `DataInputStream` and `DataOutput-Stream`.

Problem

Draw a figure corresponding to Figure 11.5 for a variable of the type `int` that contains the number 15, and a variable of the type `char` that contains the character '3'.

11.9 Random Access to the Contents of a File

Up to this point, our programs have worked their way through a file sequentially. We have read files from the beginning onward, line by line. In much the same way, we have written to files in sequential order. We started writing at the beginning of the file, or we wrote after what was already in the file. We have not been able to move forward and backward in the file, nor have we been able to open a file for both reading and writing at the same time.

An instance of the class `RandomAccessFile` is linked to a file that can be opened for both reading and writing, and we can move the *file pointer* to any position whatsoever in this file. Reading and writing start where the file pointer is located. The file pointer follows the reading and writing. After the operation has been performed, the file pointer is positioned after the data value that was written or read.

This sounds great, but we have to remember that we are referring to a stream of bytes, and it is the programmer who has to calculate how far forward or backward the file pointer should be moved. The calculation must start with the number of bytes a variable of a given type takes up.

Program listing 11.3 shows a simple example of how random access to a file might work. We start by opening the file for both reading and writing:

```
RandomAccessFile file = new RandomAccessFile("DirectFile.dat", "rw");
```

The last argument can be `"rw"` for reading and writing, or just `"r"` for reading.

The program writes the numbers 0, 1, 2, ..., 9 to the stream. The method `writeInt()` is used to write an integer:

```
for (int i = 0; i < 10; i++) file.writeInt(i); // position 1 in figure 11.6
```

Each number takes up four bytes. Therefore, the length of the file is 40 bytes. We get the length with the method `length()` and write it on the screen.

```
long fileLength = file.length(); // the length() method returns long
System.out.println("The file is " + fileLength + " bytes long.");
```

Now the file pointer is sitting after the last number that was written to the file. For example, we move it to the seventh number and read it:

```
file.seek(6 * 4); // moves past 6 integers of 4 bytes each, to position 2 in figure 11.6
int number = file.readInt(); // position 3 in figure 11.6
```

We multiply the number by 10 and write it back again. In order to rewrite the number in the right place, we have to move the file pointer back to position 2 in the figure. Note that we always give the position relative to the beginning of the file.

```
number *= 10;
file.seek(6 * 4); // moves the filepointer "back"
file.writeInt(number);
```

After writing, the file pointer is in position 3 again. Finally, the program reads the whole file and writes the data on the screen for inspection. Before reading, we have to remember to move the file pointer to the beginning of the file:

```
file.seek(0);  // moves to the beginning of the file
try {
  while (true) {  // stops when EOFException is thrown
    int t = file.readInt();
    System.out.println(t);
  }
}
catch (EOFException e) {
}
file.close();
```

This loop is complicated because the method `readInt()` does not return any definite value at the end of the file. (What should it be? All possible return values are valid integers.) Instead, it throws an `EOFException`. Therefore, we have to let the input happen in a loop where the loop condition is always true. Thus, the loop is exited directly from `readInt()` when the `EOFException` is thrown. We have to handle this exception right outside the loop, so that the file is closed when the input is finished.

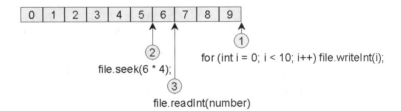

Figure 11.6 The positions of the file pointer during the running of the program in listing 11.3

Program Listing 11.3

```java
/*
 * DirectAccessFile.java   E.L. 2001-08-16
 *
 */
import java.io.*;
class DirectAccessFile {
  public static void main(String[] args) {

    try {
      RandomAccessFile file = new RandomAccessFile("DirectFile.dat", "rw");

      /* writes 10 integers to the file */
      for (int i = 0; i < 10; i++) file.writeInt(i);
      long fileLength = file.length();
      System.out.println("The file is " + fileLength + " bytes long.");

      /*
       * moves the file pointer to integer no. 7, reads i,
       * multiplies it by 10, and rewrites it to the file.
       */

      file.seek(6 * 4); // moves past 6 integers, each 4 bytes
      int number = file.readInt();
      number *= 10;
      file.seek(6 * 4); // moves the filepointer "back"
      file.writeInt(number);

      /* reads the whole file */
      file.seek(0);  // moves to the beginning of the file
      try {
        while (true) {  // stops when EOFException is thrown
          int t = file.readInt();
          System.out.println(t);
        }
      }
      catch (EOFException e) {
      }
      file.close();
    } catch (Exception e) {
      System.out.println("Error: " + e);
    }
  }
}

/* Example Run:
The file is 40 bytes long.
0
1
2
3
```

```
4
5
60
7
8
9
*/
```

 ## API Reference

The java.io.RandomAccessFile class

This class is a direct subclass of the `java.lang.Object` class. It implements the interfaces for binary data transfer, `DataInput` and `DataOutput`.

Constructors:

```
public RandomAccessFile(String fileName, String mode)
public RandomAccessFile(File file, String mode)
```

The constructors make file streams where you can read and potentially write to a random position in the stream. The `mode` is either "`r`" (read only) or "`rw`" (read and write). The file has to exist in advance if it is opened for read only.

Methods (all the methods can throw IOExceptions):

```
public long getFilePointer()
```

This method returns the position of the file pointer.

```
public void seek(long pos)
```

This method moves the file pointer to the stated position, calculated as the number of bytes from the beginning of the file.

```
public long length()
```

This method returns the length of the file in a number of bytes.

```
public void close()
```

This method closes the file.

```
public char readChar()
public int readInt()
public double readDouble()
public void writeChar(int v)
public void writeInt(int v)
public void writeDouble(double v)
```

These methods are used for binary transfer of data. `readChar()` and `writeChar()` read and write Unicode characters (2 bytes per character).

```
public String readLine()
```

This method reads bytes from the file until a newline is encountered. Every individual byte is converted to a two-byte Unicode character. This means that only a part of the Unicode character set is supported in this method. The method returns `null` if the file pointer is at the end of the file.

```
public void writeChars(String text)
```

This method writes a string with two bytes (Unicode) for every character.

Finally, a brief example shows that the methods `readLine()` and `writeChars()` are not symmetrical:

```
file.writeChars("Text\n");
System.out.println("Length: " + file.length());
file.seek(0);
System.out.println(file.readLine());
```

The output is as follows:

```
Length: 10
T e x t
```

A length of 10 shows that `writeChars()` uses two bytes per character. The last two bytes are the newline character in MS-DOS/Windows. In a UNIX system, the length will be 9, because the newline character is a single character. The spaces in the output show that `readLine()` creates a character from each one of the 10 bytes.

Problems

1. Find out what happens if the text is rewritten to a file after the input in the last example above.

2. Suppose that you are going to store groups of integers in a binary file. Every group contains an unknown number of integers. How will you keep the groups apart?

11.10 Serialization

Suppose we need to store objects in a file. Let's look at the `RenovationProject` class in Program Listing 10.1. We want to store information about surfaces and paint types from program run to program run.

What do we have to do to save all this information in a data file?

For the sake of simplicity, let's limit ourselves to the surfaces. We have to make a loop that runs through all the elements in the array list `allSurfaces`. For every surface, we have to store the name, length, width, and paint. The last is a reference, where we have to obtain the paint name and store it. To simplify the input, we should store every individual data value on one line:

```
/* for each surface */
printer.println(name);
printer.println(length);
printer.println(width);
printer.println(paint.getName());
```

When we're ready to input the data again, we have to run the loop. The numbers have to be converted from text to numerals. For every new surface, we have to make an instance of the `Surface` class and store this in the array list. This is a rather cumbersome method.

As an alternative, Java offers *serialization* for storing objects. The advantage is that our whole object (the large instance of the `RenovationProject` class) can be stored with a single statement. The disadvantage is that the data file cannot be read in an editor. We can relocate any text data there might be, but the numbers cannot be read. And there is a lot of other information stored in binary form mixed in with the text data.

Program Listing 11.4

```java
/*
 * SerializeWrite.java   E.L. 2001-08-16
 *
 */
import java.io.*;
class SerializeWrite {
  public static void main(String[] args) throws IOException {
    Paint m1 = new Paint("Extra", 10, 3, 10);
    Paint m2 = new Paint("Super", 8, 2, 12);
    Surface f1 = new Surface("Wall in children's room", 4, 3);
    Surface f2 = new Surface("Ceiling in the corridor", 6, 3);
    f1.setPaint(m1);
    f2.setPaint(m2);

    RenovationProject myApartment = new RenovationProject("My apartment");
    myApartment.addNewPaint(m1);
    myApartment.addNewPaint(m2);
    myApartment.addNewSurface(f1);
    myApartment.addNewSurface(f2);

    FileOutputStream outstream = new FileOutputStream("apartment1.ser");
    ObjectOutputStream out = new ObjectOutputStream(outstream);
    out.writeObject(myApartment);
    out.close();

    outstream = new FileOutputStream("apartment2.ser");
    out = new ObjectOutputStream(outstream);
    out.writeObject(f1);
    out.writeObject(f2);
    out.writeObject(m1);
    out.writeObject(m2);
```

```
      out.close();
    }
  }
  /*
   * SerializeRead.java   E.L. 2001-08-16
   *
   */
  import java.io.*;
  class SerializeRead {
    public static void main(String[] args) throws Exception{
      FileInputStream instream = new FileInputStream("apartment1.ser");
      ObjectInputStream in = new ObjectInputStream(instream);
      RenovationProject myApartment = (RenovationProject) in.readObject();
      in.close();

      System.out.println("Apartment data read from the file apartment1.ser:");
      for (int i = 0; i < myApartment.getNoOfSurfaces(); i++) {
        System.out.println(myApartment.getSurface(i));
      }

      for (int i = 0; i < myApartment.getNoOfPaints(); i++) {
        System.out.println(myApartment.getPaint(i));
      }

      System.out.println("Surface and paint data, read from the file apartment2.ser");
      instream = new FileInputStream("apartment2.ser");
      in = new ObjectInputStream(instream);
      try {
        while (true) { // stops when EOFException is thrown
          java.lang.Object obj = in.readObject();
          System.out.println(obj);
        }
      }
      catch (EOFException e) {
      }
      in.close();
    }
  }

  /* Output with input made by the SerializeWrite program:
  Apartment data read from the file apartment1.ser:
  Surface: Wall in children's room, length: 4.0 m, width: 3.0 m
  Surface: Ceiling in the corridor, length: 6.0 m, width: 3.0 m
  Paint: Extra, no. of coats: 3, no. of sq.m./liter: 10.0, price: $10.0
  Paint: Super, no. of coats: 2, no. of sq.m./liter: 12.0, price: $8.0
  Surface and paint data, read from the file apartment2.ser
  Surface: Wall in children's room, length: 4.0 m, width: 3.0 m
  Surface: Ceiling in the corridor, length: 6.0 m, width: 3.0 m
  Paint: Extra, no. of coats: 3, no. of sq.m./liter: 10.0, price: $10.0
  Paint: Super, no. of coats: 2, no. of sq.m./liter: 12.0, price: $8.0
  */
```

Program Listing 11.4 shows first a program that writes serialized objects to a file, then a program that reads these objects. We will go through these programs. The code bit below links an object stream to a file, writes all the data in the object myApartment to this stream, and then closes the stream.

```
FileOutputStream outstream = new FileOutputStream("apartment1.ser");
ObjectOutputStream out = new ObjectOutputStream(outstream);
out.writeObject(myApartment); // (class constants and class variables are not stored)
out.close();
```

The input is just as straightforward:

```
FileInputStream instream = new FileInputStream("apartment1.ser");
ObjectInputStream in = new ObjectInputStream(instream);
RenovationProject myApartment = (RenovationProject) in.readObject();
in.close();
```

The return type from the method readObject() is Object. Therefore, we have to cast to the RenovationProject class if we are going to use RenovationProject's methods on the object. The input object contains information about its own class. If we try to cast to the wrong class, a ClassCastException is thrown.

What's required for us to be able to store objects so easily? The classes we store all have to implement the interface java.io.Serializable. This is a very simple interface. It doesn't contain any methods. Therefore, it's enough to write implements java.io.Serializable in the class head. In this example, we have to change the class heads as follows:

```
class Surface implements java.io.Serializable {
class Paint implements java.io.Serializable {
class RenovationProject implements java.io.Serializable {
```

These classes use the predefined classes java.util.ArrayList and java.lang.String. By looking them up in the online API documentation, we find out that these classes implement java.io.Serializable. The vast majority of the classes that go with SDK implement this interface.

The program that reads the data file prints the data on the screen for inspection. The program runs through all the surfaces and prints information about every individual surface in the apartment:

```
for (int i = 0; i < myApartment.getNoOfSurfaces(); i++) {
    System.out.println(myApartment.getSurface(i));
}
```

The method getSurface() returns a reference to a Surface object. When we put that into a println() method, a call to the method toString() will be implied. Thus, the body of the preceding loop can be written in the following manner:

```
Surface f = myApartment.getSurface(i);
System.out.println(f.toString());
```

The program runs through all the Paint objects the same way.

The second part of the first of the two programs in Program Listing 11.4 shows an alternative version, where we treat the Surface and Paint objects individually. First we write:

```
outstream = new FileOutputStream("apartment2.ser");
out = new ObjectOutputStream(outstream);
out.writeObject(f1);
out.writeObject(f2);
out.writeObject(m1);
out.writeObject(m2);
out.close();
```

We have to input the same way as we wrote, i.e., one object at a time. Either we can assume that we know that exactly two Surface objects and two Paint objects are stored in the file, or we can let the program find out the type of object, and then finish inputting when the end of the file is reached:

```
instream = new FileInputStream("apartment2.ser");
in = new ObjectInputStream(instream);
try {
  while (true) { // stops when EOFException is thrown
    java.lang.Object obj = in.readObject();
    System.out.println(obj);
  }
}
catch (EOFException e) {
}
in.close();
```

In the same way as the method readInt() in the RandomAccessFile class, the method readObject() also does not return any definite value at the end of the file. Therefore, we also have to handle EOFExceptions here.

We see that we can send the object directly to the println() statement without casting to the right object type. The reason for this is that the method toString() is declared in the Object class. Since the method is also implemented for the Surface and Paint classes, this version will be used, and not the standard version that we find in the Object class.

What if we had wanted to use methods declared in the Surface or Paint class? Then we would have had to check the object type before casting:

```
if (obj instanceof Surface) {
  Surface s = (Surface) obj;
  ...send messages to the object s..
} else if (obj instanceof Paint) {
  Paint p = (Paint) obj;
  ...send messages to the object p...
}
```

Java Core

The instanceof operator

instanceof is a binary operator that takes a reference to an object as its first operand and a class or an interface as its second operand. The value for the expression is true if the object is an instance of the class, or of a subclass of the class. If the second operand is an interface, the object has to be an instance of a class (or of a subclass of a class) that implements this interface. The operator has the same priority as the other comparison operators.

We will look briefly at what serialization means.

We write to a stream of bytes. The stream itself knows nothing about how a class is constructed. The serialization process therefore stores information about the class every individual object belongs to. The values for the instance variables are written to the stream. Class constants and class variables are not stored in a serialization procedure.

In the example above we store two Surface objects and two Paint objects. Every object that is written to the stream gets its own serial number (hence the name serialization). Every Surface object has a reference to a Paint object. Notice nonetheless that it works well to store the Surface objects before we store the Paint objects. The program would also work if we only stored the Surface objects. All objects get their serial numbers and are stored the first time they are encountered. On later occasions only the object's serial number is stored. That means that the Paint object "Extra" is stored in connection with the first Surface object that is stored. After that, only the object's serial number is stored.

The file keeps track of which version of a class was being used when it was written. If this class has changed before reading occurs, an exception is thrown. For example:

```
java.io.InvalidClassException: Surface; Local class not
compatible:
stream classdesc serialVersion UID=-7026669327769092791
local class serialVersion UID=8895152082615953301
```

Problems

1. What do we have to do with the Merchandise class from [URL Java book], chapter 10, for instances of the class to be serialized?

2. Make an array of the Merchandise class with room for five elements. Give these elements values. Test whether you can write the whole array as one object to the file i.e., find out whether arrays like this can be serialized if the elements in the array can be serialized.

3. Also try to serialize an array of integers. Hint: you cast an object to an array of integers by writing `(int[])`.

11.11 New Concepts in This Chapter

Concept	Brief Explanation
binary transfer of data	The data is transferred between internal and secondary memory without conversion.
buffer	Intermediate storage for data transport between internal and secondary memory.
close file	To bring the connection between a stream and a physical file to an end.
file pointer	Keeps track of where the next read or write statement starts. The file pointer changes value gradually as the read or write process is performed.
instanceof	Comparison operator with an object as its first operand and a class or an interface as its second operand. The expression has the value true if the object is an instance of the class, or of a subclass of the class. If the second operand is an interface, the object has to be an instance of a class (or of a subclass of a class) that implements this interface. The operator has the same priority as the other comparison operators.
native	Used about methods that are written in platform-dependent code. native is a modifier found in method heads, see for example the online API documentation for the RandomAccessFile class.
open file	To link a stream object to a physical file.
random access to the contents of a file	Reading and writing can occur to any specified location, and the file pointer can be positioned anywhere in the file.
serialization	A technique for storing *whole* objects in a file, including other objects that are referred to.
stream	An abstraction that hides the details of data transfer between the internal memory and the disk or other secondary memory.
text transfer of data	Data in binary form is converted to text when writing to a secondary memory. When reading, the data is converted from text and back to binary form.

11.12 Review Problems

1. Suppose we open a file for writing. Will the writing occur after what is already in the file from before, or will we write over this?

2. What happens if the file we open doesn't exist in advance?

3. Is is possible to open a file for both reading and writing?

4. Explain the difference between text and binary data transfer.

5. What is the advantage of text data transfer over binary transfer? Are there any disadvantages?

6. What is the purpose of buffering?

7. Why is it important to close a file (a stream)?

8. Set up code lines that read a decimal numeral from a file and store it in the variable oneNumber.

9. What can we use the StringTokenizer class for?

10. Suppose that we want to consider the console to be a file. What is the file name?

11. How do we write a complete file name, including path, in Java?

12. What types of streams give us access to manipulate the file pointer? What can we do with it?

13. A program that reads from a file has to stop reading when it comes to the end of the file. How can the program check that it has reached the end of the file?

14. What does the concept "to serialize an object" mean?

15. Explain how we use the operator instanceof.

11.13 Programming Problems

Problem 1

Use the Month class from chapter 9.

Make a class Year that contains an array with 12 months. The class will calculate a number of statistics for the year as a whole:

- Find the wettest month

- Find the driest month

- Find the average precipitation per day in the summer half of the year (April–September)

- Find the average precipitation per day in the winter half of the year (October–March)

Read the precipitation from a file and print precipitation statistics for each of the 12 months and for the year as a whole.

Test the program by using a file that contains the same precipitation every day of the year. The data file is easy to make with a little program.

You might get more realistic data by generating random numbers for the precipitation.

Problem 2

Create a program that encrypts a text. The text is read from a file. The results are written to another file. The file names are read from the user. The program will also be able to take a file in encrypted format and convert it back to "readable" form.

Only the letters will be encrypted. Every letter will be replaced by a different letter. Enter the codes as a string. The first character in the string is the letter that 'A' will be replaced by, the second character the letter that 'B' will be replaced by, etc. If you start with a capital letter, the result should be a capital letter; if with a lower-case letter, the result should be a lower-case letter. Punctuation marks are kept unencrypted.

The codes are read from a file that the user has to provide the name for.

Example:

The letters BAN have the codes GHY. The word "banana" is then coded to "ghyhyh," while "Banana" is coded to "Ghyhyh."

Problem 3

Use the `Account` class from programming problem 1 in chapter 6.

Create a program that maintains a bank account.

The previous balance is in the file *balance.txt*. Recent transactions are in a file. The file contains one line per transaction. Every line contains a letter that explains what type of transaction it is and an amount.

Transaction codes: W for withdrawal, D for deposit.

After the transaction file is treated, the new balance is placed in the file *balance.txt*.

Individual transactions that mean the account has a negative balance are all right. (Change the class `Account` so that this is possible.) If the net result at the end is such that the balance is negative, however, the whole transaction file will be rejected. No transactions will be recorded in this case.

Example: Starting balance: $5,460.70. The transaction file has the following contents:

```
W 450
D 567.80
D 4000.00
W 500
```

Result: New balance is $9078.50.

Problem 4

Suppose that we have two data files of numbers. The numbers are sorted in ascending order. Create a program that generates a third file where all the numbers from both of the files are sorted in ascending order. (We say that we are "merging" the two files.)

Example:

File 1: -23 12 12 67 678

File 2: 67 676 756

The new file will look like this: -23 12 12 67 67 676 678 756

Problem 5

Make a simple birthday registry. The registry is in a file. The registry will not be input into the internal memory in its entirety, but will be maintained directly in the file. For each person, the first name, last name, and date of birth are stored in the file. For simplicity's sake, you can assume that both the first and last name each take up 15 characters. Use an array of char, possibly the StringBuffer class.

The user will be able to get the date of birth for a person when she types in the name. It should be possible to expand the registry by more names. You can assume that a person's name is unambiguous and that the user enters both the first and last name.

12

Inheritance and Polymorphism

Learning goals for this chapter

The following concepts have been mentioned previously in the book. We will now look more closely at what they mean:

- Subclass, superclass, inheritance, and the keyword `extends`. The keywords `interface` and `implements`

The following new concepts are introduced in this chapter:

- Generalization, specialization, abstract method, abstract class, the keyword `abstract`, and the access modifier `protected`

- Polymorphic operation, polymorphism

- The keyword `super`. The keyword `final` in connection with classes and methods

- Overriding/hiding an inherited member

You will be able to:

- Program class trees and polymorphic operations

You will understand:

- The difference between associations and class trees

- What inheritance means and how polymorphism works; when it should be used, and when it shouldn't be used

- The difference between classes and interfaces and how you use interfaces

In Section 4.6, you were introduced to the class tree in Java. We made subclasses for the `JPanel` and `JApplet` classes by using the keyword `extends`. In this chapter, we will take a detailed look at what making subclasses means

Figure 4.7 shows how the objects that belong to a subclass form a subset of the objects that belong to the superclass. Another way of saying this is to use the concepts of "specialization" and "generalization."

The concept of polymorphism is central to class trees and inheritance. It means that a client object can send the same message to different server objects, and these objects know all on their own how they will perform the service requested. We have a simple example when we print a document to different printers. As the user (client), we send the message "Print this document", and the individual printer knows how to do the printing all by itself. In practice, the different drivers are responsible for the job, but for us as users this is hidden.

12.1 Generalization and Specialization

In our renovation project we have three types of materials: paint, flooring, and wallpaper (see Figure 12.1). We see that these classes have a fair amount in common. All of them have a name and price as attributes, and they also have several equivalent operations.

Flooring	Paint	Wallpaper
name price widthOfFlooring	name price noOfCoats noOfSqMPerLiter	name price lengthPerRoll widthPerRoll
getName getPricePerM getWidth getNoOfMeters getTotalPrice	getName getPricePerLiter getNoOfCoats getNoOfSqMPerLiter getNoOfLiters getTotalPrice	getName getPricePerRoll getLengthPerRoll getWidthPerRoll getNoOfRolls getTotalPrice

Figure 12.1　Classes that describe different types of materials for use in renovation (UML)

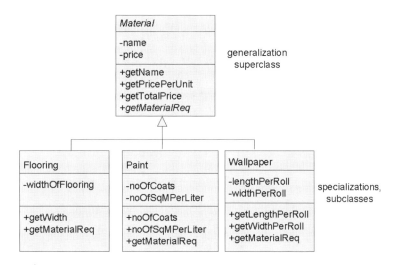

Figure 12.2 The material class represents a generalization of the flooring, paint, and wallpaper classes (UML)

In Figure 12.2, we've collected what these three classes have in common into the `Material` class. We say that the `Material` class represents a *generalization* (superclass) of the `Flooring`, `Paint`, and `Wallpaper` classes. On the other side, `Flooring`, `Paint` and `Wallpaper` classes are *specializations* (subclasses) of the `Material` class. The operations `getNoOfMeters()`, `getNoOfLiters()`, and `getNoOfRolls()` are collected under the common name `getMaterialReq()`. We have made a class tree.

Attributes and operations have a - and + before them respectively. Minus means a private member. Plus means a public member. This corresponds to the access modifiers `private` and `public`, which we use when we program the classes. Once we start exploring what the concept of inheritance involves, we will also see that it's important to distinguish between access levels in the class diagram.

Generalization always expresses an "is-a" relationship. From Figure 12.2, we therefore read the following in the direction of the arrow:

- Flooring *is* a material.

- Paint *is* a material.

- Wallpaper *is* a material.

We can also, as mentioned earlier, look at the objects that a subclass describes as a subset of the objects the superclass describes:

- All types of flooring are a subset of all materials.

- All paints are a subset of all materials.

- All wallpapers are a subset of all materials

If we cannot say that an instance of a subclass *is also* an instance of the superclass, we probably don't have a true generalization and we should instead model the relationship between the classes in another manner.

Don't confuse associations with generalization/specialization!

An association (Section 10.5) between two classes means that there is a connection between the instances of the two classes. Generalization/specialization does not express a relationship between instances of the involved classes, but between the classes (the object descriptions) *per se*. The objects that belong to a specialized class comprise a subset of the objects that belong to the general class.

Problem

A dentist has many patients. Most of them belong to the category permanent, but a few are random. Only the permanent patients are grouped by sex. Draw a tree that shows a generalization/specialization between the classes `Patient`, `Permanent`, `Random`, `Male`, and `Female`. Expand the class diagram so that it also shows that the information about all the patients together makes up an association between a `PatientRegister` class and one of the classes above (which one?).

12.2 Inheritance

Now that we are going to look at the concept of inheritance, it can be beneficial to consider it from the client side: see Figure 12.2. The client has access to the members marked with a +.

What are the consequences for the client that the class `Flooring` is a subclass of the class `Material`? This means that the client can send the following messages to a `Flooring` object:

- All the messages inherited from the class `Material`: `getName()`, `get-PricePerUnit()`, `getTotalPrice()`, and `getMaterialReq()`.

- All new messages declared in the `Flooring` class. Here that means that the message `getWidth()` will come in addition to the messages mentioned before.

- That we find the message `getMaterialReq()` again in the `Flooring` class simply means that this class makes its own version of this operation. This is not of any interest to the client.

Hence, a class does not inherit private members of a superclass. However, it's important to be clear that objects of the subclass have the data contents that these members represent, but the concept of inheritance is linked to the accessibility of the members, and the members that are private in the superclass are not directly accessible in the subclass. For example: an instance of the `Flooring` class has name and price information in it, but this information can only be reached through the methods `getName()` and `getPricePerUnit()`.

We note that the operation `getMaterialReq()` is written in italics in the `Material` class. The method is also repeated in all the subclasses, but now in upright text. What does this mean?

All types of materials offer this service, therefore it belongs in the `Material` class. But every individual type of material has its own way of calculating the materials required, so it also has to be written in every individual subclass. Since it's not possible to find a common way of calculating the materials needed, the operation will not have any implementation in the `Material` class. We say that it is *abstract*.

It is not possible to create instances of classes that contain abstract operations, which is reasonable (because how would we be able to calculate the materials needed for an instance of the `Material` class?). A class that contains at least one abstract operation becomes abstract itself.

Even if we don't have any implementation of the operation `get-MaterialReq()` in the `Material` class, it's correct to have it there anyway. It says something very important—namely, that we can send the message `getMaterialReq()` to *all* types of materials. The individual material type knows all by itself how it should calculate the quantity required, because after all, the calculation formulas are in these classes.

According to the dictionary the word *polymorphous* means "the quality or state of being able to assume different forms" [URL Merriam-Webster]. The operation `getMaterialReq()` is polymorphous. It occurs in many forms, one for each type of material. Polymorphism is supported by a central principle in object-orientation—that every object will take care of itself. In this case, the object itself knows how to calculate the materials required (see Figure 12.3)

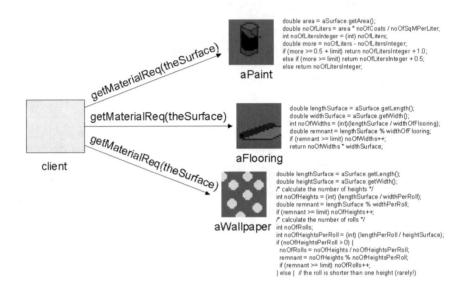

Figure 12.3 The operation `getMaterialReq()` is polymorphous

 Abstract operations and abstract classes are marked with italics in the class diagram. Concrete (i.e. non-abstract) operations and classes are written in regular text. All pertinent implementations of an abstract operation will be shown in the class diagram.

Problems

In a computer manufacturing company there are several categories of employees: customer consultants, technical personnel, system developers, and administrative employees. Some of the last group are secretaries. The following applies:

- All employees have the attributes name, position, and telephone number. A client will be able to get all the data, and it will be able to change the position and telephone number.

- The salary is calculated for all employees, but the algorithm is different depending on which category of employee you belong to.

1. Draw a class tree that shows the connection between these classes. Include attributes and operations. Use + and - to show the level of accessibility for the different members.

2. Should any of the operations you specified be polymorphous? Explain why and describe how the polymorphism can be used in this case.

3. Explain what is inherited from one class to another in your model.

12.3 The Material Class with Subclasses

Program Listing 12.1 shows all four of the classes.

From the class diagram we know that the `Material` class is abstract with an abstract method. The class becomes abstract when we put the modifier `abstract` in the class head:

```
abstract class Material {
```

The compiler protests if we try to make an instance of an abstract class.

We also use the modifier `abstract` in the head for the abstract method:

```
public abstract double getMaterialReq(Surface aSurface);
```

Pay special attention to the semicolon after the head. An abstract method has no body, not even an empty body (`{ }`).

Each of the subclasses has its own implementation of this abstract method.

We've created a constructor in the `Material` class:

```
public Material(String initName, double initPrice) {
```

If we make an instance of a subclass, we will use this constructor to make the "`Material` portion" of the object.

We see that the `getTotalPrice()` method calls the abstract method `getMaterialReq()`. This is possible because the `getTotalPrice()` method will always be called on behalf of a concrete object, and this object must be an instance of a concrete class (i.e., a class that implements the method `getMaterialReq()`). Or, in other words, a client will never send the message `getTotalPrice()` to an instance of the `Material` class for the simple reason that such an instance does not exist. The client will send the message to instances of the class `Flooring`, `Paint`, or `Wallpaper`, and all of these classes have an implementation of the method `getMaterialReq()`.

The rest of the `Material` class should be familiar.

The `Flooring` class is a direct subclass of the `Material` class:

```
class Flooring extends Material {
```

We make subclasses using the keyword extends. Classes that are declared without using extends (for example, the Material class) become direct subclasses to the java.lang.Object class. This is the reason that we can talk about one, and only one, class tree in Java. The Object class is always at the top of the tree. All other classes are subclasses (direct or indirect) of this class.

Let's look at the constructor for the Flooring class:

```
public Flooring(String initName, double initPrice, double initWidth) {
    super(initName, initPrice);
    widthOfFlooring = initWidth;
}
```

Constructors are not inherited. Even if we hadn't given a start value for the width of the flooring, we would still have had to program the constructor in the Flooring class. It would have looked like this:

```
public Flooring(String initName, double initPrice) {
    super(initName, initPrice);
}
```

The keyword super is used to call the constructor for the superclass. The parameters initName and initPrice are sent along as arguments with the call for the constructor in the superclass.

If we don't call a specific constructor in the superclass, the constructor with no arguments will be used. In our example, this will give a compile-time error, since there is no such constructor. Maybe now is a good time for a little review. If we don't make any constructors at all in a class, a default constructor will be made automatically. The default constructor is like a constructor with empty parameter list and empty body. If, on the other hand, we make our own constructors, which we usually do, the default constructor is not created automatically. If we want a constructor with empty parameter list to exist, we have to create it ourselves.

The compiler requires that a possibly super() call must be the first statement in the constructor body. Little else is new in the rest of the Flooring class. We only program the things that distinguish this class from the superclass:

- the attribute widthOfFlooring with associated get method

- the implementation of the method getMaterialReq()

The Paint and Wallpaper classes are created the same way as the Flooring class.

Program Listing 12.1

```
/*
 * Material.java   E.L. 2001-08-17
 *
 */
```

```
abstract class Material {
  private String name;  // identifies the material
  private double price; // price per unit

  public Material(String initName, double initPrice) {
    name = initName;
    price = initPrice;
  }

  public String getName() {
    return name;
  }

  public double getPricePerUnit() {
    return price;
  }

  public double getTotalPrice(Surface aSurface) {
    return getMaterialReq(aSurface) * price;
  }

  public abstract double getMaterialReq(Surface aSurface);
}
/*
 * Flooring.java   E.L. 2001-05-17
 *
 */
class Flooring extends Material {
  private static final double limit = 0.02; // limit for one more width
  private double widthOfFlooring;    // meter

  public Flooring(String initName, double initPrice, double initWidth) {
    super(initName, initPrice);
    widthOfFlooring = initWidth;
  }

  public double getWidth() {
    return widthOfFlooring;
  }

  /*
   * We are going to calculate the amount which is needed to cover one surface.
   * The flooring is always placed crosswise relative to the length of the surface.
   * If you want to find the amount the other way, you have to change
   * width and length in the surface argument.
   */
  public double getMaterialReq(Surface aSurface) {
    double lengthSurface = aSurface.getLength();
    double widthSurface = aSurface.getWidth();

    int noOfWidths = (int)(lengthSurface / widthOfFlooring);
    double remnant = lengthSurface % widthOfFlooring;
    if (remnant >= limit) noOfWidths++;
```

```
      return noOfWidths * widthSurface;
  }
}
/*
 * Paint.java   E.L. 2001-08-15
 *.
 */
class Paint extends Material {
  private static final double limit = 0.02;  // limit to buy 0.5 liters more
  private int noOfCoats;
  private double noOfSqMPerLiter;

  public Paint(String initName, double initPrice, int initNoOfCoats,
      double initNoOfSqMPerLiter) {
    super(initName, initPrice);
    noOfCoats = initNoOfCoats;
    noOfSqMPerLiter = initNoOfSqMPerLiter;
  }

  public int getNoOfCoats() {
    return noOfCoats;
  }

  public double getNoOfSqMPerLiter() {
    return noOfSqMPerLiter;
  }
/*
 * This method calculates the amount of paint required to cover the surface.
 * The result is rounded upward to the nearest 0.5 liters.
 */
public double getMaterialReq(Surface aSurface) {
  double area = aSurface.getArea();
  double noOfLiters = area * noOfCoats / noOfSqMPerLiter;
  int noOfLitersInteger = (int) noOfLiters;
  double more = noOfLiters - noOfLitersInteger;
  if (more >= 0.5 + limit) return noOfLitersInteger + 1.0;
  else if (more >= limit) return noOfLitersInteger + 0.5;
  else return noOfLitersInteger;
  }
}
/*
 * Wallpaper.java   E.L. 2001-05-17
 *
 */
class Wallpaper extends Material {
  private static final double limit = 0.02; // limit for one more width
  private double lengthPerRoll; // meter
  private double widthPerRoll; // meter
```

```
public Wallpaper(String initName, double initPrice, double initLengthPerRoll,
    double initWidthPerRoll) {
  super(initName, initPrice);
  lengthPerRoll = initLengthPerRoll;
  widthPerRoll = initWidthPerRoll;
}

public double getLengthPerRoll() {
  return lengthPerRoll;
}

public double getWidthPerRoll() {
  return widthPerRoll;
}

/*
 * This method calculates the number of rolls needed to paper a surface.
 */
public double getMaterialReq(Surface aSurface) {
  double lengthSurface = aSurface.getLength();
  double heightSurface = aSurface.getWidth();

  /* calculate the number of heights */
  int noOfHeights = (int) (lengthSurface / widthPerRoll);
  double remnant = lengthSurface % widthPerRoll;
  if (remnant >= limit) noOfHeights++;

  /* calculate the number of rolls */
  int noOfRolls;
  int noOfHeightsPerRoll = (int) (lengthPerRoll / heightSurface);
  if (noOfHeightsPerRoll > 0) {
    noOfRolls = noOfHeights / noOfHeightsPerRoll;
    remnant = noOfHeights % noOfHeightsPerRoll;
    if (remnant >= limit) noOfRolls++;
  } else { // the roll is shorter than one height (rarely!)
    double totalNoOfMeters = noOfHeights * heightSurface;
    noOfRolls = (int) (totalNoOfMeters / lengthPerRoll);
    if (totalNoOfMeters % lengthPerRoll >= limit) noOfRolls++;
  }
  return noOfRolls;
  }
}
```

See Figure 12.4. The data contents are provided by the instance variables in the Wallpaper class and in the superclass. The superclass has two instance variables, name and price. Since these are private in the superclass, we cannot get to them from the Wallpaper class in any way other than by using the get methods. But it's important to be clear about the fact that they're there. When we make an instance of the Wallpaper class, room is also set aside for these variables. We give them value by calling the constructor in the superclass.

What does inheritance mean in a Java program?

A class inherits nonprivate members from the class directly above it in the class tree (also members that this class has inherited itself). An inherited member can be used as if it were declared in the class. Access (public/package) to inherited members is the same as in the class the members were inherited from. Constructors are not inherited.

All the methods in the `Material` class are public. These methods therefore also become public in the `Wallpaper` class. For example, we can write:

```
String name = theWallpaper.getName();
```

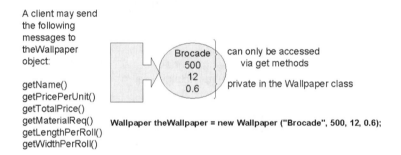

Figure 12.4 An instance of the `Wallpaper` class

Problems

1. Make a new subclass for the `Material` class. The class will be called `Parquet`. Parquet flooring is delivered in packages, and a package of parquet covers a given number of square meters. The materials needed for a surface will be the area of the surface divided by the number of square meters per package, rounded up to the closest whole number of packages. Make a little test program for the class.

2. Program the classes from the problem in Section 12.2. To save on the writing work, you can make do with two categories of employees. The `Employee` class will be abstract and have an abstract method `calculateSalary()`. The algorithm for calculating salary is different for each individual category. You will not program these algorithms here—you will only get ready to program them. You do this, for example, by having the method for technical personnel print the

following text: "An algorithm to calculate the salary for technical personnel is not implemented yet."

3. Change the program so that the text "Salary is calculated in the standard way" prints out if the method `calculateSalary()` is not programmed in a subclass.

4. What messages can a client send to instances of the various classes? Make a client program that tests this.

12.4 Handling Instances of Subclasses as a Whole

Program Listing 12.2 makes an array that contains references to different material-instances. The program runs in a loop and sends messages to these instances.

The array contains five references of the `Material` type. A reference of the `Material` type can be set to refer to instances of the `Material` class (if we were able to make such instances, which we are not), or to instances of subclasses of `Material`. This is an important trait of references, and it makes it possible to handle different types of objects as a whole, as we do in the `for` loop in Program Listing 12.2.

Why is it this way? See Figure 12.5. On the left side of the figure is a reference to each of the pertinent types. In the middle we have depicted instances of the pertinent classes. The name suggests which class the specific object is an instance of.

The arrows between the references and the objects tell which are valid assignments. A reference of the `Material` type can be set to refer to any of the objects. This is correct, because:

- Every paint, wallpaper, and flooring object *is* a material.

- All messages that we can send to a material, we can also sent to paint, wallpaper, and flooring objects.

In the lower right corner of the figure, there's an example of an invalid assignment. We cannot set `paintRef` to refer to an instance of the class `Wallpaper`, because:

- Wallpaper *is not* a paint.

- There are messages declared in the `Paint` class that have no meaning for wallpaper instances—for example, `getNoOfSqMPerLiter()`.

Let's look more closely at the short program in Program Listing 12.2. In the printout, we do not distinguish between liters and meters. Purely and simply, we write "units".

Program Listing 12.2

```
/*
 * TestPolymorphism.java   E.L. 2001-08-17
 *
 */

class TestPolymorphism {
  public static void main(String[] args) {
    Material[] materials = new Material[5];
    materials[0] = new Paint("Heimdal Super", 20, 2, 10);
    materials[1] = new Wallpaper("Brocade77", 50, 12, 0.6);
    materials[2] = new Paint("Heimdal Extra", 10, 3, 10);
    materials[3] = new Flooring("Wool-Gold", 45, 5);
    materials[4] = new Flooring("Soft-Gold", 30, 5);
    Surface aSurface = new Surface("testSurface", 4, 5);
    for (int i = 0; i < materials.length; i++) {
      String name = materials[i].getName();
      double req = materials[i].getMaterialReq(aSurface);
      double price = materials[i].getTotalPrice(aSurface);
      System.out.println("Name: " + name + ", Requirement: "
        + req + " units, Price $" + price);
    }
  }
}

/* Example Run:
Name: Heimdal Super, Requirement: 4.0 units, Price $80.0
Name: Brocade77, Requirement: 4.0 units, Price $200.0
Name: Heimdal Extra, Requirement: 6.0 units, Price $60.0
Name: Wool-Gold, Requirement: 5.0 units, Price $225.0
Name: Soft-Gold, Requirement: 5.0 units, Price $150.0
*/
```

In order to be able to give the right designation, we have to know what type of material we are dealing with. We can write:

```
String unit;
if (materials[i] instanceof Flooring) unit = " meters";
else if (materials[i] instanceof Paint) unit = " liters";
else unit = " rolls";
System.out.println("Name: " + name + ", Requirement: " + req + unit + ", price $" + price);
```

We covered the `instanceof` operator in Section 11.10.

What if now we find out that we want to add parquet as a new type of material? Of course, we have to make a new subclass for the `Material` class, but we also have to expand the `if-elseif` list. In this case it's feasible, but it's not hard to imagine that in larger systems this can be a very complex process.

There is a more elegant solution to this. We have to let the classes themselves (`Flooring`, `Paint`, etc.) assume responsibility for this as well. We don't put the printout statements in the classes, but make methods that return suitable strings that the client can choose to print out or search in, as it wishes.

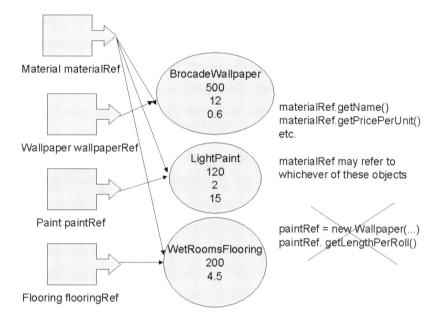

Figure 12.5 A reference can be set to refer to an instance of the class, or to an instance of a subclass to the class

In our example, we need an abstract method in the `Material` class:

```
public abstract String getUnit();
```

In the `Flooring` class, the implementation will look like this:

```
public String getUnit() {
  return "meters";
}
```

We will have equivalent implementations in other subclasses. If we have that, we can get the right units to print out by expanding the loop body with the statement:

```
String unit = materials[i].getUnit();
```

Problems

Continue working with the employee classes from the previous problems.

1. Make a client program similar to the example in this section. Send the message `calculateSalary()` to all employee objects.

2. Replace the array with an array list.

3. Expand the program by printing the category that the individual employee belongs to. Use the `instanceof` operator.

4. Do problem 3 again without using `instanceof`. Hint: expand the classes with a method `getClassname()`.

12.5 The Renovation Case with Many Surfaces and Many Materials

Now we are ready to expand the renovation case from Section 10.6 to many different materials.

See Figure 12.6. Out of space considerations we had to omit the get methods in the class diagram. Instead, we have introduced the designation {frozen} in the attributes. An attribute with the characteristic {frozen} cannot be changed by a client. Only a get method is linked to an attribute of this type. Attributes without this characteristic have associated set and get methods. In UML notation we say that they are {changeable}. Since we make the classes immutable as long as that works reasonably, we have no attributes of this kind in the diagram.

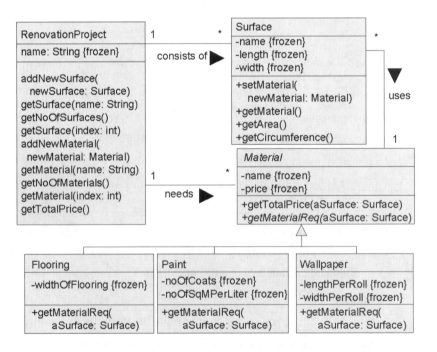

Figure 12.6 Class diagram for renovation project with many surfaces and many materials (UML)

In practice, the differences in the program code are small with respect to the example in chapter 10. We replace references to `Paint` objects with references to `Material` objects. A reference to `Material` can refer to an instance of any subclass of `Material` whatsoever.

Figure 12.7 shows an excerpt of a run of the new version of the program. We see that three surfaces are entered (ceiling, floor, and walls). The ceiling is painted. We put flooring on the floor and wallpaper the walls. The currency format is as in chapter 10 according to the running environment. To us this means Norwegian crowns (kr). To you it possibly means euros or dollars. If we want to change the materials for one of the surfaces, we click on it and the window on the right comes up. All the registered materials are shown here, and we can also enter a new type of material (new paint, new flooring, or new wallpaper).

We will look at some of the concrete changes in the source code. The classes `Material`, `Flooring`, `Paint`, and `Surface` are shown in Program Listing 12.1. Otherwise the following classes are included in the system (for complete programs see [URL Java book]):

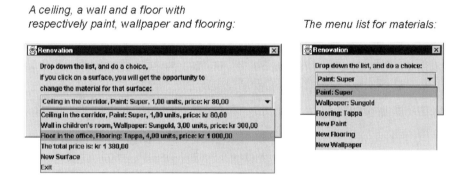

Figure 12.7 User interface with many surfaces and many material types

The `Surface` class:

A one-to-many association from `Material` to `Surface` means that we get an instance variable of the type `Material` in the class `Surface`. Earlier we linked a specific type of paint to a surface, thus:

```
public void setPaint(Paint newPaint) {
    paint = newPaint;
}
```

This method will now look like this:

```
public void setMaterial(Material newMaterial) {
    material = newMaterial;
}
```

As arguments for this method, instances of any subclass whatsoever of the `Material` class will work. Example:

```
Flooring aFlooring = new Flooring("XXX", 200, 5);
theFloor.setMaterial(aFlooring);
```

The reason for this is that a reference to a class can be set to point to an instance of any subclass whatsoever of the class.

The `RenovationProject` class:

Here we replace references to `Paint` with references to `Material`. In addition, the names of methods and variables have to be suited to this change. For example, the method `getPaint()` changes its name to `getMaterial()`.

The `ReaderRenovationCase` class: No changes.

The `ProjectChap12` class:

Most of the changes are in this class, which is responsible for presenting the menus and letting the user make the selections. We will look at the differences compared to Program Listing 10.2.

References to `Paint` are replaced with references to `Material`, and of course, user instructions and other texts have to be adjusted.

Let's look at the list on the left in Figure 12.7. A class name is printed after the surface name. Then comes the data, the same as before. We get the name of the class that the object is an instance of:

```
String classname = theMaterial.getClass().getName();
```

Here `theMaterial` is the reference to the object. The `getClass()` method is declared in the `Object` class (see the online API documentation) and it returns a reference to an instance of the `Class` class. This object represents the class that the object in question is an instance of. By sending the message `getname()` to the `Class` object, we get the class name as a string.[1]

The method `getPaint()` is replaced with the method `getMaterial()`, which out of necessity must be a little more complicated since instances will be made of different classes.

The list on the right in Figure 12.7 is written out in the method `getMaterialIndex()`. Here also, we include the class name in every line. As before, we retrieve all registered materials, but the list has to be expanded by three choices, compared to the previous one: "New Paint," "New Flooring," "New Wallpaper". The `getMaterial()` method receives the selection the user makes and further handles it. Either we get a reference to an already registered material, or we create a new object.

As previously mentioned, you'll find complete programs at [URL Java book]. Meanwhile, it is important to be clear that the differences between this and the

---

1. Other uses of the `Class` class are outside the scope of this book. If you're interested, refer to more advanced Java literature, for example [Horstmann, Cornell 1999].

example in chapter 10 are minimal, despite the fact that our program now handles many types of materials. The reason for this is that we are using inheritance and polymorphism. We are handling all types of materials as a whole by working with references to the `Material` superclass.

Problems

The example in this section covers the classes in Program Listing 12.1 and Program Listing 7.3. In addition, print out the files *Surface.java*, *RenovationProject.java*, and *RenovationChap12.java* from chapter 12 at [URL Java book]. Now you will have a complete program listing of all the classes in the example.

1. Explain the purpose of the constants `newPaint`, `newFlooring`, and `newWallpaper`.

2. In the method `setOptions()` (the `RenovationChap12` class), we retrieve the class name for an object in the following way:

    theMaterial.getClass().getName()

    The chances of your being able to figure out this method on your own might not be very good. However, it's not so difficult to create program code that does precisely this job. There are two main ways to do it. What are the two ways and how does the source code look in those two cases?

3. In a problem in Section 12.3 you made the `Parquet` class. Where do you have to make changes in the renovation example to include the material type parquet? Make the changes and run the program.

12.6 What if Polymorphism Didn't Exist?

What does polymorphism do for us? In this example, it lets us handle different types of materials as a whole. We send the message `getMaterialReq()` to an object that is an instance of a subclass of `Material`, and the object itself knows how it should calculate the materials needed.

What if the objects themselves didn't know how the need should be calculated? Then somewhere or other we would have had to make an `if-else-if-else` sequence (something like this):

```
if (material instanceof Paint) {
    ....formulas for calculating paint requirements
}
else if (material instanceof Flooring) {
    ....formulas for calculating covering requirements
}
else {
    ....formulas for calculating wallpaper requirements
}
```

Consider one more time if you think you need to use `instanceof` combined with an `if-else-if-else` sequence. To do this, evaluate if it is better to make an abstract method in a common superclass for the classes involved and thus let every individual class get its own implementation for the method.

When do we need to use the operator `instanceof`? The serialization use in Section 11.10 is special. Is there any use for this operator in finding out what class an object is an instance of? We need to use `instanceof` in conjunction with class trees in those cases where we will send a message to only one part of a subtree. See the tree in Figure 12.8.

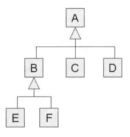

Figure 12.8 A class tree (UML)

Assume that `method1()` is abstract in the class A. It is implemented in the classes B, C, and D. In the class B, we also find the abstract method `method2()`. It is implemented in the classes E and F.
    We create the following objects:

```
A object1 = new C();
A object2 = new E();
```

We can safely send the message `method1()` to both of the objects:

```
object1.method1();
object2.method1();
```

We can only send the message `method2()` to subclasses of the class B. We therefore have to make sure that the object is an instance of a class of this type before we send the message:

```
if (object1 instanceof B) { // corresponding program code for object2
    /* casting is necessary before we can send a B message to the object */
    B anObject = (B) object1;
    anObject.method2();
}
```

Now, of course, we can argue against this test since we know that `object1` is an instance of the class C, and `object2` is an instance of class E. However, circumstances aren't usually so easy to grasp as in this example, and then the test is necessary.

The entire program is shown in Program Listing 12.3.

Program Listing 12.3

```java
/*
 * TestInstanceof.java   E.L. 2001-08-18
 */
abstract class A {
  public abstract void method1();
}

class C extends A {
  public void method1() {
    System.out.println("C: method1");
  }
}

abstract class B extends A {
  public void method1() {
    System.out.println("B: method1");
  }

  abstract void method2();
}

class E extends B {
  public void method2() {
    System.out.println("E: method2");
  }
}

class TestInstanceof
  public static void main(String[] args) {
    A object1 = new C();
    A object2 = new E();
    object1.method1();
    object2.method1();
    if (object1 instanceof B) {
      B anObject = (B) object1;
      anObject.method2();
    }
    if (object2 instanceof B) {
      B anObject = (B) object2;
      anObject.method2();
    }
  }
}
```

```
/* Example Run:
C: method1
B: method1
E: method2
*/
```

Problems

1. Download the program in Program Listing 12.2. Change the printout in the loop such that all the attributes are printed. The printout will differ, therefore, depending on the type of object. Use the `instanceof` operator.

2. Make the method `toString()` for each of the classes `Paint`, `Wallpaper`, and `Flooring` (see also Section 10.4). How will you solve problem 1 now?

12.7 The Protected Access Modifier

First, a little review—the access for constructors and members outside the class they belong to is determined by the access modifiers `private` and `public`:

```
public class Surface {
    private String name;  // for identification purposes
    ....
    public Surface(String initName, double initLength, double initWidth) {
      ...
    }
    public String getName() {
      ...
    }
```

The instance variable `name` is private. We can refer to it only in the `Surface` class. The constructor and the method `getName()` are public. They are accessible from anywhere, assuming that the class they belong to is public. This is the case in this example.

If we don't use an access modifier, then package access applies. Then the member (or the constructor) is accessible in the package the class belongs to:

```
String name;  // for identification purposes
....
Surface(String initName, double initLength, double initWidth) {
  ...
}
String getName() {
  ...
}
```

We get a fourth possibility using the keyword `protected`. This is an intermediate between package access and public access. The class itself, the package it belongs to, and all subclasses regardless of package have access to *protected constructors and members.*

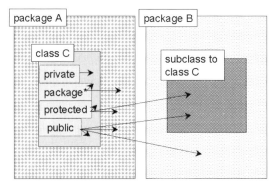

*) package means no access modifier

Figure 12.9 The access for constructors and members declared in the class

See Figure 12.9. This figure shows the access for members and constructors declared in the class C. Follow the arrows from the access modifier of interest. There we see, for example, that a member with the modifier `protected` can be reached from all locations in package A, and from all subclasses of the class C regardless of which package they belong to. There is, however, another limitation on using a protected member or a protected constructor outside the package: we only have access to this on behalf of an object in the code that is responsible for the implementation of the object. Let's illustrate this with an example:

`TestClass1` is declared in `packageA`:

```
package packageA;
public class TestClass1 {
  private int a;
  protected TestClass1(int newA) {
   a = newA;
  }
  public TestClass1() {
  }
  protected void method1() {
    System.out.println("Method1")
  }
}
```

`TestClass1` is public. In other words, you can basically make instances of the class wherever you want. It has a protected constructor and a public constructor, and it has a protected method.

Use of access modifiers

We recommend the following (these are *recommendations*; for rules, look elsewhere in the book):

- Instance variables and class variables are always private.

- Constants are usually public, but can be private if they are not of interest outside the class.

- Constructors are usually public.

- Methods are usually private or public.

- Constructors and methods can be protected if there is no point in using them outside subclasses.

As a point of departure, classes have package access (no access modifier). This also limits the access to public constructors and members of the class. Classes that will be taken into general use are made public and added to a named package. Then all public constructors and members will also automatically become public.

Let's look at TestClass2 in another package:

```
import packageA.*;
class TestClass2 extends TestClass1 {
  public TestClass2(int a) {
    super(a); // ok, protected
  }
  public void method2(TestClass1 obj1, TestClass2 obj2) {
    method1(); // ok, protected
    obj1.method1(); // not ok
    obj2.method1(); // ok
  }
}
```

TestClass2 is a subclass of TestClass1. Inside TestClass2, we can call protected members and constructors in TestClass1. method2() takes two arguments, an instance of TestClass1 (obj1), and an instance of Test-Class2 (obj2). We can send the message method1() to obj2, but we can't send this message to obj1. The reason for this is that obj1 is an instance of a class we are not responsible for declaring here.

By no means do we have access to use protected members in other packages outside subclasses:

```
public static void main(String[] args) {
  TestClass1 object1 = new TestClass1(10); // not ok, protected constructor
  TestClass1 object1 = new TestClass1(); // ok
  TestClass2 object2 = new TestClass2(20); // ok,
  object2.method1(); // not ok, protected
  object2.method2(object1, object2); // ok
}
```

The `protected` access modifier is relatively complicated to understand, and we will only use it to a limited degree in this book. In those cases where we use it, the point will be that the constructors and members are accessible in subclasses regardless of package.

Problems

With packages, it may happen that it doesn't work to compile and run from the editor. In that case, you have to compile and run from the command prompt. Example:

The file *Tests.java* includes classes that belong to `packageA`. The file is placed in a directory with name *packageA*. You compile and run the file *Tests.java* in `packageA` in this way:

```
C:\EXAMPLES\EXCHAP12>javac packageA/Tests.java
C:\EXAMPLES\EXCHAP12>java packageA/Tests
```

The current directory is *not packageA* but the directory immediately above. Note the direction of the slash!

1. Input the classes `TestClass1` and `TestClass2` and position them correctly with respect to each other. Omit statements marked "not OK." The class `TestClass1` has to be located in a subdirectory named *packageA* with respect to the other class.

   The client program will be in the same directory as `TestClass2`.

   Compile and run.

   Check that the results are reasonable based on what's in the text. Try some of the statements that are marked "not OK." Try to understand the error messages you receive.

2. Suppose that we add the following classes to `packageA`:

```
package packageA;

class TestClass3 extends TestClass1 {
  public TestClass3(int a) {
    super(a);
```

```
    }
    public TestClass3() {}
    protected void method3() {
      System.out.println("Method 3 in TestClass3");
    }
    public void method1() {
      System.out.println("Method 1 in TestClass3");
    }
  }

  class Tests {
   public static void main(String[] args) {
      TestClass1 obj1 = new TestClass1(20);
      obj1.method1();
      obj1.method3();
      TestClass3 obj2 = new TestClass3(20);
      obj2.method1();
      obj2.method3();
      TestClass3 obj3 = new TestClass3();
      obj3.method1();
      obj3.method3();
    }
  }
```

Describe the members of the class TestClass3. Which members are inherited?

One of the statements in main() gives a compile-time error. Which one?

Remove this statement (e.g. by commenting it) and possibly statements that depend on it. What will be output when the program runs?

12.8 Two Levels of Inheritance

We will look at a revised version of subclasses of the Material class (see Figure 12.10). The difference is that we have made a somewhat modified Flooring2 class, and this has itself got two subclasses, one for first-sort coverings and one for second-sort coverings. The difference between these types is that when buying second-sort coverings you get a discounted price and you must also count on using some extra material because of a greater risk of waste.

The class name Flooring2 is written in italics. This means that the class is abstract (i.e., that instances will not be made from this class). The objects will be instances of one of the subclasses. We don't *have to* do it this way. As we see, the FirstSortFlooring class doesn't differentiate itself from the Flooring2 class in any way. We can say that a covering object that is of the first-sort quality is classified as Flooring, while the ones of poorer quality are classified as SecondSortFlooring. It is still common to make a class tree so that all objects can be classified with respect to classes on the lowest level.

Program Listing 12.4 shows the class Flooring2 and the two subclasses. You will write a short client program as the solution to a problem at the end of this section.

In the Flooring2 class, as an example, we have placed the modifier final before the method getWidth(). This means that potential subclasses are not allowed to have their own versions of this method.

Using final methods makes the execution of the program more efficient because the Java interpreter doesn't need to pay attention to the fact that the method can be overridden in a subclass.

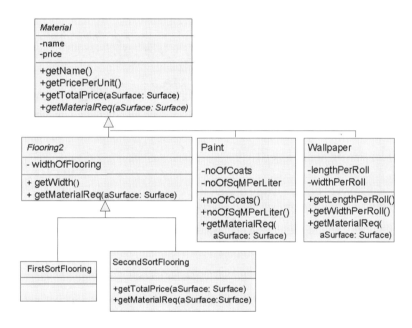

Figure 12.10 Two levels of inheritance (UML)

Program Listing 12.4

```
/*
 * Flooring2.java   E.L. 2001-08-18
 *
 */

abstract class Flooring2 extends Material {
   private static final double limit = 0.02; // limit for one more width
   private double widthOfFlooring;   // meter
   /*
   * This class is abstract, and so it is not possible to create instances of the class.
```

```
 * The constructor is needed in subclasses.
 */
protected Flooring2(String initName, double initPrice, double initWidth) {
  super(initName, initPrice);
  widthOfFlooring = initWidth;
}

public final double getWidth() {
  return widthOfFlooring;
}

public double getMaterialReq(Surface aSurface) {
  double lengthSurface = aSurface.getLength();
  double widthSurface = aSurface.getWidth();

  int noOfWidths = (int)(lengthSurface / widthOfFlooring);
  double rest = lengthSurface % widthOfFlooring;
  if (rest >= limit) noOfWidths++;
  return noOfWidths * widthSurface;
}
}

/*
 * FirstSortFlooring.java   E.L. 2001-08-18
 *
 */

final class FirstSortFlooring extends Flooring2 {

  public FirstSortFlooring(String initName, double initPrice, double initWidth) {
    super(initName, initPrice, initWidth);
  }
}

/*
 * SecondSortFlooring.java   E.L. 2001-08-19
 *
 */

final class SecondSortFlooring extends Flooring2 {
  public static final double limitHighDiscount = 5;
  public static final double highDiscount = 0.7;
  public static final double lowDiscount = 0.5;
  public static final double materialAddendum = 1.2; // factor because of risk for waste

  public SecondSortFlooring(String initName, double initPrice, double initWidth) {
    super(initName, initPrice, initWidth);
  }

  public double getTotalPrice(Surface aSurface) {
    double basicPrice = super.getTotalPrice(aSurface);
    double req = getMaterialReq(aSurface);
```

```
      if (req > limitHighDiscount) return basicPrice * (1.0 - highDiscount);
      else return basicPrice * (1.0 - lowDiscount);
    }

    public double getMaterialReq(Surface aSurface) {
      double basicReq = super.getMaterialReq(aSurface);
      return basicReq * materialAddendum;
    }
  }
```

Since `final` sets limits on what can be done in the subclasses, we should think about it carefully before we declare a method `final`. Still, it's usually safe to declare the simple set and get methods as `final`.

Both of the subclasses in the example are declared as `final` in their entirety. The modifier `final` is placed first in the class head. That means that it's not possible to make subclasses for this class. Other examples of `final` classes are the wrapper classes `Integer`, `Double`, etc.

Constructors are not inherited. Therefore, we have to make constructors in the subclasses, even if these constructors' only task is to send the parameters on as arguments for the constructor in the class above.

What happens if we do not create a constructor in the `FirstSortFlooring` class? We remember that if we don't make a constructor at all, a default constructor will be made automatically. This type of constructor will require the existence of an equivalent constructor (i.e. a constructor with empty parameter list, default or not-default) in the class above. In the `Flooring2` class we do not have such a constructor, and we'll therefore get a compile-time error.

When creating an instance of the `FirstSortFlooring` class, we want to supply information about name, price and width. So the constructor should be as follows:

```
    public FirstSortFlooring(String initName, double initPrice, double initWidth) {
      super(initName, initPrice, initWidth);
    }
```

In the `SecondSortFlooring` class, we redefine two inherited methods. The new definitions replace the inherited versions for instances of the `SecondSortFlooring` class.

• The method `getTotalPrice()` replaces the method inherited from the class `Material` through the class `Flooring2`. This method is based on the original price and gives discounts depending on how much covering the customer is buying. The amount of covering is calculated based on the new version of `getMaterialReq()` (see below). If the customer buys more than 5 meters of covering, she receives a discount of 70%; otherwise the discount is 50% off compared to the price for first sort covering.

- The method getMaterialReq() replaces the method getMaterial-
  Req() inherited from the Flooring2 class. The materials requirement
  calculated in the superclass is multiplied by a factor.

We use the keyword super to call the method as declared on the level above.
Example:

```
public double getMaterialReq(Surface aSurface) {
  double basicReq = super.getMaterialReq(aSurface);
  return basicReq * materialAddendum;
}
```

If we don't use the word super, the method will call itself and the program will
continue to run until the memory is full.

Of course, we can refrain from calling the method declared on the level above
when making a replacement for it. We saw examples of this in Section 10.4, where
we made our own versions of the methods equals() and toString().

Notice the difference between using super in constructors and methods:

- In a constructor, a call to super() has to be the first statement. Constructors
  are not inherited. One contructor for each of the classes up to the top of the class
  tree is called. The use of super() means that a special constructor in the direct
  superclass should be used. Otherwise a constructor with empty parameter list
  has to exist and is used for the direct superclass. This continues up until the top
  of the class tree.

- super can be used as a qualifier to refer to methods in a superclass. The method
  in the superclass can be declared there or it can be inherited from a class further
  up in the class tree.

Problems

1. Make a simple client program according to the following specifications:

   Make an array with room for three references to Material objects.

   Make an instance of the FirstSortFlooring class and two instances of the
   SecondSortFlooring class. Set the references in the array to point to these
   instances.

   Make a Surface instance and send the messages getTotalPrice() and
   getMaterialReq() to the three instances. Check the responses.

2. Make the method toString() for the classes Material, Flooring2,
   FirstSortFlooring, and SecondSortFlooring. Let the method in a
   subclass call the method on the level above, like this: super.toString().

   Expand the client program from problem 1 to test the new methods.

12.9 Rules and Syntax

Here we'll go through the most important rules for subclasses and inheritance. You'll find other rules for classes in Section 4.4. For a more thorough description of the topic with lots of examples, we recommend [Gosling, Joy, Steele 1996].

Java Core

Declaring a subclass

Syntax:

> *modifiers* class *nameOfSubclass* extends *className* {
>   *constructors and members*
> }

modifiers can be public, abstract, and/or final.

The class will be a direct subclass of the *className* class.

A class can have only one superclass, but many subclasses.

Inheritance

The members of a class are either declared in the class or inherited from the superclass. A subclass can use the inherited member as it is or make its own version (overriding or hiding, see below).

The level of access for an inherited member is also inherited.

Subclasses don't inherit private members.

Subclasses in the same package inherit members with package access, protected members, and public members.

Subclasses in other packages inherit protected and public members.

Constructors aren't members, and therefore they aren't inherited.

The abstract modifier

Example of an abstract class:

> abstract class Material {
>   ......*etc.*

It's not possible to make instances of an abstract class.

An abstract class doesn't need to contain or inherit abstract methods.

An abstract method consists of the modifier abstract followed by the rest of the method head and a semicolon:

> abstract *methodHead*;

A class that inherits, or declares on its own, an abstract method, has to be declared as abstract.

An abstract class can contain both abstract and concrete methods.

The super keyword

super can be used in two ways:

- We can use the keyword super in a constructor to call the constructor directly above in the class tree. The call to super() has to be the first statement in the constructor we make. The argument list for super() has to be in accordance with the parameter list for a constructor in the superclass.

- We can use super as a qualifier in any method in a subclass if we want to refer to a hidden or overridden name (see below) in a superclass.

We cannot write super.super() or something like that to call a constructor or method more than one level above in the class tree.

Constructors

If we don't call a specific constructor in the direct superclass by calling super(), a constructor with no arguments will be called. If this doesn't exist, the compiler will give an error message.

If the intent is not to make instances of a class, this can be prevented in two ways:

- Make the class abstract. This is used if the class has or can have subclasses.

- Make all constructors private. This is used if the class cannot have subclasses (it is final, see below). java.lang.Math is an example of a class with only private constructors.

References and casting

The examples in this section use the classes in Program Listing 12.4, with the difference that the class Flooring2 is not abstract. It is opened by removing the modifier abstract in the class head. With this, it will be possible to make instances of the class Flooring2.

A reference to a class can be set to point to instances of a subclass to the class. It cannot be set to point to instances of a superclass. Examples:

```
Material aMaterial = new FirstSortFlooring("SuperDuper", 140, 5);  // ok
FirstSortFlooring fineFlooring = new SecondSortFlooring("SuperDuper2", 140, 6);  // not ok
FirstSortFlooring veryFineFlooring = new Flooring2("SuperDuper1", 140, 5); // not ok
```

Assume that we have a reference to an object. The reference can be cast to the class the object is an instance of, or to superclasses of this class. It's not allowed to cast the reference to a subclass of the class that the object is an instance of. Invalid casting gives a ClassCastException. Examples:

```
Object anObject = new Flooring2("SuperDuper", 140, 5);  // ok
Flooring2 aFlooring = (Flooring2) anObject; // ok
```

FirstSortFlooring fineFlooring = (FirstSortFlooring) aFlooring; // not ok
FirstSortFlooring veryFineFlooring = (FirstSortFlooring) anObject; // not ok

The final modifier

We can declare a simple method or a whole class as `final`:

- We can't override or hide a method that is declared `final` (but we can hide a variable that is declared `final`).

- We can't make subclasses for a class that is declared `final`.

Overriding or hiding a name

We can declare names in a subclass that overrides or hides an inherited name. Then the new meaning of the name will apply to instances of the subclass. We use the concept *override* about instance methods, and *hide* about variables and class methods.

We distinguish between the following cases:

- Overriding an inherited instance method

   If a class declares an instance method, this declaration will override any inherited method there might be with the same signature. The compiler gives an error message if the return type is not right and/or the level of access is less strict than in the overridden method. An instance method cannot override an inherited class method.

- Hiding an inherited variable name

   If a class declares a variable with the same name as an inherited variable, this name will hide the inherited variable. This applies to both instance variables and class variables.

- Hiding an inherited class method

   A class method hides an inherited class method with the same signature. A class method cannot hide an inherited instance method.

   By using the keyword `super` inside the class where the overriding/hiding is occurring, we can refer to the overridden/hidden version of the name. `super` is used as a qualifier.

   Outside a class, we can refer to a name of a class variable or method by using the class name as a qualifier. This is true regardless of whether the name is hidden in subclasses of this class.

   If a client sends a message to an object, the class which the object is an instance of will decide which version of the method in question applies. Thus, a client cannot ask that an overridden version of an instance method be used.

12.10 Interface

We encountered the concept of interface in Section 10.7. An interface was presented there as a collection of method heads. These method heads are abstract methods, as we have become acquainted with the concept in this chapter. In Section 10.7 we saw how by implementing the interface `java.lang.Comparable` in a class we can use the ready-made sorting methods in the classes `java.util.Arrays` and `java.util.Collections`. This interface contains only one abstract method, and implementing the interface thus means implementing the following method:

```
public int compareTo(Object obj)
```

Thus, the ready-made sorting methods can use the method `compareTo()` to compare objects. If the objects are instances of a class that doesn't implement the interface, the exception `ClassCastException` will be thrown.

We are also familiar with the interface `Serializable` (Section 11.10), which doesn't contain any methods but is used as a mark to tell that instances of the class in question can be serialized.

Program listing 12.5 shows two interfaces and a class that implements both of them. Instead of a common comparison method as in the interface `Comparable`, here we have declared three different methods: `greaterThan()`, `lessThan()`, and `equal()`.

For variables in interfaces, it holds true that the modifiers `public`, `static`, and `final` are implied and it's not recommended that these modifiers are stated.[2] Thus, all variables in an interface should be considered as public class constants (or "interface constants"). The `Constants` interface demonstrates a practical way to use interfaces. Constants that are common for many classes can be collected in an interface, and classes that need to use these constants implement the interface. Thus all the constants are automatically accessible through inheritance, and qualification isn't necessary to get hold of them.

The class `FourDigitsNumber` implements both of the interfaces. A class can implement as many interfaces as is desirable.

Interfaces have certain traits in common with classes. However, an interface can *only* contain abstract methods and constants. For the class that uses these constants, they will work as if they were class constants. The same way that we can't make instances of abstract classes, we also can't make instances of interfaces. A reference can be of an interface type. In this case, the reference must be set to refer to an instance of a class that implements the interface:

```
MyComparable number = new FourDigitsNumber(1000); // ok
MyComparable number = new MyComparable(); // not ok
```

2. In this book, we include the modifier `public` in the API reference where interfaces are described. We do this because we know from experience that it's very easy to forget to write `public` before the method in the class that is implementing the interface when you're sitting with a description in front of you that doesn't say `public`.

Except in Chapter 19, we will make very few interfaces of our own in this book. Little by little, however, we will start using many of the interfaces that come with SDK, especially in conjunction with programming graphical user interfaces.

Program Listing 12.5

```
/*
 * ExInterface.java   E.L. 2001-08-18
 *
 */

interface MyComparable {
  /* public abstract is implied for methods */
  boolean greaterThan(Object obj);
  boolean lessThan(Object obj);
  boolean equal(Object obj);
}

interface Constants {
  /* public static final is implied for variables */
  int min = 1000;
  int max = 9999;
}

class FourDigitsNumber implements Constants, MyComparable {
  private int value;

  public FourDigitsNumber(int initValue) {
    if (initValue < min) value = min;
    else if (initValue > max) value = max;
    else value = initValue;
  }

  public int getValue() {
    return value;
  }

  public boolean greaterThan(Object obj) {
    FourDigitsNumber number = (FourDigitsNumber) obj;
    return (value > number.getValue());
  }

  public boolean lessThan(Object obj) {
    FourDigitsNumber number = (FourDigitsNumber) obj;
    return (value < number.getValue());
  }

  public boolean equal(Object obj) {
    FourDigitsNumber number = (FourDigitsNumber) obj;
    return (value == number.getValue());
  }
}
```

```
class ExInterface {
  public static void main(String[] args) {
    FourDigitsNumber number1 = new FourDigitsNumber(700);
    FourDigitsNumber number2 = new FourDigitsNumber(1700);
    FourDigitsNumber number3 = new FourDigitsNumber(70000);
    System.out.println(number1.getValue());
    System.out.println(number2.getValue());
    System.out.println(number3.getValue());
    System.out.println(number1.greaterThan(number2));
    System.out.println(number1.lessThan(number2));
    System.out.println(number1.equal(number2));
  }
}

/* Example Run:
1000
1700
9999
false
true
false
*/
```

Java Core

Interface

Syntax:

> *accessModifier* interface *interfaceName* {
>   *constants*
>   *methodHeads*
> }

or:

> *accessModifier* interface *interfaceName* extends *superInterface1, superinterface2, ..* {
>   *constants*
>   *methodHeads*
> }

An access modifier for the interface can be `public` or it can be left out (package access).

All the members in an interface are publicly accessible (`public`). This is overruled by potential package access for the interface as a whole.

In the constant declarations, the modifiers `public`, `static` and `final` are implied, and they will not be stated.

The method heads end with a semicolon and the modifiers `public` and `abstract` are implied and will not be stated.

Every interface is abstract—i.e., we cannot instantiate objects from an interface. An object can only be an instance of a class, and that class might implement an interface.

A reference of an interface type can refer to an object that is an instance of a class that implements the interface.

An interface can represent an extension of one or more super interfaces. An interface inherits the members in all its super interfaces.

Classes that implement interfaces

Syntax:

> *modifiers* class *className* implements *interface1*, *interface2*, .. {
>
>   ...
>
> }

or:

> *modifiers* class *className* extends *superClass* implements *interface1*, *interface2*, .. {
>
>   ...
>
> }

A class can only have one superclass, but it can implement one or more interfaces. The class inherits the members of all the interfaces it implements.

A class that implements an interface has to implement all the methods in the interface, otherwise the class will be abstract.

"Interface" is the interface, while the class is the implementation!

In more advanced software development, Java interfaces are used in a different way than this brief introduction gives the impression of. A Java interface represents an object's general interface, while the class that implements the interface is the implementation. The use of the keywords `interface` and `implements` is not unintentional.

In chapter 3, an object's interface was defined as follows: "A description of the messages that can be sent to an object. The description of a method contains return type, method name, and a parameter list." But these are just the abstract methods that a Java interface can contain.

Client program developers work with interfaces. They don't see the implementation (the class) that contains a number of things of a more private nature, such as, for example, instance variables and methods with a lower visibility level than `public`.

Using a Java interface is also a way of making mutable classes immutable.[3] We make a Java interface that contains only the access methods in the class. This is the

---

3. [Warren, Bishop 1999, p. 54]

interface that is presented to the rest of the world. The class, which in addition to access methods also contains mutation methods, can therefore be reserved for use by a narrower circle of programmers.

Client programmers, meanwhile, have to use constructors when they are going to make objects, and these constructors are not located in the interfaces, but in the classes. If you don't want client programmers to use the constructors, you can offer instantiation methods through the interface—for example, `createPaint()`. In the class, this method will be implemented by the class making an object on its own and returning this to the client:

```
public Paint createPaint(String initName, double initPrice, int initNoOfCoats,
    double initNoOfSqMPerLiter) {
    return new Paint(initName, initPrice, initNoOfCoats, initNoOfSqMPerLiter);
}
```

These kinds of methods are often called *factory methods*.

In chapter 19, we will create distributed systems. The client and server will run on different computers and then the client will work with an interface as described above.

Problem

In the online API documentation, look up the `Cloneable` interface. Also read about the `clone()` method in the `Object` class.

1. What are the concepts of deep and shallow copy? Can you demonstrate the difference by explaining what it means concretely for instances of the class `Surface`?

2. What does the standard version (the one that is inherited from `Object`) of `clone()` do?

3. Try the standard version of `clone()` on instances of the class `Surface`. What do you find out?

4. Make your own version of the method `clone()` in the class `Surface`. Try it out.

12.11 New Concepts in This Chapter

Concept	Brief Explanation
abstract	Modifier that declares abstract classes or abstract methods.
abstract class	A class with the modifier `abstract` in the class head. It is not possible to instantiate objects from an abstract class.
abstract method	A method with the modifier `abstract` in the method head. The method consists of just the head followed by a semicolon. It has no body.

Concept	Brief Explanation
factory method	A method that creates an instance of a class. Clients may use these methods instead of constructors.
final	Keyword that can be used, among other things, as a modifier in a method head (that then means that the method cannot be overridden in subclasses) or a class head (that means that the class cannot have subclasses).
generalization	[Rumbaugh, Jacobson, Booch 1999, p. 287]: "A taxonomic relationship between a more general element and a more specific element. The more specific element is fully consistent with the more general element and contains additional information. An instance of the more specific element may be used where the more general element is allowed." In our situation, an "element" is equivalent to a class.
hide a name	A name in a subclass may hide an inherited name of a class method or a variable. The class method must have the same signature as the inherited class method.
inheritance	Members that a class inherits from a superclass can be used in the same way as if they were declared in the class. Inside the very same package, all nonprivate members are inherited. Outside the package, public and protected members are inherited, protected members under certain conditions. Constructors are not members and are therefore not inherited.
override a name	A name in a subclass may hide an inherited instance method. The method must have the same signature as the inherited method.
polymorphic operation	An operation with many different implementations. The operation is declared in a class that is a common superclass for the classes with the various implementations.
polymorphism	We can send the same message to different types of objects; they know on their own how to handle the message. The message is a polymorphic operation.

12.12 Review Problems

1. What is the relationship between superclasses, subclasses, generalization, and specialization?

2. Why do we say that generalization expresses an "is-a" relationship?

3. How can we show in a UML diagram that some members are private while others are public? Why is it especially important to show this in a class tree?

4. What is an abstract class? What is an abstract method? How is this shown in UML? How are these concepts related?

5. What does the concept of polymorphism include? What is the relationship between polymorphism and abstract methods?

6. The keyword `extends` is used to make a subclass. Among other things, this means that the subclass inherits from its own superclass. What does the subclass inherit?

7. What does it mean for the programming that a class inherits members from another class?

8. How do we use the keyword `super`?

9. When should we use the operator `instanceof`, and when should we not use this operator?

10. Java offers four levels of access for constructors and members in a class. What four levels are there? How do we declare them? And what do they imply?

11. Explain recommended guidelines for using access modifiers.

12. What type of inherited name can we override in a subclass? What type of inherited name can we hide in a subclass? What is the difference between overriding and hiding?

13. How do we declare that a method cannot be overridden in a subclass? Are there any advantages to this?

14. What does the modifier `final` do in a class head?

15. What is a Java interface? Describe similarities and differences between interfaces and classes.

16. Explain how to use the ready-made interfaces we have been through in this book.

17. Explain what is implied by a class implementing an interface. Can a class implement more than one interface at a time? Can implementation of an interface contribute to a class becoming abstract?

12.13 Programming Problems

Problem 1

Triangles, circles, and squares are all geometric figures. It should be possible to calculate the area of all geometric figures.

Draw a class tree.

Then write the program code for the classes and make a simple test program: set up an array of references to geometric figures, enter information into it, and use it to call the methods to calculate the area of different types of figures.

Problem 2

A newsstand sells different types of reading materials—for example, magazines, books, newspapers, and periodicals. The books are either single or part of a series. The class diagram for a register of the reading material is shown in Figure 12.11.

The title and publisher are of interest for all reading materials. In the "periodical" group, we collect all the reading materials that come out at regular intervals—for example, newspapers, magazines, and periodicals. We register the number of publications per year as well as the type of reading material (newspapers, magazines, or periodicals) and subject area/genre (sports, travel, photography, family, youth, etc.).

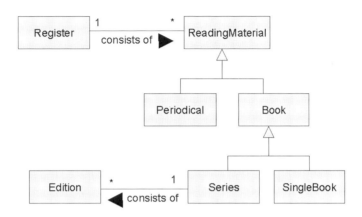

Figure 12.11 A register of reading materials (UML)

The author is always of interest for books. For books that are part of a series, we will include information about all the publications (date and title of the individual publication). Single books can come out in several editions. We will stick to keeping track of the number of editions, and not the year every single edition came out.

Both the title and publisher must be given to identify any reading material.

Do the following:

(a) Suggest instance variables and possible constants for every single class.

(b) Make a constructor for the class `Series`. This constructor will take all pertinent information about a series, as well as information about the first edition in the series, as arguments.

It should not be possible for a client to register a new series without registering the first edition in the series at the same time.

(c) Make `toString()` methods for all the classes in the problem except the class `Register`.

(d) Write a method that changes the status to a specific book from a single book to a series. This book will then become the first in the series. The date and subtitle will be parameters for the method. The method can also have other parameters. The method will belong to the class `Register`.

(e) Write a method that finds information about all periodicals within the same genre. The genre will be a parameter and the method will return all the information as a text that it's suitable to print.

(f) Create whatever is necessary in terms of other constructors and methods so that you can finally make a client program that tests what you have answered in a) through e).

Problem 3

A doctor's office can be organized such that patients who want it can be called in for routine checkups once a year. These patients are called "permanent patients".

For all patients, both permanent and nonpermanent, the patient's name, address, and social security number must be stored.

For permanent patients, test results are stored in the data system. For the sake of simplicity, we say that test results can be represented with decimal numerals. Together with each test result, the name of the test and date are stored.

The system you create must provide the following functions:

- Register a new patient

- Obtain all of a patient's information, given the social security number

- Change a patient's status from one-time to permanent

- Record test results for a patient

Make a class diagram and program the system. The client program will be menu-driven.

Problem 4

A car company wants a registry of its customers. The company has both private and corporate customers. For all types of customers, they want to register the customer's name, address, and telephone number. For corporate customers, the name and telephone number of the contact person will also be stored.

When a car is sold, information about it (sales date, make of car, and price) will be entered for the right customer, so that the car company has a summary at any time of all the cars sold to a specific customer. For used cars, the model year and a short description of the car's condition at sale will also be recorded. Note: For new cars, the model year is the same as the sales year if the sale occurred in September or earlier. For sales in October through December, the model year being sold is the next year's model. Therefore, for new cars, the model year will not be stored, but calculated when needed.

Pertinent services that the registry can offer:

- Record new customers

- Record sales

- Change customer data

- Find all cars a customer has bought

- Find out how much a customer has paid for cars

- Find the average age of the cars a customer has bought. The age is calculated as the difference between the sales year and the model year (but it must not be negative!).

  Draw a class diagram. Program the classes.
  Make a simple test program that tests each one of the classes.

Problem 5

A class diagram for a card-key system at a college can be designed as shown in Figure 12.12.

Card-locks are mounted on a certain number of doors. Access to the buildings will be controlled by the following levels of detail:

- Employees have access to all doors between 7 a.m. and 11 p.m.

- Employees have access to a limited number of doors at night. At night, a code must be used in addition to the card.

- Students only have access during the day, from 7 a.m. to 11 p.m., and then only to a limited number of doors.

- Course participants have access to specific doors during specific time intervals and on specific dates, but never at night between 11 p.m. and 7 a.m. Over the course of a day, the course participant has access during only one period—for example, from 8 a.m. to 3 p.m.

A card is associated with a specific person and this person is identified by a number. In this problem, you will not keep track of the connection between names and numbers.

An instance of the class `CardRegister` will offer a client the following services:

- Register a new card

- Block, and possibly repeal, a card

- Find out which doors a person has access to at a specific time

- Find out who has access to a specific door at a specific time

- Find out if a specific person will gain access to a specific door at a specific time

Expand the class diagram with attributes and operations, and possibly new classes if you need to.
Program the classes. Make simple test programs that test each of the classes.

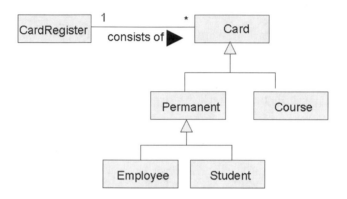

Figure 12.12   A card-key system (UML)

GUI Programming and Events

Learning goals for this chapter

After completing this chapter you will understand the following concepts:

- Event, source of the event, and listeners for the event

- GUI components, containers for GUI components

- Layout managers

- Panels

- Inner classes

You will be able to:

- Create an applet with a user interface that consists of pushbuttons and texts

- Handle events that are fired when the user presses a button on the screen, or when she presses the Enter key after having typed text in a text box

- Use inner classes

- Use the following layout managers:
  FlowLayout, BorderLayout, and GridLayout

- Divide a window into several panels, where every panel has its own layout manager

Graphical User Interface (GUI) programming builds on a technique called *event-driven programming*. The program is guided by events that the user initiates. Examples of events include menu selections and closing windows.

Even the smallest GUI program will require you to program event handling. Thus, that will be the primary topic in this chapter. We will create applets with pushbuttons and texts and see how we arrange the components in the window.

We create a GUI using the Swing library. This chapter and the next two chapters discuss some of the possibilities that Swing offers to GUI programmers. If you need more material, refer to one of the weighty books written about Swing.[1] There is also quite a bit on Sun's Web pages on the Internet.

GUI programming requires solid knowledge of most of the things we've covered up to this point. The GUI library is part of the large class tree that forms the Java SDK, and using this requires that you understand and are able to use the concept of inheritance for methods and variables, and you must also be able to use ready-made interfaces.

13.1 GUI Components

You're familiar with many different types of GUI components, such as pushbuttons, listboxes, windows, etc. You can make most of them using Java SDK. The best way to find out what GUI components are available in Java SDK is to run the demo program that comes with the compiler (see Figure 13.1). You can run it, for example, by starting the *html* file with appletviewer:

> `>appletviewer SwingSet2.html`

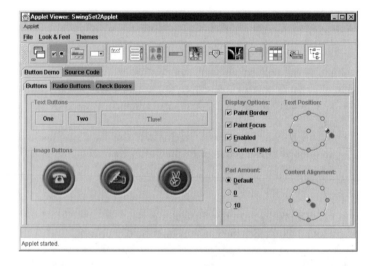

Figure 13.1   The demo program at jdk1.4/demo/jfc/swingset2/swingset2.html

---

1. See, for example, [Eckstein, Loy, Wood 1998] or [Walrath, Campione 1999].

Figure 13.2 shows an excerpt of the class tree with the Object class at the top. This excerpt covers several packages:

- The java.lang package: the Object class.

- The java.awt package: the classes Color, Font, Component, Container, and Panel.

- The java.applet package: the Applet class.

- The javax.swing package: the rest of the classes, also the JApplet class.

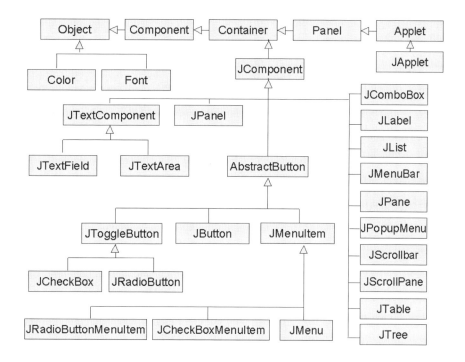

Figure 13.2 An excerpt from the class tree (UML)

SDK provides two sets of classes for creating GUI components. The older one is part of the Abstract Windowing Toolkit (AWT), and these are the classes named Checkbox, List, Button, etc. All of these classes are under the Component class. Swing is newer and, to avoid naming conflicts, these classes all have names starting with a capital J. Most of the Swing components are subclasses of the JComponent class.

Remember the J!

Remember that most of the classes that describe Swing GUI components have names starting with a J. It's easy to forget this and then use a class in AWT instead. Combinations of AWT and Swing components don't always work so well together in programs.

In this book, the GUI components are depicted for the user according to a standard for appearance and behavior called "Java look and feel". If you've worked with window systems on different platforms, you've discovered that they look a little different and they also behave a little differently. It's possible to indicate that the graphical user interface you are creating will look like and behave according to "Motif Look and Feel" or "Windows Style Look and Feel". Try the different choices in the "Look and Feel" menu in the demo program in Figure 13.1. However, you will discover that the windows' appearance is always consistent with the platform you're running on; it's just the contents of the windows that adjust to the "Look and Feel" you want. "Windows Style Look and Feel" is only permitted on the Windows platform.

A central concept for GUIs is *focus*. A component in focus is the active component. The active component is the one which reacts to our mouse and keyboard activities. On the screen this is usually indicated in some way or other—for example, with a darker frame around a window, a vertical bar cursor in a text field or a thicker frame around a button. As users we may shift focus from one component to another, for example by clicking with the mouse on the other component.

We use inheritance a great deal when we program GUIs. Therefore, it's important to have a certain familiarity with the class tree. You'll find this tree when you search in the online API documentation, and you'll also see which methods the class in question inherits from classes further up the tree. For example, look up the `JTextField` class. You find that this class inherits many methods from `JComponent`, `Container`, and `Component`.

In this section we will include an excerpt from the API reference for the `Component` class. This excerpt is, as with all the classes in this book, and especially for the GUI classes, not complete.

If you haven't already discovered how useful the online API documentation is, you certainly will now that you're ready to program GUIs. You will probably discover that it's indispensable.

API Reference

The java.awt.Component class

This class is abstract and a superclass for all GUI components.

Methods:

    public void addFocusListener(FocusListener listener)

This method registers a listener object that will listen for whether the component loses or gains focus.

    public Color getBackground()
    public Color getForeground()

These methods get a reference for the component's background and foreground colors, respectively.

    public Font getFont()

This method gets a reference to the font used in this component.

    public Container getParent()

This method gets a reference to the container that this component is in.

    public boolean hasFocus()

This method returns `true` if the component has the focus.

    public void repaint()

This method repaints the component. This happens automatically as necessary for all ready-made components (for example, when the window is moved). If a component contains an image that we drew ourselves, we have to make sure to repaint it in the event of changes. See, for example, Figure 13.10 and Program Listing 13.8.

    public void requestFocus()

This method gives this component the focus.

    public void setBackground(Color newColor)
    public void setForeground(Color newColor)

These methods set the background and foreground colors respectively.

    public void setFont(Font newFont)

This method sets a new font to apply to the component.

The javax.swing.JComponent class

The `JComponent` class is a superclass for all the Swing components. This class creates its own versions of many of the methods in the `Component` class.

13.2 Pushing a Button

Download the applet *PushbuttonApplet.java* from [URL Java book] (examples, chapter 13) and run it. Every time you push the button, a text appears in the console window. See Figure 13.3.

It's the HTML code that determines the size of an applet. If you run applets directly from an editor, all the applets will probably be the same size. The applets that are presented in this book are adjusted to a suitable size by stretching the window frame once they are presented by the appletviewer.

What's happening here? What sets everything in motion is the *event* that fires when you press the button. Every time you press the button, the same thing happens. The text "You pushed the button!" is printed to the console.

As users we can initiate many types of events in a GUI program. We can give a command by pressing a button (as we did here) or we can ask to have a menu selection carried out; we can leave an input data field or we can close a window, to mention some typical events. Every single event means that the program reacts in some way: data is checked when we leave an input data field, a calculation is performed when we press a button, our document is printed when we make a menu selection, etc.

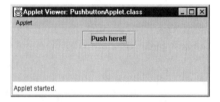

One line to the console
for every button push:

```
You pushed the button!
You pushed the button!
You pushed the button!
```

Figure 13.3 An applet with a pushbutton

How is this programmed?

Picture an "endless loop". This loop contains an enormous `switch` statement:

```
while (true) {
  switch (event) {
  case passwordInput
    check password
    break;
  case print
```

```
      print the document
      break;
    case the button "Calculate Tax" is pushed
      calculate tax
      break;
    case ...

      ...
    }
  }
```

The event determines which case block will be performed. The loop runs "indefinitely" and listens the whole time for new events.

Consider that this loop is running inside the Java interpreter, and we as programmers only deal with the contents of each individual case block.

In addition to the events that directly affect the contents of our program, we have all the events that cause the entire screen or portions of it to be repainted (for example, the event of a window closing). This event also has many other consequences, including the contents of the window no longer being accessible in the program. The Java interpreter takes care of almost all of this event handling. We rarely need to think about it.

To put it another way, a program with a graphical user interface is very complicated. What is the main difference between the programs we've written up to this point and programming with a graphical user interface?

The programs we wrote up to this point are characterized by the fact that *the program* controls the user's activities. The program asks for data in a specific order, and the user has to input that data or he won't get any further in the program. The program can offer the user a limited menu, but it's the program that decides when the menu will be offered.

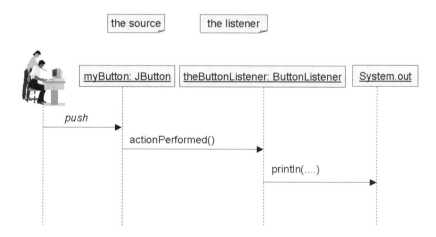

Figure 13.4 Handling the event "a button is pushed" (UML)

People who work with machines like to feel they control the machine, not the opposite. A good graphical user interface will give the user this sense. The user can choose the order of the activities and how (for example, choosing between the mouse and the keyboard) they will be performed. He has many more choices than the user of the first type of program. This places much more complicated demands on us as programmers.

With this in the back of our minds, we'll take a closer look at our little program with a simple pushbutton. Follow along in Figure 13.4. The button is an object in the program. It's called myButton and is an instance of the JButton class. By pressing the button, the user generates an event and this event is also represented as an object (not shown in the figure). This object is administered by the Java interpreter and therefore we don't have any name of our own for this object, but we know that it is an instance of the ActionEvent class. We've left out the vertical rectangles that represent that an object is active, because that would over-complicate the presentation here, especially because objects that aren't shown in the figure are involved.

The button is the *source* of the event.

In order for something to happen after this event is fired, there have to be objects that *listen* to the event. We create these objects in our program and also have to register that they will listen to events from specific objects. In this example, we have an object of this type called theButtonListener, and it is an instance of the ButtonListener class.

When a specific event occurs, the Java interpreter takes care of sending a specific message to all listeners that are registered. In this case, the Java interpreter sends the message actionPerformed() to theButtonListener object.

The class the listener is an instance of, therefore, has to implement a method with this name, and the handling of the event is inside this method. In our example, the method looks like this:

```
public void actionPerformed(ActionEvent event) {
    System.out.println("You pushed the button!");
}
```

A summary of what happens:

1. The user presses the button. The button is the *source* of an event.

2. The Java interpreter creates an instance of the ActionEvent class.

3. The Java interpreter sends actionPerformed() messages to all registered *listeners*.

4. The contents of the actionPerformed() method are carried out.

And then the Java interpreter waits for the next event to take place.
Now let's go through the applet's source code. See Program Listing 13.1.

We need two classes—one that describes the applet (the PushbuttonApplet class) and one that describes the listener (the ButtonListener class).

Program Listing 13.1

```
/*
 * PushbuttonApplet.java  E.L. 2001-08-18
 *
 */
import java.awt.*;
import java.awt.event.*;
import javax.swing.*;

public class PushbuttonApplet extends JApplet {
  public void init() {
    Container guiContainer = getContentPane();
    LayoutManager layout = new FlowLayout();
    guiContainer.setLayout(layout);

    JButton myButton = new JButton("Push here!!");  // creates the button
    guiContainer.add(myButton);  // puts it in the container
    ButtonListener theButtonListener = new ButtonListener(); // creates a listener
    myButton.addActionListener(theButtonListener); // links the listener to the button
  }
}

class ButtonListener implements ActionListener {
  public void actionPerformed(ActionEvent event) {
    System.out.println("You pushed the button!");
  }
}
```

When you start the applet, the `init()` method is called. We place the construction of the user interface in this method. This type of user interface consists of one or more windows with pushbuttons, text fields, listboxes, etc. We can think of a window as a *container for GUI components*.

We always have to start by getting a reference to this container:

```
Container guiContainer = getContentPane();
```

Here, the applet sends the message `getContentPane()` to itself. This method is declared in the `JApplet` class.

`Container` is a class that belongs to the `java.awt` package.

The way the different GUI components are laid out in the window is determined by a *layout manager*. We will come back to more details on these later; for now we just have to say that if we don't designate a particular layout manager, our button will cover the whole window in this case and that's not the idea. Therefore, we set the layout manager to "flow layout":

```
LayoutManager layout = new FlowLayout();
guiContainer.setLayout(layout);
```

Now we create a pushbutton and put it in the GUI container:

```
JButton myButton = new JButton("Push here!!");  // creates the button
guiContainer.add(myButton);  // puts it in the container
```

JButton is a class that belongs to the `javax.swing` package.

We create a listener object and tell it to listen for events that occur with the button:

```
ButtonListener theButtonListener = new ButtonListener(); // creates a listener
myButton.addActionListener(theButtonListener); // links the listener to the button
```

`addActionListener()` is a predefined message that can be sent to many types of GUI components.

Now let us turn our attention to how the `ButtonListener` class looks. As we've said, the class has to implement the `actionPerformed()` method. Gradually we'll see that there are many different types of listeners. Every type of listener requires that we implement its own set of methods. Java arranges this by insisting that different interfaces be implemented. We remember that an interface contains a collection of method heads. A class that implements the interface has to implement all the methods in the interface. If the class doesn't, it becomes abstract and it's not possible to make instances of it.

A class that is going to describe objects that listen for ActionEvents has to implement the `ActionListener` interface. The interface belongs to the `java.awt.event` package and it contains only one method, the `actionPer-formed()` method.

The `ButtonListener` class looks like this:

```
class ButtonListener implements ActionListener {
  public void actionPerformed(ActionEvent event) {
    System.out.println("You pushed the button!");
  }
}
```

Note that the method head has to be public and exactly the same as the one described in the `ActionListener` interface. Therefore, we also have to include the parameter even if we don't make use of the information that's in the `event` object.

API Reference

The javax.swing.JApplet class

Method:

```
public Container getContentPane()
```

This method returns a container that can be filled with GUI components.

The java.awt.Container class

This class describes a container that can hold GUI components. The components are placed in a list. The order of the list determines the order in the window when the user shifts focus from one component to the next using the Tab key.

Method:

> public void setLayout(LayoutManager newLayoutManager)

This method determines which type of layout manager will apply for this container.

> public Component add(Component comp)

This method places a GUI component in the container. Pertinent GUI components include buttons, lists, text fields, etc. All of these belong to subclasses of the `Component` class. This method returns the reference to the component.

The javax.swing.AbstractButton class

This class is a superclass for, among others, the classes `JCheckBox`, `JRadioButton`, `JButton`, and various menu classes (see Figure 13.2). Thus these classes inherit the methods declared in this class.

Methods:

> public void addActionListener(ActionListener aListener)

This method registers a listener for the button. The listener is alerted every time the button generates an `ActionEvent`. That happens when the user presses the button.

> public void setMnemonic(char mnemonic)

This method sets a "mnemonic" (from Greek: mneme = memory) for the button. This is a keyboard alternative to pressing the button. The underlined letter is the "mnemonic"—for example, the letter S in Save.

> public void setEnabled(boolean open)

If the argument is `false` the button is locked—in other words, the user can't press it. An argument value of `true` enables the button again.

> public void setText(String text)

This method sets the text on the button. We use this method if we used the constructor with no arguments to create the button.

The javax.swing.JButton class

This class is a subclass of `AbstractButton` and inherits all methods from that class.

Constructors:

> public JButton()
> public JButton(String text)
> public JButton(Icon icon)
> public JButton(String text, Icon icon)

The constructors can create buttons with text and/or icons on them. For an example of buttons with icons, see Figure 13.9 and Program Listing 13.7.

The java.util.EventObject class

This class is a superclass for all the event classes.

Method:

```
public Object getSource()
```

This method returns the reference to the object that generated the event. For an example of its use, see Problem 1 at the end of Section 13.4.

The java.awt.event.ActionEvent class

An object that is an instance of a subclass of the `AbstractButton` class can generate events of the `ActionEvent` type. The `JTextField` class (text box) generates an event of this type when the user presses the Enter key.

The event is described in an object that is created by the Java interpreter. This object is an argument for the `actionPerformed()` method (see the description of the `ActionListener` interface below). We can send messages to the object from within the `actionPerformed()` method.

Method:

```
public String getActionCommand()
```

This method returns the text of the GUI component that generated the event.

The class inherits the `getSource()` method from the `EventObject` class (described above).

The java.awt.event.ActionListener interface

Classes that are going to handle ActionEvents have to implement this interface.

Method:

```
public void actionPerformed(ActionEvent event)
```

Problems

In Problems 2–4 you have to use methods described earlier in the API reference.

1. Expand `PushbuttonApplet` with another button. Link `theButton-Listener` object to this button. This listener object is now linked to both of the buttons. Check that the printout to the console is the same regardless of which button you press.

2. Create keyboard alternatives for both of the buttons. Check to see that they work. As a user, you have to hold the Alt key down at the same time as the selected "mnemonic".

3. Test the `setEnabled()` method with `false` as a parameter. Check to see that it works.

4. Test the `getActionCommand()` method.

13.3 Inner Classes

The example in Section 13.2 is very simple The example becomes somewhat more complicated if we require that pushing the button will change something in the applet. As an example, let us change the background color. We have to do this in the `actionPerformed()` method in the `ButtonListener` class. The message `setBackground()` has to be sent to `guiContainer`. How are we going to accomplish that, when we're dealing with two different classes? We can send `guiContainer` as an argument for the constructor. See Program Listing 13.2. Notice the differences from the previous example: the `ButtonListener` class got an instance variable and a constructor with the reference to the container as its parameter.

We also took a little shortcut to set the layout manager. Instead of writing:

```
LayoutManager layout = new FlowLayout();
guiContainer.setLayout(layout);
```

we just write:

```
guiContainer.setLayout(new FlowLayout());
```

We don't use the `layout` reference more than once, so it's not necessary to name it. This type of shortcut is used frequently in GUI programming.

Program Listing 13.2

```java
/*
 * ColorButtonApplet.java  E.L. 2001-08-18
 *
 */
import java.awt.*;
import java.awt.event.*;
import javax.swing.*;

public class ColorButtonApplet extends JApplet {
  public void init() {
    Container guiContainer = getContentPane();
    guiContainer.setLayout(new FlowLayout());
    JButton myButton = new JButton("Push here!!");
    guiContainer.add(myButton);
    ButtonListener theButtonListener = new ButtonListener(guiContainer);
    myButton.addActionListener(theButtonListener);
  }
}
```

```
class ButtonListener implements ActionListener {
  private Container theGuiContainer;
  public ButtonListener(Container initContainer) {
    theGuiContainer = initContainer;
  }

  public void actionPerformed(ActionEvent event) {
    theGuiContainer.setBackground(Color.red);
  }
}
```

The procedure in Program Listing 13.2 is relatively clumsy and now we'll see how we can use inner classes to simplify the programming.

Often with graphical user interfaces, we don't need listeners in classes other than the class from which we're administering the user interface. In the example above, we don't need the button listener outside the `ColorButtonApplet` class. By declaring the `ButtonListener` class inside the `ColorButtonApplet` class we gain direct access from the `ButtonListener` class to all the variables declared in the `ColorButtonApplet` class. Therefore we don't need to send, for example, the GUI container over as an argument for the constructor. On the other hand, some of the local variables in the `init()` method are moved out of the method and become instance variables, so that we can access them in the inner class.

Program Listing 13.3 shows the alternative version of the applet. The simplifications with respect to the earlier version are in the implementation of the `ButtonListener` class. It can now send messages directly to `guiContainer` because it's an instance variable in the applet class.

A class within a class (an *inner class*) is considered as a member of the class, similar to variables and methods.

An instance of an inner class always belongs to a specific instance of the outer class. If we create two instances from the `ColorButtonApplet2` class (something that is very unlikely, since these are applets), these will each have their own `ButtonListener` object.

Program Listing 13.3

```
/*
 * ColorButtonApplet2.java  E.L. 2001-08-18
 *
 */
import java.awt.*;
import java.awt.event.*;
import javax.swing.*;

public class ColorButtonApplet2 extends JApplet {
  private Container guiContainer;

  public void init() {
    guiContainer = getContentPane();
```

```
        guiContainer.setLayout(new FlowLayout());
        JButton myButton = new JButton("Push here!!");
        guiContainer.add(myButton);
        ButtonListener theButtonListener = new ButtonListener();
        myButton.addActionListener(theButtonListener);
    }

    private class ButtonListener implements ActionListener {
        public void actionPerformed(ActionEvent event) {
            guiContainer.setBackground(Color.red);
        }
    }
}
```

Access to the inner class is controlled by any access modifier in the class head. In this example, the class is private and that will be the case in most of our examples. In this book, we'll use inner classes in connection with programming graphical user interfaces. Inner classes also have other applications, but we'll leave it at that for now.[2]

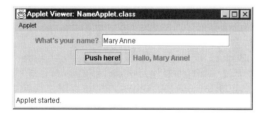

Figure 13.5 An applet with texts

Let's look at an example where the user enters her name. Pressing the button elicits a greeting to the user. See Figure 13.5 and Program Listing 13.4. The figure shows the window after the user has entered her name and pressed the button.

Let's look at two new classes for generating GUI components:

- The `JLabel` class is used to create objects that contain texts that the program can print on the screen. The objects `nameLabel` and `greeting` are both instances of this class. The object `nameLabel` gets its text content when it's created, while the object `greeting` doesn't get its value until after the user has pressed the button.

- The `JTextField` class is used to create a single-line field that the user can enter a text in. These types of fields are usually called *text boxes*. The object `nameField` is an instance of this class. The length 20 is stated as the argument for the constructor. It's completely possible to enter texts that are longer. The

_____

2. There's a thorough treatment of inner classes in [Flanagan 1997].

`actionPerformed()` method sends the message `getText()` to this object to get the text.

Program Listing 13.4

```
/*
 * NameApplet.java  E.L. 2001-08-18
 *
 */
import java.awt.*;
import java.awt.event.*;
import javax.swing.*;

public class NameApplet extends JApplet {
  private Container guiContainer;
  private JTextField nameField = new JTextField(20);
  private JLabel greeting = new JLabel();

  public void init() {
    guiContainer = getContentPane();
    guiContainer.setLayout(new FlowLayout());

    JLabel nameLabel = new JLabel("What's your name?");
    guiContainer.add(nameLabel);
    guiContainer.add(nameField);

    JButton myButton = new JButton("Push here!");
    guiContainer.add(myButton);
    ButtonListener theButtonListener = new ButtonListener();
    myButton.addActionListener(theButtonListener);

    guiContainer.add(greeting);
  }

  private class ButtonListener implements ActionListener {
    public void actionPerformed(ActionEvent event) {
      String name = nameField.getText();
      greeting.setText("Hallo, " + name + "!");
    }
  }
}
```

API Reference

The javax.swing.JLabel class

This class describes a text field that the user cannot move to.

Constructors:

```
public JLabel()
public JLabel(String text)
public JLabel(String text, int horizontalAdjusting)
```

The last parameter in the last constructor makes it possible to justify the text in a specific way. The standard is left justified. The possibilities are given as class constants inherited from the SwingConstants interface. The most common are CENTER and RIGHT. Remember to qualify these if they are going to be used. For example, JLabel.RIGHT.

Method:

```
public void setText(String text)
```

This method sets a value for the text.

The javax.swing.JTextField class

This class describes a text box. The user can write in the box. However, the program can block the text box for user input.

Constructors:

```
public JTextField()
public JTextField(String text)
public JTextField(int noOfColumns)
public JTextField(String text, int noOfColumns)
```

The number of columns determines the width of the box. If the font is proportional, a column is about the width of the letter 'm'. The text can be wider than the box.

Methods:

```
public void setHorizontalAlignment(int horizontalAdjusting)
public int getHorizontalAlignment()
```

These methods handle the alignment of the text in the text box. The default is left justified. Other possible alignments are JTextField.CENTER and JTextField.RIGHT.

```
public void setFont(Font newFont)
```

This method changes the font in the text box.

```
public void addActionListener(ActionListener aListener)
```

This method registers a listener for the text box. The listener reacts when the user presses the Enter key.

This class is a subclass of the JTextComponent class and inherits all of this class's methods.

The javax.swing.text.JTextComponent class

Methods:

```
public String getText()
public void setText(String text)
```

These methods set and get the text respectively.

```
public void setEditable(boolean open)
```

With an argument of `false`, the method will block the text from being edited on the user's side. An argument of `true` opens the text to editing again.

One more example: see Figure 13.6 and Program Listing 13.5.

Here we've created three buttons, each with its own color. Clicking one of the buttons will change the color of the text. We link all three buttons to the same listener. The `actionPerformed()` method starts by finding out which of the buttons was the source of the event.

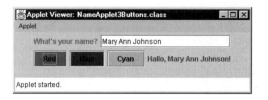

Figure 13.6 Texts and three buttons

Program Listing 13.5

```java
/*
 * NameApplet3Buttons.java  E.L. 2001-08-18
 *
 */
import java.awt.*;
import java.awt.event.*;
import javax.swing.*;

public class NameApplet3Buttons extends JApplet {
  private Container guiContainer;
  private JTextField nameField = new JTextField(20);
  private JLabel greeting = new JLabel();

  public void init() {
    guiContainer = getContentPane();
    guiContainer.setLayout(new FlowLayout());

    JLabel nameLabel = new JLabel("What's your name?");
    guiContainer.add(nameLabel);
    guiContainer.add(nameField);
    /*
     * Creates three buttons with color according to the text on the buttons.
     * Puts all the buttons in the guiContainer.
```

```
        */
        JButton buttonRed = new JButton("Red");
        buttonRed.setBackground(Color.red);
        guiContainer.add(buttonRed);

        JButton buttonBlue = new JButton("Blue");
        buttonBlue.setBackground(Color.blue);
        guiContainer.add(buttonBlue);

        JButton buttonCyan = new JButton("Cyan");
        buttonCyan.setBackground(Color.cyan);
        guiContainer.add(buttonCyan);
        /*
         * Creates a listener and links all the buttons to the same listener.
         */
        ButtonListener theButtonListener = new ButtonListener();
        buttonRed.addActionListener(theButtonListener);
        buttonBlue.addActionListener(theButtonListener);
        buttonCyan.addActionListener(theButtonListener);

        guiContainer.add(greeting);
    }
    private class ButtonListener implements ActionListener {
        public void actionPerformed(ActionEvent event) {
            String colorName = event.getActionCommand();
            Color color;
            if (colorName.equals("Red")) color = Color.red;
            else if (colorName.equals("Blue")) color = Color.blue;
            else color = Color.cyan;
            greeting.setForeground(color);
            String name = nameField.getText();
            greeting.setText("Hallo, " + name + "!");
        }
    }
}
```

Problems

You will need the last API reference to solve these problems. You will make changes
to the program in Program Listing 13.5. Start with the original program when you
begin each problem.

1. Modify the program so that the user can't write anything in the text box after
   she's pressed one of the buttons for the first time.

2. Modify the program so that the user can't press the same button more than three
   times.

3. Modify the program so that the pushbuttons contain the names of three different
   fonts. Clicking one of the buttons will change the font for all the text in the
   window.

4. Currently, the program outputs the greeting when the user presses a button. Modify the program so that the greeting appears if the user presses Enter in the text box. Then focus will be set to the first of the three buttons.

13.4 Managing the Layout

Managing the layout consists of controlling the placement and size of the GUI components in a window on the screen. It's possible to set this in pixels. Then the screen resolution will determine the size of the components. The size of all the components will be fixed.

However, it's desirable to avoid counting pixels when you're going to lay out GUI components in a window. Run the example in Program Listing 13.5 in appletviewer. Modify the size of the window using the mouse. Notice how the buttons and texts move and constantly adjust to the new size of the container they're in.

There are several different layout managers. In this chapter, we will look at three of the simplest ones.

In the previous examples, we used FlowLayout:

```
guiContainer = getContentPane();
guiContainer.setLayout(new FlowLayout());
```

We send an instance of the `FlowLayout` class as an argument for the `setLayout()` method. Then we've specified that this object will control the layout in this container. See Figure 13.7.

If we don't set a particular layout manager for a container, a layout manager called BorderLayout applies. This gives us cause to specify a north/south/east/west/ center location for a component. If we try to place several components in the same place, they wind up on top of each other. If we only indicate some of the locations, the components expand in width or height. See Figure 13.8. The program that was used to create these figures is presented in Program Listing 13.6.

A third type of layout manager is GridLayout. This lays the components out in a grid with a given number of columns and rows. Every cell takes the same amount of room. The size of the window adjusts the size of the cells. Two examples of this layout manager are shown in Figure 13.9. The programs that make these applets are shown in Program Listing 13.7.

A brief comment on the *TestGridLayout.java* program: in the `init()` method, we create a `label` reference and set it to point to an instance of the `JLabel` class:

```
JLabel label = new JLabel("Name:", JLabel.RIGHT);
```

A few lines further down in the program, we set `label` to point to another instance of the `JLabel` class:

```
label = new JLabel("Address:", JLabel.RIGHT);
```

The first object has not disappeared. The statement `guiContainer. add(label);` made sure that this object was added to the list of GUI components that `guiContainer` administers.

The left part of Figure 13.9 shows how we can use GridLayout to input data. Because all the cells are the same size, we choose to right justify the background texts so they won't be too far away from the text box they belong to.

The figure on the right shows ten pushbuttons with icons on them. The icons are from *jdk1.4/demo/applets/Animator/image*s.

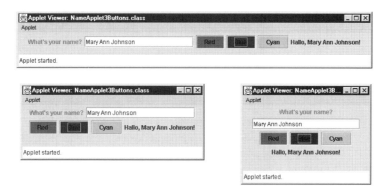

Figure 13.7 FlowLayout lays the components out from left to right, centered on the lines

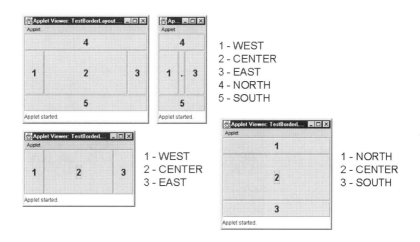

Figure 13.8 BorderLayout divides the components between north-south-east-west-center

Program Listing 13.6

```
/*
 * TestBorderLayout.java  E.L. 2001-08-18
 *
```

```
 * BorderLayout is default layout manager for applets.
 */
import java.awt.*;
import javax.swing.*;

public class TestBorderLayout extends JApplet {
 public void init() {
   Container guiContainer = getContentPane();
   Font big = new Font("SansSerif", Font.BOLD, 20);

   JButton buttonOne = new JButton("1");
   buttonOne.setFont(big);
   guiContainer.add(buttonOne, BorderLayout.WEST);

   JButton buttonTwo = new JButton("2");
   buttonTwo.setFont(big);
   guiContainer.add(buttonTwo, BorderLayout.CENTER);

   JButton buttonThree = new JButton("3");
   buttonThree.setFont(big);
   guiContainer.add(buttonThree, BorderLayout.EAST);

   JButton buttonFour = new JButton("4");
   buttonFour.setFont(big);
   guiContainer.add(buttonFour, BorderLayout.NORTH);

   JButton buttonFive = new JButton("5");
   buttonFive.setFont(big);
   guiContainer.add(buttonFive, BorderLayout.SOUTH);
 }
}
```

Figure 13.9 Two examples of GridLayout in use

Program Listing 13.7

```
/*
 * TestGridLayout.java  E.L. 2001-08-18
 *
 */
import java.awt.*;
import javax.swing.*;
```

```java
public class TestGridLayout extends JApplet {
  private JTextField name = new JTextField(15);
  private JTextField address = new JTextField(15);
  private JTextField phone = new JTextField(15);
  private JTextField eMail = new JTextField(15);

  public void init() {
    Container guiContainer = getContentPane();
    /*
     * The GridLayout constructor takes the following arguments:
     * No. of rows, no. of columns, horizontal and vertical gap between the cells.
     */
    guiContainer.setLayout(new GridLayout(4, 2, 5, 5));

    JLabel label = new JLabel("Name:", JLabel.RIGHT);
    guiContainer.add(label);
    guiContainer.add(name);
    label = new JLabel("Address:", JLabel.RIGHT);
    guiContainer.add(label);
    guiContainer.add(address);
    label = new JLabel("Phone:", JLabel.RIGHT);
    guiContainer.add(label);
    guiContainer.add(phone);
    label = new JLabel("E-mail:", JLabel.RIGHT);
    guiContainer.add(label);
    guiContainer.add(eMail);
  }
}

/*
 * TestGridLayout2.java  E.L. 2001-08-18
 *
 */
import java.awt.*;
import javax.swing.*;

public class TestGridLayout2 extends JApplet {
  public void init() {
    Container guiContainer = getContentPane();
    guiContainer.setLayout(new GridLayout(2, 5, 5, 5));

    /*
     * The images have to be in the directory Beans,
     * and the files have the names T1.gif, T2.gif, etc.
     */
    String nameOfImage = "Beans/T";
    for (int imageNo = 1; imageNo <= 10; imageNo++) {
      String imageFilname
        = nameOfImage.concat(imageNo + ".gif");
      ImageIcon icon = new ImageIcon(imageFilname);
      JButton button = new JButton(imageFilname, icon);
```

```
        guiContainer.add(button);
      }
    }
  }
```

API Reference

The java.awt.FlowLayout class

FlowLayout is a layout manager that places the components line by line from left to right.

Constructors:

```
    public FlowLayout()
    public FlowLayout(int adjustment)
    public FlowLayout(int adjustment, int horizontalGap,  int verticalGap)
```

If justification is not indicated, the components will be center justified. We can specify that the justification should be `FlowLayout.LEFT` or `Flow-Layout.RIGHT`.
   If we don't specify the gap between the components, it is set to five pixels.

The java.awt.BorderLayout class

BorderLayout lets us lay the components out according to a north/south/east/west/center format. If we place several components in the same place, they wind up on top of each other.

Constructors:

```
    public BorderLayout()
    public BorderLayout(int horizontalGap, int verticalGap)
```

If we don't indicate a horizontal and vertical gap between the components, the gap will be 0.

The java.awt.GridLayout class

The layout manager lays the components out row by row in the specified number of rows and columns. Every component gets the same amount of room.

Constructors:

```
    public GridLayout()
    public GridLayout(int noOfRows, int noOfColumns)
    public GridLayout(int noOfRows, int noOfColumns,  int horizontalGap, int verticalGap)
```

If we don't indicate a horizontal and vertical gap between the components, the gap will be 0.

Dividing a GUI container into several small containers (panels)

Every individual layout manager mentioned above distributes the components throughout one container. If we're creating large windows with lots of components, we may divide the outer container into several small containers and use a suitable layout manager for each of them. We use *panels* (the JPanel class) to create these small containers.

Figure 13.10 and Program Listing 13.8 show an example where we've divided the outer container into three panels. The components in the upper panel are laid out using a GridLayout manager, while the two lower ones follow FlowLayout, which is the default for panels. The middle panel contains a drawing. The user enters the attributes for this ellipse in the upper panel. Then she clicks on the button with the desired color and the ellipse is painted.

We'll go through the DrawApplet class.

As usual, the applet is initiated when the init() method is performed. We get a reference to "the content pane", and fill this container with the three panels:

```
UserInputPanel north = new UserInputPanel();
guiContainer.add(north, BorderLayout.NORTH);
theDrawing = new Drawing(x, y, width, height);
guiContainer.add(theDrawing, BorderLayout.CENTER);
ButtonPanel south = new ButtonPanel();
guiContainer.add(south, BorderLayout.SOUTH);
```

The classes UserInputPanel, Drawing, and ButtonPanel are all subclasses of the JPanel class. They represent different specializations of the more general JPanel. It's a matter of judgment whether we will place these classes outside or inside the DrawApplet class. We've placed the drawing outside, while the two others have been placed inside the class. We did this so the drawing can be used in other contexts, while the upper and lower panels are linked specifically to this presentation of the drawing.

The constructor in the UserInputPanel class lays out background texts and text boxes the same as in the example in Program Listing 13.7. Note that the panel sends the messages setLayout() and add() to itself.

The constructor in the ButtonPanel class also contains little new. The three color buttons are laid out, and they are linked to the very same listener object.

The Drawing class paints an ellipse. The attributes x, y, width, and height come in as parameters for the constructor and they can be changed using set methods. We have chosen to let the client objects send the numbers in as strings. The reason for this is that they come from text fields. We use Integer.parseInt() to convert from strings to numbers. If this doesn't work smoothly (Number-FormatException), we print a little message to the console and the attribute in question is set to 0. This treatment is in the private method convertText().

The event handling is in the ButtonListener class. New ellipse attributes are fetched from the input fields and sent to the drawing. We also set a new color for the drawing.

Finally, we paint the whole window again with `repaint ()`; see the API reference for the `Component` class in Section 13.1.

The default layout manager for applets is BorderLayout, where we can place components in the north, south, east, west, or center.

The default layout manager for panels is FlowLayout, where the components are placed line by line, center justified.

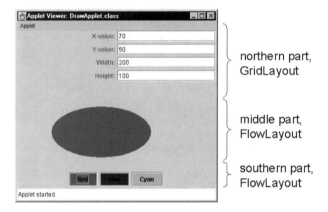

Figure 13.10   We divide the container into three smaller containers (panels)

Program Listing 13.8

```
/*
 * DrawApplet.java  E.L. 2001-08-18
 *
 */
import java.awt.*;
import java.awt.event.*;
import javax.swing.*;

public class DrawApplet extends JApplet {

    /* These ellipse attributes will be used the first time the ellipse is drawn */
    private static final String x = "70";
    private static final String y = "50";
    private static final String width = "50";
    private static final String height = "100";

    /*
     * The following variables will be used in the init() method,
```

```
      * in the listener class, and in the UserInputPanel class.
      */
     private Container guiContainer;
     private Drawing theDrawing;
     private JTextField xField = new JTextField(x);
     private JTextField yField = new JTextField(y);
     private JTextField widthField = new JTextField(width);
     private JTextField heightField = new JTextField(height);

     public void init() {
       guiContainer = getContentPane();

       UserInputPanel north = new UserInputPanel();
       guiContainer.add(north, BorderLayout.NORTH);

       theDrawing = new Drawing(x, y, width, height);
       guiContainer.add(theDrawing, BorderLayout.CENTER);

       ButtonPanel south = new ButtonPanel();
       guiContainer.add(south, BorderLayout.SOUTH);
     }

     /* Listens for button pushes */
     private class ButtonListener implements ActionListener {
       public void actionPerformed(ActionEvent event) {

         /* Gets new ellipse attributes and sends them to the drawing object */
         theDrawing.setX(xField.getText());
         theDrawing.setY(yField.getText());
         theDrawing.setWidth(widthField.getText());
         theDrawing.setHeight(heightField.getText());

         /* Gets the color of the button */
         String colorName = event.getActionCommand();
         Color color;
         if (colorName.equals("Red")) color = Color.red;
         else if (colorName.equals("Blue")) color = Color.blue;
         else color = Color.cyan;

         /* Sets the foreground color for the drawing */
         theDrawing.setForeground(color);

         /* Repaints the whole window */
         guiContainer.repaint();
       }
     }

     /* This class describes the northern panel. */
     private class UserInputPanel extends JPanel {
       public UserInputPanel() {
         /* The Gridlayout constructor takes the following arguments, in order:
            No. of rows, no. of columns, horizontal and vertical gap between the cells. */
         setLayout(new GridLayout(4, 2, 5, 5));
         JLabel label = new JLabel("X-value:", JLabel.RIGHT);
         add(label);
         add(xField);
```

```java
      label = new JLabel("Y-value:", JLabel.RIGHT);
      add(label);
      add(yField);

      label = new JLabel("Width:", JLabel.RIGHT);
      add(label);
      add(widthField);

      label = new JLabel("Height:", JLabel.RIGHT);
      add(label);
      add(heightField);
    }
  }

  /* This class describes the southern panel. */
  private class ButtonPanel extends JPanel {
    public ButtonPanel() {
      ButtonListener theButtonListener = new ButtonListener();

      JButton redButton = new JButton("Red");
      redButton.setBackground(Color.red);
      redButton.addActionListener(theButtonListener);
      add(redButton);

      JButton blueButton = new JButton("Blue");
      blueButton.setBackground(Color.blue);
      blueButton.addActionListener(theButtonListener);
      add(blueButton);

      JButton cyanButton = new JButton("Cyan");
      cyanButton.setBackground(Color.cyan);
      cyanButton.addActionListener(theButtonListener);
      add(cyanButton);
    }
  }
}

/*
 * This class describes the drawing of an ellipse where the ellipse attributes
 * may be changed by the user. The class receives the attributes as texts.
 * If it is not possible to convert the text into a number, the corresponding
 * attribute gets the value 0. A litte message is sent to the console.
 */
class Drawing extends JPanel {
  private int x;
  private int y;
  private int width;
  private int height;
  public Drawing(String initX, String initY, String initWidth, String initHeight) {
    x = convertText(initX);
    y = convertText(initY);
    width = convertText(initWidth);
```

```
      height = convertText(initHeight);
    }
    public void setX(String newX) {
      x = convertText(newX);
    }
    public void setY(String newY) {
      y = convertText(newY);
    }
    public void setWidth(String newWidth) {
      width = convertText(newWidth);
    }
    public void setHeight(String newHeight) {
      height = convertText(newHeight);
    }
    public void paintComponent(Graphics window) {
      window.fillOval(x, y, width, height);
    }
    private int convertText(String text) {
      try {
        return Integer.parseInt(text);
      } catch (NumberFormatException e) {
        System.out.println("It's not possible to convert " + text + " into integer.");
        return 0;
      }
    }
  }
```

API Reference

The javax.swing.JPanel class

We use panels to divide a window with many GUI components into smaller pieces.
We lay the components out in every individual panel, then we place the panels in
the window. We can also divide each panel into even smaller pieces, which are also
panels. We can keep doing this as long as we want. In particular, we use panels
when we are going to add a drawing to our window.

Constructors:

```
    public JPanel()
    public JPanel(LayoutManager newLayoutManager)
```

If a layout manger is not specified, FlowLayout applies.

Problems

Modify the program in Program Listing 13.8. Use the original version of the program for each problem.

1. Modify the program so that `getSource()` is used instead of `getAction-Command()`. (See the `java.util.EventObject` class, Section 13.2.)

2. Modify the southern panel so that it uses GridLayout. The user should be able to choose between all the predefined colors in the `Color` class. It's most practical to use arrays when there are so many buttons.

13.5 New Concepts in This Chapter

Concept	Brief Explanation
AWT	Abstract Windowing Toolkit, the library for graphics and GUI programming from JDK 1.0. Many of the classes are still pertinent (examples: `Color`, `Font`, and the various layout managers), but we use the Swing library to create GUI components.
event	Used in connection with GUI programming about the result of a user activity—for example, pressing on a button, leaving a data input field, closing a window. The Java interpreter creates an object that contains information about the event. The object becomes an argument in a message that is sent to registered listeners. Events can also occur in ways other than as the result of a user activity.
event-driven program	A program that is controlled by events. In a GUI, these events are usually initiated by the user. Therefore we can also say that the programs are user-driven.
focus	A component in focus is the active component. The active component is the one which reacts to our mouse and keyboard activities. On the screen this is usually indicated in some way or other—for example, with a darker frame around a window, a vertical bar cursor in a text field or a thicker frame around a button.
GUI	Graphical User Interface
GUI component	The different parts that make up a graphical user interface. Most of the GUI components belong to a subclass of the `Component` class. Exceptions are the menus in the AWT library.
GUI container	An object that is an instance of the `Container` class, or a subclass of this class. We can fill the container with components using the `add()` method.
inner class	A class that is declared inside another class. The inner class is regarded as a member of the class, and it has direct access to the outer class's variables and methods. An instance of an inner class always belongs to an instance of an outer class.
layout manager	An object that determines the way the GUI components will be laid out in the window.
listener	An object that implements a listener interface. Objects of this type can be registered as listeners for source objects.

Concept	Brief Explanation
listener interface	An interface that defines a collection of methods that a listener class has to implement. Different types of events require different types of interfaces.
panel	An instance of the `JPanel` class usually used to edit the location of the GUI components when there are many components to lay out in the same window. The window is divided into several panels. Every individual panel has its own layout manager. If desirable, each individual panel can be divided further.
pushbutton	A button that the user can press to perform a command. The button is an instance of the `JButton` class.
source, source object	The GUI component that fired the event, usually because of user activity.
Swing library	The classes in the `javax.swing` package form the Swing library. Most of the GUI components belong to subclasses of the `JComponent` class. `JComponent` is a subclass of the `Container` class. Therefore these Swing components are also GUI containers. The `javax.swing` package also contains classes for windows (`JFrame`) and applets (`JApplet`).
text box	A one-line box that the user can write in. A text box is an instance of the `JTextField` class.

13.6 Review Problems

1. Explain the relationship between the user, source objects, and listener objects when the user presses the button in Figure 13.3. In which way is the `ActionEvent` instantiated, and what is it used for?

2. It's the Java interpreter that sends messages to the listener objects. However, we have to program the class that a listener object is an instance of. How can the Java interpreter know the names of the methods we put in the listener class?

3. Explain the primary differences between an event-driven program and a traditional program (like the ones we've written up to now).

4. Why is it practical to use inner classes in conjunction with GUI programming?

5. What does a layout manager do?

6. Explain the differences between the three types of layout managers: FlowLayout, BorderLayout, and GridLayout.

7. What do we use panels for?

13.7 Programming Problems

Problem 1

Create an applet that converts dollars to euros. At time of writing, 1 euro costs 0.918 dollars.

Problem 2

Create a very simple calculator. The calculator will have a pushbutton for each individual digit. It will only be able to handle two numbers. It will be possible to add, multiply, divide, or subtract the numbers from each other. The user will be able to choose whether she wants to enter the numbers directly into text boxes or press on the number buttons.

Problem 3

Create an applet that lets the user try to create a magic squares. The square will consist of 4×4 cells. The user enters numbers in the cells. The numbers 1–16 will be used. Every time the user presses a pushbutton the applet will find out if the square fulfills the requirements. The requirements for a magic square are that the sum in the vertical, horizontal and diagonal directions will be the same.

Problem 4

Create a simple reservation system for a concert hall. You can assume that the rows are all the same length. Let every seat be represented by a pushbutton on the screen. The pushbutton will have the seat and row number displayed on it. If the seat is available, the button will be green. The user reserves the seat by pressing on it. Then it turns red. If the seat is reserved, pressing on it will make it available again.

Text, Choices, and Windows

Learning goals for this chapter

After completing this chapter, you will be able to create:

- Text areas of several lines and password fields

- Check boxes, radio buttons, and lists

- Primary windows (instances of the JFrame class)

- Focus listeners, window listeners, and listeners to list selections

   You will also know when to use the different GUI components to create the best possible user interface.

We are continuing to look at several GUI components.

   In addition to the text box we are already familiar with, we will see that Swing also offers text fields that can consist of several lines. A separate class for password fields is included, too.

   Often we want the user to choose between different alternatives. We will go through three different types of components from which choices may be made:

- Check boxes are used if the user is going to make none, one, or several choices from a few alternatives.

- Radio buttons are used if the user is going to make exactly one choice from a few alternatives.

- List: If there are a large number of alternatives (more than 5–7), we should consider using lists. Swing provides both single choice and multiple choice lists. A single choice list will correspond to radio buttons, while multiple choice lists correspond to a group of check boxes.

Most of the examples in this chapter, as in the previous chapter, are applets. At the end of the chapter, we will look at how we make application windows.

14.1 Text Components and Focus Listeners

Text components are subclasses of `JTextComponent`, see Figure 14.1. The `JTextComponent` class offers services that are common to all text components, such as methods for setting and getting the text (`setText()` and `getText()`), marking the text, and copying to and from the clipboard. In this book, we limit ourselves to the following three specializations of the `JTextComponent` class:

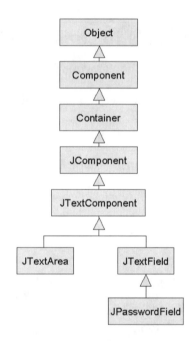

Figure 14.1 Text components (UML)

- The `JTextField` class: A one-line text. Pressing the Enter key leads to an ActionEvent, the same type of event as pushbuttons, but the focus won't move out of the field. That has to be programmed.

- The `JTextArea` class: A text of several lines. Pressing the Enter key leads to a new line.

- The JPasswordField class: The text the user enters here will be hidden by asterisks. Pressing the Enter key has the same effect as for JTextField.

It's possible to create listeners that will register all potential changes made in text fields (see DocumentListener in the online API documentation). However, it's rare that we need this since we usually handle text using menu choices and/or pushbuttons.

 Shortcuts for copying, pasting, and cutting are implemented in the Swing classes. For Windows and Java Look and Feel the shortcuts are Ctrl+C, Ctrl+V, and Ctrl+X.

Figure 14.2 and Program Listing 14.1 show examples of the three types of text components. The user will enter a username (JTextField) and password (JPassword). If these are correct, he is permitted to change the text in the large text area in the middle of the window (JTextArea). The password in the password field should be checked when this field loses focus. We have to make a focus listener. This will react by checking the username and password, and setting focus back to the username field if the contents of either one of the fields is invalid.

If, after having changed the text, the user presses the button marked "Print," the text will be written to the console.

First:

Username, password and some text are entered:

Pushing the print button gives the following text at the console:

```
Here is the text:
Ok, now I am here, and allowed to enter text. You are allowed to
enter text here, if you input the correct password.
```

Figure 14.2 Examples of different text components

Program Listing 14.1

```java
/*
 * TextApplet.java  E.L. 2001-08-20
 *
 */
import java.awt.*;
import java.awt.event.*;
import javax.swing.*;
import java.util.*;
public class TextApplet extends JApplet {

private static final String defaultText =
   "You are allowed to enter text here, if you input the correct password.";
private JTextField usernameField = new JTextField(15);
private JPasswordField passwordField = new JPasswordField(15);
private JTextArea textArea = new JTextArea(10, 20);
private JButton printButton = new JButton("Print");

 public void init() {
  Container guiContainer = getContentPane();
  guiContainer.setLayout(new BorderLayout(5, 5)); // gaps between the panels
  guiContainer.add(new LoginPanel(), BorderLayout.NORTH);
  guiContainer.add(new TextAreaPanel(), BorderLayout.CENTER);
  guiContainer.add(new ButtonPanel(), BorderLayout.SOUTH);

   usernameField.requestFocus();
   }
   /* Describes northern panel */
   private class LoginPanel extends JPanel {
   public LoginPanel() {
    setLayout(new GridLayout(2, 2, 5, 5));
     add(new JLabel("Username:", JLabel.RIGHT));
     add(usernameField);
     add(new JLabel("Password:", JLabel.RIGHT));
     add(passwordField);
     PasswordListener thePasswordListener = new PasswordListener();
     passwordField.addFocusListener(thePasswordListener);
   }
 }
  /* Describes middle panel */
  private class TextAreaPanel extends JPanel {
   public TextAreaPanel() {
    textArea.setLineWrap(true);
    textArea.setWrapStyleWord(true);
    textArea.setEditable(false);
    textArea.setText(defaultText);
    JScrollPane scrollPane = new JScrollPane(textArea);
    add(scrollPane);
```

```
      }
    }
    /* Describes southern panel */
    private class ButtonPanel extends JPanel {
      public ButtonPanel() {
        ButtonListener theButtonListener = new ButtonListener();
        printButton.addActionListener(theButtonListener);
        printButton.setEnabled(false);
        printButton.setMnemonic('P');
        add(printButton);
      }
    }

    /*
     * The objects of this class listen for changes in focus.
     *
     * The program reacts after the user has left the password field.
     * Username and password are checked. If ok, focus is moved to the text area,
     * and the user is allowed to edit the text. If not ok, focus is moved
     * to the username field, and the user may re-enter username and password.
     */
    private class PasswordListener implements FocusListener {
      public void focusLost(FocusEvent event) {
        String user = usernameField.getText();
        char[] password = passwordField.getPassword();
        if (okPassword(user, password)) {
          showStatus("Ok. You may edit the text.");
          printButton.setEnabled(true);
          textArea.setEditable(true);
          textArea.requestFocus();
        } else {
          showStatus("Username/password not valid.");
          printButton.setEnabled(false);
          textArea.setEditable(false);
          usernameField.requestFocus();
        }
      }
      public void focusGained(FocusEvent event) {
      }

      private boolean okPassword(String username, char[] password) {
        /*
         * Here the password is shown.
         * This is of course not safe enough, but ok for this example program.
         */
        char[] correctPassword = {'t', 'e', 's', 't'};
        if (username.equals("test") && Arrays.equals(password, correctPassword)) {
          Arrays.fill(password, ' '); // clears the password entered by user
          return true;
```

```
      }
      else return false;
    }
  }
  /* Describes objects which listen for button pushes */
  private class ButtonListener implements ActionListener {
    public void actionPerformed(ActionEvent event) {
      String text = textArea.getText();
      System.out.println("Here is the text: ");
      System.out.println(text);
    }
  }
}
```

First, the `init ()` method is performed. After the three panels are laid out in order, we make sure that the field where the username will be entered gets the focus.

```
usernameField.requestFocus();
```

The `LoginPanel` class is constructed in the same way as the northern panel in Program Listing 13.8. The `PasswordListener` class describes a focus listener (more about this class very soon). We make an instance of this class and link this to the password field:

```
PasswordListener thePasswordListener = new PasswordListener();
passwordField.addFocusListener(thePasswordListener);
```

The `TextAreaPanel` class makes use of the following methods that are particular to the `JTextArea` class.

The messages `setLineWrap(true)` and `setWrapStyleWord(true)` take care of automatic carriage returns and make sure that words are not broken between lines when text is entered into the large text field in the middle of the window. The text field is locked to input until the user has entered a correct username and password:

```
textArea.setEditable(false);
```

If the text is long, we might want a scroll bar on the sides so that the user easily can move forwards and backwards in the text. In order to accomplish this, we need to put the text area into an instance of the `JScrollPane` class:

```
JScrollPane scrollPane = new JScrollPane(textArea);
```

It is this object and not the text object that is placed in the container:

```
add(scrollPane);
```

The southernmost panel, the `ButtonPanel` class, adds a listener for the button:

```
ButtonListener theButtonListener = new ButtonListener();
printButton.addActionListener(theButtonListener);
```

We disable the button until later: `printButton.setEnabled (false) ;`
We have also created a keyboard alternative for the button:

printButton.setMnemonic('P');

After the panel classes, there are two inner classes that describe listeners.

The first one is the PasswordListener class: An instance of this class is registered as a listener to passwordField. A listener of this type has to handle the messages focusLost() and focusGained() (the contents of the FocusListener interface). In our case, the focusGained() method is not of any interest. However, we have to program all the methods in the interface, and therefore the focusGained() method will be empty. The focusLost() method takes care of checking the password. The getPassword() method returns the password as an array of char. There are security reasons for the method not returning a String object. An array of char can be "zeroed" after the password has been checked. We can't "zero" a String object, since an object of this type is immutable. Our program is not especially secure anyway, because the password is sitting in clear text in the source code.

To check the username and password, we have written the okPassword() method. Notice that we are using two class methods from the java.util.Arrays class (Section 9.6).

If the username and password are correct, the following happens:

- We open the pushbutton: printButton.setEnabled(true);

- We open the text field for editing: textArea.setEditable(true);

Figure 14.3 shows how messages are sent to the different GUI components to have the tasks carried out. Out of space considerations, we have left out the dotted arrows that show returns from method calls. In professional contexts, it's actually more common to leave the dotted return arrows out than to include them.

If the username and password are not right, the following occurs:

- We write a message in the status line at the bottom of the applet: showStatus("Username/password not valid.");

- We disable the push button: printButton.setEnabled(false);

- We disable the text field: textArea.setEditable(false);

- We set the username field to have the focus: usernameField.requestFocus();

The disablings are set "for security's sake". Theoretically, after having edited the text field, we can go back and enter the username and password again (and do it wrong this time!). It's better to set a block for too many things than for too few.

The second inner class is the ButtonListener class. This contains little new. If the user presses the button, the text is printed to the window in the console.

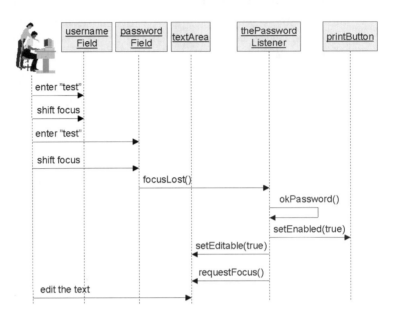

Figure 14.3 Message exchange when running the textapplet (UML)

API Reference

The javax.swing.JTextArea class

This class describes a GUI component that is a text area consisting of several lines.

Constructors:

```
public JTextArea()
public JTextArea(String text)
public JTextArea(int noOfRows, int noOfColumns)
public JTextArea(String text, int noOfRows, int noOfColumns)
```

Methods:

```
public void setLineWrap(boolean autoNewLine)
```

As default, the text is printed without automatic new lines. This is seldom desirable. Use this method with an argument set to `true` to get automatic new lines.

```
public void setWrapStyleWord(boolean wholeWords)
```

If automatic new lines is turned on, the lines can be broken in the middle of a word if no message to the contrary is given. Use this method with the argument set to `true` to avoid words being split.

The class is a direct subclass of the `JTextComponent` class (see Section 13.3) and inherits methods from this class.

The javax.swing.JTextField class

See Section 13.3.

The javax.swing.JPasswordField class

Constructors:

```
public JPasswordField()
public JPasswordField(int noOfColumns)
```

Method:

```
public char[] getPassword()
```

This method returns the text in the field as an array of `char`. For security reasons, `String` should not be used. The `getText()` method inherited from `JTextComponent` is therefore deprecated.

The java.awt.event.FocusListener interface

An object that will listen for changes in focus has to be an instance of a class that implements this interface.

Methods:

```
public void focusGained(FocusEvent event)
public void focusLost(FocusEvent event)
```

The event that is generated is an instance of the `FocusEvent` class. The methods in this class are of little interest to us.

Problem

Look up the `JTextComponent` class in the online API documentation. Find out which method has to be used if a text is to be marked. Change the program above so that the text in the text field is selected when the user enters the field. Then whatever the user writes will be written over this text.

14.2 Giving the User a Choice Between Alternatives

If it's possible, we should give the user a choice between alternatives rather than letting him enter text in response to our questions. In `JOptionPane`, we have the multiple choice version of the `showInputDialog()` method. We will see how to make a list of this type from the bottom up, and we will also make groups of radio buttons and check boxes. Figure 14.4 shows how the different components look.

check boxes

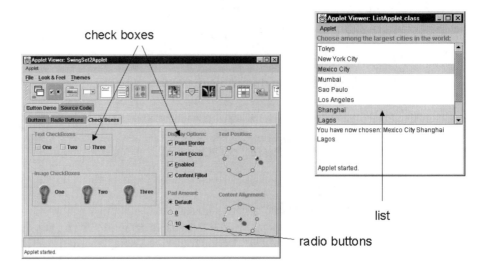

list

radio buttons

Figure 14.4   Check boxes and radio buttons from SwingSet2,[1] list from Program Listing 14.4

Class names for sources and listeners are given in table 14.1. We can make more types of listeners than are included in the table.

Table 14.1 GUI components for choices (there are more types of listeners than those listed here.)

GUI component	Class	Listener will implement the interface
Check box	`javax.swing.` `JCheckBox`	`java.awt.event.` `ActionListener`

Radio button	`javax.swing.`
	`JRadioButton,`
	usually placed in a
	`javax.swing.`
	`ButtonGroup`
		`java.awt.event.`
		`ActionListener`

List	`javax.swing.`
	`JList,`
	usually placed in a
	`javax.swing.`
	`JScrollPane`
		`javax.swing.event.`
		`ListSelectionListener`

1. Run *sdk1.4/demo/jfc/SwingSet2/SwingSet2.html* in appletviewer.

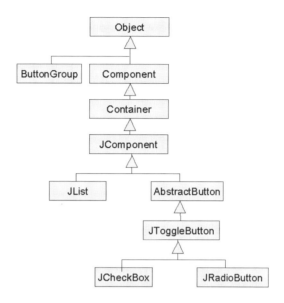

Figure 14.5 GUI components for choices: `JList`, `JCheckBox`, and `JRadioButton` (UML)

Both check boxes and radio buttons generate Action Events. This is the same type of event we are familiar with from the pushbutton examples earlier. A listener object therefore has to be an instance of a class which implements the `ActionListener` interface (in other words, the `actionPerformed()` method we know so well).

A list generates a `ListSelectionEvent`, which we will come back to in our discussion of lists.

The class tree is shown in Figure 14.5.

14.3 Choices Using Check Boxes

We use the `JCheckBox` class to make check boxes.

For example, see Figure 14.6 and Program Listing 14.2. The check boxes are independent from each other in that none, one, or several of the boxes can be checked. You will eat both lunch and dinner, or only one of the meals, or none of the meals.

The program creates two check boxes (`dinner` and `lunch`) and places them in the middle panel. A single listener object is linked to both buttons. (We can also conceive of cases where each check box has its own listener object.) When the user clicks on one of the buttons, the message `actionPerformed()` is sent to the listener object. This method checks the status of both boxes. If the box is checked, a message is printed to the console.

It's preferable to collect check boxes that go together in a group box. In this case, the box is called "Meals". We already have the check boxes in a panel of their own. From before, we know that the borders between the panels in a window are not visible. Thus, simply put, a panel is not a group box. We have to make a border around the panel for it to be a group box. There are many different types of borders in Swing. We have chosen to use one of them in this book.[2] The following statement makes a group box with the title "Meals":

```
SoftBevelBorder border = new SoftBevelBorder(BevelBorder.RAISED);
Border groupBox = BorderFactory.createTitledBorder(border, "Meals");
setBorder(groupBox); // links the group box to the panel we're in
```

The `setBorder()` method is declared in the `JComponent` class and can therefore be used on all Swing components.

Be aware of the fact that a group box does not serve any purpose besides making the GUI more visually attractive.

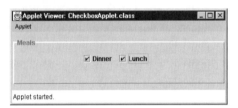

The user first clicks on the dinner check box, then on the lunch check box. An ActionEvent is generated for every click.

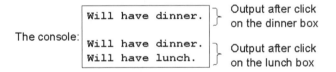

Figure 14.6 Two check boxes inside a group box

Program Listing 14.2

```
/*
 * CheckboxApplet.java  E.L. 2000-01-04
 *
 */
import java.awt.*;
```

2. You can find information about the other variants in the online API documentation: see the `javax.swing.border` package.

```
import java.awt.event.*;
import javax.swing.*;
import javax.swing.border.*;

public class CheckboxApplet extends JApplet {
 private JCheckBox dinner = new JCheckBox("Dinner");
 private JCheckBox lunch = new JCheckBox("Lunch");

 public void init() {
  Container guiContainer = getContentPane();
  /*
   * To make the group box around the checkboxes visible,
   * we have to put one empty panel in north and one in south.
   */
  guiContainer.add(new JPanel(), BorderLayout.NORTH);
  guiContainer.add(new JPanel(), BorderLayout.SOUTH);

  SelectionPanel middle = new SelectionPanel();
  guiContainer.add(middle, BorderLayout.CENTER);
 }

 /* Describes the panel with the checkboxes */
 private class SelectionPanel extends JPanel {
  public SelectionPanel() {
   add(dinner);
   add(lunch);
   CheckBoxListener listener = new CheckBoxListener();
   dinner.addActionListener(listener);
   lunch.addActionListener(listener);

  /* We make a group box by surrounding the boxes with a border, or more correctly:
     make a border around the panel which contains the check boxes */
   SoftBevelBorder border = new SoftBevelBorder(BevelBorder.RAISED);
   Border groupBox = BorderFactory.createTitledBorder(border, "Meals");
   setBorder(groupBox);
  }
 }

 /* Describes listeners, which fires on every change in a check box */
 private class CheckBoxListener implements ActionListener {
  public void actionPerformed(ActionEvent event) {
   System.out.println();
   if (dinner.isSelected()) System.out.println("Will have dinner.");
   if (lunch.isSelected()) System.out.println("Will have lunch.");
  }
 }
}
```

API Reference

The javax.swing.AbstractButton class

See also Section 13.2.

Methods:

```
public boolean isSelected()
public void setSelected(boolean selected)
```

These methods are of interest for check boxes and radio buttons. The first is used to find out whether a button or a box is selected. The second is used to set a button or a box as selected or as not selected.

The javax.swing.JCheckBox class

Constructors:

```
public JCheckBox()
public JCheckBox(Icon icon)
public JCheckBox(Icon icon, boolean selected)
public JCheckBox(String text)
public JCheckBox(String text, boolean selected)
public JCheckBox(String text, Icon icon)
public JCheckBox(String text, Icon icon, boolean selected)
```

The constructors can take strings and/or icons as arguments (use the `Icon` class, see Program Listing 13.7). We can also declare whether the box will be checked to begin with or not. If we don't declare anything, the box will not be checked.

The class is a subclass of, among others, the `AbstractButton` class (see above) and thus inherits methods from this class.

Problems

Expand the program above as follows:

1. Make a new check box for breakfast.

2. Let the printout appear in the text area under the group box, instead of on the console.

14.4 Choices Using Radio Buttons

We use the `JRadioButton` and `ButtonGroup` classes to make radio buttons.

Figure 14.7 and Program Listing 14.3 show an example of radio buttons. The radio buttons are collected in a group box with the name "Sex". Unlike checkboxes, radio buttons are mutually dependent on each other. Like the preset radio buttons in old cars, there can never be more than one button pressed in at a time, hence the name radio buttons.

Radio buttons that go together are linked to an instance of the `ButtonGroup` class. To get the buttons into a visible group box, you have to use "borders", as described for checkboxes.

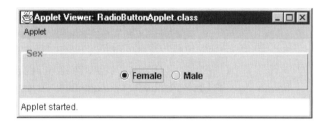

Figure 14.7 Two radio buttons in a group box

Program Listing 14.3

```java
/*
 * RadioButtonApplet.java  E.L. 2001-08-22
 *
 */
import java.awt.*;
import java.awt.event.*;
import javax.swing.*;
import javax.swing.border.*;

public class RadioButtonApplet extends JApplet {
  private JRadioButton female = new JRadioButton("Female", true);
  private JRadioButton male = new JRadioButton("Male", false);

  public void init() {
    Container guiContainer = getContentPane();

    /* The container is constructed in the same way as in the CheckBoxApplet */
    guiContainer.add(new JPanel(), BorderLayout.NORTH); // a little space
    guiContainer.add(new JPanel(), BorderLayout.SOUTH); // a little space
    SelectionPanel middle = new SelectionPanel();
    guiContainer.add(middle, BorderLayout.CENTER);
  }

  /* Describes the panel with the radio buttons */
  private class SelectionPanel extends JPanel {
    public SelectionPanel() {
      ButtonGroup group = new ButtonGroup();
      group.add(female);
      group.add(male);
```

```
    add(female);
    add(male);
    RadioButtonListener listener = new RadioButtonListener();
    female.addActionListener(listener);
    male.addActionListener(listener);

  /* We make a group box by surrounding the boxes with a border, or more correctly:
      make a border around the panel which contains the check boxes */
    SoftBevelBorder border = new SoftBevelBorder(BevelBorder.RAISED);
    Border groupBox = BorderFactory.createTitledBorder(border, "Sex");
    setBorder(groupBox);
  }
}

/* Describes listeners, which fires every change in the radio button group */
private class RadioButtonListener implements ActionListener {
  public void actionPerformed(ActionEvent event) {
    String sex = event.getActionCommand();
    if (sex.equals("Female")) System.out.println("Female is selected");
    else System.out.println("Male is selected");
  }
 }
}
```

API Reference

The javax.swing.JRadioButton class

Constructors:

```
public JRadioButton(Icon icon, boolean selected)
public JRadioButton(String text, boolean selected)
public JRadioButton(String text, Icon icon, boolean selected)
```

Remember that exactly one of the buttons in a group should always be selected.

The class is a subclass of, among others, the AbstractButton class and inherits methods from it. See Sections 13.2 and 14.3.

The javax.swing.ButtonGroup class

An instance of this class is used to make a group of radio buttons.

Constructor:

```
public ButtonGroup()
```

Method:

```
public void add(AbstractButton button)
```

This method links a button to the group.

Problems

Change the program from before as follows:

1. The middle panel will contain a group box with the title "Type of Residence". This group box will be in addition to "Sex", and it will contain radio buttons for apartment, condo, townhouse, and house. Handle the selections the same way you did for "Sex".

2. We assume that the changes in problem 1 have not been made. Add a pushbutton in the bottom panel. Move the handling of the choice from the radio buttons to this pushbutton. When the user pushes the pushbutton, the choice will be written to the console.

14.5 Choices Using Lists

If the number of alternatives is more than, let's say, 6 or 7, we should use a list instead of radio buttons or checkboxes. Swing offers very flexible lists. Here we will look at the very simplest form, a list of texts where the user can choose one or more of them. We will also look at an example where the contents of the list are changed along the way.

We use the JList class to make lists. If we are going to change the contents of the list, we also have to use the DefaultListModel class.

Figure 14.8 and Program Listing 14.4 show an example. The applet consists of three GUI components. Therefore, we don't need to use panels. We put the components directly into the applet: in the north we have a prompt, in the middle a list, and in the south we have a two-line text area.

The contents of the text area change gradually as the user makes his choices. This is a multiple-choice list. In other words, the user can choose more than one value. We can make single-choice lists by setting this up in the constructor for the list (see the API reference below).

Technique for choosing more than one line in a list:

Hold the Ctrl key down while you click on the line with the mouse. If you are going to choose a contiguous area, hold down the Shift key as you click on the line that will be the last one in the area.

We make the list in four steps:

1. We set up an array of strings that are the lines that will be added to the list:

```
static final String [] cities =
    {"Tokyo", "New York City", "Mexico City", "Mumbai", "Sao Paulo", "Los Angeles",
     "Shanghai", "Lagos", "Calcutta", "Buenos Aires"};
```

2. We make the list:

```
JList cityList = new JList(cities);
```

3. Usually we want the list to have a scroll bar on the side. Therefore, we put the list into a scroll bar in the following manner:

```
JScrollPane scrollPaneWithList = new JScrollPane(cityList);
```

4. Finally, we put the scroll bar into the GUI container:

```
guiContainer.add(scrollPaneWithList, BorderLayout.CENTER);
```

A choice is an event that sends the message `valueChanged()` to the listener object. If you put a print statement in the method, you will see that each choice sends the message more than once. It's possible to prevent that, but that's not something we need to consider in this example.

The `valueChanged()` method gets the selection by sending a suitable message to the `cityList` object. The values are printed in the text area.

Figure 14.8　A multiple-choice list

Program Listing 14.4

```
/*
 * ListApplet.java  E.L. 2001-08-20
 *
 */
import java.awt.*;
import java.awt.event.*;
import javax.swing.*;
import javax.swing.event.*;
```

```
public class ListApplet extends JApplet {
  static final String [] cities =
    {"Tokyo", "New York City", "Mexico City", "Mumbai", "Sao Paulo", "Los Angeles",
     "Shanghai", "Lagos", "Calcutta", "Buenos Aires"};
  private JTextArea text = new JTextArea("You haven't chosen cities yet.", 4, 20);
  private JList cityList = new JList(cities);

  public void init() {
    Container guiContainer = getContentPane();
    JLabel label = new JLabel("Choose among the largest cities in the world:");
    guiContainer.add(label, BorderLayout.NORTH);
    JScrollPane scrollPaneWithList = new JScrollPane(cityList);

    guiContainer.add(scrollPaneWithList, BorderLayout.CENTER);
    ListListener listener = new ListListener();
    cityList.addListSelectionListener(listener);

    text.setLineWrap(true);
    text.setWrapStyleWord(true);
    guiContainer.add(text, BorderLayout.SOUTH);
  }

  class ListListener implements ListSelectionListener {
    public void valueChanged(ListSelectionEvent event) {
      java.lang.Object[] values = cityList.getSelectedValues();
      String newText = "You have now chosen: ";
      for (int i = 0; i < values.length; i++) {
        newText += (String) values[i] + " ";
      }
      text.setText(newText);
    }
  }
}
```

API Reference

The javax.swing.JList class

Constructors:

```
public JList()
public JList(Object[] data)
```

As we see from the second constructor, the contents of the list can be something other than strings. The objects' `toString()` method is then used to generate the list items.

Method:

```
public void addListSelectionListener(ListSelectionListener aListener)
```

This method adds a listener that is alerted every time there is a change in selections.

> public void setSelectionMode(int selectionMode)

This method decides which type of selections the user will be able to make. The argument should be SINGLE_SELECTION, SINGLE_INTERVAL_SELEC-TION, or MULTIPLE_INTERVAL_SELECTION. All of them have to be qualified by the ListSelectionModel interface name. The last alternative applies if we don't state anything else.

> public void clearSelection()

This method removes the selections that were made. The message valueChanged() is sent to all registered ListSelection listeners.

> public int getSelectedIndex()

This method gets the index for the selection that was made. If several selections were made, it gets the index for the first one. If no selection was made, the method returns -1.

> public int[] getSelectedIndices()

This method returns an array with indices for the selections that were made. The indices are in ascending order.

> public Object getSelectedValue()

This method returns a reference to the selection that was made. If no selection was made, null is returned.

> public Object[] getSelectedValues()

This method returns an array of references to the selections that were made.

> public boolean isSelectedIndex(int index)

This method returns true if the line with the stated index was selected.

> public boolean isSelectionEmpty()

This method returns true if no selection was made.

> public void setSelectedIndex(int index)
> public void setSelectedIndices(int[] indices)

These methods make it possible to set one or more selections.

> public void setSelectedValue(Object selected, boolean scroll)

This method makes it possible to set a specific object as selected. The last argument is set to true if the list will scroll, so that the selection comes into view.

> public boolean getValueIsAdjusting()

Every selection sends several valueChanged() messages to the listener object. If it's important for us to handle only one of them, we can use this method. It returns `true` for all messages, except the last one in a selection. For usage example, see Program Listing 14.5.

The javax.swing.event.ListSelectionListener interface

Method:

> public void valueChanged(ListSelectionEvent event)

This message is sent to listener objects when selections are made in the list. The selection can be made by the user or, for example, using the `setSelectedIndex()` method.

The javax.swing.event.ListSelectionEvent class

The argument to the `valueChanged()` method is an instance of this class. The class inherits the `getSource()` method from the `EventObject` class. The class itself has no methods that are of interest to us.

Now we will see how we can add and remove elements to and from the list.

We have to make changes in what Swing calls the "model" for the list. The word "model" is used here in a somewhat specialized sense. Pure and simple, it refers to the data contents of the list. The word writes itself from a theoretical architecture for user interfaces called the Model-View-Controller architecture (MVC):

- Model: The model represents the data that will be displayed.

- View: That same data can be displayed in different ways. Therefore, we can have several views for the same model.

- Controller: The controller decides how the GUI component will handle the events that occur.

In Swing, View and Controller stick close together. The controller part is in the listener classes.

We recognize again the same point that we emphasized earlier: It's important to distinguish the classes that describe the problem area we are dealing with (for example, wallpaper, paint, renovation) from classes that have to do with the user interface. This makes it easy to change the user interface, something we have seen an example of in the renovation project, among other things.

As mentioned, in Swing this principle applies to the user interface itself. For example, there are many types of buttons: pushbuttons, check boxes, and radio buttons. All of them have the same data content, but they look different on the screen. The data content is a boolean value that tells whether or not the button is selected.

We don't normally need to think about the division between data and the presentation of the GUI components we go through in this book. The exception is if we're going to change the contents of a list. Then we have to work with the class that represents the "model", namely the `DefaultListModel` class. The methods for handling the individual elements in the list are about the same as for handling the elements in an array list.

Figure 14.9 and Program Listing 14.5 show an example. The list consists only of the selection "New name" when it starts. If the user clicks on this choice, a little dialog box comes up to enter the name in. After the user has written the name and pressed the OK key, the name shows up in the list. If the user clicks on a name, this name will be deleted. The message box on the right comes up.[3]

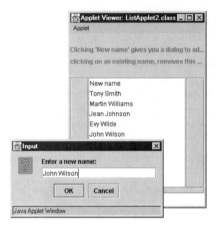

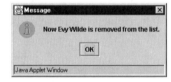

Clicking on the line
with "Evy Wilde" gives:

Figure 14.9 Dynamic change to name list

Program Listing 14.5

```
/*
 * ListApplet2.java   E.L. 2001-08-22
 *
 */
import java.awt.*;
import java.awt.event.*;
import javax.swing.*;
import javax.swing.event.*;

public class ListApplet2 extends JApplet {
  private DefaultListModel data = new DefaultListModel();
  private JList list = new JList(data);
```

3. The alert "Warning: Applet Window" appears at the bottom of the dialogs. This alert appears if an applet presents a dialog. This is a reminder to the user that the data she enters will be handled by an applet, which is usually downloaded from a "foreign" machine.

```java
public void init() {
  Container guiContainer = getContentPane();
  guiContainer.add(new TextPanel(), BorderLayout.NORTH);
  guiContainer.add(new ListPanel(), BorderLayout.CENTER);
  guiContainer.add(new JButton(), BorderLayout.SOUTH);  // a little space
}

private class TextPanel extends JPanel {
  public TextPanel() {
    setLayout(new GridLayout(4, 1, 5, 5));
    add(new JLabel(" "));  // a little space
    add(new JLabel("Clicking 'New name' gives you a dialog to add a new name, "));
    add(new JLabel("clicking on an existing name removes this name from the list."));
    add(new JLabel(" "));  // a little space
  }
}

private class ListPanel extends JPanel {
  public ListPanel() {
    /* It's difficult to control the list width. We cheat a little...*/
    setLayout(new BorderLayout());
    add(new JButton(), BorderLayout.WEST);  // fills up on the left side...
    data.addElement("New name");
    list.setSelectionMode(ListSelectionModel.SINGLE_SELECTION);
    JScrollPane scrollPaneWithList = new JScrollPane(list);
    add(scrollPaneWithList, BorderLayout.CENTER);
    list.addListSelectionListener(new ListListener());
    add(new JButton(), BorderLayout.EAST);  // ...and on the right side
  }
}

private class ListListener implements ListSelectionListener {
  public void valueChanged(ListSelectionEvent event) {
    /* All messages except the last shall be ignored */
    if (!list.getValueIsAdjusting()) {
      int selection = list.getSelectedIndex();
      if (selection >= 0) {
        list.clearSelection();
        if (selection == 0) {  // 'New name' is selected
          String newName = JOptionPane.showInputDialog("Enter a new name: ");
          if (newName != null) data.addElement(newName);
        }
        else {  // removes an existing name
          String nameToBeRemoved = (String) data.get(selection);
          data.remove(selection);
          JOptionPane.showMessageDialog(null, "Now " + nameToBeRemoved +
            " is removed from the list.");
        }
      }
    }
  }
}
```

```
        }
      }
    }
```

In order to be able to change the contents of the list, we have to make the list based on the model:

```
DefaultListModel data = new DefaultListModel();
JList list = new JList(data);
```

We manipulate the contents of the list by sending messages to the `data` object:

```
data.addElement("New name");
data.remove(selection);  // selection is the index of the element which will be removed
```

The following loop prints the contents of the list to the console:

```
for (int i = 0; i < data.size(); i++) {
  System.out.println(data.get(i));
}
```

This can be useful in debugging.

API Reference

The javax.swing.DefaultListModel class

The class maintains a list of the data content in a GUI component of the `JList` class.

Constructor:

```
public DefaultListModel()
```

Methods:

Methods with index as a parameter throw an `ArrayIndexOutOfBounds-Exception` if the index is less than 0 or greater than or equal to `size()`.

```
public void add(int index, Object obj)
```

This method makes room for a new reference by moving all references down a position, starting with `index`. The new reference is put in the `index` position. `index` can be equal to `size()`. That means that the reference is added at the end of the list.

```
public void addElement(Object obj)
```

This method inserts a reference to an object at the end of the list.

```
public Object get(int index)
public Object remove(int index)
public Object set(int index, Object obj)
public int size()
```

These methods correspond to methods with the same signatures in the class `java.util.ArrayList`; see Section 10.2.

Problem

The populations of the urban areas in Program Listing 14.4 are as follows:[4] Tokyo - 28 million, New York City - 20.1 million, Mexico City - 18.1 million, Mumbai - 18 million, São Paulo - 17.7 million, Los Angeles - 15.8 million, Shanghai - 14.2 million, Lagos - 13.5 million, Calcutta - 12.9 million, Buenos Aires - 12.5 million.

1. Change the program so that only one city can be selected. The selection will lead to a dialog box that comes up with population information.

2. We are assuming you've done problem 1. Change the program so that the user can add more cities and populations.

14.6 Windows

Figure 14.10 shows different types of windows.

- A *primary window* is also called a *top-level window*. The user's "main window" for the program will be a primary window. However, there's no reason why an application should not have many primary windows. The frame around the primary window always conforms to the platform the program is running on. What's inside the frame, however, conforms with the "Look and Feel" we have selected (see Section 13.1). If we are running on a Windows platform, the frame looks like the one in the figure. A primary window in Windows has a title line and buttons for minimizing, maximizing, and closing the window. In Swing, a primary window belongs to the `JFrame` class.

- A *secondary window* is also shown with a frame that conforms to the platform the program is running on. A dialog box is an example of a secondary window. A dialog is an instance of the `JDialog` class. A secondary window is normally linked to a parent window. The exception can be in test programs and our use of the `JOptionPane` class. The parent window can be a primary window or another secondary window. If the parent window is closed, all the "child windows" will also be closed.

  We have already made dialogs without parent windows by using the class methods in the `JOptionPane` class. The class methods in `JOptionPane` hide the `JDialog` objects to us.

---

4. According to http://geography.miningco.com/library/weekly/aa072897.htm

- *Internal windows* are windows that have to be entirely inside other windows. If necessary they are clipped when displayed. They belong to the `JInternalFrame` class, and have to be used if we are going to make what are called MDI applications in Windows. *MDI* stands for Multiple Document Interface. We have several windows inside a main window. Every window displays a document. Most word processors and editors are MDI applications. The opposite of MDI is *SDI* (Single Document Interface). An SDI application can only display one document at a time. Windows Notepad is an example of an SDI application.

- We can create *plain windows* (windows without frames) with the `JWindow` class.

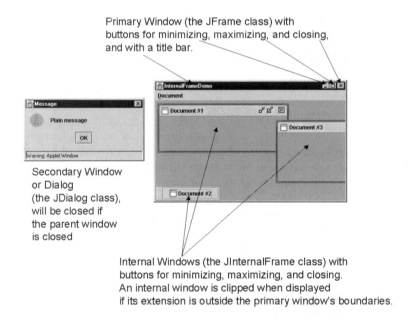

Primary Window (the JFrame class) with buttons for minimizing, maximizing, and closing, and with a title bar.

Secondary Window or Dialog (the JDialog class), will be closed if the parent window is closed

Internal Windows (the JInternalFrame class) with buttons for minimizing, maximizing, and closing. An internal window is clipped when displayed if its extension is outside the primary window's boundaries.

Figure 14.10   Examples of windows in java[5]

Up to this point, we have created applets. The window where we put our GUI components belonged to the browser. We will now see how we can make applications with their own primary windows. In the next chapter, we will create specially adapted dialog windows. We don't cover internal windows in this book. We also don't create plain windows based on the `JWindow` class.

Figure 14.11 shows the window classes in the class tree.

---

5. You'll find the example that shows internal windows by going into the `JInternalFrame` class in the online API documentation.

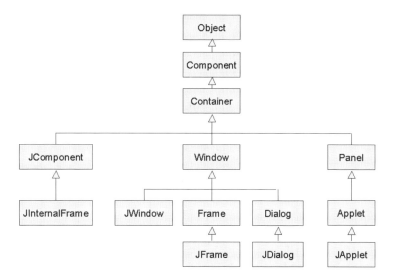

Figure 14.11 The class tree for the window classes (UML)

14.7 Making a Window

We will use the class `javax.swing.JFrame` and try the following:

```
import javax.swing.JFrame;
class TestJFrame {
  public static void main(String[] args) {
    JFrame myFirstWindow = new JFrame("My First Window");
    myFirstWindow.setVisible(true);
    myFirstWindow.setSize(300, 200); // the size in pixels
  }
} // this program does not work correctly
```

We get a nice little window without contents (see Figure 14.12). We close the window, but discover that the console window doesn't close itself. The Java interpreter keeps running.

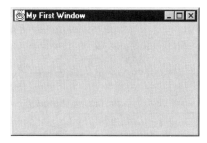

Figure 14.12 Our first window

We can stop the Java interpreter with the message:

```
System.exit(0);
```

We try adding this statement at the end of main(), but that just leads to the program running quickly from start to finish and the window just flickering past.

Instead we want the program to stop in this way when the user closes the window. We obtain that by simply adding one more statement to main():

```
import javax.swing.JFrame;
class TestJFrame {
  public static void main(String[] args) {
    JFrame myFirstWindow = new JFrame("My First Window");
    myFirstWindow.setVisible(true);
    myFirstWindow.setSize(300, 200); // the size in pixels
    myFirstWindow.setDefaultCloseOperation(JFrame.EXIT_ON_CLOSE);  // NB!
  }
} // this program works correctly
```

But what if we want to do some work, for example save data in a file, after the user has clicked on the close button, but before the program stops? Then we have to handle the event of the user closing the window.

A listener that will listen for window events has to be an instance of a class which implements the WindowListener interface. This interface contains many methods:

```
void windowActivated(WindowEvent event)
void windowClosed(WindowEvent event)
void windowClosing(WindowEvent event)
void windowDeactivated(WindowEvent event)
void windowDeiconified(WindowEvent event)
void windowIconified(WindowEvent event)
void windowOpened(WindowEvent event)
```

Now we'll implement the windowClosing() method. The other methods will be empty:

```
private class MyWindowListener implements WindowListener {
  public void windowClosing(WindowEvent event) {
    ...insert the code here...
  }
  public void windowActivated(WindowEvent event) {
  }
  public void windowClosed(WindowEvent event) {
  }
  public void windowDeactivated(WindowEvent event) {
  }
  public void windowDeiconified(WindowEvent event) {
  }
  public void windowIconified(WindowEvent event) {
  }
```

```
    public void windowOpened(WindowEvent event) {
    }
  }
```

Situations like this are common. Therefore, an *"adapter class"* was created where all the methods in the `WindowListener` interface are implemented as empty methods. We find the `WindowAdapter` class in the `java.awt.event` package:

```
package java.awt.event;
public abstract class WindowAdapter implements WindowListener {
  public void windowOpened(WindowEvent event) {}
  public void windowClosing(WindowEvent event) {}
  public void windowClosed(WindowEvent event) {}
  public void windowIconified(WindowEvent event) {}
  public void windowDeiconified(WindowEvent event) {}
  public void windowActivated(WindowEvent event) {}
  public void windowDeactivated(WindowEvent event) {}
}
```

Instead of letting our `MyWindowListener` class implement the `Window-Listener` interface, we let it be a subclass of the `WindowAdapter` class. Then the class will inherit all the empty methods. It can make its own versions of the methods that will have contents:

```
private class MyWindowListener extends WindowAdapter {
  public void windowClosing(WindowEvent event) {
    ....Here we may write to data files, etc.....
    System.exit(0); // Remember this!
  }
}
```

Adapter classes have been made for all the listener interfaces in the `java.awt.event` package that contain more than one method.

A little example application is shown in Program Listing 14.6. Try it! Instead of saving data to a file, we print a little text to the console window. As you see, the GUI is composed in the `JFrame2` constructor. In the next section we are going to take a closer look at the differences between applets and applications.

Program Listing 14.6

```
/*
 * TestJFrame2.java   E.L. 2001-08-22
 */
import java.awt.*;
```

```
import javax.swing.*;
import java.awt.event.*;

class JFrame2 extends JFrame {
  public JFrame2() {
    Container guiContainer = getContentPane();
    guiContainer.setLayout(new FlowLayout());
    guiContainer.add(new JLabel("This window handles closing. Close the window!"));
    addWindowListener(new MyWindowListener());
  }

  private class MyWindowListener extends WindowAdapter {
    public void windowClosing(WindowEvent event) {
      System.out.println("Here we may write to data files, etc.");
      System.exit(0); // Remember this!
    }
  }
}

class TestJFrame2 {
  public static void main(String[] args) {
    JFrame mySecondWindow = new JFrame2();
    mySecondWindow.setTitle("My Second Window");
    mySecondWindow.setSize(400, 100);
    mySecondWindow.setVisible(true);
  }
}
```

API Reference

Figure 14.11 shows the relationship between the classes described in this API reference. Remember the inheritance of members!

The javax.swing.JFrame class

Constructors:

```
public JFrame()
public JFrame(String title)
```

To start with, the window is invisible.

Methods:

```
public Container getContentPane()
```

This method returns a container that can be filled with GUI components.

```
public void setDefaultCloseOperation(int operation)
```

This method determines what will happen when the user closes the window by pressing on the close button in the upper right corner. The default is for the window to be hidden. If we want the application to stop (by `System.exit()`), we use the method with the argument `JFrame.EXIT_ON_CLOSE`.

The java.awt.Frame class

Methods:

```
public Image getIconImage()
public void setIconImage(Image image)
public String getTitle()
public void setTitle(String title)
```

These methods set and get the window's title and icon (when minimizing). The API reference in Section 15.1 shows a method for linking a menu bar to the frame.

The java.awt.Window class

Methods:

```
public void addWindowListener(WindowListener aListener)
```

This method registers a listener for the window.

```
public void pack()
```

This method adjusts the window's size for the components that will be displayed there.

```
public void show()
public void hide()
```

These methods can be used for windows instead of `setVisible()`.

The java.awt.Component class

See also Section 13.1.

Methods:

```
public void setVisible(boolean visible)
```

This method sets the component to be visible if the argument has the value `true`.

```
public void setSize(int width, int height)
```

This method sets the size of the component to a number of pixels. This method is pertinent for use with windows where `pack()` doesn't work satisfactorily, for example if the window includes drawings. For regular GUI components, this method only works if we don't use the layout manager (`setLayout(null)`).

```
public void setLocation(int x, int y)
```

This method places the component such that the upper left corner ends up in the stated position.

Problems

1. Which listener interfaces have we gone through up to this point? Which one of these, in addition to `WindowListener`, has an ancillary adapter class? Change one of the earlier examples so that you try this adapter class.

2. Create `JFrame3` as a subclass of `JFrame`. The constructor for `JFrame3` will take the size and location of the window as arguments, in addition to the window's title line. Write a little program that tests the new class.

3. You find out that `JFrame3` can be useful in many contexts. Make the changes that are necessary so that you can put the class into `myLibrary`.

14.8 Differences Between Applets and Applications

Program listing 14.7 shows an application with the same functionality as the applet in Program Listing 13.3. We notice the following differences between the applet and the application:

- The applet is a subclass of `JApplet`. The application is a subclass of `JFrame`.

- An applet must be a public class. The most practical thing to do when we make applications is not to let any of the classes be public. This limits the use of the classes to the package where they are declared, but usually that's fine. If classes are going to have uses beyond this, they should be placed in a named package.

- In the applet, the construction of the user interface is in the `init()` method. In the application, it's in the constructor.

- The browser (or applet viewer) takes care of starting the applet. To start an application, we have to program `main()`. In the example, `main()` contains four statements:

```
ColorButtonApplication myWindow = new ColorButtonApplication("My Window");
myWindow.pack();
myWindow.setVisible(true);
myWindow.setDefaultCloseOperation(JFrame.EXIT_ON_CLOSE);
```

After we've created the window, we send the message `pack()` to the window. This method makes sure that every individual component gets a suitable size. Thus, we avoid setting a fixed size for the window. Then we send the message `setVisible(true)` for the window so that it becomes visible.

Figure 14.13 shows the application version of some of the applets we have created so far. The window size is set with `pack()`.

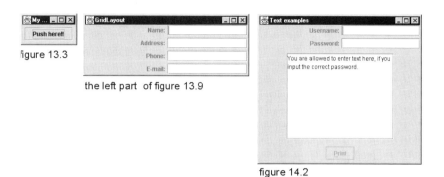

figure 13.3

the left part of figure 13.9

figure 14.2

Figure 14.13 Some of the Applets as Applications

Program Listing 14.7

```
/*
 * TestColorButtonApplication.java  E.L. 2001-08-22
 */

import java.awt.*;
import java.awt.event.*;
import javax.swing.*;

class ColorButtonApplication extends JFrame {
  private Container guiContainer;

  public ColorButtonApplication(String title) {
    super(title);
    guiContainer = getContentPane();
    guiContainer.setLayout(new FlowLayout());
    JButton myButton = new JButton("Push here!!");
    guiContainer.add(myButton);
    ButtonListener theButtonListener = new ButtonListener();
    myButton.addActionListener(theButtonListener);
  }

  private class ButtonListener implements ActionListener {
    public void actionPerformed(ActionEvent event) {
      guiContainer.setBackground(Color.red);
    }
  }
}

class TestColorButtonApplication {
  public static void main(String[] args) {
    ColorButtonApplication myWindow
        = new ColorButtonApplication("My Window");
```

```
        myWindow.pack();
        myWindow.setVisible(true);
        myWindow.setDefaultCloseOperation(JFrame.EXIT_ON_CLOSE);
    }
}
```

Problem

Change the program in Program Listing 14.4 into an application with a primary window.

14.9 Other Ways to Program Listeners

We have programmed listeners as regular classes (for example, Program Listing 13.2) and as inner classes (for example, Program Listing 13.3). In reading other literature, you will probably also encounter two other techniques. Here, we'll look briefly at these techniques. They are not used elsewhere in this book.

The window as listener

We modify Program Listing 13.3 so that the window itself becomes a listener for the events generated by the button:

```
public class ColorButtonAppletThis extends JApplet implements ActionListener {
    private Container guiContainer;
    public void init() {
        guiContainer = getContentPane();
        guiContainer.setLayout(new FlowLayout());
        JButton myButton = new JButton("Push here!!");
        guiContainer.add(myButton);
        myButton.addActionListener(this);
    }
    public void actionPerformed(ActionEvent event) {
        guiContainer.setBackground(Color.red);
    }
}
```

What are the differences?

- The class that describes the applet implements `ActionListener` on its own.

- In this way the applet itself becomes the listener, and it is registered as a listener object:

  ```
  myButton.addActionListener(this);
  ```

- Thus, the inner class `ButtonListener` is gone.

An anonymous class

We often have only one listener per object, but there's also nothing wrong with making one listener for each object that will be listened to. In that case, it's not unusual to let the listener be an instance of an *anonymous class*. An anonymous class is a class without a name. Study the source code below and Figure 14.14.

```
public class ColorButtonAppletAnonym extends JApplet {
  private Container guiContainer;
  public void init() {
    guiContainer = getContentPane();
    guiContainer.setLayout(new FlowLayout());
    JButton myButton = new JButton("Push here!!");
    guiContainer.add(myButton);
    myButton.addActionListener(new ActionListener() {
      public void actionPerformed(ActionEvent event) {
        guiContainer.setBackground(Color.red);
      }
    });
  }
}
```

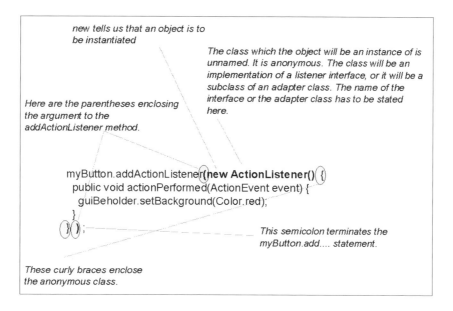

Figure 14.14 The listener is an instance of an anonymous class

14.10 New Concepts in This Chapter

Concept	Brief Explanation
adapter class	Among other things, used of classes that implement all the methods in a listener interface as empty methods.
anonymous class	A class without a name. There can't be more than one instance of the class. This instance is also without a name. Anonymous classes are especially used in connection with registering listener objects.
check box	See Figure 14.4. A check box is an object of the JCheckBox class. None, one, or several of the check boxes shown can be pressed in at a time. The boxes can be collected in a group box, but they don't need to be.
group box	A border around a collection of GUI components. In Java, the components usually are collected in a panel. To make the border we use the classes in the package javax.swing.border. A group box often has a name.
internal window	Internal windows (class JInternalFrame) are windows that have to be entirely inside other windows. If necessary they are clipped when displayed.
list (GUI)	In Figure 14.8, the cities are displayed underneath each other in a list. The list is a GUI component that allows the user to select one or more alternatives. It is an instance of the class JList.
MDI	Multiple Document Interface. Window's own name for a user interface that consists of a primary window with many internal windows.
model	"Model" classes in Swing describe the data content behind a GUI component.
MVC	Model-View-Controller. A theoretical architecture for programming user interfaces. For our purposes, it's sufficient to recognize the principle behind it. The principle is to distinguish between how a GUI component looks (view) and the data content of the component (model). The controller portion will be in the listener classes.
primary window	An application window with a title line and buttons for minimizing, maximizing, and closing the window. The window is programmed as an instance of the class JFrame.
radio button	See Figure 14.4. A radio button is an instance of the JRadioButton class. The buttons have to be collected in an instance of the ButtonGroup class. The buttons can but don't have to be in a group box. Only one of the buttons in a group of radio buttons can be "pressed in" at a time.
scroll bar	See Figure 14.8. The list has a scroll bar on the right-hand side. The user can see the whole list by clicking on the up and down arrows and the field in between. A scroll bar can also be horizontal. We expand a GUI component with a scroll bar by inserting it into an instance of the class JScrollPane.
SDI	Single Document Interface. Windows' own name for a user interface that doesn't use internal windows.

Concept	Brief Explanation
secondary-window	A window that normally has another window as a "parent" (for example, a dialog box). If the parent is closed, the secondary window is also closed. A dialog box is programmed as an instance of the JDialog class. A number of standard dialogs can be made using class methods in the class JOptionPane.

14.11 Review Problems

1. Explain the difference from the user's perspective between check boxes and radio buttons.

2. When should we use a list to present the user's options?

3. Explain the difference between an instance of the JTextField class and an instance of the JTextArea class.

4. What events does a focus listener listen for?

5. What type of events do check boxes and radio buttons generate?

6. What type of events does a list generate?

7. How do we make a group box?

8. What function does the class ButtonGroup have?

9. There is a "model" class that belongs to every Swing component. What do this model class and the component we see on the screen have in common?

10. We use the JList class to make lists. If we are going to change the contents of the list, we also have to use another class. Which one?

11. The following classes are used to make windows: JFrame, JInternal Frame, JDialog, and JWindow. What are the different windows called? Briefly explain the differences between them.

12. The WindowAdapter class is an "adapter" class for the WindowListener interface. What is this class for?

13. Explain what you have to do if you are going to "convert" an applet into an application window.

14.12 Programming Problems

Problem 1

Make an application window with a drawing of, for example, a rectangle. Let the user choose the color of the rectangle by pressing a radio button. The button group will contain all the standard colors defined in the Color class. The program will be most elegant if the colors (and the buttons, too) are in an array. Because of the drawing, it may be difficult to get `pack()` to work. Use `setSize()` to set the size of the window.

When you've accomplished this, you will make a list of all the colors. The user will choose whether she wants to use the radio buttons or the list. Test whether you can synchronize the choices so that if the user chooses "red" on the list, the radio button marked "red" is also selected.

Problem 2

Make an applet to convert your own currency into several other currencies. Let the user choose a currency from a list. The user will also be able to expand the list by adding new currencies. Use the standard dialogs to communicate with the user.

Problem 3

Change the program in Program Listing 14.1 into an application. The text will be read from a file. If the user has permission to change the text, the modified text will be saved into the file when the user presses "Print". Try to distinguish the classes that handle the file as much as possible from the user interface classes.

Problem 4

Make a user interface for maintaining two lists, one list with groups, the other with persons. Every person can exist in several groups (for example, "member of the soccer team" and "member of the basket ball team").

The most important part of the user interface is two lists:

- List A will show the groups. The user will be able to choose a group in this box. If the user hasn't chosen a group, the group "All" will be selected.

- At all times, list B will display the contents of the group (the persons) that is selected in box A.

The user interface will also contain two pushbuttons:

- Button 1 will make it possible to add a new person.

- Button 2 will make it possible to add a new group. The user will choose which members the group will have by selecting all the applicable names from list B.

The user interface will consist of only one window. New groups and new persons will be input by using methods in `JOptionPane`.

It's sufficient that the data be stored in the list's "models".

15

Creating User Interfaces

Learning goals for this chapter

After completing this chapter, you will be able to:

- Make dropdown menus and toolbars

- Make modal dialog windows that edit data that belongs in the parent window

- Use the GridBagLayout layout manager

- Present data in two-dimensional tables

Now we've covered the most common GUI components and also studied the most common event types.

This chapter contains several techniques that will make it possible to create "real" graphical user interfaces for a program.

The chapter will end with the last version of the renovation case. We'll replace the user interface from chapter 12 with a proper GUI.

You will get a deeper understanding of the point of differentiating between classes that have to do with the problem we're going to solve and classes that communicate with the user. You'll know how these two groups' objects are connected.

15.1 Menus

We can create many different types of menus in Java Swing. Look up the JMenu class in the online API documentation and click on "How to use menus." Menus can have submenus. A single menu item can contain an icon in addition to or instead of a text. It can also consist of a radio button or a check box with accompanying text. We distinguish between dropdown menus and pop-up menus. A simple dropdown menu is shown in Figure 15.1. A pop-up menu is a menu that appears when the user, for example, right clicks with the mouse.

In this book, we will limit ourselves to simple dropdown menus without submenus.

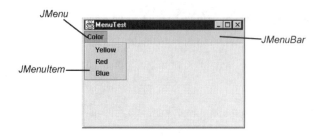

Figure 15.1 Dropdown menu with class names

Program listing 15.1 shows the source code that makes the window with the Color menu. Clicking on one of the menu entries changes the color of the window.

We have to use three Swing classes (see Figure 15.2) in order to make a menu:

1. Every single dropdown menu is an instance of the `JMenu` class:

   ```
   JMenu theMenu = new JMenu("Color");
   ```

2. Every single menu item is an instance of the `JMenuItem` class. These instances are linked to the right menu using `add()`:

   ```
   JMenuItem menuItem = new JMenuItem("Yellow");
   theMenu.add(menuItem);
   ```

3. The menu bar is an instance of the `JMenuBar` class. Every single menu has to be linked to this instance:

   ```
   JMenuBar menuBar = new JMenuBar();
   menuBar.add(theMenu);
   ```

   Finally, the menu bar has to be linked to the window:

   ```
   setJMenuBar(menuBar);
   ```

Notice that we send the message `setJMenuBar()` to the window and not to `guiContainer`. The `setJMenuBar()` method is declared in the `JFrame` class. The method is also declared in the `JDialog` class. Therefore, we can make menus in both primary and secondary windows.

We have to create an object that can listen for the user's menu choice. The event that occurs with the choice is an ActionEvent, and the message that is sent is `actionPerformed()`. This is familiar from before—refer to the program listing for further details on the listener class.

Program Listing 15.1

```
/*
 * MenuTest.java  E.L. 2001-08-22
 *
 */
import java.awt.*;
import javax.swing.*;
import java.awt.event.*;

class WindowWithMenu extends JFrame {
  private Container guiContainer;

  public WindowWithMenu() {
    setTitle("MenuTest");
    setDefaultCloseOperation(JFrame.EXIT_ON_CLOSE);
    guiContainer = getContentPane();

    MenuListener theListener = new MenuListener();

    JMenu theMenu = new JMenu("Color");
    JMenuItem menuItem = new JMenuItem("Yellow");
    theMenu.add(menuItem);
    menuItem.addActionListener(theListener);

    menuItem = new JMenuItem("Red");
    theMenu.add(menuItem);
    menuItem.addActionListener(theListener);

    menuItem = new JMenuItem("Blue");
    theMenu.add(menuItem);
    menuItem.addActionListener(theListener);

    JMenuBar menuBar = new JMenuBar();
    menuBar.add(theMenu);
    setJMenuBar(menuBar);
  }
  private class MenuListener implements ActionListener {
    public void actionPerformed(ActionEvent event) {
      String command = event.getActionCommand();
      if (command.equals("Yellow")) guiContainer.setBackground(Color.yellow);
      else if (command.equals("Red")) guiContainer.setBackground(Color.red);
      else guiContainer.setBackground(Color.blue);
    }
  }
}

class MenuTest {
  public static void main(String[] args) {
    WindowWithMenu window = new WindowWithMenu();
    window.setSize(300, 200); // pack() gives a very little window!
    window.setVisible(true);
  }
}
```

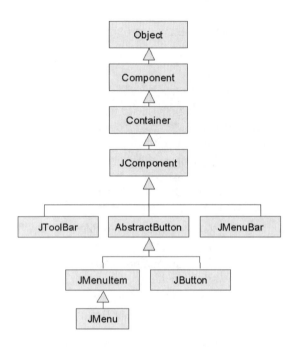

Figure 15.2 An excerpt from the class tree with classes for menus and toolbars (UML)

 API Reference

The javax.swing.JMenuBar class

This class manages the menu bar in a window.

Constructor:

> public JMenuBar()

Method:

> public JMenu add(JMenu newMeny)

This method adds a new dropdown menu to the menu bar.

The javax.swing.JMenu class

This class manages an individual dropdown menu in a menu bar.

Constructor:

> public JMenu(String text)

Methods:

> public JMenuItem add(JMenuItem menuItem)
> public JMenuItem add(String text)

These methods add a new menu item to the menu. The latter method generates an instance of the `JMenuItem` class and is actually a shortened form for creating new menu entries.

> public void addSeparator()

This method adds a line as a division in the menu.

The javax.swing.JMenuItem class

This class manages an item in a menu.

Constructors:

> public JMenuItem(Icon icon)
> public JMenuItem(String text)
> public JMenuItem(String text, Icon icon)
> public JMenuItem(String text, int mnemonic)

A menu item can consist of a text or an icon, or both. We can also add a mnemonic to go along with the menu choice. In the menu, the mnemonic character will be underlined.

The class is a subclass of the `AbstractButton` class and inherits all the methods from this class (see Sections 13.2 and 14.3).

The java.awt.Frame class

Method:

> public void setMenuBar(MenuBar menubar)

This method positions the menu bar in the window.

See Section 14.7 for more methods in the `Frame` class.

Problems

1. Modify Program Listing 15.1 so that all the standard colors are shown. With so many choices, it's practical to use arrays to make the menu and handle the selections.

2. Expand Program Listing 15.1 with a dropdown "Help" menu. The menu will have two entries: "Help" and "About the program". The first item will print out

a message about what the program does, and the second will print out the date and author.

15.2 Toolbars

Figure 15.3 and Program Listing 15.2 show the same example as above, but now the menu is replaced by a row of buttons, a so-called toolbar.

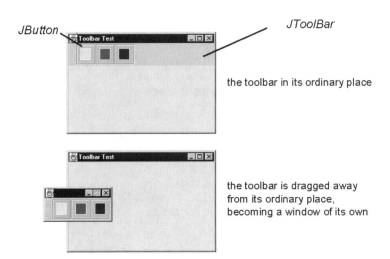

Figure 15.3 Toolbar with class names

Program Listing 15.2

```
/*
 * ToolbarTest.java  E.L. 2001-08-23
 *
 */
import java.awt.*;
import javax.swing.*;
import java.awt.event.*;

class WindowWithToolbar extends JFrame {
  private Container guiContainer;
  private JButton yellowButton;
  private JButton redButton;
  private JButton blueButton;

  public WindowWithToolbar(){
    setTitle("Toolbar Test");
    setDefaultCloseOperation(JFrame.EXIT_ON_CLOSE);
    guiContainer = getContentPane();
```

```
                    ButtonListener theListener = new ButtonListener();
                    JToolBar toolbar = new JToolBar();
                    Icon icon = new ImageIcon("yellow.gif");
                    yellowButton = new JButton(icon);
                    yellowButton.addActionListener(theListener);
                    toolbar.add(yellowButton);

                    icon = new ImageIcon("red.gif");
                    redButton = new JButton(icon);
                    redButton.addActionListener(theListener);
                    toolbar.add(redButton);

                    icon = new ImageIcon("blue.gif");
                    blueButton = new JButton(icon);
                    blueButton.addActionListener(theListener);
                    toolbar.add(blueButton);

                    guiContainer.add(toolbar, BorderLayout.NORTH);
                }
                private class ButtonListener implements ActionListener {
                    public void actionPerformed(ActionEvent event) {
                        JButton button = (JButton) event.getSource();
                        if (button == yellowButton) guiContainer.setBackground(Color.yellow);
                        else if (button == redButton) guiContainer.setBackground(Color.red);
                        else guiContainer.setBackground(Color.blue);
                    }
                }
            }
            class ToolbarTest {
                public static void main(String[] args) {
                    WindowWithToolbar window = new WindowWithToolbar();
                    window.setSize(300, 200);
                    window.setVisible(true);
                }
            }
```

Here's how we make a toolbar:

1. The toolbar is an instance of the JToolBar class:

    ```
    JToolBar toolbar = new JToolBar();
    ```

2. Every individual button is an instance of the JButton class, a class we're familiar with already. The button can show an image, a text, or both. The arguments for the constructor tell what the button will look like. Every individual button has to be linked to the toolbar. Example:

    ```
    toolbar.add(yellowButton);
    ```

3. After all the buttons are in place, we have to install the toolbar in the guiContainer:

```
guiContainer.add(toolbar, BorderLayout.NORTH);
```

And then we should not forget to register a listener for the buttons:

```
ButtonListener theListener = new ButtonListener();
yellowButton.addActionListener(theListener);
```

We let the same object listen for all the buttons. The `actionPerformed()` method handles the event and sets the right background color.

Here we've used `getSource()` instead of `getActionCommand()` to find the source of the event. The reason for this is that we only have an image on the buttons, and not a text which we need when we use `getActionCommand()`. (Alternatively, we could have set this text by sending the message `setActionCommand()` to the buttons.)

It's usually safer to use `getSource()` than `getActionCommand()`. But it's a little more labor-intensive and maybe a little more difficult to understand. The reason that `getSource()` is preferable is that it requires that we compare variable names and not strings. We write

```
if (button == yellowButton) ...
```

and not

```
if (source.equals("yellow"))...
```

If we write the variable name `yellowButton` wrong, we get an error message from the compiler. We don't get any message if we write `"yellow"` differently here than when we defined the button. A good solution if we prefer to use `getActionCommand()` is to store all the pertinent strings in an array. Then we avoid the inconsistency problem (cf. naming constants, Section 2.5).

 Notice that a menu bar is placed directly in the window (`setMenuBar()`), while a toolbar is placed in the GUI container ("content pane") the same way that other GUI components are, using the `add()` method.

 ## API Reference

The javax.swing.JToolBar class

Constructor:

```
public JToolBar()
```

Method:

```
public void setFloatable(boolean floats)
```

The default is for a toolbar to "float", in other words, the user can move it. It then becomes a window like the one shown at the bottom of Figure 15.3.

    public void addSeparator()

This method adds a separator to the toolbar.

This class is a subclass of the `JComponent` class and inherits, among other things, the `add()` method from there.

Problems

Make the following changes to Program Listing 15.2:

1. Test the `addSeparator()` method. What does the separator between the buttons look like?

2. Link tool tips to each individual button. Use the online API documentation to find out how to do that.

3. Replace the icons with texts and mnemonics.

15.3 Dialog Windows

A graphical user interface without dialogs is nothing to brag about. It's normal to use dialog windows for user input. If the windows are small, we usually call them dialog boxes.

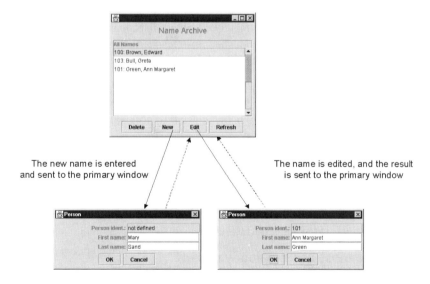

Figure 15.4   A parent window with dialogs for changing data in a database

As mentioned before, a dialog window is usually a secondary window—in other words, it's linked to a parent window. If the parent window is closed, all the "child windows" close automatically.

We distinguish between *modal* and *nonmodal* dialog windows. A modal dialog window prevents the user from accessing other windows as long as the window is open. This can be irritating for the user, especially if the windows are large. At the same time, permitting access to multiple windows at the same time places greater demands on the programmer. Making sure that the information in all the windows is updated correctly is often a demanding job. Therefore, we're limiting ourselves to modal windows in this book.

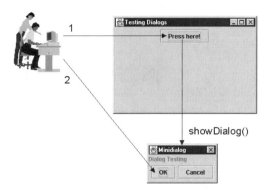

Figure 15.5 The Most Basic Dialog Window

We're already familiar with the standard dialogs in the `JOPtionPane` class. These are well suited for short messages and user responses to an individual question.

We make dialog windows in much the same way that we make other windows. An important difference that we have to keep in mind, however, is the communication with the parent window. The parent window controls when the dialog window is shown. Once the user has entered his data and closes the window, the data usually has to be sent back to the parent window. Figure 15.4 shows a parent window with a name registry. The user can maintain the name registry by pressing one of the buttons. The "New" command results in a dialog box with no data coming up on the screen so that the name of a new person can be entered. The "Edit" command displays the selected name so that the user can modify it. In the last part of this section, we'll program and test the little name dialog while postponing programming the parent window until chapter 20, where we'll connect this user interface to a database.

The most basic dialog window

The most basic situation of all is shown in Figure 15.5. The parent window comes up with a push button. The user presses this and the little dialog window is shown. The user presses the OK button and the dialog window disappears.

The source code is shown in Program Listing 15.3. Many classes are involved. We'll start at the bottom of the source code:

- The `TestMinidialog` class contains `main()`, which establishes an instance of the `ParentWindow` class and displays it on the screen.

- The `ParentWindow` class is a subclass of `JFrame`. This is a normal window with a pushbutton and an inner class that describes a listener for this button.

- The `MiniDialog` class, like all dialog windows, is a subclass of the `JDialog` class. It describes the dialog box with two pushbuttons and an inner listener class.

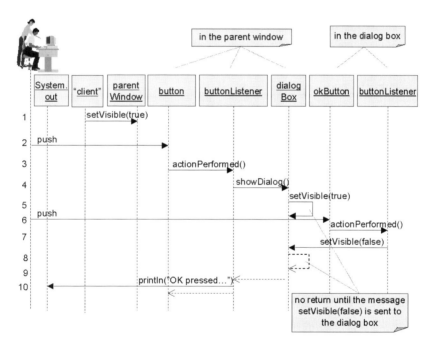

Figure 15.6 The Course of Events from the Displaying of the Parent Window on the Screen until the Printout Appears on the Console (UML)

We'll go through the source code details by looking at what happens if the user runs the program and presses the OK button. Follow along with the sequence diagram in Figure 15.6 as well (the numbers below refer to the numbers on the left of the figure):

1. The `TestMinidialog` class contains `main()` ("client" in the figure), which sets up the `parentWindow` object and sends the message `setVisible(true)` to this window. The window appears on the screen.

2. The user presses the button.

3. The message `actionPerformed()` is sent to the `buttonListener`. We are still in the parent window.

4. Now we're inside the `actionPerformed()` method and the `showDialog()` message is sent to the `dialogBox`.

5. Focus now shifts to `dialogBox`. Inside the `showDialog()`, the dialog box sends the message `setVisible(true)` to itself. *This message doesn't return before the message `setVisible(false)` is sent to the box.* This characteristic of `setVisible()` in a modal dialog box prevents the user from accessing other windows as long as this window is displayed. This is precisely what distinguishes modal dialogs from nonmodal ones.

6. The user presses the OK button in the dialog box.

7. The `actionPerformed()` message is sent to the listener object in the dialog box. The instance variable `ok` thus gets the value `true`.

8. The `actionPerformed()` method ends with the dialog box sending the message `setVisible(false)` to itself. This also ends `setVisible(true)` in point 5. The dialog box disappears from the screen.

9. The control is back in the `showDialog()` method. The value of the instance variable `ok` is returned to the parent window.

10. The text "OK pressed...." is printed to the console.

Program Listing 15.3

```
/*
 * TestMinidialog.java  E.L. 2001-08-23
 *
 * Closing the dialog behaves as if the Ok button was pressed.
 */

import java.awt.*;
import java.awt.event.*;
import javax.swing.*;

class MiniDialog extends JDialog {
  private boolean ok;
  private Container guiContainer;

  public MiniDialog(JFrame parent) {
    super(parent, "Minidialog", true);
    guiContainer = getContentPane();
```

```
        guiContainer.add(new JLabel(), BorderLayout.NORTH);
        guiContainer.add(new JLabel("Dialog Testing"), BorderLayout.CENTER);
        guiContainer.add(new ButtonPanel(), BorderLayout.SOUTH);
        pack();
      }

      private class ButtonPanel extends JPanel {
        public ButtonPanel() {
          ButtonListenerDialog buttonListener = new ButtonListenerDialog();

          JButton okButton = new JButton("OK");
          add(okButton);
          okButton.addActionListener(buttonListener);

          JButton cancelButton = new JButton("Cancel");
          add(cancelButton);
          cancelButton.addActionListener(buttonListener);
        }
      }

      private class ButtonListenerDialog implements ActionListener {
        public void actionPerformed(ActionEvent event) {
          String command = event.getActionCommand();
          if (command.equals("OK")) ok = true;
          else ok = false;
          setVisible(false);
        }
      }

      public boolean showDialog() {
        setVisible(true);
        return ok;
      }
    }

    class ParentWindow extends JFrame {
      private MiniDialog dialogBox = new MiniDialog(this);
      private Container guiContainer;

      public ParentWindow() {
        setTitle("Testing Dialogs");
        setDefaultCloseOperation(JFrame.EXIT_ON_CLOSE);
        guiContainer = getContentPane();
        guiContainer.setLayout(new FlowLayout());
        JButton button = new JButton("Press here!");
        guiContainer.add(button);
        ButtonListenerParent buttonListener = new ButtonListenerParent();
        button.addActionListener(buttonListener);
      }

      private class ButtonListenerParent implements ActionListener {
        public void actionPerformed(ActionEvent event) {
          if (dialogBox.showDialog()) System.out.println("OK pressed....");
```

```
      else System.out.println("Cancel pressed....");
    }
  }
}
class TestMiniDialog {
  static public void main(String[] args) {
    ParentWindow parentWindow = new ParentWindow();
    parentWindow.setSize(300, 200);
    parentWindow.setVisible(true);
  }
}
```

Summary: Making a modal dialog window

1. A dialog window is always a subclass of `JDialog`. What we have to provide is a constructor that calls one of the `JDialog's` constructors with `modal` parameter. If we do not do this, the constructor with empty parameter list will be used. And that constructor creates a nonmodal dialog window. The argument to the `modal` parameter has to be `true`, for example:

   ```
   super(parent, "Minidialog", true);
   ```

2. Each individual dialog has a method with the name `showDialog()` (or something similar). We find the call `setVisible(true)` inside the method.

3. All activity in the dialog has to end with the call `setVisible(false)`. With this, the dialog is closed, and the program then goes on to the first statement after `setVisible(true)`.

4. Let the dialog window be an instance variable in the parent window.

An ordinary OK-Cancel dialog

Most of the dialogs we will create will contain OK and Cancel buttons at the bottom. If the user presses OK, that means that the changes entered in the dialog window will apply. If she presses Cancel, that means that none of the changes will be recorded.

We will create an ordinary dialog that manages these buttons. Later we'll let each individual special dialog be a subclass of this class.

The `MyDialog` class is in the `myLibrary` package and the source code is found in Program Listing 15.4.

Let's look at this class. There's a lot to understand here, including some new ideas.

This is one of very few classes in this book where we use the `protected` access modifier. We restrict the access to apply within the `myLibrary` package and subclasses in other packages, the latter under specific conditions (see Section 12.7). This is natural since the `MyDialog` class doesn't mean anything except in a subclass.

The class has two instance variables:

- The boolean variable ok keeps track of whether the data the user has entered should be saved or should be ignored. The variable has both a set and get method to be used in subclasses.

- theButtonPanel variable is a reference to a panel that contains the buttons OK and Cancel. The panel is made in this class, but the subclass decides where in the dialog window it will be located. A subclass gets the reference for the panel with the getButtonPanel() method.

The class has a method called okData(). It returns true. It's not very exciting, but the point of the method is that subclasses that require control of the input data can create their own version. If the data is not all right, focus is typically shifted to the input field where the error occurred. We will see examples of this later in this chapter.

The constructor calls the superclass's constructor. Then a window listener is registered. As opposed to Program Listing 15.3, here we have to manage closing the window. What does the user mean when she wants to close the window? Does she mean OK or Cancel? If she means OK, the data has to be checked with the okData() method. Let's look at the WindowsClosingListener class:

If the user tries to close the window by pressing the × in the upper right corner, a Yes/No box comes up: "Do you want input data to be saved?". If the user says "Yes," the window is *only* closed if the okData() method returns true. Hence, we control the window's closing ourselves. We do this by sending the message setDefaultCloseOperation() to the window with DO_NOTHING_ON _CLOSE as its argument.

The panel contains two buttons. A listener object is linked to the buttons. If the OK button is pressed, the validity of the data is checked using the okData() method. If this method returns true, the variable ok is set equal to true. In all other cases, it is set to equal false. Then the dialog window is closed and the program control goes back to the parent window (see the CommandListener class).

Acceleration keys are linked to the buttons. These are not the same as the mnemonics we looked at earlier. A mnemonic is an underlined letter in the command. To issue the command, the user presses the letter together with the Alt key. It's unusual to use mnemonics in conjunction with OK and Cancel keys. It is, however, common for OK to be associated with the Enter key and for Cancel to be associated with the Escape key. We've programmed the dialog so that the OK key has to have the focus for the Enter key to work. The Escape key, on the other hand, works whether the Cancel key has the focus or not.

We won't go into the details of defining acceleration keys—we'll just take a quick look at the source code for this example:

```
KeyStroke escapeKey = KeyStroke.getKeyStroke(KeyEvent.VK_ESCAPE, 0);
cancelButton.registerKeyboardAction(buttonListener, "Cancel", escapeKey,
                JComponent.WHEN_IN_FOCUSED_WINDOW);
```

First we have to instantiate an object that describes the acceleration key. This object is from the `javax.swing.KeyStroke` class. The names of the different keys (for example, VK_ESCAPE) are defined in the `java.awt.event.KeyEvent` class. The other argument for `getKeyStroke()` can be a button that is pressed together with the first one, for example `InputEvent.SHIFT_MASK` or `InputEvent.ALT_MASK`.

Then we send the message `registerKeyboardAction()` to the button. In order, we send the following as arguments: the listener object, the command linked to the button, the acceleration key, and finally the condition for this key to work. For the Enter key, we used `WHEN_FOCUSED`, for the Cancel key, `WHEN_IN_FOCUSED_WINDOW`. For further documentation of classes and methods involved in this process, refer to the online API documentation.

Program Listing 15.4

```
/*
 * MyDialog.java  E.L. 2001-08-23
 *
 * A dialog with OK and Cancel button.
 */
package myLibrary;

import java.awt.*;
import java.awt.event.*;
import javax.swing.*;

public class MyDialog extends JDialog {
  private boolean ok = false; // is input data ok?
  private ButtonPanel theButtonPanel = new ButtonPanel();

  protected MyDialog(JFrame parent, String title) {
    super(parent, title, true);
    addWindowListener(new WindowsClosingListener());
    /* We want to handle the event WindowClosing in the program. */
    setDefaultCloseOperation(JDialog.DO_NOTHING_ON_CLOSE);
  }

  protected boolean isOk() {
    return ok;
  }

  protected void setOk(boolean value) {
    ok = value;
  }

  /*
   * Subclasses have to get a reference to the button panel, to position it correctly
   * in the guiContainer. The return type from getButtonPanel() cannot be ButtonPanel,
   * because that class is private. Instead we use JPanel. That's ok because
   * ButtonPanel is a subclass of JPanel.
   */
```

```
protected JPanel getButtonPanel() {
  return theButtonPanel;
}
/*
 * If data control should be made before everything is ok, a subclass can have
 * its own version of the okData() method. This method is checked when the user
 * closes the window (see the WindowsClosingListener class).
 */
protected boolean okData() {
  return true;
}
private class ButtonPanel extends JPanel {
  public ButtonPanel() {
    CommandListener buttonListener = new CommandListener();

    JButton okButton  = new JButton("OK");
    JButton cancelButton = new JButton("Cancel");
    add(okButton);
    add(cancelButton);
    okButton.addActionListener(buttonListener);
    cancelButton.addActionListener(buttonListener);

    /* Acceleration keys are defined for the two buttons. */
    KeyStroke enterKey = KeyStroke.getKeyStroke(KeyEvent.VK_ENTER, 0);
    okButton.registerKeyboardAction(buttonListener, "OK", enterKey,
      JComponent.WHEN_FOCUSED);
    KeyStroke escapeKey = KeyStroke.getKeyStroke(KeyEvent.VK_ESCAPE, 0);
    cancelButton.registerKeyboardAction(buttonListener, "Cancel", escapeKey,
      JComponent.WHEN_IN_FOCUSED  WINDOW);
  }
}

private class CommandListener implements ActionListener {
  public void actionPerformed(ActionEvent event) {
    String command = event.getActionCommand();
    if (command.equals("OK")){
      if (okData()) { // closing requires ok data
        ok = true;
        setVisible(false);
      }
    } else { // the user has pressed Cancel, the window is closed
      ok = false;
      setVisible(false);
    }
  }
}

private class WindowsClosingListener extends WindowAdapter {
  public void windowClosing(WindowEvent event) {
    int answer = JOptionPane.showConfirmDialog(null,
```

```
                "Do you want input data to be saved? ", "Closing the Dialog",
                JOptionPane.YES_NO_OPTION);
              if (answer == JOptionPane.YES_OPTION) {
              if (okData()) {  // closing requires ok data
                ok = true;
                setVisible(false);
              }
            } else {  // the window is closed without saving
              ok = false;
              setVisible(false);
            }
          }
        }
      }
```

Transferring data between the parent and dialog windows

Now we'll look at how to use MyDialog in an example: see Figure 15.7 and
Program Listing 15.5. (Note that the classes Person and PersonDialog are in
myLibrary.)

The principles are shown in Figure 15.5, but there are two primary differences:

- The dialog is a subclass of MyDialog.

- Data is transferred from the parent window to the dialog and back.

Starting with the latter of those two: it's most practical to have the data that will
be sent back and forth in an object. Usually we create a dialog for each class in the
problem area we're dealing with (for example, person, account, loan, etc.). Then we
already have the classes in place. In this example, we need the Person class, which
is shown first in the program listing.

Let's look at the PersonDialog class. The constructor takes the parent
window as its parameter and sends this on to the superclass with the title of the
dialog:

```
        super(parent, "Person");
```

Then we position the components throughout the window. We put the
buttonpanel at the bottom.

The showDialog() method is now relatively comprehensive. It takes a
person object as its argument. The data in this object is presented in the dialog. The
user can choose to change this data. The dialog doesn't have its own ok variable,
but maintains the one that belongs to the MyDialog class.

Just as before, the program control is waiting in the setVisible(true)
method. It will wait until setVisible(false) is called. This happens in the
MyDialog class, and the next step is to check the value of ok. If the user pressed
OK, change the data contents for thePerson object:

```
if (isOk()) {
  thePerson.setFirstName(firstNameField.getText());
  thePerson.setLastName(lastNameField.getText());
  return true;
}
return false;
```

We want to check that the user enters both a first and a last name, and this check is placed in the `PersonDialog` class's own version of the `okData()` method.

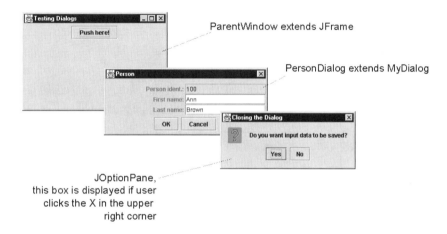

Figure 15.7 Running the `TestPersonDialog` program

The parent window is described in the `ParentWindow` class. There isn't much new here, aside from the fact that the person object has to be sent with the call for `showDialog()`, and it also has to be handled after the call. Here, we'll stick to printing a text to the console.

Finally, we'll mention that it's possible to find out how a dialog looks without linking it to a parent window. The following little program shows the name dialog:

```
static public void main(String[] args) {
  PersonDialog test = new PersonDialog(null);   // "null" as argument
  test.setLocation(500, 500);
  test.setVisible(true);
  System.exit(0);  // remember this when there is no parent window!
}
```

This can come in handy during the testing phase.

Program Listing 15.5

```
/*
 * Person.java  E.L. 2001-06-14
```

```
 * The class is mutable. First name and last name may be changed.
 */

package myLibrary;
import java.io.Serializable; // needed in chapter 19

public class Person implements Serializable {
  private int persIdent;
  private String firstName;
  private String lastName;

  public Person(int initPersIdent, String initFirstName, String initLastName) {
    persIdent = initPersIdent;
    firstName = initFirstName;
    lastName = initLastName;
  }

  public void setFirstName(String newFirstName) {
    firstName = newFirstName;
  }

  public void setLastName(String newLastName) {
    lastName = newLastName;
  }

  public int getPersIdent() {
    return persIdent;
  }

  public String getLastName() {
    return lastName;
  }

  public String getFirstName() {
    return firstName;
  }

  public String toString() {
    return persIdent + ": " + lastName + ", " + firstName;
  }
}

/*
 * PersonDialog.java   E.L. 2001-08-23
 *
 * The person-identification field is locked for editing.
 * The dialog has two common uses:
 * A. To edit data about an existing person.
 *    The identification is shown, and cannot be edited.
 * B. To register new data.
 *    The identification field contains the text "not defined".
 *    After data input, the client has to determine the new id.
 * The showDialog() method has a reference to a Person object as argument.
 * If the ident. in this object is negative, it means case B above.
```

```
       *
       */
      package myLibrary;
      import java.awt.*;
      import java.awt.event.*;
      import javax.swing.*;
      import java.text.*;

      public class PersonDialog extends MyDialog {
        private JTextField persIdField = new JTextField(8);
        private JTextField firstNameField = new JTextField(15);
        private JTextField lastNameField = new JTextField(15);

        public PersonDialog(JFrame parent) {
          super(parent, "Person");
          Container guiContainer = getContentPane();
          guiContainer.add(new JPanel(), BorderLayout.NORTH);  // a little space
          guiContainer.add(new DataPanel(), BorderLayout.CENTER);
          guiContainer.add(getButtonPanel(), BorderLayout.SOUTH);
          pack();
        }

        private class DataPanel extends JPanel {
          public DataPanel() {
            setLayout(new GridLayout(3, 2));
            add(new JLabel("Person ident.: ", JLabel.RIGHT));
            add(persIdField);
            persIdField.setEditable(false); // the ident. cannot be edited
            add(new JLabel("First name: ", JLabel.RIGHT));
            add(firstNameField);
            add(new JLabel("Last name: ", JLabel.RIGHT));
            add(lastNameField);
          }
        }

        public boolean showDialog(Person thePerson) {
          if (thePerson.getPersIdent() < 0) persIdField.setText("not defined");
          else persIdField.setText("" + thePerson.getPersIdent());
          firstNameField.setText(thePerson.getFirstName());
          lastNameField.setText(thePerson.getLastName());
          setOk(false);
          pack();
          setVisible(true);
          if (isOk()) {
            thePerson.setFirstName(firstNameField.getText());
            thePerson.setLastName(lastNameField.getText());
            return true;
          }
          return false;
        }
```

```
  protected boolean okData() {
    String firstName = firstNameField.getText().trim();
    String lastName = lastNameField.getText().trim();
    if (firstName.equals("") || lastName.equals("")) {
    JOptionPane.showMessageDialog(null, "You have to fill out both first and last names!");
     if (!firstName.equals("")) lastNameField.requestFocus();
     else firstNameField.requestFocus();
     return false;
    }
    return true;
  }
}

/*
 * TestPersonDialog.java   E.L. 2001-08-23
 *
 */
import java.awt.*;
import java.awt.event.*;
import javax.swing.*;
import myLibrary.*;  // Person and PersonDialog

class ParentWindow extends JFrame {
  private Person aPerson = new Person(100, "Ann", "Brown");
  private PersonDialog personDialog = new PersonDialog(this);
  private Container guiContainer;

  public ParentWindow() {
    setTitle("Testing Dialogs");
    setDefaultCloseOperation(JFrame.EXIT_ON_CLOSE);
    guiContainer = getContentPane();
    guiContainer.setLayout(new FlowLayout());
    JButton button = new JButton("Push here!");
    guiContainer.add(button);
    button.addActionListener(new ButtonListener());
    personDialog.setLocation(550, 550);
  }

  private class ButtonListener implements ActionListener {
    public void actionPerformed(ActionEvent event) {
      if (personDialog.showDialog(aPerson)) System.out.println("OK is pressed....");
      else System.out.println("Cancel is pressed....");
      System.out.println(aPerson); // toString() is used
    }
  }
}

class TestPersonDialog {
  static public void main(String[] args) {
    ParentWindow test = new ParentWindow();
```

```
    test.setSize(300, 200);
    test.setLocation(500, 500);
    test.setVisible(true);
  }
}
```

API Reference

The javax.swing.JDialog class

Constructors:

    public JDialog(Dialog parent, String title, boolean modal)
    public JDialog(Frame parent, String title, boolean modal)

The constructors create a new dialog, with the existing dialog, or an existing primary window as parent ("owner"). The last argument will be `true` for modal dialog windows.

Methods:

    public Container getContentPane()

This method returns a container that can be filled with GUI components.

    public void setLayout(LayoutManager layoutManager)
    public void setJMenuBar(JMenuBar menuBar)

These methods are used to set the layout manager (BorderLayout is default) and menu bar.

    public void setDefaultCloseOperation(int operation)

This method determines what will happen when the user closes the window by pressing on the upper right corner. The default is for the window to be hidden. If we want to control the windows' closing ourselves, we set the argument to equal `JDialog.DO_NOTHING_ON_CLOSE`.

Problem

Modify Program Listing 15.3 so that `MiniDialog` contains a text field the user can write in. Modify `showDialog()` so that it returns this text as a string to the parent window if the user presses the OK button. If the user presses the Cancel button, the method will return `null`. The parent window will print the text out right under the pushbutton.

15.4 GridBagLayout as Layout Manager

Now we're ready to make the last version of our renovation program. We'll use the classes from Chapter 12, but replace the user interface section with classes that create a graphical user interface as shown in Figure 15.8. We have a parent window with four dialog windows: a dialog for surface, one for paint, one for flooring, and one for wallpaper.

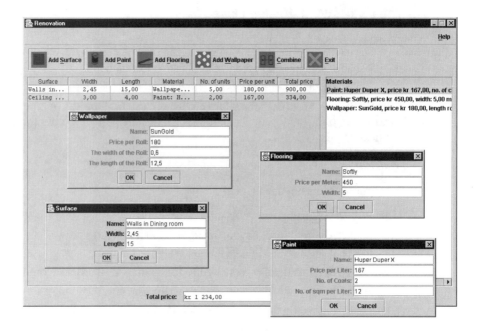

Figure 15.8 The renovation case: A parent window with dialogs. Only one of the dialogs is shown at a time.

At the top right of the parent window is a small Help menu. The menu has two choices: "Help" and "About the Program". Both of the choices print texts in text boxes.

The toolbar in the parent window offers the following functions:

- Register a new surface

- Register a new type of paint

- Register a new type of flooring

- Register a new type of wallpaper

- Combine a surface with a material (only possible if a line in each of the lists is selected)

- Exit

The large list on the left is an instance of the `JTable` class. It works more or less like a regular list, but we can set the data up in columns with their own column headers. We will come back to this type of GUI component later.

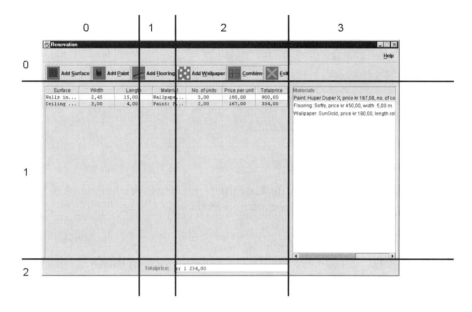

Figure 15.9 The parent window divided into cells for use by gridbaglayout

The list on the right is a `JList` type, which we're familiar with from before.

The total sum is printed out at the bottom: a regular background text followed by a regular text box.

We'll use the most general of all the layout managers to create the primary window. The layout manager is called `GridBagLayout`. It is different from the other layout managers in that it requires detailed planning. It's not suited for the trial and error method. There are many parameters and an error in one of them can yield unpredictable results.

We'll begin by creating an outline of the window. Use pen and paper! Then we divide the window up into cells using horizontal and vertical lines, such that each cell contains no more than one component. But a component may well cover several cells: see Figure 15.9. Notice that columns and rows don't necessarily have a uniform width.

Based on this figure, we'll set up the requirements for each individual component. The requirements for one component are stored in an instance of the GridBagConstraints class. This class has a set of *public* instance variables that we assign values to directly, without using set methods. We'll go through these variables in an API reference.

API Reference

The java.awt.GridBagConstraints class

An instance of the class describes the requirements for a GUI component that is laid out according to the layout manager GridBagLayout.

Constructor:

    public GridBagConstraints()

Public instance variables:

    public int gridx
    public int gridy

These two variables indicate the position of the upper left cell that the component covers. The cells are numbered as shown in Figure 15.9.

    public int gridwidth
    public int gridheight

These two variables contain the number of cells the component covers—the width and height, respectively.

    public int fill

This variable is used if the component's size is less than the space that results from the intended grid. The variable can have the following values (all the values are class constants in the GridBagConstraints class): HORIZONTAL - expand the component so that it fills the cells in the horizontal direction, VERTICAL - expand the component in height, BOTH - expand the component in both directions, NONE - don't expand the component in any direction.

    public int ipadx
    public int ipady

By declaring values for these variables we can indicate how much larger (in pixels) than the minimum value the component will be in the x and y directions.

    public Insets insets

This is an instance of the java.awt.Insets class. We use it to indicate how much room we want around the component. We can set the variable's value in the following manner:

    insets = new Insets(5, 5, 5, 5);

Here we are asking for five pixels in each direction. The order of the arguments for the `Insets` constructor is: top, left, bottom, right.

    public int anchor

Here, if the component doesn't fill its space completely (see the `fill` variable above), we tell which direction it should be "anchored" in: CENTER, NORTH, NORTHEAST, EAST, SOUTHEAST, SOUTH, SOUTHWEST, WEST, or NORTHWEST. All of these values are class constants in the `GridBagConstraints` class.

    public double weightx
    public double weighty

These are the most difficult variables to assign values to. They are useful if the user changes the size of the window. Then the size of the components should change in an equivalent fashion. The variables will have a value between 0.0 and 1.0. The consequences of the different values are beyond the scope of this book.[1] Here, we use the value 0.5 for both variables. We can also avoid problems by setting it so that the user cannot change the size of the window by sending the message `setResizable(false)` to the window.

Table 15.1 GridBagConstraints for the GUI components in Figure 15.9

	Toolbar	Table on the left	List on the right	Background text at the bottom	Text box at the bottom
gridx	0	0	3	1	2
gridy	0	1	1	2	2
gridwidth	4	3	1	1	1
gridheight	1	1	1	1	1
fill	NONE	BOTH	BOTH	NONE	HORIZONTAL
anchor	WEST	CENTER	CENTER	EAST	WEST

Now let's use this for the renovation window. We can set up an outline as shown in Table 15.1. In the constructor that lays out the GUI components, we have to program it this way:

```
Container guiContainer = getContentPane();
guiContainer.setLayout(new GridBagLayout()); // don't forget this!
```

---

1. For more information, refer to [Walrath, Campione 1999].

```
GridBagConstraints constraints = new GridBagConstraints();

/* The following variables are fixed for all components */
constraints.insets = new Insets(5, 5, 5, 5); // space around and between the components
constraints.weightx = 0.5;
constraints.weighty = 0.5;

/* Then each component has to be handled according to table 15.1 */

/* The Toolbar */
constraints.gridx = 0;
constraints.gridy = 0;
constraints.gridwidth = 4;
constraints.gridheight = 1;
constraints.fill = GridBagConstraints.NONE;
constraints.anchor = GridBagConstraints.WEST;
guiContainer.add(toolbar, constraints);
```

The `toolbar` object is created elsewhere in the constructor.

We get the equivalent for the other GUI components. The complete source code is shown later in Program Listing 15.9.

To summarize:

1. Make a table that corresponds to Table 15.1.

2. Set the layout manager for the window to GridBagLayout by sending the message `setLayout(new GridBagLayout())` to the window.

3. Create an instance of the `GridBagConstraints` class:

    ```
    GridBagConstraints constraints = new GridBagConstraints();
    ```

4. Assign a value to any variables that will be constant for all the components, for example `insets`, `weightx`, and `weighty`.

5. Assign a value to the other variables for each individual component.

6. Put the component into the container using the following version of the `add()` method:

    ```
    public void add(Component comp, Object constraints)
    ```

How to set the size of the components

You may have discovered that the `Component` class offers a method called `setSize()`. We've already used this method to set window sizes. But if we try to set the size, for example, of a pushbutton with this method, it doesn't seem to have any effect. And that's correct. `setSize()` is only effective if we don't use any layout manager. In that case we position all the components with coordinates expressed in pixels.

But what about the methods `setMaximumSize()`, `setMinimumSize()`, and `setPreferredSize()` in the `JComponent` class? It depends on which layout manager we're using:

- BorderLayout and GridLayout do not consider any of the wishes.

- FlowLayout and GridBagLayout consider a component's "preferred size."

- BoxLayout (see online API documentation) considers all the wishes.

All of these methods take an instance of the `java.awt.Dimension` class as their argument. The constructor for this class takes two arguments—the component's width and height, respectively. For example:

```
list.setPreferredSize(new Dimension(500, 300));
```

15.5 The Table GUI Component (the JTable Class)

It's frequently useful to present data in a tabular form with columns and rows. In the renovation case, we will present the surface data with costs for materials in tabular form. The `javax.swing.JTable` class can be used for this. If we're not going to present just a static table, we need to maintain the data in the table. Just as for lists (Section 14.5), we have to use the underlying model.

Tables are made up of rows and columns. They are much more complex than lists. Books on Swing devote anywhere from 20 to 80 pages on the topic. We're going to create a table with certain limitations:

- The table has a fixed number of columns with fixed column names.

- The user can adjust the width of the individual columns in the table. This results in the other columns becoming narrower.

- The user can't adjust the size of the table (the overall width and height of the table).

- The user can't change the data in the table.

- The program can insert and delete rows in the table. In order to change the data, the program can delete a row and insert a new row in its place.

- The user can select individual rows in the table. The program determines whether or not multiple rows can be selected, just as with lists.

- The program handles the selection by having the user push a pushbutton, not by listening to row selections.

Most people will be able to make do with this type of table for quite a while. A dialog window can be used if the data is going to be changed.

Unfortunately, the default versions of the data model under JTable require that the user be able to edit the data directly in the table cells. Managing this requires programming that we're choosing to avoid. Instead, we have to make sure that the user can't edit the data. To accomplish this, we have to create our own data model class. This may sound difficult, but doesn't require anything other than creating a subclass of the DefaultTableModel class and programming our own version of the isCellEditable() method there. We also have to make a constructor that goes with DefaultTableModel. We call it MyTableModel class and put it in the myLibrary package (see Program Listing 15.6).

API Reference

This only includes the few constructors and methods that are used in the renovation example in the next section. There are many more: refer to the online API documentation and textbooks devoted to Swing.[2]

The javax.swing.JTable class

Constructor:

> public JTable(TableModel data)

The argument has to be an instance of a class that implements the TableModel interface, for example myLibrary.MyTableModel (see Program Listing 15.6).

Methods:

> public int getSelectedRow()

This method returns the index for the selected row.

> public void setSelectionMode(int mode)

See the method with the same name under the JList class in Section 14.5.

> public void setPreferredScrollableViewportSize(Dimension size)

This method sets the size of the area the table will be displayed in. The parameter is an instance of the java.awt.Dimension class and may be created as follows (the width and height are indicated in a number of pixels): Dimension dim = new Dimension(width, height);

> public void setRowSelectionInterval(int fromIndex, int includingIndex)

This method sets the indicated interval as selected. It throws an Illegal-ArgumentException if the index is invalid.

---

2. [Horstmann, Cornell 2000], [Walrath, Campione 1999], [Eckstein, Loy, Wood 1998]

The javax.swing.table.DefaultTableModel class

The `myLibrary.MyTableModel` class is a subclass of this class.
Constructor (used in `MyTableModel`):

public DefaultTableModel(Object[] columnNames, int noOfRows)

The first parameter is an array with column titles, the second parameter is the number of rows (the value 0 is used in `MyTableModel`).
Methods:

public void addRow(Object[] dataForOneRow)

This method registers a new row of data. The argument has to be an array with an object for every column in the table.

public void insertRow(int rowNo, Object[] dataForOneRow)

This method inserts a row in the position indicated by `rowNo`. The other rows in the table are moved over a position. Remember that the row numbers start with 0. The argument has to be an array with an object for each column in the table.

public void removeRow(int rowNo)

This method removes the row with the indicated number from the table. Remember that the row numbers start with 0.

public int getRowCount()

This method returns the number of rows in the table.

Program Listing 15.6

```
/*
 * MyTableModel.java   E.L. 2001-08-23
 *
 * By default, all cells in a table may be edited by the user.
 * To prevent this, we have to make our own table model, as
 * a subclass of DefaultTable Model.
 */
package myLibrary;

import javax.swing.table.*;
public class MyTableModel extends DefaultTableModel {
  public MyTableModel(String[] columnNames) {
    super(columnNames, 0);
  }
  public boolean isCellEditable(int row, int column) {
    return false;
  }
}
```

15.6 GUI for the Renovation Project

We're now at the stage where we can go through the GUI for the renovation project (see Figure 15.8). You'll find all the files included in this version of the program in a separate subdirectory under Chapter 15 at [URL Java book].

The classes for the problem are the same as in Chapter 12: `RenovationProject`, `Surface`, `Material`, `Flooring`, `Wallpaper`, `Paint`. All the material classes have `toString()` methods.

The GUI classes are found at the following files:

- The *Dialogs.java* file contains a dialog window for each of the "main objects" in the problem: `SurfaceDialog`, `PaintDialog`, `WallpaperDialog`, and `FlooringDialog`.

- The *Constants.java* file contains an interface with many of the constants used in the different windows. Example constants are the names of commands, menu items, and the lengths of text fields. By collecting the constants that are used in several classes into an interface, classes that need the constants can access them by implementing the interface.

- The *RenovationChap15.java* file contains the `ProjectChap15` class which describes the primary window, as well as a little class with `main()`.

We also use the following classes from `myLibrary`: `MyDecimalFormat` (see Section 8.3), `MyNumberFormatInput`, `MyTableModel`, and `MyDialog`. The `MyNumberFormatInput` class offers simple utility methods that take a string as its argument and converts it to a decimal or integral numeral. The methods don't handle sign characters. The decimal separator is determined by the environment settings.

Program Listing 15.7 shows the constant interface.

We save the command names in an array. The button descriptions ("tool tips"), button mnemonics and icon names are sorted in arrays that are parallel to the first one. That means that we'll find information about the same command at the same index in all the arrays. For example, at index 1, there's information about the "Add Paint" command. The description of this command is "Register a new type of Paint," the mnemonic is "P", and the icon is in the file *NewPaint.gif*. Later on we'll see how easy it is to input all this in `guiContainer` when we insert the information into parallel arrays this way. (We could also have used a class where each instance of the class describes a command.)

The `columnNames` array contains column headings for the surface table.

Program Listing 15.7

```
/*
 * Constants.java   E.L.2001-08-23
```

```
     *
     * Constants to be used in the class RenovationChap15
     * and the supporting dialog classes.
     */
    import java.awt.Dimension;
    import java.text.NumberFormat;
    import myLibrary.*;
    interface Constants {
      String[] buttonCommand = {"Add Surface", "Add Paint",
         "Add Flooring", "Add Wallpaper", "Combine", "Exit"};
      String[] buttonDescription = {"Register New Surface",
        "Register a new type of Paint", "Register a new type of Flooring",
        "Register a new type of Wallpaper",
        "Combine a surface with a material", "Exit the program"};
      int combineIndex = 4;
      char[] buttonMnemonic = {'S', 'P', 'F', 'W', 'C', 'E'};
      String[] iconfile = {"NewSurface.gif", "NewPaint.gif",
        "NewFlooring.gif", "NewWallpaper.gif", "Combine.gif", "Exit.gif"};
      String iconDirectory = "icons" + java.io.File.separator;

      String menuName = "Help";
      char menuNameMnemonic = 'H';
      String[] menuItem = {"Help", "About this program..."};
      char[] menuMnemonic = {'H', 'A'};

      String[] columnNames =
        {"Surface", "Width", "Length", "Material", "No. of units", "Price per unit", "Total price"};

      int windowX = 200;  // The location of the primary window, ...
      int windowY = 300;  // ...., upper left corner
      int dialogX = 300; // The location of the dialogs, ...
      int dialogY = 400; // ...., upper left corner
      int textFieldLength = 15;  // in the dialogs
      int fieldLengthSum = 5; // in the sum field in the bottom of the primary field
      Dimension sizeSurfaceListWindow = new Dimension(600, 400);

      MyDecimalFormat outputFormat = new MyDecimalFormat(5,2); // see myLibrary
      NumberFormat currencyFormat = NumberFormat.getCurrencyInstance();
      MyNumberFormatInput numberFormat =  new MyNumberFormatInput(); // see myLibrary
    }
```

The dialogs are all constructed the same way. The `SurfaceDialog` class is shown in Program Listing 15.8. This dialog is constructed about the same way as the `PersonDialog` class in Program Listing 15.5. The `showDialog()` method is a little different. Since the dialog won't be used to change existing data, it's not necessary to have a reference as a parameter. The new `Surface` object is simply returned from the method. If the user presses `Cancel`, `null` is returned.

We've created the `okData()` method that checks if the number fields really contain numbers. `numberFormat` is declared in the `Constants` interface as an instance of the `myLibrary.MyNumberFormatInput` class. The `parse-`

`PositivDouble()` method takes a string as its argument and return a decimal numeral. If the string can't be interpreted as a decimal numeral, a `Parse-Exception` is thrown.

This method, `okData()`, replaces the `okData()` method inherited from the `MyDialog` class. The method is called when the dialog is being closed. That is taken care of in the `MyDialog` class.

Program Listing 15.8

```
/*
 * Dialogs.java    E.L. 2001-08-23
 *
 * Dialogs for use in the Renovation Example in Chapter 15
 */

import java.awt.*;
import java.awt.event.*;
import javax.swing.*;
import java.text.*;
import myLibrary.*;

class SurfaceDialog extends MyDialog implements Constants {
  private JTextField nameField = new JTextField(textFieldLength);
  private JTextField lengthField = new JTextField(textFieldLength);
  private JTextField widthField = new JTextField(textFieldLength);
  private double length;
  private double width;

  public SurfaceDialog(JFrame parent) {
    super(parent, "Surface");
    Container guiContainer = getContentPane();
    guiContainer.add(new JPanel(), BorderLayout.NORTH);
    guiContainer.add(new SurfaceDataPanel(), BorderLayout.CENTER);
    guiContainer.add(getButtonPanel(), BorderLayout.SOUTH);
    pack();
  }

  private class SurfaceDataPanel extends JPanel {
    public SurfaceDataPanel() {
      setLayout(new GridLayout(3,2));
      add(new JLabel("Name: ", JLabel.RIGHT));
      add(nameField);
      add(new JLabel("Width: ", JLabel.RIGHT));
      add(widthField);
      add(new JLabel("Length: ", JLabel.RIGHT));
      add(lengthField);
    }
  }

  protected boolean okData() {
    try {
```

```
            length = numberFormat.parsePositivDouble(lengthField.getText());
            width = numberFormat.parsePositivDouble(widthField.getText());
         } catch (ParseException e) {
         JOptionPane.showMessageDialog(null,
             "Number input could not be converted, Try again!");
         widthField.requestFocus();
         return false;
         }
         return true;
      }
      public Surface showDialog() {
         nameField.setText("");
         widthField.setText("");
         lengthField.setText("");
         setOk(false);
         setVisible(true);
         nameField.requestFocus();
         if (isOk()) return new Surface(nameField.getText(), length, width);
         else return null;
      }
   }
      /* The other dialogs are constructed in the same way, see the file Dialogs.java */
```

Finally, let's take a look at the primary window (see Program Listing 15.9). This is, of course, a very large and comprehensive class with many instance variables, two inner listener classes, and several private help methods. Let's start at the beginning and go through the different parts of the program listing.

- Instance variables

  Many of the GUI components are instance variables. That means that we may refer to them from multiple methods. There's also a reference for each individual dialog. And, perhaps most important of all, there's a reference to the theProject object that is an instance of the RenovationProject class. This is the important link between the user interface classes and the classes that describe the problem we're going to solve.

- The ProjectChap15() constructor

  Notice that the initProject reference is a parameter for the constructor. Skim to the very end of the program listing for a second. There you'll find the statements that bind an instance of the RenovationProject class to an instance of the ProjectChap15 class:

RenovationProject myProject
                = new RenovationProject("The last version of the Renovation Case!");
ProjectChap15 window = new ProjectChap15(myProject);

There's little new in the rest of the constructor. Notice that we set the layout manager to `GridBagLayout`.

- The `ButtonListener` class describes objects that can listen to the buttons in the toolbar. After finding the index for the command, we let a `switch` statement determine which operations will be executed. Every single `case`-block, except for "Cancel", communicates with `theProject` object. The models behind the lists in the window (`surfaceData` and `materialData`) are also updated. Choices 0–3 display the right dialog window and receive a new surface or a new material from this window. The new object is registered in `theProject` object. Choices 1–3 use the help method `recordMaterial()`. This is a private method in the `ButtonListener` class. Choice 4 combines surface and material.

- The `MenuListener` class describes objects that can listen to the menu choices "Help" and "About the program...."

- In addition there are many private help methods in the `ProjectChap15` class: see the comments for the individual methods.

Program Listing 15.9

```
/*
 * RenovationChap15.java   E.L. 2001-08-23
 *
 * The data are stored in array lists, in an instance of the class RenovationProject.
 * This instance is declared as "theProject".
 *
 * The surface data are displayed in the surfaceList object, which is an instance of
 * the JTable class. The model behind is named "surfaceData" and is an instance of
 * myLibrary.MyTableModel.
 *
 * Information about the materials is displayed in the materialList object, which is
 * an instance of the JList class. The model behind is an instance of the
 * DefaultListModel, and it is declared as materialData.
 *
 * The row numbers in the displayed lists should be the same as the indexes in
 * "theProject".
 *
 * Many of the variables are declared in the Constants interface.
 */

import java.text.*;
import java.awt.*;
```

```
import java.awt.event.*;
import javax.swing.*;
import myLibrary.*;

class ProjectChap15 extends JFrame implements Constants {
  private Container guiContainer;
  private JToolBar toolbar = new JToolBar();
  private JButton[] button = new JButton[buttonCommand.length];

  /* Material data */
  private DefaultListModel materialData = new DefaultListModel();
  private JList materialList = new JList(materialData);
  private JScrollPane scrollMaterialList = new JScrollPane(materialList);

  /* Surface data */
  private MyTableModel surfaceData =
        new MyTableModel(columnNames); // from myLibrary
  private JTable surfaceList = new JTable(surfaceData);

  private JTextField sum = new JTextField(fieldLengthSum);

  private SurfaceDialog theSurfaceDialog = new SurfaceDialog(this);
  private PaintDialog thePaintDialog = new PaintDialog(this);
  private FlooringDialog theFlooringDialog = new FlooringDialog(this);
  private WallpaperDialog theWallpaperDialog = new WallpaperDialog(this);

  private RenovationProject theProject;

  public ProjectChap15(RenovationProject initProject) {
    setTitle("Renovation");
    setDefaultCloseOperation(JFrame.EXIT_ON_CLOSE);
    theProject = initProject; // N.B.! the link to the problem domain object

    guiContainer = getContentPane();
    initLists();
    createToolbar();
    createMenu();

    guiContainer.setLayout(new GridBagLayout());
    layoutGUI();

    theSurfaceDialog.setLocation(dialogX, dialogY);
    thePaintDialog.setLocation(dialogX, dialogY);
    theFlooringDialog.setLocation(dialogX, dialogY);

    theWallpaperDialog.setLocation(dialogX, dialogY);
    setLocation(windowX, windowY);
    setResizable(false); // the user is not allowed to change the size of the window
  }
  /* This class describes the listeners to the toolbar buttons */
  private class ButtonListener implements ActionListener {
    public void actionPerformed(ActionEvent event) {
      String command = event.getActionCommand();
```

```
/* gets the command's index */
int index = 0;
boolean found = false;
while (index < buttonCommand.length && !found) {
 if (command.equals(buttonCommand[index])) found = true;
 else index++;  // if not found, increase the index
}

if (index == buttonCommand.length) {
 System.out.println
    ("Inexplicable error in the ButtonListener class in ProjectChap15");
 return;
}

switch (index) {
 case 0:  // new surface
  Surface newSurface = theSurfaceDialog.showDialog();
  if (newSurface != null) {
   Surface theSurface = theProject.addNewSurface(newSurface);
   if (theSurface == newSurface) {
    surfaceData.addRow(createRowData(newSurface));
    } else JOptionPane.showMessageDialog(null,
              newSurface.getName() + " is already registered.");
  }
  break;
 case 1:  // new paint
  Paint newPaint = thePaintDialog.showDialog();
  recordMaterial(newPaint);
  break;
 case 2:  // new flooring
  Flooring newFlooring = theFlooringDialog.showDialog();
  recordMaterial(newFlooring);
  break;
 case 3:  // new wallpaper
  Wallpaper newWallpaper = theWallpaperDialog.showDialog();
  recordMaterial(newWallpaper);
  break;
 case 4: // combine surface and material, calculate sum
  int surfaceIndex = surfaceList.getSelectedRow();
  Material material = theProject.getMaterial(materialList.getSelectedIndex());
  if (surfaceIndex < 0 || material == null) {
   JOptionPane.showMessageDialog(null,
     "You have to select both surface and material before combining them!");
   } else {
   Surface theSurface = theProject.getSurface(surfaceIndex);
   theSurface.setMaterial(material);
   surfaceData.insertRow(surfaceIndex, createRowData(theSurface));
   surfaceData.removeRow(surfaceIndex + 1);
   sum.setText(currencyFormat.format(theProject.getTotalPrice()));
```

```
        }
        break;
      case 5:
        System.exit(0);
        break;
      default:
        System.out.println("The program control should not enter this point!");
        break;
    }
    if (surfaceData.getRowCount() > 0 && materialData.size() > 0) {
      button[combineIndex].setEnabled(true);
    }
  }

  /* Help method, is used in the switch-statement above */
  private void recordMaterial(Material newMaterial) {
    if (newMaterial != null) {
      Material theMaterial = theProject.addNewMaterial(newMaterial);
      if (theMaterial == newMaterial) materialData.addElement (newMaterial.toString());
      else JOptionPane.showMessageDialog(null, newMaterial.getName()
                        + " is already registered.");
    }
  }
}

/* This class describes listeners which react to the menu choices */
private class MenuListener implements ActionListener  {
  public void actionPerformed(ActionEvent event) {
    String command = event.getActionCommand();
    if (command.equals(menuItem[0])) {
      /* A very simple help */
      JOptionPane.showMessageDialog(null,
        "This program calculates the material requirement and cost for renovation\n"
      + "of an apartment. The apartment has to be input as a set of rectangular\n"
      + "surfaces. Each surface has to be covered with only one type of material.\n"
      + "You may choose between paint, wallpaper and flooring. You have to input\n"
      + "data about the surfaces (length and width) and the materials (price, etc.).\n"
      + "Use the toolbar or the menu to get input dialogs.\n"
      + "Click on 'Combine' to link a surface to a material.\n"
      + "The information in the window is continuously updated.");
    } else {
      JOptionPane.showMessageDialog(null,
        "This program is one version of a continuous case in the book\n"
      + "'Java the UML Way, Integrating Object-Oriented Design and Programming'\n"
      + "written by Else Lervik and Vegard B. Havdal,\n"
      + "published by John Wiley & Sons, Ltd. 2002");
    }
  }
}
```

```java
/* This private method creates a row with data customised to the surfaceData object */
private java.lang.Object[] createRowData(Surface theSurface) {
  java.lang.Object[] columns = new java.lang.Object[columnNames.length];
  columns[0] = theSurface.getName();
  columns[1] = outputFormat.format(theSurface.getWidth());
  columns[2] = outputFormat.format(theSurface.getLength());
  Material theMaterial = theSurface.getMaterial();
  if (theMaterial != null) {
    columns[3] = theMaterial.getClass().getName() + ": " + theMaterial.getName();
    columns[4] = outputFormat.format(theMaterial.getMaterialReq(theSurface));
    columns[5] = outputFormat.format(theMaterial.getPricePerUnit());
    columns[6] = outputFormat.format(theMaterial.getTotalPrice(theSurface));
  }
  return columns;
}

/* This private method initiates the surfaceList and materialList objects*/
private void initLists() {

  /* A non proportional font */
  Font defaultFont = surfaceList.getFont();
  Font newFont = new Font("Monospaced",
    defaultFont.getStyle(), defaultFont.getSize());
  surfaceList.setFont(newFont);
  sum.setFont(newFont);

  surfaceList.setSelectionMode(ListSelectionModel.SINGLE_SELECTION);
  materialList.setSelectionMode(ListSelectionModel.SINGLE_SELECTION);

  /* The size of the window in which surfaceList is shown*/
  surfaceList.setPreferredScrollableViewportSize(sizeSurfaceListWindow);

  /* Heading for the material list */
  JViewport jvp = new JViewport(); // see the online API documentation
  jvp.setView(new JLabel("Materials"));
  scrollMaterialList.setColumnHeader(jvp);
}

private void createToolbar() {
  toolbar.setFloatable(false);
  ButtonListener theButtonListener = new ButtonListener();
  for (int i = 0; i < buttonCommand.length; i++) {
    Icon icon = new ImageIcon(iconDirectory + iconfile[i]);
    button[i] = new JButton(buttonCommand[i], icon);
    button[i].setToolTipText(buttonDescription[i]);
    button[i].setMnemonic(buttonMnemonic[i]);
    button[i].addActionListener(theButtonListener);
    toolbar.add(button[i]);
  }
  button[combineIndex].setEnabled(false);
}
```

```java
private void createMenu() {
  MenuListener theMenuListener = new MenuListener();
  JMenu menu = new JMenu(menuName);
  menu.setMnemonic(menuNameMnemonic);
  for (int i = 0; i < menuItem.length; i++) {
    JMenuItem menubar = menu.add(menuItem[i]);
    menubar.setMnemonic(menuMnemonic[i]);
    menubar.addActionListener(theMenuListener);
  }
  JMenuBar mbar = new JMenuBar();

  /* Changes the layout manager to get the menu on the right hand side */
  mbar.setLayout(new FlowLayout(FlowLayout.RIGHT));
  mbar.add(menu);
  setJMenuBar(mbar);
}

private void layoutGUI() {
  GridBagConstraints constraints = new GridBagConstraints();
  constraints.insets = new Insets(5, 5, 5, 5);// space around and between the comp.
  constraints.weightx = 0.5;
  constraints.weighty = 0.5;

  /* The toolbar */
  constraints.gridx = 0;
  constraints.gridy = 0;
  constraints.gridwidth = 4;
  constraints.gridheight = 1;
  constraints.fill = GridBagConstraints.NONE;
  constraints.anchor = GridBagConstraints.WEST;
  guiContainer.add(toolbar, constraints);

  /* The surfaceList table */
  constraints.gridx = 0;
  constraints.gridy = 1;
  constraints.gridwidth = 3;
  constraints.gridheight = 1;
  constraints.fill = GridBagConstraints.BOTH;
  constraints.anchor = GridBagConstraints.CENTER;
  guiContainer.add(new JScrollPane(surfaceList), constraints);

  /* The materialList */
  constraints.gridx = 3;
  constraints.gridy = 1;
  constraints.gridwidth = 1;
  constraints.gridheight = 1;
  constraints.fill = GridBagConstraints.BOTH;
  constraints.anchor = GridBagConstraints.CENTER;
  guiContainer.add(scrollMaterialList, constraints);
```

```
        /* The background text */
        constraints.gridx = 1;
        constraints.gridy = 2;
        constraints.gridwidth = 1;
        constraints.gridheight = 1;
        constraints.fill = GridBagConstraints.NONE;
        constraints.anchor = GridBagConstraints.EAST;
        guiContainer.add(new JLabel("Total price: "), constraints);

        /* The sum textbox */
        constraints.gridx = 2;
        constraints.gridy = 2;
        constraints.gridwidth = 1;
        constraints.gridheight = 1;
        constraints.fill = GridBagConstraints.HORIZONTAL;
        constraints.anchor = GridBagConstraints.WEST;
        guiContainer.add(sum, constraints);
      }
    }
    class RenovationChap15 {
      public static void main(String[] args) {
        RenovationProject myProject
            = new RenovationProject("The last version of the Renovation Case!");
        ProjectChap15 window = new ProjectChap15(myProject);
        window.pack();
        window.setVisible(true);
      }
    }
```

Problem

The classes in the *Dialogs.java* file have a great deal in common. Propose a class structure that uses inheritance. Make a class tree starting with the `MyDialog` class. Make new versions of the dialog classes. Test the classes by replacing the *Dialogs.java* file with the new classes. Remember to recompile.

15.7 New Concepts in This Chapter

Concept	Brief Explanation
acceleration key	A key or combination of keys that executes a command.
dialog	See dialog window.
dialog box	This term is used for small dialog windows.

Concept	Brief Explanation
dialog window	A dialog window is a secondary window—in other words, it's connected to a parent window. A dialog window is an instance of the JDialog class.
dropdown menu	The menu appears when the user clicks on the menu name. Normally the menu is shown under the menu name (hence the designation dropdown menu), but if there's no room there, it's shown above the menu name.
menu	In this book, we're only including dropdown menus. A dropdown menu is an instance of the JMenu class.
menu bar	See Figure 15.1. A menu bar is an instance of the JMenuBar class.
menu item	See Figure 15.1. A menu item is an instance of the JMenuItem class.
modal dialog window	A dialog window that doesn't allow the user to access other windows as long as it's open. The modal dialog itself can open its own dialogs.
nonmodal dialog window	A dialog window where the user has unrestricted access to all other windows in the application.
toolbar	A collection of pushbuttons. The buttons are gathered into an instance of the JToolBar class. The toolbar is displayed at the top of a window, but can also be presented in its own window.

15.8 Review Problems

1. Explain how to make a dropdown menu. Which classes do we use? What type of event is generated by a menu selection?

2. What is the relation between an instance of the JToolBar class and pushbuttons of the JButton class?

3. What classes are used to make a dialog window?

4. How do we transfer data between a parent window and a dialog window?

5. A dialog is always a subclass of the JDialog class. We make a modal dialog by passing the argument true to the superclass's constructor. Which method behaves differently when a window is modal? And what happens?

6. Outline how we use the GridBagLayout layout manager.

7. What needs to happen for the message setSize() to work when we send it, for example, to a text box?

8. Describe the characteristics of the GUI component table (an instance of the JTable class) as we've used it in this chapter.

15.9 Programming Problems

All the problems except problem 3 are based on previous programming problems in which you made a textual user interface or just a simple test program. Change as little as possible in the classes you created before.

Problem 1

Start with programming problem 1, Chapter 9.

Make a user interface that shows the prices of all the products. Use an instance of the JList class, where every line shows the product number (the array index) and price.

Make a toolbar and menu that offer the following possibilities:

- Change the price of a selected product

- Register a new product

- Remove a product (here you have to expand the class from Chapter 9 with a suitable method)

Problem 2

Start with programming problem 1, Chapter 10.

Create a GUI that shows all the information about all the employees. Use an instance of the JTable class.

The primary window will also show the number of employees and the average salary.

The window will have a pushbutton that makes it possible to register a new employee. A dialog window to register all the data must appear and the pertinent data in the primary window has to be updated once the new employee is registered.

Problem 3

In problem 4, Chapter 13, you made a simple reservation system for seats in a concert hall. Link this user interface to data stored in a file.

You can assume that there's enough room in the internal memory for all the data in the file.

The file will contain data about several different shows. There will be many performances of each show. You can assume that it's possible to reserve seats seven days in advance. Every time the program starts, data that is older than today's date will be removed.

Create a suitable class that communicates with the data file (use serialization). The user interface in turn will communicate with this class.

Hint: use the MyDate class from programming problem 1, Chapter 8 (you'll find the solution at [URL Java book]).

Problem 4

Start with programming problem 2, Chapter 10, and make a GUI to maintain the registry. Decide on the design yourself.

Problem 5

Start with programming problem 5, Chapter 12, and make a GUI to maintain the cardkey registry. Decide on the design yourself.

Threads

Learning goals for this chapter

After completing this chapter, you will understand the meaning of:

- Thread and process

- Context switch

- The different states a thread can be in in Java

- Synchronization, in the context of threads in Java

You will be able to:

- Program simple threads in your programs

- Implement simple communication between them, like join and synchronization

---

When we start a program (for example, a Java program we have programmed ourselves), we often say that we are starting a *process* on the computer. Normally it's when we're studying the way the operating system internally organizes different programs that we say process. All modern data systems *multitask*. From the user's perspective, this means that several processes appear to be running concurrently. For example, if we have Windows NT we can run a word processing program and a browser at the same time on our PC. Now we'll see that we can have several operations that seem to run concurrently inside an individual program. We call these threads, and they get that name because we can look at these operations as bands of processing that exist side by side.

16.1 Threads in Processes

As a rule, small computers of the PC type have one processor, but you don't have to move up much in size before you encounter machines with more than one processor. When that's the case, the operating system—and in certain cases the programmer—have the job of distributing the different processes to the various processors so that they can be used in the best way possible.

If we have a computer with one processor, which multitasks, the operating system has the job of distributing the processor's time so that it works a little with one program, then a little with the next, etc. Because the processor is so fast, the user has the impression that the programs are running concurrently. When the processor switches from working with one program to another, this is called *context switching*. This uses a good deal of time and resources in relative terms, but there's not much to be done about that when one processor has to run many separate processes.

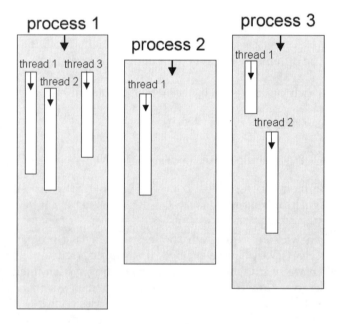

Figure 16.1 Processes and threads

Threads follow the same principle as multitasking on a slightly smaller scale. A *thread* is a miniprocess, which is part of a process. A process can contain several threads that run concurrently. In our context, that means that in a single Java program, we can have many small jobs that run at the "same" time. Many operating systems include threads as an integral component, and Java lets us make use of this. Figure 16.1 illustrates the concept. Think of the time axis as being oriented downwards so that the boxes' different heights indicate that processes and threads start and stop at uneven intervals. Each process can correspond to a Java program that is running its own interpreter.

The fact that we have numbered the processes is close to reality: in most systems, all processes are allotted a PID, *Process ID*. An important difference between a thread and a process is that the processes have their own version of a larger amount of information and resources. Both threads and processes have their set of variables, objects, and the like that are uniquely their own, but the processes have a great deal more. For the processes' part, this is information that has to be stored away every time there's a context switch. When the processor is going to finish spending time on one process and start on another, it needs to remember what the first one was doing when its turn comes around again. There's a similar problem for threads, but the point is that threads in a process usually have less of their own information and share more of the process's resources. Hence, a thread is sometimes referred to as a *lightweight process*, an LWP. Threads make it relatively easy and efficient for us to program multitasking in a program.

In many systems there is a distinction between system processes and user processes, and user threads and kernel threads, but we will not go into that.

For certain UNIX type operating systems, the process-thread model has been adjusted so that context switching for threads actually takes longer than context switching for processes, but we're sticking with a thread as a conceptual "small" process within a process.

All Java programs have at least one thread. For example, when we program GUIs, we use several threads without even knowing it. There is a single thread that keeps track of events that happen in the GUI, to name one. So, even if *we* program without threads, the final program can have several.

Threads in UML

The activity diagrams in UML can be used to visualize parallel jobs like this. If we imagine that at a given point in time a thread starts a new thread that it will later have to wait for, this can be visualized in UML as shown in Figure 16.2.

Figure 16.2 shows a thread that performs different activities (boxes). At a given time, thread number two is started and performs an operation before that side finishes. The time axis is vertical. The thick horizontal lines are an "intersection" where the program execution divides itself up into several threads, or where one or more threads end. The line where the program execution divides itself is called a *fork line*, fork being the designation for what is happening internally in an operating system when one process turns into two. We don't run into this concept in Java, but we'll see *join* soon. That is also the name of the line where two threads combine together into one. As a rule, this happens when one is waiting for the other to finish.

16.2 Dividing Time Between Threads

Because threads will share the time in a program, time has to be divided up in some manner. There are two ways a switch between two threads can take place: 1) A thread says that it can take a break for a while, or 2) A mechanism takes the program's attention away from the thread by force in one way or another. This is done differently from platform to platform, and that is extremely important to remember when working with threads. Newer Java interpreters for UNIX and Windows NT use the latter variant: the Java interpreter controls the division of time between the threads with a "firm hand". If the operating system the interpreter is running on has this kind of functionality built in, it is used. This is what is called *preemptive multitasking*: An external mechanism divides the time between the threads. "Preemptive" means preventing something by taking action.

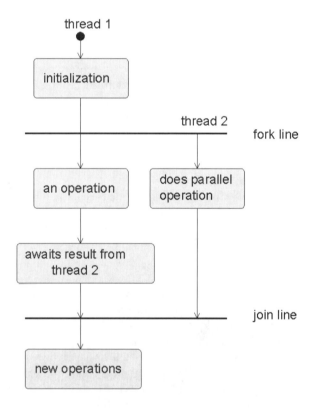

Figure 16.2 Running two threads (UML)

If we look at a platform where the Java interpreter does not have the same mechanism, such as in UNIX earlier, then it's dependent on the fact that all the threads cooperate on their own by giving up the baton at regular intervals. What happens if we have a thread that wasn't written with this in mind? Well, if it doesn't let others have a chance on its own, and the Java interpreter doesn't force it to, other threads don't get to run. As simple as that. The thread can be called selfish. Thread switching can occur now and then. For example, if one of the interpreter's internal system threads (which might be able to get priority over ours) has to run, one of ours can take its turn once it's done.

Java makes it straightforward for us to program threads that aren't selfish. We'll come back to that. It will be necessary to do this when we don't know what kind of platform our program will be used on.

16.3 Example of Threads in Use

We will look at an example, Program Listing 16.1, where we have five threads inside our program, and every thread is a small piece of code that runs in an endless loop and prints out a single number indefinitely. The five threads each write their own number.

Program Listing 16.1

```
/*
 * ShowerOfNumbers.java VBH 2001-08-12
 *
 */
class NumberPrinter extends Thread {
  private int numberToPrint;

  public NumberPrinter(int number) {
    numberToPrint = number;
  }

  public void run() {
    while (true) {
      System.out.print(numberToPrint);
      System.out.print(" ");
    }
  }
}
class ShowerOfNumbers {

  public static void main(String[] args) {
    NumberPrinter printer1 = new NumberPrinter(1);
    NumberPrinter printer2 = new NumberPrinter(2);
    NumberPrinter printer3 = new NumberPrinter(3);
    NumberPrinter printer4 = new NumberPrinter(4);
    NumberPrinter printer5 = new NumberPrinter(5);
    printer1.start();
    printer2.start();
```

```
        printer3.start();
        printer4.start();
        printer5.start();
    }
}
```

We have called the example ShowerOfNumbers because it outputs so many numbers to System.out. We see that, in addition to that class, we have a NumberPrinter class that subclasses the Thread class. This class has a method called run(), and that method is paramount when dealing with threads since the code that will be run in the thread is placed in such a method. In this example, it is the Thread objects' own run() that contains the code that will be run, but it can also be done another way that we will come back to.

Every instance of the NumberPrinter class bears the responsibility for outputting one number to System.out all the time. Every time it outputs a number, it is followed by a space character. We see that this happens in the run() method. It contains a loop of the type while (true). The loop runs endlessly. The constructor for the class takes an integer, the number the object will output. These threads are selfish. They output numbers as long as they can.

We see that five NumberPrinter objects are instantiated that will write the numbers 1 through 5. Then their start() method is called, which is the same as running the threads.

API Reference

The java.lang.Thread class

Method:

```
    public void run()
```

When we subclass Thread, we put the code that will be executed in run(), and when the thread is going to be run, start() is called. Don't call run() directly. start() does the initiating, and then starts run().

We will return to several methods in this class later in the chapter.

What happens when the program runs? We (and possibly you) get a printout similar to this:

```
    . . .

    3 3 3 3 3 3 3 3 3 3 3 3 3 3 3 3 3 3 3 3 3 3 3 3 3 3 3 3 3
    3 3 3 3 3 3 3 3 3 3 3 3 3 3 3 3 3 3 5 4 1 2 5 4 1 2 5 4 1
    2 5 4 1 2 5 4 1 2 5 4 1 2 41 2 41 2 41 2 41 2 41 2 41 2
    41 2 412 5 12 5 12 5 12 5 12 5 12 5 12 5 12 5 12 5
```

```
12  5  12  5  12  5  12  2  2  2  2  2  2  2  2  2  2  2  2  2  2  2  2  2  2  2
2  2  2  2  2  2  2  2  2  2  2  2  2  2  2  2  2  2  2  2  2  2  2  2  2  2  2  2
2  2  2  2  2  2  2  2  2  2  2  2  2  2  2  2  2  2  2  2  2  2  2  2  2  2  2  2
2  2  2  2  2  2  2  2  2  2  2  2  2  2  2  2  2  2  2  5  5  5  5  5  5  5  5  5
5  5  5  5  5  5  5  5  5  5  5  5  5  5  5  5  5  5  5  5  5  5  5  5  5  5  5  5
5  5  5  5  5  5  5  5  5  5  5  5  5  5  5  5  5  5  5  5  5  5  5  5  5  5  5  5
5  5  5  5  5  5  5  5  5  5  5  5  5  5  5  5  5  5  5  5  5  5  5  5  5  5  5  5
5  5  5  5  5  5  5  5  5  5  5  5  5  5  5  5  5  5  5  5  5  5  5  5  5  5  5  5
5  5  5  5  5  5  5  5  5  5  5  5  5  5  5  5  5  5  5  5  5  5  5  5  5  5  5  5
5  5  5  5  5  5  5  5  5  5  5  5  5  5  5  5  5  5  213  4  213  4  213  4  23
4  23  4  23  4  23  4  23  4  23  4  23  4  23  4  23  4  23  4  23  4  23  4
1  34  1  34  1  34  1  34  1  34  1  34  1  34  1  34  1  34  1  34  1  34  1
34  1  34  1  34  1  41  41  41  41  41  1  1  1  1  1  1  1  1  1  1  1  1  1
1  1  1  1  1  1  1  1  1  1  1
. . .
```

This is an excerpt from the output data for this program after it has run for a while. The first thing we notice is that this must have been run on a system where the interpreter is forced to divide time between the selfish threads. If not, we would only have seen thread switches very rarely, and it's quite possible we would only have seen one number.

The other thing we can observe is that there's no discernible system in the hail of numbers, and that illustrates an important point when we're working with threads: as long as we haven't set things up for the threads to cooperate, we can never assume anything about what kind of order the threads will run in. In principle, for example, there's no guarantee that the thread that writes "1" gets to run first, then the one that writes "2", and so on. We also never know when each thread will be terminated to make it the next one's turn. The only thing we can assume is that these five threads get to run for about the same amount of time once they've started, assuming that the Java interpreter divides the time. We have to pay attention to this when we are writing programs with threads.

The method the NumberPrinter objects are running writes its number and then a blank space. Based on the sample printout above, we can also observe that the threads don't necessarily get to run the method they are in to completion when they are interrupted. In a few spots, several numbers appear in a row without blank spaces between them. This means a thread was terminated between the statement that writes the number and the one that writes the space.

The example also illustrates the quality of threads that we pointed out in our introduction; the threads have their own data (like objects always have), but they also share the accessible portions of the program's data—other variables. The NumberPrinter objects' instance variables belong solely to the threads, in this example numberToPrint. Common data used by the threads is System.out, which is an instance variable of the System class. All the threads send the message println() to out.

Threads with Runnable

In Program Listing 16.1, we put the thread's code into the Thread objects' own method, run(). In that case, the Thread objects were created with a default constructor. However, we can also create a Thread with another object reference as its argument. Then it will be this object's run() that becomes the thread's code.

 A Thread can be created with another object as its argument for the constructor. Then this object's run() method is used, and the Thread object's run() isn't used for anything. The object we send in as an argument has to be an instance of a class that implements the Runnable interface.

From the point of view of many programmers, the main purpose of Runnable will be the following. If our thread objects are going to inherit from another class, we have problems, because then they can't inherit from Thread. We solve that by implementing the Runnable interface instead of subclassing Thread. Runnable contains the method run(), but not the rest of the methods we have seen, and classes that implement the interface are not threads. Therefore, they need to contain a Thread object, which is started. But as we've mentioned, these Thread objects can be created with another object as their argument, so that this object's run() method is called. Thus we have a connection between the thread that is started and our class. Study Program Listing 16.2.

Program Listing 16.2

```
/*
 * OurThread.java VBH 2001-08-12
 *
 */

class SuperClass {

}

class TheThread extends SuperClass implements Runnable {
  private Thread thread;

  public TheThread() {
    thread = new Thread(this);
    thread.start();
  }

  public void run() {
    while (true) {
      System.out.println("Am alive...");
    }
```

```
    }
  }
  class OurThread {

    public static void main(String[] args) {
      TheThread thr = new TheThread();
    }
  }
```

Here we see a very simple skeleton example. The `TheThread` class inherits from a superclass, `SuperClass`, so it can't also inherit from `Thread`. Instead it implements `Runnable` and has a `Thread` object `thread` inside. This is created with `this` as its argument—in other words, the pertinent instance of the class `TheThread`. That assures that it is *this* object's `run()` that is started when the thread is started. The rest of the examples in this chapter use the first method we learned, where we inherit from `Thread` directly.

API Reference

The java.lang.Runnable interface

Methods:

> public void run()

Instances of classes that implement this interface can be used as arguments when creating a `Thread`. The object's `run()` will then be the thread's code. To put it another way, when we create a `Thread` we can say to it, "Take this object and use the object's `run()` method instead of your own." This is useful when a class is going to "form" the thread—that is to say, contain `run()`—but can't subclass `Thread` itself.

Problem

Modify Program Listing 16.1 so that `Runnable` is used to actually print out the numbers.

16.4 Thread States

In Java, a thread in a program can be in five states:

- *New:* This is the state the thread is in before and while we are starting it by calling `start()`. Once we have created the `Thread` object, the thread is in this state. It can't do anything–we haven't started it yet. And we can't do anything other than call `start()`. Once `start()` is finished and `run()` begins, the thread leaves this state and changes over to Runnable.

- *Runnable:* The thread is alive and will run when it can. It's worth pointing out that this state doesn't necessarily mean that the thread is working and running. It can also be a thread that's able to run and which is thus a candidate for being started when a context switch occurs. So, both a thread that's running and a thread that has been stopped "against its will" by the interpreter are Runnable. The name of this state has no strong connection to the `Runnable` interface.

- *Blocked (not Runnable):* We will come back to the fact that threads can give themselves a break with the message `sleep()` or by sending the message `wait()` to any object. In addition, the thread enters this state if it, for example, has to wait for the user to enter something in a stream; this is generally called blocking IO (input/output).

- *Dead:* A thread enters this state when the `run()` method finishes on its own. When the thread is dead, it cannot be started again. A new `Thread` object has to be created. There is one big difference between a dead thread and a thread that is in the state New, and that is that the latter can be started.

Earlier methods for switching states

Earlier versions of the standard API for Java had some methods in the `Thread` class that were used to switch states for a thread. They are all deprecated because they could lead to the threads getting stuck while waiting for signs of life from each other. Hence these have been cut out to avoid a common source of errors. The methods `suspend()` and `resume()` are for taking a thread into and out of the Blocked state, and `stop()` to stop the thread by force before `run()` is finished.

`suspend()`, `resume()`, and `stop()` from the `java.lang.Thread` class should not be used, but you may encounter them in programs written for earlier versions of the Java API.

16.5 Communication Between Threads

We have seen that it's safest for a thread to think about other threads that might be running and let them have a chance. If not, the other threads are at the mercy of the hope that the Java interpreter has a mechanism that divides time, something that isn't always the case. A thread has the methods `sleep()` and `yield()` at its disposal to give itself a break and let others have a chance.

In code where we could benefit from making a short break in time, the `sleep()` method is often used. It's a class method in `Thread` that gives the current thread a break for a certain length of time. This can be a good way of adjusting the speed of a graphic animation—the thread sleeps a little before the next image is drawn.

We also have a method that can be used if a thread needs to wait until a certain other thread dies. The method is called `join()`, and now it's important to distinguish between the thread we are sending the message from and the thread we are sending the message to. If we find ourselves in a method in thread `thread1` and call `thread2.join()`, `thread1` will wait until `thread2` dies. The whole thing reminds us that the two threads are combined into one at an intersection. `thread1` only continues when `thread2` is finished. In the activity diagram in Figure 16.3, we have tried to illustrate this with some explanatory text inside the activity boxes.

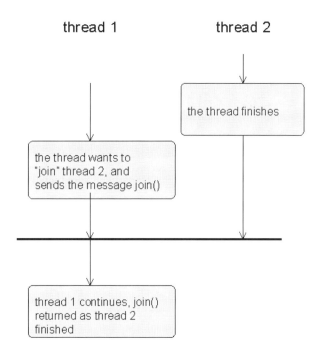

thread 1   thread 2

the thread finishes

the thread wants to "join" thread 2, and sends the message join()

thread 1 continues, join() returned as thread 2 finished

Figure 16.3 Joining Two Threads (UML)

So, what if we call `join()` on the same thread that we are in? Then the thread is waiting for itself to die, so we are risking that it might have to wait a very, very long time.

API Reference

The java.lang.Thread class

Class methods:

```
public static void sleep(long milliseconds)
public static void sleep(long milliseconds, int nanoseconds)
```

These class methods send the thread that is currently running into the Blocked state for a number of milliseconds, and possibly nanoseconds, that are arguments for the method. When the thread is Blocked, other threads get a turn.

```
public static void yield()
```

This method gives other threads a chance. When this class method is called from a thread, the thread doesn't switch states from Runnable, it just announces that it can take a break and if other threads are waiting, they get to run. `yield()` is much less drastic and comprehensive than `sleep()`.

Instance methods:

```
public final void join()
public final void join(long milliseconds)
public final void join(long milliseconds, int nanoseconds)
```

These methods make the thread sending the message come to a standstill until the thread receiving the message dies. We can also indicate a maximum number of milliseconds and nanoseconds that the calling thread can wait before it continues. It only makes sense to call a thread's `join()` from outside the thread.[1]

    `sleep()` and `join()` can throw exceptions of the `InterruptedException` type. We will explain this later.

    Several methods in this class are explained in Sections 16.3 and 16.7.

16.6 Locks and Synchronization

Synchronization is an important field in data processing and especially in programming. Now we have seen that a set of threads in a program has access to the program's other objects and classes, simultaneously. An important problem surfaces then—the unfortunate consequences that can arise from several threads working with the same object (that is to say, running methods), approximately at the same time. We know that it's possible for a thread to be interrupted in the middle of a method, so it can call a method in an object that it shares with other threads and is unable to finish. When it's been interrupted, other threads can call

1. This can definitely seem confusing!

the same method in the common object, but it cannot be assumed that everything is working properly there, because another thread has been stopped in the middle of a method.

In Figure 16.4 we have illustrated three threads that all send messages to the same object. We have called the method they are calling `printSequence()` because we will use it in an example shortly. It's possible for thread 2 to call the method before it's finished running for thread 1, and the classic synchronization problem (in Java form) is that the common object is in such a condition when thread 1 is interrupted that things are completely wrong after all the threads have finished with the method. In other words, the method won't tolerate being interrupted and having other threads in turn send the same message to the object.

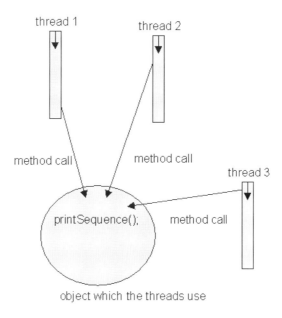

Figure 16.4 The synchronization problem

Program Listing 16.3

```
/*
 * ShowerOfNumbersSync.java VBH 1999-12-14
 *
 */
class SequencePrinter {

  public void printSequence() {
    System.out.print("1 ");
```

```
        System.out.print("2 ");
        System.out.print("3 ");
        System.out.print("4 ");
        System.out.print("5 ");
    }

}

class NumberPrinter extends Thread {
  private SequencePrinter thePrinter;

  public NumberPrinter(SequencePrinter printer) {
    thePrinter = printer;
  }

  public void run() {
    while (true) {
      thePrinter.printSequence();
    }
  }
}

class ShowerOfNumbersSync {
  public static void main(String[] args) {
    SequencePrinter aPrinter = new SequencePrinter();
    NumberPrinter printer1 = new NumberPrinter(aPrinter);
    NumberPrinter printer2 = new NumberPrinter(aPrinter);
    NumberPrinter printer3 = new NumberPrinter(aPrinter);
    NumberPrinter printer4 = new NumberPrinter(aPrinter);
    NumberPrinter printer5 = new NumberPrinter(aPrinter);
    printer1.start();
    printer2.start();
    printer3.start();
    printer4.start();
    printer5.start();
  }
}
```

Program Listing 16.3 shows program code for another shower of numbers. Once again we have five threads. What's new is that they use a common instance of the SequencePrinter class. This class has a method that writes the numbers 1 to 5 in order. It does this with five calls to System.out.print(). We will avoid doing the obvious (collecting this into a single call) to illustrate the point. When running this, the outcome will be similar to that below. We have extracted part of the job output after the program has run for a while. The very first number can be expected to be the number 1.

. . .

```
4 5 1 2 3 4 5 1 2 3 4 5 1 2 3 4 5 1 2 3 4 5 1 2 3 4 5 1
2 3 4 5 1 2 3 4 5 1 2 3 4 5 1 2 3 4 5 1 2 3 4 5 1 2 3 4
5 1 2 3 4 5 1 2 3 4 5 1 2 3 4 5 1 2 3 4 5 1 2 3 4 5 1 2
```

```
3 4 5 1 2 3 4 5 1 2 3 4 5 1 2 3 4 5 1 2 3 4 5 1 2 3 4 5
1 2 3 4 5 1 2 3 4 5 1 2 3 4 5 1 2 3 4 5 1 2 3 4 5 1 2 3
4 5 1 2 3 4 5 1 2 3 4 5 1 2 3 4 5 1 2 3 4 5 1 2 3 4 5 1
2 3 4 5 1 2 3 4 5 1 2 3 4 5 1 2 3 4 5 1 2 3 4 5 1 2 3 4
5 1 2 3 4 5 1 2 3 4 5 1 2 3 4 5 1 2 3 4 5 1 2 3 4 5 1 2
3 4 5 1 2 3 4 5 1 2 3 4 5 1 2 3 4 5 1 2 3 4 5 1 2 3 4 5
1 2 3 4 5 1 2 3 4 5 1 2 3 4 5 1 2 3 4 5 1 2 3 4 2 2 1 1
5 3 3 2 2 1 4 4 3 3 2 5 5 4 4 3 1 1 5 5 4 2 2 1 1 5 3 3
2 2 1 4 3 3 2 5 4 4 3 1 5 5 4 2 1 1 5 3 2 2 1 4 3 3 2 5
4 4 3 1 5 5 4 2 1 1 5 3 2 1 4 3 2 5 4 3 1 5 4 2 1 5 3 2
1 4 3 2 5 4 3 1 5 4 2 1 5 3 2 1 4 3 2 5 4 3 1 5 4 2 1 5
3 2 1 4 3 2 5 4 3 1 5 4 2 1 5 3 2 1 4 3 2 5 4 3 1 5 4 2
1 5 3 2 1 4 3 2 5 4 3 1 5 4 2 1 5 3 2 1 4 3 2 5 4 3 1 5
4 2 1 5 3 2 1 4 3 2 5 4 3 1 5 4 2 1 5 3 2 1 4 3 2 5 4 3
1 5 4 2 1 5 3 2 1 4 3 2 5 4 3 1 5 4 2 1 5 3 2 1 4 3 2 5
4 3 1 5 4 2 1 5 3 2 1 4 3 2 5 4 3 1 5 4 2 1 5 3 2 1 4 3
2 5 4 3 1 5 4 2 1 5 3 2 1 4 3 2 5 4 3 1 5 4 2 1 5 3 2 1
4 3 2 5 4 3 1 5 4 2 1 5 3 2 1 4 3 2 4 3 5 4 1 5 2 1 3 2
4 3 5 4 1 5 2 1 3 2 4 3
. . .
```

We see that little by little, the number sequences become incorrect, and now we know why. The threads are being interrupted in the middle of their calls to printSequence() and other threads are coming in and starting again. Now, what if this was serious? If it is critical that the program only outputs 1 2 3 4 5 in the correct order, then the problem is clear. What we have to do is ensure that the method gets to run all the way to the end before other threads can call it, and the modifier synchronized takes care of this. If we put synchronized before the method, we are ensured that it will get to run to completion before any other thread can call the same method or any of the object's other synchronized methods.

One thing that's important to remember is that synchronized does not guard against the method being interrupted by a context switch. That can happen. What we are protected from is the method being interrupted and started again from another thread, or starting another of the object's synchronized methods.

When a thread gets a turn and is able to run a synchronized method, we say that it has the object's *lock*—it locks everything that is synchronized in the object to other threads.

If we synchronize the printSequence() method in our example, we get the output we want:

```
public synchronized void printSequence() {
  System.out.print("1 ");
  System.out.print("2 ");
  System.out.print("3 ");
  System.out.print("4 ");
```

```
        System.out.print("5 ");
    }
```

This results in this output, which is never wrong:

```
1 2 3 4 5 1 2 3 4 5 1 2 3 4 5 1 2 3 4 5 1 2 3 4 5 1 2 3
4 5 1 2 3 4 5 1 2 3 4 5 1 2 3 4 5 1 2 3 4 5 1 2 3 4 5 1
2 3 4 5 1 2 3 4 5 1 2 3 4 5 1 2 3 4 5 1 2 3 4 5 1 2 3 4
5 1 2 3 4 5 1 2 3 4 5 1 2 3 4 5 1 2 3 4 5 1 2 3 4 5 1 2
3 4 5 1 2 3 4 5 1 2 3 4 5 1 2 3 4 5 1 2 3 4 5 1 2 3 4 5
1 2 3 4 5 1 2 3 4 5 1 2 3 4 5 1 2 3 4 5 1 2 3 4 5 1 2 3
4 5 1 2 3 4 5 1 2 3 4 5 1 2 3 4 5 1 2 3 4 5 1 2 3 4 5 
. . .
```

We have synchronized the access to our instance of the `SequencePrinter` class: one thread gets to call the `printSequence()` method at a time and all the others that want to must wait until the lock is free.

Using `synchronized` will slow down our program run a little. The Java interpreter has to initiate a mechanism of its own to synchronize the methods, so this isn't without a certain cost in performance.

We can also synchronize blocks of code inside a method. Then we also have the ability to specify which object's lock will be taken. We mention this briefly in the following Java Core box.

Java Core

Synchronizing methods

Syntax:

```
accessModifier synchronized returnType methodName() {
    contents
}
```

The `synchronized` modifier before a method synchronizes the method.

This ensures us that only one thread will be able to run this method for a given object at a time. If it's a class method, `static`, we are ensured that only one thread will run the method at a time. In addition, no other synchronized methods for this object or this class will be able to start.

Synchronizing blocks

Syntax:

```
synchronized (object) {
    contents
}
```

We can also synchronize a block of code—that is to say, a unit smaller than a method.

When a thread comes to this block, it has to have the specified object's lock before it starts. Usually the block will perform operations on the same object, but this isn't any kind of requirement. It will be the same as if the contents of the block were in a method that belonged to the specified object.

Problem

Modify Program Listing 16.3 so that you use block synchronization instead of synchronizing the method.

16.7 More Control: wait(), notify(), and notifyAll()

Java provides us with even more control for synchronizing and locking objects than what we have seen thus far. Suppose a thread has the lock for an object—in other words, that it's inside one of the object's synchronized portions. Suppose, furthermore, that it comes to a point in the method where it's necessary to wait for a thread to make some changes in the object first. In other words, another thread should have been in here first. But, of course, no other threads get a chance. That's why we have the wait() method. When we use that, the thread relinquishes the object's lock and sends itself into the blocked state. So it stops there. If any other threads are waiting, one of them then gets a turn and the first thread ends up in a waiting queue. The methods that can wake up a thread that has run wait() are notify() and notifyAll().

API Reference

The java.lang.Object class

Methods:

```
public void wait()
public void wait(long milliseconds)
public void wait(long milliseconds, int nanoseconds)
```

These methods relinquish this object's lock, possibly for a specific amount of time, at the same time that the execution of code in the calling thread is stopped.

```
public void notify()
```

This method wakes up a thread that has called wait() for this object. Then it will have the opportunity to continue where it left off.

```
public void notifyAll()
```

This method wakes up all the threads that have called wait() for this object. A maximum of one of them gets to take the object's lock.

A thread that has called `wait()` for an object is not automatically awakened when no other threads are working with the object, so `notify()` or `notifyAll()` *must* be called.

The methods are declared in `java.lang.Object`, and are consequently inherited by all classes.

`wait()` throws an `InterruptedException`, which has to be caught. We will come back to this shortly.

Why is `notifyAll()` necessary when only one can take the object's lock anyway? A typical situation is that several threads are waiting for the object's lock, but not for the same reason. One thread has sent the object the message `wait()` anticipating one change in the object, another thread has sent the message for another reason. We can imagine that in due course all the newly awakened threads check on whether the thing they are waiting for has been fulfilled, and a thread that already has what it wants will continue.

When a thread calls `wait()`, as we've mentioned, it's usually because it needs to give other threads a chance to change the object's condition. So, it's natural that as soon as it's awakened it checks yet again whether this condition has changed, and if not uses `wait()` again. This is the case in the example we have illustrated this with. It's still a meaningless output example, this time with a text. If you study the example carefully, you will be in a position to understand the use of the mechanisms `wait()` and `notify()`.

The example in Program Listing has five threads of the `TextPrinter` class and one instance of the `Printer` class. The threads share this one instance as before. The `Printer` class has a method that prints a text. The user can input what the text will be, and it is set by a method `newTextFromUser()`.

Program Listing 16.4

```
/*
 * ShowerOfText.java VBH 2001-08-12
 *
 */

import javax.swing.JOptionPane;
/*
 * Objects of this class print out a given text.
 */
class Printer {
  private String textToPrint = "";

  public synchronized void newTextFromUser() {
    /* Reads a new text through dialog box */
    textToPrint = JOptionPane.showInputDialog("Enter new text: ");
    if (!textToPrint.equals("")) {
      notifyAll();
```

```
        }
      }
      /* The method prints the object's text, if it's not empty. If it
       * is, wait() is called, to wait for another thread to insert a text.
       */
      public synchronized void printText() {
        while (textToPrint.equals("")) {
          try {
            wait();
          } catch (InterruptedException e) {
          }
        }
        System.out.print("Text is: ");
        System.out.println(textToPrint);
        notifyAll(); // Finished, may wake the others.
      }
    }


    class TextPrinter extends Thread {
      private Printer thePrinter;

      public TextPrinter(Printer printer) {
        thePrinter = printer;
      }

      public void run() {
        while (true) {
          thePrinter.printText();
        }
      }
    }

    public class ShowerOfText {
      public static void main(String[] args) {
        Printer aPrinter = new Printer();
        TextPrinter printer1 = new TextPrinter(aPrinter);
        TextPrinter printer2 = new TextPrinter(aPrinter);
        TextPrinter printer3 = new TextPrinter(aPrinter);
        TextPrinter printer4 = new TextPrinter(aPrinter);
        TextPrinter printer5 = new TextPrinter(aPrinter);
        printer1.start();
        printer2.start();
        printer3.start();
        printer4.start();
        printer5.start();
        aPrinter.newTextFromUser();
      }
    }
```

```
/* Printout from this program is nothing, until the user has entered a
 * text in the dialog box. After that, that text is printed time and again.
 */
```

Informally, we can summarize the program execution this way:

All five of the threads send the message `printText()` to the object `aPrinter` all the time. However, that method is written such that nothing is written as long as the registered text is empty, "". Therefore, we have a `while` loop that checks whether the text is different from "". As long as it is, `wait()` is called so that the thread waits.

It does that until something calls `notify()` or `notifyAll()`, and that doesn't happen soon in this example. So what probably happens first is that all five of the threads go right into `wait()`, because the object `aPrinter` is initiated with "" as its text.

Finally, at the same time, in `main()` we call the method in `aPrinter` that inputs a new text. A dialog box will appear on the screen. As soon as the input is done, the method does a `notifyAll()`. That wakes up all the threads, which each continue in their own `while` loop, but they immediately find out that now the object has a text that is not equal to "", if the user didn't enter an empty text again.

With that, the threads get started, writing this text over and over again. Even if it doesn't show in the output, it's one thread at a time that gets a chance in the `aPrinter` object. When one is finished outputting, `notifyAll()` is called to alert the others and give another one a chance.

Interrupting wait(), sleep(), and join()

We remember that these methods threw an `InterruptedException`, which we have to catch. All three calls have in common the fact that we can easily think of cases where the threads get stuck for a long time—maybe longer than we'd like, and therefore all the threads have a method called `interrupt()`. If it's called, the thread ends up in a type of substate, *interrupted*. The thread that receives the `interrupt()` message can either wait in a `wait()`, `sleep()`, or `join()`, or not.

If the thread is waiting in a `wait()`, `sleep()`, or `join()`, the waiting is interrupted and an `InterruptedException` is thrown. This leads to the thread immediately leaving the interrupted state again. Effectively, what we've done is to wake the thread up from a deadlocked condition.

When it receives `interrupt()` (if the thread doesn't wait in one of the three methods, but continues working as usual), it still ends up in the interrupted state. If that's the case, we can check whether anything else has called `interrupt()` and put the thread in the interrupted state by calling the thread's `isInterrupted()`. We can also check whether the thread that's running right now is interrupted using the `interrupted()` class method. It is only the latter that sends the thread out of the interrupted state. If we send a thread the message `isInterrupted()` to check, it remains interrupted.

In connection with the calls to `sleep()`, `wait()`, and `join()`, we add code in the `catch` statement in the usual way to handle the exception that the threads are interrupted. If we use `interrupt()` in our programs, it is important that we make sure that the threads that are interrupted bear the consequences of this.

API Reference

The java.lang.Thread class

Methods:

    public void interrupt()

This method gives this thread a signal to interrupt the waiting that it might be doing.

    public boolean isInterrupted()

A method that tests whether this thread (this `Thread` object) has received the message `interrupt()`. The method doesn't change the thread's interrupted state.

    public static boolean interrupted()

This class method checks if the thread that is running now has received the message `interrupt()`. If the thread is in the interrupted state when the method is called, it now leaves the state.

You'll find several methods in this class in Sections 16.3 and 16.5.

As we have outlined it here, `interrupt()` will primarily be a tool for interrupting threads that have become hung up and are waiting. But sending `interrupted()` to a thread can also be seen as a request for the thread to stop running—in other words, the thread's `run()` will quit. If we plan for the `interrupt()` message to have this meaning, all threads have to check frequently whether they have received this message, and be able to react to it by terminating themselves.

16.8 Peeking at the Threads with JDB

The tool Java Debugger (JDB) is a part of the SDK that we haven't used yet. However, it's handy for getting some insight into what types of threads are running and the state they are in. We will use it to look at the details of the program `ShowerOfText`.

A *debugger* is a tool that allows us as developers to start a program we are working with and run it step by step, keeping up with the contents of an individual variable, or stopping it at a given location. A debugger has many other areas of application besides looking at threads, which is what we are going to do now. JDB is a text-based tool, but integrated development tools often have a graphical debugger, where we can follow along line by line where the program is in its run. With JDB, we can start by running a class exactly as when we are running a program the usual way. Then we can start and stop the program along the way, look at what kinds of threads are running, and much more. Let's take an example, point by point, and assume that we are running in an MS-DOS window:

1. We start debugging `ShowerOfText` by running JDB on the class we are going to work with:

   ```
   c:\javaprogrammer> jdb ShowerOfText
   ```

2. Notice how similar this is to starting the program in the usual manner. The program will send a message that it has been initiated and then produce this output:

   ```
   0xaa:class(ShowerOfText)
   >
   ```

3. That means that the class is loaded, and that JDB is now waiting for input from you. If you write *help* or *?*, you get a help text about legal commands for JDB. Try it.

4. Run the program with *run*. In a while the dialog box will come up as it would if you were running the program normally. It's not so strange that it's going so slowly—after all, the whole run is taking place in the framework of JDB.

5. When you see the dialog box, go into the JDB window and write *threads* to see which threads are running then and there. Those last two steps give a printout like this:

   ```
   > run
   run ShowerOfText
   running ...
   main[1] threads
   Group ShowerOfText.main:
   1. (sun.tools.agent.MainThread)0xe1 main cond. waiting
   2. (java.awt.EventDispatchThread)0xe4 AWT-EventQueue-0
   cond. waiting
   3. (sun.awt.PostEventQueue)0xe6 PostEventQueue-0 cond.
   waiting
   4. (java.lang.Thread)0xe7 AWT-Windows running
   5. (TextPrinter)0xe9 Thread-1 waiting in a monitor
   6. (TextPrinter)0xea Thread-2 waiting in a monitor
   7. (TextPrinter)0xeb Thread-3 waiting in a monitor
   8. (TextPrinter)0xec Thread-4 waiting in a monitor
   9. (TextPrinter)0xed Thread-5 waiting in a monitor
   ```

```
10. (sun.awt.ScreenUpdater)0xef Screen Updater cond.
waiting
11. (java.lang.Thread)0xf0 TimerQueue cond. waiting
main[1]
```

6. We see that the *threads* command gives us 11 threads. We don't understand all of this, but we manage to recognize the five `Printer` threads in the program as the threads 5 to 9. It says that these threads are waiting in a *monitor*. Basically, this is another word for a lock. At the same time, we see some of the Java interpreter's internal threads that we have mentioned. The ones with `awt` in the name all belong to the graphical user interface. After all, we're looking at a dialog box here.

Problem

Do a similar investigation using JDB on one of the other programs in this chapter, and also on the same program as in the example: `ShowerOfText`.

16.9 New Concepts in This Chapter

Concept	Brief Explanation
context switch	When the computer changes from one process to another, or from one thread to another.
debugger	Utility for running a program during development while at the same time keeping an eye on the values of variables, which threads are started, and many other things. You can also start and stop the program along the way.
fork	When a process creates a new one, so that we end up with two.
interrupted	State when a thread receives the message `interrupt()`, as a request that it should stop waiting for other threads or sleeping. If desirable, it can also be interpreted as a request for the thread to stop running. The thread itself then has to take responsibility for this.
join	When two threads/processes "meet," one waiting for the other one finish. Done by sending the message `join()` to a thread in Java.
lock	A logical concept for something a thread gets when it gains access to a synchronized resource. Only one thread can have the lock at a time.
LWP	Lightweight process. Another term for "thread".
monitor	Another word for lock.
multitasking	When a computer seems to do many things at the same time. Often the lone microprocessor in a small computer does all this by changing from task to task.
PID	Process ID. An identification number that all processes are allotted by the operating system.
preemptive multitasking	An external mechanism—like, for example, the computer's operating system—controls the distribution of time between the threads and/or processes.

Concept	Brief Explanation
selfish thread	A thread that never voluntarily lets other threads have a chance.
synchronization	In this context: to implement a mechanism such that only one thread has access to a resource at a time.
synchronized	Modifier that indicates that a method will be synchronized. That means that as soon as a thread calls the method, no other thread can call it or any of the other synchronized methods for the object in question. `synchronized` can also be used before a block of code that is delimited by { and }. Then the block will be synchronized.
thread	A small process inside a process. Inside a Java program we have many threads, and we can make our own too. See also the table of concepts at the end of chapter 1.

16.10 Review Problems

1. What is a thread? What is it for?

2. What distinguishes a thread from a process?

3. Use an example to explain why synchronization can be important.

4. What is a debugger?

16.11 Programming Problem

Problem 1

Write a small program that starts more and more threads endlessly. It may be a little like Program Listing 16.1, but use a loop instead of making five objects explicitly. For example, put all the threads in an array list as you make them. This ensures that they are not cleaned up by the garbage collection.

Preferably add a little time delay between each time you make and start a new thread object. You do this by calling `Thread.sleep(500);` for 500 milliseconds. The call to the class method makes the current thread go to sleep. Remember that you have to catch `InterruptedException`.

Study the computer's behavior when you start this program. Here you can gain a little insight into how many threads the operating system and the machine can tackle before the performance is seriously affected.

Data Structures and Algorithms

Learning goals for this chapter

After completing this chapter, you will:

- Be able to recognize the following data structures: graphs, lists, and trees as well as simple algorithms for them

- Know what the Java API gives you to work with in this context

- Know what a hashtable is

When we introduced object-orientation earlier in the book, we emphasized that an object contains data and ancillary algorithms in a single structure. We consider this a means of preventing errors in the programs we write, since we have a high degree of control over how data is treated and changed. This is as opposed to having, for example, *global variables* in our programming language. Global variables are data that can be accessed from anywhere in the program system. In this case, there is a low degree of control over where and how this data is changed. Programmers have a great deal to keep track of, and serious errors can occur quickly.

Algorithms are "a limited and orderly set of well-defined rules for solving a problem."[1] In other words, algorithms are the way we solve problems, the kind of idea that serves as the basis for a bit of program code. See also Section 2.3.

Algorithm theory is not tied to any specific form of programming language, such as object-oriented languages. The way we solve problems is constantly in motion, moving over and under the systematism found in the language itself. Language becomes a tool for implementing an algorithm. Something algorithm theory *is* strongly linked to, on the other hand, is advanced data structures. In this chapter we will study some of these data structures, and also go through some of the central algorithms that apply in conjunction with them.

---

1. [Hofstad, Løland, Scott 1997, p. 19]

17.1 Graphs

In the Java language, we operate with primitive variables, arrays, classes, and objects. As a point of departure, this is what we have to work with for storing data in the memory, and we do fine with it thanks to encapsulation in classes. A given object can contain quite a bit of strange data that, from the outside, you avoid knowing the details of, but simply send the object the defined messages. Array lists illustrate this point: a array list is an object that serves as a container for many other objects, and putting data into it and extracting data from it presupposes that we can use the `ArrayList` class. However, array lists are usually used as "internals" for classes that we then use in our program. We have illustrated a scenario like this in Figure 17.1.

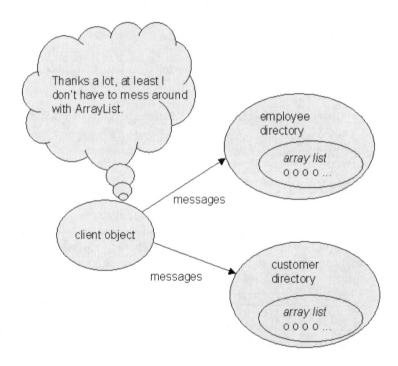

Figure 17.1   Encapsulation

Figure 17.1 shows a client object that is happy to avoid having to use an `ArrayList`. That is done inside the classes for the employee and customer directories. We see that the client object simply sends a few "nice" messages to the objects in question.

The data structures we will look at now will be somewhat similar to array lists—slightly elaborate things that nonetheless have qualities that will make them useful to us.

Definition of graphs

A *graph* is formally defined as a collection of *vertices* and *edges*. The edges connect the vertices so that the graph becomes a network. The vertices are also called *nodes*. Graphs are easy to visualize—that's one of their great advantages.

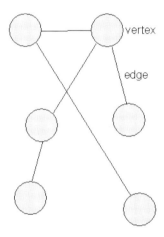

Figure 17.2 Graph

Figure 17.2 shows a simple graph with six vertices and five edges. This simple data structure has countless applications. We will name just a few:

- Visualizing a data network. We can view the vertices as computers or units in a data network, and the edges as the communication between them. Graph theory algorithms are used in the Internet's infrastructure to route traffic the fastest way available.

- Logistics. We can view the vertices as cities and the edges as roads between them. A transport company would be interested in knowing the shortest path between two cities.

- Formal mapping of an object-oriented program system. The vertices can be objects and the edges connections to other objects (i.e., object references). The graph tells us which objects are sending messages to which other objects. This application will presuppose that the graph is "directed", one of several terms we will define now.

Normally we add more elements to the very simple data structure we just presented. The graph is often defined as *directed*, which is to say that the edges have a direction, which we represent visually with arrows. Be careful not to confuse this with the arrows in UML. Some of the figures in UML can be viewed as graphs, but in this chapter, we are illustrating graphs in general. In a directed graph, an edge represents a unidirectional connection between two vertices. If the connection is going to be bi-directional, we use two edges, one for each direction.

It's also possible to use a value for each edge, called a *weight*. It could be a number that represents time use in the data communication, the distance between the cities, etc. When we introduce these additions, the graph might look like Figure 17.3.

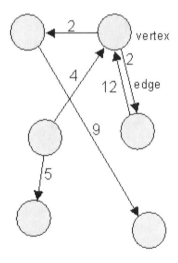

Figure 17.3 Directed and weighted graph

When we go to work with graphs in practice, the vertices and edges will also need some type of identifiers.

17.2 Lists

We looked at arrays and array lists earlier. These are data structures for data that can be ordered sequentially one after the other. With arrays, we also had multidimensional cases—for example, two-dimensional arrays. But that was an array where every element was a new array.

For every data structure of this type, there are some operations that it makes sense to perform:

- We want to add data into the data structure, be it first, last, or in a specific position. With arrays, this was easy. It was just a matter of using an index to specify a position in the array.

- In addition, we can imagine wanting to sort the data structure by one criterion or another. In that case it would be appropriate to put an element in the right place in terms of the sorting.

- We want to remove a given element from the data structure.

- We want to go through the elements in the data structure, for example in connection with a search, or if we want to print out all the data.

One such data structure or graph form you often encounter in programming is *lists* or *linked lists*. These are graphs that can be drawn in a straight line and are used as storage for data. The data is inside the vertices in this graph and it is no great secret that in practical terms they are objects in Java. The storage size is variable as are the number of vertices. Here we can see clear similarities with arrays and array lists. But there are some differences that are significant to performance.

We have chosen to call the vertices in a linked list "elements" to be consistent with much of the other literature and the term we use in conjunction with arrays. Furthermore, the links in a linked list can also be referred to as references when we implement them in Java as references between objects.

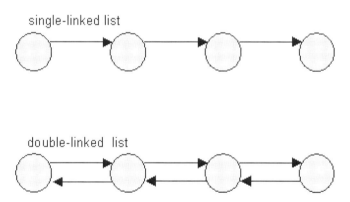

Figure 17.4 Single-linked and double-linked lists

The links in this type of list tell us something about how we can move when we deal with the list. Namely, we can't get hold of a given element directly in a linked list the way we can in arrays. As a rule, we will only know where the start and maybe the end are, since seen from the outside, we have a reference to where the first and possibly the last element are.

We distinguish between single-linked and double-linked lists, according to whether the list runs in one or both directions.

Figure 17.4 shows one of each type, both with four elements. The point to a double link is that we can easily access a given vertex's predecessor.

Now we'll delve into the operations that we mentioned in our introduction:

- Adding a new element to the list. If we want to add an element to the end, the current final element also needs a reference (a new arrow in Figure 17.4) to the new one. If it's a double-linked list, the new element needs a reference back to the preceding element.

- Deleting an element from the list. When this happens, the references have to be manipulated such that you link "around" the element that's going to be removed. This operation will typically be quick in linked lists, because we are only moving some references and not moving or copying objects.

- Searching for a given element in the list. A possible result from a search will be a reference to the right element if it's found, `null` otherwise. We may instead want a `boolean` value as a result to indicate whether or not the element we were searching for was found in the list.

- Sorting the list by, for example, last name, if every element is an object that contains a `String lastName`.

How will we do this with the references between the objects in practice? Here is an example of that for a single-linked list. First we need a class for each one of the elements the list contains, then a class that comprises the list itself.

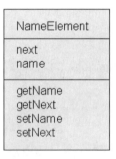

Figure 17.5 Class diagram (UML)

Figure 17.5 shows a class diagram for one such class, `NameElement`. Every element in the linked list will be an instance of this class. The source code is shown in Program Listing 17.1.

Program Listing 17.1

```
/*
 * NameElement.java VBH 2001-08-13
 *
 * The class is to be an element in a single-linked list containing
 * some names.
 *
 */

class NameElement {
  private NameElement next;
  private String name;

  public NameElement(String initName) {
    name = initName;
    next = null;
  }

  public NameElement(String initName, NameElement initNext) {
    name = initName;
    next = initNext;
  }

  public String getName() {
    return name;
  }

  public NameElement getNext() {
    return next;
  }

  public void setName(String newName) {
    name = newName;
  }

  public void setNext(NameElement newNext) {
    next = newNext;
  }
}
```

The class contains only two instance variables: a text name, which is the data that is linked to each element, and a reference to a new instance of the NameElement class. In addition, we have get and set methods, as well as a small selection of constructors. What may seem surprising here is that we have a reference to an instance of the same class that the reference is in, but that's fine. Every object has data, in this case a text, and a reference to the next element in the list. For the last element in the list, the next value is null. It stops there. Figure 17.6 shows how the reference next points on to the next element in the list.

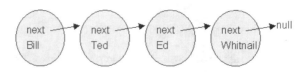

Figure 17.6 Four instances of the `NameElement` class in a list

So where does the whole thing start? How does the class that surrounds the whole list come to be? We show it in Figure 17.7 and Program Listing 17.2.

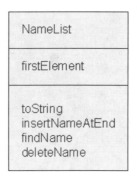

Figure 17.7 Class diagram (UML)

Program Listing 17.2

```
/*
 * NameList.java VBH 2001-08-13
 *
 * The class encapsulates a linked list where each element contains a text.
 *
 */
class NameList {
  private NameElement firstElement;

    /*The method returns the contents of the list in textual form. */
    public String toString() {
      String listText = "";
      NameElement auxReference = firstElement;
      while (auxReference != null) {
        listText = listText + auxReference.getName() + "\n";
        auxReference = auxReference.getNext();
```

```
    }
    return listText;
  }

  public void insertNameAtEnd(String newName) {
    NameElement auxReference = firstElement;
    NameElement auxReferenceRightBehind = null;
    /* We start by moving to the end of the list. */
    while (auxReference != null) {
      auxReferenceRightBehind = auxReference;
      auxReference = auxReference.getNext();
    }
    if (auxReferenceRightBehind == null ) {
      /* This happens if the list was empty from before. */
      firstElement = new NameElement(newName);
    } else {
      /*
       * This happens if there was at least one element in the list
       * from before. auxReferenceRightBehind is now referring to
       * the last element.
       */
      auxReferenceRightBehind.setNext(new NameElement(newName));
    }
  }

  public boolean findName(String textToFind) {
    NameElement auxReference = firstElement;
    while (auxReference != null) {
      if (auxReference.getName().equals(textToFind)) return true;
      auxReference = auxReference.getNext();
    }
    return false;
  }

  /*
   * This method deletes all occurrences of the given text from the
   * list.
   */
  public void deleteName(String nameToDelete) {
    NameElement auxReference = firstElement;
    NameElement auxReferenceRightBehind = null;

    /* We start by iterating through the list. */
    while (auxReference != null) {
      if (auxReference.getName().equals(nameToDelete)) {
        /*
         * auxReference is referring to an element to be removed. We
         * need a special case if this is the first element in the list.
         */
        if (auxReferenceRightBehind != null) {
```

```
        auxReferenceRightBehind.setNext(auxReference.getNext());
      } else {
        firstElement = auxReference.getNext();
      }
      auxReference = auxReference.getNext();
    } else {
      auxReferenceRightBehind = auxReference;
      auxReference = auxReference.getNext();
    }
  }
 }
}
```

The `NameList` class has a very simple set of operations. We can print out all the elements in the list, add a new name to the end of the list, search to find out if a specific name is in the list, and remove all occurrences of a specific name from the list.

Most of the operations on lists like this take place using a help reference of the same type as the elements in the list. Using that, we jump from element to element by using `getNext()` on the objects.

Also notice that a `while` loop is being used because we don't know the number of elements in advance. With arrays, we usually know the number of elements and then we use `for`.

There's a test program for the class in Program Listing 17.3.

Program Listing 17.3

```java
/*
 * NameListTest.java VBH 2001-08-13
 *
 * Test client for the class NameList.
 *
 */

class NameListTest {

  public static void main(String[] args) {
    NameList aList = new NameList();
    System.out.println("Printout of empty list: ");
    System.out.println(aList.toString());
    aList.insertNameAtEnd("Larry");
    aList.insertNameAtEnd("Winston");
    System.out.println("Printout of two men: ");
    System.out.println(aList.toString());
    System.out.println("Is Bucky in the list: " + aList.findName("Bucky"));
    System.out.println("Is Larry in the list: " + aList.findName("Larry"));
    System.out.println("Is Winston in the list: " + aList.findName("Winston"));
    System.out.println("Inserts an extra Larry...");
    aList.insertNameAtEnd("Larry");
```

```
        System.out.println("Printout with two Larries: ");
        System.out.println(aList.toString());
        System.out.println("Deleting Larry and Winston...");
        aList.deleteName("Larry");
        aList.deleteName("Winston");
        System.out.println("Printout of empty list: ");
        System.out.println(aList.toString());
    }
}
/* Example Run:
Printout of empty list:

Printout of two men:
Larry
Winston

Is Bucky in the list: false
Is Larry in the list: true
Is Winston in the list: true
Inserts an extra Larry...
Printout with two Larries:
Larry
Winston
Larry

Deleting Larry and Winston...
Printout of empty list:

*/
```

So, you may ask yourself what the point to a linked list is, when we have arrays and array lists with approximately the same functionality. It is a matter of efficiency, in specific situations. Take the operation of deleting an element from the middle of the list. For a array, first you have to remove the element you're going to get rid of, then the ones that come after it have to be copied back into place. This is because the elements are located next to each other in the computer's memory.

To remove an element from a linked list, we just adjust the next reference for the previous element to point past the one that is being removed. This is significantly faster and that can be important if there is a large amount of data.

On the other hand, if we are going to access an element in the list frequently from a specified position, then it actually goes quite slowly since all we can do is keep moving forward until we come to the right one. So if the performance is important for the operation of accessing element number n, an array list will be a far more suitable data structure.

It's not easy to understand the type of reference manipulation that the NameList class makes by simply studying the program list, so we recommend the following problems.

Problems

1. Use a pen and paper and sketch what happens when we remove an element from a linked list. Remember that it's a matter of "linking past" the element that's being removed.

2. Use a pen and paper. Start with a sketch of the list like the one in Figure 17.4 and draw in where the references `auxReference` and `auxReferenceRightBehind` point to at each point during the run of the methods in the `NameList` class. At any rate, do this for the methods `insertNameAtEnd()` and `deleteName()`.

3. Expand our example so that the list is double-linked. Every element then has to have a reference to `previous`. The `deleteName()` method changes. Make this change.

17.3 The Solution: Collection, List, and LinkedList

We looked at a code example for a very simple single-linked list with only a few operations. We can think of many desirable expansions. For example:

- Possibility of adding an element first in the list, or to a specific position in the list

- Possibility of finding the number of elements in the list

- Possibility of putting the contents of one list into another list

We could have done some of these expansions in our example relatively easily. Others would have taken more time. We will use the time to look at the Java API's possibilities instead. Even if we're tying the classes and interfaces to our example here, they have many other applications.

Collection

We find the `Collection` interface in the `java.util` package. Classes that implement this interface have the characteristics of a collection of elements of different types. In and of itself the interface doesn't say anything about how this collection is organized or what types of objects it consists of. The interface dictates some methods that this type of collection of elements must provide.

Such collections of elements can theoretically be divided into four, depending on two parameters: whether several objects in the collection can be the same or not, and whether the collection is ordered in any way. "Ordered" means that the elements can be viewed in a specific order.

In Figure 17.8 we see that there are four different "outcomes" when we have these two parameters. We have mentioned one type of collection for each outcome. We'll come back to what a hashtable is.

	Ordered	Not ordered
Duplicates allowed	List	Multiset
Duplicates not allowed	Hashtable (the table itself in many cases)	Set

Figure 17.8 Collections that are ordered or not ordered, and with and without duplicates

The Java API's own `Collection` interface is so general that it fits in all the variants. Of course, the collection may not contain multiple references to precisely the same object since it's either going to contain this element or not. Furthermore, it *may* be that you can't add a reference to an object that has identical data as an object that is already in the collection from before. When this is the case, then typically `newObject.equals(anObject)` will be `true` where `newObject` is the object we're trying to add a reference to, and `anObject` is some object or other that was in the collection from before. This presupposes that `equals()` is implemented for the applicable classes. The result is that the collection contains only different elements. On the other hand, it may be applicable to permit duplicates of this type.

Normally it isn't reference similarity that determines whether something will be removed or whether a search is successful, but similarity between the content of the objects, determined by the `equals()` method. `equals()` has to be implemented for the class in question. The standard version from `Object` only checks reference similarity. We can imagine an example with texts, where we remove a text this way:

    myCollectionOfTexts.remove("Vegard");

This removes a `String` object that contains Vegard. We don't provide any reference to the same `String` object that the collection has, just a similar object, the anonymous object "Vegard". This assumes that `equals()` is implemented correctly.

If the collection is going to be ordered, that has to be implemented in the classes, or determined by a sub-interface, just as with `List`, which we will come to shortly.

API Reference

The java.util.Collection interface

This is an interface for a general collection of elements. We will mention some central methods. Many of the methods leave it to the implementation (of both the `Collection` class and the elements) to determine what elements are similar and whether such similar elements are allowed in the collection.

Methods:

    public boolean add(Object anObject)

This method adds an element to the collection. The parameter is from the `Object` class. In other words, every object can be an argument for the call, and in principle all types of objects can be added. Classes that implement the interface can choose not to permit references to objects with similar data, in which case the method will return `false`. If the reference was added without difficulties, `true` is returned.

    public boolean contains(Object anObject)

This method checks whether the collection contains objects with the same data as the argument refers to. "Does the collection contain an element like this?". As mentioned, it is the implementation that determines how the comparison will occur.

    public boolean containsAll(Collection aCollection)

This method checks whether the collection contains all the elements that the collection in the argument contains. In other words, is everything in the `aCollection` collection included in this collection?

    public boolean remove(Object anObject)

This method removes an object that is similar to the specified one from the collection, and returns `true` if such an object was found and removed.

    public boolean removeAll(Collection aCollection)

This method removes all elements in the specified collection from this collection. `true` is returned if at least one element was removed, otherwise `false`.

    public int size()

This method returns the number of elements in the collection.

List

A list is a sub-interface of `Collection`. In other words, it retains the requirements that `Collection` dictates and adds additional requirements. What's new in `List` is that there is an ordering of the elements. The elements will have their positions in the collection. `Collection` has no such requirements. Two methods that `List` comes with illustrate this.

API Reference

The java.util.List interface

This interface expands `Collection` by requiring that the elements have reciprocal order. As a result, there are index variables to indicate a position on the list. Some of the interface's methods throw an `IndexOut OfBoundsException` if we try to use an index that is too high compared to the number of elements, or less than 0.

Methods:

    public void add(int position, Object anObject)

This method adds the specified element in the specified position on the list. The positions of the elements after this one are increased by one. The positions start at 0, precisely as they do for arrays.

    public Object set(int position, Object anObject)

This method replaces the element in the specified position on the list with a new one. The old element is returned.

    public Object remove(int position)

This method removes the element in the indicated position from the list. The method returns the object that was removed.

    public Object get(int position)

This method returns the element in the specified position without changing the list.
    The `ArrayList` class implements this interface. See Section 10.2.

Lists will typically permit us to have multiple objects with identical data. If we have a strip of data where everything has its position, it doesn't seem so strange that some elements have the same data. Note that the interface itself cannot dictate this. It depends on how the `add()` method is implemented. For example, `ArrayList` permits this and even multiple references to the same object.

LinkedList

Now we've reached the class we are going to use. This class is in the `java.util` package and implements, among other things, `List` and therefore `Collection`. In other words, the class bears the mark of being a collection of elements arranged in an order, and that obviously fits into the linked list data structure.

We are allowed to insert all kinds of objects into a `LinkedList`; the class takes care of the rest (i.e., the references between the objects). The documentation says that the class has the performance one expects from a double-linked list. We can assume that that means that deleting an element from the list goes relatively quickly, while accessing an element number n goes a little more slowly than for a array list.

API Reference

The java.util.LinkedList class

This class implements a linked list where the elements are arbitrary objects. We recognize the methods from the `Collection` and `List` interfaces—for example, `add()`.

Methods:

        public void add(int position, Object anObject)

This method adds the specified object to the specified position.

        public void addFirst(Object anObject)
        public void addLast(Object anObject)

These methods insert the specified object into the list's first or last position, respectively.

        public boolean remove(Object anObject)

This method removes an object from the list that is similar to the specified object. Even if there should be several that fit, only one is removed, the first in the list. `equals()` is used. This method returns `false` if no suitable objects are found and removed.

        public Object removeFirst()
        public Object removeLast()

These are methods that remove the first and last element from the list, and return references to the removed elements.

Problem

Rewrite Program Listing 17.3 so that it uses `LinkedList` instead of our "homemade" list class.

17.4 Queues and Stacks

A *queue* is an ordered collection of data where the data is put in and taken out at a specific place. Suppose we are going to model the waiting time for cars approaching a tollbooth. Two central events will be that a car enters the line of waiting cars and that the car leaves the line. Then, it may be of interest to calculate the average length of the line or the length of the line during rush hour.

FIFO queue

A line of cars waiting to go through the tollbooth is an example of a *FIFO queue*, First In, First Out queue. It gets that name because the first car into the line is the first car to leave it. FIFO queue is sometimes used synonymously with queue. In a data program, a data structure for a FIFO queue has to provide two operations: taking out and putting in an element. We see an operation to find out the number of elements in the queue in a possible support operation.

The LinkedList class is flexible enough that we can use it as the basis for a queue data structure. We've seen that LinkedList has methods for inserting data first and last in the list. A natural thing to do is to compose a class for a queue that encapsulates a LinkedList object, and makes use of a couple of its methods. That is a very short bit of code:

```java
class FIFOQueue {
  private LinkedList list = new LinkedList();
  public void insertElement(Object anObject) {
    list.addLast(anObject);
  }
  public Object removeElement() {
    return list.removeFirst();
  }
  public int findNumberOfElements() {
    return list.size();
  }
}
```

The Java API doesn't provide a class for a queue and when you see how easily we can make one ourselves with the existing class for a linked list, you'll understand why. Actually, you're asked to do it this way in the documentation for LinkedList. Our class FIFOQueue can have all types of objects in the queue since Object is a parameter for the methods.

Stack

A *stack* is also called a LIFO queue, Last In, First Out queue. A stack is also a queue, but it has the characteristic that the element we take out will be the last one that was put in. Picture a stack of plates. The first plate we put into the stack will be the last to leave it, if it's taken out at all. A stack is First In, Last Out in addition to Last In, First Out. Just as easily as with a FIFO queue, we can construct a data structure like this using LinkedList:

```java
class Stack {
  private LinkedList list = new LinkedList();
```

```
public void insertElement(Object anObject) {
  list.addLast(anObject);
}

public Object removeElement() {
  return list.removeLast();
}

public int findNumberOfElements() {
  return list.size();
}
}
```

Again we see that it has to do with a simple limitation on a linked list. Putting an element into a stack is also called *pushing*, and retrieving and deleting an element is called *popping*. There is also a stack implementation in the API, see `java.util.Stack`.

A very common application for stacks is in calculators and other adding machines. Suppose the adding machine is going to find the value for this expression:

$$\frac{(34 + 5) \times 56}{(5 \times 89) + (9 - 3)}$$

This is long division, with compound expressions above and below the fraction line. We can imagine that the adding machine first calculates the expression under the fraction line and that this is stored on a stack. Then the machine calculates the expression over the fraction line and possibly stores this on the stack as well. Then the calculation can be completed with the division involving the two uppermost numbers on the stack.

Problem

In the last example with the compound expression, it would also be natural for the same stack to be used when the expressions above and below the fraction line are going to be calculated together. Explain how.

17.5 Recursion

Before we continue and look at more data structures, we will go through the programming technique called *recursion*.

It happens that we can effectively solve a problem by starting at one end, solving a little bit of the problem there, and then doing precisely the equivalent operation to the rest of the problem. Finally there's nothing left of the original task, and the problem is solved.

A normal technique for doing this is for a method to call itself, and that's what recursion is. This is how it might look:

```
void myMethod() {
  /* Some lines of code ...*/
```

```
myMethod();
/* Maybe some more ... */
}
```

In the middle of the `myMethod()` method there's a new call to `myMethod()`. How can this work well? The first thing you think is that if this is permitted at all in the first place (which it certainly is), then this program bit must get stuck indefinitely. The key is recursion's *stop condition*. If the method unconditionally calls itself in all situations, it will get stuck and stop only when the program cannot use any more memory, and an `OutOfMemoryError` is thrown. An *error* is more serious than an exception, but makes itself known in a similar way. We may catch them with `try` and `catch` (see Section 8.5). But it's so serious that we can't handle them the way we handle an exception. If our program throws a subclass of `Error`, generally there's no hope left for a continued reasonable program run.

Back to recursion. For this to stop somewhere, the method has to have a condition that determines that now the method will *not* be called again. Then the recursion stops. We illustrate this with an example where we calculate the value n!, n factorial for an integer n. n factorial is defined as: n! = 1 * 2 * 3 * ... * n. For example, 3! equals 6. The following method calculates n! recursively:

```
public int factorial(int n) {
  if (n <= 1) return 1;
  else return n * factorial(n-1);
}
```

What happens? If we call the method with a negative number as an argument, then it returns 1, something that is mathematically wrong. Our method is only correct for non-negative numbers.

If we call the method with an argument of 0, it returns 1, which is correct since 0! is specially defined to be 1.

If we call it with an argument of 1, it returns 1, which is correct.

If we call the method with the argument of 2, then the method goes to the `else` statement and returns 2 * factorial(1), which is to say, an extra call to the method. That call returns 1, and the answer will be 2 * 1, which is equal to 2.

Notice how small and elegant the solution is (although in practice it can be relatively slow, depending on the Java interpreter). We'll see the same thing in the chapter on trees, where searches are performed recursively.

Problems

1. Go through the `factorial()` method step by step for the argument 3, and check that it returns the correct value, which is 6.

2. Make a method that takes a text as its argument. The method will return `true` if the text is a palindrome, otherwise `false`. A text is a palindrome if it reads the same forward and backward—for example, "Otto" or "A man a plan a canal Panama." Ignore blank spaces and capitalization. Use recursion.

17.6 Trees

We're familiar with the idea of a class tree from before. Now we will look at trees as a data structure and one special instance of a graph. A *tree* in this context is a graph with some additional characteristics. A tree cannot contain *cycles* or round trips in the graph. Figure 17.9 illustrates this.

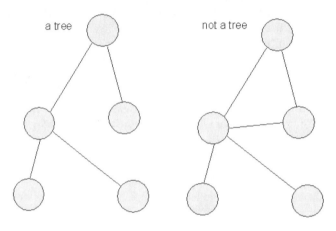

Figure 17.9   Tree

Furthermore, we require that the graph sticks together, that there aren't several bits of it. Note that this means that there is always exactly one path between two vertices. As a rule, we operate with a vertex that is designated as *root*. The tree spreads outwards from this vertex and there is always exactly one path from a vertex home to the root. We have drawn the root at the top of the tree in Figure 17.9, but note that all the other vertices *could* have been the root (just turn the book a little bit). So the root has to be defined. A *subtree* is a smaller tree that makes up part of the entire tree.

Binary search trees

This is a very familiar and much used version of trees. Like lists, the key is data storage with quick operations. Here we set up the following rules:

- Every vertice except the root have a vertex that is called the *parent*.

- Every vertice can have up to two more vertices that they are the parent for. These are called *children*. The children comprise the root in the left and right subtrees. A vertex without a child is called a *leaf*. Figure 17.10 illustrates these terms.

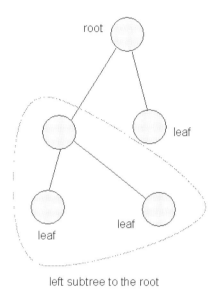

Figure 17.10 Tree with a root, leaves, and subtree

The data structure we have just defined is called a *binary tree* because there's a maximum of two children, but we don't stop there.

- Data belongs to all the vertices and the data is located in the tree such that every vertex's left child's data is "less than or equal to" the parent's, and the right child's data is "greater than" the parent's data. "Less than or equal to" and "greater than" can have many types of meanings, even if a few are quite obvious. In addition to a vertex's child having these characteristics, all the other vertices in the right and left subtrees will also have the corresponding characteristics.

Figure 17.11 shows a binary search tree, with the root at the top and the children below. We see that the condition that the child on the left will have a lower value and the child on the right will have a larger one is fulfilled, so this is a valid tree when "greater than" has the usual mathematical meaning. It won't be permissible to place 16 as the right child to 14, since this is wrong with respect to 15.

The Java API provides a class `java.util.TreeMap` that implements this data structure. Before we go through it, we will present a homemade example that is very simple. We have chosen to implement the data structure itself with two classes, `BinarySearchTree` and `SubTree`. Every vertex is a `SubTree` object, but the objects contain methods that take care of the whole subtree from the subtree's root vertex down. Data in every vertex is an integer.

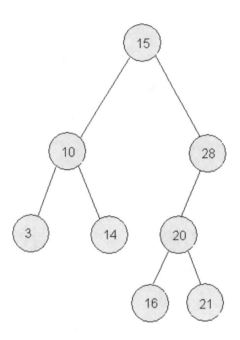

Figure 17.11　Binary search tree

Program Listing 17.4

```
/*
 *
 * BinarySearchTree.java VBH 2001-08-16
 *
 * Class for a binary search tree.
 *
 */
class BinarySearchTree {
  private SubTree root;

  public String toString() {
    if (root != null) {
      return root.toString();
    } else {
      return null;
    }
  }
  /*
   * Each time we insert a value, we have to check if there is
```

```
 * something in the tree from before. That is not especially
 * elegant.
 */
public void insertValue(int value) {
  if (root != null) {
    root.insertValue(value);
  } else {
    root = new SubTree(value, null);
  }
}

/* Returns true if the value is in the tree. */
public boolean searchForValue(int valueToFind) {
  if (root == null) return false;
  return root.searchForValue(valueToFind);
}
}
```

Program Listing 17.4 shows the `BinarySearchTree` class which is the one clients will use. The class encapsulates the whole tree. The class diagram in Figure 17.12 shows that we will implement the functionality of inserting a new value in the tree, retrieving a textual description, and searching for a value in the tree.

Figure 17.12 Class diagram (UML)

We've left out the function of deleting a value from the tree. The reference `root` points to the root of the tree, if there is one. If it has the value `null`, of course the tree is empty. You'll find a class diagram for the `SubTree` class in Figure 17.13.

We note that the operations are the same. Wouldn't that mean that we could have dropped the whole `BinarySearchTree` class, and used a `SubTree` object to represent the whole tree? We could have. But in the `BinarySearchTree` class, we are dealing with the special cases where the tree exists, but doesn't contain a single vertex. Then we get a special case in the operation for search and insert a new value. When we come to the comparable operations in the `SubTree` objects, we know that every object contains data.

You'll find the source code for SubTree in Program Listing 17.5, and here we get recursion.

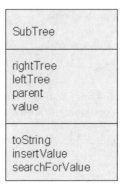

Figure 17.13   Class diagram (UML)

Program Listing 17.5

```
/*
 * SubTree.java VBH 2001-08-16
 *
 * Class for parts of a binary search tree. The subtrees, including
 * the leaves, consist of new objects of the class.
 *
 */
class SubTree {
  private SubTree rightTree = null;
  private SubTree leftTree = null;
  private SubTree parent = null;
  private int value = 0;
  public SubTree(int initValue) {

    value = initValue;
  }
  public SubTree(int initValue, SubTree initParent) {
    value = initValue;
    parent = initParent;
  }
  /*
   * The method inserts a new value into this (sub)tree.
   */
  public void insertValue(int newValue) {
```

```java
/* If the value for this node is larger than the new
 * value, the new value is going into the left subtree.
 */
if (value >= newValue) {
  if (leftTree != null) {
    leftTree.insertValue(newValue);
  } else {
    leftTree = new SubTree(newValue, this);
  }
} else {
  if (rightTree != null) {
    rightTree.insertValue(newValue);
  } else {
    rightTree = new SubTree(newValue, this);
  }
}
}

/*
 * The method traverses the tree infix, and returns a text with the
 * contents, separated by spaces.
 */
public String toString () {
  String returnText = "";
  if (leftTree != null) {
    returnText = leftTree.toString() + " ";
  }
  returnText = returnText + value;
  if (rightTree != null) {
    returnText = returnText + " " + rightTree.toString();
  }
  return returnText;
}

/*
 * The method returns true if the given value exists in the tree.
 *
 */
public boolean searchForValue(int valueToFind) {
  if (valueToFind == value) return true;
  if (value > valueToFind) {
    if (leftTree != null) {
      return leftTree.searchForValue(valueToFind);
    } else {
      return false;
    }
  } else {
    if (rightTree != null) {
      return rightTree.searchForValue(valueToFind);
```

```
      } else {
        return false;
      }
    }
   }
  }
```

The `searchForValue()` method is recursive and illustrates the idea of recursion very well while not being difficult to understand. When we send this message to a `SubTree` object, we will know about whether the value is found in this subtree or not. The following is what happens then:

1. If the value we're searching for is equal to the value in the top vertex in the subtree, `true` is returned. Then the value is found.

2. If the value is not equal, then it checks if the top vertex's value is greater or less than the search value. If the top vertex's value is greater, then it checks whether there is a left subtree. *In that case, the value must be there*. If so, the method is called recursively in this tree. If a left subtree does not exist, `false` is returned. Then we know that the value is not found in the tree.

3. A corresponding operation occurs if the value is not found and the top vertex's value is less than the search value. Then it's the right subtree where the recursive call is done, if there is a right subtree.

When we understand this algorithm, we understand that the recursion cannot get stuck indefinitely as long as the tree is not infinitely large. Sooner or later there has to be a subtree that doesn't have any children—in other words, a leaf. Then the recursion stops.

The method for inserting a value in a subtree is also recursive and very similar. First, the value that's going to be inserted is checked against the value that's on the top of the subtree in question. If the value is less than or equal to it, it goes in the left subtree. If it's equal to `null`, then a new object is established, which becomes a leaf with the new value. If the left subtree is not empty, the method is called again for the left subtree.

If the value we're going to insert is greater than the one on the top of the subtree, then the equivalent operation happens with the right subtree.

The `toString()` method also has recursion, and it's an example of what we call *traversing* the tree. Traversing is generally processing a tree with some criteria or other, in a manner where every vertex processes itself, and in addition, doing this recursively to both children. We can also talk about traversing if we are treating a list in the same, step-by-step manner. Our method will return a text with the contents of the tree sorted, and the idea is the following: for one subtree, this consists of adding the contents of the left subtree to the text, then the root's contents, and then the right subtree. Taking into consideration the binary search tree's characteristics, we understand that this will be a sorted printout of the tree.

`toString()` does this, and it's called *infix* traversing when the method handles its own data (in this case, a text is added) in between the two recursive calls. *Postfix* traversing is when the handling of its own data occurs after both the recursive calls, and with *prefix* traversing the calls come as the end.

We test the classes we've made with the test program in Program Listing 17.6.

Program Listing 17.6

```
/*
 * BinarySearchTreeTest.java VBH 2001-08-16
 *
 * Test client for binary search tree.
 *
 */

class BinarySearchTreeTest {
  public static void main(String[] args) {
    BinarySearchTree tree = new BinarySearchTree();
    tree.insertValue(5);
    tree.insertValue(3);
    tree.insertValue(1);
    tree.insertValue(2);
    tree.insertValue(4);
    tree.insertValue(7);
    System.out.println("The tree in sorted order: " + tree.toString());
    System.out.println("Is 2 in the tree: " + tree.searchForValue(2));
    System.out.println("Is 6 in the tree: " + tree.searchForValue(6));
  }
}

/* Example Run:
The tree in sorted order: 1 2 3 4 5 7
Is 2 in the tree: true
Is 6 in the tree: false
*/
```

Problem

1. Sketch a binary search tree on paper, like the one in Figure 17.11, or sketch in the book. Picture two calls for the `searchForValue()` method with the arguments 14 and 23. For each of the two calls, go through the method in your head and use your pencil to point to which subtree is under the magnifying glass at each point in time. Remember that there are several calls to the same method inside each other.

Creating a method that removes a value from our data structure will be a programming assignment at the end of the chapter, since it's a little more comprehensive.

What do we gain with binary search trees?

What we still haven't exactly addressed is why we would want to store our data in a tree structure like this. The operations we have to work with are reminiscent of the ones we get with a linked list.

If we want to search in a linked list for data, in the worst case we'll be forced to search through the whole list. It may happen that the object we were searching for is absolutely the last one in the list. In other words, the time it takes to search through a list of n elements in the worst case is proportional to n.

It usually goes somewhat faster with a search tree. Searching for an element there means going down through the whole tree until we find the right object or we reach the bottom. And it's not as far as it would have been if all the objects were lined up one by one in a linked list.

We say that the tree is *balanced* if it's as symmetrical and straight as possible. If there's a long subtree hanging all the way down on the right, then the tree is poorly balanced. A balanced tree is always best—then we save the most time in our search.

It's possible to show that if the tree is balanced, then the worst conceivable time it takes to search for a value is proportional to log(n). Remember that log(n) is always less than n. This means that it saves time to store data in a well-balanced tree compared to a list that isn't sorted.

If we use a sorted, linked list, the search can be performed faster, but it takes longer to enter the data into the list. The same is true of a sorted array or a array list.

The point of a binary search tree is that it speeds up searching for a specific value. As a rule, it's slower to enter data *into* a binary tree than a double-linked, unsorted list.

17.7 Trees in the API

As with lists, the Java API provides ready-made classes for the data structures we've explained here. They've implemented a binary search tree to be a *map*. A map takes care of a connection between some *keys* and data. A map contains only unique keys and all the keys are connected to exactly one value.

The applications for this include all types of data storage where a quantity of data is identified with a unique key. Slightly beside the point is the fact that retrieving the data connected to a key is fast. Maps in Java are implemented the same way as collections—using a Map interface, which has some subinterfaces and classes that implement them.

API Reference

The java.util.Map interface

This interface contains the basic functionality for a data structure that connects a key and data (or a value). Both keys and data are arbitrary objects. A single key can only be part of the map once and is connected to exactly one object with data. Keys that are different objects but counted as the same by `equals()` are fine.

Methods:

> public Object get(Object key)

This method retrieves the object that is connected to this key, or `null` if there is no connection for this key.

> public Object put(Object key, Object data)

This method adds a new connection between this key-value pair. If this key was connected to an object previously, this object is returned.

> public Object remove(Object key)

This method removes the key-value pair that this key is part of. The object the key was connected to is returned. If the key was not part of the map, `null` is returned.

The class that implements a binary search tree is called `TreeMap`. The numbers we used as examples of data in each vertex would have been keys in `TreeMap`. So, having an object connected to every vertex in the search tree gives us a clear bonus in functionality.

A minor obstacle is that the keys in a map have to be objects. In our homemade tree structure, we used variables of the type `int`. We have to be in a position to compare them for the search tree to be of any use. Luckily, the wrapper class `Integer` implements the `Comparable` interface (see Section 10.7). `TreeMap` requires this and uses the interface's methods. So we use `Integer` objects instead of variables as keys and then we're on target.

`TreeMap` also uses a mechanism called red-black ordering[2] to ensure that the tree is always reasonably well balanced. We won't go into how this is accomplished here, but the mechanism costs us a little extra time when we go to insert data into the tree.

---

2. [Cormen, Leiserson, Rivest 1997]

API Reference

The java.util.TreeMap class

This class implements a binary search tree, kept well balanced with red-black ordering. Every vertex in the tree contains a key that is connected to an object that comprises the vertex's data. First, here are the three most important methods from the Map interface.

Methods:

        public Object get(Object key)

This method retrieves the object that is connected to this key, or null if there is no connection for this key. Because we're talking about a tree, this method will answer the message relatively quickly.

        public Object put(Object key, Object data)

This method adds a new connection between this key-value pair. If this key was connected to an object previously, a reference to this object is returned. The tree is updated with the new value.

        public Object remove(Object key)

This method removes the key-value pair that this key is part of. The object that the key was connected to is returned. If the key was not included in the map, null is returned. The tree is updated so that it's still valid.

        public Object firstKey()
        public Object lastKey()

These methods return the smallest and the largest key in the tree. In an object that only implements Map there won't be any largest or smallest, so here we see a specialization. This specialization is due to the TreeMap class implementing SortedMap, which is a subinterface of Map.

Example

In the example in Program Listing 17.7, we use key values from Figure 17.11, and some names as data values. The names are String objects.

Program Listing 17.7

```
/*
 * TreeMapTest.java   VBH 2001-08-21
 * The key values in the tree are the nodes in figure 17.11
 * The data values are names.
 *
 */
```

```
import java.util.*;
class TreeMapTest {
 public static void main(String[] args) {
   TreeMap treeExample = new TreeMap();
   treeExample.put(new Integer(15), "Rick");
   treeExample.put(new Integer(10), "Rob");
   treeExample.put(new Integer(28), "Melissa");
   treeExample.put(new Integer(3), "Harry");
   treeExample.put(new Integer(14), "Ted");
   treeExample.put(new Integer(20), "Mildred");
   treeExample.put(new Integer(16), "Edina");
   treeExample.put(new Integer(21), "Patsy");

   System.out.println("Contents of the tree: " + treeExample.toString());
   String test = (String) treeExample.get(new Integer(11));
   if (test == null ) System.out.println("11 is not there");
   else System.out.println("11 is there: " + test);

   test = (String) treeExample.get(new Integer(10));
   if (test == null ) System.out.println("10 is not there");
   else System.out.println("10 is there: " + test);

   System.out.println("Lowest key value: " + treeExample.firstKey());
   System.out.println("Highest key value: " + treeExample.lastKey());
 }
}
/* Example Run:
Contents of the tree: {3=Harry, 10=Rob, 14=Ted, 15=Rick, 16=Edina, 20=Mildred,
21=Patsy, 28=Melissa}
11 is not there
10 is there: Rob
Lowest key value: 3
Highest key value: 28
*/
```

Problem

Implement our simple binary search tree using `TreeMap`.

17.8 Hashtables

A *hashtable* is also a data structure for storage and searches. It distinguishes itself from binary search trees by having essentially no order in the elements in the table. It distinguishes itself from a linked list in that the search goes faster.

Among other things, hashtables are used behind the scenes in many operating systems to keep track of files in a directory.

There are a number of *slots* in a hashtable. When we go to store an element in the table, we have to calculate the right slot for the element. The slots are usually ordered, and duplicates are not permitted. There has to be a *hash function*, which can take the element as an argument, and tell us which slot it should go in. The point is that when we search for an element, we use the hash function to decide which slot such an element will be in if it's in the table. Then we have to search through the slot to see if it's there. It's a fairly small job in relative terms compared to searching through all the elements in the data structure. There is a sample hashtable in Figure 17.14.

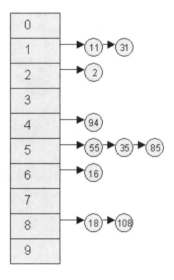

Figure 17.14   Hashtable

Elements in our hashtable are integers of random size. There are ten slots, numbered from 0 to 9. It's not an absolute requirement that the number of slots be constant, but we'll assume that here. We haven't used any complicated math or logic as our hash function. A value hashes to the slot that corresponds to the last digit in its value. It should be quick to find the last digit in an integer, so this is a fast hash function.

Several numbers remain in every slot. We have to be able to have numbers that end in the same last digit in the data structure. There are different technical ways to solve this. For example, we can envision a linked list belonging to each of the slots, containing the elements in the slot.

If we're going to search for the number 35, we proceed this way:

1. Calculate the right slot with the hash function. That will be slot 5.

2. Search through slot 5 for the value. This takes a relatively short amount of time. We find the value as element number 2 in the slot's list.

It's not much harder to insert a new value:

1. Calculate the right slot for the new value.

2. Add the new value to the list that goes with this slot—for example, at the end.

We can certainly also implement a sort for the list that belongs to each slot in order to decrease the search time within the slot. It's even faster to search in a sorted list. However, you may risk sinking all your gains into an extra mechanism like this.

A hashtable's *load factor* at any given time is defined as the number of elements divided by the number of slots. If this is high, the search will take a long time since every slot contains many elements. If this is low, the hashtable will take up a lot of space since there are a lot of slots, each with only a few elements.

Hashtable in the API

The Java API provides us with a ready-made hashtable. The class is called `Hashtable` and, among others, implements `Map`. Like `TreeMap`, we plug keys into the hashtable. They are the object of the hashing. The keys are connected to data. When we add an element into the hashtable, we add a key-value pair. The hash function for instances of a class is programmed by declaring the method `int hashCode()` in the class. The method will return an integer (can be negative), and replace the default version that is inherited from the `java.lang.Object` class. The return value may well be bigger than the number of slots. Then we simply divide the value by the number of slots, and let the remainder be the slot. The default version that is inherited from `Object` is based on the key's memory address. This can be unfortunate because the same key value can give different hash values. Hash functions are implemented for many of the classes in the Java API, for example the `String` classes and the wrapper classes `Integer`, `Double`, etc.

The capacity in a `Hashtable` is variable. The data structure sustains a desirable load factor of 0.75. If the number of elements increases, so that the load factor gets to be too high, an operation called a rehash is performed and the number of slots is increased. That takes time. We can state the number of elements we expect to have in the hashtable in the constructor, and also, if desirable, the load factor we want. This way we can let the object receive an instruction about what type of use it can expect when we set it up.

Look at Figure 17.14 again. When we use `Hashtable`, the objects for the numbers 11, 31, and so forth are the keys. The data-objects are objects that belong to every number. They are not shown in the figure. Clients of a `Hashtable` don't deal with the slots and the table itself.

API Reference

The java.util.Hashtable class

This hashtable class behaves just like a general map. It's the way it's implemented that is specific.

Constructors:

```
public Hashtable()
public Hashtable(int capacity)
public Hashtable(int capacity, float loadFactor)
```

Methods:

```
public Object put(Object key, Object data)
```

This method adds a key-value pair to the table. The location is determined by the key. This is where the data object goes. The return value is the object this key was connected to before, or `null` if the key is new to the hashtable.

```
public Object get(Object key)
```

This method searches for this key's data in the hashtable. If it finds it, the data-object is returned. If not, `null` is returned.

```
public Object remove(Object key)
```

This method removes the object that is connected to this key in the hashtable. At the same time, the object reference is returned.

Example

In the example in Program Listing 17.8 we set up a hashtable like the one in Figure 17.14. We use some names as `String` objects as the accompanying data values for every element in the table.

Program Listing 17.8

```
/*
 * HashTest.java   VBH 2001-08-21
 * The key values are shown in figure 17.14.
 * The data values are names.
 *
 */
import java.util.*;

/* The class Ident describes the hash function used in figure 17.14. */
class Ident {
  private int value;

  public Ident(int initValue) {
    value = initValue;
  }

  /* Gets the last numeral in the value */
  public int hashCode() { // redefines the hashCode() inherited from Object
    int power = 10;
```

```
      while (value / power > 10) power *= 10;
      int remaining = value % power;
      while (remaining > 10) {
        power /= 10;
        remaining %= power;
      }
      System.out.println("Value " + value + " gives code " + remaining);
      return remaining;
    }
    public String toString() {
      return "" + value;
    }

    public boolean equals(java.lang.Object obj) {
      return ((Ident) obj).value == value;
    }
  }
  class HashTest {
    public static void main(String[] args) {
      Hashtable hashExample = new Hashtable(10);  // to fit the figure
      hashExample.put(new Ident(2), "Matt");
      hashExample.put(new Ident(11), "Tony");
      hashExample.put(new Ident(16), "Celine");
      hashExample.put(new Ident(18), "Baldrick");
      hashExample.put(new Ident(31), "Arnie");
      hashExample.put(new Ident(35), "Vinnie");
      hashExample.put(new Ident(55), "Quentin");
      hashExample.put(new Ident(85), "Alexander");
      hashExample.put(new Ident(94), "Pat");
      hashExample.put(new Ident(108), "Put");

      System.out.println("The contents of the hashtable: " + hashExample.toString());
      String test = (String) hashExample.get(new Ident(11));
      if (test == null ) System.out.println("11 is not there");
      else System.out.println("11 is there: " + test);

      test = (String) hashExample.get(new Ident(6));
      if (test == null ) System.out.println("6 is not there");
      else System.out.println("6 is there: " + test);
    }
  }
  /* Example Run:
  Value 2 gives code 2
  Value 11 gives code 1
  Value 16 gives code 6
  Value 18 gives code 8
  Value 31 gives code 1
  Value 35 gives code 5
  Value 55 gives code 5
```

```
Value 85 gives code 5
Value 94 gives code 4
Value 108 gives code 8
The contents of the hashtable: {108=Put, 18=Baldrick, 16=Celine, 85=Alexander,
35=Vinnie, 55=Quentin, 94=Pat, 2=Matt, 11=Tony, 31=Arnie}
Value 11 gives code 1
11 is there: Tony
Value 6 gives code 6
6 is not there
*/
```

17.9 New Concepts in This Chapter

Concept	Brief Explanation
balanced binary tree	A binary tree that is as symmetrical as possible, not lopsided.
binary search tree	A tree structure with special limits on the vertices' locations and the number of neighboring vertices. The number of neighboring vertices is at most three: a parent and up to two children.
cycle	A "round trip" in a graph.
directed graph	A graph where all the links have one direction.
edge	"Line" that connects two vertices.
element	In the context of lists: a vertex in a linked list.
FIFO queue	First In, First Out queue. When something leaves the queue, it's the first that entered it.
global variables	Variables that can be reached from anywhere in a computer program. They don't exist in Java.
graph	Data structure/logical structure where vertices are connected by edges.
hashtable	Data structure where data is stored in different slots. Every value will belong to exactly one slot, so that's where you go to search for that value.
infix traversing	Treating a binary tree by treating the left subtree first, then the root vertex's data, and finally the right subtree.
leaf	A binary tree vertex that has no children.
LIFO queue	Last In, First Out queue. See stack.
linked list	Data structure with vertices that are linked together in a line. The vertices contain data.
load factor	Factor that says something about the average number of elements per slot in a hashtable.
map	A set of connections between keys and data.

Concept	Brief Explanation
ordering	When elements have a mutual order because greater-than and less-than have a meaning.
pop	The act of retrieving and removing an element from a stack.
postfix traversing	Treating a binary tree by treating the left subtree first, then the right subtree and finally the root vertex's data.
prefix traversing	Treating a binary tree by treating the root vertex's data first, then the left subtree, and finally the right subtree.
push	Adding an element into a stack.
queue	A data structure where elements can be added and removed according to a given system.
recursion	Programming technique where a method calls itself and this typically repeats itself until a condition is fulfilled.
root	Vertex defined as the top of a tree (or the bottom of a tree, if we draw them the other way).
stack	A type of queue. When something leaves the queue, it's the one that most recently entered it.
subtree	Part of a tree that is itself a tree.
traversing a tree	Going through a tree by treating data for each vertex, in addition to recursive calls to each subtree.
tree	A continuous graph without cycles.
vertex (plural vertices)	Junction in a graph. Usually depicted with a circle.
weighted graph	A graph where the edges have an associated numerical value.

17.10 Review Problems

1. What is an algorithm?

2. Describe what the vertices and the edges are in a graph. Name examples of what they can model.

3. Evaluate the following three data structures for storage based on the criteria of search time, time required for updating, and space usage: linked list, binary search tree, and hashtable.

17.11 Programming Problems

Problem 1

Consider our simple binary search tree in Program Listing 17.5. Try to think of an algorithm for removing a value from the tree, and implement it. This is a rather difficult problem. To remove a vertex, you have to find it first. Once you've found it, there are four possibilities: 1.) the vertex has no children; 2.) the vertex only has a child on the left; 3.) the vertex only has a child on the right; 4.) the vertex has children on the left and right. For possibilities 1–3, it shouldn't be a problem. For possibility 4, it's a little more complex.

Problem 2

Experiment with taking out and putting in large quantities of data in a linked list and a binary search tree. Look at the difference in time. One way of measuring time is to call `System.currentTimeMillis()` when you start and stop, and then take the difference.

More about Applets

Learning goals for this chapter

After completing this chapter, you will understand the meaning of:

- Malicious logic

- An applet's security model

- Swing applets versus AWT applets

You will be able to:

- Program more advanced applets that communicate with the browser they are running in, read parameters etc.

We used applets earlier in the book as examples of programs with graphical user interfaces. In this chapter we will build on what we've covered up to this point about applets and the Web. Appendix E gives a brief introduction to using applets in HTML documents. The goal here is to prepare the user to try out a few applets.

18.1 What Applets Do on the Web

The World Wide Web is a very simple network, which is part of the reason that it works as well as it does. A Web server's main job is responding to clients' requests to hand over files. In addition, it will sometimes receive data or files from clients. Data is perhaps submitted as input data for an external program that will carry out an operation, or maybe the file the client sent is to be stored. In practice it's relatively rare to see files uploaded this way over the Web. Typically, data is sent via the Web server to an external program on the server side using the CGI (Common Gateway Interface) protocol, which is quite widespread. For example, when you write in a guest book or contribute to a Web-based discussion forum, data is often updated through an external program that the server calls up. Even more useful is the JSP/Servlet technology which you can read about in chapter 21.

Regardless of what the server does every time a client asks about something, an operation is executed, and then the request is forgotten by the server. We say that the Web server is *stateless*. We might compare this to the Web server being an object without any variables. There are a number of mechanisms to make up for this statelessness, but the point is that the HTTP protocol, which the Web uses, has this quality. When you're sitting and working on the Web, there's a long series of questions about data and responses sent between you and the various Web servers.

Data that you receive from a Web server will often be passive information such as text documents and images. (It may be a result of computations by the server, though: see chapter 21.) Your Web client presents this to you in more or less the manner it was intended. The idea behind a Java applet is that data retrieved via the Web is an active bit of code that starts its own operations on the client side. This is an example of *distributed processing*. The total amount of operations to be performed is divided between several machines. Processing on the Web is already distributed as well—the clients have the considerable task of visualizing Web documents with images and layout. In an applet context, we can think of the client machine taking an even greater part of the overall job in that it's the one running the applet. Java applets are not the only technology of this kind developed for the Web. One example is ActiveX from Microsoft, which is a framework that allows smaller Windows programs and program segments to be downloaded via the Web and run.

Another related technology is Shockwave Flash. Many Web pages, especially those that emphasize visually striking presentations, use ready-made Flash objects. Similar to Java applets, they are small programs integrally linked to the Web document that are downloaded and run. Animation and sound are in the seat of honor here.

18.2 Security

One problem has to be solved, or at least pointed out: when you distribute programs the way applets are distributed on the Web, the danger is what we call *malicious logic*. This is a general, collective term for programs or parts of programs that do things we don't want and don't know about.

Most people using computers today are using some version of Microsoft Windows. Windows 95/98 are essentially *single-user systems*: When you turn on your computer and load your operating system, you have access to all areas on your hard disk right away (for example, *C:\Windows* where the operating system is installed). As a consequence of this, all the programs you start will also have access to these important directories. If a program you click on wants to damage important files on your PC, there's not much standing in its way. Security is based on the idea that of course the programs we start up will be useful and not harmful. And in the vast majority of cases, this is not a problem.

Other operating systems, like all UNIX variants and Windows NT/2000, are based on the idea that everyone using the machine will have a user identity and must log in with a password before anything can take place. Each user only has access to a clearly defined portion of the machine's disks—typically a home directory with subdirectories—and the access control is strict. Ideally, it will be impenetrable, and in practice it often is. There is also a user called the administrator, the root, or something similar. Only this user has access to all areas on the machine's disk, including the important sections where the operating system and shared software is located. Regular users can run the shared software, but often cannot overwrite the program files. It is important that only experienced individuals use the administrator-user so that accidents don't occur, hostile programs aren't run, etc. If one of the regular users were to run malicious programs, they would only affect the user's own files and programs, and not threaten the rest of the computer.

In spite of this, Windows NT/2000 is most often *used* as a single-user system. In other words, everyone who uses the same machine uses the same user identity and has access to the entire hard disk. It is extremely common for Windows applications to save configuration files in the hard disk's system directory, and then the applications must be able to access these files.

Viruses are a widely reported type of malicious logic. They are small program segments that manage to attach themselves to normal programs, inflict some kind of damage or other, and also spread themselves to other programs. Viruses are almost uniquely found on single-user systems like Windows 98 or Amiga. To a large extent, this is due to the fact that there the worst viruses can destroy the entire disk if that's their goal (as far as that goes, something so drastic would prevent spreading) and otherwise there are few limitations on their access to the machine. In addition, it's obvious to assume that the danger of viruses increases with the popularity of the operating systems.

It wasn't unusual that when Java applets were launched most people immediately thought of the possibility of malicious applets. Should you just let your Web browser run a program you stumbled across on the Web, with everything that might imply? Sun's developers solved this with the *sandbox model*. The applet can run, but mechanisms in the Web browser will prevent it from gaining any access at all to files on the machine it's running on. This is called the sandbox model because the applet gets to play in a little sandbox by itself, and ideally it has impenetrable walls. Figure 18.1 shows how a potentially damaging applet only gains access to the machine it's running on through some limited classes, interfaces, and objects. For example, it can't access a directory on the hard disk.

The browser is responsible for implementing the sandbox, and this is done through Java's security model.

A running Java program can have a *security manager* installed, in the form of an instance of the `SecurityManager` class. When a method is going to perform an operation that might be a security risk, it will ask the security manager if it has permission to do so. So, the ready-made classes that, for example, read files, create a network connection, or retrieve data from the clipboard in Windows, contain this. It shouldn't be possible for us to write our own code that will do anything risky without *having* to go through methods in the API that perform the necessary inspections. An "inspection" means that the security manager checks whether the thread that will perform an operation has the right *permission* to do so. Remember that every code that runs, runs in a thread. Every thread that is started in Java is assigned a set of permissions. These correspond to many subclasses of the `java.security.Permission` class, which can be accessed collectively in an instance of the `java.security.Policy` class. A `Policy` object corresponds to a series of permissions.

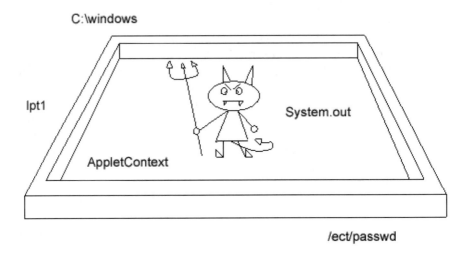

Figure 18.1 The suspicious applet does not gain access to many resources on the computer

 Every thread running in Java has a set of objects which are instances of `Permission` subclasses. When the thread attempts an operation that it might not have permission for, the installed `SecurityManager` (if there is one) always checks the thread's permissions for the operation in question.

We can send messages to the installed security manager, and we can also install a new one. So, you may ask yourself if it's possible for hostile Java code to set up a security manager of its own that is much more liberal than the original one. That won't work since one permission has to do precisely with inserting one's own security manager. It's not surprising that an applet doesn't have permission to do this. An applet cannot change the security manager that governs it.

A violation of the installed security rules will lead to an exception of the SecurityException type being thrown. This is the security manager's way of saying "no".

API Reference

The java.lang.System class

Methods:

> public static SecurityManager getSecurityManager()

This class method gets the current security manager. If no security manager is installed, null is returned.

> public static void setSecurityManager(SecurityManager newSecurityManager)

This class method sets a new security manager.

The java.lang.SecurityManager class

Example of a method:

> public void checkWrite(String fileName)

This method checks if the current code (thread) has permission to write to the file named. In other words, if we use one of the API's own methods to write to a file, this method will definitely call checkWrite() if a security manager is installed. The method throws a SecurityException if we don't have permission to write to the file.

The SecurityManager class contains about 30 different associated check methods for checking whether or not code has permission to do something. Something that is slightly unusual is that we rarely call these methods ourselves. The other parts of the API call them, when they're required.

Problem

Go through the API documentation for SecurityManager and look over what types of permissions can be checked against.

18.3 Programming an Applet

A Swing applet is a subclass of the javax.swing.JApplet class. This subclasses java.applet.Applet, which is the class for applets with the previous graphics library, AWT. When we include an applet as a *class* file in the

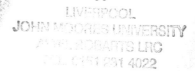

HTML file, the browser will expect to find a class that is a `JApplet` or an `Applet` there, or a subclass. If this is not the case, the browser will issue an error message. Most browsers have a little text window you can look at, called the Java console. Text messages appear there. An applet's `System.out` will also be sent to this window.

An applet is also a subclass of the GUI classes `Component`, `Container`, and `Panel` (see Figure 13.2). We make a mental note of two things:

1. An applet is not a subclass of the `Frame` class. In other words, it doesn't have the traits that a `JFrame` or `JWindow` has. For example, we cannot send an applet the message `setResizeable(true)`. This is all because an applet is visually inside a Web document and not its own window. See Section 14.9.

2. Swing is not supported by very many browsers. This will hopefully change.[1] For this chapter at [URL Java book] you have the choice between applets with and without Swing. We don't cover GUI programming—and, as part of that, applets—without Swing in this book.

The life cycle of an applet is slightly more complicated than a normal GUI application. If you've worked with the Web, you know that you look up a document, click through to a new page and then maybe go back to the first one using the Back button. The browser, among other things, will send messages to the applet every time the user goes into or out of the document where the applet is. The applet keeps running in the browser, even if the user leaves it. Thus, for example, it makes sense that it doesn't care about displaying anything when the user isn't actually looking.

The messages the applet receives from the browser in this context are as follows:

- `init()` is called when the applet is loaded into the browser.

- `start()` is called when it starts to run, and every time it gets going again after having been stopped.

- `stop()` is called when the user, for example, leaves the Web document the applet is on.

- `destroy()` is called before the applet is removed by the browser—for example, when quitting the browser.

We make our own versions of these methods if we have our own operations to do when the applet is removed or loaded, or if a user leaves the document or returns to it. We illustrate the life cycle of an applet in Figure 18.2.

---

1. This was written in August 2001.

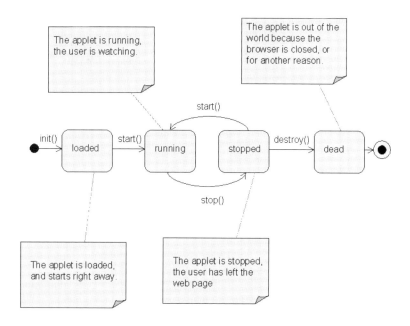

Figure 18.2 An Applet's Life Cycle (UML)

We see that the first time an applet is loaded into the browser, the browser sends the message init() to the applet object. (The identity of this object is given implicitly; the object is instantiated by the browser, as an instance of the class that is linked to in the Web document.) When the user clicks in and out of the applet's Web document, the applet gets the messages start() and stop(). It also gets start() the first time it's started—it's sent immediately after init(). When you quit the browser, the applets that are active will receive the message destroy(), so that they can undertake any terminating operations that are necessary. stop() always comes before destroy(). The methods are summarized below.

API Reference

The javax.swing.JApplet class

These are methods we often make our own versions of.

Methods inherited from `java.awt.Applet:`

    public void init()

This method is called by the browser when the applet is loaded for the first time and is ready to start. It isn't called again as long as the applet is in the browser's memory. Therefore, we add code to this that will be executed one time during the applet's life cycle.

> public void start()

This method is called by the browser every time the applet is to start running, including right after init ().

> public void stop()

This method is called by the browser when the applet is not up in a visible Web document; in practice, the user has clicked away from it.

> public void destroy()

This method is called by the browser at the end of the applet's life—for example, when the browser is quit.

We use an instance of the JPanel class as a painting surface for the applet inside the browser. This is placed in the applet's "content pane." Every time the window is painted graphically, the message paintComponent () will be sent to the painting surface so that the applet is painted. So, if we have permanent graphics that will appear in the applet's window, we could well draw them here. We do the same thing in Program Listing 18.1, and in addition, we've defined the methods we just went through.

Program Listing 18.1

```
/*
 * LifeCycle.java VBH 2001-08-21
 *
 * Applet which demonstrates methods the browser calls during the
 * applet's life
 */
import java.awt.*;
import javax.swing.*;

public class LifeCycle extends JApplet {
  private Container contents = getContentPane();

  public void init() {
    contents.add(new Drawing());
    System.out.println("The applet has been loaded into the browser.");
  }

  public void start() {
    System.out.println("The applet is starting.");
  }
```

```
    public void stop() {
      System.out.println("The applet is stopping.");
    }
    public void destroy() {
      System.out.println("The applet is quitting.");
    }
  }
  class Drawing extends JPanel {
    public void paintComponent(Graphics g) {
      super.paintComponent(g);
      System.out.println("The applet runs paint().");
      g.drawString("This is the applet. Look in Java Console in your browser!", 5, 50);
    }
  }
```

The following HTML file displays this applet:

```
<html>
<head>
</head>
<body>

<h1>Applet which demonstrates its life cycle</h1>

<object classid="java:LifeCycle.class" width="400" height="100">Your browser does
not support applets, or it's turned off.
</object>

</body>
</html>
```

You can find this document at [URL Java book]. If you open it in a browser, or download it to your own disk and look at it with appletviewer, you'll see that the applet gives you a little text message about where it is. What's interesting in this context is what is written to `System.out`, so go to the Java console window in your browser, or the console window if you're using appletviewer. There you'll in addition see any error messages the applet might send, as we'll soon see in some examples. Experiment with going into another Web page and then coming back again.

 `<object>` in HTML is a generalization of the older `<applet>`. If you have an old browser (for example, Netscape 3), you'll have trouble looking at the applets at [URL Java book]. We recommend that you use a newer browser.

Problem

What happens if you press Reload in your browser to get the Web document again? Look at the Java console when you do this.

18.4 Security in Practice

Now let's look at an example of how the sandbox principle looks in practice, and then see how an applet is not permitted to modify its own security manager.

The first example is an applet that's trying to open the file *config.sys* when it runs, and damage it by writing a little text. We've named this applet `Suspicious`.

Program Listing 18.2

```java
/*
 * Suspicious.java VBH 2000-03-12
 *
 * Applet which attempts to damage an important file, config.sys, on
 * the machine running the browser.
 *
 */

import javax.swing.*;
import java.awt.*;
import java.io.*;

public class Suspicious extends JApplet {
  private RandomAccessFile fileToBeDamaged;
  private Container contents = getContentPane();

  public void init() {
    contents.add(new Drawing());
    try {
      fileToBeDamaged = new RandomAccessFile("C:\\config.sys", "rw");
    } catch (Exception e) {
      System.out.println(e.toString());
    }
    try {
      fileToBeDamaged.writeChars("The suspicious applet has been here!");
    } catch (Exception e) {
      System.out.println(e.toString());
    }
  }
}

class Drawing extends JPanel {
    public void paintComponent(Graphics g) {
      super.paintComponent(g);
      g.drawString("This is the applet. Look for error messages in Java Console.", 5, 50);
```

```
      }
  }
  /*
  Typical printout in Java Console:

  java.security.AccessControlException: access denied
  (java.io.FilePermission C:\config.sys write)
  java.lang.NullPointerException
  */
```

In Program Listing 18.2 we see that the applet, when it's initialized, tries to gain access to read and write to *config.sys* using `RandomAccessFile`. Both instantiating an object like this and writing text to it throw exceptions that we catch here and print out to see what happens. If you go to [URL Java book] and try this applet, or download it and run it with appletviewer, you'll see that a `SecurityException` is thrown when we try to instantiate the `RandomAccessFile` object. When we try to write to the file, a `NullPointerException` is thrown because the object was never instantiated in the first place.

The wording of the exceptions that are thrown will vary somewhat from Java interpreter to Java interpreter, but the consequences of what happens are the same.

In Program Listing 18.3 we see an applet called `Sly`, which tries to set its own security manager to `null`. We catch possible exceptions that this attempt leads to (there is reason to expect them), and print out information about the exception.

Program Listing 18.3

```
/*
 * Sly.java VBH 2001-08-21
 *
 * Applet which attempts to turn off the running security handler, by
 * setting it to null.
 *
 */

import javax.swing.*;
import java.awt.*;

public class Sly extends JApplet {
  private Container contents = getContentPane();

  public void init() {
    contents.add(new Drawing());
    try {
      System.setSecurityManager(null);
    } catch(Exception e) {
      System.out.println(e.toString());
    }
  }
}
```

```
class Drawing extends JPanel {
  public void paintComponent(Graphics g) {
    super.paintComponent(g);
    g.drawString("This is the applet, look for error messages in the Java Console.", 5, 50);
  }
}
```

When you try this, the Java console will immediately report that a `SecurityException` has occurred. You should be pleased about this, because it would have been risky to work on the Web if the browser had not ensured this.

18.5 Communication Between Applet and Browser

Even if the sandbox model ensures an extremely watertight bulwark between a running applet and the machine the browser is running on, the Java API provides a few mechanisms for communication between the applet and the browser.

Applet context

The applet can get a reference to the environment it's running in through a context object. This corresponds to the document the applet is in. We can't know what type of object this is before the applet runs, because that will depend on the browser and operating system. What we do know is that this object is an implementation of the `AppletContext` interface. So if the browser is going to provide a representation of itself through an object, it will be through an instance of a class that has specific methods. The `AppletContext` interface is a message to the browser's creator, not to us, the applet programmers.

There aren't many methods that are dictated by this interface. We'll go through some of them.

API Reference

The java.applet.AppletContext interface

Methods:

       public void showDocument(URL url)

This method gives the browser a message to show the document the argument specifies. URL is a class in the `java.net` package. The class represents a URL—i.e., a Web address.

       public Applet getApplet(String name)

A Web document can contain more than one applet and this method makes it possible for us to retrieve a reference to a random `Applet` object that's running in the same Web document—i.e., within the same context. The applets are given a text name when they are linked to the HTML file using `name`:

```
<object name="applet1" classid="java:MyApplet.class" width="100" height="100">
```

Using `getApplet()`, *another* applet can get a reference to this applet object, which is called `applet1`. The prerequisite is that they are on the same HTML page.

```
public void showStatus(String statusText)
```

This method prints a new text in the status line, which is the line at the bottom of the browser where it usually says, "Host contacted, waiting for reply..." or something to that effect. The application for this is very limited since you don't have any guarantee that this text won't immediately be replaced by something new when the user drags his mouse over a link, etc.

The javax.swing.JApplet class

Method inherited from `java.applet.Applet:`

```
public AppletContext getAppletContext()
```

This method returns a browser-dependent object that implements the `AppletContext` interface. If we run the applet in appletviewer, the object that's returned may be from the `sun.applet.Appletviewer` class. If we're running in Netscape, the class is called `netscape.applet.MozillaAppletContext`.

Parameters for the applet

We can give the applet a set of parameters[2] when we link to it. This way, we can affect its run every time we link to it from HTML. This is done using the HTML element called `param`. It's probably easiest to see it in use:

```
<html>
<head>
</head>
<body>

<h1>Applet which demonstrates use of parameters</h1>

<object classid="java:Parameter.class" width="500" height="100">
<param name="name" value="Wally">
<param name="telephone" value="12 34 56 78">

Your browser does not support applets, or it's turned off.
</object>

</body>
</html>
```

The source code for the applet we're using here is in Program Listing 18.4.

---

2. Here we use the word "parameter" in a slightly different way than other places in the book.

Program Listing 18.4

```
/*
 * Parameter.java VBH 2001-08-21
 *
 * Applet which demonstrates use of parameters from the HTML document.
 *
 */
import java.awt.*;
import javax.swing.*;

public class Parameter extends JApplet {
  private Container contents = getContentPane();
  private String name;
  private String telephone;

  public void init() {
    name = getParameter("name");
    telephone = getParameter("telephone");
    contents.add(new Drawing(name, telephone));
  }
}

/*
 * This JPanel is told the parameters the applet has got, through the
 * constructor.
 */
class Drawing extends JPanel {
  private String name;
  private String telephone;

  public Drawing(String appletName, String appletTelephone) {
    name = appletName;
    appletTelephone = appletTelephone;
  }

  public void paintComponent(Graphics g) {
    super.paintComponent(g);
    g.drawString("Name sent into the applet: " + name, 5, 50);
    g.drawString("Phone number sent into the applet: " + telephone, 5, 65);
  }
}
```

This demonstrates how an agreement should be established between the applet and the HTML document about what types of parameters the applet will receive. Our applet is programmed to receive two parameters, called "name" and "telephone". We see how the get Parameter () method is used to get the value of the parameter of a given name, in the form of a String object. In the HTML document, we state which types of parameters we'll send in to the applet, with param elements that contain pairs of names and values.

API Reference

The javax.swing.JApplet class

Method inherited from `java.applet.Applet`:

    public String getParameter(String parameterName)

This method returns the value for the parameter named, if it was declared in the HTML code. If the parameter named was not sent, `null` is returned.

Problem

Expand the example in program listing 18.4 so that the applet can add two numbers. You'll send the numbers in as parameters and the applet will print out the sum. Remember that the parameters are text; the type has to be converted.

18.6 New Concepts in This Chapter

Concept	Brief Explanation
`<applet>` and `<object>`	The old and new HTML tags that link to an applet. `<object>` is also intended to be used for other distributed program segments besides applets.
ActiveX	Windows technology similar to Java applets.
applet context	An object that represents the Web document that the applet is running in. Its class varies from browser to browser.
applet parameter	A value that is sent into the applet from the HTML document. A parameter has a name and a value.
AWT applet	An applet made with the old AWT graphics system.
CGI	Common Gateway Interface. Interface for sending data from a browser, via the Web server, to an external program on the server machine.
distributed processing	Multiple computers share the total quantity of work.
malicious logic	Computer program or section of a program that intentionally inflicts damage when it runs.
sandbox model	A virtually blocked-off area in a computer from which programs can't gain access to important resources.
security manager	Object that a Java program can have "installed". It decides what the program has permission to do.
Shockwave Flash	Web visual technology that's related to Java applets.

Concept	Brief Explanation
single-user system	Everyone using the computer has the same access to all areas on the hard disks and to other resources.
stateless	A quality of Web communication. A client requests a service from the server, and then it's forgotten by the server.
Swing applet	Applet that uses the Swing library's GUI components.
virus	A segment of a computer program that can attach to other computer programs on the same machine to spread itself. They also usually cause damage.

18.7 Review Problems

1. What is the sandbox principle for an applet?

2. How is an applet sent from the Web server to the client?

3. Describe the life cycle of an applet. Who calls which methods?

4. What differentiates the HTML tags `<applet>` and `<object>`?

5. What is an applet context?

6. How can an HTML document give an applet parameters?

18.8 Programming Problems

Problem 1

Write a calculator applet. It should have two text fields where the user enters two numbers, and four buttons, one for each arithmetic operation. When one of the buttons is pressed, the answer (for example, to 6 + 19) should be printed in a result field.

Problem 2

This is a little continuation of *SoundAndImage.java* in Section 8.3. Write an applet that alternately displays two images at regular intervals. The titles of these images will be declared as parameters in the HTML file, for example `<param name="image1" value="car.jpg">`. Here, `image1` is the appointed name of the first image, and `image2` of the second. In principle, if these images are on the same Web server that the applet came from, you are allowed to download them to the applet; otherwise, the sandbox model is strict about this point.

See Section 8.3 for some hints on how to input images to your applet.

Drawing an image is often done as a separate thread in the windows system. That means that you can do things in your program where you assume that an image is already drawn, when actually it isn't. Therefore, it's beneficial to call the `sync()` method in a `Toolkit` object to bring your program into synchronization with the windows system. See the `java.awt.Toolkit` package for details. Take note of `getDefaultToolkit()`.

Problem 3

Create a continuation of the applet in problem 1 of Section 13.7, with exchange rates and currencies as parameters. It should thus be able to convert between different currencies, as specified by the HTML document where the applet is.

Distributed Systems with Socket Programming and RMI

Learning goals for this chapter

After you've completed this chapter, you will understand the following concepts:

- Socket

- Remote object

- Bootstrap registration service

- Proxy object (stub object) and marshalling

- Callback object

You will be able to:

- Perform simple socket programming using the class `java.net.Socket` and streams

- Use Remote Method Invocation (RMI) to make distributed systems based on objects collaborating over a network

---

Let's repeat some of the central definitions from chapter 1:

A *distributed system* consists of several programs that are running on several computers and that communicate with each other.

A *client* is a program or a computer that asks for services from a server, usually over a network.

A *server* is a program or a computer that performs tasks requested by clients.

Client and server are *roles* that programs and machines play. The reason we designate a machine as a client or a server is that we run a client or server program on it. We can run both types of programs on one and the same machine, in which case that machine is playing both of these roles. A program can also play both roles.

It receives queries from other programs, and it sends queries to other programs. Compare this to collaboration between objects in Chapter 7.

In this chapter, we will look at how we make client and server programs and how we get them to communicate with each other.

19.1 Sockets

Computers communicate with each other when data is sent from one machine to another over a network. A *protocol* is a set of rules that tells how this data stream will be sent from the sender and interpreted by the recipient. The Internet Protocol (IP) describes how computers will communicate with each other over the Internet.

For machines to be able to communicate with each other, they have to be identifiable. Computers connected to the Internet are identified using an *IP address*.

Examples of IP addresses are 186.45.34.100 and 156.76.50.237. To avoid dealing with these numbers, a machine usually also has a name. Examples of names are java.sun.com and mary.marysHome.dk. If we use the name, the network software in the computer will look up the corresponding IP address on the Internet's *name service*. A database matching names and IP addresses is distributed on the Internet, and the individual machines know where they should turn for this type of material.

A *socket* consists of an IP address and a port number, usually separated by a colon (for example, mary.marysHome.dk:100). We use the *port number* to identify a specific server application that is running on the machine. Thus, a port in this context is not a physical port but an entrance to a specific program that is running on a machine. Familiar server applications like Web servers and database servers run on specific ports.[1]

Figure 19.1 shows how a client program sends data to a server program on another machine. The network operating system gets the stated IP address and thus finds its way to the machine that is running the server program. The port number further identifies the program that the data will be sent to.

We will write a very simple server program that communicates with an equally simple client program. The programs each run on their own machines. The goal is to show that text the user enters on the one machine can be displayed on the screen of the other machine. The functionality is as follows:

1. The server program is started on machine A. It waits for queries from a client program.

2. The client program is started on machine B. It contacts the server program.

3. The server program sends an introductory message to the client program, which the client program displays on the screen of machine B.

---

1. Examples of so-called "well-known port numbers" are 80 for Web servers (HTTP), 21 for FTP (file transfer protocol), 23 for Telnet, and 1521 for Oracle databases. On a UNIX machine, port numbers under 1000 are reserved for the "super user" root—a regular user cannot use these.

4. The client program runs in a loop on machine B, and the user inputs lines of text. Every individual line of text is sent as a string to the server program. The server program outputs the text on the screen on machine A.

We use these same classes (`InputStreamReader`, etc.) when a program is going to send and receive data over a network as when it writes and reads data to a data file.

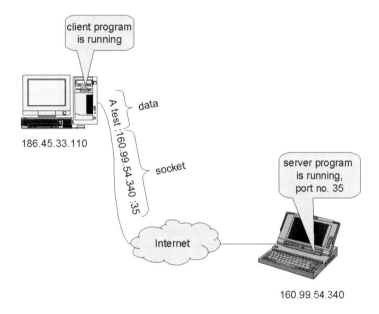

Figure 19.1 A client program sends data to a server program over a network

The link between client and server programs is created by instantiating an object of the `java.net.Socket` class. Just as with file handling, we link streams to the `Socket` object. A program that is going to send data writes to the stream. A program that is going to receive data reads from the stream.

Program Listing 19.1 shows the server and client programs previously described (see also Figure 19.2). Notice that the whole program is inside a `try-catch` block. This is necessary because quite a bit can go wrong when programs running on different machines communicate. For example, it can happen that the server program that the client wants to contact isn't running at all, or maybe the machine isn't even turned on.

 During a test phase, client and server programs can each run in their own Java interpreter on the same machine. In practice, the machine has to have a network card installed since the software connected to this is also used when both of the programs are running on the same machine.

To test the programs, first you should run them both on the same machine. When that functions perfectly, you should run the two programs on each machine. Nothing in the source code has to be changed.

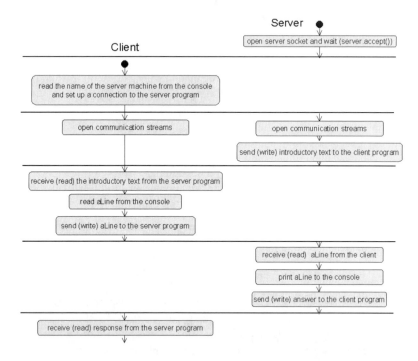

Figure 19.2 Server and client programs communicate with each other (UML)

When running on the same machine, the two programs each have to run in their own window. We assume in the following section that the console window is an MS-DOS window. If you start the programs from an editor, they will probably start in their own windows on their own. If you start them from the command line, you have to write the following to get a separate window to open for the server program:

```
>start java SocketServer
```

You run the client program in the window that is already open:

```
>java SocketClient
```

If the server window just flashes past, that probably means that an error has occurred. Then you have to run the program in the active window so that you will see the error message.

We'll start by going through the server program. The first statement in this program says that it will communicate via port 1250. The next statement, except for a `println()` statement, is `server.accept()`. This means that the program is waiting for someone to contact it. In other words, the program *doesn't continue until it is contacted by another program* at port 1250.

We start the client program. The client program starts by inputting the name of the machine that is running the server program. If the programs are running on the same machine, the response here is `localhost`.

Then, the client program contacts the server program by stating both the machine name and port number.

Now both of the programs will continue on their own until streams are opened for communicating with the other program. Follow along in the figure:

The server sends an introductory message to the client:

```
Hello, you are connected to the server side!
Write what you want, then I will repeat it. End with a
carriage return.
```

Take note of the order:

1. The server sends (writes) the message:

```
toClientWriter.println("***Hello, you are connected to the server side!");
```

2. The client receives (reads) the message:

```
String intro1 = fromServerReader.readLine();
```

Program Listing 19.1

```java
/*
 * SocketServer.java  E.L.  2001-08-25
 */

import java.io.*;
import java.net.*;

public class SocketServer {
  public static void main(String[] args) {
    try {
      ServerSocket server = new ServerSocket(1250);
      System.out.println("Log for the server side. Now we wait...");
      Socket connection = server.accept();  // waits until someone contacts us
```

```
      /* Opens communication streams to the client side program */
      InputStreamReader readConnection
        = new InputStreamReader(connection.getInputStream());
      BufferedReader fromClientReader = new BufferedReader(readConnection);
      PrintWriter toClientWriter = new PrintWriter(connection.getOutputStream(), true);

      /* Sends introductory text to the client side program */
      toClientWriter.println("***Hello, you are connected to the server side!");
      toClientWriter.println("***Write what you want, then I will repeat it. " +
                "End with a carriage return.");

      /* Receives data from the client side program */
      String aLine = fromClientReader.readLine();  // receives one line with text
      while (aLine != null) {  // the client side program has shut down the connection
        System.out.println("A client wrote: " + aLine);
        toClientWriter.println("***You wrote: " + aLine);  // sends answer to the client
        aLine = fromClientReader.readLine();
      }

      connection.close(); // shuts down
    } catch (Exception e) {
      System.out.println("Error at the server side: " + e);
    }
  }
}


/*
 * SocketClient.java  E.L.  2001-08-25
 */
import java.io.*;
import java.net.*;

class SocketClient {
  public static void main(String[] args) {
    try {
      /* Input will be read from the console, see Section 11.7 */
      InputStreamReader readingConnToConsole = new InputStreamReader(System.in);
      BufferedReader fromConsoleReader =
      new BufferedReader(readingConnToConsole);

      /* Inputs name of the server machine from the user*/
      System.out.print("The name of the machine where the server program is running: ");
      String serverMachine = fromConsoleReader.readLine();

      /* Contacts the server program */
      Socket connection = new Socket(serverMachine, 1250);
      System.out.println("Now the connection to the server program is established.");

      /* Opens streams to the server program */
      InputStreamReader readConnection =
                  new InputStreamReader(connection.getInputStream());
```

```
            BufferedReader fromServerReader = new BufferedReader(readConnection);
            PrintWriter toServerWriter = new PrintWriter(connection.getOutputStream(), true);

            /* Receives the introductory text from the server, and prints it to the console */
            String intro1 = fromServerReader.readLine();
            String intro2 = fromServerReader.readLine();
            System.out.println(intro1 + "\n" + intro2);

            /* Inputs one line of text from the console (the user) */
            String aLine = fromConsoleReader.readLine();
            while (!aLine.equals("")) {
              toServerWriter.println(aLine);  // sends the text to the server program
                String response = fromServerReader.readLine();  // receives response from the
                                                                // server
              System.out.println(response);
              aLine = fromConsoleReader.readLine();
            }
            connection.close();  // shuts down the connection

          } catch (Exception e) {
            System.out.println("Error on the client side: " + e);
          }
        }
      }

      /* Example Run from the two programs

      Output at the server side:
      Log for the server side. Now we wait...
      A client wrote: Hello, this is a test!
      A client wrote: Yes, I did! It works!


      Output at the client side:
      The name of the machine where the server program is running: mary.marysHome.dk
      Now the connection to the server program is established.
      ***Hello, you are connected to the server side!
      ***Write what you want, then I will repeat it. End with a carriage return.
      Hello, this is a test!
      ***You wrote: Hello, this is a test!
      Yes, I did! It works!
      ***You wrote: Yes, I did! It works!
      */
```

This is how clients and servers exchange, send, and receive strings. Both send, and both receive. Once in a while, both of the programs write to the console (`System.out`).

It's common for a single server program to serve several clients. The server program plods along running constantly while clients all over the network connect and disconnect themselves. We can accomplish this elegantly in Java by assigning every individual client its own server thread. The server program will run in an endless loop in the following manner:

```
ServerSocket server = new ServerSocket(250); // or another port number
while (true) {
  Socket connection = server.accept();
  Thread clientThread = new ThreadClientHandler(connection);
  clientThread.start();
}
```

We will not go further into socket programming, however.[2] Instead, we will look at a completely different way of programming distributed systems. Still, we have to remember that socket programming is always the basis.

Problem

Change the programs above so that the client enters a series of numbers, one on each line, and the server calculates the sum of these numbers. The sum will be displayed on both the server side and the client side (hint: the final criteria in the server-side `while` loop can be something other than what is used in program listing 19.1).

19.2 Objects That Collaborate over a Network

This book is about object-oriented programming. Let's repeat what we said in chapter 3:

"Client and server are roles that objects play. Objects collaborate when a client object requests a service by sending a message to a server object. The server carries out an operation as a reaction to the message. The server can send responses back to the client."

Now we will see that the objects that communicate with each other can be on different machines. Put pure and simply, we are going to adjust the programming technique we have used up to this point so that different parts of the program system can run on different machines. As an example, we will program Figure 4.4. We will make an instance of the class `YesNoCounter` (program listing 4.3) and put it on one machine. We do this by writing a server program (a class that contains `main()`) that instantiates the object and makes it accessible to client programs that are running on other machines.

There are several techniques for programming objects working together but located on physically distinct machines. We will look at the technique that is built into Java. The technique is called *Remote Method Invocation* (RMI). As the name indicates, we will see how we call "remote" methods, or, more precisely, how we call methods on remote objects. A *remote object* is an object that is running in a Java interpreter on another machine, or in another Java interpreter on the same machine.

---

2. The loop structure for handling multiple clients is derived from [Horstmann, Cornell, 2000], page 159. A complete example of this type of server program is also included there.

First we will see what the programs look like, then we will take a look at what happens behind the scenes and how the relevance to the socket programming becomes clear. For now, much of what happens at the lower levels will happen automatically for us so that we can concentrate on objects and messages the way we're used to.

Java `interfaces` that specify the interface for remote objects

- The interface must be a subinterface of `java.rmi.Remote`. In this way we tell that it's an interface for a *remote* object.

- Every method in the interface has to be able to throw a `java.rmi.Remote-Exception` or an exception higher up in the class tree. The reason for this is that errors can occur at any time in a distributed system, independent of the source code we write.

Classes that implement these interfaces

- The class must be a subclass of `java.rmi.server.UnicastRemoteObject`. An object that is an instance of such a class is accessible over a network.

- If the class is mutable, its methods should be `synchronized`. In this way there won't be conflicts if several clients are dealing with the same object.

- The default constructor is not sufficient in such a class. All constructors have to be able to throw `RemoteExceptions`.

- An instance of such a class is automatically given its own thread, to keep the object alive indefinitely (or until the program that the object belongs to is aborted). The object is a server object that waits for queries from potential clients.

A client that is going to send messages to an object has to know the interface for the object. An interface is specified in a Java `interface` (cf. Section 12.10). At the very beginning of Program Listing 19.2, we find the interface that specifies the counter in Figure 4.4. The implementation (the class) comes immediately thereafter. Notice the names: the interface is called `YesNoCounter`, while the implementation is called `YesNoCounterImpl`. In each of the methods, we have inserted a print statement that gives us a server-side printout each time a client does something with an instance of this class. When developing distributed systems, it's always sensible to insert many print statements so that you can trace the activity precisely on both the server side and the client side.

Program Listing 19.2

```
/*
 * YesNoCounter.java   E.L. 2001-08-25
 *
 */
import java.rmi.*;
interface YesNoCounter extends Remote {
  void increaseNumberOfYes() throws RemoteException;
  void increaseNumberOfNo() throws RemoteException;
  void increaseNumberOfYes(int increase) throws RemoteException;
  void increaseNumberOfNo(int increase) throws RemoteException;
  int getNumberOfYes() throws RemoteException;
  int getNumberOfNo() throws RemoteException;
}

/*
 * YesNoCounterImpl.java   E.L. 2001-08-25
 *
 */

import java.rmi.*;
import java.rmi.server.*;

class YesNoCounterImpl extends UnicastRemoteObject implements YesNoCounter {
  private int numberOfYes = 0;
  private int numberOfNo = 0;

  public YesNoCounterImpl() throws RemoteException {
  }

  public synchronized void increaseNumberOfYes() throws RemoteException {
    System.out.println("The number of yes votes was increased by 1");
    numberOfYes++;
  }

  public synchronized void increaseNumberOfNo() throws RemoteException {
    System.out.println("The number of no votes was increased by 1");
    numberOfNo++;
  }

  public synchronized void increaseNumberOfYes(int increase) throws RemoteException {
    System.out.println("The number of yes votes was increased by " + increase);
    numberOfYes += increase;
  }

  public synchronized void increaseNumberOfNo(int increase) throws RemoteException {
    System.out.println("The number of no votes was increased by " + increase);
    numberOfNo += increase;
  }

  public synchronized int getNumberOfYes() throws RemoteException {
    return numberOfYes;
  }
}
```

```
public synchronized int getNumberOfNo() throws RemoteException {
  return numberOfNo;
 }
}
```

Distinguishing between interface and implementation

Thus, when we use a Java `interface` to describe an object's interface and a class to describe the implementation, we usually use the class name *only* after the keyword `new`. We let the reference type be the interface:

```
YesNoCounter counter = new YesNoCounterImpl(); // like this
YesNoCounterImpl counter = new YesNoCounterImpl();  // not like this
```

In this way we can be sure that we are not sending other messages to the objects than those that are specified in the interface. If we try this, the compiler will protest (even if the methods we're using are included in the class `YesNoCounterImpl`).

Program Listing 19.3 shows the server program and a very simple client program.

As mentioned earlier, its own thread keeps the object `counter` active for the present. A client that sends a message to this object has to locate the object. RMI provides a *bootstrap* (= start-up, which makes it possible to start something else afterwards) *registry service* for this purpose. For simplicity's sake, we call this registry the *RMI registry*.

Once the client has found one object, it can instantiate more objects by sending messages to the first object. We can also register more than one object in the bootstrap registry.

Now we will run these programs. Download the whole subdirectory *YesNoCounter* from [URL Java book] chapter 19. Open a console window (assume in the following that this is an MS-DOS window), and move into this directory.

Compile all the programs. The easiest thing to do is to enter:

```
>javac *.java
```

Before we run the server program, we have to start the registry service. Enter the following:

```
>start rmiregistry
```

Rmiregistry is a program located in the same directory as java and javac. Be careful that the program is started from the same directory where you have all the YesNoCounter files.

A separate window opens. And nothing else appears to happen. But the program RMI registry is running in this window without outputting anything. The RMI registry is running on port 1099.[3]

Then you can start the server program. You can either do that from the editor, the way you're used to doing it, or continue to work in the console window:

```
>start java CounterServer
```

As in socket programming, it is important to start the server program in its own window, since this program's main task is to handle queries from any possible clients. The output from the program looks like this before any client has connected:

```
We'll make a server object
Now it's made!
Now we are just waiting for someone to increase our
counters...
```

While the thread is what the object `counter` is running in so that the program doesn't stop by itself, the following statement is what registers the object in the bootstrap registry:

```
Naming.rebind("CountingsLtd", counter);
```

The name "CountingsLtd" (note: no spaces) is linked to the `counter` object by using the `rebind()` class method in the `Naming` class. If the name was previously linked to another object, this link is terminated. We could also have used the method `bind()`. It would have thrown an exception if the name was used before.

Now we can run the client program:

```
>java CounterClient
```

The output from the client program will be:

```
Number of Yes: 1 Number of No: 1
Number of Yes: 11 Number of No: 21
```

At the same time, there is more output in the window where the server program is running:

```
The number of yes votes was increased by 1
The number of no votes was increased by 1
The number of yes votes was increased by 10
The number of no votes was increased by 20
```

The client program gains access to the object by looking up the name "CountingsLtd" in the registry on the machine that is running the server program. Here it is "localhost", but any machine name or IP address at all can be entered. The object's complete name in our case is "rmi://localhost/CountingsLtd".

---

3. You might also state the port number—for example, `start rmiregistry 1098`.

Run the client program several times. What happens? If there are problems, it's safest to restart both the server program and the registry. In an MS-DOS window, you stop a program by pressing Ctrl+C, or by closing the window.

Program Listing 19.3

```java
/*
 * CounterServer.java   E.L. 2001-08-25
 */

import java.rmi.*;
class CounterServer {
  public static void main(String[] args) {
    try {
      System.out.println("We'll make a server object");
      YesNoCounter counter = new YesNoCounterImpl();
      System.out.println("Now it's made!");
      Naming.rebind("CountingsLtd", counter);
      System.out.println("Now we are just waiting for someone to increase our counters...");
    } catch (Exception e) {

      System.out.println("Error: " + e);
    }
  }
}
/* Example Run:
We'll make a server object
Now it's made!

Now we are just waiting for someone to increase our counters...
The number of yes votes was increased by 1
The number of no votes was increased by 1
The number of yes votes was increased by 10
The number of no votes was increased by 20
*/

/*
 * CounterClient.java   E.L. 2001-08-25
 */
import java.rmi.*;
import java.rmi.server.*;

class CounterClient {
  public static void main(String[] args) {
    String url = "rmi://localhost/";
    try {
      YesNoCounter counter = (YesNoCounter) Naming.lookup(url + "CountingsLtd");
      counter.increaseNumberOfYes();
      counter.increaseNumberOfNo();
      System.out.println("Number of Yes: " + counter.getNumberOfYes() +
        " Number of No: " + counter.getNumberOfNo());
```

```
        counter.increaseNumberOfYes(10);
        counter.increaseNumberOfNo(20);
        System.out.println("Number of Yes: " + counter.getNumberOfYes() +
        " Number of No: " + counter.getNumberOfNo());
      } catch (Exception e) {
        System.out.println("Error: " + e);
      }
    }
  }
  /* Example Run:
  Number of Yes: 1 Number of No: 1
  Number of Yes: 11 Number of No: 21
  */
```

API Reference

The java.rmi.Naming class

This class provides methods for registering and retrieving objects in the RMI registry. The registry has to be started by having the RMI registry program running. If nothing else is declared, the registry runs on port number 1099.

The methods can throw several different types of exceptions. They are included as part of the method heads in the description below.

Class methods:

```
public static Remote lookup(String url)
        throws NotBoundException, MalformedURLException, RemoteException
```

This method looks up a name (`url`) in an RMI registry. Provided that the registry is running on the default port, we have the following examples of names:

```
rmi://mary.marysHome.dk/MarysLinks
rmi://localhost/Oslo
```

The method returns a reference to a proxy object (more about proxy objects in the next section), which the client can send messages to. The proxy will forward the messages for the real object on the server machine.

```
public static void bind(String name, Remote obj)
        throws AlreadyBoundException, MalformedURLException, RemoteException
public static void rebind(String name, Remote obj)
        throws RemoteException, MalformedURLException
```

These two methods register an object in the RMI registry. The first method assumes that the name is not registered from before. The second method binds the name to the new object regardless of whether it was previously bound to another object. The methods throw an `AccessException` (a subclass of `RemoteException`) if they're being called by a program that is not running on the same machine as the registry.

```
public static void unbind(String name)
        throws RemoteException, NotBoundException, MalformedURLException
```

This method takes an object out of the RMI registry.

```
public static String[] list(String url) throws RemoteException, MalformedURLException
```

This method returns an array with the names that are registered in the RMI registry. The argument has to be in the same form as for the method `lookup()` before.

Problems

1. Change the server program from before so that two counters are registered in the RMI registry.

2. Make a client program with a graphical user interface that does the following: The names of all the registered counters (use the method `list()` in the class `Naming`) will be displayed in a list. The user will be able to choose which counter he wants to update by a certain number of votes. After an update, the program will retrieve the total number of registered yes and no votes for this counter. The user interface can, for example, look like the one in Figure 19.3. The number of votes can be input using a standard dialog.

   Run several versions of this client program, and pay attention to the change in the number of yes and no votes.

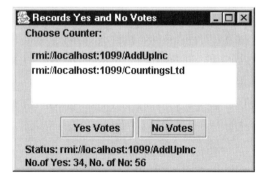

Figure 19.3 A client deals with several counters

19.3 How Does Communication Between the Objects Occur?

By now we hope you have the RMI programs to run. What happened, and what is the link to socket programming?

The following occurs when a client sends a message to a remote object:

1. The message is sent to a client-side object that functions as a *proxy*. This object is created automatically.

2. The message for this proxy is implemented such that the following information is *sent over the network*: an identification of the remote object, the name of the method that will be called, and the arguments for the method. Here is the link to socket programming.

3. On the server side, the information is read and the right message is sent to the real object.

4. If the client is to have a return value, the server will send that to the client-side proxy.

5. The proxy will send the return value on to the real client.

The proxy is an object that is an instance of the `YesNoCounterImpl_Stub` class. For this reason, it is also often referred to as a *stub object*. The class `YesNoCounterImpl_Stub` is in a file with the same name. This file is generated by a Java tool called rmic. For how to use this tool, see the checklist near the end of this section. However, as long as you run the examples, you download the stub files together with the other files, and you do not need to think about generating these files. We'll now take a little look at the contents of the stub file:

- The class `YesNoCounterImpl_Stub` implements the interface `YesNo-Counter`. In other words, we can find all the familiar methods (`getNumberOfYes()`, `getNumberOfNo()`, etc.) here.

- The contents of the familiar methods are very strange. For example:

```
public int getNumberOfYes() throws java.rmi.RemoteException {
  try {
    java.lang.Object $result =
        ref.invoke(this, $method_getNumberOfYes_0, null, 3436357891686025302L);
    return ((java.lang.Integer) $result).intValue();
  } catch (java.lang.RuntimeException e) {
    // exception handling
```

The message `invoke()` is sent to the object `ref`. This method takes care of sending the necessary data to the machine where the object is located. The process of converting a method call into a form that can be sent over a network is called *marshalling*. The word "marshalling" means ordering or arranging. Here we can talk about the fact that method calls and arguments are ordered or arranged in series and sent over the network. Conversely, we have a process called *unmarshalling*. The series is dismantled, and the actual method call is performed on the real object.

The method `invoke()` waits for a server-side response (`$result`). The method will not return before the server side has sent this value over the network (cf. the programs from Section 19.1). When this response has come, it is converted to an integer and thus becomes the return value from the method `getNumberOfYes()`.

Passing arguments

If client and server are running in the same Java interpreter, the argument *values* are always passed in a method call (Section 7.4). Accordingly, values are returned from a non-`void` method. If the data type is a primitive data type, the method will work with a copy of the argument. If the data type is a reference type, the method will get a copy of the reference but not of the object itself. Therefore, the method can change this object, which generally has its home in the client program.

This works differently when the arguments are passed from one Java interpreter to another:

- If a remote object (an object that is an instance of (a subclass of) the `java.rmi.server.UnicastRemoteObject` class) is going to be passed, a proxy object is passed. The recipient can send messages to the actual object through the proxy.

- Objects that are instances of "non-remote" classes are passed by serialization. As stated in Section 11.10, serialization is a process used to store objects in a file. For serialization to be possible, the classes have to implement `java.io.Serializable`. But, if they can be stored in a file as shown in Section 11.10, then they can also be sent over the network. A client that receives such an object thus receives a *copy* of the server-side object. The client can change the object without affecting the server-side object.

Here we see that we can pass both remote and non-remote objects from one Java interpreter to another. It is then natural to ask the following question:

When do we need remote objects, and when are serializable objects enough?

We have to make remote objects if we want a client to be able to send messages to the object over a network (from one Java interpreter to another). All the clients (and the server) are dealing with the same object.

We can make do with serializable objects if the different Java interpreters can each work with their own copy of the object.

The file *Member.java* contains two interfaces:

- The interface Member describes a remote object where a client can change and retrieve name and address. Parameters and return types are of the classes Person and String. None of these classes are remote classes. Both of the classes implement java.io.Serializable, and the objects will therefore be passed by copies being sent over the network using serialization.

- The goal of the interface MemberFactory is to make it possible for the client to make server-side objects. The factory method instantiateMember() returns a reference to Member. Here the real object will be a remote object, and the method therefore returns a proxy object. Here, serialization is not used.

Otherwise, the implementations as well as the server and client programs contain nothing new. The purpose of the client program is to show the two different types of argument passing.

Program Listing 19.4 shows examples of passing remote and non-remote objects. The class Person is the one shown in Program Listing 15.5. This class is a non-remote class. It implements java.io.Serializable so that it will be possible to send instances of the class over a network.

Program Listing 19.4

```
/*
 * Member.java   E.L. 2001-08-25
 *
 */
import java.rmi.*;
import myLibrary.Person;
interface Member extends Remote {
  Person getPerson() throws RemoteException;
  void setPerson(Person newPerson) throws RemoteException;
  String getAddress() throws RemoteException;
  void setAddress(String newAddress) throws RemoteException;
}

interface MemberFactory extends Remote {
  Member instantiateMember(Person initPerson, String initAddress)
```

```
                                    throws RemoteException;
}
/*
 * MemberImpl.java   E.L. 2001-08-25
 * This class is mutable. All data may be changed.
 */
import java.rmi.*;
import java.rmi.server.*;
import myLibrary.Person;

class MemberImpl extends UnicastRemoteObject implements Member {
  private Person thePerson;
  private String theAddress;

  public MemberImpl(Person initPerson, String initAddress) throws RemoteException {
    thePerson = initPerson;
    theAddress = initAddress;
  }

  public synchronized Person getPerson() throws RemoteException {
    return thePerson;
  }

  public synchronized void setPerson(Person newPerson) throws RemoteException {
    thePerson = newPerson;
  }

  public synchronized String getAddress() throws RemoteException {
    return theAddress;
  }

  public synchronized void setAddress(String newAddress) throws RemoteException {
    theAddress = newAddress;
  }
}

class MemberFactoryImpl extends UnicastRemoteObject implements MemberFactory {

  public MemberFactoryImpl() throws RemoteException {
  }

  public Member instantiateMember(Person initPerson, String initAddress)
                       throws RemoteException {
    return new MemberImpl(initPerson, initAddress);
  }
}
/*
 * MemberServer.java   E.L. 2001-08-25
 */
import java.rmi.*;
import java.rmi.server.*;
```

```java
class MemberServer {
  public static void main(String[] args) {
    try {
      MemberFactory factory = new MemberFactoryImpl();
      Naming.rebind("MemberFactory", factory);
      System.out.println("Waiting for someone asking for Member objects...");
    } catch (Exception e) {
      System.out.println("Error: " + e);
    }
  }
}
/* Example Run:
Waiting for someone asking for Member objects...
*/

/*
 * MemberClient.java   E.L. 2001-08-25
 */
import java.rmi.*;
import java.rmi.server.*;
import myLibrary.Person;
class MemberClient {
  public static void main(String[] args) {
    String url = "rmi://localhost/";
    try {
      MemberFactory factory = (MemberFactory) Naming.lookup(url + "MemberFactory");
      Person person1 = new Person(100, "Anne", "Smith");
      Member member1 = factory.instantiateMember(person1, "7001 Trondheim");
      person1.setLastName("Johnson");  // does not change thePerson variable in
                                                            // member1
      Person person2 = member1.getPerson();
      System.out.println(person2.getFirstName() + " " + person2.getLastName());
      person2.setLastName("Nilson"); // does not change thePerson variable in member1
      member1.setPerson(person2);  // does change thePerson variable in member1
      Person person3 = member1.getPerson();
      System.out.println(person3.getFirstName() + " " + person3.getLastName());
    } catch (Exception e) {
      System.out.println("Error: " + e);
    }
  }
}
/* Example Run:
Anne Smith
```

Anne Nilson
*/

Checklist: creating a simple distributed system

1. Find out which objects are desirable for a client to be able to send messages to over the network. It's the classes that these objects are instances of, that have to be handled specially as explained in points 2 and 3 below. Classes that are used only as parameter type or return type in methods that will be called over the network have to implement `java.io.Serializable`. With other classes, we don't need to do anything special.

2. Make the interface and implementation. Remember the requirements placed on both the interface and implementation class. (See Section 19.2.) Compile.

3. Run rmic to generate a stub class. Example run:

```
>rmic -v1.2 YesNoCounterImpl
```

If you forget to write -v1.2, a "skeleton" file will also be created. You don't need this file as long as you're not using the older JDK 1.1. The rmic command makes the *java* file first and then compiles it into a *class* file.

4. Make the server program. The easiest thing to do is to let it be in the same directory as the interface and implementation from step 2. Compile.

5. Make one or more client programs. A client program needs a compiled interface and a compiled stub class. The easiest thing to do is to have these files in the same directory as the client program. Compile the client program.

6. Start the registry from the same directory the server program will be running in:

```
>start rmiregistry
```

7. Start the server program.

8. Run any client programs.

Hints for program development

Insert a lot of print statements on both the server side and the client side to log the activity.

Restart the registry every time the server program has to be restarted.

Remember to run rmic again if the interface has changed.

Problem

What would the output from the client program in Program Listing 19.4 be if none of the objects had been remote objects and everything had run in the same Java interpreter?

Test this by redoing the classes `MemberImpl` and `MemberFactoryImpl` into non-remote classes. Combine the server and client programs into one program, and run everything inside a single Java interpreter.

19.4 RMI and Applets

The client program in Program Listing 19.2 can be run from any machine that is connected to the Internet. The prerequisite is that a compiled interface and a compiled stub class are accessible on the client side.

We can also download an applet on the client side, which contains calls to remote objects. Like other clients, the applet will also need a compiled interface and a compiled stub class. It's most practical to let these be in the same directory as the applet. The client-side browser will retrieve these classes when it discovers that they're needed.

As we know, an applet doesn't have access to resources in places other than where it was downloaded from. The RMI registry and the server objects therefore have to run on the same machine as the Web server.

At any rate, you will be able to test applets using appletviewer without a Web server running on the same machine.

If you want your applet to access, for example, a database at another machine, it may do it via an RMI object. As long as you hide the database connection inside the RMI object, the applet doesn't care. You'll learn about database programming in the next chapter.

Problem

Make a simple applet that counts the number of yes and no votes.

19.5 Deployment Diagram

A distributed system consists of several parts that are running on different computers. The machines communicate with each other, and the different parts are dependent on each other such that, for example, the server program has to be started up before a client can run.

In UML, we use a *deployment diagram*[4] to show the lines of communication between the different machines ("nodes"), and how the different programs, objects, and components that are running on these machines are dependent on each other. We see that the word "component" is showing up in a new context: a *component* is, in terms of the UML definition, "A physical, replaceable part of a system that packages implementation and conforms to and provides the realization of a set of interfaces."[5] It can be difficult to distinguish between the concepts of an object and a component:

---

4. The word "deploy" means "to spread out, utilize, or arrange especially strategically" [URL Merriam-Webster].

5. [Rumbaugh, Jacobson, Booch 1999, p. 216]

- In many ways, a component is "bigger" than an object. It usually consists of several objects.[6]

- A component is almost independent of other components. It is a physical unit that, together with other components, constitutes a larger system.

- A component never works completely alone. It has to be used inside a specific architecture or technology.

- A component can be replaced with another component that supports the same interface.

Our examples are small; therefore the components in our examples are also relatively small.

Figure 19.4 shows an excerpt of the notation that is used in a deployment diagram. With the exception of the uppermost box, this notation is also used in other types of diagrams in UML.

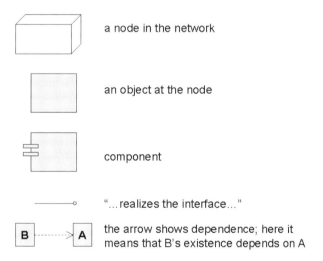

Figure 19.4 The most common notation in a deployment diagram (UML)

Figure 19.5 shows a deployment diagram for our simple distributed system. "CountingsLtd" is the component with an interface declared by `YesNoCounter`. We draw the other programs we have to run for our system to work as objects. They have no particular interface for us to deal with.

The dependence (the arrows) between the components and the objects is important. We read the following from the figure:

---

6. A component doesn't need to consist of objects at all. In that case it's usually source code written in a non-object oriented language that is "wrapped in" as a component.

- The CounterServer object assumes that the RMI registry exists.

- "CountingsLtd" assumes that the CounterServer object exists.

- The application on the client PC assumes that both "CountingsLtd" and the RMI registry exist.

This tells us something about the order the different programs have to be started up in. It also tells us whether some of the parts can be removed without this having consequences for the other parts in the system. These are parts that none of the others depend on. In this case, it is only the application on the client PC.

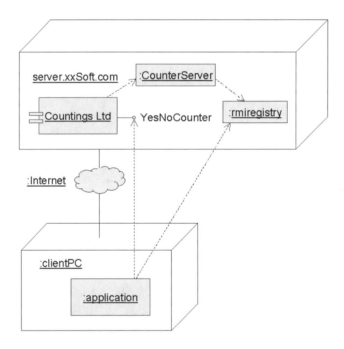

Figure 19.5 A client PC communicates with an RMI register and the component "CountingsLtd" on the machine server.xxSoft.com (UML)

Problem

Expand Figure 19.5 with a client PC that is running an applet for "CountingsLtd". The applet is considered to be an object inside the browser object.

19.6 A Distributed System with Callback

We will make a new variant of the system in Figure 4.4. Now we will make it so that every time yes or no votes are increased, all the clients will be alerted. Figure 19.6 shows the user dialog when a client connects. Then the user interface on the client side looks like the top of Figure 19.7. At the bottom, the log-in on the server side is shown. First, Peter connects. His windows are shown at the top left of the figure. Then Ann Margaret connects. See the top right of the figure. If we run everything on the same machine, the commands will look like this in an MS-DOS window:

```
>start rmiregistry
>start java CounterServer
>start java CounterClient
>start java CounterClient
```

The main difference from the example in Section 19.2 is that the server sends messages to the clients. This type of message is called a callback and means that there are objects on the client side that act as servers. Such objects are called *callback objects*. Now we will have remote objects on both the server side and the client side.

Figure 19.6 The first dialogs when a client start

The server-side program now has to keep track of which clients are connected. Therefore, a client must always begin by registering itself. When the server receives increases in the number of yes or no votes, it has to send a message to all clients about this.

We could have expanded the interface and implementation from Section 19.2. However, we are choosing to keep the class YesNoCounter "pure" and instead make a new interface on the server side, the interface YesNoCounterFront. An implementation of this interface uses an instance of the class YesNoCounter from Chapter 4 to keep track of the votes. We don't need to use the "remote" variant from Section 19.2, since the class YesNoCounterFront takes care of all communication with the clients.

The first part of Program Listing 19.5 shows the interface for the client-side object. The server uses this object in the following way:

- The message getName() is used to find the name of the client such that, for example, the text "Now Anne is registered" can be displayed in the server window.

- The message `printStatus()` is sent to all registered clients when the number of yes or no votes increases. This leads to the text in the client's status window being changed.

The second part of Program Listing 19.5 shows the interface `YesNoCounterFront`. We recognize all the methods from the interface `YesNoCounter`. In addition, a client has to be able to do the following:

Figure 19.7 Two clients and a server

- It has to be able to register itself. As an argument to the method `registerMe()`, it passes a reference to an instance of the class `Client`, so that the server can send messages to it.

- It should remember to exit before it disconnects from the connection. The method `resignMe()` takes care of this.

Program Listing 19.5

```
/*
 * Client.java, E.L. 2001-08-25
 *
 * Here is the interface of the client object. The counter addresses its request to such
```

```
 * objects, when all clients are to be alerted about changes in the number of votes.
 */

import java.rmi.*;
import java.rmi.server.*;

public interface Client extends Remote {
  String getName() throws RemoteException;
  void printStatus(String status) throws RemoteException;
}

/*
 * YesNoCounterFront.java   E.L. 2001-08-25
 *
 * Here is the interface presented to the client programs.
 * For more information, see the implementation YesNoCounterFrontImpl.java.
 */

import java.rmi.*;
import java.rmi.server.*;

interface YesNoCounterFront extends Remote {
  void registerMe(Client theClient) throws RemoteException;
  void resignMe(String clientName) throws RemoteException;
  void increaseNumberOfYes() throws RemoteException;
  void increaseNumberOfNo() throws RemoteException;
  void increaseNumberOfYes(int increase) throws RemoteException;
  void increaseNumberOfNo(int increase) throws RemoteException;
  int getNumberOfYes() throws RemoteException;
  int getNumberOfNo() throws RemoteException;
}
```

Program Listing 19.6 shows the contents of four files:

- The class `ClientImpl` implements the interface `Client`. Every time a client connects, an instance of this class is created. The instance runs on the client side.

- The class `YesNoCounterFrontImpl` implements the interface `YesNo-CounterFront`. The class maintains an array list of references to proxy objects that represent the various clients. When a client registers itself, a new reference is inserted in the array list. When the client exits, this reference is removed. The class contains implementation of all the known methods for counting yes and no votes. These methods forward requests to the instance variable `counter`, in addition to reporting the increase to the console. Every single one of the methods also makes sure that all clients are alerted by calling the method `alertAll()`. This is a private method that runs through all the references in the array list `allClients`. If the connection to a client is broken, the client will automatically be removed from the array list. The method `composeMessage()` creates the status message that will be sent to each individual client.

- The class CounterServer contains the server program.

- The interface Constants contains a number of shared constants for several of the classes. On the server side, however, it's just counterName that is used.

Program Listing 19.6

```
/*
 * ClientImpl.java   E.L. 2001-08-25
 *
 */

import java.rmi.*;
import java.rmi.server.*;
import javax.swing.*;

public class ClientImpl extends UnicastRemoteObject implements Client {
  private String name;
  private StatusWindow theStatusWindow  = new StatusWindow();

  public ClientImpl(String initName) throws RemoteException {
    name = initName;
    theStatusWindow.setVisible(true);
  }

  public String getName() throws RemoteException {
    return name;
  }

  public void printStatus(String status) throws RemoteException {
    theStatusWindow.setStatus(status);
  }
}

/*
 * YesNoCounterFrontImpl.java   E.L. 2001-08-25
 *
 * Here is the "front" implementation at the server side. The clients communicate with
 * instances of this class. These instances forward the messages on to instances
 * of the YesNoCounter class from ch. 4. The YesNoCounter class is not known
 * to the clients.
 */

import java.rmi.*;
import java.rmi.server.*;
import java.util.*;

class YesNoCounterFrontImpl
    extends UnicastRemoteObject implements YesNoCounterFront {
  private YesNoCounter theCounter = new YesNoCounter();
  private ArrayList allClients = new ArrayList();
```

```
public YesNoCounterFrontImpl() throws RemoteException {
}

/* Adds a new client. */
public synchronized void registerMe(Client theClient) throws RemoteException {
  try {
    allClients.add(theClient);
    System.out.println("Now " + theClient.getName() + " is registered.");
    theClient.printStatus(composeMessage());
  } catch (Exception e) {
    System.out.println("Error in registerMe: " + e);
  }
}

/* Resigns a client. Nothing happens if a client with the given name doesn't exist. */
public synchronized void resignMe(String clientName) throws RemoteException {
  boolean found = false;
  int clientIndex = 0;
  while (clientIndex < allClients.size() && !found) {
    Client thisOne = (Client) allClients.get(clientIndex);
    if ((thisOne.getName()).equals(clientName)) {
      found = true;
      allClients.remove(clientIndex);
      System.out.println("Now " + clientName + " is removed.");
    } else clientIndex++;
  }
}

public synchronized void increaseNumberOfYes() throws RemoteException {
  System.out.println("The number of yes votes was increased by 1");
  theCounter.increaseNumberOfYes();
  alertAll();
}

public synchronized void increaseNumberOfNo() throws RemoteException {
  System.out.println("The number of no votes was increased by 1");
  theCounter.increaseNumberOfNo();
  alertAll();
}

public synchronized void increaseNumberOfYes(int increase) throws RemoteException {
  theCounter.increaseNumberOfYes(increase);
  System.out.println("The number of yes votes was increased by " + increase + ".");
  alertAll();
}

public synchronized void increaseNumberOfNo(int increase) throws RemoteException {
  theCounter.increaseNumberOfNo(increase);
  System.out.println("The number of no votes was increased by " + increase + ".");
  alertAll();
}
```

```java
public synchronized int getNumberOfYes() throws RemoteException {
  return theCounter.getNumberOfYes();
}

public synchronized int getNumberOfNo() throws RemoteException {
  return theCounter.getNumberOfNo();
}

private synchronized String composeMessage() {
  java.util.Date now = new java.util.Date();
  java.text.DateFormat timeFormat =
              java.text.DateFormat.getTimeInstance(); // see online API doc.
  return "Now the time is " + timeFormat.format(now) + ", the no. of Yes votes is " +
            theCounter.getNumberOfYes() + ", the no. of No votes is " +
                          theCounter.getNumberOfNo() + ".";
}

private synchronized void alertAll() throws RemoteException {
  System.out.println("All clients will be notified of the changes");
  String message = composeMessage();
  int clientIndex = 0;
  while (clientIndex < allClients.size()){
    Client thisOne = (Client) allClients.get(clientIndex);
    try {
      thisOne.printStatus(message);
      clientIndex++; // updates index only if contact with the client
    } catch (ConnectException e) { // the client program is shut down
      System.out.println("No contact with the client with index " + clientIndex + ": " + e);
      /*
       * Removes the client at this index. No index updating.
       */
      allClients.remove(clientIndex);
      System.out.println("This client is now removed from our list. We continue...");
    }
  }
}
}

/*
 * CounterServer.java   E.L. 2001-08-25
 *
 * Here is the main() program at the server side.
 */

import java.rmi.*;

class CounterServer implements Constants {
  public static void main(String[] args) {
    try {
      System.out.println("Status at the server side.");
      YesNoCounterFront counter = new YesNoCounterFrontImpl();
      System.out.println("Now the counter is made.");
```

```
                    Naming.rebind(counterName, counter);
                    System.out.println("Now we're just waiting for someone to update our counters...");
                } catch (RemoteException e) {
                    System.out.println("Error in main() at the server side: " + e);
                } catch (java.net.MalformedURLException e) {
                    System.out.println("Invalid URL: " + counterName);
                }
            }
        }

        /*
         * Constants.java   E.L. 2001-08-25
         */

        interface Constants {
          String counterName = "MarysCountingOffice";
          int locationStatusWindowX = 200;
          int locationStatusWindowY = 500;
          int widthStatusWindow = 500;
          int heightStatusWindow = 80;
          int locationCountWindowX = 200;
          int locationCountWindowY = 200;
        }
```

Let's look a little more closely at the client side. We have already gone through the interface `Client` and its implementations. Let's start with the main program. It's shown in Program Listing 19.7. The program starts by letting the user enter the name of the machine where the server is running. It's easy to enter the wrong machine name. Therefore, we have been extra careful with exception handling here, and we also let the program run in a loop until we successfully contact the server. Then the client will enter its own name. These two dialogs are shown in Figure 19.6.

Further on, we create an instance of the class `ClientImpl`:

```
    Client thisClient = new ClientImpl(clientName);
```

The server will use this object when it goes to send messages back to the client. We don't need to register this object in any RMI registry. We will send it over to the server as an argument when we register ourselves there:

```
    counter.registerMe(thisClient);
```

Therefore, in this distributed system it's sufficient that an RMI registry is running on the machine where the server program is running, even if we also have remote objects on other machines.

Finally, in `main()` we get the registration window as shown in Figure 19.7.

Program Listing 19.7

```
        /*
         * CounterClient.java   E.L. 2001-08-25
```

```
*
* Here is main() at the client side.
* Contact with the server side is established, and callback object is created.
*/

import java.rmi.*;
import java.rmi.server.*;
import javax.swing.*;

class CounterClient implements Constants {

  public static void main(String[] args) throws Exception {
    YesNoCounterFront counter = null;
    boolean counterFound = false;
    do { // try to establish contact with the server
      try {
        String nameServerMachine = JOptionPane.showInputDialog(null,
          "What's the name of the server machine? ");
        String url = "rmi://" + nameServerMachine + "/";
        counter = (YesNoCounterFront) Naming.lookup(url + counterName);
        counterFound = true;
      } catch (NotBoundException e) {
        JOptionPane.showMessageDialog(null, "The Counter object is not found, " + e);
      } catch (UnknownHostException e) {
        JOptionPane.showMessageDialog(null, "Unknown machine, " + e);
      } catch (java.net.MalformedURLException e) {
        JOptionPane.showMessageDialog(null, "Invalid name format, " + e);
      } catch (Exception e) {
        JOptionPane.showMessageDialog(null, "Error: " + e);
      }
    } while (!counterFound);

    try {
      String clientName = JOptionPane.showInputDialog(null, "What's your name:");
      System.out.println("Status for " + clientName);

      /* This object runs in its own thread which receives messages from the server. */
      Client thisClient = new ClientImpl(clientName);

      counter.registerMe(thisClient);

      /* Sets up the input window */
      CounterWindow window = new CounterWindow(counter, thisClient);
      window.setLocation(locationCountWindowX, locationCountWindowY);
      window.pack();
      window.setVisible(true);
    } catch (Exception e) {
      System.out.println("Error in main(): " + e);
    }
  }
}
```

Program Listing 19.8 shows the two classes that handle the user interface. The classes don't contain anything new. However, we program the window closing ourselves:

```
setDefaultCloseOperation(WindowConstants.DO_NOTHING_ON_CLOSE);
```

The closing event is handled as follows:

- In the class `CounterWindow`, closing will lead to the client exiting the registry that the counter maintains. Then the whole program is stopped with `System.exit(0);`

- In the class `StatusWindow`, nothing will happen if the user tries to close the window. The user has to quit the program by closing the counter window.

Program Listing 19.8

```java
/*
 * CounterWindow.java   E.L. 2001-08-25
 *
 * This window is used as input window at the client side.
 * The connection to the server has to be established already.
 * It's disconnected when the user closes the window.
 */

import javax.swing.*;
import javax.swing.border.*;
import java.awt.event.*;
import java.awt.*;
import java.rmi.server.*;
import java.rmi.*;

class CounterWindow extends JFrame implements Constants {
  private JTextField number = new JTextField(8);
  private JRadioButton yesButton = new JRadioButton("Yes Votes", true);
  private JRadioButton noButton = new JRadioButton("No Votes", false);
  private JButton saveButton = new JButton("Save");
  private YesNoCounterFront counter;
  private Client theClient;

  public CounterWindow(YesNoCounterFront initCounter, Client initClient) {
    try {
      setTitle("Window for Client " + initClient.getName());
      addWindowListener(new WindowsClosingListener());
      setDefaultCloseOperation(WindowConstants.DO_NOTHING_ON_CLOSE);
      counter = initCounter;
      theClient = initClient;

      Container guiContainer = getContentPane();
      guiContainer.add(new JLabel(), BorderLayout.NORTH);
```

```java
    guiContainer.add(new InputPanel(), BorderLayout.CENTER);
    guiContainer.add(saveButton, BorderLayout.SOUTH);

    ButtonListener buttonListener = new ButtonListener();
    saveButton.setMnemonic('S');
    saveButton.addActionListener(buttonListener);

    number.requestFocus();
   } catch (Exception e) {
    System.out.println("Error in the CounterWindow constructor: " + e);
   }
  }

  /* Describes the middle panel */
  private class InputPanel extends JPanel {
   public InputPanel() {
    setLayout(new GridLayout(2, 2));
    add(new JLabel("No. of Votes: "));
    add(number);
    ButtonGroup group = new ButtonGroup();
    group.add(yesButton);

    group.add(noButton);
    add(yesButton);
    add(noButton);
    yesButton.setMnemonic('J');
    noButton.setMnemonic('N');
    SoftBevelBorder border = new SoftBevelBorder(BevelBorder.RAISED);
    Border box = BorderFactory.createTitledBorder(border, "Enter Votes");
    setBorder(box);
   }
  }

  private class ButtonListener implements ActionListener {
   public void actionPerformed(ActionEvent event) {
    int noOfVotes = 0;
    try {
     noOfVotes = Integer.parseInt(number.getText());
    } catch (NumberFormatException e) {
     JOptionPane.showMessageDialog(null, "Invalid Number");
     number.requestFocus();
    }
    try {
     if (yesButton.isSelected()) counter.increaseNumberOfYes(noOfVotes);
     else counter.increaseNumberOfNo(noOfVotes);
    } catch (Exception e) {
     System.out.println("Error in the listener to the Save button: " + e);
    }
    number.setText("");
    number.requestFocus();
```

```
      }
    }
    private class WindowsClosingListener extends WindowAdapter {
      public void windowClosing(WindowEvent event) {
        System.out.println("Tries Resigning");
        String name = "";
        try {
          name = theClient.getName();
          counter.resignMe(name);
        } catch (Exception e) {
          System.out.println("Error in WindowsClosingListener: " + e);
        }
        System.exit(0);
      }
    }
  }
  /*
   * StatusWindow.java   E.L. 2001-08-25
   *
   * This window is used at the client side for showing status information,
   * received from the server side. It's not possible to close the window. The user has to
   * exit the application by closing the CounterWindow, then he is disconnected
   * from the server, too. And this window is closed.
   */

  import javax.swing.*;
  import javax.swing.border.*;
  import java.awt.event.*;
  import java.awt.*;

  class StatusWindow extends JFrame implements Constants{
    private JLabel text = new JLabel("No message from the server yet.");
    public StatusWindow() {
      setTitle("Status");
      setDefaultCloseOperation(WindowConstants.DO_NOTHING_ON_CLOSE);
      Container guiContainer = getContentPane();
      text.setForeground(Color.black);
      guiContainer.add(new JLabel(), BorderLayout.NORTH);
      guiContainer.add(text, BorderLayout.CENTER);
      guiContainer.add(new JLabel(), BorderLayout.SOUTH);
      setLocation(locationStatusWindowX, locationStatusWindowY);
      setSize(widthStatusWindow, heightStatusWindow);
    }
    public void setStatus(String newStatus) {
      text.setText("   " + newStatus);
    }
  }
```

Problems

1. Expand the functionality of the programs in this section so that a client can access the names of all connected clients. Test this in the simplest way.

2. In addition, make it possible for a client to send a message to another client. Test this in the simplest way.

19.7 New Concepts in This Chapter

Concept	Brief Explanation
bootstrap	Start-up—something that makes it possible to start something else afterwards.
callback (object)	An object on the client side that makes it possible for the server to send messages back to the client.
component	A UML component is in many ways "bigger" than an object. It forms a physical unit that, together with other components, makes up a larger system. It can be replaced by another component that supports the same interface.
deployment diagram	A UML diagram that shows the lines of communication between the different machines (the nodes) in a distributed system, and how the different programs, objects and components that run these machines are dependent on each other.
IP	Internet Protocol—the protocol that applies for transferring data between machines on the Internet.
IP address	A series of numbers separated by periods that identifies a machine in the large network that forms the Internet.
marshalling	To package object identification, method calls, and arguments so that they can be sent over a network.
name service	A service that makes it possible to use names instead of numbers—for example, to identify the different machines on the Internet.
node	"Node" is used in UML and usually symbolizes a computer.
port	A number that can be used from outside to identify a program that is running on a machine.
protocol	A set of rules that for example tells how a data stream will be sent from the sender and interpreted by the recipient.
proxy (object)	This is an object that is used on the client side to send method calls and arguments over to the real object on the server side. The object is created automatically, and whoever is programming the client can deal with the proxy as if it were the real object.
remote object	An object that is an instance of (a subclass of) the class `java.rmi.server.UnicastRemoteObject`.

Concept	Brief Explanation
RMI	Remote Method Invocation. A technique in Java that makes it possible to let objects communicate with each other over a network.
RMI registry	The registry runs as a server program and contains references to named remote objects. It is usually used to identify an object that makes it possible for a client to access this and other objects over a network.
socket	Consists of an IP address (or name) and a port number; identifies a program that is running on a machine in a network.
stub (object)	See proxy (object).
unmarshalling	Unpacking the object identification, the method call, and the arguments that have come in over a network; the opposite of marshalling.

19.8 Review Problems

1. Explain what a socket is and what we can use it for.

2. What do socket programming and file handling have in common in Java?

3. What is RMI?

4. What do we use an RMI registry for? Why is it usually enough to register only one object for each server program?

5. What requirements do we place on an object so that it will be possible to send messages to it over a network (a remote object)?

6. Why should methods in mutable remote classes be `synchronized`? (By "remote class" we mean a class that is a subclass of `UnicastRemote-Object`.)

7. What is the purpose of a proxy object?

8. Why is marshalling necessary?

9. How does passing arguments in a distributed system based on RMI take place?

10. What do we use a callback object for?

19.9 Programming Problems

Problem 1

Use socket programming to solve the following task:

On the server side there is a simple name registry (first + last name, one line per name) in a file.

A client will be able to connect to a running server program and choose between printing out the whole file and inserting new names.

Let the server program run in an endless loop, where each run-through waits for a client to connect. Test what happens if several clients try to connect at the same time.

Problem 2

Adapt the class `Calculator` from Section 5.1 so that it can run on the server side in an RMI system. Make whatever is necessary to test the class.

Problem 3

Make a simple lending system for books. Use RMI.

A book is identified by its ISBN, and we can have several copies of each book. The class that describes the book will also contain the title and author.

We need to have a book registry on the server side.

For the sake of simplicity, we will not have an author registry or a registry of borrowers.

Make a separate client program to register new books and new copies of books that are already registered.

Make another client application that takes care of lending out and returning books:

- When a book is loaned out, the librarian will enter the ISBN, copy number, and name of the borrower. If the book is already out on loan, the librarian will get a message about this. The book can be reserved by one person. Note that the reservation is made for the book and not for a specific copy of it.

- When a book is returned, the librarian will enter the ISBN and copy number. If the book is reserved, information will come up about that so that the client can set the book aside.

Assume that reserved books are not sitting out, available for borrowing.

Problem 4

Make a chat program using RMI.

The server program will keep track of who is participating in the conversation and send out information to the individual client about what the others are saying (use callback).

A user that wants to participate in the conversation starts the client program and registers with a name.

The client program has to quit the conversation before the program exit.

Problem 5

Make a distributed system using RMI. The system will make it possible to play Mastermind over a network.

You will make a server program that can play Mastermind with several clients at the same time. A client program will also be created, preferably with a graphical user interface.

Brief review of the rules:

Mastermind is for two players. The two have different roles, the one (that we are calling the server here for obvious reasons) will set up pegs with different colors. The client cannot see the pegs. Altogether there are 8 different peg colors. Then the client will try to guess the pattern by setting up series of 4 pegs. There is a column of approximately 20 such series. The point is to guess the pattern as soon as possible and at least by the time this column of 20 series is used up.

Each time the client sets up a series of 4 pegs, the server will respond by setting out a black peg (these pegs have a slightly different appearance) for every peg that is the right color *and* in the right place. After that, the server will put out a white peg for every peg that is the right color, but *not* in the right place. In other words, if the server puts out 4 black pegs, this is equivalent to the client having solved the puzzle. If the server does not put out any pegs, this means that none of the 4 pegs the client put out are the right color. The server's black and white pegs are a hint to the client about how close to the answer she is.

For each series the client puts out, there are 4 response holes on the side for the server's response pegs.

If this is still unclear, maybe you can ask someone who has played Mastermind.

The functionality in the client and server:

The client will connect to a Mastermind server and ask to play a game. The server will then think up, but not reveal, a color combination for this client, and give the client a ready signal to start. When it's ready, the user on the client side will enter a combination of 4 colored pegs. The server will respond to this with the right combination of black and white pegs. This continues until the client has the right combination.

Variations in the rules:

In the first place, you can choose to play such that the client can have several pegs of the same color for every series she sets up. This is used frequently. If she, for example, puts out 4 red pegs, this is a good way to check if a red peg is part of the winning combination.

In the second place, there is nothing wrong in principle with the number of possible colors, number of pegs in a series, and number of tries the client gets being set for each game.

Programming with Databases

Learning goals for this chapter

After having completed this chapter, you will understand the following concepts:

- Database driver

- JDBC

- Three-layer architecture

You will be able to:

- Register a driver and establish a connection to the database

- Send SQL statements for database queries and updates, and interpret what you get back

- Use the right Java data type compared to the SQL data type used

- Make a graphical user interface that communicates with a database using a specially created database class

---

Quite a few of today's software systems work with one or more databases. Users retrieve data, modify data, and add new data. Systems like this almost always use what we call Database Management Systems (DBMS), or "database systems" for short. A database system does a great deal more than "keep track of data"—large parts of the system also take care of different types of security.

Visual tools such as "point and click" and "drag and drop" are often used to set up the connection between a user interface and a database when developing software that uses a database system. Microsoft Access is an example of a combined tool and database system. These visual tools also usually require a good deal of programming to get the system the way we want it.

This chapter is an introduction to Java Database Connectivity (JDBC). JDBC is neither a visual tool nor a database system. A visual tool created in Java will use JDBC to contact the database. JDBC is the part of the Java API that provides classes and methods that make it possible to send SQL (Structured Query Language) statements to a database and get a result back.

This chapter assumes that you are familiar with relational databases and SQL. SQL is a standardized language used to communicate to relational databases. In order to write programs that work with databases, you should also know about security and transaction handling. You should also have a knowledge of data modeling and know about the relationship between the relational model and the object model. These topics are not covered in this book. There are many database books available (for example, try [Connolly, Begg, Strachan 1999]).

20.1 Database Drivers

JDBC consists of many classes and is part of the Java API. A Java program that will work with a database uses these classes, independent of the underlying database system. The Java program uses these classes to send SQL statements to the database and then receives a response back from the database. There are many different database systems available and they all have their own API towards the outside world. The API is seldom written in Java but often in C, for example. We need something that can receive JDBC calls and convert them to method calls that fit in with the database system we're going to use. We call this type of converter a *database driver*.

An equivalent problem is familiar from the Microsoft platform. Open Database Connectivity (ODBC) is the name of the software that makes it possible for Microsoft Windows to communicate with just about any database system available. If we get our Java program to communicate with ODBC, the road is automatically opened to a great many database systems.

There are two primary types of database drivers for Java (see Figure 20.1):

• The driver is an adaptor from JDBC to ODBC. ODBC takes care of the communication with the database. This sort of driver is called a *JDBC-ODBC Bridge*.

• The driver is specially created for the database system we are programming for.

There is a summary of available database drivers at [URL Database Drivers].

In this book, we are using a driver of the latter type that is communicating with an Oracle7 database. We downloaded the driver from Oracle's Internet site—it's called *classes111.zip*. CLASSPATH has to be expanded so that the name of this zipped file is included. If the file is at *c:\prog\classes111.zip*, CLASSPATH has to contain c:\prog\classes111.zip.

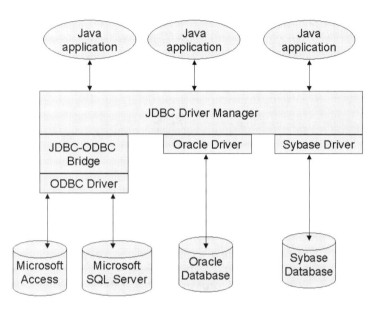

Figure 20.1 A java program communicates with a database through a database driver. A slightly revised version of the figure 23-2, p. 528 in [Orfali, Harkey 1998]. Reproduced by permission of John Wiley & Sons, Inc.

20.2 Establishing Contact with a Database

In this chapter, we're using a database created with the following SQL script:

```
create table person(
 identno    integer primary key,
 firstname  varchar(30) not null,
 lastname   varchar(30) not null);

insert into person values (100, 'EDWARD', 'BROWN');
insert into person values (101, 'ANN MARGARET', 'GREEN');
insert into person values (102, 'JOHN', 'JOHNSON');
```

Thus the whole database consists of a single table with three columns. We defined the identno field as primary key—that means that the database system will refuse to put in two people with the same identification number.

To begin with, we've stored three rows of data in the table. We're choosing to store all text as capital letters. Even if Java provides a method called equalsIgnoreCase(), we can't count on the database system providing anything equivalent. Searching for a person named "Edward Brown" doesn't happen in the Java program now, but in the database system. If we store both capital and lower-case letters, "Edward Brown" and "edward Brown" will be considered two different people by the database system, even if the latter was probably just a typo.

Program Listing 20.1 shows a Java program that connects to the database and retrieves all the data stored there. (See the printout at the bottom.)

Program Listing 20.1

```
/*
 * DatabaseContact.java   E.L. 2001-08-26
 */

import javax.swing.*;
import java.sql.*;
class DatabaseContact {
  public static void main(String[] args) throws Exception {
    String databaseDriver = "oracle.jdbc.driver.OracleDriver";
    Class.forName(databaseDriver);

    String userName = JOptionPane.showInputDialog("User Name: ");
    String password = JOptionPane.showInputDialog("Password: ");
    String databaseName = "jdbc:oracle:thin:@loiosh.stud.idb.hist.no:1521:orcl";
    Connection conn
      = DriverManager.getConnection(databaseName, userName, password);

    Statement statement = conn.createStatement();

    ResultSet res = statement.executeQuery("select * from person");
    while (res.next()) {
      int idNo = res.getInt("identno");
      String firstName = res.getString("firstname");
      String lastName = res.getString("lastname");
      System.out.println(idNo + ": " + firstName + " " + lastName);
    }
    res.close();
    statement.close();
    conn.close();
    System.exit(0);
  }
}

/* Example Run:
100: EDWARD BROWN
101: ANN MARGARET GREEN
102: JOHN JOHNSON
*/
```

Let's go through the code line by line. The classes we use in connection with database management are in the java.sql package:

```
import java.sql.*;
```

We see that `main()` throws any possible exceptions on without handling them. This (or `try-catch`) is necessary because all database calls can throw `java.sql.SQLException`.

First we have to register the driver we're going to use. The easiest way to do that is:

```
String databaseDriver = "oracle.jdbc.driver.OracleDriver";
Class.forName(databaseDriver);
```

The `forName()` method is a class method in the `Class` class. It says that we will load in a class named `oracle.jdbc.driver.OracleDriver`. (If we look at the contents of the file collection *classes111.zip*, we'll find the file *OracleDriver.class* in the *oracle/jdbc/driver* subdirectory, which conforms to the class name.)

The next step is to set up a connection to the database:

```
String userName = JOptionPane.showInputDialog("User Name: ");
String password = JOptionPane.showInputDialog("Password: ");
String databaseName = "jdbc:oracle:thin:@loiosh.stud.idb.hist.no:1521:orcl";
Connection conn
    = DriverManager.getConnection(databaseName, userName, password);
```

We input the user name and password from the user and open the connection to an Oracle database that's running on port 1521 on a machine named `loiosh.stud.idb.hist.no`.

Using other database drivers

If you use a different database driver than we're using, you have to change the name of the driver file (the `databaseDriver` string) and the name of the database (the `databaseName` string). See the documentation that comes with the driver. Also remember to change CLASSPATH.

Many of you will use Access or other databases that are contacted via ODBC. In that case, you don't need to download a special driver. SDK includes a JDBC-ODBC bridge. We can establish contact with a database like this in a Java program as follows:

```
String databaseDriver = "sun.jdbc.odbc.JdbcOdbcDriver";
Class.forName(databaseDriver);

/* The database has the name "MyDatabase" in ODBC */
String databaseName = "jdbc:odbc:MyDatabase";

/* In this case, neither user name nor password is set, but they'll be the two last
   arguments to the getConnection() method */
Connection conn = DriverManager.getConnection(databaseName, "", "");
```

Now we're done with the database system specific aspect. The program will retrieve all the data in the person table and display it on the screen. The following SQL statement does the job:

```
select * from person;
```

We'll send this statement to the database. We have to begin by instantiating a Statement object linked to the database connection:

```
Statement statement = conn.createStatement();
```

SQL statements that manipulate data are usually divided into two groups: the select statement that's used to search in the database, and the other statements (insert, update, and delete) which are used to change the contents of the database. The latter group of statements can be executed by sending the message executeUpdate() to the Statement object. We'll see an example of this in the next section. Now we'll execute a select statement by sending the message executeQuery() to the Statement object:

```
ResultSet res = statement.executeQuery("select * from person");
```

res is an instance of the ResultSet class. The result from a select statement is usually several rows of data. We use the next() method to run through all the rows:

```
while (res.next()) {
  int idNo = res.getInt("identNo");
  String firstName = res.getString("firstname");
  String lastName = res.getString("lastname");
  System.out.println(idNo + ": " + firstName + " " + lastName);
}
```

Notice that we also have to use next() to get hold of the first row. For every row we have to retrieve the data value in each individual column. We use getString() for strings, getInt() for integers, getDouble() for decimal numerals, etc. Table 20.1 shows the relationship between data types in SQL and in Java, and also which getxxx() method should be used in the various situations.

The last thing we do is to release the database resources:

```
res.close();
statement.close();
conn.close();
```

Table 20.1 The relationship between SQL data type, java data types, and getxxx() methods

SQL data type	Java data type	getxxx()
CHAR, VARCHAR, LONGVARCHAR	`String`	`getString()`
NUMERIC, DECIMAL	`java.math. BigDecimal`	`getBigDecimal()`
BIT	`boolean`	`getBoolean()`
TINYINT	`byte`	`getByte()`
SMALLINT	`short`	`getShort()`
INTEGER	`int`	`getInt()`
BIGINT	`long`	`getLong()`
REAL	`float`	`getFloat()`
FLOAT, DOUBLE	`double`	`getDouble()`
BINARY, VARBINARY, LONGVARBINARY	`byte[]`	`getBytes()`
DATE	`java.sql.Date`	`getDate()`
TIME	`java.sql.Time`	`getTime()`
TIMESTAMP	`java.sql. Timestamp`	`getTimestamp()`

Even now we can suspect that problems arise because we're not working with an object database. To save a person object, we have to take it apart into identification number, first name, and last name, and make table rows from these. To retrieve an object, we have to retrieve each individual data value and create an object from these data values. Here, we only write out the values, but we could also create an object, like this:

```
Person aPerson = new Person(identNo, firstName, lastName);
```

There are pure object databases and there are also object-like extensions of many of the traditional database systems. This makes it possible to deal with the object model when we save data as well (cf. serialization). But there is very little to suggest that the use of relational databases is diminishing; therefore we are prioritizing this type of database in this brief introduction to the topic of "programming with databases".

API Reference

All of the methods throw an SQLException if an error code is returned from the database system or another error occurs in connection with the database management.

The java.sql.DriverManager class

This class manages the database drivers. It's possible to have multiple database drivers registered (see the online API documentation).

Method:

```
public static Connection getConnection(String databaseUrl,
                      String userName, String password)
```

This method tries to establish a connection to the database indicated and choose an appropriate database driver from the drivers that are registered. The method returns a reference to a Connection object (see below).

The java.sql.Connection interface

This interface is implemented in the database driver.

Methods:

```
public void close()
```

This method closes the connection to the database. Any Statement and ResultSet object that's open is also closed. Associated database resources are released.

```
public Statement createStatement()
```

This method creates a Statement object that can be used to send SQL statements to the database.

In the API Reference in Section 20.6, you'll find more methods for this interface.

The java.sql.Statement interface

This interface is implemented in the database driver.

Methods:

```
public void close()
```

This method closes the `Statement` object and also any open `ResultSet` objects. Associated database resources are released.

    public ResultSet executeQuery(String sqlStatement)

This method closes any open `ResultSet` objects, executes a select statement, and returns the result in a new `ResultSet` object.

    public int executeUpdate(String sqlStatement)

This method executes an insert, update, or delete statement. The number of table rows affected is returned. We can also use this method to execute SQL statements that don't return anything, for example "create table." In these cases, the method will return 0.

The java.sql.ResultSet interface

This interface is implemented in the database driver. An instance of a class that implements this interface will contain the result from a select statement (see the `executeQuery()` method above).

Methods:

    public void close()

This method closes the `ResultSet` object with associated database resources.

    public boolean next()

This method moves the row pointer forward a row in the result set. Before the first call to `next()`, the row pointer is positioned *before* the first row. Thus, `next()` has to be called once in order to access the first row.

    public xxx getxxx(String columnName)

See table 20.1 for a synopsis of xxx's possible values. The methods retrieve a value from the row the pointer is pointing to (see the description of the `next()` method above). The column name determines which value will be retrieved. If the value is SQL NULL (an empty field in the database) `0`, `null`, or `false` is returned, depending on the data type.

    public xxx getxxx(int columnNo)

This is equivalent to the method above, but takes the column number instead of the column name as its argument. The columns are numbered starting with 1.

    public Object getObject(String columnName)

In a way, this replaces all the `getxxx()` methods. It retrieves the value and saves it in a wrapper object of a suitable type (`Integer`, `Double`, etc.).

    public boolean wasNull()

This method returns `true` if the last value read was SQL NULL. It might be necessary to use this if, for example, the `getInt()` method returns 0. (Otherwise, would that mean that the field in the database contained the value 0, or was the field empty?)

Problem

1. The SQL statement

    select identno, firstname from person where lastname = 'JOHNSON';

    gives us the identification number and first name of all persons with the last name Johnson. Change Program Listing 20.1 so that the program executes this SQL statement. Remember, the SQL-string has to contain single quotes.
2. Then change the program so that it runs in a loop and inputs different last names from the user.

20.3 A Bigger Example

We will make a class to maintain the person database: see Figure 20.2. We see that the class resembles the interface for the `RenovationProject` class in Figure 10.7. That's reasonable—then our registry consisted of array lists in the computer's internal memory, now it's a table in a database. The operations are primarily the same, regardless of how the data is stored.

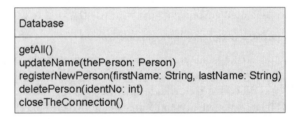

Figure 20.2 A class to maintain the person database (UML)

The class and test program are shown in Program Listing 20.2. Let's go through the `Database` class. The class is in the `myLibrary` package, and it uses the `Person` class (Program Listing 15.5) in the same package.

The constructor sets up the database connection and creates a `Statement` object. The database connection is, and has to be, an instance variable. All the operations to the database use the same database connection. The `Statement` object is an instance variable for efficiency reasons. In our case it's not necessary to instantiate a new `Statement` object every time an operation to the database is going to be executed. If, however, we need to handle several sets of results in parallel, for example, there has to be a `Statement` object for every result set.

The constructor and all the methods throw any exceptions that come up on to the client. Then it's up to the client to handle them.

All the methods print the SQL statement that is sent to the database. This makes it easy to follow along with the activity to the database.

The `getAll()` method retrieves all the rows in the table sorted by last name and instantiates `Person` objects from them. The `Person` objects are put in an array list, which is returned to the client.

The next method, the `updateName()` method, is the first method that changes the data contents in the `person` table. The method starts by converting the two strings to capital letters. Then the string that comprises the SQL statement is created:

```
String sqlStmt = "update person set firstname = '" + newFirstName +
                 "', lastname = '" + newLastName + "' where identno = " + identNo;
```

Text constants in an SQL statement are enclosed in single quotes, not in double quotes. In our case, both first and last names are in `String` objects. We join these together with the rest of the statement the usual way by using +. What may look like three single quotes is one double quote and one single quote. Which one is first, you have to see from the context, or you may take the source code into an editor and inspect the characters in detail there. If we're going to change the name "Edward Brown" to "Edward Red" for person with identification number 100, the SQL statement will look like this:

```
update person set firstname = 'EDWARD', lastname = 'RED' where identno = 100;
```

Then we send the `executeUpdate()` message to the `Statement` object. The finished SQL statement is the argument. If `executeUpdate()` returns 0, that means that no rows have been changed. In this case, our method returns `false`. In practical terms, this means that there weren't any people registered with this number in the database.

The rest of the methods in the `Database` class are constructed in an equivalent manner.

The client program starts by printing out all registered names. Then it inserts a new person, changes the person's first name and then changes her last name in order to finally delete her from the database. All the data prints out in between the changes.

Program Listing 20.2

```
/*
 * Database.java   E.L. 2001-08-26
 */
package myLibrary;
import java.util.*;
```

```java
import java.sql.*;
import myLibrary.Person;

public class Database {
  private static final String databaseDriver = "oracle.jdbc.driver.OracleDriver";
  private static final String databaseName
    = "jdbc:oracle:thin:@loiosh.stud.idb.hist.no:1521:orcl";
  private Connection conn;
  private Statement statement;

  /* The code if one tries to store more than one person with the same ident.no.*/
  private static final int code = 1; // Oracle return code

  /*
   * Establishes the database connection.
   */
  public Database(String userName, String password) throws Exception {
    Class.forName(databaseDriver);
    conn = DriverManager.getConnection(databaseName, userName, password);
    statement = conn.createStatement();
    System.out.println("** From the Database class: " +
            "A connection to the database is established.");
  }

  /*
   * Shuts down the connection.
   */
  public void closeTheConnection() throws SQLException {
    if (statement != null) statement.close();
    if (conn != null) conn.close();
    System.out.println("** From the Database class: " +
            "The connection to the database is closed.");
  }

  /*
   * Returns an array list with all the data from the person table.
   * The list is sorted with respect to the last name.
   */
  public ArrayList getAll() throws SQLException {
    ArrayList all = new ArrayList();
    String sqlStmt = "select * from person order by lastName, firstName";
    System.out.println("** From the Database class: " + sqlStmt);
    ResultSet res = null;
    try {
      res = statement.executeQuery(sqlStmt);
      while (res.next()) {
        int identNo = res.getInt("identno");
        String firstName = res.getString("firstname");
        String lastName = res.getString("lastname");
        Person thePerson = new Person(identNo, convert(firstName),
                convert(lastName)); // convert, private method, see below
```

```
      all.add(thePerson);
    }
  } finally { // the statements below are executed regardless of exceptions thrown
    /* Releases database resources, in every case, also if exceptions are thrown. */
    if (res != null) res.close();
    return all;
  }
}
/*
 * updates the name of a person in the database.
 * Returns false if no persons with this identno. exist.
 */
public boolean updateName(Person thePerson) throws SQLException {
  int identNo = thePerson.getPersIdent();
  String newFirstName = thePerson.getFirstName().toUpperCase();
  String newLastName = thePerson.getLastName().toUpperCase();
  String sqlStmt = "update person set firstname = '" + newFirstName
    + "', lastname = '" + newLastName + "' where identno = " + identNo;
  System.out.println("** From the Database class: " + sqlStmt);
  if (statement.executeUpdate(sqlStmt) == 0) return false;
  else return true;
}
/*
 * Stores a new person in the database.
 * Identno. is assigned by the method. If this is the first person to be registered,
 * she'll get number 1. Other persons get a number equal to 1 + max. no. until now.
 * (Data may be deleted, this method may therefore give holes in the number
 * sequence.)
 */
public Person registerNewPerson(String firstName, String lastName)
                                  throws SQLException {
  firstName = firstName.toUpperCase();
  lastName = lastName.toUpperCase();
  int newIdentNo = 1; // if no persons in the database
  boolean ok = true;
  do {
    ResultSet res = null;
    try {
      String sqlStmt = "select max(identno) as maxno from person";
      res = statement.executeQuery(sqlStmt);
      if (res.next()) newIdentNo = res.getInt("maxno") + 1;
      sqlStmt = "insert into person values(" + newIdentNo + ", '"
          + firstName + "', '" + lastName + "')";
      System.out.println("** From the Database class: " + sqlStmt);
      statement.executeUpdate(sqlStmt);
    } catch (SQLException e) {
      /* If the error code means that a person with this no. already exists,
```

```
    another client must have stored this person in between our two sql statements.
    We therefore rerun the do loop. (This happens very rarely.) */
    if (e.getErrorCode() == code) ok = false;
    else throw e;
  } finally {
    if (res != null) res.close();
  }
} while (!ok);
return new Person(newIdentNo, firstName, lastName);
}

/*
 * Deletes a person with a given identno.
 */
public boolean deletePerson(int identNo) throws SQLException {
  String sqlStmt = "delete from person where identno = " + identNo;
  System.out.println("** From the Database class: " + sqlStmt);
  if (statement.executeUpdate(sqlStmt) == 0) return false;
  else return true;
}

/*
 * Converts a name from the database (only capital letters) into a string
 * having a capital letter at the beginning of each word (as usual for names).
 */
private String convert(String text) {
  String newText = "";
  StringTokenizer theText = new StringTokenizer(text);
  while (theText.hasMoreTokens()) {
    String s = theText.nextToken();
    newText += s.substring(0, 1);
    if (s.length() > 0) newText += s.substring(1).toLowerCase() + " ";
  }
  newText = newText.trim();
  return newText;
}
}

/*
 * DatabaseTest.java   E.L. 2001-08-26
 */

import javax.swing.*;
import java.util.*;
import myLibrary.*;  // Person and Database

class DatabaseTest {
  public static void main(String[] args) throws Exception {
    String userName = JOptionPane.showInputDialog("User Name: ");
    String password = JOptionPane.showInputDialog("Password: ");

    Database db = new Database(userName, password);
```

```
System.out.println("Get all:");
Person aPerson = null;
ArrayList all = db.getAll();
for (int i = 0; i < all.size(); i++) {
  aPerson = (Person) all.get(i);
  System.out.println(aPerson);
}

System.out.println("Will store Ann Morris in the database:");
Person thePerson = db.registerNewPerson("Ann", "Morris");
int idNo = thePerson.getPersIdent();
System.out.println("She got ident. no.: " + idNo);

System.out.println("All the persons, after Ann Morris are stored:");
all = db.getAll();
for (int i = 0; i < all.size(); i++) {
  aPerson = (Person) all.get(i);
  System.out.println(aPerson);
}

System.out.println("Updates her first name from Ann to Greta:");
thePerson.setFirstName("Greta");
if (db.updateName(thePerson)) System.out.println("Her first name is updated.");
else System.out.println("Not possible to update the first name");

System.out.println("Updates her last name from Morris to Bull:");
thePerson.setLastName("Bull");
if (db.updateName(thePerson)) System.out.println("Her last name is updated");
else System.out.println("Not possible to update the last name");

System.out.println("Will delete the newly inserted person from the database");
if (db.deletePerson(idNo)) System.out.println("Person " + idNo + " is deleted");
else System.out.println("Person " + idNo + " is not deleted");

System.out.println("All the persons in the database after updates and deleting:");
all = db.getAll();
for (int i = 0; i < all.size(); i++) {
  aPerson = (Person) all.get(i);
  System.out.println(aPerson);
}

  db.closeTheConnection();
  System.exit(0);
 }
}
/* Example Run, the person table contains the data from the script in Section 20.2.
** From the Database class: A connection to the database is established.
Get all:
** From the Database class: select * from person order by lastName, firstName
100: Brown, Edward
101: Green, Ann Margaret
102: Johnson, John
```

Will store Ann Morris in the database:
** From the Database class: insert into person values(103, 'ANN', 'MORRIS')
She got ident. no.: 103
All the persons, after Ann Morris are stored:
** From the Database class: select * from person order by lastName, firstName
100: Brown, Edward
101: Green, Ann Margaret
102: Johnson, John
103: Morris, Ann
Updates her first name from Ann to Greta:
** From the Database class: update person set firstname = 'GRETA', lastname =
'MORRIS' where identno = 103
Her first name is updated.
Updates her last name from Morris to Bull:
** From the Database class: update person set firstname = 'GRETA', lastname =
'BULL'
where identno = 103
Her last name is updated
Will delete the newly inserted person from the database
** From the Database class: delete from person where identno = 103
Person 103 is deleted
All the persons in the database after updates and deleting:
** From the Database class: select * from person order by lastName, firstName
100: Brown, Edward
101: Green, Ann Margaret
102: Johnson, John
** From the Database class: The connection to the database is closed.
*/

Problem

Make a method in the Database class that finds all the different last names.

20.4 A Database Application

Here we'll create an application with a user interface as shown in Figure 20.3

The code is shown in Program Listing 20.3. The program consists of the classes DatabaseGUI and DatabaseApplication. The latter class contains main(). The user name and password are input in main(), and the connection to the database is established by creating an instance of the Database class. If this goes well, the window shown in the figure is made:

DatabaseGUI theApplication = new DatabaseGUI(theDatabase);

The database object is sent along as argument.

The contact with the database is primarily in the ButtonListener class, where the various button presses are handled. The "Delete," "New," and "Edit" buttons result in the contents of the database being changed. If it succeeds, the contents of the list on the screen are also changed. Because more than one person can work with the database at the same time, it's still not definite that the list will reflect the exact contents of the database. The "Refresh" button fills the list with "fresh" data from the database.

Figure 20.3 User interface, maintaining the name registry

The application uses `PersonDialog` from Program Listing 15.5.

The database object throws all exceptions on to the client. It's always an advantage for the client side to get error messages that are as accurate as possible. Here the messages are handled by being output—in professional systems we should handle more thoroughly the individual message. A database error will be an instance of the `java.sql.SQLException` class and this class gives us the opportunity to analyze the individual database error exactly (see the online API documentation).

Program Listing 20.3

```
/*
 * DatabaseApplication.java  E.L. 2001-08-26
 *
 * The primary window in this GUI application shows all the data in the person table.
 * The user may choose to update data, delete data or add new data to the database.
 * If updates were accepted by the database, they are also reflected in the primary
 * window. To reflect database updates done by other users, the user has to click on
 * the "Refresh" button.
 */

import javax.swing.*;
import java.awt.*;
import java.awt.event.*;
import java.util.*;
import java.text.*;
import myLibrary.*;
```

```java
class DatabaseGUI extends JFrame {
  private Database theDatabaseContact;

   private Container guiContainer;
  private DefaultListModel listData = new DefaultListModel();
  private JList list = new JList(listData);

  private JButton deleteButton = new JButton("Delete");
  private JButton newButton = new JButton("New");
  private JButton editButton = new JButton("Edit");
  private JButton refreshButton = new JButton("Refresh");

  private PersonDialog personDialog = new PersonDialog(this);

  public DatabaseGUI(Database initDatabase) {
    theDatabaseContact = initDatabase;

    setDefaultCloseOperation(JFrame.DO_NOTHING_ON_CLOSE);
    addWindowListener(new WindowClosingListener());

    guiContainer = getContentPane();
    guiContainer.add(
    new HeadingPanel("Name Archive"), BorderLayout.NORTH);
    guiContainer.add(new ListPanel(), BorderLayout.CENTER);
    guiContainer.add(new ButtonPanel(), BorderLayout.SOUTH);

    fillListWithData();  // see below.
    personDialog.setLocation(300, 400);
    setLocation(300, 300);
    pack();
  }

  /* Help method: Retrieves data from the database and fills the list in the primary
     window.*/
  private void fillListWithData() {
    try {
      listData.clear();
      ArrayList all = theDatabaseContact.getAll();
      for (int i = 0; i < all.size(); i++) listData.addElement(all.get(i));
      if (listData.size() > 0) list.setSelectedIndex(0); // default selection
      else { // no data, the Edit and Delete buttons should be locked
        deleteButton.setEnabled(false);
        editButton.setEnabled(false);
      }
    } catch (Exception e) {
      JOptionPane.showMessageDialog(null, "Error retrieving data.\n" + e);
    }
  }
  /*
   * Here follow the three panels describing the user interface.
   */
  private class HeadingPanel extends JPanel {
```

```java
    public HeadingPanel(String heading) {
      Font defFont = getFont();
      Font bigFont = new Font(defFont.getName(), defFont.getStyle(), 18);
      JLabel text = new JLabel(heading);
      text.setFont(bigFont);
      add(text);
    }
  }

  private class ListPanel extends JPanel {
    public ListPanel() {
      list.setPreferredSize(new Dimension(300, 300)); // FlowLayout allows for this
      list.setSelectionMode(ListSelectionModel.SINGLE_SELECTION);
      JScrollPane scrollWithList = new JScrollPane(list);

      /* List heading */
      JViewport jvp = new JViewport(); // see online API doc.
      jvp.setView(new JLabel("All Names"));
      scrollWithList.setColumnHeader(jvp);

      add(scrollWithList);
    }
  }

  private class ButtonPanel extends JPanel {
    public ButtonPanel() {
      ButtonListener theListener = new ButtonListener();
      deleteButton.addActionListener(theListener);
      newButton.addActionListener(theListener);
      editButton.addActionListener(theListener);
      refreshButton.addActionListener(theListener);
      add(deleteButton);
      add(newButton);
      add(editButton);
      add(refreshButton);
    }
  }

  /*
   * This class handles all the button clicks.
   */
  private class ButtonListener implements ActionListener {
    public void actionPerformed(ActionEvent event) {
      JButton source = (JButton) event.getSource();

      if (source == deleteButton) { // Deletes a person
        Person thePerson = (Person) list.getSelectedValue();
        try {
          boolean deleted = theDatabaseContact.deletePerson(thePerson.getPersIdent());
          if (deleted) {
            listData.remove(list.getSelectedIndex());
            if (listData.size() == 0) {
```

```
      deleteButton.setEnabled(false);
      editButton.setEnabled(false);
    }
    else list.setSelectedIndex(0);
  } else {
    JOptionPane.showMessageDialog(null, "Not possible to delete this person." +
                    "Other clients may have done it already.");
  }
 } catch (Exception e) {
   JOptionPane.showMessageDialog(null, "Error when deleting: " + e);
 }
}

else if (source == editButton) { // updates a name
  Person thePerson = (Person) list.getSelectedValue();
  int index = list.getSelectedIndex();
  if (personDialog.showDialog(thePerson)) { // thePerson object will be updated
    try {
      if (theDatabaseContact.updateName(thePerson)) {
        listData.set(index, thePerson); // updates the list in the window
        list.setSelectedIndex(0);
      } else JOptionPane.showMessageDialog(null,
            "No data updated. The person may be deleted by others.");
    } catch (Exception e) {
      JOptionPane.showMessageDialog(null, "Error when changing data: " + e);
    }
  }
}

else if (source == newButton) { // Stores new person.
  Person thePerson = new Person(-1,"", "");
  if (personDialog.showDialog(thePerson)) {
    try {
      thePerson = theDatabaseContact.registerNewPerson(
        thePerson.getFirstName(), thePerson.getLastName());
      JOptionPane.showMessageDialog(null,
              "The person gets ident. no. " + thePerson.getPersIdent());
      listData.addElement(thePerson);
      if (listData.size() == 1) { // this was the first person in the database!
        deleteButton.setEnabled(true);
        editButton.setEnabled(true);
        list.setSelectedIndex(0);
      }
    } catch (Exception e) {
      JOptionPane.showMessageDialog(null, "Error storing data: " + e);
    }
  }
}
```

```
        else if (source == refreshButton) { // Refreshes the data in the list
          fillListWithData();
        }
      }
    }

      private class WindowClosingListener extends WindowAdapter {
      public void windowClosing(WindowEvent event) {
        listData.clear(); // empties the list
        try {
          theDatabaseContact.closeTheConnection();
        } catch (Exception e) {
          System.out.println("Error when disconnecting: " + e);
        }
        System.exit(0);
      }
    }
  }

  class DatabaseApplication {
    public static void main(String[] args) {
      Database theDatabaseContact = null;
      try {
        String userName = JOptionPane.showInputDialog("User Name: ");
        String password = JOptionPane.showInputDialog("Password: ");
        theDatabaseContact = new Database(userName, password);
      } catch (Exception e) {
        JOptionPane.showMessageDialog(null,
          "Problems when establishing database connection, " +
          "the user name or the password may be invalid. \nError: " + e);
        try {
          // disconnects what may be disconnected
          theDatabaseContact.closeTheConnection();
        } catch (Exception e1) {
        }
        System.exit(0);
      }
      DatabaseGUI theApplication = new DatabaseGUI(theDatabaseContact);
      theApplication.setVisible(true);
    }
  }
```

Problem

Assume that the names (in addition to the numbers) in our person database are unambiguous. Expand the Database class with the method

```
int getPerson(String firstName, String lastName)
```

which returns the identification number of the person with this name, if found in the database. If not found, the method should return a negative number.

Write an application that inputs a name from the user and finds out whether it's registered in the database. If it's not registered, it will be inserted into the database.

20.5 The Three-Layer Architecture

Figure 20.4 shows the deployment diagram for the example above. The system consists of three parts:

1. The physical database, running on the machine loiosh.stud.idb.hist.no

2. The component (in this case a single object, named "theDatabaseContact"), which communicates with the database

3. The user interface component which communicates with "theDatabaseContact".

There is no direct communication between the user interface and the database. This delegation of responsibility is very common, and it conforms to the object orienting principles.

This division with a database on the bottom and a user interface on the top is in general called *"The Three-Layer Architecture"*. The middle layer is often divided further in, for example into one layer with the close database contact (sql statements) and the other with problem domain classes at a higher level.

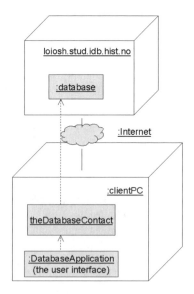

Figure 20.4 The distribution of the components in the database application (UML)

In our case, we have two of the layers running on the same machine. This is a rather "thick client". Often the layers are distributed on different machines. RMI may help us with this distribution. With an applet running in an Internet user's browser, we then have an example of the three layers on three different machines. This gives us a thinner client. We get an even thinner client if the Web browser only receives an HTML page. This is possible if the Web server creates a specially designed HTML page every time the user sends a database request. This may sound bothersome, but we'll see in the next chapter how to make programs that accomplish this.

Problems

1. Convert the `Database` class in this chapter into an RMI interface `Database` with the class `DatabaseImpl` as the implementation. Test this by doing minor changes in the program on the file *DatabaseTest.java*.

2. Do the necessary changes such that the components "theDatabaseContact" and ":DatabaseApplication" in Figure 20.4 may now run on different machines.

3. Draw a new deployment diagram.

20.6 Transactions and Compiled SQL Statements

Transactions

A transaction is a logical unit of work and can consist of multiple update statements to the database. For example, if money is going to be transferred from one account to another, it's important that the balances in both of the accounts change. If an error occurs, we can't risk that only one of the accounts changes its balance. We define the transaction, therefore, to consist of the two update commands. If an error occurs before both of the commands are successfully executed, the whole transaction is rolled back (a "rollback") so that the database remains unchanged. If everything was successful, the transaction will be committed by permanently saving the changes in the database.

Usually every individual SQL statement is a transaction unit. In situations like the ones mentioned here we have to be able to expand the size of a transaction unit. Methods in the `Connection` interface make it possible for us to control this (see the API reference below).

A transaction causes part of the database to be locked until the transaction is finished. An update means that other database connections can't access the affected data at all. Reading from the database makes it so that other database connections have read-only access to the data. Because of this it's important to remember to finish transactions that have been started. The exact amount of the database that is reserved in a transaction varies from database system to database system.

It's not always necessary to define a transaction even if multiple statements have to be executed without interruptions. It depends on what the statements do. In the `registerNewPerson()` method in the `Database` class in Program Listing 20.2, we handle this another way. We find the identification number that the new person who will be added to the database will have. We use the SQL function max() to find the largest number up to this point. The new number will be 1 larger than this. Now if another client succeeds in registering a new person before we've inserted ours, our number will already be taken in and the database system will protest. An exception object is thrown and we set ok equal to false. Then the program will ask the database once more for the largest number used so far.

This method of handling transactions builds on the fact that the probability of two or more clients accessing the same data at the same time is negligible. This solution therefore requires very few resources.

But notice that the method can't always be used. The account update example demonstrates this. The program code for the account example is shown as the solution to problem 1 after this section.

Compiled SQL statements

An SQL statement has to be compiled by the database system before it is run. The database system also sets up a plan so that the search can be done in the most efficient way possible. If you send the same statement many times, you'll save time by making these preparations only once. We can replace constant values in the statement without compiling it again.

We can make a compiled Statement object using the PreparedStatement class: see Program Listing 20.4.

The SQL statement contains two question marks:

```
select * from person where firstName like ? and lastName like ?
```

Here we get the persons that satisfy specific search criteria. The program runs in a loop and constantly asks the user for new first and last name search criteria. We put in the search criteria in place of the question marks:

```
statement.setString(1, searchCritFirstName.toUpperCase());
statement.setString(2, searchCritLastName.toUpperCase());
```

The first question mark is number 1. We can use the wildcard symbol in the search criteria. % means any sequence of characters, while _ means exactly one character.[1] The search criteria ___ (three underline characters) for the first name and h% for the last name give us all the names that have first names with exactly three letters and last names that start with H.

API Reference

The java.sql.Connection interface

See also the API reference in Section 20.2.

---

1. These wildcard symbols are standard SQL, but not all database systems follow the standard exactly on this point.

Methods:

> public void setAutoCommit(boolean autocommit)

We turn autocommit off by sending this message with the argument `false` to the database connection. It's important to remember to turn autocommit on again (same message with the argument `true`) when we no longer need to deal with transactions that consist of more than one SQL statement.

> public void commit()

This method makes all the changes that have occurred since the last `commit()`/ `rollback()` permanent. All the locks that this connection holds are released. This method should only be used if autocommit is turned off.

> public void rollback()

This method cancels all changes since the last `commit()`/`rollback()`. All the locks this connection holds are released. This method should only be used if autocommit is turned off.

> public PreparedStatement prepareStatement(String sql)

This method makes a compiled SQL statement. If the same statement is going to be executed more than once, it pays to compile it first.

The java.sql.PreparedStatement interface

The database driver implements this interface. The interface is a subinterface of `java.sql.Statement`.

Methods:

> public ResultSet executeQuery()

This method executes the compiled select statement. The result is returned as an `ResultSet` object.

> public int executeUpdate()

This method executes the compiled insert, update, or delete statement. It returns the number of table rows affected. This method can also be used to execute SQL statements that don't return anything—for example, create table. In these cases, the method will return 0.

> public void setInt(int questionMarkNo, int x)
> public void setLong(int questionMarkNo, long x)
> public void setString(int questionMarkNo, String text)

These are three of the methods in a family of methods used to give values to the question marks (called parameters) in the SQL statement. The first question mark has number 1. For the relationship between the SQL data types, Java data types, and method names, see table 20.1.

Program Listing 20.4

```
/*
 * PreparedStmtTest.java   E.L. 2001-08-26
 */

import javax.swing.*;
import java.sql.*;
class PreparedStmtTest {
  public static void main(String[] args) throws Exception {
    String databaseDriver = "oracle.jdbc.driver.OracleDriver";
    Class.forName(databaseDriver);

    String userName = JOptionPane.showInputDialog("User Name: ");
    String password = JOptionPane.showInputDialog("Password: ");
    String databaseName = "jdbc:oracle:thin:@loiosh.stud.idb.hist.no:1521:orcl";
    Connection conn =
      DriverManager.getConnection(databaseName, userName, password);
    String sqlStatement = "select * from person where firstName like ? and lastName like ?";
    PreparedStatement statement = conn.prepareStatement(sqlStatement);

    do { // infinite loop for test purposes
      String searchCritFirstName
        = JOptionPane.showInputDialog("Search Criterion, First Name: ");
      String searchCritLastName
        = JOptionPane.showInputDialog("Search Criterion, Last Name: ");
      statement.setString(1, searchCritFirstName.toUpperCase());
      statement.setString(2, searchCritLastName.toUpperCase());

      System.out.println(
        "\nThe Search Criteria: " + searchCritFirstName + " " + searchCritLastName);

      ResultSet res = statement.executeQuery();
      while (res.next()) {
        int identNo = res.getInt("identNo");
        String firstName = res.getString("firstName");
        String lastName = res.getString("lastName");
        System.out.println(firstName + " " + lastName);
      }
      res.close();
    } while (true);
  }
}

/* Example Run:

The Search Criteria: % _____
EDWARD BROWN
ANN MARGARET GREEN

The Search Criteria: % %n
EDWARD BROWN
```

ANN MARGARET GREEN
JOHN JOHNSON
*/

Problems

1. Write an SQL script that sets up a table of accounts in a database. It should contain account numbers, names, and balances. Put in three accounts. Then make a single program that tests the transaction example described above.

2. Modify the `Database` class in Program Listing 20.2 so that all SQL statements are compiled beforehand.

20.7 New Concepts in This Chapter

Concept	Brief Explanation
database driver	Software that makes it possible to use JDBC on a specific database system.
DBMS	Database Management System. "A software system that enables users to define, create, and maintain the database and provides controlled access to this database." [Connolly, Begg, Strachan 1999, p. 16]
JDBC	Java Database Connectivity. The part of the Java API that's used to communicate with relational databases.
JDBC-ODBC Bridge	An adaptor from JDBC to ODBC. ODBC takes care of the communication with the database.
ODBC	Open Database Connectivity. An API for database systems, created by Microsoft.
relational database	A database where the data is organized in table form.
SQL	Structured Query Language. Standard query language for relational databases.
three-layer architecture	The principle of dividing a software system into three layers; often the bottom layer is the database, and the top layer is the user interface. In between we have software for the problem domain, which may be divided further ("n-layer architecture") . One layer communicates only with the layer directly above and/or below, not with the others.
transaction	A group of database operations that have to be executed as a unit.

20.8 Review Problems

1. What's the purpose of a database driver?

2. What's JDBC, or to put it more correctly, what *isn't* JDBC?

3. Briefly explain the use of classes that implement the `ResultSet` interface.

4. What's the difference between `Statement` and `PreparedStatement`?

5. What is meant by three-layer architecture? What is meant by n-layer architecture? Give examples.

20.9 Programming Problems

These problems require relational database and SQL skills beyond those shown in the examples in this chapter.

Problem 1

Change the loan system from programming problem 3, Chapter 19 so that the book information is in a database. You need a table of book information and one with information about the copies. Add the database contact to a single class. The system will still be a distributed system based on RMI.

Problem 2

In the problems at the end of Section 14.5, there's a list of the populations of the ten largest urban areas in the world. Put these into a database. Assume that city name is unique.

Make a class that offers the following operations for this database:

- Register a new city with a given population

- Find all cities with more than a given number of inhabitants

- Find all cities with fewer than a given number of inhabitants

- Find the population of a specific city

- Change the population of a given city

  Write a simple test program.

Problem 3

Create the following database (primary keys are underlined):

    student(student number, first name, last name, address)
    course(course number, course name, description)
    grade(student number, course number, grade, year)

A student can take a course more than once. The best grade counts.
There will be two types of clients:

1. One client that has all the privileges including updating, modifying and deleting all data. This client logs in as an ordinary database user.

2. One client that can only look at the grades. This could be a student. Each student has his own password and is only allowed to look at his own data.

What each individual has access to can be controlled by creating an SQL view and setting privileges and a password linked to these. Find out what you can accomplish with the database system you're using. In a test phase you can input the student's password as an extra column in the student table. In this case, database log-in can be hard coded (!) in the program.

Make a class (or classes) that communicates with the database. Test the class by writing a simple test program.

Think of a suitable user interface for both types of clients. Emphasize simplicity. Implement the user interface.

Problem 4

(This problem was written by Simon Thoresen.)

Use `javax.swing.JOptionPane` to program a database client. This client will be able to execute any SQL statement entered by the user.

It should be "transparent" to the user how the program sends the call to the database (`executeQuery()` or `executeUpdate()`).

The client has to be able to produce a reasonable output for a query (select statements) with the right headers for each column. The `ResultSet` class provides a `getMetaData()` method that returns a `ResultSetMetaData` object. This object contains the necessary information about the table columns.

For updates, it's enough to print out the return value from `executeUpdate()`.

Web Programming with JavaServer Pages

Learning goals for this chapter

After completing this chapter you will understand the following concepts:

- Server-side versus client-side Web programming

- Servlets and JSP: pages, expressions, scriptlets, declarations, and comments

- Client-side versus server-side validation

- Cookies and sessions

You will be able to create *jsp* files that:

- Handle data the user enters into an HTML `form` element

- Work with a database (retrieving, inserting, deleting, and updating data)

- Maintain state information for the client (cookies) and the server (session object)

Despite the fact that Java's usability on the Internet led to its enormous popularity, very few of the programs in this book have been specially designed for this purpose. We've focused on creating ready-made classes that can be used in many different contexts. The client program could be a simple test program, or a traditional menu-driven program, or we can place a graphical user interface over the classes. Of course this graphical user interface can be an applet, and then we instantly have a program that is specially designed for the Internet.

You have certainly used the Internet to find hotels, for example. You enter the city and get back a list of possible hotels. The source code for this page shows the names of the hotels in plain text. Why doesn't the page contain program logic that searches for the hotels in a database? The answer is that the HTML code is specially adapted. The Web server receives your query for hotels in a specific city, sends this query to a program that searches the database, and generates HTML code with the applicable hotels. This code is then sent to the client in response to the query.

Compared to applets, this requires a completely different way of programming. The program runs on the Web server, not in the client's Web browser. These types of programs are the main topic of this chapter. We are still using our ready-made classes, but now with a new type of client program.

Consider this chapter an introduction, and refer to [Annunziato, Kaminaris 2001] and [Hall 2000], for example, to study the topic in more detail.

21.1 Different Ways of Programming for the Web

As you know, an applet is a program written so that it can be downloaded to a Web client in connection with an HTML page. The user notices this because the download takes a little longer than is normal, and the browser prints an alert in the status line that Java is being started. In return, the user gets a page with far greater functionality than a purely static HTML page offers.

To begin with, applets used to be about the only way to bring a Web page to "life". Various *scripting languages* have gradually made simple dynamics possible without costing too much in download time. A script describes what order things should happen in. In programming contexts, a scripting language is unique in that it doesn't need to be compiled. Each line in the source code is interpreted and performed as it comes up. An example of a scripting language is the language we use when we create an MS-DOS *bat* file. Such a file primarily contains a collection of MS-DOS commands, but can also contain other elements like for loops and if statements. The scripting language most commonly used with HTML is JavaScript. The language's syntax is similar to Java. Later in this chapter we will provide a brief example of what JavaScript code looks like. For more complicated functionality, applets are still preferable.

The dynamics described above, whether created using scripts, applets, or in some other way, take place in the client's Web browser. The user can study the source code (the HTML file) in its entirety with a menu selection in the Web browser (for example, View/Page Source). Here you'll find the HTML code including any JavaScript code and object tags to include applets.

We're used to searching for information by filling in fields on Web pages. In the HTML page's source code, these fields are found in what we call the form elements. The content we enter into the fields is sent to the Web server when we hit the "Send" button. There's a program on the Web server that handles this data. As explained in the introduction to this chapter, this handling often involves specially creating HTML pages that are sent back to the client.

The programs on the Web server can be written in several different languages. We'll write our programs in Java, or, more accurately, we'll use something called JavaServer Pages (JSP). The majority of the code we write is Java, and the results will be converted automatically into something called servlets, which are pure Java code.

21.2 Installing Software

To run the examples in this chapter, you must have access to a Web server that supports servlets and JSP. In a training and testing situation, the most practical thing to do is run the Web server on your own work station. You'll find a summary of Web servers on the market at [URL Web servers].

In addition to a Web server, you need the API online documentation for the servlet and JSP classes. You can download this from [URL Servlet info].

We've chosen to use LiteWebServer (LWS) from Gefion Software [URL Gefion]. It's free for our purposes, it's small (420 kB), and easy to stop and start. That last thing is especially important when it comes to debugging. It's often hard to register updates without stopping and restarting the Web server. The rest of this section is about using version 2.2.1 of the LWS Web server.

To install and test LWS, refer to the instructions ("Reference Manual," Chapter 4), which you'll find in the *doc* subdirectory after the files in the downloaded *zip* file are extracted. Installing on a PC requires familiarity with *bat* files in MS-DOS. For the examples in this chapter to work, CLASSPATH has to contain the path to myLibrary and to the database driver you used in Chapter 20.

If the Web server and the browser are running on the same machine, then the Web server installation can be tested by specifying *http://localhost:9090/* as the URL in the browser. Users on other machines who want to communicate with your Web server, however, have to use the computer name or IP address, e.g. *http:// marysMachine.marysCompany.com:9090/* or *http://160.99.54.340:9090/*.

A Web server can be configured and adapted in many ways. We'll stick to LWS's standard setup with two exceptions:

- As we will see, a *jsp* file will be converted to a Java servlet class. The servlet's source code is in a *java* file, which is compiled automatically. The compilation errors refer to the line number in the *java* file, and therefore it's beneficial for these not to be deleted. You avoid this by opening the *<LWS-home>/config/ examples/servlets.properties* file in an editor and changing keepgenerated=false to keepgenerated=true (at the very end of the file).

- In Section 21.9, we'll create pages that maintain state information without using cookies. Line 8 in the *<LWS-home>/config/examples/session.properties* file looks like: enable.urlrewriting=false You should change false to true here as well.

A server program has to know where the files it will use are. For LWS, the following apply if you don't make special adjustments in the configuration files:

- *jsp* files will be in the *<LWS-home>/html/examples* subdirectory, or possibly in subdirectories within this directory. For example, the URL for a JSP can be: *http:/ /localhost:9090/examples/chap21/time.jsp*

- *java* files that contain servlets will be in the *<LWS-home>/servlets* subdirectory. Note that the URL for a servlet contains the word "servlet", not "servlets": *http://localhost:9090/servlet/test*

- The *java* files generated automatically from translating the *jsp* files will be placed in the *<LWS-home>/work/examples* subdirectory.

- You'll have the other *java* files you use, such as for example the `Database` class from Chapter 20, in the `myLibrary` package. You'll be reminded of this when the time comes to run the examples.

Problems updating a page in the browser?

You will certainly experience cases where the browser doesn't keep up with your updates, regardless of how many times you press "Reload". In these cases, try the following:

- Stop the Web server. Remember to use the admin page (*http://localhost:9090/admin*, press "Shutdown") if you're using LWS.

- Delete automatically generated *java* and *class* files. LWS: Look at the *<LWS-home>/work/examples* directory. Remember that nothing will happen if you delete too many of these files. They will be recreated as necessary.

- Start the Web server again. LWS: If you've followed the installation instructions, entering *lws* in the command line should suffice.

21.3 Servlets

A *servlet* is a Java program that runs on a Web server. Servlets have certain traits in common with applets. While the browser creates the applet objects, the servlet objects are created by the Web server. Both types of objects have an `init()` method that is run once. When the user moves in and out of the Web page that contains an applet, the messages `stop()` and `start()` are sent to the applet object (see Figure 18.2). Every time a client requests a servlet object, the `service()` message is sent to the object in question (see Figure 21.1). There is, however, a substantial difference:

- An applet object is created and lives inside the client's browser and is therefore used by only one user.

- A servlet object is created by the Web server and is running there. The same object can therefore be used by many clients.

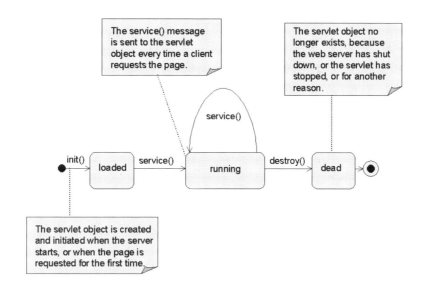

Figure 21.1 The life cycle of a servlet (a servlet object)

All servlets belong to a subclass of `javax.servlet.GenericServlet`. A direct subclass of this class is `HttpServlet`, which describes servlets that are used over the HTTP protocol. The vast majority of servlets are used this way, and all the ones we'll look at in this book certainly will be.

Like an applet, a servlet has to be an instance of a public class because it has to be accessible from all over.

The `init()`, `service()`, and `destroy()` methods have their own default versions that are used if we don't create our own versions. In particular, it's worth mentioning that the `service()` method normally shouldn't be redefined. Instead, we program the `doPost()` and/or `doGet()` methods. Every request to a servlet generates a call to the `service()` method, which interprets the request and then calls `doGet()` or `doPost()`.

The three methods, `service()`, `doGet()`, and `doPost()`, all take two arguments in the call. The one contains information about the request (the request object) and the other about the answer the Web server will send back (the response object).

Note that all the clients work with the same servlet object. Therefore, any instance variables there might be can be updated by multiple clients. Methods that work with the instance variables should therefore be synchronized.[1] In particular it should be mentioned that the java.util.ArrayList class is not synchronized. Instead, the roughly identical, but synchronized, java.util.Vector class should be used.

When a servlet is initialized, a *pool* of threads is usually generated that the service() method runs in. In LWS, the starting size of this pool is equal to 10. That means that 10 threads are created that are offered to clients as needed. A client that demands the servlet (and thereby the service() method) will be assigned its own thread. This thread is returned to the pool after use. If a thread is requested and the pool is empty, the client has to wait, or the pool can be expanded. By using a pool of threads, we avoid resource-intensive initialization every time a request comes from a client.

API Reference

The javax.servlet.GenericServlet class

This class is abstract and describes a protocol-independent servlet. Use the HttpServlet subclass (see below) if the servlet is going to be used over the HTTP protocol.

Methods:

```
public void destroy()
public void  init()
public abstract  void service(ServletRequest request, ServletResponse response)
```

The use of these methods is shown in Figure 21.1. The abstract service() method is implemented by the HttpServlet class.

The javax.servlet.http.HttpServlet class

This class is a subclass of GenericServlet. It's abstract and made concrete in a subclass that describes a real servlet.

Methods:

```
protected void service(HttpServletRequest request, HttpServletResponse response)
```

---

1. Which is to say that the code will be "thread safe". Servlet code should have this trait for efficiency reasons. The page directive (see Section 21.5) can be used if the code does not have this trait: <%@ page isThreadSafe="false" %>.

This method is called by the Web server and it interprets the query and then calls `doGet()` or `doPost()`.

> protected void doGet(HttpServletRequest request, HttpServletResponse response)
> protected void doPost(HttpServletRequest request, HttpServletResponse response)

These methods are called by the `service()` method.

Program Listing 21.1 shows a servlet that prints out the date and time in the client-side browser (see Figure 21.2).

The example uses the `response` object to indicate that it's HTML code that is being sent, and also to retrieve a `PrintWriter` object that can be used to send data back to the client. Notice how the HTML codes are created with `out.print()` and `out.println()`. The new line, which is a result of `println()`, will be included in the HTML code that results. To get a new line to appear in the browser, we have to send the HTML element "`<br>`" to the `out` object:

> out.print("
This text is on a line of its own.
");

We could also use "`<p>`" for a new paragraph.

For the example to generate something more than a static HTML code, we've included the time on the server machine:

> out.println("This page was downloaded: " + new java.util.Date());

This is sent in plain text to the `out` object: see the result in the figure.

We've not used the `request` object in the example, but it contains information about the client and also, for example, data the user has entered into data fields.

Program Listing 21.1

```java
/*
 * SimpleServlet.java E.L. 2001-08-27
 */
import java.io.*;
import javax.servlet.*;
import javax.servlet.http.*;

public class SimpleServlet extends HttpServlet {
  public void doGet(HttpServletRequest request, HttpServletResponse response)
    throws ServletException, IOException {
  response.setContentType("text/html");
  PrintWriter out = response.getWriter();
  out.print("<html>");
  out.print("<head>");
  out.print("<title>An example of server side programming</title>");
  out.println("</head>");
  out.println("<body>");
```

```
    out.println("This page was downloaded: " + new java.util.Date());
    out.println("</body>");
    out.println("</html>");
  }
}
```

```
public class SimpleServlet extends HttpServlet {
  public void doGet(HttpServletRequest request, HttpServletResponse response)
    throws ServletException, IOException {
    response.setContentType("text/html");

    PrintWriter out = response.getWriter();
    out.print("<html>");
    ...see program listing 21.1...
    out.println("</html>");
  }
}
```
source code
at the server side

```
<html><head><title>An example of server side programming</title></head>
<body>
This page was downloaded: Mon Aug 27 10:54:14 GMT+02:00 2001
</body>
</html>
```
the request from the
client generates this
HTML source code

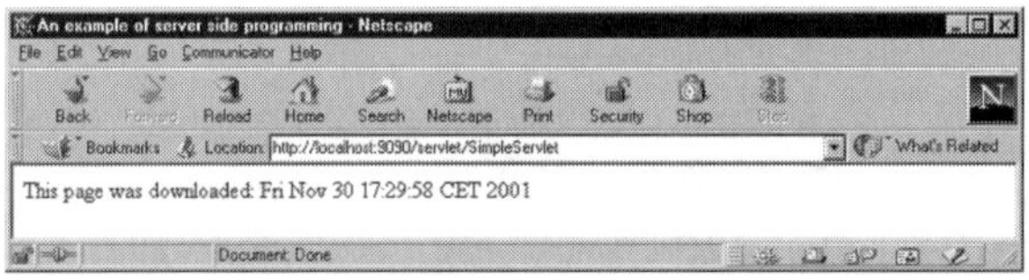

the browser
displays
the page

Figure 21.2   Example of server-side programming

Problems

The main goal of these problems is for you to understand what's involved in the concept of server-side Web programming. You run the Web server on your own machine and you will also be able to test all the servlets by opening all the pages in the browser on your own machine. In addition, it will be beneficial to download the pages at least once on another machine besides your own. This will allow you to see on your own that this does work over the Internet.

1. Copy the source code in Program Listing 21.1 to the right location on your computer. It should go in the directory for servlets. Compile.[2] Then open the servlet in your browser. Make sure that you understand what's happening on the server side and what's happening on the client side. Check the source code in the browser.

---

2. It may happen that you have to make sure that CLASSPATH contains *servlet.jar*. The *servlet.jar* file is located where the Web server is.

2. Change the source code so that, in addition to the time, it outputs five random numbers. For your change to take effect, you have to stop the servlet from problem 1 and start it again. To find out how to do this, you need to study the documentation for the Web server. Alternatively, you can stop the Web server and start it up again.

3. When a browser requests a Web page, it sends along some information about itself, for example the name of the computer it's on. The computer name can be accessed by sending the message `getRemoteHost()` to the `request` object. Try this and output the result on the server side using `System.out.println()`.

21.4 JavaServer Pages (JSP)

We're not going to develop servlets directly. Instead, we will make what is called *JavaServer Pages*. These are, to put it simply, HTML code with elements of Java code. The file extension will be *jsp*. The user requests the *jsp* file directly. If this is a first request for this file, it will be converted to a servlet. The servlet is compiled and started automatically. The result of the servlet's `service()` method will be an HTML page that is sent to the client and presented in the client's browser. A *JSP page* is thus an HTML page that is created by a servlet based on a *jsp* file. A *jsp* file equivalent to the servlet in Program Listing 21.1 is shown in Program Listing 21.2.

Program Listing 21.2

```
<!--
    Time.jsp E.L. 2001-08-27
 --!>
<html><head><title>An example of server side programming</title></head>
<body>
This page was downloaded: <%= new java.util.Date() %>
</body>
</html>
```

You'll find the Java code that runs on the server side between <% and %> in the third line from the bottom.

As we mentioned, a *java* file[3] is generated that contains a servlet. This servlet is far more complicated than Program Listing 21.1—that is because it is created automatically and also contains initializations for a number of standard objects that we can choose to use if we need to. The servlet class in the generated file is a subclass of the `HttpJspBase` class. Therefore the contents will be somewhat different than in our servlet class. However, we recognize the `request` and

---

3. Our Web server, LWS, creates a file that we will find in the *work/examples* subdirectory. The file name is long and detailed, but for this example, it includes the text "time_JSP", because the *jsp* file is named *time.jsp*. If you have several files like this, look at the dates to find the most recent one.

`response` parameters. We also find the variable `out`, which is used in writing the HTML codes.

Right from the start it may seem as if most of the advantage to using JSP instead of writing our own servlets is not having to write `out.println()` around the HTML elements.

A *jsp* file will, for the most part, contain HTML code. As with other HTML files, therefore, the *presentation* will be the main purpose. In several places in this book, we have demonstrated the importance of differentiating the user interface from the problem we are solving. The same problem can be presented with several different user interfaces. A potential user interface can be specified by HTML codes. We can also imagine other "markup" languages (see Appendix E.1). One example is *Wireless Markup Language*, WML, for use on mobile phones that support *Wireless Application Protocol*, WAP.

By using JSP, we can let Web designers use their own tools to generate an appealing design while we can create regular Java classes that cover most of the programming. Only smaller "snippets" of Java code are needed in the *jsp* file. With a few programming skills, Web designers can learn to put some of these in place themselves.

The examples in this book, however, will emphasize the JSP code over design. Most of the examples will therefore contain more JSP than HTML.

Nevertheless, to understand the examples and to solve the problems in this chapter, you'll need to know more about HTML than Appendix E tells you. You probably will need a reference such as [URL W3C] and perhaps a textbook like [Deitel, Deitel, Nieto 2000].

That having been said, it's not a disadvantage, of course, that the quantity of code we need to write when we write a *jsp* file is quite a bit less than for an equivalent servlet. And this is true not just for generating the HTML code. We will see that JSP also offers us several other "shortcuts".

Problems

1. Insert the sample file from Program Listing 21.2 into the right place and retrieve it in your browser. Check that you're finding the automatically generated *java* file. Open it in an editor and check to see that you recognize some of the code.

2. Change one of the texts in the sample file and check that you can see the change in the browser. This should work on its own. If you have problems, see the last part of Section 21.2.

21.5 What Does JSP Consist of?

It's important to hold on to the fact that the contents of a *jsp* file are converted into a servlet. Running the servlet generates an HTML page that is sent to the client. The HTML code in the *jsp* file therefore becomes `out.write()` or `out.print()` statements in the servlet. But a *jsp* file also contains other things. We distinguish among expressions, scriptlets, and declarations. In addition, there are directives and actions. However, we'll begin with an overview of predefined objects.

Predefined objects

When we write JSP code, we can use the following objects directly:

```
request
```

This object describes the client's request, and it belongs to the `HttpServletRequest` type, which is a subinterface of `ServletRequest`. The most important methods are described in the API references in Section 21.6 and 21.9.

```
response
```

This object describes the response the Web server will send to the client, and it belongs to the `HttpServletResponse` type. We don't use this object much (see the online API documentation for more information).

```
out
```

This object is an instance of the `PrintWriter` class and makes it possible to write directly to the client's HTML page (API reference, see Section 11.5).

```
session
```

This object describes the client's session (see Section 21.9) and it belongs to the `HttpSession` type. The most important methods are described in the API reference in Section 21.9.

JSP expressions

In Program Listing 21.2, we have a *JSP expression*:

This page was downloaded: <%= new java.util.Date() %> // *N.B.! No semicolon!*

The expression is surrounded by <%= and %> and the value of the expression is calculated before it is sent to the client in an `out.print()` statement. Here the value of the expression is a reference to an instance of the `Date` class. As you know, `print()` will look for an object's `toString()` method and use this.

Another example:

The server calculates 17 * 7 and gets <%= 17 * 7 %>

This gives the following on the client side:

The server calculates 17 * 7 and gets 119

Or we can use a predefined object:

The client machine is: <%= request.getRemoteHost() %>

JSP scriptlets

A *scriptlet* is surrounded by <% and %> and can contain larger sections of Java code:

Five random numbers in the interval [1, 100]:
<%
int sum = 0;

```
for (int i = 0; i < 5; i++) {
  int number = (int) (100 * Math.random() + 1);
  out.println("<br>" + number);
  sum += number;
}
out.println("<br>" + "The sum is " + sum);
%>
```

The client output looks like this (depending of course on which random numbers are drawn):

```
Five random numbers in the interval [1, 100]:
86
7
43
91
3
The sum is 230
```

Here we use `out.println()` to send HTML codes to the client. We do this because the codes are an integral part of the scriptlet. We could also have done it this way:

```
Five random numbers in the interval [1, 100]:
<%scriptlet - begin
int sum = 0;
for (int i = 0; i < 5; i++) {
  int number = (int) (100 * Math.random() + 1);
  %>scriptlet - end
  <br> <%= number %>HTML element and JSP expression
  <%scriptlet  - begin
  sum += number;
}
%>scriptlet  - end
<br> The sum is <%= sum %>HTML element and JSP expression
```

JSP declarations

In the example above, we declared the local variables `sum`, `i`, and `number`. We can also declare variables and methods that are located outside the `service()` method. These are instance variables and instance methods in the servlet class. We enclose these types of declarations in <%! and %>. For example:

```
<%! private int noOfVisits = 0; %>
```

Since all clients deal with the same servlet object, these variables will be common for all the clients. (Of course, we could declare class variables and class methods as well.)

The following example demonstrates the difference between variables declared in <%! %> and variables declared in <% %>.

```
<%! private int noOfVisits = 0; %>          instance variable, same for all clients
<% noOfVisits++; %>
No. of visits since servlet started = <%= noOfVisits %>
<br>
<% int counter = 0; %>                      local variable, every client has its own variable
<% counter++; %>
Counter = <%= counter %>
```

The first time the servlet is accessed, we get this printout in the browser window:

```
No. of visits since servlet started = 1
Counter = 1
```

The next time it looks like this:

```
No. of visits since servlet started = 2
Counter = 1
```

And so on:

```
No. of visits since servlet started = 3
Counter = 1
```

Every time the servlet restarts, the variable noOfVisits is set to zero.

Comments

We can use regular Java comments in the Java code.

In addition, we can use *JSP comments* to document the JSP code:

```
<%-- this is a JSP comment, it can be several lines long --%>
```

The JSP comments are not sent to the browser. If we want the comments to be sent to the browser, we use HTML comments:

```
<!-- this is an HTML comment, it can be several lines long -->
```

JSP directives

A *JSP directive* controls the construction of the servlet that is created from the *jsp* file. A directive is enclosed between `<%@` and `%>`. There are three types of directives: page, include, and taglib.

The page directive has many possibilities. In this book, we will only use the import version of this directive. Not surprisingly, it will be converted to an import declaration in the servlet. For example:

```
<%@ page import="myLibrary.Book, java.text.NumberFormat" %>
```

page directives can be located anywhere in the *jsp* file, but we prefer to put them at the top, just before the first JSP declaration or scriptlet.

The include directive is used to insert the contents of another file into the location where the directive is. The text of the other file is copied in before the *jsp* file is converted to a servlet. The drawback is that if the other file is changed, the servlet won't know. Therefore, in this case, you have to make sure that a new servlet is generated and compiled (see the last part of Section 21.2). For example:

```
<%@ include file = "PersonForm.jsp"%>
```

We don't use the `taglib` directive in this book.

See, for example, [Hall 2000] for more information on JSP directives.

JSP actions

JSP actions are used to connect *jsp* files to Java Bean components and applets (see [Hall 2000]).

Problems

1. Write a *jsp* file that retrieves today's date and prints it out in red if today is Sunday, otherwise in blue. If today is Saturday or Sunday, the word "weekend" should also be written. Hint: The following HTML lines will cause the text "Sunday - weekend" to appear in red:

   ```
   <font color = "red">Sunday - weekend</font>
   ```

2. Write a *jsp* file that calculates and displays a table of square roots for the numbers 1–20. Use a `<table>` element to display the table. For an example of `<table>`, see Figure 21.8.

3. Write a *jsp* file according to the following specifications: It declares three instance variables: `counter`, `allNumbers`, and `sum`. `allNumbers` is an instance of the `java.util.Vector` class, while `counter` and `sum` are integer variables. `counter` will be increased by 1 every time the page is downloaded, while `sum` will be increased by a random number in the interval [1, 100]. The random numbers will be stored in the object `allNumbers`. All the numbers will be written out every time the page is accessed. The `java.util.Vector` class is similar to the `java.util.ArrayList` class, but has synchronized methods. Since instance variables of this type can be simultaneously accessed by multiple clients, synchronized methods should be used.

21.6 Inputting Data from the User

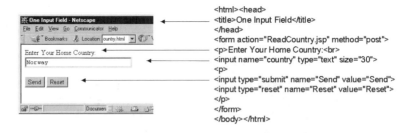

Figure 21.3   Inputting data using HTML

We use the HTML `form` element to read in data from the user (see Figure 21.3). Let's look at the HTML code.

`<form>` and `</form>` enclose the HTML elements that describe the part of the page that contains data that will be sent to the Web server. In addition to the usual formatting elements (`<p>`, `<br>`, etc.), there are different types of `input` elements; here we have text fields and pushbuttons. An input element receives data from the user.

The attributes[4] in `<form>` are responsible for the further handling of the input data. In the example we have:

```
<form action="ReadCountry.jsp" method="post">
```

The value of the `action` attribute gives the URL for the program that will receive the data. `method` indicates the way the data will be sent. In our case, `action` will always refer to a *jsp* file, while the method will usually be "post." The closest alternative is "get." Before we look at the difference between "post" and "get," however, we will look at what else happens.

The form includes three input elements, one of which is a text field. The two others are a submit button ("Send") and a reset button ("Reset"). Figure 21.4 shows what happens if the user presses "Send." The *ReadCountry.jsp* file runs. The source code that is sent to the browser is shown in the bottom right of the figure.

ReadCountry.jsp

```
<html><head><title>Feedback</title></head><body>
<%
String theCountry = request.getParameter("country");
if (theCountry != null) {
  theCountry = theCountry.trim();
  if (theCountry.equals("")) out.println("You have to enter data!");
  else out.println("Hallo, you are from " + theCountry + "!");
}
%>
<p>
<a href = "Country.html">Back</a>
</body></html>
```

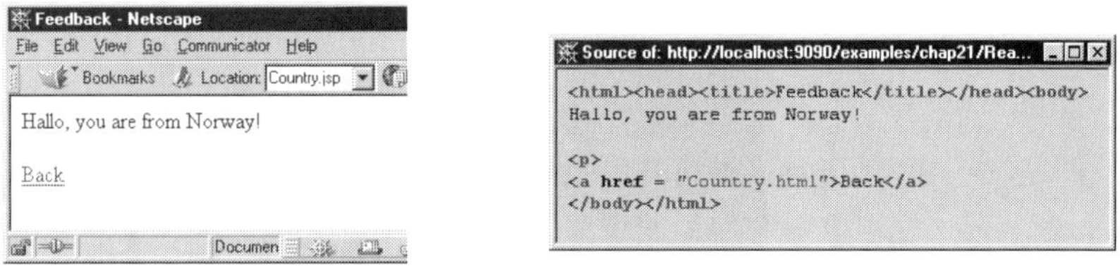

Figure 21.4 What happens after the user presses the send button

---

4. Attributes in an HTML element give a more precise description of the element.

The input elements in an HTML form have names. These become *parameters*[5] in the `request` object. The value of a parameter is what the user enters; alternatively it is the value that is indicated as `value` in the input element. The parameter names are case sensitive—in other words, "Country" and "country" are two different parameters.

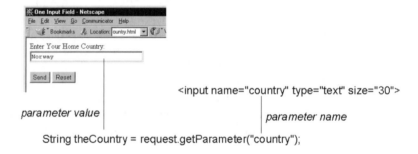

Figure 21.5   Parameter name and value

We get an input element's value by sending the message `getParameter()` to the `request` object (see Figure 21.5).

We have inserted a data check into the *jsp* file in Figure 21.4 so that we check whether the user has entered data. How does this work in practice? If the user doesn't write any text in the input field, a page with the following contents will appear in the browser:

> You have to enter data!
> <u>Back</u>

The user has to press "Back" to get to the page with the input field.

This is inconvenient for the user. It's more practical if the error message appears on the same page as the input field. We can accomplish this by putting the scriptlet with the data check in the same file as the input field (see (and try) Program Listing 21.3). The first time the file is downloaded in the browser, `request.getParameter("country")` will return `null` and neither an error message nor the "hallo" will print out. When we press the "Send" button, the *ReadCountry2.jsp* file will be activated again, a new HTML page will be created and

---

5. Note that the word "parameter" is being used with a somewhat different connotation than it has been up to this point.

sent to the client. This time, the country parameter will have a value—it will either be blank because the user didn't enter anything or it will contain a text.

Program Listing 21.3

```
<!--
    ReadCountry2.jsp  E.L. 2001-08-27
-->
<html><head><title>An Input Field with Error Check</title></head>

<form action="ReadCountry2.jsp" method="post">

<p>Enter Your Country:
<br><input name="country" type="text" size="30">

<p>
<input type="submit" value="Send">
<input type="reset" value="Reset">
</form>
<p>
<hr>
<%
String country = request.getParameter("country");
/* country is null the first time the page is downloaded by a user */
if (country != null) {
  country = country.trim();
  if (country.equals("")) out.println("You have to enter data!");
  else out.println("Hallo, you are from " + country + "!");
}
%>
</body></html>
```

What if we'd used "get" instead of "post"?

In the HTML file we now write:

```
<form action="ReadCountry.jsp" method="get">
```

The data the user entered is now attached to the URL so that it shows in the browser's address field (see Figure 21.6). The treatment in the *ReadCountry.jsp* file is the same as for transfer using post. Because the data is attached to the URL at get, there is a limit to the number of characters. In terms of sending data, there is usually no reason to use get instead of post. And in particular:

Always use post transfer if the user is entering sensitive data. When transferring particularly sensitive data, encryption must also be used. That is not covered in this book.

Figure 21.6 Keyed-in data shows up again as part of the URL if "get" is used

A larger example with many different input elements

See Figure 21.7 and Program Listing 21.4. The treatment of the data is in the *jsp* file shown in Program Listing 21.5. The user evaluations are written consecutively to a text file.

The *jsp* file contains a method declaration. The `composeOneString()` method becomes an instance method in the servlet class.

Aside from this, the contents of the *jsp* file should not require further comments.

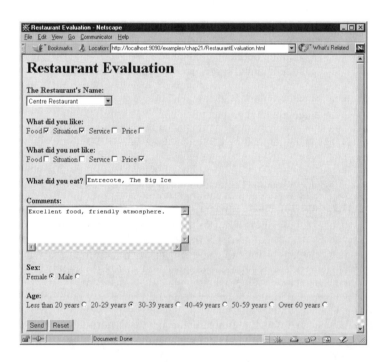

Figure 21.7 Many different input elements are used

Program Listing 21.4

```
<!--
   RestaurantEvaluation.html  E.L. 2001-08-27
-->
<html><head><title>Restaurant Evaluation</title></head>
<body bgcolor="wheat" text="black" link="darkgreen" vlink="steelblue" alink="darkblue">

<h1>Restaurant Evaluation</h1>

<form action="RestaurantEvaluation.jsp" method="post">

 <p><strong>The Restaurant's Name:</strong><br>
   <select name="nameRestaurant">
    <option>Tom's Brasserie and Bar
    <option>Café Just Now
    <option>Café Just Here
    <option>Chinahouse
    <option>Cecilie Food House
    <option>Centre Restaurant
    <option>The Big House Restaurant
    <option>Italian Ristorante
   </select>

   <p><strong>What did you like:</strong><br>
   Food<input name="like" type="checkbox" value="food">
   Situation<input name="like" type="checkbox" value="situation">
   Service<input name="like" type="checkbox" value="service">
   Price<input name="like" type="checkbox" value="price">

   <p><strong>What did you not like:</strong><br>
   Food<input name="notLike" type="checkbox" value="food">
   Situation<input name="notLike" type="checkbox" value="situation">
   Service<input name="notLike" type="checkbox" value="service">
   Price<input name="notLike" type="checkbox" value="price">

   <p><strong>What did you eat?</strong>
   <input name="menu" type="text" size="30">

   <p><strong>Comments:</strong><br>
   <textarea name="comments" type="textarea" rows="4" cols="40"></textarea>

   <p><strong>Sex:</strong><br>
   Female<input name="sex" type="radio" value="female" checked>
   Male<input name="sex" type="radio" value="male">

   <p><strong>Age:</strong><br>
   Less than 20 years<input name="age" type="radio" value="less20" checked>
   20-29 years<input name="age" type="radio" value="twenty">
   30-39 years<input name="age" type="radio" value="thirty">
   40-49 years<input name="age" type="radio" value="forty">
   50-59 years<input name="age" type="radio" value="fifty">
   Over 60 years<input name="age" type="radio" value="sixty">
```

```
<p>
<input type="submit" name="Send" value="Send">
<input type="reset" name="Reset" value="Reset">

</form>
</body></html>
```

Program Listing 21.5

```
<!--
    RestaurantEvaluation.jsp   E.L. 2001-08-27

    This jsp file is activated from the RestaurantEvaluation.html.
    Data entered into the form is fetched, and saved to a text file.
    New evaluations are appended to the evaluations already saved.
-->
<%@ page import="java.io.*" %>
<%! String fileName = "EvalRest.txt"; %>

<%--
    A help method composing an array of strings into one single string.
--%>
<%!
String composeOneString(String[] values) {
  String text = "";
  if (values != null) {
    for (int i = 0; i < values.length - 1; i++) text += values[i] + ", ";
    text += values[values.length - 1];
  }
  return text;
}
%>

<%
if (request.getParameter("Send") != null) {
  String output =
    "Restaurant: " + request.getParameter("nameRestaurant") + "\n" +
    "Pleased with: " +
      composeOneString(request.getParameterValues("like")) + "\n" +
    "Not pleased with: " +
      composeOneString(request.getParameterValues("notLike")) + "\n" +
    "The guest ate: " + request.getParameter("menu") + "\n" +
    "Comments: " + request.getParameter("comments") + "\n" +
    "Sex: " + request.getParameter("sex") + "\n" +
    "Age: " + request.getParameter("age") + "\n" + "\n" + "\n";
  /* Printing to file: It is important to print all the output in one
     single print statement. This prevents other clients to intervene.
     If you have installed LWS as explained in Section 21.2,
     the data file will be in the examples directory. */
  String fileName = application.getRealPath(nameOfFile);
  FileWriter writeConnToFile = new FileWriter(fileName, true);
  PrintWriter printer = new PrintWriter(new BufferedWriter(writeConnToFile));
```

```
        printer.print(output);
        printer.close();
        out.println("<P>Your evaluation is saved.");
    }
%>

<%--
After one evaluation the file may contain the following:
Restaurant: Centre Restaurant
Pleased with: food, situation
Not pleased with: price
The guest ate: Entrecote, The Big Ice
Comments: Excellent food, friendly atmosphere.
Sex: female
Age: twenty
--%>
```

 ## API Reference

The javax.servlet.http.HttpServletRequest interface

JSP standard object `request` is an instance of a class that implements this interface.

This is a subinterface of `javax.servlet.ServletRequest` and thus inherits all its methods (see below).

The following method is also relevant:

    public String getQueryString()

This is relevant in transferring using `get`. This method returns the part of the URL that contains the parameters with values.

The API Reference in Section 21.9 shows more methods for this interface.

The javax.servlet.ServletRequest interface

Methods:

    public String getParameter(String name)
    public String[] getParameterValues(String name)

These methods return the value(s) for a parameter with the indicated name. If there is no parameter with that name, `null` is returned. The parameter name is case sensitive. Remember to use `getParameterValues()` if there is the slightest chance that the parameter might contain more than one value.

    public java.util.Enumeration getParameterNames()

This method returns a list of all the parameter names; for examples of its use, see below.

    public String getRemoteAddr()
    public String getRemoteHost()

These methods return the IP address and the name of the host computer the request came from, respectively.

As you can see, the getParameter() and getParameterValues() methods are used to get the individual data values. If we want all the data values, a loop will work:

```
java.util.Enumeration parameterNames = request.getParameterNames();
while (parameterNames.hasMoreElements()) {
  String name = (String) parameterNames.nextElement();
  String value = composeOneString(request.getParameterValues(name));
  System.out.println("Parameter " + name + ": " + value);
}
```

Enumeration is an interface. An instance of a class that implements this interface generates a series of elements, one at a time. The nextElement() method generates a new element. In the example, the elements will be references to String objects.

API Reference

The java.util.Enumeration interface

Methods:

> public boolean hasMoreElements()

This method returns true if more elements can be generated.

> public Object nextElement()

This method returns the next element.

The java.util.Iterator interface

Newer implementations use Iterator instead of Enumeration.

Methods:

> public boolean hasNext()
> public Object next()
> public void remove()

Problems

1. Try the example shown in Figures 21.3 and 21.4. Change the example so that first and last names can be read in, in addition to country. Also include radio buttons to indicate sex.

2. (Difficult) you're going to expand the large example from above. Make a new *jsp* file that writes out all the data that's been keyed in by the user. If the user accepts the data, it's saved. If not, the user will return to the original page to change the data.

21.7 Client-Side Validation with JavaScript

In the little example above (Figure 21.4), we inserted a check of the user input this way: The data is sent to the Web server, it is checked there, and an error message is returned if there is one.

A better solution is to check the data before it's sent to the Web server. To accomplish this, we have to expand our HTML code with script code. JavaScript is the *de facto* standard for client-side script programming. We won't cover JavaScript in this book, just offer an example of how a client-side data check might look. Program Listing 21.6 shows the revised HTML file. Let's consider the parts of the file that contain JavaScript code.

Program Listing 21.6

```
<!--
   Country3.html  E.L. 2001-08-27
-->
<html><head><title>An Input Field with JavaScript data control</title>

<script language="JavaScript">
function checkData() {
  if (window.document.countryInput.country.value == "") alert("You have to enter data!");
  else window.document.countryInput.submit();
}
</script>

</head>
<form name="countryInput" action="ReadCountry.jsp" method="post">

<p>Enter Your Home Country:
<br><input name="country" type="text" size="30">

<p>
<input type="button" value = "Send" onClick = "checkData()">
<input type="reset" name="Reset" value="Reset">
</form></body></html>
```

The following line appears near the bottom:

```
<input type="button" value = "Send" onClick = "checkData()">
```

The Submit button is replaced with an input element of the "button" type. This is not HTML, but JavaScript. Handling of the "onClick" event is linked to the button. If this event occurs, the `checkData()` function (a function is the same as a "method" in Java terminology) will be executed. This function is at the top, after the `title` element. The function is placed inside the `script` element.

What, for example, does `window.document.countryInput.country` mean? When we program JavaScript, we have access to a vast quantity of pre-defined hierarchically organized objects. `window` represents the browser window that among other things contains the `document` object, which describes the document that is displayed. The HTML code shows what objects a document contains. For example, these could be images, applets, and forms. In our case, it is a single form, which in contrast to earlier, has been given a name, `countryInput`:

```
<form name="countryInput" action="ReadCountry.jsp" method="post">
```

We can refer to the individual parts of a form, and to get the value of the `value` attribute in the `country` input field, we write: `window.document.countryInput.country.value`. The `checkData()` function checks whether the field contains a blank text—if that is the case, a brief message appears on the screen (`alert(..)`); if not, everything is alright and the `submit()` message is sent to the `window.document.countryInput` object. Also notice that in JavaScript we use the `==` operator to compare texts.

JavaScript makes it possible to alert the user of errors right after he's made them. This is clearly an advantage compared with receiving all the error messages after all the data has been sent to the server. It also reduces network traffic. Therefore, we should add a client-side data check where it makes sense.

We won't devote any more time to JavaScript in this book. Therefore, you will need references to use JavaScript: see [URL JavaScript], or if you prefer a textbook, try [Deitel, Deitel, Nieto 2000].

In addition, there should always be a server-side error check. We may run into Web developers who don't run the requisite data check when developing their pages. On the flip side, the pages should be built so that they also work for users who have turned JavaScript support off on their browsers. Alternatively, these users should be advised that the page will not work.

Of course, we may use applets as an alternative to forms and JavaScript on the client side.

21.8 Databases

We're going to make an Internet version of the example from Chapter 20. We will start as simply as we did there with a *jsp* file that retrieves data from a table in the database. Refer to Figure 21.8 with the *jsp* file in Program Listing 21.7.[6] Notice that the data is retrieved from the database and is then inserted as plain text into the HTML file that is sent to the browser.

---

6. Note that we have to qualify the `Statement` name. The reason is that the resulting servlet imports the `java.beans` package, which contains a `Statement` class. We have to qualify this to avoid name conflict.

For the sake of simplicity, we are putting the password directly into the source code in the *jsp* file. As you can see, the Java code is like Program Listing 20.1. The only new thing here is probably the HTML element `table`. To summarize, `<tr>` is a table row, `<th>` is a table head, and `<td>` is table data.

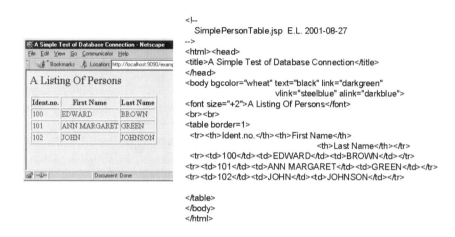

Figure 21.8 Data from the person table with the generated HTML code on the right

Program Listing 21.7

```
<!--
    SimplePersonTable.jsp  E.L. 2001-08-27
-->
<html><head><title>A Simple Test of Database Connection</title></head>
<body bgcolor="wheat" text="black" link="darkgreen" vlink="steelblue" alink="darkblue">
<font size="+2">A Listing Of Persons</font>
<br><br>
<%@ page import="java.sql.*" %>
<table border=1>
  <tr><th>Ident.no.</th><th>First Name</th><th>Last Name</th></tr>
  <%
  try{
    Class.forName("oracle.jdbc.driver.OracleDriver");
    Connection conn = DriverManager.getConnection
      ("jdbc:oracle:thin:@loiosh.stud.idb.hist.no:1521:orcl", "username", "password");

    java.sql.Statement statement = conn.createStatement();
    String sql = "select * from person";
    ResultSet resSet = statement.executeQuery(sql);
    while (resSet.next()) {
      out.print("<tr><td>" + resSet.getString("identno") + "</td>");
      out.print("<td>" + resSet.getString("firstname") + "</td>");
```

```
        out.println("<td>" + resSet.getString("lastname") + "</td></tr>");
      }
      if (statement != null) statement.close();
      if (conn != null) conn.close();
    } catch (Exception e) {
      out.print("Error, database connection: " + e);
    }
    %>
  </table>
  </body>
  </html>
```

Then we'll make a Web-based version of the database application in Section 20.4. We use the `Database` class from Program Listing 20.2.[7] Figure 21.9 shows the user interface as it looks in the browser.

The Web application consists of many files: see Figure 21.10 and Program Listing 21.8. We will go through the *jsp* files in the order they are shown in the program listing.

The introductory file, *NameArchive.jsp*, is shown at the top center of Figure 21.9. This shows all the names recorded. The user chooses between three different submit buttons depending on what is going to be done.

The *HandleSelection.jsp* file is activated. The `request` object contains information about which submit button the user presses. `getParameter()` returns `null` for the buttons that weren't pressed. Depending on the user's selection, either the *DeletePersonData.jsp* or the *PersonForm.jsp* file is included. The `include` directive makes sure that the source code in the file in question is inserted in place of the directive before the page is converted into a servlet. The effect is the same as if the source code had been there from the beginning.

The *PersonForm.jsp* file is used both to change existing data and to record new data. However, there are two differences between these situations.

The identification number is unknown when you go to enter a new person. In this case, as in Chapter 20, we've chosen to fill the "Ident. No." field with the text "not defined". If we go to change the data, the selected person's number will be displayed in the field. What will be displayed is determined in *HandleSelection.jsp*. That text will be stored in the `idNo` variable. *PersonForm.jsp* gets this:

```
      <td align = left>Ident.no.:</td>
      <td align = left><strong><%=idNo%></strong></td>
```

The database operation itself also differs depending on whether data is going to be changed or entered for the first time. You'll find the two operations in the files *UpdatePersonData.jsp* and *AddPersonData.jsp*. In other words, the submit button in *PersonForm.jsp* will activate different files. Again we use a local variable:

---

7. LWS: You have to update the *lws.bat* file such that CLASSPATH contains the path to `myLibrary` and to the database driver you used in Chapter 20. See LWS Reference Manual

```
<form action="<%=managingFile%>" method = "post">
```

The following line appears in *PersonForm.jsp*

```
<input type = "hidden" name = "identNo" value = "<%=idNo%>">
```

Here we are using a hidden field (type = "hidden") to transfer the identification number to the right file. A hidden field is different from other fields in that it is not displayed in the browser. It is only used to transfer data.

The handling files, *DeletePersonData.jsp*, *AddPersonData.jsp* and *UpdatePersonData.jsp*, are put together the same way:

```
establish a database connection
do a database operation
close the database connection
```

Of course this is not a particularly efficient way of dealing with a database. The whole thing can be very sluggish with many requests to the database.

Professional systems should maintain a pool of database connections and distribute these among the clients as needed. Several books include code for a Connection class of this type (see for example Section 18.7 in [Hall 2000]). Many database drivers [URL Database Drivers] also have built-in "connection pooling".

In our example, we can add this service to the Database constructor and the closeTheConnection() method. The rest of the code then remains unchanged.

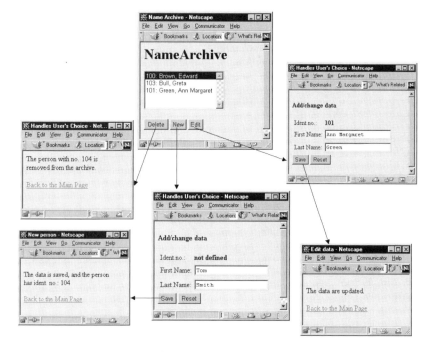

Figure 21.9 A web application that works with a database

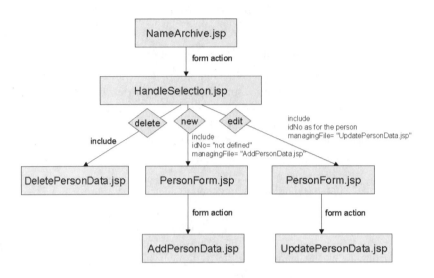

Figure 21.10 The order the various files are requested in

Program Listing 21.8

```
<!--
    NameArchive.jsp     E.L. 2001-08-27
    Main Page, maintenance of a person registry.
-->
<html><head><title>Name  Archive</title></head>
<body bgcolor="wheat" text="black" link="darkgreen" vlink="steelblue" alink="darkblue">
<h1>NameArchive</h1>

<form action = "HandleSelection.jsp" method = "post">
 <select name = "persons" size = 5>
  <%
  try {
   myLibrary.Database theDatabase =
                               new myLibrary.Database("username", "password");
   java.util.ArrayList all = theDatabase.getAll();
   out.println("<option selected>" + all.get(0));
   for (int i = 1; i < all.size(); i++) {
    out.println("<option>" + all.get(i));
   }
   theDatabase.closeTheConnection();
  } catch (Exception e) {
   out.print("Error, database connection: " + e);
  }
  %>
 </select>
```

```
  <p>
  <input name = "delete" type = "submit" value = "Delete">
  <input name = "new" type = "submit" value = "New">
  <input name = "edit" type = "submit" value = "Edit">
  </form>

  </body></html>

  <!--
     HandleSelection.jsp    E.L. 2001-08-27
     This is a part of the Name Archive System.
     Here we handle the choice the user has made in NameArchive.jsp.
  -->
  <html><head><title>Handles User's Choice</title></head>
  <body bgcolor="wheat" text="black" link="darkgreen" vlink="steelblue" alink="darkblue">
  <%@ page import="java.util.StringTokenizer" %>
  <% /* Deletes a person from the archive */
   if (request.getParameter("delete") != null) {
    String selectedPerson = request.getParameter("persons");
    StringTokenizer text = new StringTokenizer(selectedPerson, ":, ");
    int identNo = Integer.parseInt(text.nextToken());
  %>
   <%@ include file = "DeletePersonData.jsp"%>
   <%
   }

      /* Adds a new person to the archive*/
   if (request.getParameter("new") != null) {
    String idNo = "not defined";
    String firstName = "";
    String lastName = "";
    String managingFile = "AddPersonData.jsp";
    %>
    <%@ include file = "PersonForm.jsp"%>
   <%
   }

     /* Changes the name of a person in the archive */
   if (request.getParameter("edit") != null) {
    String selectedPerson = request.getParameter("persons");
    StringTokenizer text = new StringTokenizer(selectedPerson, ":, ");
    String idNo = text.nextToken();
    String lastName = text.nextToken();
    String firstName = text.nextToken();
    int noOfWordsLeft = text.countTokens();  // handles the middle name
    for (int i = 0; i < noOfWordsLeft; i++) firstName += (" " + text.nextToken());
    String managingFile = "UpdatePersonData.jsp";
    %>
    <%@ include file = "PersonForm.jsp"%>
   <%
```

```
       }
%>
</body>
</html>


<!--
   DeletePersonData.jsp     E.L. 2001-08-27
   This file is a part of the Name Archive System.
   The file is included in the HandleSelection.jsp file,
   if a person should be removed from the archive.
-->
<%
try {
  myLibrary.Database theDatabase = new  myLibrary.Database("username", "password");
  if (theDatabase.deletePerson(identNo)) {
    out.println("The person with no. " + identNo + " is removed from the archive.\n");
  }
  else out.println("Not possible to delete data about this person. " +
  "Other clients may have done it already.\n");
  theDatabase.closeTheConnection();
} catch (java.sql.SQLException e) {
  out.println("Error when deleting from the database: " + e);
}
%>
<p><a href = "NameArchive.jsp">Back to the Main Page</a></p>

<!--
   PersonForm.jsp     E.L. 2001-08-27

   This file is a part of the Name Archive System.
   The file is included in the HandleSelection.jsp file,
   if data should be added or updated.

   Here we use four local variables (idNo, managingFile, firstName and lastName),
   which are given values in the HandleSelection.jsp file.
-->
<br><strong>Add/change data</strong>

<form action="<%=managingFile%>" method = "post">
  <table>
    <tr>
     <td align = left>Ident.no.:</td>
     <td align = left><strong><%=idNo%></strong></td>
     <input type = "hidden" name = "identNo" value = "<%=idNo%>">
    </tr>
    <tr>
     <td align = left>First Name:</td>
     <td align = left><input type = "text" name = "firstName" size = "20"
                                value = "<%=firstName%>"></td>
    </tr>
```

```
        <tr>
          <td align = left>Last Name:</td>
          <td align = left><input type = "text" name = "lastName" size = "20"
                                    value = "<%=lastName%>"></td>
        </td>
      </table>
      <input type = "submit" name = "save"  value = "Save">
      <input type = "reset" name = "reset" value = "Reset">
</form>

<!--
   AddPersonData.jsp     E.L. 2001-08-27
   This file is a part of the Name Archive System.
   The file is activated from the PersonForm.jsp if data should be added.
-->
<html><head><title>New person</title></head>

<body bgcolor="wheat" text="black" link="darkgreen" vlink="steelblue" alink="darkblue">
<%@ page import="myLibrary.*" %>
<%
Database theDatabase = new Database("username", "password");
try {
  String firstName = request.getParameter("firstName");
  String lastName = request.getParameter("lastName");
  Person thePerson = theDatabase.registerNewPerson(firstName, lastName);
  out.println("<br>The data is saved, and the person has ident. no.: " +
  thePerson.getPersIdent() + "\n");
} catch (java.sql.SQLException e) {
  out.println("Error saving data: " + e);
}
theDatabase.closeTheConnection();
%>
<p><a href = "NameArchive.jsp">Back to the Main Page</a>

</body>
</html>

<!--
   UpdatePersonData.jsp     E.L. 2001-08-01
   This file is a part of the Name Archive System.
   The file is activated from the PersonForm.jsp if data should be updated.
-->

<html><head><title>Edit data</title></head>
<body bgcolor="wheat" text="black" link="darkgreen" vlink="steelblue" alink="darkblue">

<%@ page import="myLibrary.*" %>
<%
Database theDatabase = new Database("username", "password");
try {
  int pNo = Integer.parseInt(request.getParameter("identNo"));
  String firstName = request.getParameter("firstName");
```

```
String lastName = request.getParameter("lastName");
Person thePerson = new Person(pNo, firstName, lastName);
if (theDatabase.updateName(thePerson)) out.println("<br>The data are updated.");
else out.println("No data updated. The data may have been deleted by others.");
} catch (java.sql.SQLException e) {
  out.println("Error when updating data: " + e);
}
theDatabase.closeTheConnection();
%>
<p><a href = "NameArchive.jsp">Back to the Main Page</a>
</body>
</html>
```

Problems

1. Change the *SimplePersonTable.jsp* file so that the number of people is printed out under the table.

2. Change the *SimplePersonTable.jsp* file so that the user can enter a last name and the list only shows people with that last name. Try to do this on the same page.

3. Change the system in Figure 21.9 so that the messages about changes appear on the start page. In other words, the number of different pages should be reduced from six to three.

21.9 Storing State Information

As explained in Section 18.1, HTTP is a stateless protocol. The same client can send request after request to the Web server, which handles each individual request completely independently of all the other requests.

In this chapter, we've seen several examples where pages are "connected" to each other. We've transferred information from one page to the next using the submit button and then interpreting the request object. The data that's transferred is what the user has entered into the form fields. In one case, we've used a hidden field (Program Listing 21.8, the *PersonForm.jsp* file, the identNo field).

These methods of transferring data place significant limitations on the practical possibilities. Therefore, other mechanisms have been developed to store data between the requests. If the data is not going to be sent back and forth using hidden fields, it has to be stored, either on the client side or on the Web server side.

Client-side storage takes place in small informational units called *cookies*. A browser can usually handle up to 300 cookies, 20 per Web server. The size of one cookie must not exceed 4 kB. Cookies often store personal information such as name and address or username and password. This way you don't have to enter the same information every time you shop in your everyday Web store. The information is sent to the store along with the URL you write in the address field.

You will almost certainly find a lot of cookies on your computer (if you haven't configured your browser not to accept cookies). Search for directories with the name *cookies* and files with the name *cookies.**. You may be surprised at how many you find. Many of the places you have visited recently on the Internet have left traces on your computer. Not all of them are immediately readable—long, cryptic numbers could be session identifications (see below). That said, we should also point out that this is the only thing the Web server can do to your computer, i.e. leave a little snippet of text in a specific location. It does not have access to other locations on your disk, nor can it deposit other types of files. In other words, cookies let the server recognize you, but not identify you.

Programs on Web servers, however, should not depend on cookies working. Cookies should be an *option* for the client and not the only solution.

The alternative to store state information at the client side is to store it on the server. In that case, it's normal for the client to be assigned a *session ID* when the *session* starts, i.e. when contact is established between the client and the server. The data is stored in a *session object* on the server, while the session ID is normally stored as a cookie on the client. But as we'll see later, it is possible to use sessions without using cookies.

Let's look at an example of how cookies and session objects can be used. You log onto an Internet store to order pizza and soda and are assigned a session ID, which is stored on your computer as a cookie. At the same time, you are assigned a session object on the Web server. This happens without your being aware of it. You browse here and there and check out different types of pizza toppings and side dishes. Every time your computer asks for a new file from the Web server, the session ID is sent along with the URL. If you place an order, it is saved in the associated session object on the server. If the Web server has already saved your name, telephone number, and delivery address in cookies on your computer, you will be asked to confirm that they are correct before your order is confirmed. Or you may have to enter this information and then they will be saved automatically in cookies so that you don't have to enter them again later. If you decide to forget the whole order and make do with what you have in the fridge, the session object will be deleted from the Web server after a given period of time. It's standard for the object to be deleted if the client is inactive for 20–30 minutes. This can, however, be controlled by the Web site's creator.

We will take a look at how we program using cookies and session objects.

Cookies

Figure 21.11 shows how cookies work. The *jsp* files are shown in Program Listing 21.9. Try them by downloading *CookiesTest.jsp* into the browser. The page should look like the one on the left of the figure. (If it shows cookies, restart the browser to remove the cookies.) Type in your name, and then press the "Save" button. You'll get the following message:

> Have found: Mary Johnson
> Now the cookies are stored.
> Push the 'Back' button and 'Reload' the previous page.

Then, follow the instructions ("Back" and "Reload") and you'll get a page similar to the one on the right side of the figure. This means that your name is stored on your computer as a cookie, between the downloadings.

If, when running these programs, you check if new cookies really were saved on your computer, you will probably find that this is not the case. Cookies are temporarily saved for a time before they are permanently saved on your disk, if they're saved permanently at all. The cookies in this example disappear when the user closes the browser. This you may utilize when testing the programs. If you want the cookies removed, simply restart the browser.

Now, let's look at the source code. The *CookiesTest.jsp* file starts by getting the cookies that are stored for this Web site. Nothing is stored the first time you download the page. Then you enter your first and last name and press "Save", and control is transferred to the *SaveNameAsCookies.jsp* page. The cookies are recorded in the `response` object:

```
response.addCookie(cookie1);
response.addCookie(cookie2);
```

This is how cookies are sent to the client. Now if you reload the previous page, the name and the session ID are found as cookies. Hence, a session is automatically established when a client contacts a Web server without anyone having to ask for it.

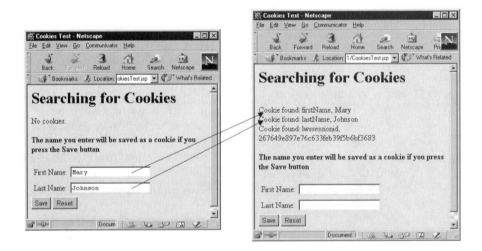

Figure 21.11   Examples of cookies

Program Listing 21.9

```
<!--
    CookiesTest.jsp  E.L. 2001-08-28
-->
```

```
<html><head><title>Cookies Test</title></head>
<body bgcolor="wheat" text="black" link="darkgreen" vlink="steelblue" alink="darkblue">
<h1>Searching for Cookies</h1>
<%
  Cookie[] cookies = request.getCookies();
  if (cookies == null || cookies.length == 0) {
      out.println("<p>No cookies.<br><br>");
  }
  else {
    for (int i = 0; i < cookies.length; i++) {
      out.println("<br>Cookie found: " + cookies[i].getName() + ", " +
                            cookies[i].getValue());
    }
  }
%>
<p>
<p>
<strong>
The name you enter will be saved as a cookie if you press the Save button
</strong>
<form action="SaveNameAsCookies.jsp" method="post">
  <table>
    <tr>
      <td align = left>First Name:</td>
      <td align = left><input type = "text" name = "firstName" size = "20"></td>
    </tr><tr>
      <td align = left>Last Name:</td>
      <td align = left><input type = "text" name = "lastName" size = "20"></td>
    </td>
  </table>
<input type="submit" name="save" value="Save">
<input type="reset" name="reset" value="Reset">
</form>

<!--
    SaveNameAsCookies.jsp  E.L. 2001-08-28
-->

<html><head><title>Save the Name as Cookies</title></head><body>
<%
  String firstName = request.getParameter("firstName");
  String lastName = request.getParameter("lastName");
  out.println("<br>Have found: " + firstName + " " + lastName);
  Cookie cookie1 = new Cookie("firstName", firstName);
  Cookie cookie2 = new Cookie("lastName", lastName);
  response.addCookie(cookie1);
  response.addCookie(cookie2);
  out.println("<br>Now the cookies are stored.");
  out.println("<br>Push the 'Back' button and 'Reload' the previous page.");
```

```
%>
</body></html>
```

API Reference

The javax.servlet.http.Cookie class

This class describes a cookie, which is a small quantity of information that is sent from a Web server to a Web client and saved there. A cookie always has a name and a value, as well as other possible attributes such as, for example, a domain name and path. See the online API documentation for more information about these and other attributes.

Constructor:

    public Cookie(String name, String value)

The name can consist of alphanumeric characters (the letters from A–Z and a–z, as well as numbers from 0–9). In particular, the name cannot include special characters such as commas, semicolons, and blank characters such as space, tabs, etc. Nor can the name begin with "$". The constructor will throw an `IllegalArgumentException` if the name is invalid.

Methods:

    public String getName()
    public String getValue()
    public void setValue(String newValue)

The name is unambiguous and cannot be changed. The value, on the other hand, can be changed using the `setValue()` method.

    public void setMaxAge(int newAge)

This method makes it possible to set a cookie's maximum age. The age is given in seconds. If no maximum age or a negative one is set, the cookie will be deleted when the client closes the browser. `newAge` equal to 0 means the cookie is deleted immediately.

    public int getMaxAge()

This method gets the maximum age. A negative value means that the cookie is deleted when the client exits the browser.[8]

---

8. In the Web servers LWS 2.2.1 and Tomcat 3.2.1 this method returns -1 regardless of what value was set as the maximum age. The age still works the way it should, it's only this method that returns the wrong value.

Sessions

Figure 21.12 and Program Listing 21.10 show sessions. Download the file *SessionTest.jsp* in your browser. Then enter some data and press "Save the new attribute". Then you get a message:

> The session ID came from the client as cookie.
> Now the new attribute is stored in the session object.
> <u>Want to store more data in the session object</u>

The last line is a link to the previous page. Click on it. And you'll see your data in the attribute list. You may enter more data. Try it out!

The data contents of a session object are called *attributes*. An attribute is identified by name (for example: "City") and contains a value (for example: "London").

Now we'll look at the JSP code in Program Listing 21.10. The *SessionTest.jsp* file starts by displaying some information about the session. Test the pages with and without cookies turned on in the browser.

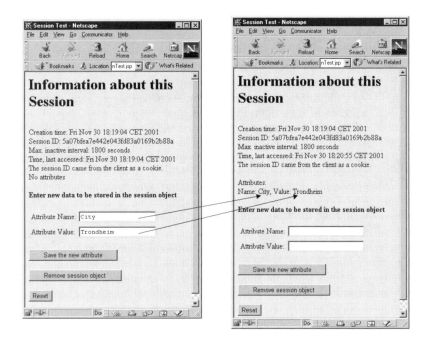

Figure 21.12 Saving data in the session object

Servlets are created so that if the client doesn't support cookies, then another method will be used. The session ID will be sent along with the URL. This assumes that all URLs on the pages that are downloaded from the Web server are run through the `response.encodeURL()` method. For example:

```
<a href="SessionTest.jsp">
```

is replaced by

```
<a href="<%=response.encodeURL("SessionTest.jsp")%>">
```

If the pages don't work without cookies, it might be that the Web server doesn't support this, or that it's not configured for this.[9]

Once the session information is written out, the scriptlet runs through all the attributes and prints out their values. The first time the page is downloaded, this list is empty: see the left side of the figure.

The user can enter an attribute with a name and value in the two fields and save it in the session object by hitting the "Save the new attribute" button. Control is transferred to the *SaveDataSession.jsp* file. Here, the session object is expanded to include the new attributes.

Program Listing 21.10

```
<!--
    SessionTest.jsp  E.L. 2001-08-28
-->
<html><head><title>Session Test</title></head>
<body bgcolor="wheat" text="black" link="darkgreen" vlink="steelblue" alink="darkblue">
<%@ page import="java.util.*" %>
<h1>Information about this Session</h1>
<p>
<br>Creation time: <%= new Date(session.getCreationTime())%>
<br>Session ID: <%= session.getId()%>
<br>Max. inactive interval: <%= session.getMaxInactiveInterval()%> seconds
<%
  if (session.isNew()) out.println("<br>This session is new");
  else {
    Date lastAccessed = new Date(session.getLastAccessedTime());
    out.println("<br>Time, last accessed: " + lastAccessed);
    if (request.isRequestedSessionIdFromCookie()) {
      out.println("<br>The session ID came from the client as a cookie.");
    }
    if (request.isRequestedSessionIdFromURL()) {
      out.println("<br>The session ID came from the client as part of URL.");
    }
  }

  Enumeration attributeNames = session.getAttributeNames();
  if (!attributeNames.hasMoreElements()) out.println("<br>No attributes");
```

---

9. LWS: See Section 21.2.

```
    else {
      out.println("<p>Attributes:");
      while (attributeNames.hasMoreElements()) {
        String name = (String) attributeNames.nextElement();
        out.println("<br>Name: " + name + ", Value: " + session.getAttribute(name));
      }
    }
%>

<p><strong>Enter new data to be stored in the session object</strong>
<form action="<%=response.encodeURL("SaveSessionData.jsp")%>" method="post">
  <table>
    <tr>
      <td align = left>Attribute Name:</td>
      <td align = left><input type = "text" name = "name" size = "20"></td>
    </tr><tr>
      <td align = left>Attribute Value:</td>
      <td align = left><input type = "text" name = "value" size = "20"></td>
    </td>
  </table>
<p><input type="submit" name="save" value="Save the new attribute">
<p><input type="submit" name="remove" value="Remove session object">
<p><input type="reset" name="reset" value="Reset">
</form>

<!--
    SaveSessionData.jsp  E.L. 2001-08-28
-->

<html><head><title>Saves data in the Session object</title></head><body>
<%
  if (request.isRequestedSessionIdFromCookie()) {
    out.println("<br>The session ID came from the client as a cookie.");
  }
  if (request.isRequestedSessionIdFromURL()) {
    out.println("<br>The session ID came from the client as part of URL.");
  }
  if (request.getParameter("save") != null) {
    String name = request.getParameter("name");
    String value = request.getParameter("value");
    if (name != null && value != null) {
      session.setAttribute(name, value);
      out.print("<br>Now the new attribute is stored in the session object.");
    }
    else out.print("<br>Name or value is missing!");
  }
  if (request.getParameter("remove") != null) {
    session.invalidate();
    out.print("<br>Session object removed");
  }
```

```
%>
<br><a href="<%=response.encodeURL("SessionTest.jsp")%>">
Want to store more data in the session object</a>
</body></html>
```

Let's look at a slightly larger example. Figure 21.13 and Program Listing 21.11 show something that could be the beginning of an Internet bookstore. Meanwhile, all the data is hard coded in the program and we're not connected to a database. It also doesn't include any information about the buyer.

The Book class is shown at the end of the program listing. This class is in the myLibrary package and it describes a book.

Look at the figure. So far, we've ordered 6 books at a value of $232.82. The page is designed such that "Update Status" or "Reset the Order" takes us back to the same page. If, for example, we also order a copy of Bergsten's book, the status line at the top of the page will be changed to:

> The number of books up to now: 7,
> Totalprice: $275.77.

Download the *BookStore.jsp* file and get familiar with the functionality!

Now we look at the code in the *jsp* file. Let's start by looking at the form element at the bottom of the file:

```
<form action = "BookStore.jsp" method = "post">
```

Note how we design the field names that are going to contain the number of books. In the source code we write

```
<td> <input type="text" name="<%="number"+i%>"
         value="<%=bookTitles[i].getNumber()%>"></td>
```

Thus the name of the fields will be number0, number1, number2, etc. Take a look at the source code in the browser to be convinced. For example, for Bergsten's book, this will be converted to the following HTML code:

```
<input type="text" name="number4" value="0">
```

The starting value of the number fields is got from the book object. The user can then change this as desired.

Data we enter is handled by *BookStore.jsp*. Therefore, this file has to handle both the case where the user is visiting the page for the first time and where she is returning to the page because she pressed one of the buttons.

Let's go to the beginning of the file. There we first find an instance variable currencyFormat and an instance method jspInit(). The book prices are real, they are found on the book covers, and they are all in US dollars, so we have to set the localization to USA to guarantee the correct currency format. This instance variable has the same value for all clients, and therefore we want to set it in the init() method of the resulting servlet. The equivalent method in JSP is jspInit(). (We also have a method jspDestroy() if we need to release resources or clear in some other way before the servlet is taken down. But don't trust 100% in the `jspDestroy()` method. It's not called if the servlet is stopped in an irregular way.)

We have one more instance method, `createBookList()`, which generates an array of books and records this as a session attribute. Note the difference between an instance variable and a session attribute. Here's how we would make the instance variable:

```
<%! private Book[] bookTitles = {
    new Book("Annunziato, Kaminaris: JavaServer Pages in 24 Hours", 29.99),
    ...
```

As the variable `currencyFormat`, this array would be common for *all* clients. This would have been fine if the array only contained the titles and prices. An instance of the `Book` class, as we have designed the class, would also come to contain information on the number of books. We choose to use the class so that this means the number of books *the individual customer* has ordered. Therefore we have to have one array, `bookTitles`, per customer. We accomplish this by declaring that as a session attribute:

```
session.setAttribute("bookList", bookTitles);
```

Now the book array will live for one session, i.e. either until the user exits the browser or until a long period of time has elapsed since she's visited the Web site. In our case, a "long time" is defined by the Web server (usually 20–30 minutes), since we haven't set any specific length.

Here we come to the active section of the file. If the `bookList` attribute does not exist, we generate it by calling the method we went through above:

```
if (session.getAttribute("bookList") == null) createBookList(session);
```

We make the attribute locally accessible:

```
Book[] bookTitles = (Book[]) session.getAttribute("bookList");
```

Then we handle the different situations we might be in when the user arrives at this page:

- If `request.getParameter("reset")` is different from `null`, that means that the user pressed "Reset the Order". We set the number to 0 for all of the books.

- If `request.getParameter("update")` is different from `null`, that means that the user has pressed "Update Status". In this case, we look for the `request` parameters whose names begin with "number". We know that these parameters contain the number of books the customer wants. For example, the parameter `number3` contains the number of books the customer wants with the index of 3, i.e. Hall's book. We get the price for the book and update the local variables `totalnumber` and `totalprice`.

- If both of these parameters are `null`, that means that the page is being visited for the first time in this session. All we do is display a little welcome message.

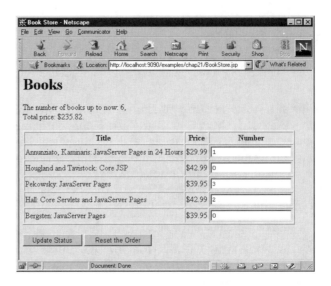

Figure 21.13 A little bookstore

Program Listing 21.11

```
<!--
  BookStore.jsp   E.L. 2001-08-28
-->
<html><head><title>Book Store</title></head>
<body bgcolor="wheat" text="black" link="darkgreen" vlink="steelblue" alink="darkblue">
<h1>Books</h1>

<%@ page import="myLibrary.Book, java.util.Locale, java.text.NumberFormat" %>

<%! private NumberFormat currencyFormat;
%>
<%! public void jspInit() { // initializations common for all clients
      Locale.setDefault(new Locale("en", "US"));  // the prices are in dollars
      currencyFormat = NumberFormat.getCurrencyInstance();
   }
%>
<%! public void createBookList(HttpSession session) {
      Book[] bookTitles = {
        new Book("Annunziato, Kaminaris: JavaServer Pages in 24 Hours", 29.99),
        new Book("Hougland and Tavistock: Core JSP", 42.99),
        new Book("Pekowsky: JavaServer Pages", 39.95),
```

```
                new Book("Hall: Core Servlets and JavaServer Pages", 42.99),
                new Book("Bergsten: JavaServer Pages", 39.95)};
                session.setAttribute("bookList", bookTitles);
            }
%>

<%
  if (session.getAttribute("bookList") == null) createBookList(session);
  Book[] bookTitles = (Book[]) session.getAttribute("bookList");
  double totalprice = 0.0;
  int totalnumber = 0;
  if (request.getParameter("reset") != null) {
    for (int i = 0; i < bookTitles.length; i++) bookTitles[i].setNumber(0);
    out.println("No books ordered.");
  }
  else if(request.getParameter("update") != null) {
    int index = 0;
    try {
      java.util.Enumeration parameterNames = request.getParameterNames();
      while (parameterNames.hasMoreElements()) {
        String name = (String) parameterNames.nextElement();
        if ((name.substring(0, 6)).equals("number")) {
          index = Integer.parseInt(name.substring(6));
          int number = Integer.parseInt(request.getParameter(name));
          totalnumber += number;
          totalprice += bookTitles[index].getPrice() * number;
          bookTitles[index].setNumber(number);
        }
      }
      out.println("The number of books up to now: " + totalnumber + ", <br>Total price: " +
                          currencyFormat.format(totalprice) + ".");
    } catch (NumberFormatException e) {
      out.println("Invalid number entered for " + bookTitles[index].getTitle());
    }
  }
  else out.println("Welcome to the Book Store!");
%>

<br>
<form action = "BookStore.jsp" method = "post">
<table border=1>
  <tr><th>Title</th><th>Price</th><th>Number</th>
  <%
    for (int i = 0; i < bookTitles.length; i++) {
      %>
      <tr><td> <%=bookTitles[i].getTitle()%></td>
        <td> <%=currencyFormat.format(bookTitles[i].getPrice())%></td>
        <td> <input type="text" name="<%="number"+i%>"
```

```
                        value="<%=bookTitles[i].getNumber()%>"></td>
      </tr>
      <%
    }
  %>
</table>
<br>
<input type="submit" name="update" value="Update Status">
<input type="submit" name="reset" value="Reset the Order">
</form>
</body></html>

/*
 * Book.java  E.L. 2001-08-28
 *
 */
package myLibrary;
public class Book {
  private String title;
  private double price;
  private int number = 0;

  public Book(String initTitle, double initPrice) {
    title = initTitle;
    price = initPrice;
  }

    public String getTitle() {
    return title;
  }
  public double getPrice() {
    return price;
  }

    public int getNumber() {
    return number;
  }

    public void setNumber(int newNumber) {
    number = newNumber;
  }
}
```

API Reference

The javax.servlet.http.HttpServletRequest interface

See also Section 21.6.

Methods:

```
public Cookie[] getCookies()
```

This method returns an array with all cookies that came in with this request. `null` is returned if there weren't any cookies.

```
public String getRequestedSessionId()
```

This method returns this session's ID.

```
public boolean isRequestedSessionIdValid()
```

This method checks if the requested session is still valid.

```
public boolean isRequestedSessionIdFromCookie()
public boolean isRequestedSessionIdFromURL()
```

These methods check where the session ID came from, either from a cookie or from the URL.

The javax.servlet.http.HttpSession interface

The JSP default `session` object is an instance of a class that implements this interface.

Methods:

```
public long getCreationTime()
```

This method gets the time the session object was created. The time is stated as a number of seconds after midnight (00:00) GMT on January 1, 1970. This can be an argument for the `Date` constructor to get the time in the date format instead.

```
public String getId()
```

This method returns the session ID.

```
public long getLastAccessedTime()
```

This method returns the time the client last sent a request in this session, as a number of seconds since midnight (00:00) GMT on January 1, 1970.

```
public void setMaxInactiveInterval(int interval)
public int getMaxInactiveInterval()
```

These methods are used to set and get the maximum number of seconds between the requests. If the number of seconds exceeds this limit, the session object is no longer valid. A negative interval means that the session will live "forever". If an interval is not specified, the default value set for the Web server is used.

```
public Object getAttribute(String name)
public void setAttribute(String name, Object value)
public void removeAttribute(String name)
```

These methods are used to maintain the contents of the session object. `getAttribute()` returns `null` if an attribute with the indicated name does not exist. The second argument to `setAttribute()` cannot be `null`. These methods throw an `IllegalStateException` if they are called in conjunction with an invalid session object.

> public java.util.Enumeration getAttributeNames()

This method gets the attribute names as an enumeration.

> public void invalidate()

This method marks the session as invalid.

> public boolean isNew()

This method returns "true" if the session is new.

The problem with Reloading Pages

Download the HTML file in Program Listing 21.4 into your Web browser. Fill inn the data, and then press "Send". Then you'll get the message "Your evaluation is saved". Click the Reload button in your browser. What happens? The data is stored in the file once more. A single user may fill up your evaluation file with repeating data.

A solution to this problem is to use a session attribute. We set the attribute for the first time after the data are saved. Before the saving section there is a check if this attribute exists. If it does, we do not save again.

The same considerations apply to updating databases, as well.
See problem 3 below.

Problems

1. Expand the code in Program Listing 21.9 with cookies for address, zip code and city.

2. Set the age of one of the cookies in Program Listing 21.9 to 24 hours, and try it from one day to the next. Check that the cookie is stored on your disk.

3. Implement the solution to "The problem with Reloading Pages" for the restaurant evaluation example, as presented above.

4. Change the code in Program Listing 21.11 after the following lines:

   Put the book information into a text file (use a text editor). The number should now tell us the total number of books ordered by all clients. All the information in this file should be read into an instance variable `bookTitles` when the accompanying servlet is initiated (put this in the method `jspInit()`).

When the servlet runs, the information should be held in the instance variable. The number of books ordered by an individual customer should be held in a session attribute.

The page should be expanded with a "Send Order" button, which updates the instance variable and saves it to the file.

The `Book` class should now have synchronized methods. Why?

21.10 New Concepts in This Chapter

Concept	Brief Explanation
attribute, HTML	HTML code can have attributes that provide additional information for an element.
attribute, session	The individual data element in a session object is called an attribute and is identified with a name. The attribute has to be of a reference type.
client-side validation	Data is checked on the client side before being sent to the server.
cookie	A small quantity of information that is stored as text on the computer where the browser is running.
JSP	JavaServer Pages—a technology that makes it possible to distinguish the Web page's dynamic contents from its design. The dynamics are isolated and surrounded with special characters. See the concepts that start with JSP below.
JSP comment	Comment surrounded by `<%--` and `--%>`. The comment doesn't show when the source code is shown in the browser.
JSP declaration	Variables and methods surrounded by `<%!` and `%>`. These will become members in the servlet created from the *jsp* file.
JSP directive	Directives that control how the servlet will be constructed. Enclosed between `<%@` and `%>`.
JSP expression	A Java expression surrounded by `<%=` and `%>`.
JSP page	An HTML page that is made by a servlet based on a *jsp* file.
JSP scriptlet	Java code surrounded by `<%` and `%>`.
parameter, the request object	In conjunction with Web programming, the word "parameter" refers to the data sent to the server as part of a `request` object (or a query string). The parameters are usually names and values from the `input` elements in HTML forms.

Concept	Brief Explanation
pool	Often used about data resources that are labor-intensive to set up. A pool is a specific quantity of this type of resources, for example 10 database connections. Clients that need one of these resources are assigned one from the pool. The resource is returned to the pool after use, without closing it. If the pool is empty, the client has to wait until one is free, or the pool can be expanded to contain more.
script language	Code written in a scripting language is not compiled, but rather interpreted line by line.
server-side validation	The data is checked on the server side.
servlet	A Java program that runs on a Web server. It is started and runs until the Web server is taken down or it is stopped in another way. Executes specific tasks every time it's accessed by a Web client.
session	The period of time during which a client communicated with a specific Web site.
session ID	A string that identifies a session. Assigned by the Web server.
session object	An object that contains data which will survive from request to request in a session.
WAP	Wireless Application Protocol—a mobile phone has to support the WAP protocol to be able to download WML files.
WML	Wireless Markup Language—a "markup" language, usually used in developing pages for mobile phones.

21.11 Review Problems

1. Outline the different ways dynamics in Web pages can be accomplished.

2. Describe the similarities and differences between applets and servlets.

3. When should instance variables in a servlet only be accessed by synchronized methods?

4. What is a JSP page?

5. Give examples of the following in use: `<%  %>`, `<%!  %>`, `<%=  %>`.

6. The *jsp* file is converted to a servlet class. How many (and which) methods do we get in this servlet class?

7. By translating a *jsp* file to a servlet class, some variables become instance variables while others become local variables. Which variables turn into instance variables? Which ones become local variables? And in which method are these variables local?

8. Among other things, by transferring data from client to server, we can use "post" or "get". What is the difference and which method should we use?

9. What do we use JavaScript for?

10. What is a cookie?

11. Explain the concept of a session, and in particular the relationship between a session and a cookie.

12. Why should we send all URLs in *jsp* files through the `response.en-codeURL()` method?

21.12 Programming Problems

Problem 1

Create a very simple calculator with a Web interface. The calculations will be done on the Web server. You could use the `Calculator` class from Chapter 5.

Problem 2

Make an archive for CDs.

The archive should be very simple and saved in a data file. It should contain one line per piece of music. Every line should contain the title of the piece, the artist, and the name of the CD. Separate the different parts with commas.

The Web interface will make it possible to display all the pieces and find pieces by one specific artist.

Create a regular Java class with the necessary operations. Use the `StringTokenizer` class to get the individual parts of a line. Then make the Web interface.

(The data file is going to be edited in a regular editor so you shouldn't create any operations for it.)

Problem 3

Start with programming problem 1 from Chapter 9.

Make a Web interface that shows all the products. Let the user change the price of a selected product, register a new product, or delete a product.

Problem 4

Make a Web interface that can be used by a client of type 2 in Problem 3 from Chapter 20. The user will enter his user ID and password.

Problem 5

Make a Web interface for the application developed as the solution to Problem 4 in Chapter 20.

Using Java SDK and WinEdit

As explained in Chapter 1, we can divide the program systems we need to program Java into two: a tool for writing, editing, and storing the files in source code, and a set of tools for compiling and running the files. In many cases, we use larger development tools, which combine these functions in one program. For example, we will use the Java SDK (Software Development Kit) package from Sun to compile and run. This is the official development tool for Java. SDK is the same package that was previously called JDK, the Java Development Kit. As of version 2 of Java, the package has been called SDK, but the name JDK is still hanging on, and the two names are used interchangeably even on Sun's Web pages.

We've used a program called WinEdit for text editing, but that's just to have an example. There are many similar programs. In addition to the primitive Notepad that comes with Windows, we can also mention UltraEdit and JPad as examples. Another tool used a great deal by advanced users is Emacs, a powerful tool with a somewhat steep learning curve. You can search for "editors" at [URL WinFiles], where there's a large selection of text editing tools that are cheap or even free.

On the book's Web pages [URL Java book], you'll find links and updated information concerning Java-related tools.

A.1 SDK

The SDK development package exists for many types of computers/operating systems. A bunch of versions come from Sun itself, but there are also SDKs for other platforms that others have made (or "ported," as we call it when you rewrite programs for operating systems other than those they were originally written for).

For those with limited experience, installing this program package can be a little complicated. A little help, for example from people who have done it before, may come in handy.

Downloading and installing

In this book, we're assuming that the reader is using Windows 95/98/NT/2000, even though we don't go as far as recommending it. The SDK for this platform is available from Sun—the URL to go to it is [URL Javasoft]. In the following, as an example, is a description of how the download works. (Sun may have modified the procedure since this was written.) Read through the whole thing before you begin, and keep in mind that small details may have been changed. The most important thing is to keep your goal in mind: to download Java 2 SDK and install it on your hard disk.

You'll come to the [URL Javasoft] front page. Here you'll find advertisements and news. You can click on Products & APIs in the menu; here you'll find the products that are available. Sun have a menu where you can choose a product to download. We want Java 2 SDK Standard Edition.

When you get to the SDK page, you can click on Microsoft Windows. Locate the download button on the following page.

Press "Agree" to agree to the terms for downloading. You see pages of terms like this all the time when downloading software, but they don't usually have any practical significance for students. One exception may be time-limited licenses.

You get to choose between an FTP or HTTP download. Choose FTP. Now your browser will ask where you want to save the file. It may be beneficial to have a directory ready on your hard disk for SDK, *C:\sdk2* or something similar.

When the file is finished downloading, it can be unwrapped by running the file. (It's a self-expanding *exe* file, which means that it will unwrap itself when you run it.) It will ask where on the disk SDK should be placed, and which modules you want. In terms of the modules, it's OK to say "yes" to whatever is being recommended.

As for the documentation, you can download it, but it's also available on the Web—you can get to it from [URL Javasoft]. We recommend that you download the entire set of documentation to your own hard disk, and read it from there. Especially in connection with programming graphical user interfaces, there will be a lot of use for it. Regardless, it's important to familiarize yourself with the documentation, because only a small portion of the program code that is available for use is discussed in this book.

The size of the program package can be a hassle for people with slow Net connections: it just takes too long to download everything. However, you need the development tools to get some work done, so this problem has to be addressed. One possibility could be downloading the package from a place with a good Internet connection.

Path

In the computer's operating system, there's something called *environmental varia-bles*. These are values or a list of values that belong to all the programs we run. They are used to keep track of the many things a program needs to know. They are exactly like Java's own variables that we cover in Chapter 2: they have names and values. But the environmental variables apply to the whole operating system, and we as users can create and delete them as needed.

When SDK is expanded and ready, it's an advantage if we can use the programs in the package regardless of where we are on the hard disk, in the console window (MS-DOS window), or in using other programs, like WinEdit. We can do this by adding the directory to the environmental variable PATH. The result of this is that, for example, we can use the program javac regardless of where we are in the console window. Often this is done automatically when SDK is installed, so it may happen that this is all taken care of once your installation is done. The section Using SDK on below describes how you check this. In the next paragraph, we'll describe how you can do this yourself.

To change PATH in Windows NT/2000, go into the control panel from the Start menu, then System and Environment. Often there's already a PATH, and in that case, all you have to do is add, for example, *C:\sdk2\bin* to the line of text that's there. (The programs themselves, the *exe* files, are in the subdirectory *bin* under SDK.) Note that the different directories in PATH are separated by a semicolon, so the new directory we add has to be as well.

Example of the contents of the PATH variable after we've made this addition:

```
C:\;C:\windows\;C:\sdk2\bin\
```

Here we see that three different directories are in PATH. For these changes to apply, you have to close the Environment dialog and start a new console window.

To do this in Windows 95/98, add this line to *C:\auotexec.bat* :

```
set PATH=C:\;C:\windows\;C:\sdk2\bin\
```

There's probably a PATH line already, and then you just edit it the way we've shown here. For the changes made in *autoexec.bat* to apply, you have to run the file by double-clicking on it.

Classpath

Another environmental variable that affects the use of SDK is CLASSPATH. While PATH is a general environmental variable that contains information about where the operating system should look for *exe* files, CLASSPATH is Java-specific and tells the Java interpreter, java, where it should look for *class* files. So there's a certain analogy between the two; the *class* files are run in conjunction with Java just as the *exe* files are run otherwise. CLASSPATH, like PATH, is a list of directories, and what is worth taking note of is that even the directory we're in has to be in CLASSPATH for the Java interpreter to look there. If you get an error message like the following one when running a Java program, and the right *class* file is definitely in the directory, it's probably CLASSPATH that's not correctly set.

```
C:\javaprograms> java PrintText
Exception in thread "main" java.lang.NoClassDefFoundError:
PrintText
```

This is an error message saying that the class definition (*class* file) was not found. What should you do if you have problems with this? It's hard to say something precise that will work every time, because there may be programs other than SDK that are using CLASSPATH, but we have the following two suggestions.

The first thing you can do is delete the whole environmental variable CLASSPATH. (If it has a value from before you shouldn't do this—read the next section instead.) In Java 2 SDK, the interpreter will then look in the directory you're in. You delete an environmental variable the same way you set it (see the section on PATH). Just remember to restart the console window under NT/2000 afterwards, and if it's Windows 95/98 it can pay off to reboot.

The other way to go about setting CLASSPATH up correctly is to add a period in the list of directories. Change CLASSPATH, for example, so that it looks like this:

```
.;C:\netscape\classes\
```

In this example, we see that there's a directory that refers to the program Netscape in CLASSPATH, and we shouldn't touch that. So we add a period to the list. This indicates that the current directory should always be included in CLASSPATH. The different directories are also separated by semicolons here.

Bear in mind that it's quite likely you won't need to touch this environmental variable.

Using SDK

Once you've done all this, you can test that you did the installation and adjusted PATH correctly by starting a console window and trying to start the compiler by writing javac:

```
C:\> javac
Usage: javac <options> <source files>
where <options> includes:
  -g                      Generate all debugging info
  -g:none                 Generate no debugging info
  -g:{lines,vars,source}  Generate only some debugging info
  -O                      Optimize; may hinder debugging or
                          enlarge class files
  -nowarn                 Generate no warnings
  -verbose                Output messages about what the
                          compiler is doing
  -deprecation            Output source locations where
                          deprecated APIs are used
  -classpath <path>       Specify where to find user class
                          files
  -sourcepath <path>      Specify where to find input
                          source files
  -bootclasspath <path>   Override location of bootstrap
                          class files
  -extdirs <dirs>         Override location of installed
                          extensions
  -d <directory>          Specify where to place generated
                          class files
  -encoding <encoding>    Specify character encoding used
                          by source files
```

```
-target <release>        Generate class files for specific
                         VM version
```

If you get something like this as a result, the installation was done correctly and you're ready to program Java. The point is that you should be able to start the compiler in a console window from any arbitrary directory. What happens here then? Well, you start the compiler javac without stating any file. It then responds by giving you some hints concerning proper usage of the program. You can also test the interpreter java the same way, but it's almost inconceivable that it won't start when javac starts.

If during your test run you get a message that the program or the command is not found, it may be PATH that is wrong, and the operating system doesn't know where to find the javac program.

As demonstrated in Chapter 1, we then compile a Java file by writing, for example:

```
C:\javaprograms\> javac PrintText.java
```

and if it works, a program can be started from a *class* file by writing

```
C:\javaprograms\> java PrintText
```

A.2 Running Applets

A third important program in SDK is *appletviewer*. It's one of two main ways to test Java applets. An applet's *class* file will always be called from an HTML document. (See Appendix E for a brief discussion of HTML and including applets on Web pages.) Appletviewer will also need an HTML file of this type, so here the call will be

```
C:\javaprograms\> appletviewer PrintTextApplet.html
```

Then you get a graphical window, where the applet will start. In a browser, the applet will run in a small field after downloading. Appletviewer plays the same role, but only displays the applet, not the HTML document that surrounds it.

In many development tools and slightly advanced text editors that are suited to Java, there will be a menu option for starting an applet directly, after compiling. The tool will then automatically generate a little HTML file and start appletviewer for you.

The other main way to test an applet is to create an HTML file that uses it, the same as in the previous section, and then open the file from the hard disk with a browser. Then we'll see the whole HTML document with the applet, as if we'd seen it on the Web.

A.3 WinEdit

The text editor we've decided to use as our example in this book is called WinEdit. You can read about it at the vendor's Web pages: [URL WinEdit]. At the time of writing, the program costs $100 (check the URL for the correct price) and you can download and install a free evaluation version as follows.

From the URL given in the previous paragraph, click on "Download". You will be given a choice between HTTP and FTP. After the program is downloaded, place it in its own directory and run the self-expanding *exe*-file. During installation, you can safely accept the options the program suggests, but it may also want to install some add-on programs which you do not necessarily need. Start it up by double-clicking on *WinEdit.exe* in the file manager, or choose the program from the start menu. In other words, install and start up work in the usual Windows fashion— several people will have done this before.

Editing text

WinEdit has the same principal functionality as Windows Notepad, but with many more options. You open, save, and close files from the File menu. If you open a *java* file, you'll notice that the program uses colors in the Java program to make programming easier. WinEdit will also apply colors to other types of files—for example, HTML. This is called syntax highlighting.

If you've written a Java file that you want to try to compile, choose Compile from the Tools menu at the top. WinEdit will then run javac for you, with the right parameters.

 For WinEdit to be able to do the compiling, SDK *must* be installed earlier, and PATH modified so that the *bin* directory for SDK is included.

A separate window in WinEdit will give you the compiling result—i.e., error messages or a message that there were no errors. If there are errors, you go into the code and try to correct them before compiling again.

After you've compiled the program without errors, you can run it by selecting Java, Run Java Application from the Macro menu. The reason this isn't under Tools is that this is done another way—the interpreter is started in its own window. In that window, you will see the dialog with the program. You may also run an applet from the Macro, Java menu. For applications, you have the choice between running console (i.e. textual) or graphical applications.

Play around with WinEdit (or the tool you decide to use) on your own, and get to know its capabilities. Editing and managing text files is an important skill for a programmer.

Keywords

These words cannot be used in any way other than as specified in the syntax of the Java language.

abstract	assert	boolean	break
byte	case	catch	char
class	const	continue	default
do	double	else	extends
final	finally	float	for
goto	if	implements	import
instanceof	int	interface	long
native	new	package	private
protected	public	return	short
static	super	switch	synchronized
this	throw	throws	transient
try	void	volatile	while

The list is from [Gosling, Joy, Steele 1996, section 3.9] except for the `assert` keyword, which has been added to the language in JDK release 1.4. The Java authors continue: "The keywords `const` and `goto` are reserved by Java, even though they are not currently used in Java. This may allow a Java compiler to produce better error messages if these C++ keywords incorrectly appear in Java programs."

Number Systems

(Written by Mildrid Ljosland)
Most number systems are based on the positional principle so that a number's value depends on where in the sequence of digits it's located. A 1 means 10 (in the base 10 system) if it comes next to last, while it means 1000 if it comes two places further forward. Roman numerals are an example of a number system that doesn't use the positional principle. The letter D means 500 regardless of where it's located. The number systems covered in this appendix use the positional principle.

Base 10 system (the decimal number system)

Ten different digits, 0 to 9. Example: $286 = 2 \cdot 10^2 + 8 \cdot 10^1 + 6 \cdot 10^0$.

Base 2 system (the binary number system)

Two different digits, 0 and 1. Example:
$$01101 = 0 \cdot 2^4 + 1 \cdot 2^3 + 1 \cdot 2^2 + 0 \cdot 2^1 + 1 \cdot 2^0 = 0 + 8 + 4 + 0 + 1 = 13$$
To convert from the base 10 system to the base 2 system, divide repeatedly by two and then take care of the remainders.

Example: Convert 123 to binary.

123 / 2 = 61 with a remainder of 1
61 / 2 = 30 with a remainder of 1
30 / 2 = 15 with a remainder of 0
15 / 2 = 7 with a remainder of 1
7 / 2 = 3 with a remainder of 1
3 / 2 = 1 with a remainder of 1
1 / 2 = 0 with a remainder of 1

When we get 0 as the answer, we're done. Then we collect the remainders—the last remainder computed is the first digit in the binary number. Here that will be 1111011. Check that this is correct: $1111011 = 64 + 32 + 16 + 8 + 0 + 2 + 1 = 123$.

Base 8 system (the octal system)

Eight different digits, 0 to 7.

Example:

$$632 = 6 \cdot 8^2 + 3 \cdot 8^1 + 2 \cdot 8^0 = 6 \cdot 64 + 3 \cdot 8 + 2 = 384 + 24 + 2 = 410$$

Converting from the base 10 system to the base 8 system works the same way as to the base 2 system.

Convert 123:

123 / 8 = 15 with a remainder of 3
15 / 8 = 1 with a remainder of 7
1 / 8 = 0 with a remainder of 1.

The answer is 173. Check if this is correct: $64 + 7 \cdot 8 + 3 = 123$.

To convert between the binary system and base 8:

We have $123_{10} = 173_8 = 1111011_2$ (the subindices indicate which number system we're talking about). The number 1 can be written in binary as 001, while the number 7 can be written 111 and 3 as 011. If we combine the three numbers (1, 7, and 3), we get 001111011, which is the binary representation of 173_8.

Every digit in the octal number is written as the equivalent binary number, with three binary digits for each octal digit. If you know the binary forms for the numbers from 0 to 7, then you can easily convert both ways by treating octal digits one at a time and binary digits in sets of three.

Because the conversion is simple, we frequently use the base 8 system when there's a use for the bit pattern. Numbers in the base 2 system have three times as many digits as numbers in the base 8 system, and it's easy to get confused with all the zeros and ones. Using the base 8 system is both easier and more succinct.

We indicate that a number is written in base 8 instead of base 10 by putting a 0 at the start of the number. This is true both for the program and for input.

Example: `int number = 027;` means the number 27 in the base 8 system, which is the number 23 in the base 10 system.

Base 16 system (the hexadecimal system)

Here we need 16 different digits. The numbers 0 through 9 are used and in addition, we use A for 10, B for 11, C for 12, D for 13, E for 14, and F for 15. We can also use lower-case letters.

Example:

2D18 =
$2 \cdot 16^3 + 13 \cdot 16^2 + 1 \cdot 16^1 + 8 \cdot 16^0 =$
$2 \cdot 4096 + 13 \cdot 256 + 1 \cdot 16 + 8 =$
$8192 + 3328 + 16 + 8 = 11544$

To convert from base 10:

Convert 11544

11544 / 16 = 721 with a remainder of 8
721 / 16 = 45 with a remainder of 1
45 / 16 = 2 with a remainder of 13 (= D)
2 / 16 = 0 with a remainder of 2

Result: 2D18.

To convert to binary: this works the same as for base 8. The difference is that now there are four binary digits for each hexadecimal digit. Example: 2D18 will become 0010 1101 0001 1000.

To convert to the octal system is done through binary:

2D18 = 0010 1101 0001 1000 = 0 010 110 100 011 000 = 026430

The hexadecimal system is used in data processing for the same reason as the octal system, and with it there are even fewer digits to keep track of. This also fits in well with a byte being 8 bits. There are exactly two digits per byte.

If we're going to indicate that a constant in a program is declared in the hexadecimal system, we start by writing 0X. Example: `number = 0X2D18;`

The Unicode Character Set

For complete specifications, see [URL Unicode]. In Windows NT you may find "Unicode Character Map" in the group Accessories useful. The table below only shows the printable characters in the part of Unicode that coincides with ASCII

value	character	value	character	value	character
32		64	@	96	`
33	!	65	A	97	a
34	"	66	B	98	b
35	#	67	C	99	c
36	$	68	D	100	d
37	%	69	E	101	e
38	&	70	F	102	f
39	'	71	G	103	g
40	(	72	H	104	h
41	)	73	I	105	i
42	*	74	J	106	j
43	+	75	K	107	k
44	,	76	L	108	l
45	-	77	M	109	m
46	.	78	N	110	n
47	/	79	O	111	o
48	0	80	P	112	p
49	1	81	Q	113	q
50	2	82	R	114	r
51	3	83	S	115	s
52	4	84	T	116	t
53	5	85	U	117	u
54	6	86	V	118	v
55	7	87	W	119	w
56	8	88	X	120	x
57	9	89	Y	121	y
58	:	90	Z	122	z
59	;	91	[	123	{
60	<	92	\	124		
61	=	93	]	125	}
62	>	94	^	126	~
63	?	95	_		

E

HTML and Applets

As we pointed out in the first chapter, Java is tied to the Web, but far from exclusively. Applets are small Java programs that are part of a Web page. Applets are a special version of Java programs. The regular programs, the applications that we work with, are a larger and more general group.

Java applets are compiled like Java programs from source code with the *.java* extension to a byte code file with the *.class* extension. So an applet takes the form of a file—for example, *SimpleApplet.class*. Here, we will briefly explain how we use this applet in a Web page, once we've covered the most important elements of HTML, Hypertext Markup Language.

E.1 HTML

The Web came to exist so that researchers could present documents in electronic form and so that they could be easily distributed on the Internet. Central to this is the *HTTP protocol*, which is the set of rules used when files containing texts, graphics, sound, etc. are linked together and transported around on the Net. In general, a protocol is a type of standardized and agreed upon set of rules, and the concept is key in the field of data networking. HTML is a language that we use to format the basic Web files, the pages that contain regular text with associated formatting and also graphics. The *hyperlinks* are also important—with these, HTML allows us to jump to a new document with, for example, the click of a mouse.

When we work on the Web, we are usually dealing with a browser, which is called a *client*. We use this to request files—for example, *english.html*—that are on a Web *server*. The Web server has a name on the Internet that makes it easy for us to look it up. *www.tisip.no* is the name of TISIP's Web server. To get a document on it, we use a URL, Uniform Resource Locator, which may look like this: *http://www.tisip.no/english.html*. Here we're saying that we're going to get the document with the file name *english.html* on the server *www.tisip.no*, and it's the HTTP protocol that's used (i.e., the regular Web).

This document, in turn, can contain references to graphics (and other things).

Below you'll find an example of how an HTML file might look. It's regular text, just like Java source code. However, it's important to remember that these aren't instructions to the computer, but a *markup*, a static description of something.

```
<html>
<head>
 <title>An example page</title>
</head>

<body>

 <h1>Welcome to our little test page</h1>

 <p>
 This is a little test page. It doesn't contain much.

 <p>
 Actually only a header plus these two paragraphs.

 </body>
</html>
```

We see that different codes are found inside < and >. These codes are called tags (for example, the body tag). The tags mark the start of different *elements* and an element is often ended with `</ ...>`. Study the example and you'll see that `<html>` and `</html>` mark the start and end of the HTML document itself, `<head>` and `</head>` mark the start and end of the head part of the document, and `<body>` and `</body>` mark the document's body. This is the basis of all HTML pages. In our example, there's a title marked with its own tag, and also header 1, or `<h1>`. `<p>` comes before a paragraph and you'll see that these aren't ended—they end when something else starts.

It's the browser—Netscape or another browser—that's responsible for displaying the data in this HTML file nicely for those who come and visit the page.

In addition to what we've presented here, there are a number of other elements we use. A common one is the element with the tag `<img>` for including graphics:

```
<img src="sunrise.gif">
```

Here, graphics from a file are inserted into the Web page. The file is assumed to be in the same directory on the Web server as the HTML document using it.

The whole point of the Web and HTML is that it can link many different types of machines together, and that many different browsers can display documents in a reasonable manner. Thus, there's a need for both HTTP and HTML to be standardized, and for those who make both Web servers and browsers to focus on the same standards. It's the World Wide Web Consortium, W3C, which bears the overall responsibility for this standardization. You can find and study the official HTML standard (at the time of printing), HTML 4.0, at [URL W3C]. There you'll see which elements are permitted (and there aren't all that many). The reason that there are relatively few elements is that it has been cleaned up from the previous version, HTML 3.2. In version 4.0, everything that has to do with presentation is formatted in a special language, CSS, which stands for Cascading Style Sheets. We won't go into any more detail on this here.

For chapter 21, you will need more HTML elements; look them up in [URL W3C] when you need to refer to them.

E.2 Including Applets

Normal Web pages are all passive. They are static information located in files that we retrieve from the Web server and which are then presented to us in our browser. Applets are small programs that are downloaded to the browser the same way a graphics file is. Then the applet is started and it fulfills its mission. We can say that this takes place inside the browser, because the browser controls it. The Java interpreter, which we're used to needing to start a Java program, is built into the browser.

Here's how you include an applet in your HTML file:

```
<object classid="java:SimpleApplet.class" width="500" height="500">
  Your browser does not support applets.
</object>
```

As with a graphics file, the `class` file has to be in the same directory on the Web server as the HTML document. (This is not required and can be changed, but we will assume that here.) Then a little text follows and the browser will show this text if it does *not* support applets. The element is closed with `</object>`. Also notice that we have to specify the width and height of the window the applet will get in the browser.

Previously, the tag `<applet>` was used to include an applet.

```
<applet code="SimpleApplet.class" width="500" height="500">
  Your browser does not support applets.
</applet>
```

If you want the applet to work on a browser that doesn't understand `<object>`, it may be wise to use `<applet>`, but then you risk that future browsers, which may only support the standardized `<object>`, can't access the applet.

When the browser downloads a document that contains a reference to an applet, the applet is downloaded as needed, and started.

Security is an important aspect here. It wouldn't be especially safe to travel around on the Web if Web pages could contain applets that downloaded and ran unintentionally, and those applets damaged our hard disks. Of course there's a mechanism that protects us against this—it's called the *sandbox model*. This means that the applet never has a chance to read or write files on the client's computer (nor can it ever find anything out about the type of machine, memory, or where in the world it's located). It only has its own small sandbox to play in. The browser, with its associated Java interpreter, is responsible for keeping the applet in the sandbox. If a Java applet tries to delete a file, the browser will send an error message and stop the applet.

In chapter 18 we cover this and other applet aspects in more depth.

A Java applet runs in a security model called the sandbox model. In practice, that means that you don't risk anything when you download a foreign applet on the Web, because it's not allowed to do anything that might damage your computer.

But doesn't this greatly limit the applet's capabilities? Yes, to an extent, but it can still display things, talk to the user through GUI components, show animations, and much more.

The quality of browsers' built-in Java interpreters is extremely variable. The level of performance is often low, and many who have tried their hand at programming applets have experienced frustration with browsers that don't support applets written in the version of Java code they used. The language itself varies minimally, but the ready-made code we use, which is included in the browsers, varies.

Exceptions to the Code Standard

[URL Coding standard] contains the code standard used in this book. We have chosen to use the standard with the following exceptions:

Point 3.1: "Each Java source file contains a single public class or interface." A file cannot contain more than one public class, but we permit a file to contain multiple classes with package access. The code standard doesn't mention classes with package access.

Point 3.1.1: We've chosen to simplify the head comment a little compared to these recommendations.

Point 4: Out of space considerations, we're only indenting two spaces instead of four.

Point 4.1: For the same reason, we allow lines longer than 70 (80) characters.

Point 5: We've included some comments for instructional reasons. These are comments that explain things that appear in the code. Normally, one would assume that the reader is familiar with Java and comments like this would be considered extraneous.

Points 5.1.3 and 5.1.4: We only use // to insert comments at the end of a line.

Point 5.2: Documentation comments are used to generate documentation like the online API documentation. We're not using documentation comments /**...*/. You can find examples of these in use (and a brief description of how they're used) in the myLibrary package.

Point 6.1: We chose the first alternative, a blank space between the data type and the name.

Point 6.3: We are putting variable declarations close to where the variables are used for the first time. This makes it easier to initialize the variables (Point 6.2) with reasonable values.

Point 7.2: We permit the brackets in if/else/while/for/do statements to be omitted if only one statement is going to be executed—and this statement goes on the same line as if/else/while/for/do. (We have our reservations about this exception, but have found that this simplification is difficult to avoid in practical programming.)

Point 7.4: Nested if might therefore look like this:

```
if (...) .....
else if (...) .....
```

```
else if (...) .....
else ...
```

"Note" at the end of the section is still important. Remember that there has to be room for the statement on the *same* line as the `if` statement.

Point 9: Only ASCII characters (A–Z, a–z, '0'–'9') are used in class names. Names of classes that are answers to problems are the exception. There we use the underline character to indicate which problem the answer is for (example `Problem5_4_3`).

We have opted to use the same naming conventions for constants as for variables.

Point 10.3: This is too severe a limitation. It must be possible to use other anonymous constants (literals) besides -1, 0, and 1 directly in the program. For example: the number 2 in the formula for the radius of a circle: `2 * Math.PI * radius`.

Point 10.5.1: We're not using extraneous parentheses in expressions containing frequently used operators. We think that the reader should learn the operator precedence, and we also think that so many levels of parentheses make the expressions difficult to read. There are, however, examples of expressions in point 10.4 and point 10.5.3 where parentheses should be used: `if ((c++ = d++) != 0)...` and `(x >= 0) ? x : -x;`. Particularly the first one is the type of expression that is best rewritten as multiple statements.

Point 10.5.2: We find the first two alternatives to be equivalent. In the second case, the code standard recommends using the conditional operator. This operator is difficult for many people, especially beginners. Therefore it's not used in this book.

References

G

Books:

Cay S. Hortsmann, Gary Cornell *Core Java 2. Volume I - Fundamentals*. Prentice Hall 1999.

Cay S. Hortsmann, Gary Cornell *Core Java 2. Volume II - Advanced Features*. Prentice Hall 2000.

Craig Larman Applying UML and Patterns *An Introduction to Object-Oriented Analysis and Design*. PTR (ECS Professional) 2000.

David Flanagan *Java in a Nutshell. A Desktop Quick Reference. 2nd edn*. O'Reilly 1997.

Grady Booch, James Rumbaugh, Ivar Jacobson *Unified Modeling Language User Guide*. Addison-Wesley 1999.

H. M. Deitel, P. J. Deitel, T. R. Nieto *Internet and World Wide Web, How to Program*. Prentice Hall 2000.

James Gosling, Bill Joy, Guy Steele *The Java Language Specification*. Addison-Wesley 1996. See [URL Language spec].

James Rumbaugh, Ivar Jacobson, Grady Booch *The Unified Modeling Language Reference Manual*. Addison-Wesley 1999.

Jose Annunziato, Stephanie Fesler Kaminaris *Sams Teach Yourself JavaServer Pages in 24 Hours*. Sams Publishing 2001.

Kathy Walrath, Mary Campione *The JFC Swing Tutorial. A Guide to Constructing GUIs*. Addison-Wesley 1999.

Knut Hofstad, Ståle Løland, Per Scott *Norsk dataordbok, 6.utgave*. Universitetsforlaget 1997. (A Norwegian book on computer terms.)

Mark Allen Weiss *Data Structures and Problem Solving Using Java*. Addison-Wesley 1998.

Marty Hall *Core Servlets and JavaServer Pages*. Prentice Hall 2000.

Nigel Warren, Philip Bishop *Java in Practice. Design Styles and Idioms for Effective Java*. Addison-Wesley 1999.

Robert Eckstein, Marc Loy, Dave Wood *Java Swing*. O'Reilly 1998.

Robert Orfali, Dan Harkey *Client/Server Programming with Java and Corba. Second Edition*. John Wiley & Sons, Inc. 1998.

Thomas Connolly, Carolyn Begg, Anne Strachan *Database Systems. A Practical Approach to Design, Implementation and Management*. Addison-Wesley 1999.

Thomas H. Cormen, Charles E. Leiserson, Ronald L. Rivest *Introduction to Algorithms*. MIT Press 1997.

URLs:

[URL Coding standard] http://java.sun.com/docs/codeconv/
[URL ColorApplet] http://www.tisip.no/JavaTheUmlWay/examples/ColorApplet.html
[URL Database Drivers] http://industry.java.sun.com/products/jdbc/drivers
[URL Gefion] http://www.gefionsoftware.com/
[URL Java book] http://www.tisip.no/JavaTheUmlWay/
[URL Java glossary] http://java.sun.com/docs/glossary.html
[URL JavaScript] http://developer.netscape.com/docs/manuals/javascript.html
[URL-Javasoft] http://java.sun.com/products/
[URL Language spec] http://java.sun.com/docs/books/jls/html/
[URL Servlet info] http://java.sun.com/products/servlet/
[URL SimpleApplet] http://www.tisip.no/JavaTheUmlWay/examples/SimpleApplet.html
[URL Unicode] http://www.unicode.org/
[URL W3C] http://www.w3.org/
[URL Web servers] http://java.sun.com/products/servlet/industry.html
[URL WinEdit] http://www.winedit.com/
[URL WinFiles] http://www.winfiles.com/

Index

Page numbers in italic refer to concept explanations. Identical terms with different capitalization are different words in Java and this is reflected in the index entries.